# The Hollies

# The Hollies

Riding the Carousel

Malcolm C. Searles

A Dojotone Publication in association with Troubador Publishing Ltd.

All lyrics quoted in this book are for the purposes of review, study or criticism.
All photographs remain the copyright of their respective owners.
Photographs printed with permission. Any credit omissions or corrections
should be directed to the author for future editions.


Matador
Unit E2 Airfield Business Park,
Harrison Road, Market Harborough,
Leicestershire. LE16 7UL
Tel: 0116 2792299
Email: books@troubador.co.uk
Web: www.troubador.co.uk/matador
Twitter: @matadorbooks


ISBN 9781800463493

British Library Cataloguing in Publication Data.
A catalogue record for this book is available from the British Library.


Typeset in 11pt Minion Pro by Troubador Publishing Ltd, Leicester, UK

Matador is an imprint of Troubador Publishing Ltd

*To my wonderful wife. Well, I've gone and done it again.*
*Thank you for hanging in there and permitting me the time*
*xx*

# CONTENTS

# Contents

# THE HOLLIES

Representation The Wilson Agency, 142, Charing Cross Road, W.C.2.
Telephone : Temple Bar 3948, or Stoke-on-Trent 22274/5.

# PREFACE

The Hollies have had a rich and varied career, and there have been many fans and collectors of the group who have travelled the equally varied path alongside them, commencing back in the early days of the 1960s. There may even be a few of you reading this who go back even further. Those who can vividly (or hazily) recall a youthful Ricky and Dane Young performing around Manchester's coffee houses and bars, when their visions of a rock 'n' roll lifestyle were but a mere dream.

The career of the five-man band that followed can subsequently be divided into three distinctive time frames – and has been split in such a way for the layout of this very tome you are now holding. With a dividing line of the high tenor vocal, Part One appropriately covers the Graham Nash years. Part Two naturally takes over with Terry Sylvester stepping into the harmony blend, whilst Part Three can be summarised as the Alan Coates and beyond era. Now, that isn't to say these fine vocalists were the defining benchmark for all that went on around them, but it neatly breaks the story into sections for the sake of compiling such a detailed story. Then again, it often appears that such a division can also break apart the loyalty within much of a group's following as well. Some fans of the band to this day mourn the loss of Allan Clarke as a frontman, failing to accept the face and voice of Peter Howarth, who currently fronts the band, or that of earlier replacements Mikael Rickfors or Carl Wayne. Why, I ask? Isn't it all about the music? This is not to put any of them down. Far, *far* from it. We all have our own favourites, for whatever reasons, but to vehemently dismiss such talented frontmen, simply because they are not the original vocalist, is, to this mind, inexcusable. Surely, as I say, The Hollies we see today are all about celebrating the music? The history? The legacy? *For Certain Because...,* *Evolution* and *Distant Light* are all wonderful collections, but then so is *Romany*. Others in turn stand by *Staying Power*. They are all examples of the ever-changing progression of this fine band, regardless of who stands out front. Of course, Allan will always be seen as a key face in the band, and justifiably so. He was there from the start and helped chart the course for much of the success that duly followed. And yet, he chose to step away for personal reasons in later years – whilst the band continued ever onwards. Sadly, the division that his departure caused, remains. Some stand up for the argument of a new face centre stage, others not so. You decide which way you fall – and that is your prerogative. We all have our own voice, and the beliefs of others must be respected. Hopefully, the following chapters will allow you to judge clearly for yourself.

Certain readers may also wish to step on and/or climb off at any particular stage as the story unfolds. Having avidly followed the band for however many years, your fanatical fandom may have waned as other interests or lifestyle changes took over, and you are now possibly reading this out of curiosity. To look back and remember those long-forgotten times of your chosen era. You may have no interest in what happened twenty years or so after you took the vow of Hollie-celibacy but, if you do feel inclined to follow this through, from cover to cover, to discover what went on in the latter years, I truly hope you enjoy the read as it develops before you. It truly is a fascinating story.

I have often wondered why there has never been a detailed retelling of the complete Hollies story. Heaven knows, many of their musical peers have had reams and reams written and published on their histories. Many of a far less worthy status. Recent years have seen a few Hollies-related publications arrive on our bookshelves, eagerly pored over by the enthusiast, devouring the tantalising glimpses and snippets of detail, and rumours abound of more to follow but, to date, none has ever quite gotten underneath the full story of what went on. Maybe this book will go some way to quenching that thirst a little more. I hope so. However much of it you decide to read.

December 2020

# INTRODUCTION

Twelve years old in 1968 and her beloved older brother has just left home. She consoles herself by playing his reel-to-reel tapes, and suddenly the opening notes of 'King Midas In Reverse' break into her melancholia. That piece of tape was an epiphany – a lifelong love affair had started.

Musicianship, harmonies, lyrics (and yes, okay, appearances!) – The Hollies brought all that to my appreciative senses. They have been a constant in a sometimes-unsettled life, reflecting all and any emotions in their songs. Songs which can, within a few notes, bring smiles or tears accordingly, evoking memories.

The thrill of seeing them on stage for the first time. Here they were, not on paper, not on vinyl, but living, breathing, just a few yards away!

The sorrow when Allan first decided to quit the group. The excitement upon hearing Mikael's tones for the first time, introduced by Alan Freeman on *Pick of the Pops*, when 'The Baby' launched over the airwaves. "Fluff" loved it so much, he played it twice!

The elation when Allan returned to the fold – even if the way I found out was slightly unorthodox – a DJ friend hit me on the head with a copy of *Melody Maker* before revealing the front page, announcing the wanderer's return!

It has been a wonderful experience to have gone through life with a backdrop of music from, unquestionably, one of the world's finest-ever groups. A life which has seen so many things changed. But one thing has never changed. Since that first day in 1968, The Hollies (and I include

Graham, Terry and all past members – but most especially Allan) have always been, and will always remain, at the heart of my music appreciation, and in the heart of this dedicated fan.

Thank you.

Janet Stevens
A devoted UK Hollies fan
May 2020

# PART ONE

---

# CHAPTER ONE

# "IT'S ONLY MAKE BELIEVE..."

*Standing in front of his new classmates, with not a familiar face amongst them, the young six-year-old schoolboy could be forgiven for not seeing fate sitting before him – but when one youngster raised his hand and offered him the seat next to his own then the journey that both would eventually be taking together was sealed. Friends for life.*

'What a trip this has been. I'm so pleased to be here, especially to honour the man I've known for over sixty-three years. One of the best lead singers a band could ever have. My dear friend and partner, Allan Clarke.'

Graham Nash
*Rock and Roll Hall of Fame Awards*
10th March 2010

Harold Allan Clarke was born on 5th April 1942, to parents John and Ann Clarke, in the city of Salford, a mere stone's throw to the west of the bubbling cauldron of Manchester, in the north-west of England. With six siblings growing up in the small family home on Cavendish Street, including elder brother, Frank, and four sisters, Lillian, Anita, Audrey and Cynthia, life was tough for the young family. A seventh sibling tragically died at an early age. Often described as the "slums of Manchester", the working-class Salford area, dark dull brickwork buildings with cobbled or bricked roads running adjacent to narrow back alleys and high-walled rear yards, was as far removed from the genteel green and pleasant countryside of England as one could imagine. The overbearing grey clouds were palpable, and the infamous Christmas Blitz, two years earlier, had reduced much of the city skyline to rubble during that notorious period, with the German Luftwaffe undertaking regular bombing raids over England's industrial heartlands. But to the youngsters growing up amongst the shattered buildings and crumbling remnants of their own decimated communities, it was a playground of discovery. A fortress of undefeated defiance where friendships were built amongst the blackened concrete and smoke-filled clouds that hovered menacingly overhead. In later years, Allan would reflect favourably on this era: 'It was great. I loved my early life at home...'

There was little in the way of music in the family household during those formative years, excepting when Ann would take her youngest son to the nearby movie theatre to see the big Hollywood musicals of the day.

In conversation on BBC Wales Radio, he recalled, 'We used to go to a Methodist church in Gravel Lane, Manchester and used to do a lot of singing, so I'm told, but I don't ever remember us having a radio in the home. But my mum used to take me to the local cinema whenever a blockbuster movie came on. I just fell in love with musicals. I couldn't get enough of Doris Day! *Annie Get Your Gun, Calamity Jane, Seven Brides for Seven Brothers...* It was pure escapism but to me the music was wonderful. I fell in love with music at that particular time...' [23]

On that fateful day during 1948, at Ordsall Board Primary School, Harold Clarke was brought into Mr Burke's infant class, having transferred over from nearby Broughton Primary, and made to stand sheepishly before his fellow pupils whilst a seat was found for him. No one could have envisaged the bond that was to develop between Harold and the thoughtful classmate who had raised his arm skywards, indicating the only vacant seat next to him.

That boy, Graham William Nash, had arrived in the world on 2nd February 1942. His parents, William and Mary, also lived in Salford, Lancashire, in a small terraced house situated on the corner of Skinner Street but, much like the neighbouring Cavendish Road, residents were still targeted by the ominous drone of the German Heinkel or a Junkers, and many were briefly evacuated during pregnancy to give their newborn a greater chance of survival. Hence, Graham's arrival at 1.50am, in the surroundings of the temporary maternity unit of the Kimberley Hotel, a vast imposing building, a short tram ride away from the glorious Pleasure Beach on Blackpool's Golden Mile, fifty miles to the north-east of their hometown. Nevertheless, despite the lack of emphasis that Hitler placed upon this idyllic northern seaside resort, Graham's sojourn in the shadow of the landmark tower was brief, and life as he knew it truthfully began shortly afterwards, alongside his two sisters Elaine and Sharon, back in the bleak but homely environment of Skinner Road.

'Growing up in Salford,' Graham would later comment in *Wild Tales*, his 2013 autobiography, 'you had to be pretty creative. There wasn't much for kids to do, except play soccer and explore the skeletons of bombed-out houses. And I enjoyed going to church. Not that I was religious, but I was happy to get out of the house and I loved singing in the choir. It was the first time I ever got to sing with people, hearing voices lift, combining in harmony. Man, what a thrill. Even at that age, I learned how to put my voice above the melody.'[1]

Once the friendship between Graham and Harold began to develop, the two began to see the similarities that ran between them. It wasn't just soccer teams and a love of exploring that bonded them.

'We liked the same football teams, the same girls. We'd grease our hair the same way, with Brylcreem. And music – that really joined us at the hip. We would do early morning sing-songs and it just seemed so natural…'[1/2]

The school assembly at Ordsall Board Primary was the first musical opportunity that the two friends had to perform together and, having heard how their two young voices blended, it was even suggested by one of the teachers that they may like to perform 'The Lord Is My Shepherd' as a duo in front of their fellow pupils at the next assembly gathering. Having been used to hearing the school choir reeling off the familiar melody in perfunctory style, with seemingly little thought or effort, it must have been a delight to hear these two youngsters perform, alone on the stage, with a glint in their eyes, singing in natural harmony. With Graham taking the higher register, the fusion of their two voices, even at such an early age, just came so effortlessly and intuitively.

Following up their debut assembly performances, the duo went on to join the school choir and then later made appearances at the Salford Lads

Club, on the corner of St. Ignatius Walk and Coronation Street, a social and recreational club where the twosome would often spend their non-school hours, playing snooker, laughing and harmonising in unbroken voices together. On occasion, they would also participate in a Minstrels act at the club.

In 1953, with their primary education drawing to a close, Graham was offered a place at Salford Grammar school, the result of him achieving a satisfactory pass mark in the 11-plus examinations (a test devised to measure aptitude for junior education and thus placing the "clever ones" into the best education facilities and those "not-so-adept" into a more suitable system). His reward for such an achievement and for the commitment to his schoolwork was that his mother presented him with his first record player. For one with whom music was beginning to make such an impression on his life, this was a particularly notable and memorable moment. In Graham's own words: 'Talk about sacrifices! I have no idea how she managed to scratch up enough to pay for it because we had absolutely no money to speak of.'[1]

Fortunately, for such an inquisitive mind, a neighbour had a number of long-playing records to spin on Graham's new turntable, and that only enhanced his increasing fascination for all things musical. Certainly, such was the financial position of the Nash family that they couldn't justify the additional costs of regular vinyl purchases, a relatively new format for pressing music onto, and an additional hardship for the family was no doubt brought about by the recent incarceration of William, Graham's father, over the dubious ownership of a camera he had recently acquired from a colleague at the foundry where he worked, P.R. Jackson & Co. Rather than own up to the law over whom had supplied him with the camera, which he believed to be a genuine purchase, William took the responsibility upon himself and was duly sentenced to twelve months in prison; an act that, in effect, broke the spirit of the man. Upon his release, one year later, he returned home, devastated, unemployed and shorn of any self-respect, despite the love and support of his family.

Unfortunately, over on Cavendish Street, Harold, as did many like him, failed to achieve the necessary score on his primary exam, and was thus placed into a lower secondary tier at Ordsall Secondary Modern.

'It wasn't because I was thick,' he later claimed. 'I was just bad at exams...'

However, the outcome of these examination results was that the two young friends were parted during subsequent schooling hours, but this only went to strengthen their bond out of term, and as they entered their teenage years the surrounding influences, and those that were gradually beginning to permeate the English youth from across the seas, also began to play a significant part in their development.

For much of the British youth culture of the 1950s, *skiffle music* was becoming a way of life. Having originated in the United States during the early years of the 20<sup>th</sup> century, the result of an amalgamation of influences between jazz, folk and blues, with the occasional dusting of country music as a topping, the key to skiffle was the combination of both manufactured and improvised instrumentation, be they percussive washboards, broom-handled strings or straight-laced jug-blown honks. The first use on record of the term was back in 1925, in the guise of Jimmy O'Bryant and his Chicago Skifflers, but by the arrival of World War II, the term skiffle had pretty much disappeared from American music. It remained a relatively obscure genre, and it may well have stayed largely forgotten if not for its revival in the UK during the early 1950s.

British skiffle grew out of the developing post-war British jazz scene, which saw a move away from swing music towards authentic trad jazz. Amongst these bands were the Bill Bailey Skiffle Group and Ken Colyer's Jazzmen, a band formed by trombonist Chris Barber. The banjo player for the Jazzmen was the Scottish-born Lonnie Donegan. During the interval breaks for the Jazzmen performances, Donegan would take to the stage and sing and play the guitar, with the accompaniment of two other members, usually on washboard and tea-chest bass. The trio played a variety of American folk and blues songs, particularly those derived from the recordings of Lead Belly, in a lively style that emulated American jug bands. These were listed on posters as "skiffle breaks" and soon enough these breaks were as popular as the traditional jazz sets.

After a series of internal disagreements, the result of which was that Ken Colyer left to form a new outfit, the band became Chris Barber's Jazz Band and it was the subsequent release of two skiffle tracks by Barber's Jazz Band, issued on Decca Records under the name of The Lonnie Donegan Skiffle Group, that transformed the fortunes of skiffle in late 1955. Donegan's up-tempo version of Lead Belly's reworking of 'Rock Island Line' was a major hit in 1956, again featuring a prominent washboard as the percussive lead, and it was this recording, along with subsequent Donegan hits (including

'Cumberland Gap', 'Gamblin' Man', 'Jack O' Diamonds'...) that became so ingrained in the psyche of the British youth that they too turned to create skiffle for themselves. By the thousand. After all, how easy was it to place a thimble along the tip of each finger and tap out a rhythm in time? And how much did it cost to drill a broom handle through an old echoey tea chest and run a length of string from top to bottom? Simple. You didn't need to be able to tell the bottom from the top... just pluck.

'We fell in love with the Lonnie Donegan sound,' Allan would later comment for an online *Strange Brew* podcast. 'It gave kids the opportunity to pick up a guitar, learn three chords and sing skiffle. It was a very exciting time.'

By the age of thirteen, in 1955, both Harold and Graham had obtained their first guitars. They took them everywhere over the next couple of years. Practising, sharing chords and bleeding fingertips, hunched over British guitar god Bert Weedon's five-shilling instructional book *Play in a Day* (first published in 1957), all whilst listening to the amazing new sounds emitting from Graham's small record deck.

By January of the following year, a new sound was beginning to take a hold on the music scene, initially over on the distant American shores of the Atlantic but, gradually, one that would creep into the UK via the industrial seaports, lined along the coastline, courtesy of the British sailors returning home from abroad, arms laden with the latest American vinyl or shellac exports. This new sound, when it eventually reached inland to the city of Manchester, would have a profound effect on the two teenagers from Salford.

On 27th January, the new release by a promising young singer out of Memphis, Tennessee was issued on the RCA Victor record label, initially as a 78rpm pressing, and subsequently on 45. The release also made its appearance in UK record stores during May of '56. Elvis Aaron Presley, born in Mississippi but raised as a teenager in Memphis, had cut this latest recording 'Heartbreak Hotel' (actually his sixth 45 single) earlier in January but upon its issue had seen it rocket up to the very pinnacle of the US *Billboard* chart listings. Across the ocean, the May release of the 78/45 also made a significant dent in the chart placings, and in the pockets of many record-buying persons, eventually peaking at the number 2 slot and remaining in the best sellers for an astonishing 22-week run. Needless to say, the impact the record also made on the eagerly listening youngsters off Skinner Street was equally as astonishing.

Graham Nash: 'Wham! – it was as though someone had slugged me. My mouth fell open as Elvis powered through that ferocious thriller…'[1]

From that moment on, they simply absorbed these imported records that made their way into the UK department stores and, occasionally, onto the weak radio signals that hailed from the European airwaves and intermittently crisscrossed the country. Elvis, Little Richard, Jerry Lee Lewis, Buddy Holly, Eddie Cochran, Gene Vincent… an unprecedented tidal wave of new "rock 'n' rollers" as they were being labelled. 'Lucille', 'That'll Be The Day', 'Whole Lotta Shakin'', 'Summertime Blues', 'Be-Bop-a-Lula'. And then there was Lonnie Donegan, still plying his trade for his loyal British audiences, making music that was so good and lively, so much fun, and yet so easy to replicate with a couple of guitars and a homemade orchestra, full of various kitchen utensils.

'Skiffle became rock 'n' roll,' suggests Allan Clarke today. 'And we all wanted to be rock 'n' roll stars.'[3]

Shortly afterwards, good fortune pressed down upon the boys as the man deemed by many to be the founding father of this new rock 'n' roll fad, a chubby kiss-curled 31-year-old hailing from the US state of Michigan, and the man behind such iconic recordings as 'See You Later, Alligator', 'Shake Rattle and Roll' and the groundbreaking quintessential rock 'n' roll recording, 'Rock Around The Clock', made a short stop-off in Manchester, England, playing one night at the Odeon Theatre on his debut UK tour.

Bill Haley and his support band, The Comets, were not typical rock 'n' rollers. Or, at least, not what rock 'n' rollers were perceived to look like. For starters, they weren't particularly young or youthful in appearance, and Haley himself was most certainly not "cool", dressed as he was in his neatly pressed checkered plaid jacket. No, sir, there was no rebellious nature in sight here but, boy, could the man put on a show. He rocked and he rolled and the two young boys, viewing the show from the upstairs balcony, were beside themselves. Not that the tousle-haired twosome were alone in their dreams either. Manchester city centre itself, just a short bus journey away from their hometown of Salford, was full of similar like-minded youngsters, all eager to pick up their affordable Levin and Goya guitars, endlessly strumming the jump from A to E to B7 and back. Shakin', rattlin' and rollin'…

The 700 Club was one of the first coffee bars to spring up in the city of

Manchester, opening in 1958, and it gradually became one of the prime haunts for the city's disgruntled youth population to congregate and hang around in. Before the rise of the 700 Club, and that of its neighbouring counterparts, there had been nowhere in particular, bar the Salford Lads Club or similar such youth establishments such as Addswood or St Georges, where the teenagers could meet regularly. All that changed once the coffee bar scene arrived. You didn't have to drink the smooth or frothy concoction, as there were always other options, and it was a strictly no-alcohol rule in the majority. Several popular locations had one-armed bandit machines or, better still, a jukebox upon which you could play your favourite tunes and share the experience with your friends. It was strictly social. The 2J's, the Astoria, the Bodega, the Raven and the Mogambo soon followed.

For the fifteen-year-old Harold Clarke, and his best friend and singing partner Graham Nash, it was only a matter of time before these locations began to develop into regular haunts on their city travels, but until that point arrived, their regular rehearsals and practices continued in earnest.

'One afternoon, while I was visiting at Clarkie's,' Graham recalled, 'his older brother Frank walked in while we were rehearsing. "I really like the way you sound," he said. "Do you mind if I suggest that you entertain at a club I belong to?"'[1]

Sensing a serious opportunity, the duo swiftly accepted the offer and were soon undertaking their first professional and *paying* gig at the Devonshire Sporting Club, situated over in nearby Higher Broughton.

'It was actually in my brother's sweet shop that my brother heard us,' adds Allan, 'and we then went on to sing 'Cumberland Gap', 'Bring Me A Little Water Sylvie', 'Rock Island Line' and other skiffle songs. We turned up in short trousers and went down a storm! They loved us for our innocence, but I'm sure we sounded diabolical. With 'Rock Island Line', whereas Lonnie Donegan just did a short, snap ending, we just carried on, and got faster and faster and faster! The whole audience was out of breath before we were! We came off stage and the guy (manager Bill Benny) gave us a ten-bob note – and asked us back to play the next weekend! It was incredible...'[5/6/23]

Gradually, and despite their youthful ages, the bookings began to start coming in and the boys bestowed upon themselves their first stage name: The Two Teens.

Graham: 'Kids our age could play the clubs as long as we weren't drinking, and my mother would occasionally chaperone Allan and me to make sure that was the case. We got a lot of jobs and our price slowly went up to two pounds! The big time! And it was to us. Playing music in clubs till two or three in the morning.'[1/2]

'Because we played and sang in nightclubs, we attracted all the girls,' adds Allan. 'So, this made us a target for rival gangs, which was a little frightening. We'd get beat up a lot, mainly because other gang members were jealous of what me and Graham were doing.

'We also did a lot of normal things, like go to church dances. The best dances were at the Catholic churches because all the best chicks were Catholic!'[2]

'Allan and I were besotted with girls,' laughs Graham. 'We weren't cool, but we hoped we had *something* going…'

It was at one of these Catholic social events, this time held at the nearby St Clements School, that the duo first heard the incredible harmony vocals of one of America's newest musical sensations. It took their breath away. Even more than the girls did that night.

Born two years apart, brothers Isaac Donald and Philip Jason Everly had grown up in the south-western US state of Tennessee, both blessed with a natural harmony pairing that, more often than not, only siblings can appreciate the true benefits of. Having relocated to the musical epicentre of country music, Nashville, in their mid-teens, the duo had secured a recording contract with Cadence Records in 1957, issuing their first release for the label shortly afterwards. 'Bye Bye Love', recorded at the RCA Studios in the famed Music City, became an instant smash hit, achieving Top 10 status in both the US and UK charts. From the driving acoustic guitar introduction through to the catchy hook line, and down to Don's lead vocal and Phil's oh-so-sweet high harmony, this was a record made for the ears of the young Two Teens. This was what two-part harmony was *really* about.

Enamoured by what he heard, Graham immediately set about purchasing all of the brothers' records that he could locate, studiously poring over their intertwining voices, adding a third harmony on top where he could see how it would fit in.

'Don and Phil were my teachers,' he summarises. 'I'd listen to their songs on the phonograph and that's where a lot of my feelings for three-part harmony came from.'[2]

Taking their newfound passion to their hearts, and into their performances, the duo began adding Everly tunes into their expanding repertoire – 'Bye Bye Love', 'When Will I Be Loved', 'Wake Up Little Susie' – even winning local talent contests along the way. However, by this stage, Allan, as he was now calling himself (having dropped "Harold"), had left secondary education and had taken on his first full-time position in an electrical engineering supply store, where his social circle was broadened considerably. Inevitably, he began to mix with other like-minded souls, and it was only a matter of time before new friends began to gather around. Opportunities to spend time with Graham gradually became fewer and far between. New acquaintances, new interests. He even took on the lead vocalist role with another local skiffle band, The Riverside Rockets, and for a number of months the pair saw little of each other. According to Graham in his *Wild Tales*, he felt abandoned by his singing partner and had 'no one to sing with for months.' Nevertheless, this parting of the ways didn't last for more than a summer and soon enough, after reconnecting one day in the street and rekindling their mutual love and respect, the duo opted to get back together and resume their harmony partnership, renaming themselves Ricky (Allan) and Dane (Graham) Young – a tip of the hat to Don and Phil Everly – and taking on more regular bookings around the city.

Shortly afterwards, Graham, having left school with six O-level passses, also took up a working position at the same company as Allan, Alexander Kenyon & Co., an engineering firm based in Ardwick, five miles away from Salford, on the opposite side of Manchester. This wasn't his first job, and he had previously been employed alongside Allan at a nearby cloth mill, but this new role cemented their close friendship further. Besides, such a responsibility helped bring in the money that was badly needed in the Nash household, his father still suffering the mental torture and lack of esteem following his incarceration. The supplementary income brought in by Ricky and Dane became crucial to the family's very existence.

On 24th November 1958, having won a recent qualifying round, the duo entered the regional finals of a popular *Star Search* talent competition, held at the vast Ardwick Hippodrome Theatre, along the Stockport Road in Manchester. For the winners, the stakes were high; direct passage to the grand finals and the opportunity to appear on a prestigious television variety show. Also appearing on the bill that night, aiming to win the favour of the judging audience, were a number of other Lancashire hopefuls, including Manchester's very own Freddie Garrity and the Liverpool-born Ronald Wycherley, both of whom would achieve far greater fame later on in their careers. Likewise, the same future beckoned for a bunch of scruffy Liverpool teenagers who had also made the journey across to the Manchester venue, performing under the name of Johnny and The Moondogs. Reportedly, they impressed all who saw them but had to leave before the evening ended, thus voiding their chances of winning, as the last public transport back home to Merseyside was scheduled to depart. In addition, the show was judged by the results of a "clapometer" which recorded the volume of applause for each act, during which the competitors gave a brief resume of their performance. Johnny and The Moondogs missed this, as they had to leave the theatre, and thus the applause would have been muted somewhat. Their rhythm guitarist, a short-sighted, sarcastic teenager from the Woolton district, picked up a guitar by the stage door as he left the building and, regardless of ownership, took it home with him, commenting in his strong scouse accent that 'the trip wasn't a total loss…'

Performing a two-part harmony rendition of Conway Twitty's 'It's Only Make Believe', Ricky and Dane Young brushed aside much of the competition with ease, their voices tuned together as one.

Their stocks rising, the duo began to widen their appeal by taking on gigs further afield than those that had locally sustained them up until now. The 2J's (later renamed the Oasis), the Three Coins, the New Rialto and later venues such as the Twisted Wheel, the Ritz and the Bolton Palais, or even venturing down south where they once performed at the legendary 2i's club in Soho. Performing a set that was mostly filled with Everly Brothers harmonies, and with the new decade commencing, Allan and Graham also saw fit to rename their act. After briefly toying with The Levins, named after Graham's Swedish-made archtop acoustic guitar, they settled on The Guyatones, a name deriving from the electric guitars that both had recently acquired. Often appearing alongside another local band, Jerry Lee and The Staggerlees, the newly electrified pairing began to develop their increasing repertoire further. The Staggerlees themselves were a relatively new band at that time, but one that was building up a solid reputation around the Manchester music scene, due no doubt to the developing abilities of the two guitarists in the band; Eric Stewart and Vic Farrell on their Rossetti Lucky 7 guitars. Such contacts would play an important role for all as their careers moved ever upward, and the context of playing within the realms of a full working band also became all the more evident.

One afternoon, The Guyatones were booked to play a set at the Bodega, a basement club located opposite the Royal Exchange in Manchester. Following the conclusion of their performance, a collection of Everly, Buddy Holly and Gene Vincent covers, Graham was approached by Joe Abrams, a young drummer in another Manchester rock 'n' roll group, Johnny Peters and The Jets.

'You and Allan are really good,' suggested the impressed youngster. 'But you need a band.'

Indicating that they would have far greater appeal if their impressive harmonies were augmented by the full guitar, bass and drum accompaniment, Abrams went on to suggest not only himself as the drummer they needed but also the talents of a fellow Jets member, Pete Bocking, on lead guitar.

'You *need* a Bocking,' was his vague description. 'He can play every solo you've ever heard. Buddy Holly, Gene Vincent, Little Richard…'

Inquisitive enough to follow the suggestion, Allan and Graham duly met up with the mysterious Bocking, a teenager who, despite his rapidly advancing hair loss and chain-smoking, more than made up for any shortfall with his dextrous abilities and the fact that he owned a Fender Stratocaster, *the* dream guitar for any budding Manchester musician back then.

'We decided to audition this guy,' laughs Allan, 'and when he arrived at Graham's house, he opened this guitar case and, lo and behold, there was this Fender Stratocaster inside, and my tongue just lolled from my mouth! Graham and I could never have afforded a guitar like that in a million years, but this guy played every solo that was possible. Buddy Holly, the Everly Brothers…'[7]

Agreeing to front this new band, with a third ex-Jets member John "Butch" Mepham filling in on bass (after the quartet went to watch him play at the Empress Ballroom in Stockport), Allan and Graham signed on and the line-up duly rechristened itself as The Fourtones or, on occasion, as either Ricky Young and The Fabulous Fourtones or Ricky and Dane and The Fourtones. For at least two performances, held at the Raven Club in Stockport and the Club Creole over in Wilmslow, they were even billed as Ricky Young, Graham Nash and The Fabulous Fourtones. A sixth member, and yet another ex-Jet, lead guitarist Derek Quinn, who later achieved success with Freddie and The Dreamers, also performed with the line-up during this period, although membership was often fluid, with both George Wilcowski and Keith Bates sitting in on the drum stool at times, and Terry Morton replacing Quinn on guitar.

Despite the responsibilities of full-time employment, either at the Alexander Kenyon engineering firm, or later (as in Graham's case) at the postal office or the Toggery clothing boutique, the music was still clearly the prime focus for the two teenagers, and none more so than on one particular evening. On 22nd April 1960, the golden voices of Don and Phil Everly graced the stage for two performances at the Free Trade Hall in Manchester during their debut UK tour. Supported by The Five Dallas Boys, Cherry Wainer, The Freddy Lloyd Five, Danny Hunter, The Flee-Rekkers and Lance Fortune, the two brothers, backed by the late Buddy Holly's band, The Crickets, ran through a succession of their popular hits, including 'Wake Up Little Susie', 'Bye Bye Love', 'All I Have To Do Is Dream', 'Be-Bop-a-Lula', 'Cathy's Clown' and "Til I Kissed You', before finishing up their short set with the irrepressible 'Bird Dog'. Needless to say, Allan and Graham were in the audience that night to see their heroes in the flesh. Allan: 'We had heard that they were on at the Manchester Free Trade Hall and Graham and I decided it was the most important thing in our lives to get to see these guys, so we queued up and we got tickets. We saw the show, which was absolutely fantastic, and we then decided that later on we'd try and find the hotel where they were staying. One of the hotels in Manchester was the Grand Hotel [the Midland Hotel] where all the big stars used to stay, so we went and stood outside and we were there for about three and a half hours. Eventually, about one o'clock in the morning, The Everly Brothers came walking up the road! They stopped and we chatted with them for about half an hour. We said, "We're two kids who love your stuff and we more or less do all of your songs on stage," and they told us to keep on doing it and one day, you never know, you may make it…'[6]

'One thing we talked about that night,' recalled Graham, 'was writing songs. The Everly Brothers already had a stash of fabulous material to their credit, so obviously Allan and I were going to give it a try. They told us not to overthink it, just let it rip. A few months later, we finally got up our nerve.'

June 1961 saw The Fourtones backing up star attraction Lance Fortune, a UK Top 10 artist from the Larry Parnes stable of performers and, as demand continued to grow, so the bookings increased. That same month they appeared at the Blackpool Festival of Pop, supporting Eden Kane, held at the Empress Ballrooms in the same seaside resort where Graham had been born. The following month they were at the Locarno Ballroom in nearby Sale, appearing on the same bill as Shane Fenton and The Fentones, Jimmy

Crawford and the increasingly popular Freddie and The Dreamers. Such was his musical ability that the latter group also featured Derek Quinn on stage with them that day.

By now, the Manchester music scene was becoming a thriving hive of activity. New rock 'n' roll bands were forming in virtually every street, alleyway and coffee house across the city. In as much as the Liverpool "Mersey Beat" was developing, thirty-five miles to the west, with the sounds of Gerry and The Pacemakers, The Remo Four, Rory Storm and The Hurricanes, The Big Three and the recently renamed Johnny and The Moondogs heading the stampede, so the Manchester sound was pounding out its vibrant heartbeat amongst the youth of the northern English metropolis. Not only were The Fourtones now leading the way, with the notable support of the Alan Arnison Publicity Agency promoting them, but they were accompanied *en route* by bands such as The Deltas, Ricky Shaw and The Dolphins, The Crestas, The Emperors of Rhythm and The Dakotas, with names such as Freddie Garrity, Wayne Fontana and the ever-youthful Peter Noone each finding their foothold. Meanwhile, it cannot be underestimated how much The Fourtones, now holding down a Monday night residency at the Bodega and a weekly Wednesday spot at the 2J's club, with and without the Ricky and Dane credit, were fast developing into one of the city's hottest figurehead bands, and their set was becoming extremely tight and proficient.

'We used to include quite a bit of Everly Brothers material,' recalled Derek Quinn, 'and we got quite a bit of attention as we used to do the Everlys' version of 'Lucille' when most people were doing the Little Richard version.'[4]

Other popular and current US hits, such as 'Stay', 'Anna', 'Poison Ivy' and 'Mr Moonlight' were also added to the performances, and it was only a matter of time before they transferred their abilities onto tape, and subsequently onto record. That event finally took place during the spring of 1962 when the band, by then consisting of Ricky and Dane Young (Allan and Graham), Pete Bocking, Derek Quinn, "Butch" Mepham and drummer Keith Bates booked a session, according to Graham in *Wild Tales*, at a small recording studio above the Johnny Roadhouse Music store in Oxford Road, Manchester. "Butch" Mepham, however, recalls the location differently, stating it as being above a Catling-Hadley office and typewriter store in nearby Princess Street, whilst a further source, Alan Lawson's excellently researched bible, *It Happened in Manchester (1958-1965),* suggested it may have even taken place down Regent Road, over in Salford.

'I'm certain it wasn't the Johnny Roadhouse Music shop, but I honestly can't remember exactly where it was…' added an equally unsure Derek Quinn, when questioned by this author, shortly before his passing in 2020. 'I always thought it was in Salford that we did the recording but wasn't sure.' The jury is out.

Nevertheless, the band taped four songs that day – a cover of The Everly Brothers' 'Crying In The Rain', 'Wimoweh' (a South African Zulu chant, popularised in the 1950s by folkies Pete Seeger and The Weavers and recently, a Top 10 hit in the UK charts for Karl Denver), a gentle thirty-second guitar instrumental entitled 'The End', credited to Bocking, Mepham and Quinn, and, of most significance, one of the very first known compositions credited to Clarke and Nash; 'Learn How To Twist'. There have also been reports to suggest that a cover of 'Wayward Wind', originally a US hit for Gogi Grant back in 1956, but more recently covered by both Gene Vincent and The Everly Brothers, was attempted, but there remains no aural evidence to back this up. Only one set of acetate discs were seemingly produced from this recording date, one for each band member, and little has been heard of this session since, but it gave the band its first taste of recording; the "feel" of running through a take and then of hearing the playback.

Certainly, listening to their faithful rendition of 'Crying in The Rain' almost sixty years after the event, with Allan and Graham harmonising closely together, only goes to highlight the enthusiasm that they must have come away with, acetate gripped firmly in their hands. And then to cut one of their own compositions, one of their very first, was another reason to feel elated. Although somewhat lyrically naïve, the recording of 'Learn How To Twist' still maintains a simplistic charm to this day.

*"You all know how to rock 'n' roll*
*You all know how to do the stroll*
*But baby, you gotta learn how to twist*
*It's not hard, it's easy to learn*
*All you gotta do is twist and turn*
*Oh baby, you gotta learn how to twist"*

'Learn How To Twist'
Music and Lyrics by Allan Clarke and Graham Nash

However, just a matter of months after hearing the results from that first session, and despite a strong and increasing following around the local music scene, the band disintegrated, simply fading away after a crash along Whitworth Street in Manchester, involving the group's van, rendered them without the use of any transport. In addition to that, promises by several record companies had led nowhere, no auditions and no deals, and that was getting the band members down. The crash was simply the final nail in the coffin. Their last performance together, held at the Three Coins Club in Fountain Street, Manchester (a venue owned by the then-popular, but more recently vilified, disc jockey Jimmy Savile), was on 28th July 1962, the day after bass player "Butch" Mepham's 21st birthday.

'For me, that group was in a league of its own,' summarises Mepham. 'Anybody can sound good on record, but it's if you can do it night after night on stage. Pete Bocking was absolutely brilliant, and as for the vocals… we could leave anybody standing!' 4

The late Derek "Lek" Leckenby, another talented musician who would later find fame as the lead guitarist for Manchester's Herman's Hermits, also recalled how impressive and important to the Manchester scene The Fourtones were: 'I had seen a lot of local bands before I thought of playing myself. Then I started going to the 2J's when the evening session was jazz, plus the Fourtones. My interest in playing music was started by watching The Fourtones. They had the best guitar player, Pete Bocking, and the best singers, Allan and Graham. I learned from them. A wonderful group…' 4

# CHAPTER TWO

## "LIKE NO PLACE ON EARTH..."

Eric John Haddock made his entrance into the world on the 3rd of February 1943, in Stockport, a large town situated seven miles outside of Manchester's city centre, sitting on the borderlines between Cheshire and Lancashire. To many, the town was perhaps most renowned for being the source of the River Mersey, although it too failed to escape the focus of the Luftwaffe bombing of the 1940s, and much of the population, including the two-year-old Eric, would have taken shelter in the now-famous tunnels, dug deep into the banks of the mighty river, that protected them from the bombing raids.

Born to Eric and Vina Haddock, Eric Jr grew up locally, although his father left the family home whilst he was still at an early age and he was brought up instead by a loving stepfather, Mike, who became a doting parent to the young boy and instilled a love of music in him. His mother, Vina, ran a traditional public hostelry, the Queen's Head in Little Underbank, and kept family life busy. Like his two sisters, Eric attended the local Vernon Park School where he excelled in the weightlifting and athletics programmes, winning trophies in various events, whilst also developing a lifelong passion for following Manchester City Football Club. However, he left school at the early age of fifteen, becoming a toolmaker in order to bring income into the family household, the result of his stepfather, Mike, sadly passing away. Nevertheless, Mike's passion for music remained in his stepson...

By his mid-teens, and inspired by the instrumental music of the increasingly popular Shadows, Eric had purchased his first guitar but soon switched to playing bass as he began to jam along with other local musicians. Rather than the customary four-stringed instrument, he pioneered the use of a six-string version, a Fender Bass IV, imported from America. In his own words, the guitar 'cost almost as much as a terraced house in Manchester,' and he took on a variety of additional jobs, including a brief spell as a rat-catcher, to pay for it.

By the turn of the 1960s, Eric was competent enough on his chosen instrument to start playing in public and, after regular practice sessions held in the family front room with a friend of his, guitarist Johnny Murphy, the duo began to put together a band. It was also around this time that Eric changed his surname, dropping "Haddock" and adopting the stage name of "Haydock" in its place.

'We got a lad named Tommy Turner and a singer called Harry Morris, and that was the basis of the band. We used to rehearse in the Farmer's Arms in Brinnington before we started appearing in public.'[4]

Initially starting as Kirk Daniels and The Dominators, the band soon rebranded themselves as Kirk Daniels and The Deltas and began picking up regular bookings, care of the popular Alan Arnison Agency. Most performances took place in and around the Stockport and Manchester areas; the Birch Park Palace, the Raven Club, St Bernadette's Theatre Club, Accrington's Conservative Club, the Tipperary Club in Reddish, the House of Bamboo, the Three Coins... although the occasional journey across county to Liverpool was also eagerly accepted.

However, as their reputation grew, so did the bizarre stage antics. Having fallen in with a local management figure, Arthur Fee, who provided them with regular transport, the band also willingly took on board his ideas when it came to their appearance on stage. Thus, was created The Flintstone Five.

'He had the idea of dressing us up in caveman outfits, with the clubs and stuff,' recounted Johnny Murphy. 'We used to do exactly the same set as when we were The Deltas, but people never seemed to realise...'[4]

Nevertheless, despite the requirements to don a tiger skin each night and prance around like Fred and Barney, the bookings increased to bigger and better venues, with establishments such as the Higher Broughton Assembly Rooms and the Palladium Variety Club in Collyhurst now appearing regularly on their schedules, as did a weekly residency at the Hi-Fi Club on Richmond Street. Then, one night in 1962, as Eric was walking along the

Cheetham Hill Road in North Manchester, he heard a sound emitting from the nearby La Ronde Club that caught his attention.

'The La Ronde was a wonderfully dark and atmospheric place,' he later commented. 'It was a great club. That night, I was walking past it and thought, "That's the nearest thing I've ever heard to the Everly Brothers!"'

Inside the newly refurbished, 600-strong capacity venue that night, performing to the teenage crowd on the small stage, were Ricky and Dane Young, harmonising together with their familiar Everly Brothers setlist. Having parted company with their former Fourtones bandmates, Allan and Graham were now back to performing sets as a duo. Two voices, two guitars. Once they'd finished their short set that night they were approached on the stage by Eric Haydock, and once Eric had introduced himself, they got talking. Within a matter of days, Allan and Graham had agreed to join up with Eric and his Delta bandmates, forming a multi-talented gathering, with their combined performances now divided into three differing factions. Firstly, the full Deltas band would play a short set, performing their standards and the rock 'n' roll hits of the day. Then the acoustic Ricky and Dane Young personas would take to the stage, running through their Everlys repertoire before, finally, The Flintstone Five, featuring the entire cast (clearly more than five), closed the show, all dressed up and bashing it out with hammer, tongs and clubs. It made for a truly bizarre experience.

'During this Deltas phase we found black American R&B to be very translatable to our particular blend of rock 'n' roll,' Allan remembered. 'We added Coasters stuff, Chuck Berry, The Zodiacs and some standard ballads.'[2]

One of their first notable showings together took place at the Manchester Festival of Music, held on the bank holiday Monday of 6th August. A prestigious local event, held at the Platt Fields Park in Fallowfield, the show drew large audiences in to see the headlining acts for the day, all compered by the popular BBC radio host Brian Matthew, presenter of such shows as *Saturday Club* and *Easy Beat*. Established names in jazz, such as Acker Bilk, George Melly and Ken Colyer, topped the bill, but the support came from a selection of chosen Manchester rock 'n' roll bands, including The Deltas, now with Graham and Allan in the ranks. It remains undocumented as to whether the tiger-skin Flintstones outfits made an appearance on the day, although, by now, the line-up within the band was fluctuating as new members replaced old, and the talent pool began to increase.

Coming in on lead guitar was a seventeen-year-old by the name of

Victor Winston Farrell. A local Manchester lad, born on the 8th of May 1945, Vic had spent a number of his early teenage years playing in bands around the city whilst also attending Openshaw Technical High School. As a member of Jerry Lee and The Staggerlees, he shared frontline guitar duties with a fellow Openshaw student named Eric Stewart (who, in turn, would become a principal member of Manchester hit-makers The Mindbenders and, much later on, 10cc). However, at Eric's suggestion, the young guitarist had changed his stage persona to become Vic Steele, a name taken from the popular 1950s TV detective series, *Shadow Squad*.

'My dad had bought me a Spanish guitar when I was about ten,' Vic reminisces today, 'and I used to listen to Radio Luxembourg. There you got all the current hits, and a lot of American records. I was influenced by Buddy Holly, Chuck Berry and Ricky Nelson, although, to me, Elvis was the King. He revolutionised the music business. He was one of the reasons I started playing rock 'n' roll.

'I remember we (Jerry Lee and The Staggerlees) did an audition at Hulme Hippodrome. The van picked Eric Stewart and me up from school and we went along. Outside, we saw two lads struggling with a big bass amp and they turned out to be John Lennon and Paul McCartney! They failed the audition like we did but the chap holding it was quite impressed by us. While we were packing away our gear, he came over and asked us where we were the following day, obviously expecting us to name some big club or ballroom. Without thinking, Eric innocently said, "Oh, we'll be at school!"'[4/76]

That band, in time, developed into The Emperors of Rhythm, who became a popular attraction on the Manchester circuit, known as "the north's best-dressed group", in their matching purple blazers, white shirts, grey checked trousers and white shoes, topped off with silver bow ties. Unfortunately, despite getting a series of regular bookings at many of the top venues across the city, and winning numerous battle-of-the-band style competitions held at the Three Coins club, along with an audition for the BBC radio show *Here We Go Again*, they simply dissolved as the various members drifted away to join new bands. At one point, in an attempt to keep the act alive, Vic offered a role in the Emperors to bass player Eric Haydock, but when that failed to materialise, Vic jumped ship himself and threw his weight, and that of his mighty new white Fender Jazzmaster, in with the Deltas, although, as Vic was later to comment, the Emperors' name did remain in place for a short period too.

'The first practices took place over the Wimpy Bar in Oxford Road in the evenings and on Sundays, and after three or four weeks, we started gigging under the name of Ricky and Dane Young and The Emperors of Rhythm, at the local dance halls, youth clubs, and coffee dance clubs. We soon got a regular Wednesday spot at the Oasis and built up a small following…'

Donald Gordon Rathbone, born on 7th October 1937 (later publicity showed it as 1942), was another who hailed from the dividing county lines, born and raised in the nearby affluent town of Wilmslow, Cheshire, eleven miles south of Manchester's busy Lancashire nightlife. His parents, Robert and Lily, also had one other son, George, born two years before Don, and Robert had followed the trade of stonemasonry as a family tradition, going back to his own grandfather, to keep an income arriving on the doorstep. He also undertook work as a registrar for the local community. Don, however, had other ideas.

Having left the nearby Wycliffe Avenue School, aged just fifteen, he took on a position at Cleggs department store in Wilmslow, whilst undertaking his other passion for drumming. An earlier attempt at piano lessons, alongside his elder brother, had not been fruitful and he subsequently responded to an advertisement he spotted in the *Alderley and Wilmslow Advertiser* in November of 1959. A local band, The Electrons, were seeking a replacement for their original drummer, Roy Tomkins, and, impressed with what they saw and heard, Don was duly offered the position. They even used his grandmother's house on Manchester Road, Wilmslow for Sunday band rehearsals.

Interestingly, The Electrons' previous incarnation, The Cestrian Skiffrocks, had appeared on the same *Star Search* stage as Ricky and Dane Young at Manchester's Hippodrome theatre twelve months earlier.

*The Electrons: They're cool Daddyo, real cool. The way they hep that swingin' jive is solid man. The livin' end.*

*Alderley & Wilmslow Advertiser*

Working as a stonemason, Robert Rathbone was able to lend Don his spacious business van, normally utilised for shifting heavy granite blocks, in order to help transport the group's equipment around from venue to venue. Clearly a beneficial factor, Don remained with the Wilmslow-based line-up for the following two years, playing his Ludwig kit with a passion, performing regular shows around the surrounding circuit, including the 800-capacity Yew Tree in Wythenshawe, the Regal Ballroom in Alderley Edge (appearing on the same bill as The Staggerlees on one occasion) and Wilmslow's Rex Ballroom. Unfortunately, despite several rave reviews, they never quite reached the same levels of success or acclaim as many of their Manchester contemporaries. Subsequently, it came to be that Don, finally tiring of the limited success that The Electrons were seeing, briefly signed on with another local band, Cliff Bowes and The Arrows, before also committing to The Deltas/Flintstones/Emperors amalgamation. What would become The Hollies' first line-up of Clarke, Nash, Haydock, Steele and Rathbone was now in place.

Early September 1962 saw Ricky and Dane Young, along with Fred and The Flintstone Five performing at the Bodega club. Shortly afterwards, as the new line-up settled in and got to know each other, the band changed its name once more, albeit briefly on this occasion. For no more than a month or two, they became known as The Dominators of Rhythm, occasionally with Ricky and Dane, sometimes without. But then, as the festive season fast approached, during the first week of December 1962, the band made a series of appearances at one of their regular haunts, the 2J's club, a favoured venue that too had recently taken up a new name; the Oasis. History suggests that their first show back on the newly christened stage was held on Sunday, 2nd December 1962.

Graham Nash recalls, 'Graham Clegg, who was the emcee [of the Oasis that night] grabbed us just before we went on. "I'm about to introduce you," he said. "What's the name of the band?" Good question. "What about The Deadbeats?" Don said, taking a cue from the family business. Clarkie, thankfully, didn't agree. "We're not Deadbeats," he said. "We're more fun than that."[1]

A brief discussion ensued before someone, and no one is quite sure who it was (although Vic Steele later indicated it was Allan), suggested they rename themselves after one of their favourite singers. That choice, accompanied by the simple fact it was the festive season and the red-berried decorations were in evidence all around, consolidated the snap decision. Informed of the choice, Clegg then stepped up to the microphone. 'Why don't you give a nice round of applause to a local band,' he announced. 'The Hollies!' History was made.

Vic: 'It was December 1962, approaching Christmas, when Allan came up with the name The Hollies. Initially, the band went out as Ricky and Dane Young and The Hollies. Ricky and Dane were, of course, Allan and Graham. The thing about The Hollies that probably set us apart from the other Manchester groups at the time was Allan and Graham's unique vocal harmony blend and the backing that was more like Chuck Berry rather than the Shadows style which was popular at the time.'[9]

However, these appearances also marked the end of their working association with the Alan Arnison booking agency.

Arnison: 'I had known them through The Fourtones period, and Kirk Daniels and everything else and they were obviously a very successful group, but they wouldn't keep still! They were forever changing personnel and it became impossible to keep up. One day I was told they'd changed their line-up again and were going to call themselves The Hollies, but by then I'd had enough, and we didn't represent them anymore…' [4]

The following week saw The Hollies reappear once again at the Oasis, performing on Tuesday the 5th and then again, the following Sunday, the 9th, on both occasions billed as either "Manchester's Latest Rockers" or "Manchester's Newest Rockers".

---

WEDNESDAY 5th DECEMBER
Evening
Manchester's Latest Rockers
THE HOLLIES

"The Beatles are coming"

---

As can be detected from the promotional flyer that circulated in advance, the focus was more on the fact that the day before their third appearance was due to take place, another popular band was scheduled to appear at the same venue. Once known as Johnny and The Moondogs, and now calling themselves The Beatles, this Liverpudlian four-piece band were making a return visit to the club, having first played there themselves at the start of the year when they were being publicised as "Polydor's Great Recording Stars!" For this, their third visit that year, having recently signed to the Parlophone label, and having just acquired a new drummer, the printed flyer that circulated simply read "Hit Recorders of 'Love Me Do'". With their debut 45 release on the EMI subsidary label still ascending to its peak UK chart position of number 17 at the time, The Beatles certainly were coming, and the Oasis was keen to announce it. It is also worth noting that, for this appearance, The Beatles were being supported by The Pete Bocking Six.

What was perhaps most apparent to those who attended the shows during that particular week was the varying differences, clearly laid out before them on the stage, between the Liverpool and Manchester bands. The persona that differed between the youth of the two cities was all too evident. Liverpudlians were often overly brash, some may say aggressive. They were loud and proud. The city had a lot higher unemployment rate than its inland neighbour and the abrasive nature of its youth reflected that. By contrast, the Manchester teen was more worldly-wise, cosmopolitan in his/her approach to life. Chalk and cheese – but both had the music to fall back on, and even though The Beatles, overseen by the polite and professional image of their manager, Brian Epstein, had restyled themselves from scruffy, leather-clad rockers to suited and booted, loveable mop-tops (well, almost), The Hollies, now decked out in leather themselves, were far more practised and "friendly" in their stage mannerisms.

Eric Haydock later added his own perspective on the scene: 'The Mersey bands tended to be more raucous than the Manchester ones. They had a strong, macho, Teddy Boy type of image, whereas the Manchester bands were more glitzy. Club owners would tell us that if we got the women in, we would get the men and they would book us again. [11]

Vic Steele also recalled that 'our stage gear was black leather jeans, leather tops and black polo neck jumpers, which were very hot on stage.'[9]

Certainly, no one could deny The Beatles' immense, uncontrollable talent, boiling underneath, but the Manchester quintet used stage patter and appeared "likeable" to the watching audiences. The Hollies made you dance and smile. The Beatles just blew your socks off with their raw energy. Not that The Hollies were immune to turning up the volume themselves. Watching audiences were often struck by the power and exuberance they delivered during live performances, with one onlooker later commenting,

'They came on and knocked shit out of the gear. It was so loud and dynamic, and the sound was wonderful because it was custom-built equipment with plenty of amplification. Vic hit some massive chords and bang; they were away. It was stunning. Their set was crystal clear, with everything – power, volume and clarity.' [4]

'We threw away the echo chambers, which were the mainstay of most groups,' remembered Vic. 'With Don, Eric's bass and myself, we had a powerful rhythm section and of course with Allan and Graham we had an absolutely unique vocal blend.'

'The sound we made onstage, the energy that came pouring off us, was fantastic,' Graham added. 'And our vocals pulled everything together in a tidy package. The songs we did then weren't anything special. Every band in England played the same basic set, but the Hollies managed to give them a unique sound…'

'Initially it was a mixture of Buddy Holly and the Everly Brothers stuff,' continued Vic, 'with the odd early Elvis or Lonnie Donegan number. But we were never fixed to a particular set. I can remember one time when the audience called out for 'Sun Arise', which was a big hit at the time. We quickly sorted out the chords and Allan sang it, and it was a pretty good version too! We later played the odd Beatles number as well, 'Please Please Me'. Graham was a big Beatles fan.' [18/76]

Graham: 'We didn't have that same kind of power [as The Beatles]. We could put on a damn good show but hadn't hit our sweet spot.' [1]

That said, by this stage, the "Fab Four" were now "professional" musicians, in as much as this *was* their day job. By comparison, The Hollies were still working their positions with their respective employers, be it tinker, tailor, engineer or toolmaker. Yet, with the hard-earned money that they were now pulling in as a group, it was surely only a matter of time. They were certainly earning their wages, spending hours and hours behind the wheel of Don's father's van, driving wherever there was a paying gig in the north of the country. Not getting home until 3am, then promptly up and out to the day job at 9.00. Stoke, Blackpool, Rochdale, Tamworth…

Allan recalls: 'We sometimes had to hire a driver to take us, and he would get more money than we did. We went on like that until we met Alan Cheetham, who became our first manager. We were getting well known in the area, in direct competition with The Beatles, and when they started having hits, the managers from down south thought they ought to go where the action was and started signing everyone up.' [12]

A fellow Mancunian, Alan Cheetham, had been associating with the band for a while and was partly responsible for helping put together the band's impressive new sound system, whilst also allowing the band to rehearse in his father's factory. Having been an integral part of the Manchester music scene, albeit from a non-performing agency role, he knew how good this particular line-up was and saw their potential. Gradually, Cheetham began to step into a managerial capacity for them. Rumours also abound that he almost joined forces with Brian Epstein in co-managing The Beatles, during Epstein's early interest in the quartet. His relationship with the Liverpool businessman didn't run smoothly, however, and he reportedly turned away from any potential partnership, instead opting to take his management skills to The Hollies and later to The Merseybeats.

Surprisingly, for one of the final shows of the year, the popular annual Christmas Eve Party Night, held at the Memorial Hall in Northwich, they remained billed as "New Recording Artists: Ricky and Dane Young – Plus The Emperors of Rhythm", as, presumably, the new band name wasn't deemed sufficient enough to generate additional ticket sales as yet but, as 1962 faded into the history books, and 1963 settled in, the gigs continued. The workload and the commitment were incessant, but it was gradually starting to pay off. At one point during this period, the new quintet booked a room at the rear of a nearby Manchester pub, and put four or five songs down onto a demo tape to use as a tool to promote themselves further. Whilst no records survive as to the actual content on the tape, Vic recalls, 'we did it in a pub, midweek. We rented the room and a guy came along [to record us]. I think it was a double track machine, but we just did it on a single track. It was really no more than a demo, just to say, "we're the Hollies". I don't remember what the songs were.'

On 26th January, The Hollies and The Beatles shared a bill at the King's Hall in Stoke-on-Trent, and word began to spread around the country that the Manchester music scene and that of the surrounding areas was something special.

Eric: 'The north was a long way away from London in those days, so we felt we needed a manager in the south as well. This guy Tommy Sanderson came to see us because everybody was looking for a northern group.'[12]

Pianist, producer and wannabe music impresario Tommy Sanderson was a former plugger for Francis, Day & Hunter music publishers, and was currently venturing into music management alongside singer Bernard Jewry (aka Shane Fenton). Acting as an agent on behalf of The Hollies, Tommy in turn alerted Ron Richards, who currently worked as a staff assistant at Parlophone Records to George Martin, who was The Beatles' new record producer. In fact, Richards himself had played a crucial role in the sessions leading up to the release of their debut 45. Ron agreed to make the long journey up from London to watch The Hollies in action, taking the opportunity to spend a full week in the north with Tommy, scouring the clubs for talent. At stake was the chance of a recording contract, and a professional career.

On 3rd February, the quintet packed the van and headed off along the A580, driving the thirty-five miles from Manchester to the city that spread itself along the banks of the River Mersey. And the venue where they were scheduled to play that evening? The mecca of the newly christened "Merseybeat" sound. Home of The Beatles, Gerry and The Pacemakers, The Merseybeats and numerous others; the Cavern Club, Mathew Street, Liverpool, where they were appearing at the Cavern's "Rhythm & Blues Marathon", alongside The Merseybeats, The Fourmost, The Swinging Blue Jeans, Kingsize Taylor and The Dominoes... and the Fabs once again.

'The Cavern was like no place on earth,' summarises Graham. 'The club was a cellar. Literally underground. No ventilation to speak of. Condensation streamed down the walls; circles of water pooled on the floor. Filled with dense cigarette smoke…'[1]

And yet it appears that not everyone was as enthusiastic about the famed cellarful of noise as the regular crowds, those who poured in every night and every day, breathing in the smell of stale sweat and fumes.

'The Cavern was a stinking filthy hole,' recalled Eric Haydock. 'Above it, they used to store vegetables. There weren't any freezers in those days, so the cabbage water ran down the walls into the Cavern. It was absolutely disgusting.'[10]

Nevertheless, their appearance in Mathew Street was to play a crucial part in the rise to success, as amongst the audience that day as they performed on the tiny stage underneath the central Cavern arch was Ron Richards.

'The walls were certainly dripping, and I couldn't believe how much noise there was,' he later recalled when reminiscing about the Cavern. 'But I was impressed [with The Hollies], so I invited them to London for a test.'[10]

What impressed Richards the most was the way that the band tackled the environment in which they were playing. It was a small location, packed to the rafters with teenagers, all tightly squeezed together, and The Hollies performed with such vigour and charisma, fast and hard, as that was the only emotion one could truly play in such a situation. He was reportedly also struck by the way that Graham Nash attacked the fretboard on his guitar until he realised that there were no strings on the instrument.

Graham: 'The night before, I'd broken my last string and I couldn't afford new ones, so I did the lunchtime show at the Cavern with my Harmony guitar – and no strings. What did it matter?'

For the five band members, the prospect of Ron's offer, and the long arduous trek down to London, wasn't something to be taken lightly. But, then again, this was what the band had been working for. The opportunity to be auditioned with the goal of a recording contract in mind. This was *serious* business. It was time to put away any doubts over their career and make a go of it. Turn professional and make music their living…

For Allan, Graham, Eric and Don, it was a relatively straightforward decision. This is what they wanted.

'My parents weren't happy when I said I was turning professional,' Eric was to say to a *Pop Weekly* journalist, during early 1963. 'They said I was silly as there was more brass to be made with a trade than in an insecure music world. Now I want to prove 'em wrong.'

For Vic Steele, however, it was a difficult call to make and one he opted against: 'We had already made a demo tape and a record company was now interested. The lads' ambitions were to become professional and seek successful careers in the music industry. At that time, as Graham would say, I had a proper job. I was also attending college studying engineering. I was tempted to stay but decided to complete my education rather than turn professional. I explained my situation to the guys and also promised to stay until they found a new guitarist.

'The other lads were really nice, trying to persuade me to stay. I think Graham was a bit more upset than the others because he was planning hard for a recording career and losing the lead guitarist was a definite problem. But it wasn't a question of falling out. I wished them well…'[18/76]

'In the north of England, there was a union hierarchy,' comments Graham. 'You apprenticed at a job and worked your way up, the payoff being a lifetime gig to support your family. Vic wasn't willing to give that up, which was too bad because he was a pretty good player.'[1]

With Vic agreeing to hold off his departure until a replacement was found, Alan Cheetham and the remaining members of the group started on the search.

# CHAPTER THREE

# "WE'RE GOING FOR AN AUDITION..."

Anthony Christopher Hicks arrived in the world on 16th December 1945, in the former northern mill town of Nelson in Lancashire. Born to Alan and Margaret Hicks, alongside his sister Maureen, he grew up into a determined young boy, attending Saints John Fisher and Thomas More Secondary School in nearby Colne.

Tony's mother was later quoted as saying: 'When he wanted something, he didn't just hint hopefully. He went out and got it, some way or other. There has never been anything he wanted that he didn't get on his own initiative. He was so determined when he was a child that he cycled eighty miles one day with the cycling club, just to prove that he could do it. He was only ten.'

'When I was a kid, I wanted to play the piano,' Tony would later recall. 'My grandmother offered to let me have her grand piano, but we couldn't get it into our house. We tried taking the windows and the doors out, but it was no use. Eventually, we gave up and I had a guitar instead – it was easier to get in and out of our house!'[35]

'When he was eleven, his auntie bought him a guitar for Christmas,' his mother continued. 'He never even had time for girls after that. He was too wrapped up in the guitar.'[13]

'The guitar thing just grew on me,' Tony was to later comment to the Hollies' *Carousel* fanzine. 'It was more the image of the guitar, with rock 'n' roll just starting. I just liked the feel of it, but I was very casual about it. I was more interested in getting out on my bike! I used to go cycling with a cycle club. That was what I was mainly into...'[18]

Gradually, as the music began to filter through to the suburbs of Manchester and the surrounding districts, Tony became fixated with the sounds of the classic American rock 'n' roll guitarists who were providing the rockin' rhythms across the ocean. It appeared that they had it all. They were better players and had better guitars than almost anything available in England at the time.

'I remember hearing 'Hello Mary Lou', he later recalled, 'and wondering who was playing that wonderful guitar.'

He also listened avidly to the early recordings of Elvis Presley, fascinated by the guitar licks that Presley's sideman, Scotty Moore, reeled off, practising hard on his acoustic model, developing his own technique of playing.

On 2nd March 1958, Tony was glued to the family's black and white television set when visiting American rock 'n' roll star Buddy Holly made an appearance, live from London, on the weekly *Sunday Night at the London Palladium* show, performing three of his hits; 'That'll Be The Day', 'Oh Boy' and 'Peggy Sue'. Then and there Tony's future was laid out before him. *That* was what he wanted to be.

In those days, he recalled, this was not a lonely fixation. 'Concerts would sell out just because of the guitars that these bands were playing,' he remembered. 'We would travel to the shows just to get a look at the guitars.'

Tony first felt the spotlight of fame bearing down on him when, at just twelve years of age, he joined a local skiffle band, Les Skifflettes, appearing on the stage alongside fellow band members Russ Lee, David Shanahan, Pat Belshaw, Frank Lord, Paul Shanahan and Keith Shackleton. Founding member of the group, Harold Russell (aka Russ Lee), later recalled for the *Lancashire Telegraph*:

'A couple of weeks before Christmas, in the winter of '57, a few mates went out carol singing. That's what young teenagers did, but what was different, was that we went out carrying guitars. Some weeks earlier, I had imparted my knowledge of the three-chord trick to both Paul and Keith, so by the time Yuletide was approaching, it seemed like a good idea to expose our newly found skills to an audience, and carol singing was the perfect vehicle. The response was amazing. I remember us standing in the driveways of the large detached houses on Halifax Road, Nelson, singing and playing our hearts out. People would come to their doors. They had never heard anything like it. "Can you play any Lonnie Donegan?" some would say. Are you kidding? Anyway, the result of all this was that Les Skifflettes came into being.'[14]

Their audiences at that time were mainly to be found in the church youth clubs, whilst the group also took to performing at local dance nights around Nelson and nearby Brierfield.

'I can't remember who brought Tony to us,' continued Harold, 'but we realised at once that this polite, well-brought-up twelve-year-old with a nice guitar and deft little fingers would be an asset to the Skifflettes. So, it was as a seven-piece skiffle group that we went on to come second in an all-Lancashire group competition held at the Empire Theatre, Burnley. Then, before we knew it, we were also off to auditions at the Ardwick Hippodrome, Manchester for the Carroll Levis *Star Search* show.'

'We were brought down from Nelson to London, and stopped for the night in the city,' added Tony, during a later interview with the *New Musical Express*. 'We thought it was the most marvellous thing that could ever happen. We were bashing away at washboards, guitars and packing-case basses. A right crew! And I remember we got about £65 between us!'

Harold continues: 'We appeared on radio and television and performed at the Palace Theatre along with the King Brothers. We also now had a manager, Lew Askew. He used to manage the Imperial Ballroom in Nelson and also the Savoy and Hippodrome Cinemas in Colne where he had us playing on stage between the feature films, much to the delight of the young audiences out front.

'By late 1959, though, Les Skifflettes had fizzled out, but Tony Hicks and Pat Belshaw went on to form The Dolphins. I was lucky enough to catch their act at the Chez Nous Club, Colne and I thought that with their smart suits, Selmer Truvoice amps and Futurama guitars, they were brilliant. With Tony and his nimble fingers playing Shadows classics, and Pat Belshaw up front, and Bernie Calvert on bass, they were the best group in the area.'[14]

As Tony's musical prominence began to increase, so did his influences as he began to refine his unique style of playing. US players in the calibre of James Burton (the guitarist on 'Hello Mary Lou') and Chet Atkins hit hard on him, as did the British session guitarist Big Jim Sullivan who, as a member of Marty Wilde's Wildcats, appeared regularly on UK TV screens, courtesy of the *6.5 Special* and *Oh Boy!* shows.

'When I was around fourteen, I went to see a show with Johnny Kidd and The Pirates,' he later recounted. 'There was Johnny Kidd and this three-piece band, and they were just incredible to hear. They played so loud and clean. That was the sound that I wanted on stage; just one guitar, one bass, and drums, with no rhythm guitar in the way.'

Whilst all of his later bands did go on to feature rhythm guitarists (to a degree, subject to Nash stringing his guitar), his comments truly emphasised the clarity of the lead guitar role. A clean sound, one that could pierce through the dark venues and reach out to the audience. No muddled mid-ground.

With Les Skifflettes having given Tony his first real taste of live performing, and with the encouragement of his parents who arranged for him to have lessons with a local music teacher, he then went on to form his next musical venture with fellow Skifflette Pat Belshaw. Combining with drummer Alan Buck and a bass player (originally on piano) named Bernard Bamford Calvert, and with Belshaw taking on the frontman pseudonym of Rick Shaw, this quartet, known as Ricky Shaw and The Dolphins, began a gradual rise to become one of Manchester's leading combos in the new "beat scene" that was developing across the city. Later joined by John Robert Shaw on rhythm guitar, clearly a compromise on Tony's behalf, and with drummer Buck being replaced by the fair-haired former skinsman from Eddie G. Marten and The Falcons, the band played extensively on the Manchester circuit, including sets at Belle Vue's Cumberland Ballroom along with the Imperial, La Ronde, El Rio's, the Chez Nous, the Birch Hall Palace and the appropriately named Dolphin Club in Colne. They even provided support as the backing band when the London-based Top 40 pop singer Doug Sheldon played several shows in the Manchester area.

'We gained plenty of experience like that and we were full of ourselves for days whenever we played with a big name!' Tony added, during his *NME* interview.

This, in turn, led to the quintet venturing down south on 12th November 1962, to the Decca Records recording studios in West Hampstead, London, where they provided the backing tracks for Sheldon's latest sessions. Unfortunately, the two tracks cut that day, the commercially sounding 'Wendy' and the Buddy Holly-styled arrangement of 'Until The Next One Comes Along', the latter featuring a punishing tom-tom rhythm, remained unreleased and, despite the proposition of further shows accompanying the singer, the offer floundered and the band returned home.

However, it was when the band began to play regular slots at the famed Oasis club that fate took a turn for the better in Tony's career.

'I remember this guy used to turn up at every gig,' recalled Bobby Elliott, the band's newly appointed drummer. 'And we knew he was trying to get Tony away from us...'

Acting on behalf of The Hollies, Alan Cheetham was doing the rounds of all the local shows, trying to find a suitable replacement for the soon-to-depart Vic Steele. It wasn't an easy task.

'There weren't many people available to replace Vic,' commented Eric Haydock. 'Pete Bocking was an immense talent. I heard him doing 'Lucille', playing Chet Atkins solos, and it completely blew my head away, but Vic projected a good macho image in the leather stage uniforms and it was for that reason that Bocking wasn't considered as a replacement...'[4]

Subsequently, an invite went out to Tony to come and see The Hollies play, although his reluctance to leave the established Dolphins line-up for a band which, at that time, was barely two months old, was reasonable. Nevertheless, on the evening of 22nd February 1963, Tony Hicks boarded the local Ribble bus from his home in Nelson and headed into Manchester.

'I knew they were playing at the Twisted Wheel, but I didn't know where that was, so I called into the Oasis, which was nearby, and the manageress gave me directions.'

Fighting through the crowds, Tony became all too aware of another attraction that was actually playing at the Oasis that night. The Beatles were back in town, and the queues were stretching for as far as the eye could see, down Lloyd Street, onto Deansgate, and round to Brazennose St, overspilling into the nearby Albert Square. In fact, Graham Nash and Vic Steele, ever keen to see and hear how the other bands were going down, even managed to briefly escape the Twisted Wheel during an interval in the band's own set, just to catch a brief glimpse of The Beatles at the Oasis.

'That occasion was on a Friday night,' recounts Vic. 'We were playing at the Twisted Wheel and The Beatles were on just around the corner at the Oasis and we were puzzled as to why our venue was packed out. Graham, myself and my girlfriend, Barbara, walked the short distance along the narrow streets to the Oasis. Apparently, Tony Hicks was walking in the opposite direction to the Twisted Wheel. The story goes that Tony waited outside near a ventilation grill to hear the band. However, he did enter the club as he briefly spoke to Barbara to say he had come to see The Hollies.

Incidentally, when myself, Barbara and Graham had entered the Oasis, The Beatles were actually on stage performing 'P.S. I Love You'. The place was packed like sardines and the atmosphere was electric...'[76]

Undaunted by the noise and excitement generated by Beatle-crowds, Tony had made the short walk to the Twisted Wheel club, just off Princess Street where, so legend tells us, he did wait outside, reluctant to enter at first. Instead, waiting for The Hollies to recommence their set, he listened intently to the sound that they were making through an open vent. Clearly, he liked what he was hearing.

Tony: 'I remember standing outside an air vent. I didn't want to get involved so I just listened for a bit. I quite liked it, so I wandered downstairs and watched them for about half an hour. When they finished, I wandered up to one of them. I didn't know them. Unfortunately, I picked Eric. I thought he would be pleased to see me, but he was never a chatty person and I remember trying really hard to make conversation with him. Then Graham came up and he was really chatty and very nice. He said, "We're going for an audition in London with EMI. Do you want to come and do it, because Vic can't make it?" I'd always wanted to do a test recording, so I went.[19]

'I was a semi-professional musician when I was a member of The Dolphins. I was also working as an electrician, so it was a risk. Initially, I had said I wasn't interested and left it at that, but what really weakened my resistance was when they asked me to go with them to London. I spoke to my parents and they said, "Well, if you love music that much then go and do it." So, I decided to join up. The boys are tremendous and play with great spirit...'[4/16]

That said, in order to link up with the newly professional band, Tony needed some reassurances, financially, before he would fully commit. He wanted confirmation that they could at least equal his current salary structure. The band responded by guaranteeing him that he would make the same, if not *more* than he was currently drawing from his engineering position. Was there also a place somewhere for his drummer friend? he reportedly asked. Sadly not. But the deal was sealed, and the early spring of 1963 saw Tony Hicks officially join The Hollies. Vic Steele, meanwhile, reverted to his given surname, rejoined a reconstructed Emperors of Rhythm line-up and continued a life outside of professional music.

'As far as I can remember, my last gig with The Hollies was around the end of April 1963,' he recalls today. 'It was shortly before my 18th birthday and it was on a Sunday evening, at the Three Coins in Fountain Street, Manchester. At the end of the evening, we said our goodbyes. I remember Allan carried my amplifier up the stairs and out to my car. We shook hands, wished each other good luck, and the rest is history.' However, Don Rathbone's surviving 1963 tour diary, which neatly lists their appearances at the popular Manchester venue, indicates that The Hollies took to the small Three Coins stage on the 10th of March, along with a later date at the beginning of May. But that too throws up an anomaly, and it suggests that Vic remained with the band, potentially playing a few final shows with them, after the subsequent events that took them down to London.

'I honestly can't remember,'" he muses, when quizzed on the subject today. 'It was almost sixty years ago now…'

There was, however, yet one further twist to the tale. The Dolphins still had one outstanding booking to fulfil, a performance at the Memorial Hall in Northwich, Cheshire, supporting hit-maker Mike Berry, who had reached the UK Top 30 with his 'Tribute to Buddy Holly' 45, two years previously. Unfortunately, Tony was no longer available to fit it into his new schedule and so, for one night only, Vic took on The Dolphins' lead guitar role.

'They called me up on the Friday and said, "Can you stand in for Tony tomorrow?"' He adds, 'Mike Berry was one of the headliners and we had to back him. With me knowing the Buddy Holly stuff, it was like second nature, to be honest. Bobby Elliott was a great drummer…'[76]

March of that year was the month that the newcomer initially began to find his feet in The Hollies, adding his distinctive playing to the established rhythm section of Eric and Don. Gigs at the Regal Ballroom in Alderley Edge and the Fire Station Dance Hall in Rochdale were mixed in with more familiar surroundings such as the Cavern and the Twisted Wheel.

On Monday, 4th March, the band squeezed into Don's father's Commer van and headed south, down the A6, towards the capital city of London. Destination (as Graham was to later recount), the De Lane Lea studios in the seedy Soho district of London, a stone's throw from the 2i's coffee bar where Ricky and Dane Young had performed a few years back. No further record of this event has been noted in print, bar a brief mention in *Wild Tales*, although it is believed the band ran through their current stage setlist for their EMI audition with Ron Richards. Suitably happy with the result, the band returned to the smoky capital, according to the band's official session logs, the first week of the following month, this time as official Parlophone recording artists. This time, they had a recording test scheduled at EMI Recording Studios, a former Georgian townhouse located at 3 Abbey Road, St John's Wood, West London.

After booking in at a nearby bed and breakfast house, the five-piece Hollies line-up, Allan, Graham, Tony, Eric and Don, reportedly entered the hallowed halls of the acclaimed studios on 4th April 1963 for the very first time.

'We were just wide-eyed and laughing,' remembers Graham. 'It was like a miraculous dream!'[2]

Back in the 1960s, the recording studio was run very much like an efficient, well-oiled business. The band simply came into the studio, watched over by a team of engineers in white laboratory coats, set up their equipment and performed. Union rules dictated the length of each session, and they had no say in the sound, the mixing or the balance. It was that clinical, but to a group of youngsters, some of whom were still in or barely out of their teens (it would be Allan's twenty-first birthday the day afterwards, whilst Don, the eldest, was now a mature twenty-five year-old), the excitement of such an occasion was profound. Could it get much better?

Opting to cut three songs chosen from their live shows, with Ron Richards deciding that a cover of The Coasters' '(Ain't That) Just Like Me' was the stronger choice, despite its nursery rhyme naivety, although Tony's stinging lead guitar solo (edited down for the forthcoming 45 release) and Eric's driving bass patterns made up for any lyrical shortcomings. However, in the eyes of one band member, their debut session didn't get off on the best footing...

Eric Haydock: 'We got to EMI after The Beatles and we obviously thought things would go the same way. But the first time we were in the studio, Ron saw Tony on lead, Graham on rhythm and me on six-string bass and he said, "Where's the bass?" He had no idea I played six-string bass and he had no idea how to record or mix it!'[4]

Accompanying Richards in the studio that day was Peter Bown, sitting in as engineer, and Ken Townsend as a technical engineer, both accompanied by a youthful Geoff Emerick as the tape operator. Two relatively new self-composed offerings from Graham and Allan subsequently made up the trio of songs taped that day, highlighting their growing confidence in their own abilities. Graham later recounted that 'Hey, What's Wrong With Me' had actually been the very first composition that the duo had written together, the direct result of their encounter with Don and Phil Everly, but it was the Everly-influenced 'Whole World Over', a delightful mid-tempo ballad, that struck a particular chord, with the combination of the two harmonising voices (Tony hadn't joined in with the harmonies as yet) and Allan's gentle harmonica riff.

With their London-based manager Tommy Sanderson watching from the sidelines, the session was deemed a success and, following completion of the three-hour session, the elated band packed their equipment back into Don's van and headed back up north.

It is worth noting at this point that, due to conflicting recollections across the many subsequent years, some have suggested that this April 4th date was, in fact, their actual EMI audition and that maybe Graham's recollections of De Lane Lea have been confused with another occasion that took place at the Soho location shortly afterwards. However, it does seem highly unlikely that EMI would authorise numerous takes of a song at audition level, with ten attempts needed to nail a satisfactory take of '(Ain't That) Just Like Me' taking ten attempts to nail a satisfactory take. Or would they?

'We were actually offered a two-hour audition at Abbey Road,' Tony would later state to broadcaster Iain Lee on BBC 3 Counties Radio, thus suggesting that this was their first London appearance with Ron Richards. 'We recorded an old Coasters song, 'Just Like Me', and a song that Allan and Graham had knocked up, and that was released.'

Ron Richards later contradicted the audition theory, commenting, 'It was normal procedure. They had a recording test at Abbey Road and we released their first single from that session,' whilst studio engineer Ken Townshend (as noted in Brian Southall's *The Hollies Story*) also added his recollections to the scenario: 'I was on holiday and everybody else in the studio had said they couldn't do it, so the manager called me on Wednesday to ask if I could come in on the Thursday night for an artists' test. It was The Hollies and I recall they did four songs that night in Studio Two…'[18/3]

Four? Only three have ever been documented for this particular date. And it is logged as taking place in Studio Three. The mystery deepens. However, to add further intrigue to the suggested dateline, research on this book threw up yet further anomalies. Don Rathbone's tour diary confirms that on 4th March, the quintet did indeed journey down to the nation's capital, spending four days in London, with a photo session in Harrow also booked in, and thus backing up Graham's recollections of an earlier audition. And yet, even the officially recognised session date of 4th April, on what is now assumed to have been the recording test, is now also brought back into question once again, with the diary suggesting that a booking at Mirlees Social Club in Stockport actually took place on that day. Did they manage to complete their EMI session *and* drive back up north in time to hit the stage, later that evening? It was a concept certainly not unheard of in those early hazy, crazy days of rock 'n' roll. Vans of all sorts, loaded with battle-weary musicians, passing in opposite directions on the darkened motorways of England.

And then, confusing matters further, Vic Steele still vividly recalls remaining with the band until they appeared at the Three Coins, which took place *after* the EMI session dates. That too remains at odds with Don's diary listings. Maybe, just perhaps, the full day-by-day timeline as it *really* occurred during the period has now been lost amongst the mists of time…

With interest in the Hollies suddenly increasing, and with a successful audition and now a recording test for EMI both on their resume, along with a steadily growing demand for their live performances, the vultures soon began circling, eager for a slice of what they could see was becoming a very lucrative pie. The management lines were becoming blurred. Tommy Sanderson (and, to a degree, Bernard Jewry/Shane Fenton – acting as a road manager), along with his colleague at the Wilson Entertainment Agency, booking agent Eddie Donoghue, continued to represent them in London and down south, with Tommy often putting the weary group up in his flat in Shepherd's Bush, whilst Alan Cheetham, responsible for the bookings in and around their home counties, was working the north. Yet, Alan was soon moved aside as the predators prowled, and another astute businessman moved in. It begs the question, where was the management line drawn? Was the legendary Blue Boar truck stop, halfway up the M1 motorway, the division between north and south and acclaimed by early 1960s bands as *the* post-gig midnight meeting point, the location where it was neutral ground for Hollies management?

One of the final acts undertaken by Cheetham, thusly documented on fading paperwork, was a contract he signed on 10th April 1963, co-signed by resident disc jockey and promoter Bob Wooler, for a residency at the Cavern

Club in Liverpool, split over the following five-month period. Listing the group as official Parlophone recording artists, at a total salary of £200.00 (£20 in cash after each evening performance), the band were required to perform twenty 90-minute shows, during both lunchtime and evening dates, during which time they were also not permitted to perform at any other venue within a five-mile radius of the club. But, hey, that's rock 'n' roll.

Wednesday, 24th April 1963: Evening + Lunchtime
Sunday, 19th May 1963: Evening only
Monday, 20th May 1963: Lunchtime only
Tuesday, 28th May 1963: Evening + Lunchtime
Wednesday, 12th June 1963: Evening + Lunchtime
Wednesday, 26th June: Evening + Lunchtime
Monday, 1st July 1963: Lunchtime only
Friday, 12th July 1963: Evening + Lunchtime
Tuesday, 23rd July 1963: Evening + Lunchtime
Friday, 2nd August 1963: Evening + Lunchtime
Tuesday, 6th August 1963: Evening + Lunchtime

Signed by Alan G Cheetham
"The Toggery"
Mersey Square
Stockport

"The Toggery" was a men's tailors and clothing store, based in Stockport, and owned by a local businessman named Michael Cohen. The Hollies used to visit the store to browse and purchase the latest clothing; Copperfield jackets, tab-collar shirts, boots, full leather and suede gear, and it was viewed as a popular fashion boutique by many of the local teenagers. Graham Nash even had a part-time job there at one early stage, rising to the role of Assistant Manager, but Cohen saw a greater future for him and his fellow bandmates.

'I didn't know much about music,' he would later admit. 'But I liked the boys and money was not an issue. I said I would back them and take care of them. I was young and it opened many doors for me.'[3]

By supporting the group financially, Cohen was installed as their new manager, and as for Alan Cheetham, who had utilised an office above the store for the purpose of supervising the band, Cohen later responded, 'Cheetham was never the manager of The Hollies but was more of a hanger-on. I was their sole manager from 1963 onwards.'[3]

Indeed, it was Cohen's signature that reportedly graced their official recording contract with EMI Records. And yet to many, including much of London's media, Tommy Sanderson was still viewed in a management capacity too:

> They are some of the swingiest guys to make up a group at any time. Their manager Tommy Sanderson thought they were terrific when he saw them and promptly rushed them into a recording studio for their first platter, a swingy chunk of wax titled 'Ain't That Just Like Me'.
>
> *Pop Weekly*
> August 1963

'I was their manager, and he became their agent, based in London,' reiterated Cohen.

'I always wanted to go with Danny Betesh,' Eric Haydock was later to comment. 'He had a great proven track record...'

> It's like a fairy godmother at times, that little spinning disc whirling on the turntable at 45 revolutions a minute. Ask The Hollies, five lads from Manchester way who decided only two months ago to twang guitars and sing for a living.
> On the strength of their first record, which doesn't even go on sale until tomorrow, they have landed a widescreen colour film with Frankie Vaughan. The Hollies, all of whom had been playing in instrumental groups in their spare time, got together at the beginning of the year. In March they got a disc contract and turned professional. On Tuesday this week they got the news that they had won the film part after the producer heard an early pressing of their record.
>
> *The Mirror*
> May 1963

It's the Hollies. Five young men who have just crash-banged the charts at the first time of asking with '(Ain't That) Just Like Me', and already the breaks are flowing fast. Piano-star Tommy Sanderson engineered their first disc. Now comes the news that they are starring in the new Frankie Vaughan film, "It's All Over Town". Producer Ben Nisbet plans to use at least one original Hollies composition in the movie.

'All happening? I should say it is.' So said spokesman Graham Nash. 'I'm spending as much time as possible on writing. I've got six numbers on paper ready for publication.'

He is a driving force in The Hollies sound – a driving sound which rejects the nice sound of the balladeers and gets down to real, earthy, meaty-beaty singing and playing.

*Pop Weekly*
June 1963


With the choice of the debut 45 A-side an easy decision for Ron Richards, and with 'Hey What's Wrong With Me' placed on the flip side, the band's first release, issued on 17th May 1963 (Parlophone R5030), gradually climbed up the UK charts, making its debut in the Top 40 on the 30th of May, before reaching its pinnacle of number 25 five weeks later. Not quite the smash hit that some of the media reports suggested, but to even *make* the Top 30 was enough of a thrill for the quintet. And with their very first recording session. To them, this was now the big time. Having only turned professional in March of that year, their livelihood now depended on achieving chart success and on taking the band to new heights. It was certainly a promising start and one that they, and their newly installed record producer, began to see a future in.

Of interest, the Top 3 UK chart positions that week were filled by Liverpool's Gerry and The Pacemakers ('I Like It'), the north/south combination of The Shadows ('Atlantis') and, holding down the number 3 slot, Manchester's very own Freddie and The Dreamers, featuring former Fourtone Derek Quinn on lead guitar (with their debut hit, 'If You Gotta Make A Fool Of Somebody').

However, such was their confidence in the abilities of The Hollies that EMI had scheduled a further series of recording sessions two days before the first 45 was even released, and on the 15th of May the boys were once again making that now-familiar journey down to Abbey Road. They worked on five new recordings that particular day, all efficiently performed for the lab-coated technicians in attendance – two lively cuts from the ever-busy pens of Graham and Allan; 'Now's The Time' and 'Little Lover', along with cover versions of Allen Toussaint's 'Fortune Teller', The Coasters' R&B chart-topping Leiber and Stoller composition, 'Searchin'' and, finally, a rockin' version of the Disney film theme, 'Zip-A-Dee-Doo-Dah'. All five cuts show the all-encompassing togetherness that was to become the essential "sound" of The Hollies over the subsequent months and how Allan, with several years' experience singing on stage and before audiences, was already an extremely confident lead vocalist when placed in front of the studio microphone.

Shortly afterwards, the quintet made their way back into central London, where they renewed their acquaintance with the De Lane Lea studios, out of Soho, who took on the role as the production company for a filmed performance of 'Little Lover', sponsored by FilmVision. The resulting product, a mere two and a half minutes in length, was produced exclusively for use on a Scopitone Jukebox, a 1960s visual version of the standard jukebox player whereupon the customer – it was predominantly aimed at the teenage market – could also view the performance of the chosen artist as well as listen to it. Unfortunately, the appeal of such a heavy piece of equipment was limited, and the popularity of the machines soon faded fast. The Hollies, dressed in smart mohair suits and performing their original composition, were one of the few pioneering rock 'n' roll bands to utilise the facility, and their surviving footage, in glorious 16mm full colour, remains a visual feast. Unless, of course, you were a particular fan of cherubic-faced drummer Don Rathbone who, for reasons unclear, was placed towards the edge of the film shot and spends most of the resulting short with just his body and arms visible. Only towards the end of the song do his fellow band members take their eyes off the twisting and gyrating blonde dancer and rally around, offering him full screentime.

It is also interesting to note in the film that the band, Tony and Eric in particular, had by now partially abandoned the "quiff" hairstyle, so popular during the closing years of the 1950s and into the new decade, and had instead adopted the "Beatle cut", with fringes (or "bangs" as the US referred to them) flopping down over the forehead. Graham, meanwhile, stuck steadfastly to his familiar backcomb, but the originality and influence of the Liverpool foursome, currently out on tour around the UK with American Roy Orbison, was clearly starting to take hold. And not just with the music.

N E W S L E T T E R  N₀.1.

### THE HOLLIES. THE HOLLIES. THE HOLLIES.
### FAN CLUB.

Dear Member,

Here is the first news letter from THE HOLLIES Fan Club.
We apologise for such a delay, but organisation of such things
takes time and concentration. We thank you for showing your
appreciation for our kind of music by joining the fan club and
as and from now, you will receive a monthly news letter and any
new photographs which the group have taken.

As you all well know, THE HOLLIES have established themselves in this new and exciting section of the show business world
not only by releasing a great new disc, but also by taking part
in a film, starring FRANKIE VAUGHAN and the team from "That Was
The Week That Was". They have also appeared in person on "Scene
at 6.30" and have had two personal appearances on Friday Spectacular on Radio Luxenburg.

The group was formed six months ago, and have really
shown great ambition to get to the top, and it seems as if they
will do it even after such a short time. Members of the group
are:-

                GRAHAM NASH - 21 - Rhythm Guitar and Singing.
                ALLAN CLARKE - 21 - Lead Singer.
                TONY HICKS - 18 - Lead Guitarist.
                ERIC HAYDOCK - 20 - Bass Guitarist.
                DON RATHBONE - 21 - Drums.

All the boys come from Manchester with the exception of
TONY who comes from Nelson. The group play strictly rhythm and
Blues numbers, which seems to be the most popular sound on the
'scene' to-day. Graham and Allan are perfect combo, as they have
been singing together since their days at Junior School, and
coupled with a really great backing group, which by the way,
includes a Fender Six String Bass, they produce a sound which is
practically unique, especially as Graham does not play or x plug
in his guitar when on stage, but uses it to do something with his
hands, but do not be mistaken, he does really play the guitar
extremely well, and for that matter so does Allan. All the
boys thoroughly enjoy their work and practice regularly to perfect
their act.

As you will have noticed THE HOLLIES are frequently out
of town playing in different venues all over the country, to get
themselves known nationally, but I am sure that when they are in
your district, you will all show them your best support, for they
really do need their fans.

HOW ABOUT THIS!!! If there are a lot of HOLLIES Fans
in your district, why not arrange for a coach tour to see your
favourite group. If any of you fancy having a coach trip somewhere where the group are playing, why not write to us and let us
know and we will see if we can arrange anything. BUT MORE ABOUT
THAT NEXT MONTH.

# CHAPTER FOUR

# "I'VE BEEN SEARCHIN'..."

In addition to the first record release, May 1963 had also seen the band make their debut appearance on the nation's television sets, promoting their debut 45 on the *Scene at 6.30* show. Filmed at the Granada TV Studios in Manchester, this was a newly launched magazine programme *for* the north and *of* the north, with a very irreverent anti-metropolitan feel. Although designated as a current affairs show, it featured guests from the entertainment sphere every night of the week, promoting the best new bands in the studio before their record had hit the charts, thus stealing a march on the opposition. It may have only received a regional airing but to the band's loyal following, in their home city, this was something special. They were one of them… and they were on television! But the boys knew it, and they were proud of their local scene. As other northern bands were all too soon to find out, the hub of the UK music business was down in London, and the constant buzz around Denmark Street and its nearby Soho counterparts just couldn't be ignored. The Hollies stayed loyal to their Manchester roots for as long as possible, returning regularly to play the local venues where they had found their newly acquired fame, with Tony often lodging the night with Don and his parents to avoid the extra hour or so travel back to his hometown of Nelson.

Throughout May and June, and into the warm summer months, they made regular appearances in the Twisted Wheel, the Cavern, the Oasis, or at nearby venues in Stockport, playing down the rivalry between the northern bands and their localised followings.

Tony Hicks: 'I think it was just good press news to make the north, Liverpool, Manchester and whatever, out to be that. There was competition, in as much as there were groups equally as good as each other. There was no jealousy. I must admit that the Liverpool groups come more to mind. As far as Liverpool goes, top of the tree was The Beatles, and then you move down with Gerry and The Pacemakers, Billy J. Kramer and then names that didn't particularly make it; The Remo Four and The Big Three. They stick out in my mind more than Manchester. We'd play at the Cavern and just wander out and see The Big Three play, which was just incredible. It was something very new, very exciting.'[12]

'We played the Cavern with The Beatles, but The Big Three were the stars for me. I just idolised that group…' adds Allan Clarke.

'[The Big Three] were the best group I ever heard in my life,' Graham was also to comment, this time to an American reporter during a mid-'60s interview. 'They had the worst equipment, but they did more to influence the Beatles, and us, and whoever you care to name, than anyone in the world. They were incredible…'[79]

On 7th June, The Hollies made one of their earliest BBC radio appearances, just one of many, on The Light Programme's *Talent Spot* show, performing the current 45 and appearing alongside The Ted Taylor Four, Mickie Most, Perry Ford and Sandra Edema, following it up, four weeks later, with a guest spot on *Go Man Go* for the same BBC station. Appearances on *Easybeat*, *Band Beat* and *Pop Inn* followed shortly afterwards. They even ventured north of the border for the first time during mid-July, travelling up on the 16th and filming on the 18th, making an appearance on the Scottish Grampian TV programme, *Joe and the Music*, widening their appeal further still.

Then, following on from two further journeys down to Abbey Road, whereupon attempts were undertaken once more at a successful cover version of the popular Leiber-Stoller tune, 'Searchin'' (it would take a fourth endeavour later that month before they cut a satisfactory rendition), they made their one and only entry into the world of the widescreen cinema, albeit for a low budget Brit-flick, featuring the comedic talents of resident British humourists Lance Percival and Willie Rushton. *It's All Over Town*, scraping in at a mere fifty-eight minutes in length, was a film with little script, little laugh value and little else, other than the brief musical appearances of Dusty Springfield, Acker Bilk, The Bachelors and The Hollies.

Directed by Douglas Hickox, and reportedly filmed in just over fifteen days, this "musical romp" was predominantly no more than a publicity short for the headliner and all-round entertainer Frankie Vaughan, who got to perform five numbers for the cameras.

'Six weeks ago, nobody knew us outside Manchester,' Graham was to comment to the press. 'Now the record and the film have meant so much to us financially. We're booked right through to September and we have the wonderful chance of working on the film with such great people as Frank and Acker Bilk. We've just travelled to London to record two of our own numbers for the soundtrack and we shall be at Elstree tomorrow for our spot before the cameras. We're looking forward to it tremendously.'[77]

Performing for the film crew on 21st June 1963, The Hollies, still relative newcomers compared to their onscreen partners, were given the opportunity of lip-synching to just one of the Clarke-Nash collaborations taped during their second visit to Abbey Road. Arriving on the set on motorcycles, dressed in black leathers, and with Don's head and arms bouncing around like a Gerry Anderson puppet *sans* strings, 'Now's The Time' offers a rare musical highlight in an otherwise forgettable cinematic experience.

*A near hour of nonsense,* ran the subsequent *New Musical Express* review of the film.

And yet, despite all of the thrills that came with movie-making, and the successes and publicity that had seemingly dropped on their doorstep of late, the late summer months of 1963 would mark a further turning point in the band's brief history, and one that would usher a new dynamic into the line-up.

The 13th of July 1963 saw the group take to the stage in a small club called the Outlook, located in Middlesbrough, up on the windswept north-east coastline. First on the bill that day had been a new upcoming quintet, driven by a love for the Chicago blues, hailing from London. The Rolling Stones.

As Bill Wyman later recounted in his book, *Stone Alone,* 'One of our first adventures north was to a small club in Middlesbrough [Wyman mistakenly refers to it as the Alcove Club]. We were support act to The Hollies, a top Manchester group. We later found out the two groups had been equally nervous of each other, [but] from that day The Hollies became one of our favourite groups and we subsequently worked with them on many occasions…'

Then, returning to London soon after, The Hollies' 23rd July recording session, held at Abbey Road, with Ron Richards firmly establishing himself in the producer's chair, resulted in the fourth and final take on 'Searchin'', a huge hit for The Coasters on the US *Billboard* charts back in 1957 and an extremely popular tune for the British bands to cover. That said, the arrangement of the song used that day, void of any notable Hicks' guitar contributions and instead utilising the distinctive barrel rolls of Tommy Sanderson on piano, certainly wasn't the most effective. As with their recently filmed appearance for the big screen, 'Searchin'' lacked much of the urgency of the band's live performances. Ron Richards, however, deemed the recording to be a suitable enough choice to be issued as the band's second single, released just three weeks after the session was completed. Paired with the pleasing 'Whole World Over', cut during their debut appearance at Abbey Road, the 45 (Parlophone R5052) managed to improve on their previous chart standings and eventually climbed to a very respectable number 12 on the UK lists, spending a total of 14 weeks in the recently expanded Top 100. That, despite it being unfavourably reviewed in both *Melody Maker…*

> I can't describe how much I hate it. It's a complete muck-up of a great R&B thing. Horrible when you know the original. This record is absolutely diabolical. I loathe it and I hope it flops.
>
> > Screaming Lord Sutch
> > *Melody Maker*
> > 1963

… and on the weekly TV show *Juke Box Jury*. Sitting on the review panel that week, US recording star Pat Boone, an artist renowned for cutting insipid covers of classic R&B hits, simply encouraged the audience to 'buy the Coasters' original version instead.'

> The Hollies: 'Searchin'' (Parlophone R5052)
> Manchester Hollies do a great treatment on this wild one from Presley's hit writers, Leiber and Stoller. The combination adds up to another strong chart-climber.
>
> > David Gell review
> > *Beat Monthly*
> > September 1963

After a long-drawn-out success with their 'Just Like Me' hit, the popular Hollies, Manchester's second-biggest chart group, seem to have another of the same calibre on their hands with their latest effort 'Searchin'. Despite the bashing that Juke Box Jury gave it the boys have still managed to make the lists with the rock standard, which they have been performing on stage for some time now. And I can't help thinking that they perform it better on stage than on disc, having heard both interpretations of the song. And it says a lot for a group when they can perform a number better on stage than they did on their HIT record, with which they have all the technical facilities available.

*Record Mirror*
September 1963

It is interesting to note the differing flipside in the above *Beat Monthly* review. Advance promotional copies were sent out to various reviewers and radio stations prior to any official release and 'When I'm Not There', a rare Tony Hicks composition recorded in two takes at an earlier 3rd July session, was initially earmarked for inclusion as the reverse of the new 45, before being substituted at the last minute, removed in favour of the slightly older Clarke-Nash tune.

August saw the group appear as guests on BBC radio's *Pop Goes The Beatles*, a short-lived weekly show hosted by the Fabs (the show had been taped the previous month), in addition to appearing on several concert bills around the country, supporting a variety of established "name" acts for the teen-filled, packed audiences. Two appearances at the Bournemouth Winter Gardens saw them listed at the bottom of the bill for shows featuring the likes of Billy Fury (the one and same Ron Wycherley, who had auditioned alongside them on the Manchester *Star Search* talent show), The Tornadoes, guitar hero Bert Weedon, former Shadows' Jet Harris and Tony Meehan, teen idol Mark Wynter and The Springfields, a trio fronted by the dynamic Dusty. Then, on the final Saturday of the month, they performed at the Stanley Greyhound Stadium in Liverpool, taking a slot at the all-day Non-Stop Beat festival, a vast gathering of (mainly Liverpudlian) performers such as local favourite Beryl Marsden along with Billy J. Kramer, Lee Curtis and The All Stars, The Big Three, Freddy Starr and The Midnighters and The Searchers. This particular event, promoted by Allan Williams (The Beatles' first manager), was also notable for featuring a relatively new local band who went by the name of The Escorts. Amongst this particular four-piece line-up was a young sixteen-year old singer-guitarist by the name of Terry Sylvester.

This show has also gone down in history as being one of the final live performances by Don Rathbone as the drummer for The Hollies. His 1963 tour diary, which still survives in his personal collection, shows that following an appearance at the Queens Hotel Theatre in Blackpool, on 15th September, Don had no further commitments with the band. Three days later, his replacement made his debut on the drum stool.

> Hi there again. Well, I suppose you thought this letter was never coming, but you see there's been a slight mix up. I had a newsletter printed and then Don gave in his notice, so I had to have a new one printed. The reason for Don leaving is that he was offered an extremely good job in London, and as he was getting a bit tired of all the rush and travel, he thought he would take on the new job. I can assure you that there is no ill feeling between Don and the group, and the boys wish Don all the best of luck for the future, as I know we all do. The new member to our group is Bobby Elliott, a very good friend of Tony's.
>
> *Hollies Fan Club Newsletter*
> Edition #2 (Version 2)

Whilst it never reached the same heated levels that the Beatles faced following the dismissal of fan favourite, Pete Best, Don still received plenty of well wishes and cards from the increasing hordes of Hollie-admirers.

'It was a shame,' Eric Haydock was to later comment when discussing Rathbone's departure, 'as Don was a very lovable, wonderful guy. He'd seen the band through the bad times, putting money in for petrol when we were short. He did most of the driving, and he just loved the scene. But after we did our first recordings there were complaints at EMI that he wasn't up to it...'[3/4]

'He was good enough for roadwork,' Allan revealed for a later interview with *Melody Maker*, 'but when we got in the studio, he just didn't come up to scratch because it showed more on record than it did on stage. We used to have a nickname for him; Paradiddle. It's a drum roll or so I'm told. We used to say "You need to do a paradiddle, Don. Y'know, merrily merrily"...'

'If anyone decided that Don Rathbone was not good enough a drummer it would have been Ron Richards and nobody else,' stated engineer Ken Townsend.[3]

Certainly, Don's abilities can be summarised as steady and reliable, if unspectacular. With a considerable age difference between the ranks – officially, Don was eight years older than the youthful Tony Hicks (even if the group publicity did knock five years off his birth date) – this was nearly a generation in the music business. He kept time in an orderly fashion but played it straight, and his backbeat was unpretentious, with few fancy frills and flourishes. Yet, in the eyes of producer Richards, his drumming capability simply wasn't up to studio recording standards. In a storyline that bears an uncanny resemblance to that of their Liverpudlian counterparts – instead of Don, read Pete – Don was invited to a meeting with Michael Cohen, and let go. With the band looking to take the next steps on the road to success, they now needed someone who could deliver the rhythm and drive the band – and not, it appears, just from behind the wheel of a Commer van.

Disappointed, but not down, Don accepted another role, taking on a position behind the scenes, alongside Tommy Sanderson. However, within the space of a few months, tired of London, he had returned back to the north, accepting the offer of a return to the drum stool for Cliff Bowes and The Arrows. This was briefly followed by a position with Remo Sand and The Spinning Tops but, resigned to the fact that the music business was no longer for him, he sold his kit and took on employment with General Motors.

'I left The Hollies with nothing except memories,' he was to later recount. 'Some were bad, as you may think. I was the only member who was able to drive so after arriving home after each gig I then had to travel some forty miles to drive the others before getting home for my sleep. The next day was the same. The money was very poor and sometimes I had to pay for petrol out of my own pocket. I'm not ashamed to say now that I was somewhat relieved when I was asked to leave…'[77]

Interestingly, Don maintained a single ownership share of the band for many years to come, before finally agreeing to sell his rights back in 1999 for the princely sum of £5,000.

With Don having moved on, Allan's elder brother, Frank, stepped in to handle the driving and roadie duties for a period until former musician Jay Vickers took on the full-time role as the ever-reliable road "crew".

\*

Graham sends special thanks to all who sent him presents and get-well cards. I don't know whether you all heard but we nearly lost him as he fell out of the van the other night, and not very gracefully slid down the road on his rear end. Actually, it wasn't very funny at the time and he quite hurt himself and was in a terrible state of shock. Who wouldn't be? We see to it that he can't fall out now, we tie him to the seat.

*Hollies Fan Club Newsletter*
Edition #2

\*

The 8th of December 1941 and the world was in shock. The previous day's events, the Japanese bomb attack on Pearl Harbour, had reverberated around the globe. Reports of this catastrophic attack filled newspapers across the western world. That said, the residents of 13 Chiltern Avenue, a typical three-bedroom, semi-detached townhouse located on the outskirts of Burnley, eastern Lancashire, may have had little time for such reading. Instead, proud parents Bob and Edna Elliott were celebrating the birth of their son, Robert Hartley Elliott.

Robert, or Bobby, grew up an only child, moving to nearby Pike Hill at the age of three when Edna purchased a shop in the area. Having attended Todmorden Road and then Holm-in-Clivinger Primary Schools, he would later comment that his best friends were, in fact, his parents, who were strongly influential in his development as a youngster.

'My parents weren't musicians,' he would later recount in an interview for *Record Collector*, 'but they were musical in the sense that the house was always full of Rachmaninov and Grieg's piano music. One of my first experiences was going to King George's Hall in Blackburn and seeing the Liverpool Philharmonic playing the Rachmaninov Piano Concerto. We were seated behind the orchestra and I was next to the tympanist. I was intrigued by the way he kept turning the heads so he would be ready for the next piece, and that got me interested in drumming.'

Whilst attending nearby Nelson Grammar School, he developed his love of jazz music, with artists of the calibre of Woody Herman, Cannonball Adderley and Duke Ellington listed amongst those he admired the most.

'My mum had a grocer's shop and I used to take biscuit tins and construct a drum kit next to the radiogram. I would play along to Gene Krupa with the Benny Goodman Orchestra. I had a chum at Nelson Grammar who encouraged me to play and told me that there was a snare drum for sale in a junk shop in Walton Lane. I got a pair of sticks, a pair of brushes, a snare drum and a stand for £2. That was the start of it and then I borrowed money from my dad to get a decent kit.'[15]

'He would play in his bedroom, and he was always very considerate of the neighbours,' Edna would say. 'He never practised after seven o'clock. We wanted Robert to study for his exams but when we looked at his homework books and found sketches of American jazz drummers, we realised we were fighting a losing battle.'

Upon leaving school, Bobby took up a mechanical engineering apprenticeship for the National Coal Board, often working down the darkened mines repairing the engines. Most evenings were spent with a group of friends, playing music in each other's houses. His first notable public appearances came courtesy of local performances at the Borough Band Club in Nelson, the Sefton Club in Colne, or at the popular Rawtenstall Jazz Club, approximately ten miles from the family home. First steps into rock 'n' roll came when he joined up with the five-piece Gerry Storme and The Falcons in 1959, which ultimately transformed into Eddie G. Marten and The Falcons once they switched lead vocalists.

Through constant practising and hard work, he soon turned semi-professional, often playing five nights a week. The following year, Bobby began performing with the Bob Price Band, a jazz quintet where he remained on and off for the next couple of years. Yet the exciting sound of the rock 'n' roll beat had begun to capture his attention. In between gigs with Bob Price he also joined up with popular Manchester band Ricky Shaw and The Dolphins, replacing founder member Alan Buck. In front of his kit now stood talented young guitarist Tony Hicks and bass player Bernie Calvert: two youths with whom the drummer was destined to spend many an evening sharing a stage in adulthood.

Bobby had first met Tony when he had noticed a Futurama guitar, a popular yet inexpensive model, sitting in his girlfriend Maureen's living room.

'I asked Maureen who it belonged to and she said it was her brother Tony's.'[18]

An introduction followed soon after...

Having built up a sizable following over a short period, The Dolphins' momentum evaporated with the departure of Tony Hicks. Headhunted by The Hollies during the spring of 1963, there was no easy replacement for the loss of one of the finest young guitarists in the north. The Dolphins were forced to fold shortly after, the other band members now looking for new opportunities. Initially, Tony had suggested that his drumming bandmate come along too, but as the then-unsigned Hollies still had a drummer in place, who also doubled as the band's driver, they couldn't justify switching members. The opportunity passed... for now. Instead, at Tony's suggestion, Bobby signed up with Shane Fenton's backing band, who were in need of a new sticksman.

'I went down and did the audition, and they said, "Yeah, that's great!" I said, "Oh, have I got the gig?" "Well, no. Can you come down to London on Monday? We've got eight other drummers to audition." So, my dad drove me down there in his little van, and we eventually found this sort of cellar place just off of Tottenham Court Road in London, and there were eight other guys queued up there. I was at the back of the queue 'cause we got lost coming down from the smoky old industrial north. But it turned out I got the gig. I was number eight, and number three in the line was Keith Moon! That was before The Who, of course.'[15]

Seated behind his reliable Trixon drum kit, Bobby remained with the Fentones for around five months, including one notable performance at the Royal Albert Hall. It was during this period that he got his first real feel for the professional circuit. Fenton had already released a series of relatively successful Top 40 singles by the time Bobby joined up and thus already had a sizeable following. A debut television appearance for the drummer on Grampian's *Joe and the Music* in Aberdeen was followed by a spot on *Thank Your Lucky Stars*, two months before The Hollies themselves (by then with Bobby behind the cymbals) guested on the show. Then, in the aftermath of The Hollies' initial success, once they could afford the luxury of paying for a roadie as well as a new drummer, Don Rathbone was removed from his responsibilities and Bobby was officially drafted in as his replacement. The first classic line-up of The Hollies was now complete – Clarke, Nash, Hicks, Haydock and Elliott.

Graham Nash: 'When I first saw Bobby play, I thought, *My God, this guy is completely on top of his game.* He was completely different from what we'd been used to because he'd been very influenced by American jazz drummers.

He was a more worldly musician than anyone I'd ever met before.'[5]

'Bobby is very unique as a drummer,' states Allan. 'His technique is very different to a lot of the other drummers around. He has a way of being able to incorporate what he hears in his head into his snare, and that makes it different to anything else anyone else does. He just added to our music in the same way that Tony's guitar did.'[17]

Joining up with the band for an 18th September show in Warrington, his first major outing as a Hollie came about with the subsequent "Beat Show of 1963" tour, performing, ironically, alongside Shane Fenton and The Fentones, who were headlining the 26-date outing. Then, on Friday, the 11th of October, on a mid-tour day off, they filmed a guest appearance for a newly launched, weekly TV broadcast on the UK independent network; *Ready Steady Go!*

'We were miming to our record 'Searchin'', Bobby recalled, 'and Rollo (Gamble, the director) instructed the five of us to walk in line, abreast, in time with the playback, around the basement studio. Right hands over eyes, looking from side to side as if we were, well, searching for something! There we were, a pop group with no drums or guitars, parading up and down like a pantomime dance troupe!'[74]

Having successfully completed the sequence, they then journeyed down to the EMI Studios in Abbey Road where, with his new bandmates, Bobby made his recording debut, letting loose on a frantic version of 'Stay', previously a 1962 US *Billboard* number one hit for songwriter Maurice Williams. The interplay between the key musicianship of Elliott, Hicks and Haydock was now clearly dynamic and the brief 15-second instrumental break in the track was, in the parlance of the day, far out…

Tony: 'The first time I went into the studio,' he says, 'I learned that something has to take precedence, and it isn't always the guitar. I realised that if I took 50% of the notes out of my solos, I ended up with something that was effective rather than clever.' [5]

Indeed, Tony's fretwork shines through in this particular session and most certainly would have made the listener sit up and take note.

Someone said 'Stay' but the lads aren't stopping. Not The Hollies certainly! With two sure-fire chart riders in succession, the boys have started to blast the charts with 'Stay', a sure-fire big-seller if ever I heard one. These boys are with-it in every conceivable way.

Hairstyles, clothes, looks, music, they're different and delightful. Behind the boys is that driving force in show biz, Tommy Sanderson, one of the brightest and ablest guys to hit the scene ever. 'They're a great group,' explains Tommy, 'and they turn out some great material music-wise. Their latest, 'Stay', is a really good recording, one that will give them a much bigger hit, I hope, than the other two.'

*Pop Weekly*
November 1963

'We were touring Scotland and Graham and I found an old record called 'Stay' in a junk shop,' Bobby recalled in a later interview with *Creem* magazine. (In an alternative interview, he also referred to being with Tony on that occasion.) 'It was obviously the Maurice Williams original. Well, we had one more gig, so we set up in the afternoon to do the sound check and we rehearsed 'Stay' for the first time. We just ran it through. As the support band were setting up, I noticed this guy playing harmonica with a bouffant hairstyle, a very mod hairstyle for those days. It was Rod Stewart with a band called Jimmy Powell's Dimensions! Anyway, when we returned to London we wanted to record 'Stay' the way we had rehearsed it.'

That same October 1963 recording date also saw them tackle yet another Coasters hit, 'Poison Ivy', the immensely popular Leiber-Stoller composition, covered by numerous artists during that era. Although two differing attempts were completed, both would remain in the can for the foreseeable future. One version (take 12) would later appear on a 1985 UK compilation, *The Hollies* (MFP 41-5727), issued on the Music for Pleasure label, whilst the second attempt (take 9, a longer variation highlighted by a rare error by Eric on bass) only ever appeared on an obscure '70s Australian collection. However, with the November single release of 'Stay' as their third EMI single (Parlophone R5077), paired with 'Now's The Time', the band culminated a year of seemingly unparalleled successes. Each release just climbed higher than the one before, and 'Stay' would go on to give the group their first Top 10 hit and remain in the Top 40 for almost four months. Unfortunately, it was not the same story on the other side of the vast ocean as the US issue of 'Stay', their debut release stateside, distributed via Liberty Records (Liberty 55674), failed to make a dent in the *Billboard* lists.

Eric Haydock popped the cork from the bottle, and they all drank the champagne with enthusiasm. 'We are now hoping beyond hope that we will be able to sell the 5,000 [sic] copies needed to earn us a Silver Disc. But that's an awful lot of copies!'

*Disc*

January 1964

1963 drew to a close in the best way possible on home soil. It was busy. Some may even say chaotic. A best-selling hit single, sold-out live performances around the country at settings such as the Cavern, and at McIlroy's Ballroom in Swindon and the California Ballroom in Dunstable (both as part of an extensive 30-date Top Rank Ballroom tour), along with a charity appearance in Streatham (co-starring comedian Tommy Cooper) and shows at larger venues such as the Matrix Hall and Colston Hall in Southport and Coventry respectively, supporting Bobby Rydell and Helen Shapiro. Paired with further TV appearances on *Thank Your Lucky Stars*, *Scene At 6.30* and *Ready Steady Go!*, the demands placed upon the group were really cranking up a level.

Then, to round the year off, the annual *New Musical Express* December readers' poll placed the group at number 11 in the Best British Vocal Group category. The Top 3 placings were unsurprisingly dominated by the leading Liverpool bands, and one wonders exactly who voted for the one-hit-wonder duo, The Caravelles at number 8, but the fact that The Hollies had broken into the lists was fantastic news for the boys and due reward for their efforts and commitment during such a crazy year.

THE *NEW MUSICAL EXPRESS* 1963 POLL WINNERS
Category: British Vocal Group

1. The Beatles
2. The Searchers
3. Gerry and The Pacemakers
4. The Shadows
5. The Springfields
6. The Rolling Stones
7. Freddie and The Dreamers
8. The Caravelles
9. Brian Poole and The Tremeloes
10. The Bachelors
11. The Hollies
12. The Dave Clark Five

'It's refreshing being at the start of something new like this,' Tommy Sanderson was to comment to *Evening News* journalist Anne Batt. 'In my business, I see pop stars who turned from being nice kids into blasé, smooth-talking show men. But these boys are completely unspoiled. In a way, they've been knocked off their feet – they're tickled pink by everything that's happened. They haven't had the time to be soured by success. I only hope they stay this way.'

1964 would only get better… and busier.

# CHAPTER FIVE

# "I THOUGHT I WAS DREAMING..."

The 1st of January, 1964...
...and a brand-new music television series aired for the very first time, broadcasting out of an old, converted church on Dickenson Road in Rusholme, Manchester. Resident northern disc jockey Jimmy Savile presented the first *Top of the Pops* show live from the Manchester studio, introducing, in order, Dusty Springfield, The Rolling Stones and The Dave Clark Five, before he turned his attention to the next band on the schedule, Manchester's very own Hollies, performing their current chart smash 'Stay' before the studio audience and television cameras. The show then went on to culminate with The Swinging Blue Jeans, followed by, of course, The Beatles (in a pre-filmed sequence) performing their current chart-topper 'I Want To Hold Your Hand'. With such a barrage from the toppermost of the poppermost, how could the show not succeed? It did, and it went on to become a staple of British society for the following forty-two years.

'Let's get this straight,' stated Bobby in more recent years. 'The Hollies were never a Manchester band. I'd moved to Nelson and Tony Hicks is from Nelson. Allan Clarke and Graham Nash are from Salford, and Eric Haydock is from Stockport. The Hollies said that they were a Manchester band so that the southern papers would understand the common denominator. It looked like a competition: "The Beatles are from Liverpool, The Hollies are from Manchester," but it wasn't like that…'[15]

As the 1960s moved into the swingin' era, and music became the very epicentre of British youth culture, television shows such as *Top of the Pops* began to play a vital role in allowing viewers each week to access their favourite recordings, and the artists and bands behind the tunes, from the comfort of their very own armchairs. From there, word spread across the school playground, the office desk or the corner shop counter about who appeared on last night's show, who looked fab and "gear", what happened where and when… and for the artists in question, it was maximum exposure to the hilt. Previously, one had to be seen at a live performance, or in the pages of a magazine, to be recognised. Now, with millions tuning in to their TV sets on a Wednesday night, *Top of the Pops* brought them directly into the nation's living rooms, albeit still in black and white (the show didn't air in colour for another five years). And didn't they all look groovy? The boys now dressed smartly in their Cuban heel "Beatle" boots, hairstyles reaching down to touch the collars of their mohair suits, fringes daringly hanging towards their eyes, guitars held chest high. And the girls? Oh, my word! Go-go boots had arrived, flip and bob hairstyles… and London was becoming the place to be seen. And not just for the music. Yes, there was the Marquee Club, the Flamingo and Crawdaddy for the nightlife but, within the year, a fashion revolution would be here.

The Hollies performed on each of the first three episodes of *Top of the Pops*, all airing in January of 1964, driving the single up to its peak position of number 8 (in a week that saw The Beatles and The Dave Clark Five vying for the top spot). That same month also saw the release of the group's debut long-playing record, appropriately entitled *Stay With The Hollies*, capitalising yet further on the single's success.

Packaged in a decidedly "pleasant-looking" sleeve, with no inklings of the raw R&B that intermittently featured within the grooves – check out the cardigan sweaters – the album was a hodge-podge of styles, clearly influenced by the American sounds that filtered across the Atlantic and featured on the stage setlists of so many Brit-bands of the era. Indeed, with not one of the fourteen selected inclusions fading at the close, one can almost imagine this as a near-perfect recorded example of the band's own live performances, such was the authenticity.

'Basically, we decided to take the best material from our two 45-minute sets and fuse it into one kick-ass hour,' recalled Graham. 'The whole thing was done in one morning session. Then, after the lunch break and a cup of tea with some biscuits, we did the same set again – the entire album in two hours flat. That was it. Ron chose the best twelve songs.'[1]

The brash 'Lucille' subsequently brushed shoulders with 'Mr Moonlight'; the rock 'n' roll of 'Do You Love Me' preceded the Everly-styled arrangements on the old Ricky and Dane Young favourite, 'It's Only Make Believe', and on it went. Throughout the eventual 35-minute running time, the thrill of hearing the group's live set was startlingly evident, void of unnecessary overdubs, bar the occasional harmonica solo. The sparse, basic recording techniques utilised in the studio only went to highlight the raw excitement they generated, and even on the slower covers – such as on Arthur Alexander's 'You Better Move On' (also covered by the Rolling Stones on their 1964 debut EP), the enthusiasm was intense. The musicianship on the album was simple, but effective and exciting, with Bobby's drums setting a solid backbeat to build upon, although one track leftover from the Don Rathbone period, 'Little Lover', also made a belated appearance. The album opener, Chuck Berry's 'Talkin' Bout You', had also been taped during Rathbone's residency but had been recut for the album once Bobby had signed on.

The rear of the sleeve, with notes that credit the management skills of Tommy Sanderson – with no mention of Michael Cohen – surprisingly give little mention, bar one sentence, of the contributions from Ron Richards, the man who, in effect, was guiding the five youngsters around the gradually familiar surroundings of Abbey Road. His importance to the band's early career cannot be underestimated. That said, EMI was clearly reluctant to offer any credit to their paid employees, as neither Richards nor George Martin received any significant printed acclaim on the early releases for The Beatles or Gerry and The Pacemakers either. It was a different story over at EMI's sister company, Columbia Records, where Adrian Clark was duly noted for his contributions to the *Session With The Dave Clark Five* LP. Then again, Adrian Clark was, in reality, Dave himself.

Ron Richards had been born Ronald Richard Pratley back in 1929, in London, and was adopted at an early age. He became a proficient pianist as a child and, after being conscripted, played the piano and saxophone for the

Central Band of the Royal Air Force. After leaving the services, at the age of twenty-three, he took a job as a song plugger in London's famous Tin Pan Alley region, working for Campbell Connelly Publishers, and was credited for discovering composer Jerry Lordan, who later wrote a series of popular instrumental recordings for Bert Weedon and The Shadows. A career switch into the recording side of the business then found Ron working at EMI's Parlophone imprint as an assistant to producer George Martin. Reportedly, he was hired because he had a solid background in publishing and was seen as a "song man", who understood the pop market.

Viewing the producer's role from a different perspective to others who worked in a similar capacity, Ron was not a "knob-twiddler", nor was he primarily a businessman. He loved great sounds and clean production, and he later began utilising the skills of established engineers to help him achieve that. To him, that was the packaging but not the essence of the product. He focussed much more on songs and the artist. The perfect pairing. He saw his role as getting the best out of the artist, not moulding them. In time, it would be his ability to identify a potential hit record that would become his greatest musical attribute.

Soon enough, not long after his appointment at Parlophone, Richards was assigned to produce a session by himself, for a northern "beat" group that George Martin had agreed to sign to the label. At Martin's request, during September of 1962, Ron had booked a session drummer to use that day, as the band's regular player, a good-looking Liverpudlian lad by the name of Pete Best, had been deemed as not up to studio standard. Although they had already employed a replacement drummer by the time the date had arrived for the session, on 11th September 1962, the hired hand was still utilised at Richards' insistence. It was a hard day's night for the new band member, left to watch from the sidelines and to randomly bang a tambourine whilst the established session muso played his part. Soon after, George Martin took back the reins for the not-yet Fab Four. Nevertheless, although Ron played an important role at the Parlophone label and was also instrumental in the early career of Gerry and The Pacemakers and later American singer P.J. Proby, it is as the mastermind of The Hollies' commercial success for which he will always be associated.

Although he was considerably older than the band members, and not quite as creatively inventive as his senior producer, Ron knew his way around the studio and was a good match for his new signings.

'Ron had a very commercial ear,' says Tony Hicks. 'He had great patience and had the knack of pulling the best performance out of people.'[5]

Bobby Elliott added, 'Our times at Abbey Road were very quick. The red light came on, count in one, two, three, four… and get the track down. First take if possible, and that was it. It was always hurried and that's the way Ron Richards worked.'[15]

Currently riding high with their biggest hit today, 'Stay', The Hollies are represented on an album of the same title. And what a stimulating album it is.

Fourteen tracks as meaty and beaty as they come. A lot of favourites are among them, plus some which soon should become very popular. It's impossible to select any track for special mention – they're all good and of a very high standard for pop fans. You'll love it.

*Record Mirror*
February 1964

Entering the charts during the second week of February, *Stay With The Hollies* spent a highly impressive twenty-five weeks in the UK Top 20 album lists, reaching a March high of number 2. (Do you *really* need to ask who held down the pole position?) Before this, during the final week of January, the group had spent two days at the Abbey Road studios, cutting their first new recordings since the album sessions were wrapped up the previous December. By the time the album was peaking, they were ready once more to launch an attack on the singles market. It was becoming an endless cycle of performing, recording and hit-making.

The live shows continued to pull in the crowds, and despite travelling the endless miles of roads in the hazardous winter weather, they rarely missed an appearance. Even when their van skidded off the snow-covered tarmac between Hastings and London, on the evening of 12th January, the show went on.

Late January saw them perform second on the bill to The Searchers at Birmingham Town Hall. Notably, the bottom of the bill that day was none other than Screaming Lord Sutch and his merry band of Savages. One wonders if his disdainful *Melody Maker* review of 'Searchin'' was discussed. Two weeks later and the band headed north of the border once more and undertook their first brief tour of the Scottish regions, performing in

Dundee, Paisley, Stirling and Glasgow. Then it was the long journey back down to London again to promote the next single, 'Just One Look', the result of the recent sessions.

> Such is the faith that The Hollies have in Ron Richards that they never make a move, recording-wise, without his consent. And they have good reason to act that way. All their hits have been waxed by Ron, and each title has been OK'd by him. 'Just One Look' is no exception to the rule.
> 'We heard the American version by Doris Troy and were knocked out by the lyrics,' exclaimed Eric. 'We knew as soon as we heard it that it would be great for us. Ron liked it and so we went ahead.'
>
> *New Musical Express*
> March 1964

'Just One Look' would go on to introduce the defining nature of The Hollies. The song would act as a true springboard for their influential trademark three-part harmonies, with Tony now joining in the vocal blend, creating a dense layer over the rhythmic backbeat that would raise them head and shoulders above many of their peers.

Allan: 'Tony was more or less just a guitarist when he joined the group, and I don't know why we said "come and sing with us." It may even have been when Graham and I were singing and Tony just sidled up and went la-de-da… but we thought, *Hang on, that sounds different. Why don't we put that in?*

'I must have been mumbling a bit too close to a microphone,' adds Tony with deadpan humour, when discussing his input into the vocal stack. 'But that's where the third lower harmony came in, and it is undoubtedly the three-way sound of The Hollies.' [17]

> 'This namby-pamby music we've had from some groups – we don't dig at all,' the ever-outspoken Graham was to comment in a *Beat Monthly* article at the time. 'What the fans want is music with guts. People with weak eardrums should stay away from us!'
> One of the brightest and probably most musical of the Manchester groups are The Hollies. Their latest, 'Just One Look', sold 80,000 in two days and sped into the charts in the first week of release. Since then they have appeared on major TV and radio shows to boost the

disc into being their fastest-selling hit. As their manager, Tommy Sanderson, told me, 'When they finish the Dave Clark tour, they will need a two-week holiday!'

Pop Weekly
March 1964

'Just One Look' had been a 1963 US Top 10 hit for Doris Troy, who was also the co-writer of the song. Although it had failed to reach a substantial audience across the Atlantic, its end-of-year *Billboard* ranking position – number 70 of the best-selling US hits of 1963 – ensured that it did reach the ears of a few significant UK record buyers. Paired with a rare Hicks-Elliott collaboration, the infectious 'Keep Off That Friend Of Mine', the new Hollies rendition (Parlophone R5104) would rise up and surpass the success of the original version, peaking at the number 2 slot in the UK charts. In addition, it would also go on to mark the introduction of the group to the US *Billboard* charts for the very first time (issued as Imperial Records 66026), albeit at the lowly number 98 spot.

Tony Hicks can step forward as the man responsible for suggesting the band record this particular song. Indeed, the young guitarist's abilities to source material for their catalogue would become an essential part of their history. In the years to come, he would often spend his downtime scouring publishers' offices, listening to demo recordings and acetates of new compositions, or avidly checking out the R&B hits, shipped in from over the ocean, before presenting them to his listening bandmates, a knowing, gleaming look in his eye.

'That one just stood out as a great song,' Tony later commented.

Familiar TV reappearances on *Scene at 6.30*, *Ready Steady Go!*, *Thank Your Lucky Stars* and *Top of the Pops* all followed in the initial wake of the 45's increasing success, with the band smiling at the cameras, clearly having a ball, dressed in their matching suits. They also made an appearance on the much-loved BBC children's TV show *Blue Peter*, performing both 'Stay' and '(Ain't That) Just Like Me', although that particular appearance, whilst still residing in the television vaults, now only survives in audio format. Such televised guest spots also highlighted the natural proficiency that Elliott now brought to the band, with his flowing fills and flourishes seemingly a world away from his predecessor's puppetry style of attack.

The subsequent 1964 package tour that followed, an extensive jaunt around the country supporting London's hit-making Dave Clark Five (alongside fellow supporting roles for Mark Wynter, The Mojos, The Trebletones and a recently formed quartet out of Muswell Hill, North London, calling themselves The Kinks), would raise the profile of The Hollies higher still, and increase their popularity vastly, particularly amongst the hundreds of young females who attended the performances each night. Screaming uncontrollably, without inhibition, at each jerk of the head, shake of the hips, or thrust of the guitar-laden pelvis.

> Young women are unfairly asked to squeeze into an impossible mould of politeness and modesty. A concert is a unique event that gives girls the rare opportunity to break out of those roles. In their day-to-day, non-concert-going lives, girls don't have a lot of permission to scream, but a concert offers an oasis from the daily rules about being good girls. Screaming is about letting go and leaving the confines of being the self-conscious pleaser.
> Screaming is a way to control a situation, but when you're a kid, and a girl, you don't have control. Young people don't have a loud voice in society, so screaming in this kind of space is a way to have a voice. Literally.
> That's one way to explain why so many concerts are filled with screaming girls instead of screaming boys.
>
> *The Washington Post*

1964 wasn't the first time that popular music had brought about such wild teenage abandon and, as the subsequent successes that would follow in later years would testify, it certainly wouldn't be the last. One can predate the early '60s pandemonium by simply going back to the initial gyrations from the previous decade that Elvis Presley had brought into his stage act, causing mayhem and hysteria amongst his adoring prepubescent following. Or back even further still, to the 1940s bobby-sox era of early Sinatra, when his audience would squeal with delight as he crooned and swayed in front of the stage lights. But by the early 1960s, teenage hysteria, nay, *female* hysteria, was taken up a notch, brought into public awareness across the world by the ensuing media. Whilst the devotion that The Hollies induced amongst their loyal following never quite reached the cataclysmic proportions of that bestowed upon their Liverpudlian peers – Yeah! Yeah! Yeah! – they still maintained a support and fan base that was certainly the equal of many of their nearest competitors. During their early months together, the band members themselves were not immune to the delights such devotion brought to them from upon their lofty chart positions. They even revealed tales of sneaking young girls up the fire exit stairwells in hotels, whist someone would distract the concierge down in the lobby. In fact, in later years, Eric Haydock went into quite explicit detail for the sake of the press into the sordid facts of such liaisons.

> He revealed how the girl-hungry super-studs hid a groupie in a wardrobe of their hotel room to beat a love ban whilst touring. Anyone who wanted sex only had to knock on the cupboard door.
> 'The girl was a local slag who was well known to pop stars of the time, but there was still a queue outside the wardrobe. It was a right laugh seeing who knocked and how many times.'
>
> *News of the World*
> September 1988

But this *was* rock 'n' roll, and these were all red-blooded young men, travelling across the country, city to city, crammed together in a small transit van.

'I doubt whether any group in the country have got such great fans as we have,' they would politely comment to *Pop Weekly*. 'Every time we've played a one-nighter there have been hundreds of members of our Fan Club always there and many of them have to travel hundreds of miles just for one show. They're a gas!'

Fellow northern acts such as Gerry and The Pacemakers, The Searchers, Freddie and The Dreamers and Billy J. Kramer and The Dakotas all induced the same amount of female frenzy that left the ears of most concertgoers ringing. Many often came away from the venue having heard little of the actual *music*, such were the deafening cries of the thousand-plus that rang on throughout each performance (although the sex appeal of Freddie was a little puzzling to many...). Likewise, the southern crescendo afforded to the thumping beat of The Dave Clark Five, Brian Poole and The Tremeloes, or the blues-influenced riffs of The Rolling Stones, was equally as thunderous, although at times the bitter rivalry that ran across the north-south musical divide was apparent for all to see, both fans and musicians alike.

'The Manchester bands and the London bands didn't really get on very well…' suggested former Fourtone Derek Quinn, by then firmly established as a Dreamer, gallantly performing each night behind the ever-exuberant antics of former milkman Freddie Garrity.

### THE FIVE AND THE HOLLIES GET FANS SCREAMING

A power failure caused a nine-minute delay before Dave Clark's act at the beginning of his tour on Sunday. During it, the audience amused itself chanting 'We want Dave!'

The Hollies opened with the beaty 'Too Much Monkey Business' and were greeted by frenzied yells and screams. Without a pause, they followed straight into 'Rockin' Robin' and had the fans going wild. For the Everly Brothers' 'So Sad', Graham Nash put down his guitar and joined Allan Clarke at one microphone for a very moving duet. The audience sensibly remained quiet until the number had finished, then they let out so much applause that it took Allan some moments before he could announce 'Memphis'.

They kept the pace – and the fans – going with 'Stay', which brought screams from all parts of the packed theatre.

The Hollies were an undoubted hit and deserve every praise for their style and cheery manner.

*New Musical Express*
April 1964

What the above review failed to mention was the fact that the power failure, just before Dave Clark and his Tottenham cohorts took to the stage, was caused by Eric Haydock in an act of cheeky northern defiance, purposely cutting the power cable following The Hollies' own set. In retaliation, the Dave Clark band later offered to take on the Manchester crew in a fistfight – five vs five – although this didn't amount to anything more than a verbal threat.

Nevertheless, despite the devotion and media attention afforded to The Hollies each night, and the subsequent temptations seemingly on offer during a gruelling national tour around the provinces, by early 1964, several members were now enjoying the comforts of a settled relationship. On 24th March 1964, just five days before the touring schedule with The Dave Clark

Five commenced, Allan Clarke tied the knot with Jennifer Bowstead (with Graham standing alongside as best man), although, for fear of upsetting the burgeoning fan base, the relationship had been kept under wraps for a while.

'We were supposed to keep our relationship secret,' Allan would later reveal to the *Sunday Express* magazine, 'like John Lennon and Cynthia. We met during a Hollies tour in 1963 [when] a friend said, "Do you fancy having a blind date with a girl I know in Leamington Spa? She's got a mate." Jeni came in her own car and when I saw how she was dressed, I thought, *She's in a different class!* She didn't have a clue who The Hollies were...

'When I said I was getting married I was fired from The Hollies, but as I was lead singer, two days later I was back in!'

Whilst strictly untrue, there were certainly some heated discussions over the pending nuptials, with fear over a loss of popularity with a married singer in their midst. The prospect of replacing Allan with Frank Renshaw, vocalist from another Manchester band, The Toggery Five, was even mooted but, fortunately, common sense prevailed.

Nevertheless, once the press found out about the forthcoming marriage, it was reported nationally:

> Next Tuesday things are going to be a bit terrifying for the Hollies singer. For Allan Clarke is going to have to face a big audience. This time they won't all be teenage fans. Some will, of course, but Mum and Dad, Uncle Bert and Aunty Ethel are going to be there too. For 21-year-old Allan, this is the end of the struggle. He's getting married.
>
> *Top Boys of the Week* Magazine
> March 1964

Graham's own marriage, to an attractive young blonde named Rose Eccles whom he had met at Manchester's 2J's club, would take place later that year in August (although Allan was reportedly upset it was a private affair, and he wasn't invited). Graham and Rose were soon living together in Graham's newly purchased flat down in London, just off Kensington, before they found a place of their own in nearby Shepherd's Bush.

Eric Haydock, too, had found love, and would ultimately go on to marry his long-time girlfriend, Pamela Done, in January 1965 after they had initially met in a popular Stockport coffee bar called the Klub Koquette.

Although Allan, Eric and Bobby all retained their northern spirit and remained living in the north of the country with their wives or families for now, Graham, followed shortly afterwards by Tony, charted a business instinct by opting to move south. The music capital was on the cusp of exploding…

With the honeymoon period seemingly on hold, the performing schedule continued relentlessly onwards. The success of the 1964 package tour, which had started on the 29th of March at the Coventry Theatre, and culminated forty-seven days later at the Granada Cinema in Kingston, only emphasised how vastly popular were these multi-act package tours. The crowds poured in, to both afternoon and evening performances, to see this plethora of top pop performers run through a collection of their most popular songs in quick succession. And if that tiring itinerary wasn't enough, with days off in between shows few and far between, The Hollies still managed to cram in recording dates for EMI when they weren't needed on stage.

The 13th of April 1964: The day after two sold-out shows at the Embassy Theatre in Peterborough, on a 24-hour break in the tour, and the quintet once again found themselves in the salubrious surroundings of Studio 2 in St John's Wood, north London where they cut four new tracks under the watchful eye of Ron Richards.

'Here I Go Again', a new composition by acclaimed US songsmith Mort Shuman in partnership with the British-born Clive Westlake, was one of the songs undertaken, as was 'Baby That's All', credited to the previously unknown Chester Mann. That second number, along with the remaining two compositions taped that day, was actually a recently written piece of work by the newly established songwriting team of Clarke-Hicks-Nash. With Tony now added into the writing spectrum of the inner circle, the fact that they were composing under a pseudonym has been thusly explained over the years:

'We were told by the record company that "Clarke, Hicks and Nash" were too many names to put on the label, as a credit, which is silly really,' recalled Tony Hicks. [7]

Allan later confirmed it as such: 'We weren't the type of writers that would turn down a song which was good for us but we were being sent stuff from all over the world and we started to realise that these guys were being well paid for writing the songs, so we started to write our own. Mostly, we were writing B-sides. But the record company was telling us that our names were too long to fit on the record, so we said to Graham, "What should we do?" He said, "We should put my grandpa's name down," which was Ransford."[5/7]

Born in 1892, Ransford John Fitton was Graham's maternal grandfather and sadly only lived to the age of thirty, leaving behind his young daughter, Graham's mother, who was only two at the time of his death. Graham would never know him personally.

Consigning the alias of "Chester Mann" to the history books, cuts three and four, 'Time For Love' and 'Don't You Know', were subsequently the first two recordings credited to one "L. Ransford", the alternative name the songwriting trio would jointly utilise for the following two years. 'I had no connection with Ransford,' continued Tony. 'I think it was a name either Allan or Graham knew...'

It is worth noting at this point that EMI Records clearly couldn't justify such a claim, seeing that another of their best-selling acts, The Shadows, featured up to four names on each record label (on the Columbia subsidiary), running at up to twenty-five letters – so were there further underlying and undisclosed reasons?

As April drew to a close, there was one further significant date pencilled into the diary. On the 26th of that month, over 12,000 music lovers crammed into the famous Empire Pool arena in Wembley, North London, the venue for the eleventh *New Musical Express* Poll Winners Concert. Appearing on the bill alongside a virtual Who's Who in UK popular music – The Beatles, The Rolling Stones, The Merseybeats, The Searchers, Gerry and The Pacemakers, The Dave Clark Five, Billy J. Kramer and The Dakotas, Cliff Richard and The Shadows, Brian Poole and The Tremeloes, Jet Harris, The Swinging Blue Jeans, Kathy Kirby, Freddie and The Dreamers, Manfred Mann and Joe Brown – The Hollies took to the stage following a rather lame opening slot from Ross McManus (father of Elvis Costello) and The Joe Loss Orchestra, and immediately got the crowds rockin' in the aisles. Introduced by compere David Jacobs as "a group who hail from up there in the north", the band entered to an outburst of screams and rapturous applause, before breaking into 'Rockin' Robin', followed by their current Top 10 hit 'Just One Look'. Although they didn't take home any of the awards at the event, the simple fact that they were invited to be the opening act at the concert spoke volumes for their emerging status. It was official; The Hollies were one of the star attractions of the UK music scene. Not that they had the time to savour the occasion. As soon as they had rushed off the stage at Wembley, it was down the busy A23 road to Brighton, along the south coast, where they rejoined the tour for a show at the Hippodrome, alongside The Dave Clark Five.

Somewhat thoughtfully, one may say, the following day they were permitted the luxury of another day off from performing as the tour took a 24-hour respite – but there was no time for relaxation, it seems, with the group opting to use the time to return to the Abbey Road studios to cut five tracks for their second upcoming album. Certainly, with such unwavering commitment, the five band members were earning their money. And yet it appeared that, despite reaping the financial rewards of success, they were seeing very little of it personally.

> As a team, they are earning roughly £13,000 to £15,000 a week. 'But I don't think we are overpaid,' said 22-year-old Graham. 'After all, we have worked for it.'
> In spite of all the money they are earning, The Hollies don't have much time to spend. They have a financial manager in Manchester who holds the purse strings.
>
> *Record Mirror*
> 1964

Having set up Hollies Limited in April 1963, their own company to take care of all of the finances, the band had little dealings themselves with any incoming assets. Overseeing such arrangements was their trusted acquaintance, local Manchester businessman Michael Cohen, still assuming a role within the band's management structure.

'Michael helped us out when we were broke,' Graham was to say in interviews, 'and he has remained a firm friend of us all. Of course, it's in our own interest, but it can get a bit embarrassing when we have to go to him for every penny.'

'Our accountant advised us to form the company, into which all our UK earnings were paid,' Cohen was to comment from behind the desk of his clothing boutique. By agreement, they also set up a separate account into which they would pay any internationally generated income. 'This was solely for tax reasons…' he added.

Cohen ran the business from the offices above his successful Toggery fashion store in Stockport, from where he also oversaw the group's ever-increasing fan club. It is also worth noting that, during this period, he financially assisted and subsequently took over the managerial reins of The Toggery Five, another popular Manchester "beat" band, named after his store, and featuring guitarist-vocalist Frank Renshaw, Allan's supposed replacement following his pending marital announcement. As with The Hollies, that band went on to sign for the Parlophone label during 1964, subsequently releasing two (unsuccessful) singles.

'Everyone wants to become friendly with you,' continued Graham. 'You have to be able to sort out which are your real friends, and which aren't. The thing to remember is not to let people impose upon you. I don't...'

*Record Mirror*
1964

### AN ABC THEATRE
# ABC - CHESTER
Managers: D. S. Baker
TWO PERFORMANCES
## ON THE STAGE
Instead of the usual film programme
Telephone 22931
FOR ONE DAY ONLY
## WEDNESDAY, 7th OCT. at 6.15 & 8.30

Kennedy Street Enterprises Ltd. in association with Tito Burns present

BRITAIN'S TOP ENTERTAINERS

# FREDDIE
and the
# DREAMERS

HIT PARADE STARS

# The HOLLIES

# TONYJACKSON with the VIBRATIONS

# MARIANNE FAITHFULL

Compere DON DWIGHT

# THE TOGGERY FIVE

# The FOUR PENNIES

## Stalls & Circle 10/6  8/6  6/6

PRINTED BY HASTINGS PRINTING COMPANY, PORTLAND PLACE, HASTINGS. TELEPHONE 2450

# CHAPTER SIX

## "HERE I GO AGAIN..."

With a subsequent return visit to Wembley's Empire Pool venue now scheduled – another prestigious slot at the Pop Hit Parade concert, to be held on 31st May, alongside The Rolling Stones, The Merseybeats, Wayne Fontana and The Mindbenders, The Swinging Blue Jeans and Adam Faith – the band were clearly in high spirits, although the constant demands were, without doubt, now weighing heavily on their tired shoulders.

As prominent music journalist Keith Altham, writing in the *New Musical Express*, noted;

Allan Clarke was busily engaged flicking holes with a rubber band through a photograph of Dave Clark in an NME which Eric Haydock held outstretched as he sprawled, seemingly asleep, on the windowsill. 'Eric slept in the van in a lay-by on the road back from Bath this morning,' informed Bobby, as Eric continued to drop off to sleep at every available point. So far, he had said nothing – as usual. I decided to try for an NME exclusive; "Eric Haydock Speaks!" As he staggered sleepily into the lift on leaving, I shouted in his ear. Eric opened one eye and, just before the doors closed, he muttered: 'I'm too tired!' But Eric HAD spoken!

A man of few words, Eric likes to get away as often as possible from the hustle and bustle that is so large a part of The Hollies life. And getting away from it all in Eric's case is roaming about on the moors with a gun, cartridges and something to shoot at.

'I've got seven guns,' he said. 'From a 12-bore automatic to a .177 slug. Often, I just go out on the moors and shoot game. If something moves – bam!'

*New Music Express*
April 1964

Clearly, opportunities for a bit of genuine downtime were greatly appreciated, but they were becoming all too few and far between.

The second half of 1964 would follow pretty much the same path as the first half had so successfully done. The next 45 release, 'Here I Go Again' b/w 'Baby, That's All' (Parlophone R5137) steadily climbed into the UK chart listings, enjoying a healthy twelve-week run, with a peak position of number 4, although, once again, the release failed to make any significant impact in the *Billboard* charts. And that was despite the recent touchdown of Beatlemania in the United States when almost anything with an anglophile accent was generating significant levels of interest.

One of my favourite rave groups, and I'll bet one of yours too, are The Hollies. They have a great sound, are good-looking and wear fab "Mod" gear. In fact, they are a great bunch of guys and are regarded as one of the most friendly groups out. They wander into recording sessions with The Rolling Stones and other artistes at any time. Their latest waxing, 'Here I Go Again', looks like being another smash-hit for the boys and should set them well-placed in a number of overseas charts, besides Britain.

*Pop Weekly*
May 1964

'We came across it almost by accident,' Graham was to comment to the *NME* when discussing the new single. 'We were doing this recording for a BBC programme and backstage we met Mort Shuman, the American composer. We chatted and joked with him before someone said, "Why don't you write a composition for us?"

'A couple of weeks later, we got this letter from Mort. He enclosed the number with his compliments and wished us lots of luck with it!'

The Hollies: 'Here I Go Again' (Parlophone R5137)
The melody has a definite appeal but is not nearly so ear-catching as 'Just One Look'. A highly polished performance though. The contagious twist beat keeps the listener moving from start to finish, and the attractively blended voices – complete with vibratos – are bang in the current idiom. It's unison vocal throughout.

*New Musical Express*
May 1964

It had been during the first week of February '64 that the Hollies/Rolling Stones alliance, as referred to in the above *Pop Weekly* article, had occurred. On 4th February, both Allan and Graham had found themselves outside the Regent Sounds recording studios, along Denmark Street, in London's Soho district. The Rolling Stones were in residency that day, working on a series of new recordings with acclaimed producer Phil Spector and singer-songwriter Gene Pitney also in attendance. Encouraged to come in and participate alongside their illustrious American guests, Graham and Allan duly offered up percussive support and backing vocals to a number of the songs cut during that lengthy session. Perhaps the most infamous was the tribute to Stones' producer Andrew Oldham, entitled 'Andrew's Blues' – a somewhat obscene rendition of 'Can I Get A Witness' that has remained officially unreleased, although bootleg copies did begin leaking out in the early 1970s.

Bill Wyman: 'For our recording session on 4th February, there were some surprise guests; Phil Spector dropped by, Graham Nash and Allan Clarke of The Hollies also came in, and Gene Pitney arrived directly from the airport. Pitney played piano while Spector and The Hollies played tambourine and maracas and banged coins in empty bottles. We recorded three songs; 'Little By Little', 'Can I Get A Witness' and 'Now I've Got A Witness' before the session degenerated into silliness. But everybody had a great time cutting 'Andrew's Blues', and 'Spector and Pitney Came Too', both of which were very rude...'[68]

'We've always had a wild image,' The Stones' co-founder Brian Jones would later suggest. 'We built ourselves on that fact. Groups like The Hollies envy our image a little.' [68]

Interestingly, Graham would again contribute to a Rolling Stones session a few months later, alongside Tony Hicks, offering up support at a demo session for several new Jagger-Richards compositions for the Andrew Oldham Orchestra.

By contrast, the pop sensibility of 'Here I Go Again' entered the UK charts on 27th May and, despite the lack of US success, the band undertook the usual round of heavy televised promotional work, with standard guest appearances on *Ready Steady Go!, Open House, Thank Your Lucky Stars* and *Top of the Pops*. They also taped a live performance, recorded at London's Royal Albert Hall for the BBC2 *Top Beat* series, which was aired that same week, before rounding off the publicity junket by filming a brief sequence at the Shepperton Film Studios, alongside a host of other Brit-pop bands (The Tremeloes, Animals and Swinging Blue Jeans) for a 30-minute music short entitled *UK Swings Again*. This glorious colour footage, aimed at cinema-goers, highlighted the impact that the rhythm section of the band was now making to the sound, with both Bobby and Eric putting in solid performances. 'Baby, That's All', a smoother offering than that which graced the A-side of the single, gave Eric in particular the opportunity to run some truly impressive patterns along the neck of his six-string Fender bass. Without question, the triumvirate of the Elliott-Haydock-Hicks instrumental partnership was now one of the strongest, if not *the* strongest of the rock 'n' roll popular music era. Certainly, the rhythm partnership continues to gather much respect to this very day:

> The quality of the low end became apparent after the original Hollies' drummer was replaced by Bobby Elliott. In him, Eric Haydock found a skin basher worthy of supporting his bass expertise. Right from the start this combination worked incredibly well, with Eric's somewhat flamboyant style and occasional burst of speed usually emanating from a trusty Fender Bass IV, a six-string baritone bass tuned an octave down from guitar. What added extra force to this section pairing was the fact that Elliot was particularly fussy about his bass drum sound, insisting that should have a good, solid recorded sound, allowing Eric to pursue avenues that might have been dangerous without that powerhouse beat behind him.
>
> *Bassist Magazine*
> 1998

Taking it one step further, at one point during the period, Eric also took ownership of the world's only prototype twelve-string bass, which 'sounded great, but was a bugger to play and impossible to keep in tune!'[10]

Utilising a popular marketing ploy of the time, Parlophone then opted to add two further Hollies vinyl releases to their catalogue, in the form of the first in a series of "extended play" (EP) 4-track issues. By including a selection of songs from the debut album, alongside a number of unreleased recordings, and filled out with both sides of the previous 45, the two mono EPs, *The Hollies* and *Just One Look*, both achieved UK chart success on their own merit, with little promotion.

July saw the group once again embarking on the by-now-familiar touring schedule, although the opening show on the list, in Clacton-On-Sea, had to be cancelled due to Allan Clarke coming down with a throat infection. However, having sufficiently recovered, Allan and his bandmates then kicked off with an eight-day tour of Scotland, playing alongside Wayne Fontana and The Mindbenders and Johnny and The Copycats. Unfortunately, a proposed appearance at the Chantinghall Ballroom in Hamilton, ten miles out of Glasgow, was cancelled when, following on from the riotous reception The Rolling Stones had received the previous month, the promoter pulled out, wary of a repeat. Hamilton magistrates even imposed a ban on travelling beat groups in the wake of the outcry. Instead, the band moved on to five days of performing in the Channel Islands in late July. Up and down the entire country, with nary a thought for scheduling. Surviving footage from a local island travelogue, featuring the quintet messing around on go-karts at a Jersey amusement park, clearly depicted a band enjoying their first trip off the British mainland.

They then joined up with Big Dee Irwin, Shane Fenton and The Fentones and Syd and Eddie (later known as comedians Little and Large) for a three-week residency at the Gaumont Theatre, located in the seaside tourist resort of Weymouth, along the southern coastline. Finally, it was back to the regular one-nighters for the Autumn '64 package tour with Freddie and The Dreamers, The Four Pennies, Tony Jackson and The Vibrations and fellow stablemates The Toggery Five. For the newly-wed Allan, however, it would be the added inclusion of the teenage Marianne Faithfull on the bill who would prove one temptation too far – although the ensuing brief extra-marital relationship didn't extend beyond a short liaison on the road (as Marianne herself later recounted in her 1994 autobiography *Faithfull*).

There was also one additional face added to the itinerary with new recruit, tour manager and lighting director Rod Shields accompanying the band on the road for the first time, replacing regular sideman Jay Vickers who, following a falling-out with Graham, was moved aside. Rod would go on to become a loyal confidant to the members for many years to come.

'This tour we're doing is a load of fun,' Bobby was to say to the *New Musical Express*. 'We're having plenty of laughs with Freddie and The Dreamers and everyone. When we finish it, we've got another to do with Heinz and Jess Conrad, but we can afford to stop at all the best hostels and transport caffs now!'

Needless to say, further scheduled visits to the tree-lined St John's Wood district of London were squeezed in amongst the continuing pandemonium, with the band's upcoming third single release of that year, 'We're Through', a new composition bearing the "L. Ransford" songwriting credit, making its studio debut during August. Initially cut utilising two alternate arrangements, the final chosen mix of the song, the faster of the two, was the first time a group credit was placed upon the lead side of any Hollies single. Following its first chart appearance on 23rd September, it would go on to reach the number 7 position during an eleven-week run. Nevertheless, whilst undoubtedly happy with the recognition it received, Ron Richards still felt the composition lacked the quality that an established songwriter could offer them and continued to encourage the group to carry on looking for outside material. Once again, however, upon its release across the ocean, Imperial Records release 66070 failed to break through into the US market. For a group whose influences lay so directly in the land of the free, and who were constantly hitting the Top 10 positions in their homeland, it must have been immensely frustrating. And without a hit record to their name in America, there were no US performing offers landing on the office desks of the Toggery.

April of that year had seen The Beatles, in the wake of their debut performances on US television, hold down the entire top five positions in the Billboard singles charts. Gerry and The Pacemakers and The Rolling Stones were to follow soon after, consolidating their newly acquired positions as Hot 100 acts, whilst The Dave Clark Five were already regular Top 10 contenders. And then came The Animals, a rough Newcastle-based quintet who would take America by storm before the summer was out with a cover of the classic folk-blues standard 'House Of The Rising Sun'. Yet, for The Hollies, there was little to crow about beyond the British coastal waters.

There had been a modicum of international success in the less-publicised chart regions of Norway, Sweden, Canada and New Zealand, whilst two Top 30 placings in Australia had started a lifelong, loyal following down under. However, outside of the United Kingdom, the USA was seen as the place to guarantee international status. Both Liberty Records and Imperial Records had Hollies releases on their catalogue in the US but, in the same way that The Beatles had initially laboured with both Vee-Jay and Swan Records, these releases saw little airplay, and a lowly number 98 placement in *Billboard* had been the lone achievement to date. One is left to seriously question this, seeing the financial weight and size of the recognisable Liberty brand (who owned the Imperial subsidiary) in comparison to the smaller, independent Beatle-related labels. With successful American artists of the calibre of David Seville, Bobby Vee, Jan and Dean, Del Shannon and Johnny Burnette on their roster, it stands as bewildering that, with the looming prospect of a full British invasion on the horizon, and with a succession of popular UK acts already lining up at London Airport to board their cross-Atlantic BEA flights, Liberty Records could initially offer so little to The Hollies.

Even the novelty aspect of fellow Manchester artists Freddie and The Dreamers, with the wacky choreography and music-hall trouser-dropping routines, would somehow strike a muted chord with the American record-buying public before they finally caught on to what The Hollies could really offer.

Back home and the publicity machine was gearing up another notch. Allan, Graham, Eric, Tony and Bobby were now featured regularly in many of the weekly music papers and teen-zines that proliferated the newsstands around the country. Rarely would a week pass by without either *Record Mirror, New Musical Express, Pop Weekly, Disc & Music Echo, Fabulous* or *Rave* running an article or a news report on the popular fivesome somewhere within their pages. More often than not, said articles, particularly those geared towards the younger female audience, would lead off with such tantalising headlines as;

HOLLIES THANK FREDDIE FOR "TIP"!
GRAHAM WANTED TO PLAY WITH SHARKS!
HOLLIES IMAGE IS A WORRY!
HOLLIES TO HOLIDAY ON THE CONTINENT!
THE HOLLIES FLIP OVER THEIR HOUND DOGS!

It therefore came as no surprise when the national *Daily Mirror* newspaper jumped on board the fast-paced Hollie-train and published a paperback book, aimed at the mass teenage market. *The Hollies Tell You How to Run a Beat Group*, a typical exploitation ploy, first appeared on the book stands during the summer of 1964 and, priced at a mere two shillings and sixpence, offered the reader all the experienced advice that the band, and co-author Anne Nightingale, could muster.

Graham Nash: 'Every group must have a leader. He is usually the one with the drive and determination to get on. When I became the leader of The Hollies, I reckoned that if we were going to set ourselves up as a good group, then we had to do the job properly…'

Tony Hicks: 'Study the pop charts regularly. That way you will be able to anticipate any requests you get…'

Allan Clarke: 'Boys in groups mustn't hesitate about using make-up for stage work. There's no need to go to the extent of using eye make-up or lipstick, but you need colouring on your face. The best is Max Factor Pan Cake No.27 for fair skin, No.28 for dark…'

From these quotes you will gain some idea of how useful this book is to those planning to form groups.

Daily Mirror Publications
1964

Nevertheless, the book failed to mention that Graham Nash and Anne Nightingale developed more than a casual writing session during their short time together.

'He had a fling with [Nightingale],' Eric Haydock would later state to the *News of the World*. 'She was writing a book about The Hollies, [but] she was so boring I don't know what he saw in her…'

The Hollies are delighted because 'We're Through' is the first of their own compositions to be used as an A-side. Recorded several weeks ago with some other titles, it was put on a shelf – but not forgotten.

A&R man Ron Richards listened to it again, liked the song, but felt it needed more time on recording. 'Let's remake it,' he decided.

'We gave it a lot of thought,' Ron tells me, 'and spent a whole afternoon in the studio working on it, giving it more beat and more polish till we were sure it was right.'

*Disc & Music Echo*
September 1964

'We did a summer season in Weymouth some time ago,' recalled Bobby. 'It meant we lived in one place for a few weeks and we had time to laze around on the beach during the day. I suppose it was the lazy atmosphere that induced Allan to write 'We're Through'.

'When he wrote it, it was a very Latin-type thing, almost a bossa nova. We didn't think about it very much, until we took a day off to go up to London to do some recording. The song came up and we decided to cut it as an LP track, but it turned out so well, in fact, the Latin flavour got lost somewhere, that we had to release it as a single.' (*New Musical Express*)

'We're Through' was a different approach for the band, certainly from an arrangement perspective. The initial opening drum fill and the intricate acoustic guitar riff that hit the listener right from the off, was a world away from the thumping beat that had opened up both 'Stay' and 'Here I Go Again'. The results demonstrated how far the Hollies-Richards partnership had come in their studio experimentation together. Ron Richards may have come from a previous generation and was set in his studio mannerisms, but he was certainly open to the ideas and arrangements the five young musicians had in mind, particularly with their own compositions.

'He held the reins,' observed Allan Clarke once, 'but he always listened to our ideas. He taught us one hell of a lot. We worked as a team, but he always had the last word. When you sang a song, you sang it to Ron. If he objected to it or didn't think it was right, we didn't do it.'[18/19]

'He had a great ear, and we relied on his judgement,' added Graham. 'The only thing he did that pissed me off was to tell me we couldn't record past 10:30 in the evening because the echo machines went off at that time. It wasn't until years later that I realised echo machines don't automatically shut off. It dawned on me that 10:30 was closing time at the pub and Ron and the engineers wanted to get a pint in before last call!'[1]

Surprisingly void of the distinctive three-part harmonies the group was developing, and set to a pulsating rhythmic pattern, the single release was yet another unqualified success, paired off with the impressive driving pace and the harmonica riffs of the self-composed 'Come On Back', perhaps a last gasp of air for the raw sounds of the northern beat boom. It appears that the group were also content to relinquish any credible promotional appearances to aid sales, as an appearance on the top-rated children's TV variety show *Crackerjack* on 23rd October would show. Rock 'n' roll it wasn't, but the rows upon rows of school children, seated amiably in the theatre audience, weren't to know that.

Late October also saw both Graham and Tony, mid-tour, active in the recording studios once again, albeit on this occasion it was taking place in Stockport, near to where they had both started their own careers. Prior to their own evening performance, they offered support at a session for The Warriors, a fellow Lancastrian band that included future Yes vocalist Jon Anderson (and, later, keyboard player Brian Chatton) in their line-up. It was reported in the media at the time that the group were cutting a version of a new Clarke-Hicks-Nash composition 'Too Much (Please Don't Feel Too Bad)', and although that particular recording remained unreleased (surviving only in a demo acetate form), both Graham and Tony had dropped by to assist in the studio that day.

'We used to play at Nelson Imperial [Ballroom] a lot,' recalls Warriors' guitarist Rod Hill. 'Our bass guitarist Dave Foster picked up with Maureen, Tony Hicks' sister, and we used to go around to their parents' house in Nelson after playing. We used to bump into them all over at gigs and became friends.

'Graham [Nash] invited us to his house in Cheshire where he played a cassette of their original material which he then gave us. We then recorded at least one track in Stockport. Graham basically produced it...'[75]

The numerous recording sessions that The Hollies somehow squeezed into their busy schedules, in between a stream of live bookings, before long allowed them to compile enough songs for a second long-playing release. Pencilled in for a late autumn issue, the chosen twelve songs, gathered together under the banner of *In The Hollies Style*, were a change of direction for the group, in as much as they perhaps now believed they knew what their style was becoming. Or did they?

Unlike the debut LP, a compilation of almost a full collection of cover versions, the new offering was heavily weighted in favour of self-composed tunes, and even then, of the five cover versions that did make the cut, only two of these (Chuck Berry's 'Too Much Monkey Business' and Rudy Clark's 'It's In Her Kiss' – aka 'The Shoop Shoop Song') were widely enough known to UK audiences to be instantly recognisable. The issue with the remaining cuts, and the reason perhaps behind the relatively fewer sales figures that followed, certainly in comparison to the longevity of the debut album, was that the Clarke-Hicks-Nash (Ransford) songwriting partnership had yet to consolidate quantity with quality. Standards of the early 1960s UK music business often dictated that the current hit singles generated by the popular bands were rarely featured on any of their long-playing releases. As these were considered the strongest cuts available, the remaining compositions, often written and worked on in dingy one-nighter hotel rooms around the country or as last-minute collaborations in the studio, were more often than not simple throwaways, with little studio crafting and nowhere near the same attributes as the 45s. It was these that were subsequently designated as mere album cuts. In 1964, the long-playing record was not the art form it would become in later years.

*In The Hollies Style* found the group still trying to work out what that actually *was*. The 45s had certainly suggested the path ahead, but the albums were lagging that little bit behind. The time constraints from such a heavy touring schedule dictated it so. That is not to write it off entirely. They had come a long way since their debut release, and of the newer compositions from the trio, 'Don't You Know', 'To You My Love' and the frantic closing 'Set Me Free' are all noteworthy cuts, as is their own version of 'Please Don't Feel Too Bad' (recently taped by The Warriors), and from a sleek production perspective it was a significant step. The assured lustre of Allan's lead vocals, the tight blending of the harmonies (notably on 'Time For Love'), with Graham's higher register smoothly sliding in without the need to veer into falsetto, show the conviction the group was now taking from their stage act and putting into a studio setting. The consistency wasn't there... yet, and the subsequent sales hesitated accordingly, with the release purportedly failing to achieve any significant official chart ranking, but the record remains a firm favourite for many in the catalogue to this day. That said, in 1964, the recognised *Record Retailer* UK LP charts did only consist of twenty placings – with The Beatles, The Rolling Stones, Manfred Mann, The Kinks and Jim Reeves holding down the top spots – whilst chart-compiling rivals, the *NME*, sourcing their sales figures elsewhere, justifiably afforded the album a respectable peak of number 6 within their own independent listings. This confirmed that the tills were ringing favourably across the country and copies of the album were shifting in notable quantities in selected outlets.

Of note, that autumn also saw the belated release of their debut album in the USA, released by Imperial Records as *Here I Go Again*. In yet another attempt to launch the group on American soil, the first album was reconstructed for an American audience, adding both 'Here I Go Again' and 'Just One Look', along with 'Keep Off That Friend Of Mine' to nine of the songs from the UK version. Packaged within a new sleeve layout, this was, arguably, a far stronger collection than either of the UK issues to date but, inexplicably, still failed to reach an audience amongst the vast overseas population.

'I don't think there's any special reason for us not making it in America,' Graham was to comment in an *NME* article during October 1964. 'We'd like to hit it big over there; it's just that we're taking things a lot easier than other groups. You see, we want to be a group that *stays*, not one that has a big hit in the States and is immediately forgotten. We think that to get ourselves known there is something that's got to be carefully planned. We haven't done much for ourselves promotion-wise over there [but] there are one or two things going on right now, which might mean an American tour, but nothing definite.'

That same article went on to comment that the band had written twenty-five new songs whilst travelling on the tour with Freddie and The Dreamers and that The Toggery Five may record one of these, 'I Can't See You Again', for themselves;

'Obviously we haven't arranged them yet, we have just the melodies and the lyrics, but we're pretty pleased with this batch. One especially, because it might be our first composition that someone else has recorded...'

Unfortunately, that particular opportunity never came to pass.

A second album from the group and most of the tracks emphasise how their musical togetherness has grown during recent months. I rate them as high as any British group but, extraordinarily, they seem to just miss the really big time. For me, The Hollies are clean-cut, disciplined yet spasmodically raw-edged, always professional in their music. Obviously, they've left nothing to chance on the Ron Richards controlled set. It'll sell really well.

*Record Mirror*
November 1964

The Hollies have that magical talent. I still can't figure out why everyone flips over The Beatles and The Stones and yet they don't go quite so crazy over the Hollies, who haven't missed the charts yet with one of their singles. These days it seems that long hair and talent have to go hand in hand if one wants more publicity. Let's hope that the shorter-haired Hollies come into the reckoning as one of the top groups of the year.

*Pop Weekly*
November 1964

On 9th November, having completed yet another extensive UK package tour alongside Heinz and The Wild Boys, Jess Conrad, The Tornadoes and The Dixie Cups, the band returned to the stage of London's Royal Albert Hall for a second appearance on the BBC *Top Beat* broadcast (airing two days later), ultimately bringing their hectic one-night touring schedule to a close for the year. There would still be a few sporadic appearances before 1964 wound down completely (an appearance at the Cavern on 24th November was subsequently taped and broadcast by Radio Luxembourg), but the break in performing allowed them to take time and spend a few more days in residence at Studio Two in Abbey Road.

The 15th December recording session saw them tackle four new songs, including a first pass at what would become the next 45rpm release, a new composition entitled 'Yes, I Will', composed by the vastly experienced New York-based songwriting team of Gerry Goffin and Russ Titelman. Brought to the group's attention by Ron Richards, courtesy of a demo version he had recently obtained featuring Goffin's wife, Carole King, the first take of the tune relied heavily on an arrangement featuring Tony's acoustic guitar. Whilst the three-part harmonies shone through on the recording, headed by Allan's immaculate phrasing, by the time further attempts were made on the song in the new year (sixteen takes in total were attempted in the studio), an alternative electrified arrangement was in place. This would go on to provide yet another Top 10 placement in the catalogue. Five in a row and counting.

With a further two Parlophone 4-track EPs – *Here I Go Again* and *We're Through* – now also on the record shelves in time for Christmas, the band closed out the year by appearing on the popular *Five O'clock Club* TV show (filmed in London's Trafalgar Square), followed by the seasonal pantomime at Liverpool's Odeon Theatre, accompanying Gerry and The Pacemakers, Cliff Bennett and The Rebel Rousers, The Fourmost, Danny Williams and Tommy Quickly in *Gerry's Christmas Cracker*. After one week, the show transferred to the Leeds Odeon and, finally, to Glasgow.

"Gerry's Christmas Cracker", a Brian Epstein presentation, opened at Liverpool's Odeon on Boxing night. The title more than justified itself – it turned out to be a cracker of a show. One weak spot is the poor comedy material, which doesn't give Gerry and the boys much to work on. The Hollies were in superb form, relaxed and professional as they gave an appreciative and packed house their hit numbers, plus the slow 'That's My Desire', the wailing 'Nobody' and 'Something's Got A Hold On Me'.

*New Musical Express*
December 1964

## THE *NEW MUSICAL EXPRESS* 1964 POLL WINNERS
Category: British Vocal Group

1. The Beatles
2. The Rolling Stones
3. The Bachelors
4. The Searchers
5. Manfred Mann
6. The Kinks
7. The Shadows
8. The Hollies
9. The Animals
10. The Dave Clark Five
11. Gerry and The Pacemakers
12. The Four Pennies

BRIAN EPSTEIN Presents
# GERRY'S CHRISTMAS CRACKER

GERRY and the PACEMAKERS

THE HOLLIES

THE FOURMOST

DANNY WILLIAMS

TOMMY QUICKLY THE REMO FOUR

CLIFF BENNETT and the REBEL ROUSERS

JOHNNY HACKETT

THE RUSTIKS

DEVISED AND PRODUCED BY PETER YOLLAND

For
Brian Epstein

Assistant producer John Lyndon
Scenic Designer Andrew Drummond
Stage Director Les Howard
Press Representative Tony Barrow

For the
Rank Organisation
Theatre Division

Booking Controller George Pinches
Production Director Stan Fishman
Stage Director Bill West
Advertising & Publicity Michael Buist

Scenery made and painted by Stage Decor Ltd., Harold Fielding Ltd., Jas. Fredricks Studios
Additional lighting equipment by Strand Electric & Engineering Co. Ltd.    Costumes by Bermans Ltd.
Additional material by Ireland Cutter, Peter Yolland and John Blythe

# CHAPTER SEVEN

---

# "IT'S ALL SO CLEAN-CUT...."

1965, and it was fast becoming a recognisable routine for Allan, Graham, Eric, Tony and Bobby. The scene going on around them was holding a familiar pattern, day in, day out, and only the points on the map, informing them of which town they were performing in, were changing. Leeds, Stourbridge, Bradford, Dunstable, Ramsey... all passed by the van window during the early months of the year as they toured up and down the country, appearing nightly in the all-too-similar-looking Odeons, ballrooms and theatres.

In between the shows, there were recording sessions in Abbey Road, followed by the obligatory rounds of television appearances promoting each new release – *Top of the Pops, Scene At 6.30, Thank Your Lucky Stars, Ready Steady Go!* – and radio guest spots – *Saturday Club, Delaney's Delight, Top Gear* – along with endless interviews with newspaper and magazine journalists. Some of these exchanges they clearly enjoyed – whilst others reflected a beat scene starting to become a little weary;

Q: How long do you think The Hollies can last?
A: That's a difficult question...
Q: Try answering it anyway.
Q: Why don't you appeal to older people, like The Beatles are doing now?

Q: Why is it that you always leave a stage door and never sign autographs? Is it because you are getting big-headed?

*"Under The Pop Searchlight"*

*Pop Weekly*

The recording session held on 3rd January had resulted in a satisfactory take of 'Yes, I Will', and the publicity rounds once again started in earnest once the disc appeared in the record stores on the 22nd (Parlophone 5232), backed with the introspective 'Nobody', one of the group's most mature compositions to date. An appearance at Manchester's Oasis Club, scheduled for 7th February, was cancelled at the last minute as Allan had been involved in a car crash that day. Fortunately for all, the lead singer wasn't seriously injured and the promotional appearances continued soon after.

Unsurprisingly, given the band's now loyal following, the single comfortably slotted into the UK Top 10, peaking at the number 9 position during a thirteen-week visit to the national hit parade.

As they took a break from the endless promotional circuit, the following month threw a different challenge in their direction. On 17th February, the group participated in a new weekly TV show, one that partially focussed on the viewer as the central participants. *Three Go Round* was a short-lived children's series, airing on the Southern TV network, that also featured a music competition in its weekly round-up. Viewers were invited to write a pop song themselves, send it in, and the best would subsequently be submitted to record companies for potential release. The competition was hosted by the successful songwriter Mitch Murray (creator of 'How Do You Do It?', 'I Like It' and 'I'm Telling You Now'), with the best entries to be announced and played by a top group on the show. Sadly, it appears there is now no record of what The Hollies performed on their first visit to the show (they would make a return visit later that same year), or of any success stories that came about as a result of winning the show itself… but it's a fascinating concept – and one that backs up the theory that any publicity is good publicity. Even if it meant appearing on *Crackerjack* (as the band were to do once again, the following month) and *Ollie and Fred's Five O'clock Club*, an equally popular children's show, hosted by two ragged glove puppets. However, in its favour, the music director of the latter show was UK blues legend Alexis Korner, who would often handpick the guest appearances himself.

Nevertheless, despite the draw of such TV publicity, the band still maintained their music credentials on the road, as a joint headlining tour with The Rolling Stones showed during the early spring of 1965. Packaged up alongside Dave Berry, The Checkmates and the American all-girl group Goldie and The Gingerbreads, the tour undertook the usual two-week jaunt around the cities and suburbs, performing in Liverpool, Manchester, Scarborough, Sunderland, Huddersfield, Rugby, Greenford, Leicester, Southend-on-Sea and Romford along the way.

'It was absolutely insane,' noted Graham at the time. 'There was an incredible difference between the depth of emotion expressed for The Stones and for us. We could certainly drive them crazy, but it went to a brand-new level when The Stones came on. It was somewhere deeper and darker than Beatlemania...'[68]

Recalled Tony Hicks (in a 2013 interview for the *Daily Mail*), 'It was expected of us, as runners-up so to speak, to close the first half of the show. But we refused, insisting we went on just before The Stones as if to challenge them to "follow that".'

With the first ten rows of the stalls on their feet screaming and the rest on their feet trying to see The Stones, a highly emotional 'Time Is On My Side' caused waves of fans to surge down the aisles at the stage only to be broken up by a breakwater of police and ushers.

During 'Route 66' and 'I'm All Right', Mick Jagger obtained hysterical reactions from a well-timed flick of the head or jerk of his body (look, Mum, no pants splitting) and impressed with a new confidence and assurance in his vocals.

The highlight of The Hollies' varied and impressive close to the first half was the folksy 'Very Last Day', which the audience were invited to 'boo us off' if they did not approve. The audience listened (no screams) and cheered it to an echo. Their other numbers were 'Here I Go Again', 'Mickey's Monkey', 'Just One Look', 'That's My Desire', 'Yes, I Will' and 'Too Much Monkey Business'. This is one package with more of a "bang" than a "pop".

Keith Altham
*New Musical Express*
March 1965

'Those Stones gigs were something else,' Graham would add. 'Mayhem to the nth degree. The first time we played with them that joint was jumping before anyone hit the stage.'[1]

Despite sharing the road and the stage with such rebellious untouchables as Jagger, Richards, Jones and company, The Hollies themselves played it quietly when it came to the immediate after-show frenzy. Or, at least, to the watching eye. In his autobiography, Graham would later confess to certain dalliances with one particular female member of the touring entourage – and that there was certainly a little "ginger" added to the mix.

'There was very little outrageous behaviour,' Tony would continue in his *Daily Mail* interview, 'although I can remember us checking out of a hotel in the morning and seeing the lounge piano balanced on the end of the diving board over the pool. Did we do that? Who knows? But we never got into the really wild stuff like throwing TVs out of the window.'

'When you are touring for weeks on end you begin to suffer from what bands call "road madness",' responded Bobby in a similar article for the *Daily Mirror*. 'You get really fed up with the faceless hotels. Once we got so bored, we wheeled out a white piano in the dead of the night and left it on the end of a diving board in the hotel's swimming pool. When we got up the next morning it was still there, gently bouncing up and down as guests lounged by the pool.'

'We'd go to parties,' added Tony, 'but they didn't really do anything for us. Our manager was a tailor by trade, and he'd turn up backstage, hoping to sell some clothes on the side. His best customer was Keith Richards, who'd buy almost everything he was shown, [but] there was no real rivalry. We knew our place. And that was immediately before they went on…'

5th March 1965: Edmonton Regal Theatre, London
6th March 1965: Empire Theatre, Liverpool
7th March 1965: Palace Theatre, Manchester
8th March 1965: Futurist Theatre, Scarborough
9th March 1965: Odeon Theatre, Sunderland
10th March 1965: ABC Theatre, Huddersfield
11th March 1965: City Hall, Sheffield
12th March 1965: Trocadero Theatre, Leicester
13th March 1965: Granada Theatre, Rugby
14th March 1965: Odeon Theatre, Rochester

15th March 1965: Odeon Theatre, Guildford
16th March 1965: Granada Theatre, Greenford
17th March 1965: Odeon Theatre, Southend-on-Sea
18th March 1965: ABC, Romford

A brief visit across the northern borders to play a few shows in Scotland followed onwards but then, as Graham had previously predicted, came the news that The Hollies had received an invite from a US-based entrepreneur named Morris Levy, founder of the Roulette Record label, to perform in America as part of a New York-based Easter show, to be held at the legendary Paramount Theatre on 43rd Street & Broadway, Manhattan. Hosted by popular comedian and TV host "Soupy" Sales, and featuring ten other "name" acts, including Little Richard, The Hullaballoos, The Detergents, Shirley Ellis, Dee Dee Warwick, King Curtis and The Exciters, this ten-day run in the Big Apple – and on Broadway no less – was what the band had been waiting for. This was their chance to show the US what they could offer! Or not.

Their initial departure from London was significantly delayed due to visa and work permit issues (a visiting "exchange" of US musicians had to take place before The Hollies were granted permission to fly) and then, upon arriving in New York, the band were left floundering from the start when no one was there to meet them at the airport. Nevertheless, upon sorting out transport, and now running behind schedule (thus missing the first two shows), they immediately headed off to the Paramount, only to be informed upon arrival that their slot on the bill would consist of just two songs – performed five times a day, starting mid-morning and running through until the late evening. Each and every day. It certainly wasn't the big promotional launching pad that the five members had envisaged but… still, this *was* America, the land that they had all dreamed about, and so they simply stood back, wide-eyed and breathed in the air, or the Manhattan taxi fumes, and took in the entire New York experience with wonder. Working alongside such luminaries as Little Richard was an experience all in itself – particularly for Graham Nash, who later recalled with particular note how the great coiffured rock 'n' roller chewed out his backing guitarist for upstaging him. That guitarist would later get his own back, surpassing the heights of his former band leader when performing under his own name – James Marshall Hendrix. That said, Little Richard swiftly fell out with

Levy over the arrangements of the show, as he was prone to overrunning his allotted two-song time frame and was subsequently removed from the bill after the second night.

Each day, starting at 10.30am, 3,000 teenagers would snake around Times Square, hoping for seats at the morning performance. The Hollies, for their part, then churned out their daily routine versions of 'Stay' and 'Mickey's Monkey' to the screaming crowds with professionalism, occasionally alternating with 'Rockin' Robin' or 'Here I Go Again', before staggering out into the neon New York nightlife after the curtain had closed for the final time that day.

More often than not, the offstage opportunities were spent relaxing at the famous Peppermint Lounge club or catching up on the local music scene, with jazz enthusiast Bobby, in particular, thrilled to see such legends as Gene Krupa, Stan Getz, Dizzy Gillespie, Cannonball Adderley and Charlie Mingus performing at nearby venues. They were also fortunate enough to watch one of the earliest performances by the newly formed Lovin' Spoonful, who were still learning their trade as a working unit, playing at the Café Bizarre in Greenwich Village. Whilst the touring party were booked in to stay at the Abby Victoria Hotel for the duration of their visit, it seems likely that, other than actual sleeping, the hotel was barely used by the excited tourists.

'Walking along Broadway gave me the chills,' Graham would suggest. 'It was just like in the movies. The lights and the people were insane. I couldn't take my eyes off the Camel billboard that blew gigantic smoke rings into the air. I was in love with the place and it kicked off my lifelong romance with the States. I couldn't get over how the taps turned on in the bathroom and hearing the phone ring like it did in the American movies. And getting take-out food. There was no such thing in England!'[1]

In addition to their live shows at the Paramount, on the 23rd of April, they also taped their first appearance for US television, performing their current UK Top 10 'Yes, I Will' on the recently launched NBC musical variety series, *Hullaballoo,* a big-budget primetime showcase for many leading bands of the day (two days of rehearsals had taken place prior to the actual filming), and created to rival the ever-popular *American Bandstand* and *Shindig!* shows. The Hollies' appearance (airing four days later) kicked off in bizarre style with a gyrating George Hamilton, acting as host, introducing the band on a small stage, amidst a gathering of twisting and frugging hipsters, go-go-ing at high speed to the slightly mid-tempo ballad. Nevertheless, the band put in an incredibly adept live performance with their three-part vocal harmonies hitting the mark perfectly. With Graham now also combing his hair across his forehead, a sign of the times (or in recognition of the American fascination for all things Brit), if one listens carefully enough, the occasional squeal of delight from the females in attendance can also be detected.

Then, on the day the appearance was aired across the nation, giving American viewers their first glimpse of The Hollies in action, the band paid a visit to the Bell Recording Studios, located on West 54th Street in Manhattan. During their downtime in the big city, Graham, Allan and Tony had worked on some new compositions together and subsequently took three of them into the studio to cut as demo recordings.

'In those days there weren't cassette players,' commented Bobby Elliott to *Rolling Stone* magazine. 'The guys had written some songs and wanted to get them down, so we didn't forget them. There was one, 'So Lonely', I remember Clarkie saying, "Oh, that'd be great for the Righteous Brothers." You can tell it's a bit tongue-in-cheek.'

In addition to the dramatic overtones of 'So Lonely', the boys also cut the folky, railroad sound of 'Listen Here To Me' and the rougher edge of 'Bring Back Your Love To Me'. Out of these recordings, only 'So Lonely' would have any further studio time spent on it once they returned to home shores. However, the taping of 'Bring Back Your Love To Me' was not completely lost either, as the song would be deconstructed at a later date and used as the basis for a completely different release two years later.

The band's US publicity drive also received a further shot in the arm during May of 1965, when the British cinema short, *UK Swings Again*, was incorporated in a package alongside an earlier featurette (not including The Hollies) and given a US cinema run. Retitled and extended as *Go-Go Big Beat*, and misleadingly featuring several Beatles songs (performed by another Liverpudlian soundalike quintet named The Cheynes), the film unfortunately disappeared from the movie houses and drive-in theatres soon afterwards, once a lawsuit by the fab four ensued.

Allan Clarke: This visit to America really was the most. We were appearing with Little Richard, The Vibrations, The Hullabaloos, The Exciters and Shirley "Nitty Gritty" Ellis. What a show!

When we tried to squeeze out of the theatre, we used to find fans following us everywhere. In the shops, along the streets... everywhere. It was like a snowball...

*New Musical Express*
June 1965

Back in England, still buzzing with the sounds of the *Star-Spangled Banner* ringing in their ears, the group immediately leapt aboard the Spring '65 package tour, alongside The Kinks, The Yardbirds and Graham's favourite ladies, Goldie and The Gingerbreads, for a two-week run around the provinces. However, that tour is perhaps recalled in rock 'n' roll history for events other than the music. Four days before the final show was due to be held, whilst playing the Capitol Cinema in Cardiff, Dave Davies of The Kinks and the band's drummer, Mick Avory, had a violent altercation on stage, directly in front of several thousand screaming teenagers, ultimately resulting in Avory crashing the hi-hat pedal and cymbal down on Davies' head.

Kinks frontman and principal songwriter (and Dave's elder brother), Ray, later recounted, 'That could have been the end of The Kinks right there, it really had a tremendous emotional effect on me. We were just kids, don't forget, and forever having a go at each other. I just guess that on that evening Mick decided to do something about it, and that meant cutting my brother's head off!'

In the chaos that followed, an unconscious Dave was rushed to Cardiff Royal Infirmary to receive stitches to his wounds, whilst Avory fled the venue and into the night, convinced he'd killed his bandmate.

The police wanted to charge the errant drummer for attempted murder, and TV's *News at Ten* even interviewed him later on that night from a "secret location".

'When they finally caught up with and arrested him, Mick tried to deny it all. But the cops turned around and said, "Mr Avory, we've got 5,000 witnesses!"'

Evidently, all charges were dropped but the result had a serious effect on the career of The Kinks, with their unsavoury reputation causing the American Federation of Musicians to refuse them permission to tour the States for the next four years, thereby cutting them off from a huge US fan base at a time when British music was at the height of its popularity there. Needless to say, the four final shows on the tour were played without

Muswell Hill's finest. Their spot on the stage was filled by the UK-based, American-born trio, the Walker Brothers.

As was often the case, any availability between live dates was frequently filled by The Hollies' management. With a show in Aldershot scheduled for 5th May, and the venue being a mere 50-mile drive from North London, a recording session at EMI studios was slotted in for that day, with plans to work on one particular new song recently brought to their attention.

Frank Renshaw from The Toggery Five later recounted on his own band's website, 'After their first two single releases had failed to bring The Toggery Five a much-desired chart entry, Wayne Fontana gave the group a Clint Ballard Jr song to record as their next single. The song was originally written for Gene Pitney, who had rejected it, as did Fontana. He said it wasn't his style. We liked it a lot, booked time at Abbey Road Studios, and recorded it with Ron Richards as producer. He then played it to The Hollies, and they stole it! They quickly recorded it themselves, then got a release date two weeks before ours, and stopped our version from being released. Our manager, Mike Cohen, who also managed The Hollies, thought that this song was so good it would be their first number one. And it was!

'I'm sure it would have made a turning point for The Toggery Five because it was such a good song...'

'I'm Alive' was rush-released to the market as The Hollies' new 45, just sixteen days after recording it. True to the faith that everyone had in it, the song topped the UK charts at the end of June, spending one week in pole position before being displaced by Elvis Presley's mournful 'Crying In The Chapel'. Not to be outdone, however, The Hollies then reclaimed the top spot seven days later, holding down the position for a further two weeks before finally succumbing to America's new hot-shots, The Byrds, who reached the UK pinnacle with the jingly-jangly sounds of 'Mr Tambourine Man'. It was fast becoming a healthy period for the British music scene, as many of America's new talents gradually began to challenge the UK dominance of the previous twelve months in the wake of "Beatlemania". 1965 would become a ground-breaking year for many.

The Hollies: 'I'm Alive' (Parlophone R5287)

Touted as perhaps the best yet from this highly talented group. Nice lyric idea, with group vocal taking a while to really get going. As ever, it's a clean-cut, decisive sort of vocal sound; and the guitar-drum backing is imaginative and solid. A very good record indeed. Flip also has most of the Hollie trademarks, but the number isn't so immediately catchy. Top Fifty Tip.

*Record Mirror*
May 1965

Parlophone's 'I'm Alive' is excellent material for The Hollies who give a distinctive performance. A medium-paced beater with a lead vocal of great impact. It is all so clean-cut and nicely produced; the finished effect is striking. Good luck, lads!

*Pop Weekly*
May 1965

Clean-cut it was then!

'The ending of 'I'm Alive', when the tempo doubles up, that's my arrangement,' states Bobby, confirming his input into the song's memorable conclusion. 'It's like a proper ending. It's not a fade. But that was the influence of our stage shows; we were still trying to create that excitement. It was teamwork. The three guys would be working out their harmonies most of the time, but I'd try and get the intros, the arrangements...' [42]

'At the end of that song it should have been all in the key of C. Well, Tony was playing in C and singing harmony in it, but I was singing and playing in G,' laughed Graham to *Disc Weekly*. 'We couldn't do anything because the red light was on, so we carried on until we'd finished and the red light went off. Then we all started swearing at each other. When we heard the playback and it sounded so good we decided to leave it in!'

'The guy who wrote 'Game Of Love' penned this,' commented Tony Hicks, when questioned by the *New Musical Express*, shortly after the single was released. 'He offered it to Wayne Fontana as a follow-up, [but] Wayne said it was rubbish and he didn't want it. We got to know of it when we were in America and we were just knocked out. We'd already recorded some material with a single in mind, but this was so good we rushed into the studio and did it instead.'

Notably, Wayne Fontana and The Mindbenders soon released another Clint Ballard Jr composition, 'She Needs Love', a song that, according to media reports at the time, The Hollies had previously turned down. The single subsequently scraped into the lower reaches of the UK Top 40.

With the final few days of May, running into the first week of June, tied down with a heavy round of promotional guest appearances – *Ready Steady Go!* (26th May), *Top of the Pops* (27th May), *Thank Your Lucky Stars* (30th May), *Scene At 6.30* (1st June) and *Discs-a-Gogo* (2nd June), followed by a second *Top of the Pops* spot (3rd June) and an appearance on the short-lived *Gadzooks! It's All Happening* show, the success of the newly issued 45 was assured. Then on 7th June, they appeared as special guests on the BBC radio show *The Beatles (Invite You to Take a Ticket to Ride)*, a show that had been taped on the same day as the *Ready Steady Go!* recording. Hosted by actor and presenter Denny Piercy, this two-hour radio spectacular (taking three and a half hours to actually capture onto tape) featured songs and interviews with the Fabs, recorded on the tiny stage at the BBC Piccadilly Studios in London. The Hollies' offering of four songs – 'Stay', 'You Know He Did', 'Nitty Gritty'/ 'Something's Got A Hold On Me' and 'I'm Alive' – were tackled with the usual enthusiasm and energy. By comparison, The Beatles sounded somewhat jaded by the whole affair, with this particular show being their 52nd and final radio appearance for the corporation. Although they still turned in solid performances of 'I'm A Loser', 'The Night Before' and an impressive 'Ticket To Ride', these new tracks reflected a growing introspection in the Lennon-McCartney partnership. At this point, the Clarke-Hicks-Nash songwriting team was still finding its feet. The Hollies were seemingly content in simply having fun, turning in lively and clean-cut performances; never turning out anything less than professional-sounding pop music.

Plans for an immediate return visit to the US were temporarily called off when, despite having an offer to tour across the country for two months as a part of the Dick Clark *Caravan of Stars* road show, the group deemed it too risky a commitment, in light of further potential visa issues, and instead they opted to schedule more touring on home soil. Explaining the concerns with David Griffiths from the *NME*, Graham summed it up:

'An American promoter wanted us to return in July and do a nationwide tour lasting two and a half months. We said we'd love to. Then we thought about it. Supposing the authorities refused our visas at the last minute as they have a nasty habit of doing. We'd have months of blank dates with little chance of filling them up in the summer. Naturally, we didn't want to take the risk of being out of work that long, so we've accepted an offer to go back to America for three weeks in September.'

All of the potential issues had come about as the result of US authorities clamping down on visiting musicians, restricting working trips. 'Americans have come over for years and made fortunes,' Graham continued. 'Now, as soon as the situation is reversed, the unions start complaining. None of it makes sense...'

It was also around this period that The Hollies crossed paths with another young, talented songwriter, firmly intent on creating his own successful path in the industry. Reportedly introduced to the band by Michael Cohen, a friend of the songwriter's mother, nineteen-year-old protégé Graham Gouldman had already achieved success by writing a recent Top 3 hit for The Yardbirds and was currently gigging around the Manchester clubs with his band, The Mockingbirds. In his *Wild Tales* autobiography, Graham Nash recalls sitting in the front room of the Gouldman house in Manchester whilst the teenager auditioned a number of potential hits on his acoustic guitar – 'Look Through Any Window', 'Bus Stop', 'No Milk Today' – a memory at odds with Gouldman's own recollections.

'The Hollies were looking for songs, and I had already written 'Look Through Any Window', but the song suited them. I actually think it was another publisher, Ronnie Beck, who got it to them,' Gouldman was to note during an interview with Rob Steen for *Rock's Back Pages*. 'I didn't know them before. They did come to my house later and I played them some songs but that was before I wrote 'Bus Stop'. With 'Bus Stop', I wrote it specifically for them in mind. The Hollies were like the kings of Manchester at that time. They were on a different level...'

Impressed with the songs they were hearing, from whatever source they originated, the band took the first of the new Gouldman compositions they encountered, 'Look Through Any Window', a co-write with fellow Mancunian Charles Silverman (Gouldman's co-manager), into the EMI Recording Studios on 30th June, shortly after returning from a week in Scotland, playing on the same bill as The Rolling Stones and The Moody Blues (the latter group fresh from their debut number one hit with 'Go Now').

'Look Through Any Window' was, without question, a song perfectly moulded to the band. From Tony's intricate twelve-string guitar introduction, coupled with Bobby's flawless flourishes and Eric's solid backing, the vocal mix brought the song to life further still, with the overlapping harmonies (including Tony with his first solo vocal on a single) adding a touch of sophistication to the arrangement.

'It will almost certainly be our next single,' Graham stated in *Disc,* during a July interview for the newspaper. 'It's different to 'I'm Alive'. We try to do something different with every single. It has a good storyline, though, and our usual harmonies. And it has a big guitar figure at the beginning and the end. ...'

'That's a Graham Gouldman song,' added Tony, 'and the demo sent to us had that intro [already] on there so I just did it on an old Vox twelve-string, which was wonderful.'[18]

As a peace offering to The Toggery Five, having stolen 'I'm Alive' from their grasp, The Hollies then offered them one of the other new compositions that Graham Gouldman had written for them. Entitled 'Going Away', the band took it into the studio but, sadly, that too failed to get a Parlophone release.

Frank Renshaw: 'The song 'Going Away' I had forgotten even existed, but a while ago I found an EMI acetate of it in the attic, a version recorded by The Hollies. It was a good song, but not as immediate in impact as some of the better-known Graham Gouldman compositions from the 1960s, and there was no way it could compensate for 'I'm Alive'.'

With a succession of Top 10 hits under their belts, two album releases and numerous sell-out shows, what could be the next medium for The Hollies to conquer? Could the silver screen be beckoning? Following in the footsteps of The Beatles (*A Hard Day's Night* and the soon-to-be-released *Help!*), Gerry and The Pacemakers (*Ferry Cross the Mersey*), The Dave Clark Five (*Catch Us If You Can*) and Freddie and The Dreamers (who had appeared in a succession of low-budget flicks), The Hollies looked certain to be the next big pop stars to make a movie. At least, according to the headlines that ran in *Disc* during July of '65. However, closer inspection revealed it was not *quite* such a big-budget affair.

Lights. Camera. Action.

# CHAPTER EIGHT

## "SMILING FACES ALL AROUND..."

HOLLIES WANT TO MAKE A FILM...

The Hollies are going to make a film... literally. By that, I don't mean they've signed with one of the big film companies to star in a major feature. No, this is one film you are unlikely to have the good fortune to see. Not unless you are a personal friend of The Hollies, that is. Why? Because The Hollies are going to shoot and edit the film themselves, from their own script.

*Disc*
July 1965

Hollywood this wasn't, with Graham then going on to elaborate that the film would portray the life of Eric Haydock, and would be filmed on their own cine camera, with assistance from Rod Shields, the band's road manager, who was an amateur film enthusiast. Certainly, as history now shows us, Rod and the boys did shoot a selection of film footage across the ensuing years, some of it later utilised for promotional work. In reality, though, this film concept was probably no more than Graham offering up a scoop to the media, with tongue firmly in cheek. It never came to pass. But it does beg the question as to why the group never followed the cinematic route. The *New Musical Express* had only recently suggested that the group *did* have plans to film a movie in America's Golden State, but Graham would later denounce that fact, stating that initial negotiations had fallen through over the overall theme of the proposition.

Other bands would later follow suit, jumping on the movie bandwagon that The Beatles had so successfully crafted, creating perfect time capsules of the era. Next in line for the silver screen would be Manchester's newest kids on the block, Herman's Hermits, led by the toothsome teenager Peter Noone. Such was their swift rise to fame that they appeared in two films in swift succession: *Where the Boys Meet the Girls* (1965) and *Hold On!* (1966). A third film would follow two years later, and they too were a band that was to benefit from the songwriting talents of Graham Gouldman.

However, maybe it was the impact made the following year by yet another Mancunian export that would define the role of pop musicians on the screen, when David Thomas Jones, a product of Manchester's Varna Street Secondary Modern School, took the world and their television screens by storm as a member of manufactured pop band The Monkees. Music, slapstick, improvisation, laughter, tears and joy – their *Emmy* award-winning television series had it all. And just maybe, it also spelt the end for the fun-loving pop music film. It all got a bit… *serious* after that.

Of note: such was the impact that The Hollies had made with their rendition of the Goffin-Titelman composition, 'Yes, I Will', that The Monkees covered it on their million-selling debut album (under the alternative title of 'I'll Be True To You'), with Jones crooning away on lead vocals, albeit without the soulfulness of Allan Clarke's delivery.

Choosing not to follow suit and tread the studio backlots and red-carpeted premieres around the globe, The Hollies settled back into their music, concentrating on developing and honing their skills as performers and songwriters of note. On 16th June 1965, they formed GRALTO Music Publishing (named after the songwriting trio of Graham, Allan and Tony), in partnership with Dick James, the man who also presided over Northern Songs Publishing, the home of The Beatles' songwriting arm. The Hollies, however, ensured they got a far better deal than that which James had given to Lennon and McCartney. Although, as one journalist would later so succinctly put it, in defence of the wheeling-dealing music publisher, back in early 1963, when Northern Songs first came into being, no one, but *no one,* knew that The Beatles would become *The Beatles*. Not one person could have foreseen the impact that this band would create. It was as much a gamble to James as it was to Epstein. For The Hollies, when it came to creating their own publishing company, two years of additional hindsight made a huge difference.

Listed as company directors for GRALTO were Graham Nash, Allan Clarke, Tony Hicks, Ron Richards and Dick James himself. Bobby Elliott had no real interest in pursuing a career as a songwriter, content in his contributions as a musician and co-arranger in the studio. Eric Haydock, on the other hand, began to find it frustrating that his input was so often disregarded and that he wasn't considered a part of the songwriting "team".

With unfulfilled visions of adding his own interpretations to their music, Eric was very much the loner of the band. Content to spend his downtime out of the spotlight, away from his bandmates, either together with his new wife or enjoying his other passions: shooting and cycling.

'Eric is a very strange guy,' Graham was to comment to *Disc*. 'Of all of us, basically he talks most sense, but he doesn't say much very often. But if it wasn't for Eric, our group would collapse. We always take the mickey out of him, and his sense of humour is so way out.'

'Eric was recently married, and we never see him,' added Tony.


As predicted, Gouldman's 'Look Through Any Window', paired with 'So Lonely', was issued as the next 45 to bear The Hollies name, appearing in music stores across the country on 27th August 1965 (Parlophone R5322). The following month, with the single comfortably nestled in the Top 40 chart, and on its smooth ascent into the Top 10 (where it would eventually peak at the number 4 slot during October), the band's third long-playing album was issued.

Simply entitled *Hollies* and recorded at various sessions held between March and July, the album came packaged in a simple yet strikingly effective sleeve, with the band's name highlighted in red above a series of individual black and white, burnt-out images of the quintet. Content-wise, it was also one step further in the constantly developing sound of the group. From the opening number, a wonderful, upbeat rendition of the gospel-tinged 'Very Last Day', composed by Noel Paul Stookey and Peter Yarrow from the popular Peter, Paul and Mary folk trio, through to the closing bars of 'Mickey's Monkey' (a regular concert staple for the band), this twelve-track collection could comfortably hold its own alongside such contemporary releases as *Help!*, *Out Of Our Heads*, *Animal Tracks* and *Kinda Kinks*. In hindsight, it does appear that *Hollies* dipped a tentative toe into exploring how far the band could stray from its formulaic sound. They weren't quite ready to be the rule-breakers as yet, and cover versions of 'Lawdy Miss Clawdy' (with a notable error from Allan on harmonica, audible on later stereo editions), 'Fortune Teller' and 'Down The Line' clearly kept a safe foothold firmly in the rock 'n' roll era.

All four of these long-playing releases, by The Beatles, The Rolling Stones, The Animals and The Kinks respectively, and now with *Hollies* firmly staking its position alongside, played a pivotal role in taking the UK music scene onto the next level in its ever-evolving journey. And they needed to. Their US counterparts were turning the screw, intent on outmanoeuvring the recent British Invasion and claiming back the rock 'n' roll mantle for themselves. Folk-rock trailblazers, The Byrds, were at the forefront of the assault, as were California's golden boys, The Beach Boys, having left the beaches and dragstrips behind, intent on exploring new themes and loves. Following on behind, stepping into the footprints created for them, The Doors, The Mamas and The Papas, The Association, Love, The Lovin' Spoonful and The Turtles were now also starting along their own journeys of discovery. It was a healthy rivalry as each act vied for position amongst the elite, and with the subsequent American LP releases of *Mr Tambourine Man, It Ain't Me Babe* and *Summer Days (and Summer Nights!!)* squaring off against the British contributions, the competition was hot. All of the artists certainly took an active interest in each other's work, and the influences bounced back and forth freely, but with Bob Dylan's groundbreaking albums, *Bringing It All Back Home* and *Highway 61 Revisited* also entering the fray, the *potpourri* of musical style and invention was scintillating.

The Hollies' third long-player, whilst staying true to the band's beat group roots, began to show signs of a growing maturity in style, production and ambition. Alongside the opening track, it was the cover of Curtis Mayfield's 'You Must Believe Me', along with the self-composed 'Too Many People' and the excellent 'Put Yourself In My Place' (the latter featuring support from ex-Checkmate and future Shadows' pianist Alan Hawkshaw) that took it onto that higher level. Their own songwriting was sharper, with the lyrics suggesting a wider social awareness, and there was a little extra sophistication added into the mix.

A later 1966 cover version of the Clarke-Hicks-Nash composition, 'Put Yourself In My Place', cut by the Australian quartet The Strangers (featuring singer-guitarist John Farrar), was an early indication that the band's own songwriting talents were beginning to get noticed worldwide. However, the inclusion of 'That's My Desire', a composition dating back to the 1930s (as written by Carroll Loveday and Helmy Kreza), was not without question, as the band themselves hadn't wanted to include it on the eventual release. Ron Richards, on the other hand, was keen they record the song, as he clearly saw The Hollies appealing to a wider, older audience and firmly implied that this was the song that could indeed aid such a development. The group had previously performed the song during their run in the *Gerry's Christmas Cracker* pantomime, and despite their combined dislike of the work, previously a hit for Frankie Laine, they duly bowed to Ron's wishes, committing the song to tape on 1st March 1965. Despite the negativity and the outdated overtones that surrounded the eventual recording, the song went on to become a major international success, reaching the number one position when issued as a single in South Africa two years later.

Nevertheless, with an overlying sheen of trademark Hollie harmonies throughout, the new LP was a noticeably refined progression from the previous releases, and one that was duly rewarded with a Top 10 position in the UK's *Record Retailer* album charts.

That summer of 1965 had seen the group also attempt to diversify their live shows and earn some lucrative income by taking to the stage of England's cabaret circuit. This renowned circuit, predominantly located in the working men's clubs of the north, was a popular source of employment for many artists of the period, although it was unusual for a serious Top 40 "pop" act to take to the small stage. Certainly, for one so high profile as The Hollies. On 30th July 1965, they trialled a 25-minute cabaret set at two venues in Manchester, one straight after the other. Then they followed this up two months later with a week-long residency at Mr Smith's, a well-established casino and cabaret haunt in the city centre. It wasn't a match particularly made in heaven, and it was at the complete opposite end of the spectrum from where many of their musical peers found themselves during this same period. Whilst The Beatles discovered 1965 to be a round of vast American shows, such as the infamous Shea Stadium performance in New York City, where they couldn't hear a note above the cacophony of noise created by 55,000 screaming teenagers, the Hollies found themselves competing with the clinking of 500 beer glasses and dinner plates as the northern punters supped warm ale, whilst watching these young rock 'n' rollers do their routine. Worlds apart.

'We were in ballrooms week after week until we were sick to death of them, running up and down the country until it drives you mad. That is why we started to branch out into cabaret. In the dates we have done so far, we have realised that the numbers are probably the least important. Getting across to the audience with a mixture of professional ability and patter is what counts. We enjoyed it.'

Radio Luxembourg Record Stars

The Hollies opened in cabaret to rave receptions. Frankly, they had been very nervous of this, their first attempt to break into wider entertainment fields. They need not have bothered. The Hollies are much too professional ever to lay an egg.

*Pop Weekly*
August 1965

One must seriously question the abilities of the management who stood behind The Hollies during this period. The mismatched Cohen-Sanderson arrangement appeared to have little vision as to where the music industry was heading. The band themselves were wanting to be a part of what was "happening", but these early years seemingly suffered from endless one-nighters, booked up and down the country, with little forethought and planning for the future. Cabaret was all very well for the coffers, but in terms of industry credibility and developing the music? For all his shortcomings, "Eppy" would never have put "his boys" through such a schedule once fame had knocked on the door of his NEMS office, and whilst it does seem unfair and unjust to make direct comparisons between the two bands – was the Lennon-McCartney songwriting partnership *really* that much stronger than the Ransford triumvirate? – it does make one speculate on the cards that the two bands were dealt. They both recorded at the prestigious EMI Studios in Abbey Road, they both dominated the upper echelons of the UK chart listings, and yet whilst The Beatles caught the emotion, the feel, the *zeitgeist* of the mid-1960s, it seemed at times that The Hollies simply caught the north London traffic congestion on the way home.

With 'Look Through Any Window' scheduled to be the next US single release on Imperial Records (sandwiched in between 45s by Johnny Rivers and Billy J. Kramer on the roster), the quintet planned their return visit to the US for September of '65, having initially scheduled a three-week tour across the American Midwest and Northeast regions. Before, this, they journeyed across to Germany for four shows, although, unfortunately, all didn't go quite as planned. As Graham was to report in *Disc*, shortly after returning home: 'We died the death! They just didn't seem to understand what we were doing. The groups had heard of us, and they were playing our records, but a German rock 'n' roll group, The German Bonds, got a much stronger reception than we did.'

Also featured on the bill for those particular dates was the Liverpool-based quartet The Escorts, whose guitarist, Terry Sylvester, later recalled, 'We played together in Munich, and they were top of the bill at a club called the Hit House, and we were supporting them. It was such a dump; you can imagine what we ended up calling it! At the end of their show, we came back on again and had a bit of a jam session, doing all Everly Brothers hits. I got to know them on sort of "Hi, how are you?" terms...'[18]

Terry would later indicate that during one of the Hit House performances, two members of The Escorts became unwell, prompting both Allan and Graham to jump on stage in their places to complete the set.

> The Hollies are off on their second American trip in September, and they are certainly not taking their Stateside success for granted.
> 'I'm a bit fed up with the way things have gone for us in America,' explains Tony Hicks. 'We just don't seem to score. I think it is a problem beyond our control, we haven't been entirely happy about our record releases there. We hope to get a chance to go to the record company and find out what they are playing at.'
> *Melody Maker*
> September 1965

With the three-week tour now reduced to two, and the majority of the visit scheduled simply for further promotional purposes, the band immediately hit a problem. As had happened with their previous Stateside visit, the appropriate visas were not issued in time, resulting in a proposed performance at the Arie Crown Theatre in Chicago being postponed.

Having successfully negotiated work permits and visas, the group then flew out to New York on 18th September and immediately transferred on up to Chicago to perform the rescheduled show, performing on the same bill as The Animals and The Yardbirds. Such was the success of the Hollies' appearance at the first show that their scheduled next single, 'Look Through Any Window', shot straight to #1 in the local Chicago airplay charts. Following the performance, the band headed back to New York City to undertake the arranged promotional work, but what ensued for the remainder of the visit remains largely undocumented. Bobby Elliott later confirmed that a meeting with the "men in shiny suits and shiny shoes" had taken place, presumably to discuss their dissatisfaction with the record releases, and whilst The Animals continued their tour out to the sun-kissed west coast, it appears that The Hollies remained on the eastern seaboard.

On 20th and 21st September, a return visit to the New York *Hullabaloo* studio set was undertaken, although the subsequent taping of 'Look Through Any Window' was held back for a few months before airing. Then, the following day, Morris Levy, the musical kingpin responsible for much of the band's early US work, booked time for them to cut some recording work at his own 4-track Roulette Records studios... at his own expense, and with a clear agenda in mind.

Three new "Ransford" demos were cut at the 1631 Broadway studios on 22nd September, in the hope that they could get the songs placed with other recording artists. Only one of these, the lively 'I Can't Get Nowhere With You', has since surfaced in its original demo form, but it was the subsequent event that followed that has created the legend surrounding the Hollies-Levy connection. Impressed by what he now knew about the three songwriters in the band, and with a nose for a business deal, Levy took the band out to an expensive Turkish restaurant in the city. It was here, whilst wining and dining the boys, and entertaining them with a dazzling show of belly dancers, he made them an offer to purchase their full publishing rights. On the spot. For $75,000. Whilst clearly astounded with the big money on offer ($25,000 each was a huge amount for the three working-class northern lads), and impressed with Levy's particular choice of entertainment, the songwriting trio nevertheless rejected the proposal, having been warned of the mogul's business dealings before they settled into their seats. Stop! Stop! Stop! Their instincts were clearly to the good, judging by subsequent events that ran through the remainder of Levy's career, and life.

Graham Nash: 'We'd heard stories of how he put his name as a writer on all of the records that Roulette released. How at one point he owned the phrase "rock 'n' roll". We heard other things that scared the shit out of us, even though he was very kind to The Hollies. So, we weren't willing to sign...'[1]

'I think he quite took a liking to these five cheeky northerners,' added Bobby Elliott.

The following year, the Michigan-raised Tommy James signed with Roulette Records, hitting the big time with 'Hanky Panky' (and later with 'Mony Mony' and 'Crimson And Clover'). Though continuing to praise Levy throughout much of his subsequent career, James unknowingly lost huge $$$ financially to the man who, it was later acknowledged, was affiliated to the mob. Convicted of extortion in 1988, Levy died weeks before he was due to be incarcerated.

Despite the intentions of Allan, Graham and Tony to have their songs covered by other performers, it was not a venture that would prove immediately successful to them, certainly during their early years of songwriting together. The first notable cover of a song they had composed was when the Embassy Records label cut a version of 'We're Through' during 1964, credited to The Typhoons. This, however, was no more than a cheap cash-in by the UK-based label, who specialised in churning out cheap imitations of the originals. Soon after, The Warriors recorded their unreleased version of 'Please Don't Feel Too Bad'. The following year saw London-based pop band The Mirage, featuring a youthful Dee Murray on guitar (later known for his role within Elton John's band), cover an otherwise unrecorded Ransford composition entitled 'Go Away'. Sadly, despite its clear commercial potential, and being adopted by the British Youth Council charity for its theme, that one too failed to register any chart success.

'We recently started a company with publisher Dick James,' Tony was reported as commenting to *Melody Maker* during 1965. 'Now we really intend to get down to writing. We hope to sell a lot of songs to other groups. I believe The Escorts, from Liverpool, may be doing something of ours for their next record.' They didn't.

With their US commitments fulfilled – a performance for the *Shindig!* TV show was aired across the fifty states on the 30th of September, but it later transpired that the footage had been shot back in London the previous July and then edited together with the dancing Shindig Girls for the actual televised airing – the band returned to UK shores. With seemingly little having changed on the national American success scale, the group completed several bookings on the calendar that had been arranged before their Stateside visit. On 3rd October, they took part in the popular ATV televised light entertainment variety spectacular, *Sunday Night at the London Palladium,* performing a fine live rendition of 'Look Through Any Window', notable for Tony not only claiming the spotlight for his exceptional lead guitar work, playing his distinctive coffin Vox Phantom guitar, but also for his all-too-rare solo vocal contributions.

---

*ALL-VOX MAN… that's TONY HICKS*
*It's no secret! The Hollies feature VOX, the Sound Equipment that gives the most, sounds the best! Tony Hicks features the VOX Phantom 12-string, partnered by the superb VOX AC50 Super Twin Amplifier.*
*If you dig The Hollies' sound… you dig VOX*

VOX Promotional advert

---

Two weeks later and it was back to prime-time children's television with yet another visit to the *Crackerjack* studio, this time to perform a rare version of Lee Dorsey's 'Ride Your Pony'. This was a song they never actually cut in the recording studio, despite also performing it on BBC radio shows such as *Saturday Club.* Following this, they undertook a run at Mr Smith's casino in Manchester, along with an appearance on *Scene At 6:30*, before having to take an enforced three-week lay-off whilst Allan recovered from a severe bout of tonsillitis, requiring hasty surgery for their removal.

The 17th of November 1965 and, having recovered sufficiently, Allan was back in the studio with his bandmates, cutting three tracks in what turned out to be one of the most controversial moments in Hollie-history. 'Don't Even Think About Changing' and the jangly country-influenced 'Running Through The Night' were both compositions from the songwriting trio, but the third song recorded that day was a version of a brand new George Harrison song that, at the time of recording, hadn't been released into Pepperland yet – or anywhere else for that matter.

The Hollies: 'If I Needed Someone' (Parlophone R5392)
Written especially for the boys by George Harrison, this is a pacey
beat ballad which gives rein to their high, rather strident (but always
distinctive) harmonies. Fine guitar bits 'n' pieces but not quite as
immediately commercial as 'Look Through Any Window'.

*Record Mirror*
December 1965

'I thought we made a damn good record of it,' Graham would later
comment, despite offering up initial resistance to cutting it (both Allan
and Ron Richards had been the creative force behind the decision). 'It was
perfectly suited to our voices, with a smart three-part harmony that gave
the song a soaring melodic virtuosity. Too bad George didn't share our
enthusiasm.' [1]

Had the song remained untouched by Beatle-hands then maybe The
Hollies wouldn't have come in for the criticism that unduly fell upon
them, following the release of the recording as the band's next single.
Unfortunately, Beatle-George felt compelled to include the version his own
band had cut (one month prior to The Hollies taking it into the studio) on
the next long-playing release by the Fabs, *Rubber Soul,* issued on the same
day The Hollies brought it out as their new 45. The 3rd of December 1965.
Perhaps unsurprisingly, when it came down to the wire, the popular vote
seemingly fell in favour of the lads from Liverpool. Not that George helped
the situation:

'I think The Hollies version of my song is rubbish,' he reportedly went on
record as saying, during a brief discussion with a journalist from the *NME*,
little realising he would be quoted as such in print. 'They've spoilt it. The
Hollies are all right musically, but the way they do their records they sound
like session men who've just got together in a studio without ever seeing
each other before...'

Whilst avoiding the obvious comparisons between the two versions of
the song, it is worth noting that Bobby Elliott's driving backbeat, and the
natural fills he intersperses throughout the recording, pushes The Hollies'
version far more than Ringo's solid patterns do in this instance. Which
version wins out? That's down to the choice of the individual listener, but
such was The Beatles god-like status by the close of 1965, when *Rubber Soul*
was the talk of the town and beyond, that it seemed near sacrilegious to

even attempt to put your own stamp onto something deemed "untouchable", without tempting fate.

Graham Nash, referring to Harrison's remarks in the *NME*, responded, 'Not only do those comments disappoint and hurt us, but we are sick and tired of everything The Beatles say being taken as law! We did this song against a lot of people's advice. We just felt that after nine records we could afford to do something like this without being accused of jumping on The Beatles' bandwagon. We thought it was a good song. George and the rest of them are entitled to their own opinions, but when things like this are said they really must believe their own publicity.

'My opinion of The Beatles hasn't changed. I still think they're great and I like their music. But knocking comments like the one about us are a load of…'

'We were given the song on a white label and George Martin said that we could do it if we wanted to,' recalled Bobby during a series of later interviews. 'We thought he'd written it especially for us. We didn't know they were going to release it. We thought that we'd been set up to be knocked down. That turned out to be wrong, as someone in The Beatles' organisation had given the press a wrong story.'[15/3]

Released as Parlophone 45 R5392, coupled with the impressive Ransford composition 'I've Got A Way Of My Own' (a song that charted on its own merit in the far-flung regions of the Philippines), the single barely scraped the UK Top 20, despite some heavy televised promotion, and swiftly disappeared altogether, just three weeks after peaking. By Hollies' standards, this was a comparative failure, and the result left a sour taste in the mouths of many. Eric Haydock, who was also against recording the song in the first place, later stated that the recording caused 'one of the biggest arguments we ever had. It just showed a lack of direction from somewhere.'

Thankfully, any negative impact that the release had on their career was short-lived, and any comments reportedly made towards them by Harrison, true or false, were soon enough in the past. For his part, Beatle-bandmate John Lennon often made snide press comments about, what he saw as, "the competition", and The Hollies were not averse to receiving his acid tongue either. However, the reaction from their peer group towards the band was, more often than not, largely positive, with many of them feeling unthreatened by their clean-cut appearance and lack of any serious image.

'They've got a real driving sound that I love. Everything they do is great, and I think that their particular appeal lies not only in their professional attitude towards music, but because they always look so happy-go-lucky.'

Tom Jones

'I don't think a produced image is important. It's the group's ability which has got them to the top.'

Keith Relf (The Yardbirds)

'I think it's tremendous that they have no image. Images are horrible things. They're one of the best groups in the country. They pick top rate songs and perform them very well.'

Jonathan King

'They have a tremendous approach to their music. It's the sort of sound that can't be excelled by anyone. They are a great bunch of guys.'

Steve Marriott (The Small Faces)

*Disc*

September 1965

Naturally, the success of their music was prevalent in the band members' minds at all times but, as with Eric's penchant for losing himself in his extra-curricular activities – cycling and shooting – both Graham and Tony also made ventures into a normal life, outside of the music business, one of which was the co-financing and opening of a fashion boutique back in their home city of Manchester, with the financial guidance of Michael Cohen. Tony Bookbinder (also known as Tony Mansfield, the drummer for fellow Manchester-based band The Dakotas) also added some input to the project.

'We felt we wanted to do something outside of the music business to occupy our minds,' said Tony Hicks at the time. Keeping it in the family, the store was run by Graham's wife, Rose, and Tony's sister (and Bobby's girlfriend) Maureen, and both group members played an active part in selecting and collecting stock for the property. *Disc Weekly* even ran a competition, offering its readers the opportunity to name the outlet, located in an old four-storey carpet warehouse in Back Pool Fold, near the city centre. Pygmalia was the subsequent chosen name and such was the illustrious financial backing it received, the store briefly became one of the hottest centres for Manchester's fashion scene, with various celebrities attending the opening launch.

Whilst all of the drama and external activity was going on at home, it couldn't have escaped the attentions of the quintet that, just maybe, something was also slowly stirring on the opposite side of the Atlantic Ocean. Somewhat belatedly, Imperial Records had issued 'Look Through Any Window' (Imperial 66134) in the wake of the band's September visit to the shores. Having witnessed the immediate impact it had made in the Chicago region, following their one live appearance, the label had seen the release gradually build up an audience in a country where radio play was seen as equally as important as sales.

Another appearance on *Shindig!* aired on US TV on 2nd December, although, as was the case with their earlier spot on the show, this had been taped in London, back in the early summer months. Then, four days later, the NBC network finally broadcast their lip-synched appearance on the *Hullabaloo* show, again promoting the 45, filmed back in September. With the five members forced to go through a staged American football-influenced introduction, with Allan being labelled as the quarterback, they then had the ignominy of listening to host, former teen-star Frankie Avalon, rally them up with mock-British cries of 'tally-ho' and 'let's win this one for Ringo!' How that must have grated.

Nevertheless, the increased December promotion aided further interest in the band and as Christmas approached, the single gradually climbed up the Hot 100 *Billboard* charts, hovering just outside the Top 40 prior to the New Year.

The year rounded out with further televised guest appearances, gamely promoting 'If I Needed Someone' – *Ready Steady Go!, Discs a Gogo, Three Go Round, Top of the Pops* and *Stramash!* (the latter being a short-lived Scottish music show) – along with a further showing alongside those damned glove puppets once again on the *Five O'clock Club*. It was a busy winter season.

On 8th December, the ATV television channel aired a pre-recorded live concert that had taken place the previous month at the Empire Pool in Wembley. Appearing amongst a wealth of headline performers, The Hollies had appeared at the show, a university charity event labelled The Glad Rag Ball, sharing the stage with The Rolling Stones, The Animals, The Who, The Merseybeats, Long John Baldry, Susan Maughan and Donovan. For reasons unclear, and disappointingly for their fans, the edited highlights broadcast failed to include any of The Hollies' numbers.

Cramming in yet further live appearances in between the TV shows, including a swift visit across to Denmark and Sweden alongside Herman's Hermits at the start of the month, and more recording sessions held at Abbey Road, it seemed as if Christmas 1965 held the same chaotic schedule as any other time of the year. There was simply no let-up for the boys.

UK audiences were treated to a little further festive cheer on one occasion when, after a spirited performance of 'If I Needed Someone 'on *Ready Steady Go!*, airing on Christmas Eve, the group launched into an upbeat rendition of the popular Bernard-Smith tune, 'Winter Wonderland', resplendent with three-part harmonies chiming out. It was a nice touch. Even if it was swiftly followed, as reported in the media at the time, by a comic appearance in the show's seasonal pantomime, with Graham and Bobby taking on the role of the panto horse... or were they?

'The Hollies were nowhere to be found when the Ready Steady Go! Christmas panto was being cast,' Bobby would later respond for *Carousel* magazine. 'I don't know who was in that panto horse, but I swear that it wasn't me, not after our earlier [1963] experience with Mr Gamble!'

With the slowly increasing US fan base receiving a bonus by way of a third spot on *Shindig!* (again, from the July London tapings), 1965 was brought to a successful close. With some northern humour thrown in for good measure. As was often the band's wont, whilst performing a rockin' rendition of 'Too Much Monkey Business' for the US airing (notable for featuring all three frontline singers performing a solo vocal), Graham broke out into a verse of The Beatles' 'I Feel Fine' mid-way through. The female audience, watching the pre-recorded film in the LA studios, duly screamed their approval, perhaps unknowing of the fact that this little interlude was, by now, a standard part of the set, often alternating with 'A Hard Day's Night' or The Who's 'My Generation'.

Happy Christmas – with tongue firmly in cheek.

### THE NEW MUSICAL EXPRESS 1965 POLL WINNERS
### Category: British Vocal Group

| | |
|---|---|
| 1. The Beatles | 7. The Walker Brothers |
| 2. The Rolling Stones | 8. The Bachelors |

3. The Seekers
4. The Animals
5. Manfred Mann
6. The Hollies

9. The Shadows
10. The Fortunes
11. The Yardbirds
12. The Who

The year finally closed out with a slight deviation in their midst when Graham briefly appeared alone on UK TV screens, guesting on a short 30-minute televised play, *Stage One Contest: The Winning Team*, aimed specifically at the younger generation. Filmed for Rediffusion, the play was taped on 28th December (airing the following week) and co-starred Manfred Mann frontman Paul Jones in a leading role. However, with little publicity, the recording soon disappeared into the annals of TV history.

# ALL-VOX MAN... that's TONY HICKS

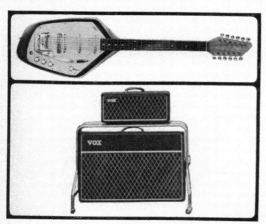

# CHAPTER NINE

## "I CAN'T LET GO..."

1966, and London was the swinging youth capital of the world.

The rain-grey town of old was now a bright, colourful fashion city, where the hip clientele that made up the city nightlife would socialise in the famous 100 Club, the Bag O'Nails or the Cromwellian, all whilst wearing the latest fashions purchased at designer stores such as Biba or Mary Quant, or at trendy boutiques like Granny Takes a Trip and Hung On You. Take a walk down the King's Road in Chelsea and there was a high chance you would see Mick Jagger, Jean Shrimpton, Terence Stamp or Twiggy perusing the many fashion emporiums, or head into nearby Carnaby Street where the latest styles would make your head spin. Miniskirts, go-go boots, bell bottoms, houndstooth… the dedicated followers of fashion. The Hollies, for their part, much like the majority of the British music scene, gravitated to this central hub of existence. Northern lads at heart but in order to stay at the forefront of any scene, you *needed* to be seen.

The band had recently employed a new publicist, Robin Britten, who had previously worked with Craig Douglas and Gene Pitney, to keep the name in the public eye, but simply by being a part of the London scene ensured publicity would court you, wherever you ended up on any particular evening.

'Yes,' stated Allan Clarke most categorically, 'it WAS me that you saw then.' I'd just told Allan that about half a million people, including myself, had seen him walking along Shaftesbury Avenue wearing a green corduroy jean jacket and matching trousers, or jeans.

'As a matter of fact, I'd bought them from Graham. He didn't like them; he'd got them made somewhere in London.'

*Record Mirror*
July 1966

Certainly, the group's stage act had loosened up a little over the preceding months. The smart matching suits and ties that the quintet had been wearing for the last two or three years were gradually left hanging on the backstage wardrobe rails as a selection of stylish, individual jackets, roll-neck sweaters and mismatched trousers (or pants) were coming into the selection, indicating the more relaxed approach that success had now afforded them.

'I think the days of everyone dressing alike are gone,' noted Allan, during an interview with *Beat Instrumental*. 'As long as you don't look scruffy, it's all right. The only time we wear identical suits is if we're doing something like the Palladium.'

Within the next eight months, The Beatles would retire completely from live performances, having tired of the endless tours around the world. For The Hollies, and the many other bands who followed along behind in the wake, the constant touring was a necessary godsend. It was a way to ensure the band stayed alive. A regular guaranteed income without the unrelenting demands that the Liverpudlian quartet had to endure; the elaborate security procedures, the hotel room trappings and the mayoral presentations of the key to a city in Nowheresville, USA.

Chatham, Ramsgate, Hassocks, High Wycombe, Stevenage and Chesterfield, along with the more exotic cities of Rotterdam, The Hague and Eindhoven, would all play host as The Hollies continued into early '66 with their relentless touring schedule – as would the Manchester cabaret circuit. It wouldn't ease up either. Unlike their more illustrious musical friends, for whom the package tour was a thing of the past, The Hollies' management kept the ball and the tours rolling along.

The 13th of January found Allan, Graham, Eric, Tony and Bobby entering the doors of the Abbey Road studios for their first sessions of the new year. Working on two songs, 'Don't You Even Care', written by Clint Ballard Jr (composer of 'I'm Alive'), along with another outside tune, written by two American songsmiths, Chip Taylor and Al Gorgoni. The twenty-five-year-old Taylor had recently seen acceptance within the industry when US rock band the Wild Ones had taken his song 'Wild Thing' into the studio. Although that version wasn't a big hit, it had made enough of an impact for the British band The Troggs to plan their own version of it in the coming weeks. The Hollies, however, focussed on another of Taylor's tunes, 'I Can't Let Go', co-written with former session guitarist Gorgoni. Tony Hicks had first discovered the song, picked up during one of his many regular visits to the publisher's offices, always in search of the next big Hollies 45.

On that particular day, whilst listening to a number of potential new songs to cover, ultimately passing over a recently released composition by US folkies John and Michele Phillips, 'California Dreamin'', Tony had come across the first recorded version of 'I Can't Let Go', by the American vocalist Evie Sands. Due to an ongoing series of legal issues surrounding her debut release, the promotion for 'I Can't Let Go' (her follow-up 45) was somewhat muted, allowing The Hollies the opportunity to swiftly record and issue it, and thus getting the edge on the song.

Another new song also offered to Tony during that period was 'Walk Away Renée', as written by Michael Brown, Bob Calilli and Tony Sansone from the New York-based band The Left Banke. Despite The Hollies never issuing a completed version for themselves, this was covered shortly afterwards by Toggery Five member Frank Renshaw, who later recalled, '[That] was a solo effort by me, which was produced by Graham Nash. The backing track had already been done by The Hollies, with an added brass section, and I sang to that. It sounded really good, but it got lost somewhere in history.'[80]

Unfortunately, it remains undocumented as to when The Hollies actually cut the track, prior to Renshaw adding his vocals, as all the EMI session sheets for that period remain missing from the archives. However, whilst the date has never been verified, nor who was involved, there is reference to a mixing session being undertaken in early January of 1966. Other than that, little is known, and Frank Renshaw's version remains unreleased. It would take the songwriters' own band, along with a later cover by The Four Tops, to successfully take the song onto the world's stage.

Now, having recorded 'I Can't Let Go' over two sessions, dated in studio logs as the 13th and 18th of January (the band were reportedly dissatisfied with the vocals from the first date and subsequently opted to rework them), within four weeks the song was mixed and pressed, ready for distribution as Parlophone 45 5409. Before that, however, there was a brief visit across to the Netherlands to perform live for a local television show, *Rooster*, followed by a flight to Reykjavik in Iceland, to play four shows at Reykjavik University.

By this time, the single release of 'Look Through Any Window' had entered the Top 40 in the American *Billboard* bestseller lists, topping out at a credible number 32 placement. It was by no means an unqualified success, but breaking into the Top 40 was a major step in the right direction, and it gave Imperial Records further impetus to release the second US Hollies album, *Hear, Hear,* which charted at #145 in the Hot 200. Essentially, this was no more than a revised version of their third UK LP, *Hollies*, with 'I'm Alive' and 'Look Through Any Window' substituting 'Fortune Teller' and 'Mickey's Monkey', all neatly packaged in a stereotypical grand English-looking sleeve design. A pre-recorded appearance on the CBS *Red Skelton Show*, filmed in the UK, and once again singing the current US hit, aired in early February, giving the drive for US success yet more focus and airtime.

However, despite the promising start that 1966 had suggested, an article that ran in a Dutch magazine that same month indicated that all was not well within the Hollies' camp. The group's finances were being brought into question following poor investments and, as a result, the situation would have long-lasting results on the quintet:

Once it was fast cars and bright spotlights, but now The Hollies have lost £20,000 and have learned their lesson. They're all profound businessmen now, unwilling to waste their money on sports cars and an expensive lifestyle.

Tony Hicks explains it like this: 'You know how it goes. A young group is used to playing at dances and clubs, they have made a top album and the money is going to their heads. That's exactly what happened to us. We signed every little paper that was shoved under our noses. The result was that we lost £20,000. That's a lot to lose, and there's no chance of getting it back ever again.'

Translated from *Looney Tunes*
February 1966

On top of that, unbeknownst to the group members themselves, the UK taxman was building a case up against them for a cool quarter of a million pounds. For one particular member of the band, bass player Eric Haydock, this was the start of him seriously questioning the financial management of the band's income. Questions that would come to a head a few months later.

'I Can't Let Go', a musical *tour de force*, with a pulsating arrangement and some stunning vocal interplay, was released in the UK on 18<sup>th</sup> February 1966, b/w 'Running Through The Night', a song from the November '65 sessions. Within two weeks, the new single had broken into the charts, spending ten weeks in total on the lists, with a peak position of three weeks at #2. Fending them off at the top spot was the Walker Brothers with 'The Sun Ain't Gonna Shine Anymore'.

> The Hollies: 'I Can't Let Go' (Parlophone R5409)
> Better than their last, this one is a very lively beater, full of the spirited vocal work that makes the Hollies stand out in any company. A rather complicated vocal harmony approach, with a sort of wave-upon-wave arrangement, and with fair shrieks of falsetto. A good song. Flip is not too distinguished, song-wise. But well done. Top Fifty Tip.
>
> *Record Mirror*
> February 1966

Then, with further live appearances looming, the band once again locked themselves away in Studio 2 at the EMI Studios in Abbey Road and knuckled down to some intense sessions, under the ever-present eyes and ears of Ron Richards.

Whilst The Hollies had been out on the road, playing to their thousands of fans across the country, Ron had quietly been occupying himself with other arrangements. The previous year, he had been out to California, with the intention of taping a live album with Gerry and The Pacemakers. Whilst on the West Coast, to his great surprise, Ron had discovered that his American counterparts received royalties on the hit records they were producing. This was unheard of in the UK where, traditionally, producers were paid for their initial work but received no further remuneration outside of their salary. Returning home, bit between his teeth, he convinced George Martin and John Burgess (EMI/Capitol Records) and Peter Sullivan (Decca) that they should establish an independent production company, AIR (Associated

Independent Recording), to rectify the issue. It was a gamble, as the big labels could so easily have turned away and committed themselves to their loyal in-house production teams, but what company would want to disturb the creative flow that Richards, Martin and friends had with their favoured artists?

Ron was an astute businessman and was also keen to push AIR into the lucrative jingles and advertising market, as well as music publishing – with a new company, Maribus, derived from their surnames. Although AIR wouldn't have a fully functioning location for another few years, until the set-up of a four-studio complex in central London, Ron continued to work with The Hollies as an independent producer, utilising the familiar surroundings of the EMI studios in Abbey Road as his base. He had also been undertaking production responsibilities for PJ Proby, Matt Monro, Johnny Scott and Rolf Harris in between his mixing desk duties for The Hollies.

The 22nd of February saw The Hollies re-record two of their songs, 'We're Through' and 'You Know He Did 'as French language versions, for marketing purposes over the English Channel. Two months earlier, they had also re-cut the vocals for 'Look Through Any Window' and 'Stewball' in French. Strangely, none ever received an official release. A French 4-track EP for the EMI-owned Odéon label was mooted in the press for a March release, but it never came to fruition, possibly an indication that the group's translated vocals were deemed unconvincing enough to appease their cross-channel fans.

'Stewball' was an old folk song, detailing the story of an 18th century racehorse (actually named "Skewball"). The basic concept of the song had been in circulation for many years, courtesy of alternative variations made famous by the likes of Leadbelly; Woodie Guthrie; Peter, Paul and Mary and Lonnie Donegan. The Hollies had cut their own rendition, initially sung in English, during September of 1965, although it had remained on the studio shelf to date. Such was its popularity during live appearances that it later achieved Top 3 status when issued as the lead song on their 1966 Swedish-only *Folk Style* EP. Of particular interest is that The Hollies credited the songwriting trio of John Herald, Bob Yellin and Ralph Rinzler as the composers of the song. However, this US threesome were simply the principal members of the New York bluegrass group The Greenbriar Boys, who were just one of many acts who had adapted and recorded this traditional folk melody and lyric in their own style, back in 1961.

Earlier that month, Allan, Graham, Eric, Tony and Bobby had made the usual rounds of the television studios, promoting the release of 'I Can't Let Go' on *Ready Steady Go!*, *Top of the Pops* and the *Five O'clock Club*, whilst also making an appearance on a brand-new BBC TV show entitled *A Whole Scene Going*. This new series was the first real teenage lifestyle programme, with regular features on Carnaby Street fashions, the London club scene and youth culture in general, and although it had a "pop music" focus, it wasn't just about the music. Fashion icon Twiggy made her first TV appearance on the show, and other performers over the twenty-four episodes filmed included Dave Dee, Dozy, Beaky, Mick & Tich; Ravi Shankar; The Who; The Yardbirds; The Koobas; Stevie Wonder; Marianne Faithfull and The Kinks. However, despite its success, the show was axed after just one six-month series, in somewhat mysterious circumstances. The Hollies made their one appearance on the 23rd of February, alongside the newly rechristened Eric Burdon and The Animals, with Eric as the sole surviving member from the original combo, and The Beatmen, an obscure group from Czechoslovakia.

Gathering themselves together once again in St John's Wood, over two successive days (28th February and 1st March), The Hollies committed an impressive collection of nine completed tracks onto tape, the majority of which would go on to make up their next studio album. One of the songs cut that day, 'Oriental Sadness', highlighted the ever-developing approach that the five-man line-up was intent in taking as they experimented in the studio. It was gentler in sound, with overdubbed percussion to the fore, and a delightfully intricate melody that wove in and out of the arrangement. With Tony's "oriental-styled" guitar riff adding to the effect, the song even generated a half-page article in the *NME*.

The Chinese Sound – that's what you'll be hearing from The Hollies in the near future! They've just recorded a song called 'Oriental Sadness' which Allan Clarke sings velly slowly while Graham Nash hits at a big dinner-gong and drummer Bobby Elliott plays the wooden blocks. Sounds sort of… well… different, doesn't it?

'It's definitely, but definitely way-out as far as we're concerned,' the ever-chatty Graham Nash told me. 'We have to make a decision for our next single, but if we don't use it for (that), it'll definitely go on the next LP.'

*New Musical Express*
April 1966

At some stage during this period, in between the overseas concerts and the ongoing group recording schedules, Bobby Elliott also found the time to liaise in the studio with fellow drummer, and long-time friend, Bob Henrit, formerly of Adam Faith's backing band, the Roulettes. In addition to his work with the early '60s hit-maker, Henrit was also a part-time session player who had recently played on Unit 4+2's 1965 chart-topper 'Concrete And Clay'. The initial intention of the two drummers was to work on a grand project together, focussing on the percussive aspect of the music but, for whatever reason, the project never ventured further than one or two early attempts.

Bob Henrit: 'It was during the mid-sixties that I thought it was time that the UK had a drum record like [American session drummer] Sandy Nelson's, so Bobby Elliott and I went into the studio to make one called 'Drum and Coke'. No adverse pun was implied in the title; it absolutely wasn't a drug reference, although we also recorded one intentionally riddled with puns. That was a music-hall type song called 'Why Won't They Let Us Drummers Sing'!'[59]

'We have run into a couple of difficulties though,' added Bobby, 'as we are both tied up with EMI, so we are going to re-record it with them. Still, it came off pretty well. We used two saxes, a piano, guitar and the two drums. We recorded the backing first and then did our bit. The B-side is a comedy number with Bob and I both singing. I've known Bob a long time and we've often talked about doing this.'

Sadly, their combined efforts remained in the vaults. Instead, Bobby's attentions focussed on the band's upcoming visit to Poland, undertaking one of the first western tours behind the so-called Iron Curtain (The Animals having broken down the borders the previous October).

'The thought of Poland is a bit frightening,' he was to say to the media. 'We don't know what to expect or how we will go down.'

The 6th of March 1966, and accompanied by the diminutive Scottish powerhouse vocalist Lulu and her four-piece backing band of Luvvers, the touring party boarded a BEA flight in London, bound for Warsaw (via Brussels and East Berlin), where they were booked on a two-week tour of the central European communist region. It certainly wasn't to everyone's pleasure that western rock 'n' roll was managing a breakthrough in such restricted areas as, prior to the band's first performance, protesters were in evidence, demonstrating with signs saying, *Long Live Chopin* and *Hollies Go Home!* Ultimately, however, whilst crowds may have filled out the grey, uninspiring venues and enthusiastically applauded the band, overall, it wasn't a pleasant experience…

'I hope we never go back,' commented a disappointed Bobby to *Record Mirror* upon their return. 'It's a terrible place. All those guards with steel helmets and machine guns everywhere. At one concert the kids ran up to the front and men started beating them with dirty great truncheons. They put all the lights on at one show when the kids wouldn't sit down, so we just walked off.'

The weather was dismal, with little to entice their interest beyond the concert stage. After a series of dates, including two shows at the 3,000-seat Congress Hall in Warsaw, followed by visits to Gdańsk, Kraków and Wroclaw, the band were happy to return home.

Nevertheless, they remained positive on their outlook and came across as so when they participated in an obscure 45 release later that month. Issued as a 7-inch flexi-disc, *Sound of the Stars* was a promotional giveaway item, offered exclusively by *Disc Weekly*, and promoted as "letting the listener overhear a series of informal, fascinatingly different conversations between top artists". Recorded alongside similar random ramblings with Cliff Richard, Cilla Black, The Beatles and others, the Hollies inclusion was no more than fifty seconds of jet-fuelled frolics, with TV host Cathy McGowan asking a series of inane questions whilst Graham, Bobby and Allan laughed and fooled about before the microphone. Openly criticising the popular TV show *Juke Box Jury* for featuring guests who knew nothing about music, they clearly overlooked the fact that Allan had actually appeared as a panel judge himself, the previous summer.

However, with the recent Polish jaunt still languishing at the back of their minds, they once again boarded an aeroplane at London's newly rechristened Heathrow Airport, on 27th March, with New York City once again earmarked as their destination. Unlike previous visits across the Atlantic, this time it would be for a fully-fledged concert tour, along with scheduled promotional appearances, with little time in between for enjoying the sights and sounds of the vast continent.

Having arrived safely in the Big Apple after the lengthy ten-hour flight, the opening few days of the visit became a rather frustrating experience for the five members and their entourage when planned TV appearances on NBC's *Hullabaloo* and the local New York station WPIX's *Clay Cole's Discotek* were cancelled due to union issues. Despite having turned up and taken part in rehearsals for the final airing of the NBC show, a series they had appeared on twice before, executives on behalf of the American Federation of TV and Radio Artists refused them permission to appear on the broadcast, citing that the show should remain an all-American affair, despite the fact that Peter and Gordon, and Chad and Jeremy, both popular UK duos, appeared in the final few episodes. At least WIPX had the decency to allow the band to be introduced from their seats in the audience for their union-led studio show.

On 1st April, the band travelled to Roosevelt Field in Long Island NY to participate in a three-day event promoting a new club, created by Murray Kaufman, a high-profile east coast-based DJ and TV presenter, better known by the nickname of "Murray the K". Ceremoniously dubbed "the fifth Beatle" by his own fair hands, during the Liverpool invasion of early '64, Murray was a prominent force in US radio, playing and promoting the music as he saw fit, often at odds with what the radio controllers specifically wanted. Subsequently, his popularity soared and by 1966 he was collaborating with the media art collective USCO to produce a huge multimedia nightclub he labelled The World. Based in an abandoned hangar in Long Island, and dubbed the first discotheque, the concept was for both live and recorded music to be playing whilst slides and moving film were projected onto the crowd. For 1966, this was big. Music acts booked to perform for the grand opening days, alongside The Hollies, were The Young Rascals, Del Shannon, The Isley Brothers and Mitch Ryder and The Detroit Wheels.

Unfortunately, the grand plan was short-lived, in large part because a month-long transit workers' strike prevented many members of his intended audience from reaching the venue, but the April promotional launch was a much-publicised event. It was what's happenin', baby…

Murray the K's World, located at Roosevelt Field in Garden City, was in a converted hangar, once a film studio. The outside walls of the hangar were painted white, with black-and-red trim, the result resembled a combination roller-skating rink and adobe pizza parlour. The inside decor resembled a gym, an art gallery and an ocean liner ballroom. Walls hung with black-and-white canvases. Around the walls, several feet above eye level, were little movie screens, while the dance floor of glossy wood was surrounded by black-upholstered benches and black linoleum-tile standing room.

Against the side walls were stands selling food & Coke, and above the stands were large free-form platforms, supported by white stilts. One contained the sound and lighting equipment, another musical instruments for entertainers. In the centre of the room was a platform loaded with movie projectors.

At 7:55pm the first customers arrived. Admission was $2.50, with a minimum age of 18. The first music played was taped rock 'n' roll, then films by underground cineastes – Stan VanDerBeek, Gerd Stern et al. were shown. A musical group called The Young Rascals and, later, one called The Hollies played. The noise was deafening, and a surging crowd had to be expelled from the lobby.

*The New Yorker*
April 16, 1966

The Hollies played on the large stilted stage for all three nights of the event, whilst also attending a press party after one show, hosted by Imperial Records in their honour and held at a local club, Clay Cole's Happening Place in Manhattan. Then, after a few days' rest and acclimatisation to life on foreign soil, during which they spent time walking around Greenwich Village observing some of the performances in the nearby clubs and, as recalled by Graham in *Wild Tales*, were introduced to songwriter Paul Simon, they prepared to head out onto the long, dark road. With eighteen dates scheduled ahead of them, and lengthy travel in between the venues – covering far more mileage than they could possibly have envisaged after the familiarity of the relatively short-haul UK tours – all downtime was duly appreciated.

The band had cut a version of the Paul Simon composition, 'I Am A Rock', a song originally appearing on the Simon & Garfunkel *Sounds of Silence* album, shortly before arriving in the States. One couldn't simply ignore the wonderful lyrical undertones that Simon used in his work. He didn't stick with the formulated boy-girl-love-kiss scenario; in his mind, that was too basic for an educated young man, and instead, he wove his personal feelings around his meticulous melodies. Unfortunately, The Hollies had caused some controversy upon recording the song, upsetting Simon in the process when they substituted the lyric "*safe within my womb*" to sing "*safe*

131

*within my room*" instead, commenting that it made it more acceptable for staid British audiences. Nevertheless, the songwriter reportedly loved the arrangement that they had created, impressed with the additional third harmony added to the composition.

Compared to the lyrical innocence of 'Look Through Any Window', it's no wonder that Graham Nash, in particular, found freedom and openness in the works of such songwriters. To be so politically challenging and worldly-wise within a 2-minute pop song was a new concept for the reserved British youngsters, and Paul Simon in particular, with the new songs he was now working on ('A Dangling Conversation', 'For Emily, Whenever I May Find Her' and the Dylan-pastiche, 'A Simple Desultory Philippic'), hit a most powerful chord.

As the tour rolled out across the Midwest, cities such as Cedar Rapids, Clear Lake, Sioux Falls, Madison, Peru, Vincennes and Saginaw all hosted the ever-confident band. In Clear Lake, Iowa, on 10th April, they performed at the infamous Surf Ballroom, playing on the same stage that Buddy Holly, Richie Valens and The Big Bopper had played on seven years previous, the evening of their fateful flight. A later stop-off in Chicago on the 22nd, to revisit the Arie Crown Theatre and support the Anglo-Scottish partnership of Peter Asher and Gordon Waller, also gave them the opportunity to visit one of the many legendary recording studios of the windy city. These were home to many of the great blues artists that had so influenced the UK beat boom during the early years of the decade. A recording session was even cautiously booked during one of the rare days off from the road. Unfortunately, that too was cancelled, reportedly due to further union rules and restrictions over the performing rights of non-resident musicians.

One further performance, scheduled for the 800-seat Devine's Million Dollar Ballroom in Milwaukee, was also withdrawn, as the show was somehow missed off the list of approved appearances for the tour – albeit as a last-minute addition. Inconceivably, this wasn't even discovered until they actually arrived in the city in preparation for the performance. Instead, the band appeared on the local TV news, being interviewed and explaining their absence.

'We're here and we're ready to play', Graham was to tell the *Milwaukee Journal*. 'But the immigration guy said in so many words that if we played, we'd be deported tomorrow.'

'We didn't tell them they couldn't play', an immigration service officer was to reply. 'But entertainers who come into the United States are not free agents. Under an H-1, less restricted visa, no clearance is needed. The top British rock groups – The Beatles, Rolling Stones, Herman's Hermits and The Animals – all have H-1 visas. The Hollies and other lesser groups have restricted H-2 visas which, in effect, protect American workers from foreign competition.'

'They're worried that Herman's Hermits are going to take over the government,' responded Graham.

Despite the frustrations resulting from the union regulations (they wouldn't be afforded H-1 status until the following year), and the obstacles that seemed to be piling up in front of them, the band were received extremely well in the cities and venues they played at, although for one member of the touring party, it was all becoming too stressful.

Eric Haydock had always been the quiet one; some may say detached at times from the remainder of the quintet. Strikingly handsome, but often portrayed with a broody, sullen image in group portraits, the prospect of yet further weeks apart from his wife back home was making him restless and unhappy, to the extent that at one point, during the first half of the tour, he threatened to walk out and return back to Manchester. However, with thoughts of just two further weeks ahead, out on the sun-kissed west coast, he decided to remain and endure the separation. For now.

On 25th April, The Hollies flew out to California for the first time, and the impression it made on them was immediate. And it wasn't just the sunshine and the sounds of the surf lapping in against the golden shoreline. Graham, in particular, was instantly struck by the vibe.

Imperial Records, in every effort to placate the band for their earlier failings, and to promote them with their recent "hit" recording, held a further champagne reception for them upon their arrival in Los Angeles. In Graham's own words, it was the typical showbusiness LA *shmoozefest*, filled with wall-to-wall music business suits, songwriters, staffers and the occasional wannabee. At one point during the event, an up-and-coming nineteen-year-old radio host named Rodney Bingenheimer approached the band unannounced and asked them if they would like to tag along with him to a nearby studio where some of his friends were recording. Unsure as to what to expect, Graham, Tony and Bobby accepted the invitation and soon found themselves at the famed Western Recorders along Sunset Boulevard, in nearby Hollywood, attending a recording session for a new folk-rock vocal quartet. One that was bathed in every aspect of sunshine harmonies and cool vibes. The Mamas and The Papas. For Bobby, it was a meeting with the legendary session drummer Hal Blaine, hit-maker extraordinaire who played on all of The Mamas and The Papas' recordings, that became a personal tour highlight. For another Hollie in attendance, however, the session would prove to be a life-changing moment.

'Rodney invited us to the session,' Tony would later recount. 'Everyone there was having a good time, all out of their minds, which was the in-thing at the time. After the session, we were invited back to one of their pads up in the Hollywood Hills. I was more interested in checking out the talent at the Whisky a Go Go club, but Graham went…'[20]

One member of the LA-based quartet, the irrepressible "Mama" Cass Elliott, stood out like no other and became an immediate confidante and source of inspiration to Graham (who had initially set out to conquer the desire of the other "Mama", the demure but strictly-off-limits Michelle Phillips). The bonding of the cheery Hollie and the equally ebullient Mama was instantaneous and no more than forty-eight hours later, the newfound friendship was on the Los Angeles freeway, with Cass having collected Graham from the Knickerbocker Hotel on Ivar Avenue where The Hollies were staying, heading up the winding hills into Laurel Canyon to meet another friend of hers.

Nash: 'I'll never forget it. We arrived at this house and Cass strode in without knocking. We went upstairs and there on a couch was this man in a blue striped tee-shirt, rolling the longest, thickest joint you've ever seen in your life. "I'd like you to meet David Crosby," she said to me. He passed the joint around, produced another, and that was it.'[20]

That meeting with The Byrds' singer-songwriter-guitarist would be Graham's entrance ticket into the free-living, free-loving, hedonistic lifestyle that would subsequently engulf him in years to come.

'I remember thinking to myself, *I'm never going back,*' Graham was to say in a later interview with journalist Harvey Kubernik. 'I just decided for some reason, whatever consciousness is running this planet wanted me to be in Los Angeles. I wasn't quite sure what was going on, you know, what my future would entail, but I trusted myself because my parents always told me and taught me to trust myself. I'm a musician, first and foremost. I'm a believer in beauty. I'm a believer in the fact that truth and justice will prevail in the end.'[21]

That said, at this particular point in time, Graham was still very much committed to The Hollies and their future, regardless of the diversions that were steadily proliferating throughout their daily routines. His introduction to marijuana, courtesy of Crosby, became a point of difference between him and his bandmates, all of whom remained in favour of only alcohol as their chosen high.

'In England, it was mainly hash and I would smoke that. I had a friend who was a William Morris agent and we shared an apartment in London and would get very high. So, I had a bit of a difference in lifestyle. I think it pushes you in different directions…'[21]

During their time in California, they performed a number of shows, although a proposed appearance at the Hullabaloo Club on Sunset Boulevard was cancelled due to scheduling conflictions. On 29th April, the band made their debut performance out on the west coast, appearing at the Starlight Ballroom in Oxnard, thirty miles to the north of Los Angeles. Following two evening shows across the state line in Arizona, the second of which saw them play at the Monterey Recreation Centre in Tucson, supported by the pre-Alice Cooper band The Spiders, The Hollies settled into a five-night residency at the popular but short-lived LA nightspot, the Trip, their name ceremoniously daubed in paint on the outside walls of the venue.

The Hollies Take Over the Beat.
They came, they saw, they created chaos…

It all started the day after they arrived on the West Coast. We met them at a champagne reception given by Imperial Records in their honour. They came up to the office the next day. It went something like this;

'I don't like Batman,' said Tony, sprawling himself across the desk. 'But I like the Beverly Hillbillies.'

He told me how proud they are that they never put anything on record that they can't reproduce exactly on stage. 'It's disgraceful not to,' he said.

He told me all about their legal problems – they had trouble getting in the country, then were denied permits to do television appearances and were only allowed a very few live appearances. At one point they were so disgusted they booked flights home and even sent their equipment home. After being talked into visiting the West

Coast, they did manage to get clearance for a few live appearances and had to borrow equipment to perform.

And so it went on, each one trying making himself at home in the middle of the desk I was trying to take notes on, all except Eric. He doesn't talk.

*KRLA Beat*
May 1966

With a non-performing appearance at the *KRLA Beat* awards show also under their belts, and with all permitted concerts fulfilled, the tour officially came to a conclusion on 8<sup>th</sup> May, 1966. As duly advised by the US Immigration Department, they swiftly departed American shores, flying back to home soil, albeit via Gatwick Airport as opposed to Heathrow, London fog causing the necessary route changes. However, all was not well. Eric Haydock was both emotionally and physically exhausted, a fact subsequently reported in the press that he was now also seeking medical treatment for his ailing health. In reality, the backbone of the issue was based upon Eric's increasing dissatisfaction over the financial concerns surrounding the group, paired with the seemingly non-stop schedule the band were being forced to endure. He began questioning management over fees payable and monies owed; a factor that had originally been raised following the investment losses of the previous year. It was all to come to a head.

# CHAPTER TEN

# "WOULD YOU BELIEVE..."

Two days after arriving home from the US tour, still tired and exhausted, the band reconvened in the recording studio. That is to say, four of them did. Eric remained at home with his wife, who was expecting their first child. In his place that day sat the Scottish-born bass player Jack Bruce, fresh from a short chart-topping stint as a member of Manfred Mann. (Within two months. he would link up with Eric Clapton and drummer Ginger Baker to form the powerhouse trio Cream.) The project that day was to record the theme song to a new United Artists feature film, *After The Fox*, starring comedian Peter Sellers in the lead role. Co-written by acclaimed American songwriters Burt Bacharach and Hal David, the theme song was a bizarre concoction of European-styled melodramatic landscaping, broken up by Sellers' own droll interludes, performed in a pseudo-Italian accent, as per his character. Burt Bacharach himself provided the keyboard accompaniment.

'We were approached by George Martin and Ron Richards,' recalled Bobby Elliott. 'George being Peter Sellers' producer and Ron being ours. Burt Bacharach wanted to meet us, and so we met him in London, and he said how much he liked our records. [He] was very meticulous but Ron was a hard man and when he felt that he had it in the can, he closed Burt down. I remember being surprised that Peter Sellers was so subdued. He came in the studio and walked to the grand piano and threatened it with a karate chop, and that was the funniest thing he did that day...'[15]

'We went to [Burt's] apartment and sat around the piano and worked out the arrangements and the harmonies,' added Graham who, at the time, was far from enamoured at taking on this semi-comedic slice of pop.[5]

A soundtrack album (United Artists ULP 1151) containing the score from the film, along with The Hollies-Sellers theme song, was to appear in stores during the August of '66. This was a full four months prior to the December launch of the production (albeit a poorly received release), although Hollies fans were able to capitalise on the band's contribution by purchasing the accompanying 45 (UP1152) instead, also issued in advance of the film during mid-September.

The following weekend, 15th May, having completed work on the Bacharach-David title track, the group were once more booked to perform on the prestigious *Sunday Night at the London Palladium* weekly TV broadcast. However, once again, Eric Haydock failed to attend. With discussions between himself and Michael Cohen over the finances clearly unsettling him, Eric chose to stay away until his concerns were resolved.

'I was buying a new house and thought I had enough money to buy it outright. I'd been working for the last three years, making hit records and touring...'[3] but when Hollies Limited, the company that Cohen oversaw on behalf of the group, responded that he needed to mortgage the new build in order to finance the cost, Haydock took a stand. Clearly, something was not right. He stayed away.

'The exhaustion was a press story,' he was to comment, offered up by The Hollies' PR agent Robin Britten to deflect any focus on the questions being raised, with *Melody Maker* duly stating that Eric was taking "indefinite leave due to nervous exhaustion and fatigue".

With the Palladium show only days away, the band were forced to bring in a substitute for the performance.

Klaus Voormann was a German-born artist and musician who had befriended The Beatles during their early 1960s residencies in Hamburg. Having relocated to London during the middle years of the decade, where he had remained in close contact with the Liverpool quartet, he was establishing a reputation for both his artwork and his solid bass playing, honed as a member of Hamburg's Paddy, Klaus & Gibson trio. Recently approached by both The Beatles and The Bee Gees to design the sleeve layouts for their forthcoming album releases (*Revolver* and *Bee Gees 1st* respectively), Voormann was more than happy to assist at short notice with

The Hollies' current predicament. That Sunday, he stepped out onto the Palladium stage with the band for their TV appearance, sharing the stage with comedian Jimmy Tarbuck, magician David Nixon and the legendary song and dance *chanteuse* Liza Minnelli.

Two further recording sessions were also scheduled for that week, and with Eric still at home in Manchester, stoically refusing to participate, stand-ins were once again called upon to supply the necessary lower register duties.

On 17th May, they cut the powerful Ransford-composed 'Don't Run And Hide', utilising the resonating bass of established session player John Paul Jones. Whilst the rhythm pairing of Bobby Elliott and the future Zeppelin superstar provided a solid enough foundation for the band to play around, the recording lacked any of the impressive six-string runs that made Eric's contributions so unique. The following day, they called upon an old friend at short notice to fill Eric's role for another new song, this time from the now established songwriting pen of Graham Gouldman.

By this time, Gouldman's own band, The Mockingbirds, were undertaking the warm-up position during the filming of the weekly *Top of the Pops* TV show, still airing from its Manchester studio. On one of the earlier occasions that The Hollies had appeared on the show, possibly the 24th February performance, Gouldman had cornered Nash, in the men's toilets, offering him the opportunity to hear another new composition he had written specifically with The Hollies in mind (although in a more recent interview, Gouldman suggests that the "meeting" took place in the toilets of Stoke Town Hall, where The Mockingbirds were supporting The Hollies).

'I played 'Bus Stop' to Graham Nash in the toilet, using a twelve-string guitar, since it was the only quiet part of the building,' smiled Gouldman. Liking what he heard, Nash suggested that the band hold back on the recording whilst the songwriter cut a demo version for them and they work out what arrangement worked best for the tune. By all accounts, they had been working on it for at least a week or two before the 18th of May recording session.

In the detailed liner notes for the US CD release of the *30th Anniversary Collection*, Tony commented that the acoustic guitar solo that featured on the final mix of the song had been inspired by the contributions of Klaus Voormann, during rehearsals for their London Palladium show.

'When Eric Haydock was having one of his walkabouts, Klaus stepped in and did a live television show with us, *Sunday Night at the London*

*Palladium*. He must have been around when we were rehearsing 'Bus Stop', because I remember him playing through the solo with me – the part where one guitar follows the other.'

'We rehearsed 'Bus Stop' with him in a little hotel in London,' confirmed Bobby. 'We needed a solo, a Bach-type thing, and he suggested one or two things that found their way into the record.'

'I played the Palladium show and then did some BBC recordings,' Klaus was to reply to this author when questioned about his brief time with the band. 'But that's all I can remember.'

Sadly, there are no records confirming precisely to which BBC shows Klaus contributed, although several sessions, including one for *Saturday Swings* (12th May), were recorded around the time he was involved.

Without question, 'Bus Stop' is one of the pivotal songs in the entire Hollies catalogue, showing the growing maturity of both arrangement and performance, whilst maintaining the pure pop sensibility that defined The Hollies' trademark sound. Lyrically, it fell a considerable way short of many of the more thought-provoking songs of that period, such as 'God Only Knows', '19th Nervous Breakdown' and 'Eight Miles High'. However, placed alongside 'Look Through Any Window', 'No Milk Today' and 'East West' (both hits for Herman's Hermits) and 'Pamela Pamela' (a Top 20 success for Wayne Fontana), Gouldman's lyrical abilities to portray the quintessentially English way of life, as seen through the listener's eyes, provided genuine hit-making material. Whilst, with hindsight, one can also look back at the overall naivety of the compositions, it is this innocent quality that today fills us with such nostalgic charm.

Also attending the 18th May Abbey Road recording session, visiting from the sunny side of America with her fellow bandmates, was "Mama" Cass Elliott. Experiencing the London scene for the first time, the gregarious singer met Mick Jagger, hung out with The Beatles and was keen to renew acquaintances with her charming new friend in The Hollies. However, unfortunately for Graham, the earlier object of his desires, Michelle Phillips, had been left behind in California, having recently been fired from the quartet by her husband, band leader John Phillips. Michelle's extra-marital affairs, firstly with bandmate Denny Doherty and then, more recently, with The Byrds' Gene Clark, led to her short-term replacement, Jill Gibson (the girlfriend of producer Lou Adler), making the trip instead.

"Bus Stop' was recorded completely in just one and a half hours,' Ron Richards later recalled for *Record Mirror*. 'Cass Elliott was in the studio at the time and just couldn't believe it! It was a classic example of the discipline under which the group works.'

Watching as the band laid down the track, Cass would also have noticed an unfamiliar face in their midst. Supplying bass guitar for the session was Tony and Bobby's former Dolphins bandmate, Bernie Bamford Calvert who, despite working in a factory during that period, had taken time off from his day job to help out his friends. He subsequently stayed around and filled in for the errant Haydock for the following month, including a subsequent visit overseas.

Bernie: 'I was working in the factory Monday afternoon and the phone rang. The charge hand came down and said, "There's a phone call. It's the Hollies' manager," and I ran to the phone and Michael Cohen, the manager, said, "Bernie, we've got a problem with the bass player. The boys are going to Scandinavia for a three-week tour. Can you join them?" Can you imagine the feeling?

'I said to the guy in charge of the factory, "Can I have three weeks' holiday?" and he replied, "The Hollies? They're famous! My daughter thinks they're great. Can you get me some autographed photos? Your job will be waiting when you come back…" And so off I went to get a visa since I didn't have a passport.[26]

'I went to London the following morning and I met the band in the BBC Studios to do a live broadcast. We then went from the studios to a hotel where we were staying for the night, and rehearsed 'Bus Stop' because they were going into the studio the following day. I nearly had a nervous breakdown when we arrived [at Abbey Road] because Ron Richards had booked a session bassist and I thought, *I'm just going to be a spectator here.* Thankfully, Tony, Allan, Graham and Bobby suggested that I did the session, so Ron paid the bassist and he went home, and I played on 'Bus Stop'.

'The speed that they worked was absolutely amazing. By tea-time we'd got the backing track, and by ten o'clock the vocals were on…'[69]

Two proposed UK performances, scheduled for the Locarno Ballrooms in Streatham and Stevenage respectively, were subsequently cancelled and, following the 18th May recording session in London, Bernie's first public appearance with the band came about three days later on 21st May in Rønne, a small town located on Denmark's island of Bornholm. This was followed immediately afterwards by a three-day run at the Hit House in Copenhagen. The band then took the short hop across the Baltic Sea into Germany and onto Yugoslavia, before finishing up with a two-week tour of Sweden.

'It all lasted for three weeks,' Bernie would later recall, 'with two shows a night, so it was an amazing baptism of fire.

'Scandinavia was amazing. We worked at these places they call folk parks, kind of open-air gigs. They have them everywhere, and they're brilliant. After a couple of weeks, the band was so tight.'[25/26]

Whilst in Germany, the reconstructed line-up appeared on the country's top-rated music show *Beat Club*, performing excellent live renditions of 'Look Through Any Window', 'Very Last Day' (promoted by Graham as their current number 2 hit in Sweden – it actually reached #1) and 'I Can't Let Go'. The absence of Eric was certainly not noticed as Bernie seemed perfectly at home, filling in with riffs and runs along the neck of his bass. With two other fellow former Dolphins band members only feet away, Bernie's return to band life could not have been made any smoother.

Sweden saw the group undertake a similar televised recording when they filmed lip-synched performances of 'Very Last Day' and 'I Can't Let Go', along with the debut TV showing of 'I've Got A Way Of My Own'. A song that had initially appeared on the flip-side of the 'If I Needed Someone' single, this would also feature on the band's upcoming fourth album. Filmed in the strange surroundings of a Swedish dockyard for the TV show *Popside*, the appearance (which didn't air until the following month) was notable for Graham's spoken introduction for each band member, including the line…

'Standing in for Eric, who's ill in Manchester at present, is our friend Bernie.'

Clearly, the band were content to play along with the exhaustion and fatigue charade. If, indeed, it was a charade. The management team reportedly ran a tight ship, with doctor's certificates requested to account for any non-appearances, and Eric always insisted in later years that he had provided these, but the unease surrounding his absence continued.

'Eric Haydock was my favourite member of the band in the early days,' admitted Bobby. 'He was a very exciting bassist. He had a certain aura about him, and he was a pioneer. He used a six-string bass long before anybody else did, but we just couldn't carry on that way.' [56]

It was backstage at the London Palladium, just prior to taking the stage on

15th May, that either Graham or Allan (depending on who is recalling the events) took a short telephone call from one of their idols. Phil Everly (or Don, subject to who…) had called to say that the brothers were currently staying at the Ritz Hotel in London, preparing to record their next album, and were enquiring as to whether they had any songs the duo could cut. Needless to say, when one of your idols calls, you tend to jump and, according to both Graham and Allan over the many ensuing years, within a matter of hours, having graced the Palladium stage with a selection of their hits, they were seated in front of Don and Phil in their plush London hotel suite, running through a selection of their new compositions.

One national newspaper report that followed, shortly afterwards, actually suggested that it was at the recording session, the following day, and not the hotel, when they presented their songs to the duo, some of which were still just ideas in their heads. According to the press report in question, Phil Everly commented, 'Some of their material is absolutely great. Some [of it] wasn't even written down. They just sang it to us at the session. We liked it and recorded it then and there. They didn't show us a bad one!

'I've never heard so many good songs all at once. I'm sure Tony and Graham are going to be another Lennon and McCartney team!'

Wherever the initial meeting took place, here's hoping that Allan Clarke wasn't reading the news over his breakfast the following day.

Nevertheless, Allan still walked away from the encounter with a certain sense of pride, later commenting that the brothers were asking him at one point, how to sing a particular phrase. The *Everly Brothers*, asking *him!* Could it get any better?

Of course, this wasn't the first time they had encountered their idols face-to-face. Other than the infamous meeting, pre-Hollies, on the steps of Manchester's Midland Hotel, Graham had previously met Don Everly (according to Don's own recollections in the sleevenotes for the brothers' 1994 *Heartaches & Harmonies* box set) in New York, whilst The Hollies had been undertaking promotional activity across the ocean. In addition, both Allan and Graham had been present at the East Ham Granada Theatre on 25th October 1965, during the Everlys' UK tour. According to British beat and harmony aficionado Tony Rivers (in his autobiography *I'm Nearly Famous: Tales of a Likely Lad*), the duo had met up with him, prior to the show, and had offered to take him backstage to meet Don and Phil in their dressing room.

Eight of the songs that appeared on the upcoming Everly Brothers disc, issued during that July under the title *Two Yanks in England*, were credited to the L. Ransford pseudonym, and some of the instrumentation was provided by the band as well, although the actual date for the sessions has been brought into question.

Of the chosen eight, six were cut in London that same week at the Decca Recording Studios in West Hampstead – 'Don't Run and Hide', 'Have You Ever Loved Somebody', 'Fifi The Flea', 'Hard Hard Year', 'Like Every Time Before' and 'Signs That Will Never Change', all featuring a session team of John Paul Jones (bass), Andy White and Dougie Wright (drums), James Patrick Page (guitar) and Arthur Greenslade (keyboards), along with a selection of uncredited (and unconfirmed) Hollies. However, if the dated session logs are correct – and how many actually are? – then the given date of 14th May throws the story of the Palladium telephone call into doubt, seeing that the show actually took place on the 15th. One can only presume that the session log was detailed incorrectly.

'When I met and worked with the Everly Brothers, I was so impressed with them,' recalled Tony during a 2013 interview. 'Their voices just blended so naturally, so ideally, and they were very professional. I ended up playing guitar on their *Two Yanks in England* album. Jimmy Page was working as a session guitarist then and he joined us, along with John Paul Jones on bass – so, basically, it was the Everly Brothers with Led Zeppelin and myself. Jimmy Page and John Paul Jones were so successful as session musicians, working all day, being chauffeured around between recording studios and earning so much money, that I was always surprised they opted out and formed Led Zeppelin – but what a good thing they did!'[22]

'I knew the guitar parts well, of course,' he continued on, in an interview for BBC radio's *They Ain't Heavy, They're The Hollies* Special. 'Jimmy was such a sweet guy and I'd be teaching him how to play certain things. He was saying, "That's good, how d'you do that?" and I'd say, "No, Jimmy. You'd find that a bit difficult. You'd better let me do that!"'

Bobby Elliott later suggested that he too supplied drums for at least one track on the album, but which one has never been clarified.

Allan Clarke in *Record Mirror*: 'Somehow the numbers we write never seem to suit the Hollies, we could never release one of our numbers as a single. But we were amazed at the results that the Everlys got. They progressed with the songs. To our mind, the Evs are the best ever vocally, and we're hoping to get a relationship in which we can be their sole writers. The fact of what they did gave us great confidence.'

The remaining two Ransford compositions, 'So Lonely' and 'I've Been Wrong Before', were cut during a later Hollie-less Stateside session, and featured such celebrated luminaries as James Burton, Glen Campbell, Jim Gordon and Larry Knechtel as the session players. It was indeed a stellar crew all round but, unfortunately, despite the quality within the grooves, the success of the release was minimal, ultimately failing to chart either side of the Atlantic.

A week after their return from the Swedish tour and having thanked Bernie publicly for his assistance (and seeing him return to his factory job), The Hollies prepared themselves for the publicity assault that would follow in the wake of the fourth album release.

*Would You Believe* appeared in the shops across the UK on 1st July, 1966 (Parlophone PMC7008), comprising twelve songs, only four of which came from within the band. As was to be expected, and following the pattern of previous LPs, the selection was a mixed affair, with the driving R&B and rhythmic drumbeat of the opening 'I Take What I Want' and Chuck Berry's 'Sweet Little Sixteen' sitting fairly uncomfortably alongside the gentle folk of 'Stewball' and Graham's own solo 'Fifi The Flea'. This latter offering, with its haunting narrative of a Shakespearian tragedy set against a deeply silly scenario (and potentially inspired in part by the band's previous roadie, Jay Vickers, who was nicknamed "Freddie Flea"), seemingly points ahead, style-wise, to the future balladeer framework he was to make very much his own in later years.

Elsewhere, reasonable covers of Paul Simon's 'I Am A Rock' and Buddy Holly's 'Take Your Time' still paled against the superior recordings of the band's original tunes 'Oriental Sadness', with (as noted by author Alan Clayson in his *Call Up The Groups*) its "spiralling vocal tangents", and 'Hard Hard Year', a song highlighted by a blistering Tony Hicks guitar solo. Overall, it made for a difficult, and at times dissatisfying, listen. Nevertheless, the addition of the hit 45 version of 'I Can't Let Go' as the album closer brought it back to a rewarding conclusion.

Recorded over an erratic six-month period, sessions here and sessions there, and packaged in a sleeve dominated by an artistic hand-drawn interpretation of the band, with rear sleeve notes by Andy Wickham (an up-and-coming music business entrepreneur who later worked at Warner/

Reprise), the album still managed a Top 20 placing in the official UK charts (and a Top 10 rank in the competing *NME* lists). June also saw the Parlophone release of *I Can't Let Go*, the sixth and final 4-track EP collection bearing the band's name.

As was to be expected and following their pattern of issuing alternative song selections on their releases, Imperial Records put out their revised US version of the album, retitled *Beat Group!* one month earlier, albeit with a far superior front sleeve design. Sadly, despite the increased interest in the band, following the success of the recent tour and the preceding 45, the album failed to chart.

> Eric Haydock, the Hollies bass player who has been resting at home with nervous exhaustion for the past few weeks, has been declared fully recovered by his doctor and returned to the group last night for TV's "Scene At 6.30".
>
> Eric was taken ill just before the Hollies trip to Germany and Sweden three weeks ago and his place in the group was taken by Bernie Calvert.
>
> *Disc & Music Echo*
> June 1966

In a somewhat surprising move, and despite his dissatisfaction over the handling of the band's finances (which remained an ongoing scenario), Eric returned to the line-up mid-June at the invitation of Michael Cohen, to fulfil promotional obligations. Forgiveness was seemingly in the air. With the 17th June release of 'Bus Stop' as the next Parlophone single, b/w 'Don't Run and Hide', Eric found himself in the strange situation of being a founder member, miming on TV to a song he hadn't actually played on. *Scene At 6.30* and *Top of the Pops*, taped days before the single was officially released, along with *Ready Steady Go!, The Five O'clock Club, Now*, and *Hey Presto, It's Rolf!* were all filmed in the wake of the release, pushing the single up into a Top 5 slot. Not that all of the publicity for the release went as smoothly as hoped...

'I bought a double-decker bus to publicise everything,' Michael Cohen later recounted. 'It was a stunt, and I wrote "The Hollies" and "The Toggery" and got art students to paint it. I couldn't get much publicity out of it, so I said to Frank Renshaw [from The Toggery Five], "Frank, drive it around and

attract people," and he went under a bloody bridge and took the top off!'[29]
*Top of the Pops*, the only surviving footage from the run of promotional TV appearances, remains interesting viewing. With a dark, moody Eric at the lip of the stage, barely offering any sign of enjoyment, the good-looking frontline trio of Tony (in Lennon-esque round sunglasses), Graham and Allan (the latter also playing an acoustic guitar) smile, laugh and fool about in their casual stage clothing. For his part, Bobby, simply decked in white tee-shirt, and topped off in his now customary flat hat, hiding the thinning thatch underneath, gamely plays along, miming along to the pre-recorded track. However, within weeks, the situation was to change yet again, and this time it was to be permanent.

The 2nd of July, and following their appearance at the art-deco Floral Hall Ballroom in Southport, Eric was reportedly called into a meeting with Michael Cohen, who informed him of the band's unanimous decision to oust him from the line-up. It caught him completely off guard. He was under the assumption that all was working out fine again and his position within the band had been resumed.

'He said that the boys had held a meeting and decided to let me go,' a bitter Haydock was to say to Brian Southall many years later. 'The truth was that the band had sacked me, voted me out, but got Cohen to fire me.' [3]

### The Hollies Dump Haydock

Usually, the bow-out amongst groups is graceful with all sides admitting a "mutual decision". However, The Hollies have gone a step beyond this with Eric and the remaining Hollies each giving contradictory views on the split.

Eric claims, 'It was a raw deal and I am consulting my lawyers. It all hinges on the fact that I wanted a few days off in November when my wife is expecting a baby. It's true that I've missed a few dates through illness but on each occasion, I have produced a doctor's certificate.'

Graham Nash emphasised that The Hollies had no gripe against Eric but that he was extremely unreliable.

*KRLA BEAT*
August 1966

'It's a real foul trick in my mind. None of the group has spoken to me. I think they used me for a mug when I re-joined. I was filling in until Bern Calvert could make it...'

*Disc & Music Echo*
August 1966

With Eric a difficult man to deal with at times, none of his former bandmates had much to say on the positive side in the wake of his departure. Clearly, Robin Britten's role in the PR department, and that of new publicity agent Alan McDougall, went into overtime.

'That's right,' Graham was to comment to the UK press. 'Eric has been dismissed. Basically, because it's been increasingly difficult to work with him. When we came back from America, we were all knocked out, but Eric just took time off. He just walked out for a month! You've got to have cohesion amongst all five. Can't have four pulling against one.'

*Disc & Music Echo*
August 1966

In the immediate aftermath of Eric's dismissal, rumours began to circulate over his next move. Stories in the press indicated that The Kinks had earlier offered him a berth in their line-up as a temporary replacement for their own bass player Peter Quaife, who had recently been hospitalised after an automobile accident. Eric had turned down the opportunity, working under the belief that all had been forgiven in Hollie-circles.

Instead, opting to continue without the comfortable surroundings of his friends alongside, Eric became intent on putting his own band together. Led by a desire to front the line-up himself, the plan was to take the music away from the formulated "pop" field that his former partners ploughed so successfully.

*

The Hollies: 'Bus Stop' (Parlophone R5469)
A very clever song, and, in some ways, as good as anything The Hollies have done. Lyrics are tight, with meaning, and the vocal

harmonies are excellent. Heavy beat, fine guitar phrases. This is high quality judged from any angle.

*Record Mirror*
June 1966

Barry: 'I like it. It's not as good as their last one, 'I Can't Let Go', but it's a hit!'

Paul: 'It's a good record. I'd like to hear it a few more times. It'll get into the Top Ten. It's a pity about their London Palladium – they didn't play very well, did they?'

Paul and Barry Ryan guest review
*Melody Maker*
June 1966

'Bus Stop' would also go on to become one of the band's most successful releases around the globe, with at least fourteen countries charting the single in their best-selling lists, seven of which placed it in their Top 3 slots, whilst in Malaysia and the ever-loyal Sweden it hit the top spot. Meanwhile, still intent on breaking The Hollies amongst the vast potential US audience, Imperial Records once again released a Hollies 45 into the mass market of America during July of 1966. However, unlike the lukewarm reception that the previous releases had garnered, this time it was to pay dividends. 'Bus Stop' began charting during late August and remained in the Top 40 *Billboard* lists for the following nine weeks, with an impressive peak position of number 5 during the first week of October. By that time, The Hollies would be part-way through their third US visit.

1 'Cherish' by The Association (Valiant)
2 'You Can't Hurry Love' by The Supremes (Motown)
3 'Beauty Is Only Skin Deep' by The Temptations (Gordy)
4 'Black Is Black' by Los Bravos (Press)
5 'Bus Stop' by The Hollies (Imperial)
6 '96 Tears' by ? and The Mysterians (Cameo)
7 'Reach Out (I'll Be There)' by The Four Tops (Motown)
8 'Yellow Submarine' by The Beatles (Capitol)
9 'Sunshine Superman' by Donovan (Epic)
10 'Cherry Cherry' by Neil Diamond (Bang)

'Imperial never gave us much encouragement,' Bobby later recalled, when reminiscing with *Goldmine* over their limited success overseas. 'I can remember meeting with some fellow over there, who told us we just weren't commercial enough in what we were doing. He told us we should try and sound more like the Association.' [12]

In the weeks prior to the next journey across the Atlantic Ocean, the band had regrouped back at EMI's Abbey Road base, alongside Ron Richards, with Bernie Calvert once again recalled to sit in on the bass guitar stool. Having made his UK performing debut with the band on 29th July at the Marine Ballroom in Morecambe, followed by shows in Blackpool and in Tony's hometown of Nelson, Bernie's potential as a permanent replacement for Eric Haydock was clearly an option the band were considering, so much so that he also appeared on TV's *Five O'clock Club* with them at the latter end of August, performing 'Bus Stop'. Then again, impressed with how Klaus Voormann had helped them out at the London Palladium show, and how he had worked alongside Tony in the early arrangements for 'Bus Stop', Klaus had also been approached to see if he would be interested in the vacancy. However, the talented musician-artist had instead opted to go with a similar offer coming in his direction from Manfred Mann, themselves high in the UK charts at that point with 'Pretty Flamingo'. Other names that reportedly crossed the minds of Allan, Graham, Tony and Bobby, but went no further, were Mike Gregory (of Liverpudlian quartet The Escorts) and ex-Searchers founding member Tony Jackson.

The 16th August sessions at Abbey Road resulted in three new recordings, all of which would end up on the band's next studio album. Then, the following day, they cut a brand-new composition from the Ransford pen, an ode looking back to their infamous meeting with Morris Levy in New York, the previous September. With a lyric inspired by the bevy of belly dancers with whom Levy had attempted to entice them, the opening riff of 'Stop! Stop! Stop!' had initially been conceived by Tony as part of an alternative song he was working on, 'Suspicious Look in Your Eyes'.

'It turned out that the intro for 'Suspicious Look' fitted perfectly into 'Stop! Stop! Stop!', so I swapped them over and played it on a six-string banjo with slapback echo.'[5]

With the banjo effect cut to sound like a *balalaika* or a *bağlama*, a range of eastern European stringed instruments akin to the traditional sounds of Turkey, the new arrangement fitted in perfectly with the lyrical visions suggested in the song, so influenced by the Arabic and Turkish style of dancing. With Bobby's crashing cymbals adding to the dramatic overtone during the chorus, it was an instantly unforgettable tune and another wonderful offering that would soon be foisted upon the group's expectant fan base. For its own part, 'Suspicious Look in Your Eyes' was also taped during that same period in its newly altered state.

## HOW A HOLLIE SPENDS HIS LOLLY

On Saturday, August 6, The Hollies appeared at the Imperial Ballroom, Nelson and received £500. This is what they had to pay out:

Promoter Tito Burns, ten per cent – £50

Financial Manager Michael Cohen, five per cent – £25

Travelling Expenses took about £2 each

Their two road managers Rod Shields and Derek Duck are paid about £20 per week, so they earned some £3 each that night

That left The Hollies with just over £400, less income tax, which was put straight into their bank account. Out of this, they draw personal living expenses of £50 per week.

Graham told me: 'Our publicity man takes £10 to £20 and we pay our fan club secretary £10 a week. If we are doing a tour of one-nighters the hotel bills cost us £40 a week each. Our executive Zodiac car cost over £1,000 and the van nearly as much. Petrol costs easily £20 a week for each.'

Bobby Elliott added: 'Our allowance of £50 per week is sometimes not enough. Last week we stayed in a hotel at £3 5s a night. Dinner was 18s 6d and breakfast 9s. Everyone was short that week!'

Graham continued: 'When we go abroad, we pay heavy airfares. Our trip to America soon will cost about £150 each way for each of us…'

*Disc & Music Echo*
August 1966

# CHAPTER ELEVEN

# "IT WAS SO FRIGHTENING..."

I t was to be £150 well spent, as the North American tour during the autumn/fall of 1966 further highlighted the growing popularity Stateside of what was, essentially, one of Britain's most successful bands on home soil of that era. Touching down at John F Kennedy International Airport in Queens, New York with them on this occasion was their recently confirmed, official new bass player, Bernie Calvert.

Bernard Bamford Calvert had been born on 16th September 1942 in the small town of Brierfield, Lancashire, located in the Borough of Pendle, and situated in between the more widely populated settlements of Burnley and Nelson. One of four children (with two brothers, Jack and Ronald, and a sister, Joan), he became a keen piano player during his formative years.

'I took piano lessons for about four years, from the time I was eight to when I was twelve,' Bernie would later remark. 'Then rock 'n' roll took over.'[26]

Whilst attending nearby Fisher-More Secondary School in Nelson, he was encouraged to pick up the bass guitar by his friend Tony Hicks, a fellow member of Ricky Shaw and The Dolphins, the popular Manchester-based rock 'n' roll outfit whom Bernie had first joined during 1958 at the tender age of sixteen.

He had remained with the band throughout their three-year tenure as one of the city's leading music attractions, whilst also training as an apprentice engineer. However, once Tony had quit the line-up to become a Hollie, joined shortly afterwards by the band's drummer Bobby, The Dolphins were no longer, leaving Bernie to consider his options. Shortly after, Calvert signed on as the bass player for the semi-professional Ivan D. Juniors, a Burnley-based quartet fronted by vocalist Ivan Dixon, who were proving immensely popular on the northern circuit for a fleeting moment. The summer of 1963 saw the band playing across the Lancashire and Yorkshire divide, with both the Cavern Club in Liverpool and King's Hall in Ilkley, along with Dewsbury Town Hall, hosting a number of their performances. That year also saw the Ivan D. Juniors appear on vinyl for the only time, issuing a 45 release on the UK independent arm of the Maurice Levy-founded Oriole Records label. John Schroeder, a producer for Oriole Records, had seen the group perform and was immediately impressed by their (then) novel use of the guitars in their music, and signed them to the label.

'Catch You If I Can' (b/w 'On My Mind'), issued as Oriole 45-CB 1874, was a beat-driven little number, albeit one that clocked in at a mere one minute and thirty-five seconds. Comprised of little more than two catchy, but simple verse-choruses, the disc was nevertheless the debut composing credit for the listed "B. Calvert". The flip side, running for a full five seconds longer, was a slightly grittier offering, suggesting some nice harmonies within the group. Ultimately, though, the release did little business outside of the band's immediate catchment area, failing to break nationally. Subsequently, seeking financial security, and despite the group making the lists for the *Billboard Who's Who in Music: International Talent Directory* for 1964, Bernie opted to leave the music behind and took a job at a nearby factory, offering himself the satisfaction of a steady income.

During Eric Haydock's self-imposed absence from the line-up, following the culmination of The Hollies' second US tour, Bernie was the first point of call when they needed a stand-in for the upcoming Scandinavian visit. Whilst his bass guitar was perhaps not quite so prominent in the band's instrumental set-up (after all, it was difficult to compete with Eric's often stunning six-string riffs and runs), he supplied a proficient, steady rhythm, aided by Bobby's flourishes and fills, whilst keeping it simple. Indeed, Ron Richards was later to pass dismissive judgement, remarking that Bernie was not a good player, technically, and that he purposely buried the bass in the mix once he joined the group. That said, both Tony and Bobby recommended his talent, reliability and his friendship, and Allan and Graham were both happy to go along with the choice, taking a liking to the quiet musician and recognising his musical ability on both bass and piano.

Bernie would later recall how the offer to become an official member came about: 'We had this old tradition in Britain at that time where we had what they called Wakes Weeks. The whole town used to close down for a couple of weeks during the summer months. It was a throwback from the cotton era when all the mills used to shut down. So, it was coming up to the Wakes Week and we were all getting ready to go away on holiday, and the phone rang, and it was Michael Cohen. He said, "The boys want to offer you the job permanently, Bernie, if you're interested." Without hesitation, I said, "Of course I'm interested." So he says, "Well, okay, you're on the payroll from now. Just bear in mind that your first gig is in September." And this was only July! So, I got the complete summer off, three months doing nothing. Well, of course, it wasn't doing nothing, really I was getting my guitar and working like crazy...

'It was so frightening. I didn't sleep for the first two weeks!' [26]

On 11th September 1966, following a last-minute meeting with Ron Richards in London to discuss their next album release, provisionally entitled *On Wax*, the five-piece band boarded their flight to New York. Having only just completed a two-night cabaret showcase the previous evening, and then having flown down from Manchester to London straight after the curtain call, the lengthy flight across the Atlantic was a chance to briefly wind down for a few hours, before they were swiftly hustled away upon arrival to Baltimore, almost two hundred miles south of the welcoming New York skyline. Subsequently, their opening appearance of the tour, held on the same day as their arrival, was at the Baltimore Civic Centre as part of a multi-act two-day festivity entitled the "Teen Bash", a twenty-four-hour extravaganza, spread across the two days, and also featuring The Yardbirds, The Young Rascals, The Cyrkle, The Happenings and an American quartet (heavily influenced by The Rolling Stones, The Who and The Kinks) known as The British Walkers. After this hasty introductory performance, they returned to New York City to begin four days of promotional work, whilst also introducing Bernie to the social delights of the Big Apple, all before starting the tour off on a three-week run of shows.

'We landed in Baltimore and went straight to a gig in the afternoon. And then we had the evening off, and so I went to a club to see the Four Seasons,' reminisced Bernie about that first trip. 'That was amazing, watching them live. It was all fantastically exciting.'[26]

'On the first day we played Baltimore with The Young Rascals,' a newly bearded Graham was to report back to the UK press, part-way through the tour. 'That was great. Then we had to go to New York and Cass [Elliott] said as they had a week off, she'd fly to New York to see us. She came across and we went to the Lovin' Spoonful's recording session for the new single, 'Rain On The Roof'. It was marvellous meeting up with them again. They were the first group we met in America, the very first time we came out.

'We then went to see Paul Simon and Art Garfunkel at their home and went on to their recording session where they were putting together their *Parsley, Sage, Rosemary and Thyme* album. We had to move from New York at the end of the week and go out on the road and Cass travelled with us on the bus. She sort of acted as our unofficial press agent. We weren't allowed to do any radio shows, so we used to send her along and all she'd do for the whole spot was talk about us!'

One other introduction that Cass made to the band before the bus rolled out into the heartlands of the Midwest, was with another good friend of hers, and a fellow folk musician, Henry Diltz. A multi-talented singer-banjo-clarinet player Henry "Tad" Diltz was a key member of the popular folk revivalist act The Modern Folk Quartet. He was also beginning to express himself creatively behind the camera lens, developing a career in photography that would, over time, overtake his musical ambitions. One of his earliest assignments, undertaken as a favour to his friend Cass, was taking a series of photographs around New York City of The Hollies. Encouraged by Graham Nash, himself a keen lensman, Diltz shot a series of iconic images of the quintet in and around the Village, on park benches, stepped entranceways and underneath the trees, partying with The Spoonful. From these photographic sessions would emerge the front cover and a selection of other shots that would feature on their next LP release.

17th September 1966: Forest Park Arena, Dayton, OH
18th September 1966: Clark County Fairgrounds, Springfield, OH
19th September 1966: McCormick Place, Chicago, IL
20th September 1966: McCormick Place, Chicago, IL
23rd September 1966: National Guard Armory, Ft. Wayne, IN
24th September 1966: J.D.'s Place, Kokomo, IN
25th September 1966: Civic Centre, Hammond, IN
28th September 1966: Prom Centre, St. Paul, MN

30<sup>th</sup> September 1966: The Coliseum, Montgomery, AL

1<sup>st</sup> October 1966: Municipal Auditorium, Birmingham, AL

2<sup>nd</sup> October 1966: Shadowland Ballroom, St. Joseph, MI

7<sup>th</sup> October 1966: State Armory, Hartford, CT

8<sup>th</sup> October 1966: Hidden Valley, Muskoka Resort, Toronto, Canada

9<sup>th</sup> October 1966: Hidden Valley, Muskoka Resort, Toronto, Canada

10<sup>th</sup> October 1966: Kitchener, Ontario, Canada

11<sup>th</sup> October 1966: Sandsabarn, Perry, NY

12<sup>th</sup> October 1966: Walt Whitman High School, Bethesda, MD

At Cass' suggestion, and at the financial expense of her producer Lou Adler, following the 25<sup>th</sup> September show in Hammond, Indiana, the group hopped onto a plane bound for Los Angeles. For the next two days, Elliott hosted the touring party at her home, high up on Lookout Mountain in Laurel Canyon. Relaxing in the sunshine state for forty-eight hours also allowed Graham to take in a visit to the Trip nightclub on Sunset Boulevard, where the band themselves had performed earlier in the year. A proposed second appearance at the venue failed to materialise, but Graham caught one of the many new, exciting "psychedelic" acts one night, shortly before the club closed down for good following an earlier, infamous sadomasochistic appearance by the Andy Warhol-managed act, The Velvet Underground & Nico. The times they were indeed a-changin'…

'In the Trip, I watched one of these [psychedelic] groups, and although it was a giggle at first I got involved and hung up on it later in the act. I don't think it will be accepted on a mass basis.'

*Disc and Music Weekly*
November 1966

Returning to the tour bus, two dates on the schedule found the group supporting one of America's own most popular and successful recording acts, The Beach Boys, for a brief series of concerts in Alabama. On 30<sup>th</sup> September, the Alabama State Coliseum in Montgomery hosted The Beach Boys, The Hollies, Peter and Gordon, Lou Christie, The Happenings, Ian Whitcomb, The Count Five and The Rocking Gibraltars for a vast evening show. Then, the following day, the party continued for three shows (2.00pm, 6.00pm and 9.00pm) at the Municipal Auditorium in Birmingham, all sponsored by WVOK Radio for their Fall Shower of Stars concert events.

'Despite the impressive roster of stars, it was The Beach Boys whom everyone had come to hear, and they obliged in high style with their repertoire of past and present hits,' thusly reported the *Birmingham News,* although it should be noted that the touring entity of The Beach Boys, minus their reluctant genius Brian Wilson, was nowhere near as musically proficient onstage as their UK counterparts. The vocally gifted Carl Wilson was a poor match on guitar for Tony's abilities, whilst Dennis, the youngest Wilson brother, with the movie-star looks, was a clubber at best behind his drum kit, devoid of the finesse and finer percussive touches that Bobby Elliott possessed. And as for any comparison between the magnetic frontman Allan Clarke and the ham-fisted approach of Mike Love...

Also, on the first day of October, a TV guest appearance on New York's *Clay Cole Show* aired on WPIX-TV. Filmed two weeks earlier during their brief four-day stopover in New York, the group were captured on film promoting the recent US release of 'Bus Stop', further aiding its steady climb up the *Billboard* charts. One week later and the group made a second US TV appearance, presumably taped before the actual airdate, guesting on the syndicated music and variety *Upbeat* show for the Ohio-based TV channel WEWS-TV. Shortly afterwards, the band flew up to Toronto, appearing for two shows at the Hidden Valley ski resort, one of which saw Graham appearing in a black priest's smock.

Meanwhile, whilst the band were on the Stateside tour, back on UK soil, a new Hollies 45 was being prepared for release. But not, on this occasion, by the Parlophone label. On 16th September, United Artists Records issued the theme song from their *After The Fox* feature film as a standalone single, b/w an instrumental Bacharach tune, entitled 'The Fox Trot' (UP1152). It didn't chart and, despite the novelty value of having The Hollies performing alongside Peter Sellers' comic interactions, failed to impress the reviewers;

Peter Sellers and The Hollies: 'After The Fox' (from the film)
What an unusual combination. Quite frankly I don't like it as much as Sellers and The Hollies on their own. Chart wise, I don't think it's got anything. It's out of context, but I could imagine it over the film titles.

I don't think this was a very good idea.

Spencer Davis guest review

*Melody Maker*

October 1966

'Sellers was a disappointment to me at the recording,' Graham was to admit to the *New Musical Express* when asked to comment on the release. 'He didn't seem to care about the vocal. During rehearsal, he was a scream, but on the disc he did nothing. We were all disappointed it was issued as a single at all.'

Confusion has blown up over the surprise release on Friday of The Hollies single 'After The Fox', written by Burt Bacharach. The label says the song is sung by Peter Sellers AND The Hollies. But the official Hollies single is the group's own composition 'Stop! Stop! Stop!', released on October 7.

*Disc & Music Echo*

September 1966

Most certainly, by the time that the promotional drive for 'Stop! Stop! Stop!' was in high gear, the impetus for the United Artists release had been swept under the carpet. Arriving back in the UK on 13th October, within two days they were back out on the road once again, this time as part of another package tour alongside Paul and Barry Ryan, The Nashville Teens, Paul Jones, Peter Jay and The New Jaywalkers, Robb Storme and The Whispers and, most controversially, current hit-makers The Small Faces. Initial plans to also have The Mamas and The Papas added to the tour never came to fruition.

With the single immediately entering the charts (Parlophone 5508, b/w the banjo-harmonica trading on the delightful 'It's You'), the tour was another guaranteed sell-out even before the initial chords were struck by opening act, Robb Storme. With guests including Graham and Allan's wives Rose and Jeni, Tony's model girlfriend Jane Lumb, along with other "name" celebrities such as Peter Noone and model Samantha Juste in attendance, the first night was an unqualified success – and that was despite the no-show of one of the tour's main attractions.

Small Faces withdrew from The Hollies tour on the opening night at

Aldershot ABC. They refused to appear on the first date unless they could close the show, after complaining that they did not have equal billing with The Hollies.

The Faces walked out, only minutes before they were due on stage to close the first half of the show. Next night, at ABC Romford, the New Vaudeville Band took The Faces' place. But on Monday night agent Tito Burns said, 'It was a complete misunderstanding that has now been straightened out and The Faces will be rejoining the tour.'

*Disc & Music Echo*
October 1966

First disappointment to tour-goers on Saturday evening was the tell-tale notice board in the foyer of Aldershot ABC. It stated the Small Faces were unable to appear, so the show went on without them.

The Nashville Teens cavorted in usual style, opening with 'Tobacco Road', still an excellent number. They gave way to the Ryan twins, in shining white suits, who looked like soap powder men. Then came the debut of Paul Jones. He shot onto the stage to much screaming and started with a number called 'Along Came Jones' which was a bit egotistical. However, Paul is a good entertainer and his solo career seems assured.

Finally came bill toppers, The Hollies. Vocal cords stretched to high pitched wails as the group roared into 'I Can't Let Go' in a blaze of colour, lights and sounds. As usual, The Hollies put on an outstandingly professional show, without ever letting go. A gas set with Bobby Elliot drumming like a tornado.

*Melody Maker*
October 1966

Wearing a collection of claret, green, white, blue and pink silk shirts, the Hollies opened their act at Romford on Sunday with 'I Can't Say Goodbye' [sic] and were immediately engulfed in waves of hysterical screams. Through Sam and Dave's 'You Don't Know Like I Know' where Allan and Graham used hand mikes and stood in opposite corners of the stage, an up-tempo version of 'A Taste Of Honey', the Capitols' 'Cool Jerk' and their latest hit, 'Stop! Stop! Stop!', The Hollies received mass adulation from the audience.

I only wish they would perform 'The Times They Are A-Changin'' as a folk number and not lay on the beat.

*Record Mirror*
October 1966

In addition to the opening nights being tainted by the Small Faces' show of self-importance, the remainder of the tour was also beset by ego and jealousy. The Small Faces' manager, Don Arden, argued that as they had recently hit the top of the charts with 'All Or Nothing', they should have headline status. He even tried to use physical force on the Hollies' road manager, Rod Shields, to get his point across. However, Shields was no shrinking violet and sorted Arden out in no uncertain manner – a rare feat in itself! Then twin-idols Paul and Barry Ryan began to demand that they be higher on the bill too, and the backstage atmosphere was reportedly uncomfortable at best, with Nashville Teens frontman Ray Phillips offering, 'I've never been on a tour like it. On all of the others, the groups mixed backstage. Maybe it would be different if everyone travelled together but The Hollies, Faces and Paul Jones all have their own cars...'

That said, following the two shows held at the Embassy Theatre in Peterborough on 22nd October, most of the touring party, including The Hollies, Small Faces and the Ryan twins, along with Samantha Juste, went out partying at a nearby nightclub into the early hours of the following morning.

'Stop! Stop! Stop!' eventually peaked at the number two slot during its three-month chart run, losing out on the top spot to The Four Tops and their rendition of 'Reach Out (I'll Be There)'. With promotional slots on the usual round of TV shows also scheduled, all seemed to be as straightforward as usual, until the band checked in for their upcoming appearance at Rediffusion's *Ready, Steady Go!* studio. Upon discovering that they were not receiving top billing themselves this time, they pulled out of the show.

'We walked out because The Dave Clark Five were topping over us on the programme. We consider this situation ridiculous since that group have not had a hit record for nearly a year...' came the official statement from The Hollies camp. The Manchester quintet certainly held no high respect for their North London rivals who, despite reaching the UK Top 40 a dozen times to date, had seen their popularity on the decline once the initial "beat boom" phase had waned.

Graham Nash: "We'd toured with The Dave Clark Five in late 1964 and, to my ears, we blew them off the stage. Dave was aloof and condescending, just a mediocre drummer. They thought they were The Beatles, and they weren't. Their songs just didn't cut it…'[1]

Instead, the band simply resumed their place on the package tour.

*

*Hollies Dolly*
*She's the Hollies Dolly! Rated No.1 on their hit parade.*
*Where she leads, men follow. And she leads, With flair. For hair.*
*Available from Boots and leading chemists*

So ran the promotional series of hairspray advertisements that The Hollies lent their name to during the autumn of 1966. With a byline, in tiny print, that added "The latest release by The Hollies – Stop! Stop! Stop!" the posing features of the five-piece band, accompanied by a silky-haired glamour model, were spread throughout the fashion magazines of late '66, taking the band outside of their usual comfort zone. Not that this was the first time that the band name had been utilised for promotional campaigns outside of the music business. Earlier contracts and financial arrangements had heard their vocals utilised on several advertisements, ranging from a Shell petrol commercial, taped at the Radio Luxembourg studios, to Wrigley's Spearmint chewing gum, but this was one of the first occurrences whereupon their good looks, as the clean-cut pretty boys of pop, were also played upon. Yet the benefits, financially, were clear to see.

Back in the US, Imperial Records were keen to continue the buzz that the recent tour and the Top 10 success of the 'Bus Stop' single had generated. October had seen the release of yet another Americanised mishmash album, *Bus Stop*, a collection of previously issued UK recordings, including 'Little Lover' from the Don Rathbone-era, along with both sides of the recent Top 5 hit single. It was far from being a strong representation of where the band were currently at, but the inclusion of 'Mickey's Monkey' and 'Sweet Little Sixteen' maintained the high intensity that their concert appearances suggested, and the collection gamely climbed into the Top 75, remaining in the Hot 200 album charts for eleven weeks.

With Bobby Elliott having recently tried his hand, and his drum kit, at a recording venture outside of the band's immediate circle, it soon became apparent that he wasn't the only Hollie-related personnel working alone in the studio during that period. Still regarded as a Hollie by many, despite his official and enforced departure from the ranks months earlier, Eric Haydock was also finding his feet in the recording studios once again.

Retained by EMI, under the subsidiary Columbia Records banner, Eric was now working with a new line-up labelled Haydock's Rockhouse, a gathering pulled from the remnants of an earlier band known as The Soul Executives.

Trumpet player Ian Brookes later recalled, 'Haydock's Rockhouse was originally a seven-piece outfit called The Soul Executives, put together in Stockport, back in 1963. The line-up was Pete Ainsworth on vocals, Bill Conway on keyboards, vibes and alto sax, Derek Taylor on guitar, Barry Worthington on tenor sax, Graham Attwood on baritone sax, Ken Knight on drums and myself on bass, doubling on trumpet. Then, when Graham left the band in 1966, after a spat with Pete, I went on trumpet full time and we advertised for a bass player. Eric Haydock, fresh from The Hollies, walked into our rehearsal and asked to join!

'With his contacts, we were offered a recording deal very quickly and, with his history, at the suggestion of the record company, we also changed the band name to Haydock's Rockhouse. In no time, we were in the Abbey Road Studio, where the producer wanted us to record the Sam Cooke number 'Cupid' – but none of us was impressed by that!'[60]

'I was a bit cautious at first,' Eric was to say in one of his first solo interviews with *Record Mirror*. 'But I took the plunge by being spurred on by Dave Berry, Herman and Wayne Fontana. They all said why shouldn't I have a go? I want to shake off the ex-Hollie tag, and I suppose that getting this group together was partly to show The Hollies that I could make it alone, but really, I want just a darned good band. I plan to play all kinds of stuff from rock to stuff from *West Side Story*. I'd hate to be labelled for one kind of music...'

Sure enough, shortly afterwards, Haydock's Rockhouse issued a debut single (Columbia DB8050), featuring their Latin-tinged cover version of 'Cupid', b/w the upbeat, self-composed 'She Thinks'. It failed to chart, and the band began disintegrating with internal friction.

'Within a week of the recording, Bill was given the shove,' adds Ian

Brookes. 'He was, without doubt, the most talented muso in the band. I fell out with everyone as a result and followed Bill's exit within days before the record was released…'

> Ex-Holly [sic] Haydock needs congratulating. He has taken Sam Cooke's gentle little number and given it the most American sound I've heard for ages. There is much whooping and whistling and handclapping and the whole thing swings gently. I don't know whether it will be a hit but it's jolly impressive.
>
> *Disc & Music Echo*

'I haven't seen Eric, but I certainly don't miss him,' the often-outspoken Graham was to respond in print when questioned about his former bandmate in *Disc & Music Echo*. 'The change has done us the world of good. It has given us a change of attitude because our new bass player can play different instruments.'

The following week's edition carried an open letter response from Eric: 'I just thought that Graham might like to know that I haven't missed him either. The change has done me the world of good, and I haven't got the worries of wondering whether I'm going to be sacked. Anyway, it was nice of him to mention my name, Merry Christmas to Bob Elliott, Tony Hicks, Allan Clarke and Bernie Calvert…'

Continuing on his conversation with *Record Mirror*, Eric summed up his feelings accordingly: 'Honestly, I hate all this knocking that has gone on between The Hollies and myself, so I hope it will end soon.'

Unfortunately, a second 45 by Haydock's Rockhouse, a cover of John Sebastian's 'Lovin' You' b/w 'Mix-A-Fix', also failed to register with the record-buying public and, following a three-song guest appearance on a BBC radio broadcast during 1967, having been dropped by EMI, they disbanded shortly afterwards. It would be almost sixteen years before Eric would resurface in Hollieland again.

"Isn't Graham Nash Britain's most changed pop star?" asked *Disc & Music Echo* in one of their regular November "Scene" columns. "Allan Clarke arrived at a business meeting with a bundle of comics. Graham Nash is currently reading the *Korean* [sic] *Book of the Dead*."

Most certainly, Graham was seeing things a little differently from the perspective that had seemed so focussed on the band a year or two back. His eyes and his mind had been opened wide by the sights, sounds and influences that so readily latched onto his "pop star" status, and filled his thoughts with so many questions, answers and, some may say radical beliefs. By far and away, he was the most outspoken member of the band, and always the spokesperson who said exactly what he thought. Graham was never one to simply back down from conversation, or confrontation, often outwardly critical of his peers – be it the Dave Clark Five, Herman's Hermits or Bob Dylan.

His mind had recently been unlocked further still by the visionary opinions of his new friends across the Atlantic; Cass Elliott, Paul Simon and, briefly, David Crosby, and he had recently experienced his first LSD trip, accompanied by Cass in Chicago. His songwriting had also become heavily influenced by the unbridled admiration he carried for Simon, John Phillips, John Sebastian, and that for the UK's very own resident think tank, Donovan Leitch.

'Pop music is moving forward at an incredible speed,' he was to say to the *New Musical Express*. 'It's not just progressing; it's running full tilt into tomorrow. I have never been so frightened, or excited, by the power which we have over young people. The Beatles, The Mamas and The Papas, The Stones, Lovin' Spoonful, The Beach Boys and Donovan are all examples of people working desperately to out-record one another on albums.

'The Beach Boys told me that they are devoting the whole of this year to recording happiness songs – trying to make people happy. That's a wonderful aim and to be in a position to do this is wonderful too.

'Donovan's new compositions to me excel Dylan's because he has this tremendous ability to transmit tenderness and kindness through his work. With Dylan, I can't reconcile the man who writes 'Blowin' In The Wind' with rubbish like 'Subterranean Homesick Blues.''

Paul Simon had recently bestowed upon him a vinyl record, simply entitled *The Music of Bulgaria*, a collection of traditional Bulgarian songs, performed *a cappella* in multi-layered harmonies. The vocals featured on the record had so struck a chord with him that he immediately began spreading the word about the recording, enthusiastically sharing it with his friends and acquaintances. As well as absorbing the thoughts of so many, he now had his own opinions and ideas that he wanted to share. And if anyone wished to listen, he was *there…*

What before were standard interviews for the music press now became deep and meaningful opportunities to impart further knowledge. He became more socially aware, and as he began to embrace this sense of amplified awareness, and his intake of various substances increased, then the gulf between him and his bandmates, often at odds with each other, grew ever wider.

'Young people are in a very beautiful position. Their minds are still open and usually pure. They haven't yet been pressured by society, custom, or tradition to think a certain way about certain things. Youth is beautiful. It's also innocent.

'The mind of the thirteen- and fourteen-year-old must be very impressionable. If pop music and its makers influence the way young people think and mature, let's stop singing about bad things. A whole feeling of love and beauty can be imparted to these kids who don't know about love and compassion. A lot of the stuff we've made hasn't pleased me, but we'll get there. It takes time and we're only just starting to realise where we're at. As we go on, we'll get the freedom to do the things we want...'

Graham Nash
*Melody Maker*

# ON the Single scene

# THE HOLLIES
## On a carousel

PARLOPHONE R 5562

A CLARKE–HICKS–NASH COMPOSITION

# CHAPTER TWELVE

# "RIDING ALONG ON A CAROUSEL..."

F*OR CERTAIN BECAUSE...* the fifth long-playing release by The Hollies was issued by the Parlophone label on 2nd December 1966 and broke the mould of all previous albums by being the first to be completely made up of self-composed Clarke-Hicks-Nash compositions (Mr Ransford's label credit now gracefully consigned to the vaults). Titled after a line in the popular children's nursery rhyme 'Teddy Bear's Picnic', which the band used to make Tony perform onstage, the twelve-song selection (recorded between August and October) was a fine affair, right from the opening 'What's Wrong With The Way I Live' (also cut by Australian band The Twilights the following December) through to the closing refrains of 'Stop! Stop! Stop!'. The growing maturity of their work simply shone brightly out of the dark vinyl. With Graham's prominent contributions aiding a series of gentle introspective numbers, 'Clown' and 'Crusader' along with a distinctive nod in the direction of where his future lay with the upbeat 'Tell Me To My Face' (a tune that had started around a simple guitar riff that Tony had thought up), this was a far more evenly produced affair throughout, devoid of any unnecessary revised American cover tunes.

Dixieland, Latin-American, Orchestral, Folk are just four of the musical moods used on the Hollies' new LP "For Certain Because…" which has been produced by Ron Richards.

The album is an important progression for the group, because it is the first on which all the numbers have been written by them, and as such is a clue to their own musical identities. The result is an imaginative, entertaining and at times disturbing fusion of talent. It is also the best album they have cut, and the only adverse criticism I would offer is that I think it a shame they could not produce two more original thoughts instead of including both sides of current hit single 'Stop! Stop! Stop!' – which many fans must already have.

Keith Altham
*New Musical Express*
November 1966

With Bernie Calvert now adding to the band's arrangement with his piano-playing on a number of the tracks, including an overdub on the late 1965 recording 'Don't Even Think About Changing' (which is the one tune that perhaps sits out of place on the collection) and Bobby's increasing percussive repertoire now including kettle drums, the overall style, as noted by Keith Altham, regularly crossed the divides of varying musical genres.

Graham's Crosby-like melody on 'Clown' found a comfortable foothold in the studio experimentations of reflective sorrow, and the Dixieland-inflections that influenced the direction of 'High Classed' meshed nicely alongside the folky 'Crusader' and the more adventurous pop-rock of 'Pay You Back With Interest' (the latter conceived by Tony in a Stockholm hotel room). 'What Went Wrong', with its big-brass showband arrangement, would have also slid silkily into the cabaret repertoire of either Tom Jones or Cilla Black, had someone told them.

'Graham writes the more sentimental, deep things,' Bobby was to summarise. 'Tony writes the commercial ones, and Allan is more of a rocker. The beat is there…'

Utilising the full spectrum of instrumentation available to them at Abbey Road, the band freely toyed around in the studio, experimenting with glockenspiels, vibraphones, tympani, a Hammond organ and differing effects, searching for the magic pieces of the puzzle. They even resorted to adding an unconventional lump of studio tape to the actual recording heads to obtain a wobbling, flange effect on the opening piano introduction to 'Pay You Back With Interest'.

Discussing the album with Altham, just prior to its December release, Tony Hicks was both positive and unsure about some of the inclusions, recognising that each member has an opinion of value.

'Suspicious Look': 'Three-part harmony. We went out to get a Byrds-type sound on this one. The lyric is more of mine on this. I try to stress the point that I'm confining myself to writing about feelings which are common to both myself and young people. It's no use doing a Yardbirds lyric – those things just spin your mind!'

'Clown': 'I don't dig this kind of thing, but I understand it. It's very effective. [I'm] not sure you have to dig this deep. Dave Berry could well make a smash hit out of it.'

'Crusader': 'Allan plays guitar on this, and we got that echoing vocal by singing from the far end of the recording studio into the mike at the other end. The marching effect is a tape from the EMI sound effects library of Beefeaters on the march.'

'What's Wrong With The Way I Live': 'It's important for the kids to feel a part of what is being written. A great deal of this so called "freak-out" music and progressive pop is way above their heads. How can you understand the LSD scene unless you take it? This is about real people, living a real life. Something that young people can grab hold of in the words and say, "I feel like that!" This just falls short of being a single.'

*New Musical Express*
November 1966

With its striking front sleeve image of the group, as portrayed through the camera lens of Henry Diltz, taken during their recent forays around Greenwich Village, the expansive EMI gatefold packaging is also notable (and not only for the Gary Leeds/Walker Brothers sleevenotes) for crediting ex-Manfred Mann guitarist and woodwind maestro Mike Vickers with the arrangements for three of the featured songs. His introduction of a Dixie jazz-styled accompaniment to 'High Classed', a song initially visualised by Allan, most certainly opened the doors and the ears of a number of Hollies followers, overly familiar with the R&B style that the band had previously played with.

And as to how and why the pseudonym of L. Ransford was discarded? That came down to the notable scenario that The Hollies were currently renegotiating their record contract with EMI Records. The main outcome of these discussions would be highly significant, as the group looked to a more secure future, controlling their own financial destiny. Hollies Ltd would own all of their future recordings, from the 45 issue of 'Stop! Stop! Stop!' onwards but would agree to lease them back to EMI for release. The label executives, sitting in their plush offices in Manchester Square, London, were clearly happy with the arrangement, not wanting to lose one of their prized assets. This was to be an extremely lucrative deal for the band, and one that would see "A Hollies Production/Recording" stamped prominently on all future issues, along with the co-credit of Clarke-Hicks-Nash on all band compositions, regardless as to how or from whom the song originated.

It also appears that the words did fit rather comfortably on a record label after all.

The week that the LP hit the record racks around the country, the band themselves were flying off once again, initially for a show in Germany at the vast Deutschlandhalle Arena in Berlin, followed by a further flight to Denmark from where they commenced a two-week Scandinavian tour at the smaller Falconer Salen Hall in Copenhagen. From there, the touring party ferried across to Sweden, all piled into a large Chevrolet truck, festooned with a Union Jack and large letters spelling out "THE HOLLIES", heading for the nation's capital of Stockholm. They then spent their first day in the beautiful coastal city romping around the streets, riding the trams that ran throughout the ancient municipality, followed by a camera crew filming their every move for an upcoming Swedish TV appearance on a local music show entitled *Drop In*.

The concert appearances over the next two weeks took in the wintry December venues of Sandviken, Gothenburg and Malmo, along with cross-border visits to Helsinki in Finland and the Norwegian cities of Oslo and Stavanger. It was whilst staying in Stavanger that Tony, composing in his hotel room after the show, first began to work on a new tune he had been toying around with. Randomly singing the lyrics *"Hey, Mister man, what's your game..."*, in due recognition of The Byrds' recent chart-topper, 'Mr Tambourine Man', the song was put on the back burner until it could be worked on further.

The 12th December performance in Stockholm, held at the impressive Konserthuset Hall, home of the prestigious *Nobel Prize* ceremonies, was a particular highlight for the band, with Bernie later commenting in the press that the show 'turned out to be the best concert of the tour.' The show was even taped for broadcast by the Stockholm-based Sveriges Radio, airing across the snow-filled nation during the following February. Somewhat surprisingly, the setlists for these shows still carried several non-originals in their midst, some of which the band never even took into the recording studio. Considering the ever-increasing success of their own compositions, and the vast tally of hit songs now under their belts, the short 30-minute performances during this era (the 90-minute full-blown extravaganza was still a long way off in concert history) were noticeably lacking in familiarity, with 'Stop! Stop! Stop!' and 'I Can't Let Go' being the two "hits" rolled out for this tour.

Faithful, slick cover renditions of 'Cool Jerk' (a recent US Top 10 hit for The Capitols), 'Reach Out (I'll Be There)' (The Four Tops) and Bob Dylan's 'The Times They Are A-Changin'' appeared throughout their Scandinavian performances, as did popular versions of 'Very Last Day', 'Stewball', 'Too Much Monkey Business' and the recently recorded 'What's Wrong With The Way I Live', the latter prematurely announced by Allan as an upcoming single.

All told, the brief tour was an outstanding success, further cementing their popularity in the chilly North European region... with Bernie's final comment in his press article summarising their opinion of their loyal fans: 'Oh, and all those lovely Swedish birds! I just can't wait to get back!'

The Swedish TV appearance on *Drop In*, directed by the acclaimed Peter Goldmann (later responsible for The Beatles' 'Penny Lane' and 'Strawberry Fields Forever' promotional footage), aired on SV-TV during late December 1966 and, alongside The Hollies, featured filmed Stockholm performances from The Small Faces, The Troggs, Manfred Mann and, reportedly, footage of The Beach Boys from their own recent Swedish visit. No material seemingly survives – excepting The Troggs' lip-synched appearance on a Stockholm subway.

### THE NEW MUSICAL EXPRESS 1966 POLL WINNERS
### Category: British Vocal Group

1. The Beatles
2. The Rolling Stones

7. The Small Faces
8. The Shadows

| | |
|---|---|
| 3. The Walker Brothers | 9. Manfred Mann |
| 4. The Hollies | 10. The Who |
| 5. The Searchers | 11. The Bachelors |
| 6. Spencer Davis Group | 12. The Kinks |

After an all-too-brief seasonal stopover at home, the never-ending touring party once again stepped into gear and the group headed back out across the Atlantic for a short winter tour of North America, accompanied on the road by Herman's Hermits – currently basking in the success of twelve Top 20 US hit singles themselves.

The pairing undertook a series of eight shows together, often adding one or two local bands to fill out the programme, starting in Tampa, Florida on 26th December, before hopping across the state lines to perform in Green Bay, Fort Worth, El Paso, Albuquerque, Charlotte, Duluth and Chicago as part of the brief schedule. A film crew from CBS-TV accompanied them for much of the tour, capturing both acts on stage and behind the scenes for an upcoming US TV Special, directed by David Oppenheim, airing during the following spring.

In a complete turnaround from the recent Scandinavian visit, the US sojourn saw The Hollies opting to fill their short set (no more than six songs apiece were performed) with a selection of their best-known hits – 'Bus Stop', 'Stop! Stop! Stop!' and 'I Can't Let Go' included – whereupon the group went down a storm, with the Wisconsin-based *Post Crescent* review acknowledging that the group was "the highlight of the show. This Liverpool [sic] quintet is as proficient a rock group as (the reviewer) has seen on stage".

That same publication had previously promoted the upcoming show with a prominent advertisement for the Hermits' appearance, with the smaller byline of "Plus! The Hollies!" underneath, clearly suggesting that the popularity of the Peter Noone-led outfit was the main draw.

The Hollies, probably England's third most popular group, behind The Beatles and The Hermits, is a lively fivesome with a brisk pace and a flair for comedy. They have a following of their own and satisfied it with a few of their million sellers, including 'Look Through Any Window' and 'Bus Stop'. Their best effort, however, was done on 'A Taste of Honey'.

The girls, who made up about two-thirds of the audience,

warmed up their lungs – and their cameras – to the offerings of The Hollies during the first half of the show, and by the time Herman came on, every girl in the place was in screaming-good tune.

*Green Bay Press Gazette*
December 1966

Returning home on 3$^{rd}$ January 1967 and, following a brief respite and recuperation, the line-up next gathered together for an 11$^{th}$ January recording session at Abbey Road, alongside Ron Richards. That same evening, Allan and Bobby both ventured out to the Bag O'Nails club, along Kingly Street in Soho where, alongside Paul McCartney, Ringo Starr, Eric Burdon, Bill Wyman, Pete Townshend, Eric Clapton, Donovan and so many others, they watched an early performance by the Jimi Hendrix Experience, currently riding high in the UK charts with their first hit, 'Hey Joe'. Over the following week, The Hollies would cut seven new songs, three of which would be held back for the next studio album. The remaining four tracks would grace two 45 releases, both issued within the next month.

The next official Hollies 45 in the UK, coinciding with a US release for the first time, pulled together two new Clarke-Hicks-Nash offerings, the first of which – started whilst the band were on tour in the US – was inspired by the old Elvis and Bill Haley songs they listened to in their younger days.

'Originally, the lyric was all about a man in a prison camp,' Graham was to tell journalist Keith Altham, for the *New Musical Express*. 'We put any kind of words to a tune, to begin with, just to hold the song together.

'When we sang it to our road manager, he said that we were always writing sad songs and we ought to try a happy one. So, we went away and came up with the idea of a fairground as a happy place. I always associated those old Presley and Haley discs with the fairs when I was a kid, and that was the kind of sound we went for. At first, we tried working "merry-go-round" into the lyrics but eventually came up with "carousel" because it sounded more musical.'

With lyrical visions of riding brightly painted carousel horses and playing fairground games (*"pulling ducks out of the water"*), the joyful sense of happiness the song created was abundant, and with Graham stepping to the fore to handle the opening solo lead vocals, a first for a 45 release, it comfortably epitomised the sounds of the swinging UK music scene of the era. Released as Parlophone R5562 and coupled with the distinctly trippy-sounding 'All The World Is Love' (cut during the same sessions), 'On A Carousel' was a sure-fire Top 10 success, peaking at the #4 spot in a March chart list that featured such musical heavyweights as the 'Penny Lane'/'Strawberry Fields Forever' double-whammy, 'Georgy Girl' (The Seekers), 'I'm A Believer' (The Monkees) and Donovan's hypnotic 'Mellow Yellow'. However, to the bewilderment of much of the country's pop music-loving public, filling out the top spot that week was the overtly grandiose sound of Engelbert Humperdinck's 'Release Me'.

Over in the US, the single (Imperial 66231) reached a pinnacle of #11 during a nine-week run in *Billboard*'s Top 40.

The Hollies: 'On A Carousel' (Parlophone R5562)
Wham Pow! Hollies' Best Record Ever. Usually, a Hollies record does not hit me first time around. I usually have to hear them a lot before I really like them. Not so this. What must definitely class as the best record they've made, done in a style which comes closer to the huge round sound of American records than any I've ever heard. An excellent record.

*Disc & Music Echo*
February 1967

It was during a recording session for this particular track, held at EMI's Studio 3 in Abbey Road, that a truly fascinating and insightful occurrence happened. On 17th January, the same day that Paul McCartney was finishing 'Penny Lane' in the adjoining Studio 2, and whilst the group were working on vocal tracks for 'On A Carousel', a Granada TV film crew, accompanied by EMI producer George Martin, walked into the studio unannounced and captured the group on film for an upcoming 30-minute TV documentary about the music business, entitled *The World Tomorrow: Sound or Music?*

Happy to participate, and for the sake of the film, the group played along to the master backing track that they had already captured onto tape during two earlier sessions (11th and 13th January), but then performed the vocal tracks live for the cameras. Granada's intrusion clearly didn't faze Graham, Allan and Tony at all, as this particular vocal take was a powerful vocal presentation.

Interestingly, the footage also suggested that the trio were performing their vocals without hearing the master track, or by utilising headphones, as no accompanying music could be heard on film. How did they do that? Graham Nash later explained:

'They had these huge speakers at EMI, called 604e's, six feet high and three feet square, on rollers, but when you point speakers at each other they cancel out in the middle. So, we were listening to the track from these giant speakers but because the microphone we were singing into was right in the middle it cancelled out the music, so it looked like we were singing without the track…'[24]

Altogether, the crew captured around twenty minutes or so of raw 16mm film, although an edited 5-minute version, interspersed with footage of the studio control room and an interview with Ron Richards, was eventually broadcast the following month (10th February) on the ITV show.

In contrast to the happy sounds within the grooves of the lead side, the accompanying flip, 'All The World Is Love', was clearly influenced by Graham's newly discovered, ever-increasing awareness and experimentations, and took the band on their first tentative steps towards pop-psychedelia. Running bass lines, with seemingly random harmonies crossing over the evocative lyrics about "secluded and floating states of mind", this was far removed from any of the familiar forms of comfort the band had held on to for so long, and it was one that would pave the route towards their next release, the fully-fledged album immersion into the golden sounds of '67. This was no simple song about a traditional boy-girl relationship, smiling faces and bus stops. This was getting deep.

'The Hollies should have world status by now. We deserve it. We haven't got it because we've played safe. There's nothing wrong in that except that it is boring – to me anyway. I don't think anyone can criticise the quality of the records we turn out, but the group are frightened to experiment. We lack stimulant. I am trying to lead the group my way because they need direction and I believe my way is best for them. I think we have come to the point where we must decide.'

Graham Nash
*Disc & Music Echo*
February 1967

The same week that 'On A Carousel' reached its chart peak, further down the UK rankings, and appearing as a new entry at the number 50 spot (before disappearing the following week) was a highly competent cover of the band's composition 'Tell Me To My Face', credited to James Keefer, who went by the simpler stage name of Keith. Issued on the Mercury label, the 45 achieved better success in the singer's US homeland where it peaked just inside the Top 40 *Billboard* charts.

Likewise, a similar chart position (#48 to be precise) had befallen another cover version, issued a few months earlier when the successful Liverpudlian band, The Searchers, normally Top 20 regulars, had opted to release their own rendition of the "L. Ransford" credited tune 'Have You Ever Loved Somebody'. Unfortunately, coinciding and thusly competing with yet another version of the same song, issued just two weeks earlier by the popular teen-twins Paul and Barry Ryan (which peaked at one position lower), dented any sales potential the single had, giving The Searchers their weakest chart placing to date. Considering the composition had already appeared on The Everly Brothers' LP *Two Yanks in England*, issued that same year, it remains puzzling why the record labels in question (Pye and Decca) couldn't foresee such a strange clash.

'That Searchers-Ryan thing was unforgivable,' Graham would subsequently comment in the *Melody Maker*. 'Somehow it all seemed to bounce back on to us. We gave the song to Chris Curtis for the Ryans...'

Clearly, Curtis, who was acting as the Ryans' producer, had a conflict of interest going... seeing that he was also the ex-drummer with The Searchers – although, reportedly, it had been Tony who had first given a demo of the song to the band's guitarist John McNally. Graham, in turn, gave one to Curtis who then initially offered to produce a version for The Searchers. For whatever reason, they declined his offer, so he took it over to the Ryan twins instead.

The Hollies' own version of this song, also recorded during the lengthy 13th January 1967 session (following on from three earlier aborted attempts, dating back to March '66), was later to surface as an album track, although they did perform a lip-synched version for French television one week after it was cut in the studio, playing it alongside the debut TV performance of 'On A Carousel' on the *A Tous Vents* show.

The second 45 release to come out of the mid-January Abbey Road sessions was the result of the group being selected as one of the UK's participants in the Sanremo Music Festival, an event held annually in the Liguria region of north-western Italy. This three-day festival consisted of a competition of previously unreleased songs, performed entirely in Italian. Each song was sung twice by two different artists, each one using an individual arrangement to illustrate the meaning of the festival as a "composers' competition" and not for highlighting the actual singers themselves. One version of the song would be performed by an Italian artist whilst the second rendition was to be performed by an international guest artist. Chosen to represent the UK alongside Marianne Faithfull, The Hollies were initially offered two spots at the festival, performing 'Non Prego Per Me' and 'Devi Aver Fiducia In Me', and they subsequently took both songs into the studio so they could familiarise themselves with the chosen works, with the initial idea of miming to the song on performance day. However, as Allan later recounted, 'We'd been taught it phonetically so we could record it. Then when we arrived in Sanremo, we were told that we had to sing it live, so I had to actually learn it! I had to remember an Italian song from start to finish when I didn't know what I was singing about!'[5]

Despite rehearsing and recording both songs, only one of the chosen entries was performed by the band during the three-day event, with the upbeat 'Devi Aver Fiducia In Me' being switched to an Italian pairing at the last minute. The song actually selected, a dramatic ballad composed by Guilio "Mogol" Rapetti and Lucio Battisti and performed by The Hollies, resplendent in their white cabaret jackets and frilled neckties, was eliminated from the competition early on, and the festival became perhaps more memorable when one of the other performers, Luigi Tenco, a popular Italian singer-songwriter, allegedly committed suicide on the second of the three days (the day after The Hollies' appearance), following the elimination of his own song. His death remains a much-rumoured conspiracy theory to this day.

Both of The Hollies' Italian recordings, cut at Abbey Road on 13th January, were subsequently issued together on an Italian-only 45rpm release (Parlophon(e) QMSP-16402), whilst an obscure appearance on Italian TV, presumably promoting the single, was also undertaken. No further details are known.

Such was the recognition for The Hollies' Italian excursion, despite the lack of success it brought, that shortly afterwards they were asked to help score the theme to an upcoming Francesco Maselli-directed comedy film, entitled *Fai in Fretta ad Uccidermi, Ho Freddo! (Kill Me Quick, I'm Cold)*. The result was another Italian-only 45 release, the English language Clarke-Hicks-Nash pairing of 'We're Alive' b/w 'Kill Me Quick', recorded on 22nd February, and another unsuccessful result.

'I'm not particularly proud of that,' Allan later commented. 'It was very cabaret-ish. The film was a flop, anyway!'[5]

However, that session was also notable in that it was undertaken without the participation of Bobby Elliott who, following a recent performance at the Jaguar Club in Herford, Germany, had been taken seriously ill and had to step away from the band for a lengthy recuperation period.

The first week of February had seen them appear on *Top of the Pops* for UK television and then travel across to Germany to participate in the recording of a local TV show, *Beat! Beat! Beat!*, in addition to the scheduled performance at the Jaguar Club. The filming had gone without a hitch and the group had performed some delightfully polished versions of 'Stop! Stop! Stop!', 'On A Carousel' and 'Bus Stop' for the cameras, before rounding off the show with an improvised take of Chuck Berry's 'Guitar Boogie'. But then, immediately after the taping was completed, Bobby was struck down, the initial symptoms of a burst appendix swiftly developing into peritonitis, requiring immediate hospitalisation in Germany.

'I remember listening to 'Strawberry Fields' with Graham and Allan, and then blacking out,' Bobby later recounted. 'When I woke up, I was in the hospital, and I was there for two weeks. In the end, they couldn't operate for three months because the whole area had swollen up so much.'[5]

Stepping into his shoes for the aforementioned recording date in North London, just ten days later, was John "Mitch" Mitchell, appointed drummer with The Jimi Hendrix Experience, who had only recently completed recording the groundbreakingly experimental 'Purple Haze'. In addition to assisting on the Italian soundtrack recordings, Mitchell also played on two other tunes that day, adding his distinctive rhythms to 'The Games We Play' and a new Graham Gouldman composition entitled 'Schoolgirl'. Naturally, all thoughts were with Bobby's well-being but, with commitments made and schedules to complete, the machine ploughed onwards.

'Schoolgirl' was a gritty number from the pen of the talented 'Bus Stop' songwriter and despite The Hollies cutting a wonderfully intricate version (completed by Hicks in later years), they opted not to release it, consigning the track to the vaults. Having failed to seal the deal with The Hollies,

Gouldman offered it to fellow Mancunian band The Mindbenders, who issued it as a single on the Fontana label. Shortly afterwards, he joined that band himself, lining up alongside former Emperors of Rhythm guitarist Eric Stewart, and forming a formidable partnership: 5cc.

Further Hollies studio sessions were soon booked in and, despite Bobby's non-participation, the remaining quartet re-entered Abbey Road during the first week of March, commencing initial work on what would become their upcoming new LP. Eleven tracks were cut over a frantic two-day period, with a further session undertaken later that same month putting the final touches to the recording. It was a hastily undertaken affair, but the quality still shone through, even if many of the tracks lacked the style of Bobby's input. Nevertheless, acclaimed session players Clem Cattini and Dougie Wright filled in behind the drum kit for these dates.

The 9th of March saw yet another unfamiliar face seated on the drum stool, as former Dakotas drummer Tony Mansfield sat in for a guest appearance on *Doddy's Music Box*, a new comedy-variety TV show hosted by Liverpool-born comedian Ken Dodd. Whilst an upcoming tour around Britain was kept on the schedule, with Tony again filling in, planned spring tours to Australia, the USA (including a pre-announced debut in Hawaii), Japan, Hong Kong and Israel, along with a rumoured visit to Pakistan, were subsequently cancelled over concerns surrounding Bobby's continuing absence. A decision that came at a price, with a reported loss of over £50,000 in potential earnings.

It was also noted in the press at the time that another stand-in drummer (the fifth), Tony Newman (founding member of the popular instrumental sextet Sounds Incorporated), helped fill the drum stool for a few appearances during this unsettled period. However, Tony himself, speaking from his home in Las Vegas, comments that, 'There was no road work. I simply played on a track for 'On A Carousel' that was used for a TV show. I think it was for *Top of the Pops,* which I also appeared on.'

Sharing the stage alongside Paul Jones, The Spencer Davis Group and The Tremeloes, the 1967 UK spring tour was another huge success, with The Hollies performing a setlist that featured a selection of recent hits… but not all. Tony Hicks was to later remark in *Beat Instrumental,* 'We never practise now unless it's for a new record. We've chucked quite a few songs out. Pretty well all of the old hits have gone, and there's a number called 'Cool Jerk' we kicked out. It got a bit of a drag playing it night after night.'

11th March 1967: Granada, Mansfield

12th March 1967: City Hall, Newcastle

13th March 1967: Odeon, Glasgow

14th March 1967: Gaumont, Doncaster

15th March 1967: Odeon, Leeds

16th March 1967: Granada, Bedford

17th March 1967: Granada, Maidstone

18th March 1967: Granada, Kingston

19th March 1967: De Montfort Hall, Leicester

21st March 1967: Odeon, Manchester

22nd March 1967: Granada, Kettering

23rd March 1967: Finsbury Park Astoria, London

25th March 1967: ABC, Blackpool

26th March 1967: ABC, Blackpool

27th March 1967: Town Hall, Birmingham

28th March 1967: Gaumont, Southampton

29th March 1967: ABC, Exeter

30th March 1967: ABC, Plymouth

31st March 1967: ABC, Gloucester

1st April 1967: ABC, Nuneaton

2nd April 1967: Empire, Liverpool

Starting with complete sell-outs at Mansfield and Newcastle, the Hollies-Paul Jones-Spencer Davis tour has settled down into one of the most entertaining yet... especially the second half.

The Hollies coped magnificently with their show-closing spot. A tremendous PA set-up, whipping up a massive storm, cheered to the echo, through 'I Can't Let Go', 'You Don't Know', 'Like A Rolling Stone', 'Stop! Stop! Stop!', 'Carousel', 'Reach Out', with Tony Mansfield standing in well for Bobby Elliott on drums.

Meanwhile, the sieges outside the theatres go on...

*Record Mirror*
March 1967

Records indicate that Bobby did try to resume his rightful position for the two shows held at the ABC Theatre in Blackpool during March but found the demand of each performance too much for his weakened state, and Tony

Mansfield returned to complete the tour. It would appear that the lack of the seasoned Hollie behind the drum kit didn't affect the overall success of the live appearances, and the solidly reliable rhythms of Mansfield, working in partnership with Bernie Calvert, comfortably supported the frontline trio.

'I must admit that in the beginning, I wasn't quite sure we'd made the right decision accepting Bernie as a bass player,' Graham would suggest to a *Record Mirror* journalist at the time. 'I wasn't sure whether he'd got as strong a personality as Eric. In actual fact, Bernie has had a great effect on us as individuals. He's been completely withdrawn from the business and he has an amazing attitude which brings us down to earthly levels…'

## CHAPTER THIRTEEN

# "I DON'T UNDERSTAND THIS PSYCHEDELIC STUFF..."

'No one has been more devoted to The Hollies than myself, but I've realised that the success was overshadowing my personal wants. I want to find a happy medium. If it doesn't happen, I'll give up either one or the other.'

Graham Nash
*Record Mirror*
January 1967

'Graham gradually became our spokesman because he is on the scene all of the time. He was always available and he's a good speaker. He started speaking out after being influenced by all the hippies and psychedelic crowd in Los Angeles.'

Tony Hicks
*Disc & Music Echo*
March 1967

The March 1967 recording sessions certainly highlighted the direction in which Graham was hoping to take the band, and the resulting album, *Evolution*, issued later that summer, suggested the effect that the so-called "summer of love" was having on many of the world's music elite. With The Beatles working on their upcoming *Sergeant Pepper's Lonely Hearts Club Band* concept in the studio next door, the fact that two of the most successful UK bands were creatively on a roll at the same time couldn't be ignored. And surely a small amount of cross-studio inspiration must have bled through the Abbey Road walls and along the corridor.

On one particular day in St John's Wood, 17th March, during which The Beatles and George Martin were working on one of Paul McCartney's new compositions, 'She's Leaving Home', in the cavernous Studio 2, The Hollies, minus Bobby, were tracking and sweetening a number of their own works, next door in Studio 3. In addition to Dougie Wright aiding with the percussion on songs such as 'Rain On The Window', 'Then The Heartaches Begin', 'Ye Olde Toffee Shoppe', 'Stop Right There', 'Water On The Brain' and 'Heading For A Fall', a young keyboard player was also reportedly drafted in to supply piano on another one of the new tunes; 'You Need Love'. Not that many would have given the bespectacled Reggie Dwight much thought, other than acknowledgement for his clear talents as a member of the band Bluesology. Confirmation of Reg's precise movements during his pre-fame career have often remained elusive but, as Bluesology were in London that day, appearing at the Marquee Club in Soho alongside Long John Baldry later that evening, the suggestion cannot be dismissed. Unhelpfully, Hollies members themselves have no recollection of this appearance, although the quiet pianist remains listed in the session details for 'You Need Love' in the EMI 6 CD-box, *The Long Road Home.*

Another significant event that signposted the band's subsequent direction also took place around this period, although such is the private nature of The Hollies' business dealings that the arranged non-disclosure notices between the parties concerned have kept the full details away from the eyes of the prying public for virtually all of the fifty years that have since followed.

In a move that saw a number of their key current backroom team reshuffled, Michael Cohen parted company with Hollies Limited. Tommy Sanderson had departed by this stage as well, replaced by Harold Davidson from the Grade Organisation, whilst Robin Britten moved up from his PR role to take over the management reins. As to whether Cohen's departure had anything to do with the previous financial irregularities, as previously mooted by Eric Haydock, or the earlier tax bill that the band had been forced to pay off, or even the £20,000 investment loss, it was open to much debate and rumour over the ensuing years. However, upon review, it was apparent how much the accounts were in a mess.

'If we were more aware of what we were doing, we wouldn't have been ripped off,' Allan was to later suggest when quizzed upon the subject. 'The things that were done to us weren't done in a way that we could sue anyone, it was done very subtly. [But] we have people who have actually taken money from us and put it into their own pockets. I don't want to name names…'[7]

'That was a horrible period for us,' added Bobby when reminiscing with the *Daily Mirror*. 'It was a new business, and we were very green. We were signing contracts that gave the managers the right to rip us off. The worst point came when we found ourselves in debt to the tune of £200,000. We learnt the hard way that a fool and his money are soon parted.'

Bobby later went further into detail for his 2020 autobiography, *It Ain't Heavy, It's My Story*, suggesting that Cohen fraudulently cashed in on their names, forging signatures, stealing blindly from the accounts, expanding his business dealings beyond his means. Caught with his fingers in the proverbial till drawer, he was swiftly removed of all responsibilities, escaping a custodial sentence only due to the band's forgiving nature.

'We knew that he had a wife and kids to take care of. Through his solicitor, he admitted his wrongdoings, [and] offered to pay us back at the rate of £10 a month. He'd been out of his depth, naive and incompetent.' [39]

One benefit that resulted from the changes was firmer handling on the live appearances, as Allan made clear to the *New Musical Express* during March that year: 'We've changed agents. The result is that we are now playing better dates and seem to be going somewhere. In the past, it was as if we were just playing ballrooms and things, and there was no end in sight. That was soul-destroying.'

With positive steps in the right direction on home soil, The Hollies' stock was also still on the rise across the ocean, where Imperial Records were capitalising on the recent chart successes in US territory. With both 'Stop! Stop! Stop!' and 'On A Carousel' reaching the higher echelons of the *Billboard* lists, it seemed only right to justify their faith and issue another LP in America. Thus came about the US *Stop! Stop! Stop!* album, a replica of *For Certain Because…* but retitled and repackaged in new artwork and released on 25th February 1967. Although it wasn't a mammoth success, spending a credible two months in the Hot 200, and peaking at #91, it certainly benefitted from the crossover sales accompanying 'On A Carousel', which was making its steady climb into the Top 20 at the same time.

Further American acceptance also soon came their way, initially via a 12-track *Greatest Hits* collection, issued by Imperial Records (LP-9350) during May, that gradually gathered momentum in the wake of the recent increased publicity, entering the charts two months later and reaching the highly desirable placement of #11 in *Billboard*. Not that this was the first such collection. That honour is generally recognised as going to a Swedish 1965 set simply entitled *The Hollies* (PMCS-309) but, certainly in the US and on home soil, the record company marketing executives were slightly slower off the mark.

Then during late April, the CBS-TV network broadcast a radical new documentary entitled *Inside Pop: The Rock Revolution*. Produced and directed by David Oppenheim, and hosted by Leonard Bernstein, this highly credible slice of TV history represented one of the first times that "pop" or "rock" music had been presented on television as a genuine art form. It was an acknowledgement that duly coincided with a newfound appreciation by cultural commentators and scholars for the current advances that both songwriters and performers of the current generation were making. By comparing The Beatles to Bach, Bernstein was raising the bar of acceptance towards the current music scene, and with due acknowledgements also paid to artists in the calibre of The Rolling Stones, Bob Dylan, The Byrds, The Association and Tim Buckley, the show gave a massive boost to the public perception of the medium. Perhaps the highlight of the 60-minute broadcast was the stunning debut of a new Brian Wilson composition featuring just Brian alone at the piano in his Bellagio house, performing a solo rendition of the inspiring 'Surf's Up'. Not to be outdone, various UK artists were also represented.

Filmed during their recent joint winter tour of America, The Hollies and Herman's Hermits were also given screen time in the special. The CBS cameras captured The Hollies performing a sparkling rendition of 'Bus Stop', with Bernstein referencing its lyrical simplicity. Bobby Elliott, Peter Noone and an accompanying Graham Gouldman were also filmed off stage, sitting in a hotel room, listening attentively whilst a wildly enthusiastic Graham Nash once again espoused his philosophies and his views for the younger generation;

'We can go in front of a television camera, we can go on the air, and say that Hitler was wrong, and that Rockwell is wrong. We can get up there and shout it to the world. So why don't we do more of it? We can stop world wars before they're even started. Do you know who start world wars? People who are over forty. People that are too old to realise that love rules the world...'

Graham Nash
*Inside Pop: The Rock Revolution*
CBS-TV 1967

By the arrival of spring 1967, the composition that Tony had initially started writing during the previous winter tour of Scandinavia had reached fulfilment. Originally conceived under the working title of 'Hey Mister Man', the concept had altered significantly and, following an initial idea to perform it as a tribute to singer Marianne Faithfull – 'Hey Marianne' – the group baulked at the idea, and altered it yet again to the similar sounding name, 'Carrie Anne'. It was under this title that the group, now with a healthier Bobby Elliott back behind the drum kit, brought the song into the recording studio on 1st May.

The previous month had seen Bobby take tentative steps back to work, gradually building up his strength and stamina after the enforced and lengthy lay-off. His first full role back, looking beyond the two appearances in Blackpool, was a taping of 'On A Carousel' and 'Stop! Stop! Stop!' for the television cameras, recorded specifically for the UK comedy duo Morecambe & Wise and the *Piccadilly Palace* variety show they hosted Stateside. The appearance would be repeated on their own weekly UK TV series later in the year.

'Bobby's so very much a part of the group,' Tony was to comment to *Disc & Music Echo* at the time. 'And it was mainly for his own mental satisfaction that we stopped [the proposed foreign tours]. He's out of hospital now, but the specialist's report shows that he was very close to death when he fell ill in Germany. Today we feel like a brand new group and are making a fresh start...'

'I was able to look at my life objectively and think about things,' Bobby was to respond in *Beat Instrumental* magazine. 'I was knocked out when the others cancelled a lot of work because of me. It's at times like that that you really discover your worth as both a musician and a person.'

Issued as the next single (Parlophone R5602) at the end of the month 'Carrie Anne' – coupled with another new Clarke-Hicks-Nash composition, the folky 'Signs That Will Never Change' – exemplifies the sound that the Hollies were renowned for. Overtly commercial, bright and cheerful, coupled with lyrics of seemingly simple reflection, it had all the right ingredients for a pop smash. However, that, in turn, raises the question as to how the band, and Graham Nash in particular, did truly perceive their act. On one hand, we had them taking their music into the new Nash-led experimental territories that would grace their next album, whilst on the other hand was this perfectly crafted yet ultimately lightweight piece of plastic. One only has to look closely at the songs that surrounded this new offering once it peaked at its eventual #3 position on the UK chart lists to understand the dichotomy it represented.

Number 1: 'A Whiter Shade of Pale' by Procol Harum
Number 5: 'Waterloo Sunset' by The Kinks
Number 8: 'Paper Sun' by Traffic
Number 11: 'Groovin'' by The Young Rascals
Number 12: 'Dedicated To The One I Love' by The Mamas and The Papas
Number 16: 'Here Come the Nice' by Small Faces

…whilst swiftly climbing up to the number 22 position was 'Strange Brew' by Cream, with Jimi Hendrix and 'The Wind Cries Mary' just one place lower. Even those former manufactured hit-makers The Monkees entered the charts that week at #30 with the self-penned 'Alternate Title (Randy Scouse Git)', arguably their first disc of real lyrical substance. Not that this was necessarily appreciated by all who heard it.

"Alternate Title' is a load of rubbish,' Allan Clarke bluntly stated when guest reviewing the latest releases in *Disc & Music Echo*. 'The song is terrible, (and) I feel the Small Faces should also be progressing, but they're not. There's nothing very special about this one. 'Fraid I also keep getting Eric Clapton mixed up with Jimi Hendrix, and that's bad, but 'Strange Brew' is a good record…'

Of interest, the Small Faces condemnation continued onwards into the following year, when the arrangement for their Top 10 hit 'Lazy Sunday' was a direct result of criticism the band had faced from The Hollies, accusing them of not singing in their native cockney accents. Mustn't grumble.

Then again, maybe 'Carrie Anne', for all its commercial success, was simply playing it safe once more – at least, from a purely melodical pop perspective. But was that any more than their deep fan base really wanted from them? A full two-month run in the Top 20 suggested so. Lyrically, however, there remained a deeper undercurrent of suggestion – playing with the older boys and prefects. What *is* the attraction in what they were doing?

Nevertheless, what is truly distinctive about the recording are the vocals of the three key frontline players within the band. The trio each took individual solo leads for the three featured verses, a first for them on a 45 release. With Graham overdubbing the harmonies himself, the other additional feature was the inclusion of a steel drum arrangement for the bridge – albeit one that perhaps hasn't stood the test of time too well. Legend tells us that it was Tony and Ron Richards who found the owner of the steel set-up during a break in recording and asked if he would assist on the track. Graham maintains to this day no one knows who he was, although Ron later clarified the events in the sleevenotes for a latter-day *Anthology* CD release.

'I went through a big steel drum phase as a producer, and I found this guy from South America who had this steel drum band and I decided to use them on this track. They were very difficult to record…'[70]

Bobby later confirmed the issues surrounding the recording, noting that, as the steel drum was out of tune with the master track, they had to attempt to adjust the sound with a hammer, before eventually resorting to varying the tape speed manually in order to compensate for their inability to fix the issue.

Bernie also recounted his recollections of the session: 'When we laid the track down, I put that little bit of percussion on the intro with this instrument that has a little stick you drag across this ridged area. It was lying around in the studio and it worked really well. It got us into that Caribbean feel. We hadn't decided when we got to the solo to put steel drums on. We just played the musical sequence and it was so obvious what was needed: steel drums.'[26]

And after all of that – how would they carry it off in live appearances? A unique approach was thus undertaken as, on various occasions, either a string section was brought in to perform the instrumental break, or a pre-recorded track was played over the sound system at the appropriate moment, with the band humorously mocking the sudden taped audio appearance.

A promotional film was also made to aid potential sales of the release, one of the very earliest "promo videos" of its type, directed by Peter Goldmann once again, and featuring a short vignette designed for each Hollie (not too dissimilar to the musical "romps" that the Monkees were now regularly using in their TV series). Allan has a staged western shootout scene with Walker Brother Gary Leeds; Graham leaps gaily through the fields dressed in his paisley-coloured kaftan; Bobby sneaks into a house to play wildly behind a strobe-lit drum kit; Tony drives along in his stylish sports car; and Bernie finds himself surrounded by a bevy of beauties.

'I didn't have much to do with the writing of this one,' confessed Allan, before later admitting that he contributed the middle eight section to the composition. 'The idea had been plaguing Tony for at least six months. He had the opening and was going berserk trying to finish it. We told him to forget about it for a while, but he wouldn't!' (*Disc & Music Echo* June 1967)

A conversation with journalist Keith Altham, printed in the *New Musical Express* shortly afterwards, appeared to summarise the differing opinions that now continuously flowed between the members of the band…

Graham: "Carrie Anne' is going to be the last of our really commercial singles. We are getting so commercial we are becoming uncommercial. It's time for The Hollies to re-group. I want to make records which say something.'

Tony: 'I think it does say something. It says something very simple; a boy-girl relationship which anyone can understand. I'm frightened of going over the heads of the kids. It's no good being progressive if people cannot understand you.'

Graham: 'All I want is for people to listen. I've had five years of playing to screamers, and now I want an audience who will listen. I believe The Hollies have tremendous potential, and I want people in Britain to hear it. I want us to move forward, do something different.'

The release of the *Evolution* album (PMC/PCS-7022), appearing in stores on 1st June, certainly gave The Hollies' audience a disc of greater artistic ambition than they had previously experienced. However, much of what they had committed to tape in the studio could no longer be easily recreated on stage, an issue that befell many guitar-based bands of the era.

Studio techniques and effects were all very well for vinyl releases, but it was not easy to duplicate the intricate sound effects, often layered on top of the initial studio tracks, or the deft vocal tricks achieved by running the microphone cable through a guitar amplifier. More often than not, live representations of these experiments and techniques were often avoided on stage by attempting to perform a basic, stripped-back rendition of the song in question. An easier option was to not even attempt to play the song at all, a fate which befell many of the songs on *Evolution*. The album did receive mostly positive reviews from the music press, however, going on to comfortably achieve a Top 20 position in the British album charts. In addition, the release also garnered significant critical radio acclaim, with popular off-shore Radio Caroline affording it the honour of "album of the week".

The Hollies must take a big bow for their latest, and best, LP "Evolution". Especially Graham Nash, Allan Clarke and Tony Hicks for composing all the twelve rousing and interesting songs.

They've also brought into it added instrumentation on nine tracks, which is mostly deep brass, directed by ex-Manfred Mann guitarist Mike Vickers. Ron Richards produced the disc for Parlophone, and the startling cover design is by Holland's surrealistic Simon and Marijke, aided by photographer Karl Ferris. Altogether an ear- and eye-opening production.

Only one question remains in my mind – as nine tracks have "extra instrumentation" behind them, can The Hollies do these on tour?

*New Musical Express*
June 1967

The high-quality songwriting, the effortless production and all-round excellence of the performances present a band still at the top of their game. Right from the opening acoustic guitar chords of 'Then The Heartaches Begin', this new twelve-inch slab of vinyl took the listener through a delightful combination of classy pop, edgier rock and watered-down psychedelia.

A selection of outstanding cuts – 'Rain On The Window', 'Stop Right There', 'Water On The Brain', right through to the driving fuzz guitar utilised on the band's own version of 'Have You Ever Loved Somebody' and the thrilling organ and heavier allusions of 'Leave Me' demonstrate a group starting to explore more introspective thoughts within their writing. Even the "poppier" commercially driven tunes, such as the Nash-led 'When Your Light's Turned On', suggest themes of infidelity and deceit. With Graham's marriage to Rose reportedly going through various personal issues during that period, it does make one question how close some of this was to reality. The album's heavier moments are nicely counterbalanced by the twee English whimsy of Graham's harpsichord-laden 'Ye Olde Toffee Shoppe' and 'Lullaby To Tim', Allan's heartwarming ballad to his young son, replete with a frustratingly distracting vocal-guitar-amplifier effect applied to Graham's lead vocal.

Packaged in multi-coloured splendour, the sleeve was designed by Dutch artists Simon Posthuma and Marijke Koger (a pairing widely known as The Fool), and photographed by their associate Karl Ferris, today best known for his iconic shots of Jimi Hendrix. The five band members are captured close-up, Tony to the fore, dressed in garish silk shirts designed specifically for them by Posthuma and Koger. Hands outstretched, the pose screams "psychedelia", but in a softer, clean-cut way. The Hollie-way…

'I don't understand half of all this psychedelic stuff. There's a lot of rubbish going around about pop stars and drugs, but you wouldn't catch me taking drugs. A good beer is strong enough for me.

'Graham talks a lot about the inner mind and psychedelic things, but to tell you the truth, I don't understand half of what he's on about. It's just weird. Sometimes he gets too deep for me, and I can't listen any more…'

Allan Clarke
*New Musical Express*
March 1967

An appearance on *Top of the Pops*, promoting 'Carrie Anne', also took place on 1st June, but further personal appearances on *Dee Time* and *As You Like It* were unfortunately cancelled when Tony was struck down with an ailment, requiring a sinus operation. Graham, meanwhile, never one to miss an opportunity to hang with the hip crowd, managed to achieve a certain level of notoriety by appearing on a televised show that, quite literally, was viewed by (estimations vary) an astonishing 500 million viewers across the planet.

*Our World* was a two-and-a-half-hour televisual extravaganza and the very first live, worldwide satellite production, broadcast on 25th June 1967. Creative artists from around the globe, representing nineteen nations, were invited to perform or appear in individual segments featuring their respective countries. Greek soprano Maria Callas and Spanish artist Pablo Picasso represented their homelands, whilst various countries undertook documentary-style features or short scientific experiments for their section of the broadcast.

For the UK segment, The Beatles were invited to perform a song that would, ultimately, bring the entire show to a fitting climax. Having permanently quit their rigorous touring schedule the previous year, the foursome agreed to have their appearance filmed at the Abbey Road studios. Cautious of a live performance before such a vast audience, the Fab Four opted to partially pre-record the rhythm track beforehand, only choosing to record live vocals for this momentous occasion. The song they had chosen to perform was a new composition that John Lennon had written specifically for the event, with simple lyrics that captured the utopian sentiments of 1967; 'All You Need Is Love'.

Adding to the colourful combination of flowers, balloons, banners and general festivities in the studio was a small orchestra (playing live) along with various friends and musical associates, seated like pawns at the feet of the mighty Liverpudlian gods. Anyone watching the broadcast would barely have noticed many of those invited to attend, but blink and you would miss the happy-clappy, smiling faces of Mick Jagger, Marianne Faithfull, Eric Clapton, Keith Richards, Keith Moon, Pattie Boyd, Mike McCartney, Jane Asher, various Small Faces, Dutch artists The Fool... and Graham and Rose Nash.

'It was insane. Paul called me on the Sunday morning and told me they were doing this telecast at Abbey Road and did I want to go?' recalled Graham.

"They were all good friends. It was a pretty mellow afternoon and evening." (*Guardian.com* 2016)

Not that this was the only time Graham would be present at a McCartney recording session. The week before the global broadcast, taping had commenced in London for the eponymous album by two members of The Scaffold, a Liverpool-based satirical comedy trio featuring Paul's younger brother, Mike (who went by the stage name of McGear), and Liverpudlian poet Roger McGough. The result was the somewhat surreal *McGough & McGear* album. At various stages during the subsequent months, a host of acquaintances and fellow rock stars passed through the studios to add their contributions – including Jimi Hendrix, Dave Mason (Traffic), Gary Leeds (Walker Brothers), Viv Prince (Pretty Things), Paul Samwell-Smith (The Yardbirds), along with Mike's famous brother and his current girlfriend, Jane Asher. Issued on the Parlophone label the following year, Graham's distinctive vocals can be heard, piercing through the introductory seconds of the song 'Ex-Art Student'.

'Graham was just a mate,' says Mike McCartney when reminiscing over the sessions. 'He would just turn up and add guitar and vocals. I'm sure he's on [the song] 'Living Room' as well. In fact, I think he may well have been on all of them...'[78]

One further slab of Nash involvement also took place when he sat in on a session with pop band Marmalade, assisting them as they recorded their self-composed summer '67, Euro-chart topper, 'I See The Rain'.

It can be said now that The Hollies, in this month of July 1967, have ARRIVED! They are the most adventurous musical force in Britain after The Beatles.

There was a time when they were thought of as very nice boys from Manchester. Not very hip, not very exciting, but steady. Now their LP's – which are, after all, a sign of what it's all about – are greeted not just with enthusiasm but with something close to awe.

*Disc & Music Echo*
July 1967

Following Allan's comments to the UK press as to how their performing agenda had changed, with better venues supporting the band as they toured around the country, he announced in *Disc & Music Echo* that their days of the one-nighter package tour were also now over.

'We're fed up with the same old round of pop shows. We want to do something entirely new. A special vehicle built around our own talent. We're not saying pop package shows are played out for other groups, but they are for us.

'What we'd like to do is tour with an orchestra, having just one act, a folk group maybe, on the first part of the bill, and then we'd do the whole of the second half. Graham has another idea. He is supposed to be writing a ballet with two friends of his. This would be something different, and we all feel the kids are ready for it…'

Touring with a poet was another option thrown into the mix. 'I don't want to see a bloody poet!' was Tony Hicks' reaction.

Recently, Graham had been stretching the boundaries of his songwriting abilities, working outside the confines of the Clarke-Hicks-Nash triumvirate. He had begun associating with Nicky James and Kirk Duncan, two struggling songwriters with whom Nash would spend many late nights together, holed up in London clubs such as the Bag O'Nails. Between them, they had tested the waters, co-writing several new compositions. As part of an arrangement with GRALTO Music, The Hollies' own publishing arm, James and Duncan were put on the payroll, and alongside Graham, they added works such as 'Reaching For The Sun' and 'Good Day' to the catalogue of songs. The trio did find success with one of their co-compositions, 'Annabella', a UK Top 30 solo hit for John Walker/Maus, following his departure from The Walker Brothers, although Graham's contribution to the writing was reportedly minimal in this instance. The trio were also partially involved in the negotiations with the Dick James Publishing house, DJM (who also looked after GRALTO), for the piano-playing session man Reggie Dwight and his new songwriting partner, Bernie Taupin. The latter duo had also been working with the struggling pair, but both Nicky and Kirk were excluded from any part of the final deal, with Graham and Ron Richards solely benefitting GRALTO with the publishing on the early Dwight-James-Duncan compositions. By late 1967, Graham's involvement with the two writers had dissolved, and both James and Duncan were removed from the company's workforce.

For The Hollies, the remainder of the "summer of love" was a muted affair. With a new album successfully selling in the stores, a hit single remaining in the Top 40 until mid-August (by which time The Beatles and Scott McKenzie were dominating the peak position in the UK charts with their odes to love, peace and flowers) and few live performances scheduled over the summer, due to the uncertainties surrounding Bobby's recovery, it was a time to bask in the glory of recent achievements, play up to the press and absorb new ideologies reshaping art and youth culture. Ever the epitome of the UK hippie-tribe, Graham took to wearing his multi-coloured kaftan at every opportunity, ignoring the mocking remarks of the press, and sharing his words of wisdom to fellow like-minded souls who graced the boutiques and nightclubs of the King's Road and Knightsbridge. Holding back from the full influences of flower power, and drawing the line at overindulging in the various mind-expanding substances so freely on offer, the remaining four Hollies dipped their toes warily into the freedom that the hippie movement offered. Beads, paisley shirts, floppy wide-brimmed hats (predominantly placed to keep Bobby's receding hairline out of sight) became the daily norm, with Allan even allowing himself the distinction of a pencil-thin 'tache on his upper lip and the merest suggestion of a wild-haired afro growing out. For his part, Tony, he of the doe-eyed, good-looking boyish charm, retained some sense of normality amongst the rainbow of garish garments that festooned the Carnaby Street brigade. A northern factory worker twelve months previously, new boy Bernie barely endeavoured to dive in, his attire often a combination of neatly pressed slacks and shiny black shoes, mismatched against the flowing scarf and lace-graced cuffs. And were they really patent leather sky-blue boots Allan was wearing, matching the flowing, flared sleeves on his colourful silk shirt?

Tentative recording sessions were undertaken during August, with an eye on the timelines for the expected follow-up to *Evolution*. Graham was constantly pushing the boundaries back, and as his own songwriting dominance began to outshine that of Allan and Tony, the chasms dividing the partnership grew ever wider. Not that Allan and Tony sat idle whilst Graham explored his freedom. Far from it; both began to develop and push their individual songwriting skills to new heights. Allan started work on a selection of new songs, including 'Try It' and 'Would You Believe', whilst Tony took it a step further with the enchanting 'Pegasus'.

Following exploratory attempts at two new works, 'Charlie And Fred' and 'Step Inside', the group pulled together for two days of graft at Abbey Road during the first week in August. The result of these sessions would not only provide the band with their next 45 single release, a highly powerful song from Allan and Graham, but would also scar the band immeasurably and start a gradual decline in the working relationships within. For all its subsequent faults, 'King Midas in Reverse', taped between the 3rd and 4th of that month, ranks as one of the band's finest artistic achievements to that point.

*Sergeant Pepper's Lonely Hearts Club Band* was *the* sound of a 1967 summer, blaring out of every open window and doorway. Whilst many other popular acts and singers tried hard to emulate the success and experimentation, very few managed to do so successfully, without sounding like a watered-down parody. Across the ocean, Brian Wilson, guiding light behind The Beach Boys, had bowed out of the race due to peer pressure and expectation, abandoning his much-vaunted *SMiLE* project, but not before hinting what might have been with the bewildering, yet stunning, vocal realisations of 'Heroes And Villains'. The Rolling Stones took an ill-advised journey into Neverland with the release of *Their Satanic Majesties Request*, whilst The Byrds were unsure of which direction to take next. Having mixed fusions of psychedelia with jazz and pop on their impressive *Younger Than Yesterday* album, they were now suffering from the interpersonal issues that consistently hounded them throughout their career (a similar tale that befell the mighty Buffalo Springfield). Meanwhile, fellow UK contemporaries such as The Kinks, The Who, The Zombies, Small Faces, Pretty Things *et al.* were still on the rocky road to their own creative peaks. Come mid-1967, and in between the sentimental offerings that Tom Jones, Engelbert Humperdinck, Des O'Connor and the Johnny Mann Singers were clogging up the charts with, The Hollies were more than ready to deliver the quality that the fickle music industry and press demanded. *Evolution* had shown them so. But the question remained: was their fan base prepared to accept this new, less commercial direction Nash wished the band to take?

*(Right) Ricky and Dane Young in perfect harmony.*
*(Below) Don Rathbone with Cliff Bowes and The Arrows*
*(Below Right) The Dolphins with Bernie Calvert, Bobby Elliott and Tony Hicks*
*(Bottom) Vic Steele, second from right, with The Emperors of Rhythm*

*(Top left) The only known image of Vic Steele as a Hollie, pictured with Eric during 1963*
*(Below) Tony Hicks joins the group*

**THE HOLLIES**
PARLOPHONE RECORDS

Photo : Philip Gotlop, London

# THE TOGGERY

MERSEY SQUARE, STOCKPORT

MANY OF THE TOP NORTHERN
RECORDING STARS INCLUDING
**THE HOLLIES**
HAVE CHOSEN
# The Toggery
FOR ALL THEIR STAGE AND LEISURE WEAR

RECORD
MAIL

A MONTHLY REVIEW AND DETAILS OF THE LATEST
'POPULAR' RECORDS ISSUED BY E.M.I RECORDS LTD.
H.M.V, Capitol, Columbia, Parlophone, Encore, Stateside,
M-G-M, Liberty, United Artists, Verve

Vol. 7. No. 6. (Published on the first Friday of each month) June, 1964

HERE THEY
GO AGAIN!

1 D.

HERE go the Hollies again—set for another trip to the charts with their latest Parlophone release, "Here I go again" (R5137).

*Bobby Elliott joins the line-up*

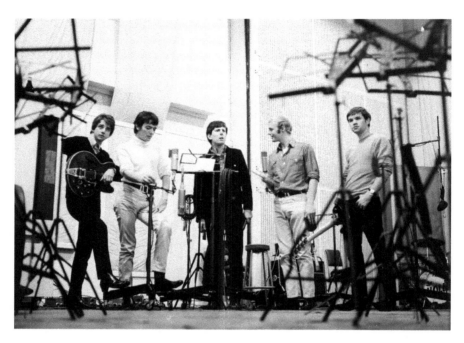

*(Above) At home in the cavernous surroundings of the EMI Recording Studios in Abbey Road*

*(Above) 1966 in the U.S., with Bernie Calvert
having taken on the bass role
(Right) The U.S. Greatest Hits release*

The Hollies' Greatest Hits

Bus Stop / Pay You Back With Interest / Here I Go Again
Memphis / Tell Me To My Face / I'm Alive / Look Through Any Window / Stop! Stop! Stop
Whatcha Gonna Do Bout It / Just One Look / I Can't Let Go / On A Carousel

THE ESCORTS

representation: Jim Godbolt Agency
15 Wardour Street, London, W.1
agent 8321-2

Management: Jim Ireland
Mardi-Gras, Mount Pleasant, Liverpool 3
Royal 4448

(Above Left) Terry Sylvester and his first group, The Escorts
(Above Right and Below) His early days as a Hollie, officially replacing Graham Nash
during January of 1969

# CHAPTER FOURTEEN

---

# "ELEVATED OBSERVATIONS..."

The Hollies: "King Midas In Reverse" (Parlophone R5637)
Pops consistent hit-makers have done it again! It must go shooting
up. Opens gently enough and builds beautifully to a really dramatic
finale with everything happening. A real mind blower!

*New Musical Express*
September 1967

The media reviews for the new Hollies 45, issued during September of
1967, were nearly all universal in their praise for this adventurous new
release, a result of the band's ever-inventive and creative songwriting.
Born out of an earlier melody that Allan had been working on, the song
simply took flight once Graham heard, and ultimately visualised, what it
could offer, and began to guide its star-bound trajectory.

Starting with his delicate acoustic guitar, the recording just grew as he
developed the idea, and the orchestral flourishes that Ron Richards oversaw,
the trilling flutes and the resonating brass, made the song just come alive.

'I wrote the melody,' Allan was to comment, 'but I couldn't get the lyrics.
But Graham said he'd think about it and came up with this idea of a character
who found everything he touched turned to dust. It was not a happy song.'

'I actually had very little to do with it,' said Tony at the time (in *Melody
Maker*). 'Graham did say I gave him the idea for the title, but I don't know

how. It's about people who feel that nothing they do ever comes right. We all feel a little like that from time to time.

'It's another departure from the old moonlight and roses idea of pop songs. There's Graham pulling like mad to move ahead and me pulling back and Allan taking another path. I am a bit dubious about moving ahead too quickly. But the whole thing adds up to a good scene for The Hollies.'

In his autobiography *Wild Tales*, Graham would recall how excited the band were with the recording. 'It was innovative,' he would say. 'A huge leap forward.'

Bobby Elliott would also later recount how Ron and the group experimented with various techniques on the track, just to find the special ingredient that made the magic work. One such instance saw them speeding up the tape recorders in order to get a distinctive sound on the drums, then by slowing them back down to normal speed, they gave a fuller, tympani-like ambience. There were simply no rules with recording back then, it was all try-it-and-see – and if there were any regulations in place, they were there to be broken.

Unfortunately, and despite the entire band's initial support for the single (paired with the throwaway summer pop of 'Everything Is Sunshine'), the public perception of the group was too straight for this radical departure in style. To the stunned surprise of all those involved, particularly Graham, who was the main protagonist in pushing the song to the outer boundaries, sales of the record floundered. Ultimately, as he would later admit, 'it was more of a Graham Nash record with The Hollies on it.'[1]

'That was a big production job,' noted Ron. 'I think I went production crazy on that record. I had a big orchestra, we had flutes, we had… you name it, we had it on it. I think as a production it's really very good but not as a commercial record.'[70]

Allan: 'All our stuff had got into the Top 10, but this one didn't. We thought we had such a set following that anything we did would get into the charts and that we could therefore experiment. We realised we didn't have this, and if they don't like one, they don't buy it. It'll be worth the experience if we don't make the same mistakes again.'

Whilst still maintaining a two-month run in the UK charts, the 45 barely scraped the Top 20, peaking at number 18 in a week that saw the Bee Gees single 'Massachusetts' knock Engelbert's million-selling 'The Last Waltz' off the very pinnacle. An appearance on *Top of the Pops* took place on

21$^{st}$ September, appearing on the show alongside The Move, The Flowerpot Men, Sandie Shaw and The Dubliners, and an eventual positional run of 45-22-18-20-19-25-30-41 was, with hindsight, certainly far harsher than the record deserved. Clearly, what drove The Hollies' loyal audience to the record stores was the usual catchy, 2-minute pop song, with a memorable melody and a strong hook. The band itself, fronted by Graham's insistent drive and force, was trying to evolve, to grow and mature, but their audience was content with what they had, thank you very much. They didn't want lyrics such as *"It's plain to see it's hopeless, going on the way we are,"* that, perhaps, came far closer to the truth than anyone realised. If you wanted the "serious", harder-edged side of the business, then take a listen to the singles that The Move, Small Faces or Traffic were offering in the same chart lists that week. The vast majority of The Hollies' record-buying fans wanted little more than more of the same...

Graham: 'The worst backlash from the record was what it did to my relationship with The Hollies. They no longer trusted my judgement. I suggested a number of songs to pursue as a follow-up, but they backed away.'[1]

A song entitled 'Sleep Song' was one of the new numbers he offered up to the band, but they recoiled at the song's suggestive lyrical content. He would also play them another new tune on which he had been working, with lyrics recounting a recent vacation he had taken to northern Africa with Rose. The trip had taken them both on an enlightening journey around Morocco, stopping off *en route* in both Casablanca and Marrakesh, but the subsequent visions and themes that Graham had passionately absorbed and worked into the new composition failed to impress his bandmates. The Hollies would later take the song into the studio to try to make it work – but to little avail. Nevertheless, despite such a setback with his envisaged direction, Graham continued to dominate the recording sessions, and his ideas, vocals and songwriting played a huge part in the development of their next album, recorded over the late summer of 1967.

A brief return visit to Sweden was one of the few runs of live concert appearances throughout the summer, with the group taking to the stage decked out in their finest paisley and open-toed sandals. Surprisingly, they continued to perform a set held together by the hits and the early songs, with little to show from their recent studio experimentations. Of the twelve featured songs on *Evolution*, only two songs made the onstage selection during that period, with 'The Games We Play' and 'Stop Right There' both, for example, being performed in Vänersborg, Sweden on 23rd August, alongside more familiar versions of 'Carrie Anne', 'On A Carousel', 'Bus Stop', 'Very Last Day', 'Stewball' and 'A Taste Of Honey'.

The *Evolution* album also saw a belated US release during the final weeks of the summer. Issued on the Epic Record label (a result of the band finally losing patience with Imperial), the LP saw a familiar pattern to those that had preceded it, with a butchered song revision crawling into the lower regions of *Billboard*. It was a relative disappointment following the recent run of successful singles, along with the strong sales for Imperial's *Greatest Hits* offering. That said, the remixing process that Epic put the recordings through prior to the release, top-heavy in both echo and reverb, took away much of the magic held within the grooves.

The apparent failure that 'King Midas In Reverse' had endured on home soil was also subsequently duplicated across the ocean with a poor #51 *Billboard* showing, giving Epic Records little payback for their initial hopes and intentions. 'Carrie Anne' had started the partnership off on a strong footing, hitting the number 9 slot, but for the remainder of the decade, all further US releases would fail to establish that firm foothold The Hollies so craved in America.

Unlike previous long-playing releases, often committed to tape within a matter of days at Abbey Road, sessions for the band's upcoming seventh album would stretch over much of September, running into early October. But, disregarding any reservations over Graham's leadership direction, the long days at Abbey Road continued, with a number of the newer works treading the boundaries of pop, rock, folk, balladry and even touching on the mysticisms of Indian raga.

In between these official Hollies sessions, the temporary hold on live appearances gave band members the opportunity to utilise their time elsewhere. October saw the release of a 7-inch single on the RCA Victor label, credited to a Swedish-based band called The Lee Kings, who had supported The Hollies during their recent visit to Scandinavia. Fronted by the Sheffield-born Mike Watson, this obscure 45 was produced by none other than the Clarke-Nash partnership, with the A-side of the release – 'Coming From The Ground' – being composed by the duo alongside the former GRALTO staff writers Nicky James and Kirk Duncan. Photographs taken during the recording session even appeared on the picture sleeve of the single but, unfortunately, the venture saw little success outside of the band's homeland.

One other non-Hollies release that also had ties with GRALTO appeared in record stores the following month, this time credited to Scottish band The Societie. On this occasion, the distinctive brown and white Deram label bore the credit: "produced by Allan Clarke for Hollies Recording Co. Ltd."

The Societie began in July '66 in Glasgow, and shortly afterwards they were heard, dug and reported to The Hollies by a showbusiness-man holidaying north of the border. When their annual British tour hit Glasgow in the spring of '67, The Hollies caught The Societie in the act at a club, much to the delight of the teenyboppers in attendance, and [they] liked The Societie very much.

'Good image, man,' said bearded Graham Nash.

'It's ridiculous, young lads like them playing their guitars so well,' said elderly Tony Hicks, aged twenty-one.

'Knockout voices! I'd like to record them,' said Allan Clarke, who knows, 'cos he's sung on eighteen big hits. And so a recording session was set for May '67. No hit record came from that session. No record at all. But it was discovered that they could write good songs, so Allan Clarke sent them back the 397 miles to write some more. The Societie returned to London in September '67 and, with Clarke at the controls, produced two groovy sides – 'Bird Has Flown' and 'Breaking Down', both group compositions.

Deram Records Promotion

1967

Despite the quality of both song and production, this wondrous slice of psych-pop also soon disappeared into oblivion, retaining only a cult status in the ensuing years.

Graham Nash, first of The Hollies to emerge from the underworld of anonymity and attempt to project himself as a pop personality is going about it in a grand manner. Mr Nash receives reporters in his well-appointed Paddington mews cottage, curled up on a couch with his legs crossed, curtains drawn, candle burning. Mothers of Invention playing and joss sticks sweetening the air.

'My main interest these days is making LPs. We've just completed an album called "Butterfly" and although we still haven't found a direction with our albums – we want to do a continuous fairytale or something – I think we're heading in the right direction. The Hollies, however, have never been trend-setters...'

*Disc & Music Echo*
October 1967

With sessions on the album winding down during the first week of October, the new LP was prepared for a November release. Packaged within a striking front sleeve, depicting the appropriate winged insect, the album was widely expected to match the success of *Evolution*, and positivity was in the air during the lead-up to the official issue.

The twelve tracks compiled together were, once again, immaculately polished and presented, with Graham to the fore on many of the songs, more so than on any previous release. From the opening bars of 'Dear Eloise' (the basis of which was written by Allan in a short burst, whilst awaiting to attend a meeting, and subsequently arranged by Bobby), with Graham's often fragile lead laid bare against a simple harmonium refrain, the album is a pure aural delight. *Butterfly* was another artistic triumph for The Hollies; tight group harmonies and whimsical arrangements offering a charming pop portrait of 1960s English psychedelia.

The Hollies: "Butterfly" (Parlophone PMC/PCS 7039)
Some interesting and weird sounds on this Ron Richards-produced album, but also a lot of good happy beat music as well. For instance, the first tune, 'Dear Eloise' is sung more or less in The Hollies' style but at the end it goes all distorted and slow. Quite effective. After that we get Oriental, churchy, outer space and other effects but I must be old-fashioned because I like to hear the happier, beatier pieces like 'Away Away Away', 'Wish You A Wish' [sic], 'Charlie And Fred' and 'Step Inside'. But I must admit interest in 'Try It', which I saw them record at EMI, complete with Bobby Elliott's brush beats recorded backwards. Good song, but then so is almost everything The Hollies do.

*New Musical Express*
November 1967

The Hollies: "Butterfly" (Parlophone PMC/PCS 7039)
Pretty is the word to describe The Hollies current music. Pretty
and tasteful, nice songs and nice arrangements. A typical track
is 'Wishyouawish' which bounces along like a lamb loose in the
countryside. Tribute must be paid to arranger and conductor Johnny
Scott and producer Ron Richards.

*Melody Maker*
December 1967

Interestingly, the stereo mix of the album (PCS-7039), overseen personally
by Graham, differed from the Parlophone mono version in the original
pressings, in as much as the tracks ran in a continuous groove on the vinyl,
without a clear gap in between the songs, making for an all-in and joyous
listening experience. There were also subtle differences in the playback – the
sound effects on both 'Postcard' and 'Wishyouawish', the fadeout on 'Dear
Eloise' and the alternate mixes on 'Elevated Observations' and the title track.
The German release of the LP, issued on the Hansa record label, featured a
further unique variation of 'Elevated Observations', being almost double the
length of the mono version, although this was almost certainly a mastering
error.

Overall, the accompanying arrangements, credited to seasoned jazz
musician and EMI arranger Johnny Scott, were certainly fuller than on
any other release, with many of the compositions lending themselves to
the woodwinds, brass or the more exotic overdubs. Notably, the Indian
sitar utilised on the extraordinary Nash-led 'Maker' was actually owned by
George Harrison, having been left in the studio one day to the obvious delight
of Tony Hicks. However, in later conversation with *Carousel* magazine, he
indicated that an unnamed session musician had actually played it on the
recording, not himself.

By contrast, the album's many sound effects and orchestral overdubs left
the album mostly bereft of the types of overtly commercial numbers the
typical Top 20 "Hollie-fan" had enjoyed on previous albums. 'Step Inside',
featuring a distinctive pop vocal from Allan, was perhaps the sole example
of the "old" Hollies sound.

Tony's enchanting childlike composition, 'Pegasus', offered up a rare
lead vocal from the writer himself – although when he wrote it (reportedly
during the *Evolution*-era), he had envisaged Allan taking the lead. The

finalised lyrics, completed during the days leading up to the session, perfectly defined the gentler, surreal images of that period. Meanwhile, Allan's own Walker Brothers-styled 'Would You Believe' was a production powerhouse, cross-pollinating with a wonderfully emotive string arrangement from Scott which, it should be noted, was recorded during the same period that George Martin was working on the strings for 'I Am The Walrus' in the studio next door. Coinciding sessions on 5th September suggest an overbearing sense of mutual admiration from either direction.

"Would You Believe' is from one of my very emotional states,' Allan was to remark in *Record Mirror*. 'It incorporates my feelings towards my wife. We have a son, Timmy, and I suddenly realised how hard it was for my wife being left alone so much, getting him off to bed, and so on. I wrote this one at home, at night.'

Interestingly, despite Graham being the Hollie most openly influenced by the psychedelic scene, Allan's current interest in astral projection produced 'Try It', the album's most "out there" inclusion.

Backward cymbals, inventive bass lines, synthesised sound effects and a droning melody conjured up mindful visions of Haight-Ashbury or other such hippie havens.

Allan: 'Everyone is supposed to be a prisoner of their own body. That's what that one is about. I read a lot of books by Labsang Ramtha, who was like a European Buddhist who was into astral projection. I've been trying ever since to do it and have failed each time.'[70]

Allan's other centrepiece, the simple singalong folk-styling of 'Charlie And Fred', placed him in more familiar-sounding territory. Nevertheless, it was Graham's infectious contributions that predominantly drove the album, with 'Away Away Away' and 'Postcard' both written during a recent solo vacation in St Tropez. Along with the trippy collaborative efforts on 'Elevated Observations', the songs all benefited from his inspired thought processes.

'Graham does something and puts it away in his brain,' continued Allan, when trying to explain his bandmate's abilities to the *Record Mirror* journalist. 'He writes about his surroundings. Things happen around him and he then incorporates it into a song. He is in a dream world of his own.'

Another fine example of Graham's singular ability was with the gloriously fully orchestrated title track, with some stunning arrangements that offered up picturesque visions of a Vaughan Williams-styled ethereal beauty.

'When you hear some of the stuff that Johnny Scott put on (the record), orchestrally… well, I just feel like crying. With happiness…'

Allan Clarke

*Record Mirror* 1967

One might scoff at the dreamlike imagery in some of the lyrics on this particular song, but then is a "*lemonade lake*" any sillier, or more profound, than, say, a "*marmalade sky*" or knowing a "*mouse who hasn't got a house. I don't know why I call him Gerald*"? – surreal wordplays that other bands were pondering over in those trippy days of 1967.

With a further co-write between Allan and Graham, 'Wishyouawish', these all offered up Nash's inimitable and instinctive ability for a deceptively lightweight, yet catchy and joyful, melody. However, at one point during proceedings, and in the aftermath of the 'King Midas In Reverse' debacle, Bobby Elliott allegedly suggested that Graham was more focussed on the sonic effects of the recordings than the actual quality of the material itself. Coupled with the scenario whereupon Graham insisted on overdubbing all the vocal parts himself on these songs, which must have antagonised Allan and Tony to a degree, you had a band working within varying degrees of harmony.

According to reports that have since surfaced in more recent years, Graham was always looking for more inventive ways to record different sounds. At various stages during these album sessions, vocals were either recorded with a metal waste bin placed over his head, in order to get a distinctive echo, or both he and Allan reverted to cutting vocals from underneath a bass drum, again achieving a hollowed effect.

'It was more or less the album he took over and decided that the songs that he'd written he wanted to sing and do the harmonies. We let him have his way. We thought *maybe this guy has something that we don't know about,* recalled Allan.[6]

Reportedly, Graham had written 'Postcard' with Jimi Hendrix in mind, encouraging his stressed friend to take a break from the increasing pressures building up on him. Graham had previously visited Jimi, bassist Noel Redding and drummer "Mitch" Mitchell during the recording dates for their *Axis: Bold As Love* album, taped a few months earlier, even offering up percussive support on 'If Six Was Nine' and vocal backing on the 'You've Got Me Floating' session. One can only imagine how 'Postcard' would have sounded had Jimi repaid the favour and plugged in on it…

Despite the credits for all of the featured songs being equally shared amongst the three principal songwriters – the Clarke, Hicks & Nash byline remained firm – it was becoming very apparent that the threesome were now splintering and working on their own compositions, but with a significantly lesser amount of creative input from their bandmates. This arrangement of co-crediting was immensely frustrating to some. By Tony's own admission he had little to do with the creation of 'King Midas In Reverse', but such was the arrangement with GRALTO Music that he still shared equal billing with its main composer, Graham Nash, and so it continued with much of the album (a later agreement, signed by all three principle songwriters, corrected these oversights and gave back credits on many of the songs, written solely as individuals). Only Graham could have related so closely with his lyrical contributions to 'Elevated Observations', discussing being high, finding your head and killing one's ego. However, even he was now beginning to realise that the whole scene was shifting once more and that the "flower power" phase was waning.

'Flower power was killed by all the people who just weren't genuine,' he was to note in *Melody Maker*. 'All the real flower people have moved out of Haight-Ashbury.'

'The basic idea was fine. Very nice. But there is all this gimmick thing and so, when the gimmick dies, the whole flower business will die,' Tony was to comment further in *Beat Instrumental*. 'Some of the flower people make themselves a laughing stock, with their hands clutching at flowers. It's a good idea which will be killed by the people who follow it.

'Progress in music? We have ideas which are very progressive. I hoped to be the first to use the Vox wah-wah pedal on disc, it's on our soon-out LP, but Jimi Hendrix beat me to it. I think it's great, but it's true that electronic devices are coming in and I suppose you can see a time when the musician will be more or less a push-button star. I'm not keen on that. But take the guitar. Soon a genuine guitar sound will be back, all the rage. And that can't be bad.'

The release of the *Butterfly* album coincided with the group jetting off across the Atlantic Ocean once again, this time for an extended four-week tour. Unfortunately, it couldn't have come at a worse time, as sales for the LP were sluggish. Despite the group and production team pulling together such a polished collection of material for the release, flowing effortlessly from track to track, the release was, inexplicably, a complete commercial disaster. *Butterfly* failed to even touch the expanded Top 40 LP charts.

Certainly, EMI's lack of promotional support affected the album's sales, failing to even feature it on their inner sleeve promotional campaign for 1967, and the lack of any recognisable band images on the front cover would have hardly aided the impact in the stores. Besides, it had only been a matter of months since *Evolution* had first appeared and maybe it was too much, too soon, lost amongst the wealth of significant LP releases put out in the second half of 1967. However, even to this day, it remains a conundrum as to where it all went wrong for this Nash-led project. The supposed "failure" of 'King Midas In Reverse' certainly raised concerns and the warning bells would have been chiming in the minds of many as to the direction in which they were being steered. For such a successful act, it is truly unfathomable as to how the new LP sold so few copies, even without the support of a hit 45 backing it. America's favourite sons, The Beach Boys, and their parent Capitol label, had considered their own work of art, *Pet Sounds*, a comparative failure when it scraped to a lowly #10 position in *Billboard* in the aftermath of a run of successful album releases. For The Hollies to follow the relative success of *Evolution* with such a poor showing was unthinkable.

'EMI never really put any work into promoting our albums,' Bobby was to state to *Shindig* magazine's Andy Morten during 2010. 'It was a case of "you're a successful band so therefore you make an album". They got their album and that was it. They'd just stick it out without any promotion.'

A major supporter of the band during earlier years had been the pirate radio stations, moored off the English coastline and broadcasting from outside territorial waters. Unhindered by the strict regimes portrayed by the BBC, stations such as Radio Caroline and Radio London were only too happy to play the deeper album cuts by the popular bands. However, once they were shut down by new legislation brought in during August of 1967, a lot of these bands, including The Hollies, lost a significant amount of airplay for their long-playing releases. The BBC tended to concentrate solely on the chart hits.

'We were undeniably known as a singles band,' Tony was to add during the same *Shindig* interview. 'And that's what confused people. They thought if they bought a new album it would be full of catchy choruses like the singles, but that wasn't really the case.'

Subsequently, having presumably discovered that scenario with previous releases, no one bothered to spend the cash this time around.

Having boarded a trans-Atlantic flight, bound for America's west coast, on 9th November 1967, their first appearance on the winter Stateside jaunt was on TV's popular *Joey Bishop Show*, broadcast on the ABC network on 13th November. Filmed in Hollywood's famous Vine Street Theatre, it was during the recording of the show that the band happened to hear fellow guest, actor Ross Martin, talk about his charity work for asthmatic children. All five members were so moved by Martin's dedication that, during their interview segment, they informed the host they had agreed to donate their entire appearance fee for the show to aid Martin's charity.

A second recording for television occurred that same week, with a guest showing on the often-controversial *Smothers Brothers Comedy Hour* (broadcast the following month). Hosted by two streetwise entertainers and comedians, Tom and Dick Smothers, both popular performers themselves on the folk music circuit during the early years of the decade, the show had been launched earlier that year, and within weeks had evolved into a programme that, as has often been stated, "extended the boundaries of what was considered permissible in television satire". It was a new, satirical, and somewhat groundbreaking comedy-variety show that, over time, gave notable airplay to many underground or new musical artists, regardless of political stance or nature. It took risks, often paying the network censorship penalty as a result, but it was a commercial success nonetheless, and was considered a "hip" alternative to the many staid shows that saturated the stations and broadcasting airwaves throughout the industry. For the good-looking, ever-cheery Hollies, it was primetime exposure, and whilst their lip-synched performance of the cheerful-sounding 'Carrie Anne' was at odds with many of the guest appearances that had graced the show, notably Buffalo Springfield, Jefferson Airplane, The Blues Magoos and fellow Brits The Who (who notoriously over-utilised a gunpowder explosion effect during the riotous climax to 'My Generation'), it was a further opportunity to share their music across the vast continent and into the central heartlands where, to date, they had made little impact. A further performance of the more *of-the-times* 'Dear Eloise' was also played out for the cameras, this time with Graham studiously "writing" with feathered quill and ink whilst a promotional film was shown alongside.

*"Dear Eloise, I am writing to say..."*

Epic Records had issued 'Dear Eloise' as a single in advance of the visit, as had a number of other countries (strangely, the UK opted not to follow suit), but despite the airtime afforded to it, and the undeniable hit potential, the 45 (Epic 5-10251) limped into *Billboard* at the lowly #50 position. The label followed this with the official US release of *Butterfly,* although, once again, the stateside executives, high up in their smoke-filled executive suites, chose to retitle, repackage and realign the entire concept of the original album. Three of the more adventurous cuts, 'Pegasus', 'Try It' and 'Elevated Observations', were all omitted with 'King Midas In Reverse' and the *Evolution* filler 'Leave Me' added in their place. The result was the far weaker 11-track *Dear Eloise/King Midas In Reverse* album. Hot on the heels of Imperial's best-selling *Greatest Hits* collection, this new Epic release failed to chart.

On 18th November, the group officially kicked off the month-long tour with a live appearance at the State Fairground Coliseum in Salt Lake City, Utah. From there, it was a journey across the states, taking in shows in Illinois, Texas, Ohio, Rhode Island, Washington DC and New York as they travelled back towards the east coast, with the flight back to London during the second week of December.

Appearing alongside such established names *en route* as Simon and Garfunkel (who they supported at the 7,800-seat G. Rolie White Coliseum in Texas), The Strawberry Alarm Clock and American Breed, along with a series of lesser known acts – The Crystal Mesh, The Mosaic Virus, The Plain Brown Wrappers, Rubber Band and New York R&B specialists, Wilmer and The Dukes, the setlist for the tour (varying between venues) was comprised of 'I Can't Let Go', 'Stop! Stop! Stop!', 'Look Through Any Window', 'The Games We Play', 'On A Carousel', 'A Taste of Honey', 'I'm Alive', 'Alice's Restaurant', 'Dear Eloise', 'Butterfly', 'Stewball', 'Carrie Anne', 'Just One Look', 'Bus Stop' and Bob Dylan's 'The Times They Are A-Changin''. Whilst the inclusion of the folkie 'Alice's Restaurant', a short cover version of Arlo Guthrie's then-recent composition, was an interesting addition, it was the inclusion of the title track from the *Butterfly* album that drew the most attention. Essentially, a Graham Nash solo performance, accompanying himself on acoustic guitar and supported by the original orchestral studio master track, this song was highlighted yet further when, during a stopover in Philadelphia, they filmed a three-song appearance on the *Mike Douglas TV Show*, with the ballad sandwiched in between versions of 'On A Carousel' and 'Dear Eloise'. Not only was Graham the highlighted vocalist on all three of these songs, but then the host of the show, along with his infatuated co-host, actress and singer Kaye Stevens, gave scant attention to his bandmates, much to the noticeable chagrin of Allan and Tony.

With Stevens pawing away at his neatly trimmed facial hair, Graham was clearly embarrassed by the overly attentive approach, but he politely accepted a series of Gold Awards, acknowledging sales for each of the 'Stop! Stop! Stop!', 'Carrie Anne', 'Bus Stop' and 'On A Carousel' singles, along with the recent Imperial *Greatest Hits* collection.

This use of the original studio tapes to aid the onstage sound on the tour was, for the time, a rarity amongst stage acts, albeit one that was to become the norm over the ensuing years as artists found it increasingly difficult to represent complex studio productions in a live concert setting. For The Hollies, in 1967, it offered up a way to represent the best sound they could, and the closest option to the original record releases for their audience.

'We got the original tapes and plugged it into the amplifiers,' explained tour manager Rod Shields to a local reporter. 'Thus, the teens heard 'Games We Play' with French horns, trumpets and violins and 'Carrie Anne' with steel drums...'

A further highlight of the visit came about when, before taking to the stage of Cleveland's Music Hall, in Ohio, the quintet paid a visit to a nearby children's hospital, entertaining the many youngsters with songs and stories.

Graham Nash of The Hollies started to sing 'Bus Stop' and the whole room came alive. Sneakers wiggled. Hands clapped. Others kept up the beat in stocking feet.

'This is wonderful. I can't believe it,' said Darren Richardson, 8.

Neither could many Clevelanders. How often does a top-flight group take the time and trouble to give an hour's free concert for crippled children? This was Rosemary Hospital. The wiggling sneakers and stockings were on bed-bound teens. The tappers and clappers were in wheelchairs or braces.

*The Plain Dealer*
Cleveland, OH
November 1967

The Hollies Have Teens Spinning
Public Music Hall, Cleveland, OH. November 24, 1967
The lights went out. Suddenly five young Englishmen were in the

spotlight singing 'I Can't Let Go'. Neither could the young audience. With the final curtain, two dozen young girls popped through police lines to hug The Hollies.

'Too much! We love you forever,' scribbled fan Reggie Sietman, 19, in her love note. She sat through the 7:00 and 9:30pm supershows, but many of the teens couldn't sit. They stood up and screamed and waved for more.

'Tuff show!' said Laurie Middleton, 14.

*The Plain Dealer*
Cleveland, OH
November 1967

Having arrived back in the UK in mid-December, the group jumped straight into the festive spirit with a short flight across the English Channel to Holland for a seasonal '67 appearance on the local *Fenklup* (Fanclub) TV series, a monthly show broadcast on the VARA television network. Rather surprisingly, some might say, the band chose to perform a version of 'Step Inside' which, whilst perhaps being the most commercial song on the recent *Butterfly* album, had only appeared as the flip-side on the Dutch 45 release of 'Dear Eloise'. To many, it was an unfamiliar composition. Nevertheless, with the festive season approaching, The Hollies also performed a singalong version of 'Jingle Bells' for the cameras.

The ever-loyal following in Sweden had also received an early Christmas present when the band contributed two minutes of madness to a festive giveaway from *Bild Journalen*, a popular teen magazine published in Stockholm. This giveaway came in the form of a 7-inch flexi-disc, comprising songs from two local Swedish acts along with a jovial Christmas message from The Hollies, incorporating an impromptu rendition of 'White Christmas' thrown in for good measure. Nothing more than a collector's curio, it remains a highly prized addition for Hollies-fans to this day.

As 1968 began, The Hollies found themselves in unsettled territory. Lower than expected 45 and LP sales of their latest product had the band questioning their next move. In one corner there was Graham, unhappy with the never-ending conveyor belt of pop hits, intent on developing the group and taking them into new and uncharted terrain. In the other corner were the rest of the band, content in knowing their boundaries and playing within them. But a lot can change in the space of twelve months... as 1968 would show.

THE *NEW MUSICAL EXPRESS* 1967 POLL WINNERS
Category: British Vocal Group

1. The Beatles
2. The Rolling Stones
3. The Hollies
4. The Bee Gees
5. The Kinks
6. The Shadows
7. The Seekers
8. The Jimi Hendrix Experience
9. The Tremeloes
10. Traffic
11. Dave Dee, Dozy, Beaky, Mick & Tich
12. The Troggs

# CHAPTER FIFTEEN

# "WHITE CHALK WRITTEN ON RED BRICK..."

The first Abbey Road recording sessions of 1968 kicked off in fine style. Between the 9th and 11th of January, two new compositions were committed to tape, and yet neither would see the significant release in the coming months that both deserved. One would appear as the B-side to the next pop-orientated 45, whilst the second would languish in the vaults for almost two years before finally seeing a public appearance.

'Open Up Your Eyes', a new Clarke-Hicks-Nash offering, was a step away from their current predicament – but in both directions. It wasn't the catchy commercial pop music that the public so craved from the group but, in turn, it wasn't in the more progressive, experimental camp that Graham desired to explore either. Yes, it contained the lyrical images of everyday life that Graham Gouldman had previously and so expertly proclaimed – the wonderful faces with their appointments, the bald-headed bankers and the pig-tailed schoolgirl with freckly nose – but the song was perfectly crafted, with tight harmonies, intermittent time patterns and Tony's catchy banjo middle eight.

'Wings', a song that reportedly evolved after repeated listening to Buffalo Springfield's majestic 1967 ballad 'Expecting To Fly', as composed by Neil Young, was an equally stunning affair.

Allan Clarke recently recalled on BBC Wales radio, 'I remember once I was in the Whisky a Go Go club [during the recent visit to Los Angeles] and Stephen

Stills and Neil Young came over to me and said, "We'd like you to listen to our album." I'd never heard the Buffalo Springfield before so they took me to their hotel and there was a big wardrobe in their room where they'd put two speakers inside, and they said, "We want you to sit in there and get the full experience." But before they closed the doors, they blew in some stuff that I was not normally used to, so you can imagine what the album sounded like! I was just blown away. 'Expecting To Fly' has always been one of my favourite songs since…' [23]

Allan took inspiration from the Californian-based quintet and then structured a similar ballad with his bandmates by simply strumming the guitar and letting the poetic words and feelings flow, although the lyrics did alternate slightly over the coming weeks. Two months after cutting the tune, the group performed a differing set of lyrics on the *David Symonds Radio Show*, taped for the BBC on 25th March.

*"Birds fly away out of tune*
*Running in circles, nowhere to turn*
*Why do we want them to walk, when they can fly?"*

'Wings'
Music and Lyrics by Allan Clarke and Graham Nash

Shortly after recording the song, the band also made a promotional film for the composition, filmed for the Swedish *Popside* television show, a moody black and white affair featuring the five members sitting around in a circle, with the camera artistically panning amongst them as they played the tune. What then makes it all the more surprising is that this wonderful recording was then returned to the vaults, unreleased, and no further announcement was forthcoming. Possibly there was a master plan to put it out as a single, or to include it on a proposed follow-up to *Butterfly*. Several other compositions were taken into Abbey Road over the coming months, suggesting a mooted successor was being considered but, having not seen a UK 45 release since September 1967, there was still nothing forthcoming for the stores.

The 25th of January saw the band still gamely promoting the 'Dear Eloise' release as a single in the European market with a further lip-synched performance on Germany's *Der Goldene Schub*. The single went on to achieve Top 10 status in many of these regions, including the #2 slot in Austria and #8 in Germany. A week later, the boys were back in the recording studios in London, intent on a belated follow-up to 'King Midas In Reverse'. Having been made all too aware as to how and what the public expected of them – bright and breezy, cheerful and clean-cut – the new composition they commenced work on was the polar opposite to the adventure and experimentation of Graham's perceived masterwork.

Taking the title of the song from the names of their other halves, Jennifer being the name of Allan's wife, and Eccles being the maiden name of Graham's wife, Rose, 'Jennifer Eccles' wasn't deliberately crafted in such a retrospective style, but they all knew that this was exactly what the public and their record label wanted from them.

'We weren't trying to go back on this. It's a new song...' Allan was to say to *Disc & Music Echo*. 'I happened to find the tune going around in my head one day and I went over to see Graham and we sorted out the lyrics. Then we recorded it in a new studio, that made a difference, and everyone liked it...'

Well, perhaps not everyone. Graham was particularly scathing about the song when offering up his recollections in *Wild Tales*.

'Puppy love in the schoolyard again. I thought we'd grown up a little, that we were past that shit. But I went for it again, which pissed me off big time!'[1]

For the first time, the group, still working alongside Ron Richards, utilised an alternative recording facility to cut the initial tracks for the song. With his independent status as an AIR producer, Ron was familiar with a great number of the studio set-ups around the capital, and the small studio above Chappell Music in Bond Street, central London, was just one of them. Subsequently, on 3rd February, The Hollies took up residency there for the day to record 'Jennifer Eccles'.

One cannot fault the commercialism of the composition. Simply put, it is an incredibly well-crafted pop song, but the novelty sound effect employed on the chorus, instigated by Ron Richards, has certainly marred the longevity of the work beyond its 1960s hit status. Using a steel guitar to mimic a wolf-whistle effect gave the song distinct originality but scarred it indefinitely. Brought in to perform this unique slide, in addition to adding accompaniment to the band (at the suggestion of band roadie and technician Dek Whyment), was Rod King, well known on the UK cabaret and television circuit for his abilities on the instrument. Rod would also later suggest that another drummer/percussionist was also in evidence that day:

'I played the steel guitar on 'Jennifer Eccles', complete with the wolf whistle. My guitar at the time was a Fender 400 that I played for years in shows all over the world. The record was done at Chappell's Studio on Bond Street and there was even an extra drummer, Clem Cattini, on the session.' (*Steel Guitar Forum*: 2006)

With a further sweetening session undertaken within the familiar environs of Abbey Road shortly afterwards, the finished recording was placed on the EMI release schedules for the following month. The group, meanwhile, keen to consolidate their newly acquired status abroad, once again packed their suitcases and boarded a flight to the USA for a spring tour that took in cross-state performances in Florida, Illinois, Wisconsin, Virginia, Minnesota and New York, as well as two shows across the border in Ottawa, Canada. However, within days of them landing on the west coast of America, before they kicked off the tour with a series of television recordings, David Crosby (who had recently been fired from The Byrds) turned up at the band's hotel on Wilshire Boulevard and whisked Graham away to the highlife – a party at 3615 Shady Oak in Studio City, just south of Ventura Boulevard, near Laurel Canyon. Owned by Monkee Peter Tork, this location was known throughout the surrounding Hollywood hills as party central and was frequented daily by the hip and the happening. Not that they needed a reason to party. Clothing was optional. The gathering was thrown to celebrate Jimi Hendrix's headlining appearance at the nearby Shrine Auditorium (Hendrix had previously supported The Monkees on a recent tour and was close friends with Tork). In the shadow of the Hollywood Hills, Graham was duly introduced to fellow singer-songwriter, and Buffalo Springfield founder, Stephen Stills, a regular houseguest of Tork's and one who had earlier auditioned but failed in his bid to become a Monkee himself. Allan had already raved about Stills' band to Graham, having met them himself during their previous Stateside visit. The bearded Hollie was already enamoured with the music and now the human connection was in place.

Both Stills and Crosby were subsequently invited to attend The Hollies' first show on the tour, a last-minute promotional appearance taking place in the very hub of Los Angeles hipness, the Whisky a Go Go club on the Sunset Strip. Performing a setlist that featured 'Stop! Stop! Stop!', 'Look Through Any Window', 'The Times They Are A-Changin'', 'On A Carousel', 'Stewball', 'Just One Look', 'I Can't Let Go', 'Butterfly', 'A Taste Of Honey', 'Carrie Anne', 'Bus Stop', 'Very Last Day' and 'Too Much Monkey Business', along with brief acknowledgements for Elvis' hit 'Teddy Bear' and The Lovin' Spoonful's

'Daydream', the performance was the usual quality production that the band had honed to perfection across the years. Also in attendance that night was a gathering of rock royalty from the city's music hierarchy and, in addition to Crosby and Stills, the show was watched by Cass Elliott and her then-beau Lee Kiefer, producer Lou Adler, Brian Wilson, Lee Hazelwood, various Monkees and Buffalo Springfield members, Eric Burdon and Johnny Weider from The Animals, Marvin Gaye, Jackie DeShannon, teen-zine editor Ann Moses and various prominent DJs from the LA radio stations.

If Wednesday was the day to turn on your heart, Wednesday evening was the night to really turn on, musically.

St. Valentine's Day saw an appearance of what was overheard to be called "the greatest performing group today". The Whisky a Go Go swung with The Hollies.

As the 10:15 showtime neared, crowds that had gathered earlier in the evening found their way through the little doorway on Sunset. Inside, as the light shows flashed and blinked in their mind-expanding splendour, patrons mingled with a list of guests that might be mistaken for a Who's Who of pop music.

As the dancers finished doing their thing to the recorded music, the lights dimmed and the only spotlight that shone on the stage revealed Micky Dolenz who smiled and said, 'Everybody, here's The Hollies...'

*Independent Star News*
Pasadena
February 1968

Later that night, high on the reception and heaven only knows what else, Graham, David and Stephen found harmony together as they drove through the illuminated city streets. By contrast, Bernie Calvert, opting for a quieter lifestyle, settled for an intimate meal with Moses.

"My time hanging around with The Hollies was brief," recalls Ann today. "I truly can't remember details, but Bernie was a sweet young man."

Having fulfilled their Hollywood obligations, including appearances at the *Hollywood Palace* variety spectacular performing 'Jennifer Eccles', alongside Phil 'The Bear Necessities' Harris, and on ABC's popular *The Dating Game,* which even featured Tony as a guest on the contest, with the band playing 'Bus Stop' at the end of the episode, the group headed out on the road.

During their performance on 16th February, whilst playing at the University of Florida in Gainesville, a local seventeen-year-old who occasionally helped out on the campus grounds offered his services for the evening as a roadie. The band duly accepted and having assisted the band in and out of the venue, Thomas Earl Petty went on his way. Also in attendance for that show, joyfully sitting and watching from just in front of the stage, was Petty's friend, a youthful Donald Felder. In later years, he would find acclaim as lead guitarist for The Eagles, and co-writer of the iconic 'Hotel California', but back in 1968 he was as much enamoured with the touring British band as those sitting around him.

'When the Hollies came to Gainesville and played a gig at the university, I jumped at the chance to go see them,' Felder later recounted in his autobiography. 'I pushed my way to the front of the crowd and watched Allan Clarke and Graham Nash singing their hit, 'Bus Stop', and was mightily impressed. They looked so different. I took mental notes on their clothes and how they wore their hair, and there was something about Graham Nash's voice that really appealed to me. He not only played well, he looked like he was having fun. When he smiled down at me in the front row, while singing, I couldn't help but smile back.'[71]

The 1st of March saw the group play a show at the Civic Dome in Virginia Beach, VA, having performed a free show earlier that day for the crew of a homecoming aircraft carrier, the USS *Independence*, fresh out of Vietnam, at the nearby US Naval base.

March 15th then saw them cross the border into Canada for a series of three appearances, and it was there, whilst performing two shows at the Capitol Theatre in Ottawa, that Graham encountered another of Crosby's many acquaintances. At a press launch held in the city, he was introduced to, and subsequently fell for, Joni Mitchell.

Five of the finest had Ottawa teens stomping their feet at the Capitol Theatre Friday night.

The Hollies, in their area debut, performed before two packed houses and proved why they have been referred to as a "group's group" by other British artists. Instrumentally, they are superb. Vocally, The Hollies are unlike most groups – they can sing. Onstage, they create an impression of relaxed professionalism. They are at home with the audience and bring a sense of personal style to the concert.

*The Ottawa Citizen*

March 1968

Unlike their recent appearance at the Whisky a Go Go, both 'Dear Eloise' and 'Jennifer Eccles' featured during their on-the-road live appearances and, whilst inwardly frustrated at having to perform the upcoming single and suffer the sickening wolf whistle each night, outwardly Graham displayed the professionalism and honesty expected, offering up exactly what the public wanted.

'We write and record simple songs because that's what people want. We tried one different song, 'King Midas In Reverse', and it bombed, so we went back to songs about girls. Every teenager can identify with 'Carrie Anne' or 'Jennifer Eccles'.

'I like some of the more intricate music of today, but obviously our fans won't go for a change in image the way they did for The Beatles. We're a happy group playing happy songs...'

Graham Nash

*The Ottawa Citizen*

March 1968

Back home, 'Jennifer Eccles' b/w 'Open Up Your Eyes' was released as the new Hollies 45 on 22nd March 1968 (Parlophone 5680). With the five members now back on home soil, the promotional bandwagon was once again rolled out, much to Graham's distaste. He now had to go out and perform, smile and lip-synch the single endlessly, maintaining an air of Hollie-clean-cut enjoyment, whilst underneath it all, becoming ever more frustrated, embarrassed, dissatisfied...

Despite such discontent within the inner circle, the group still received the plaudits from their musical peers. Peter Frampton, frontman for The Herd, recalled his first meeting with The Hollies during this period, commenting in his 2020 autobiography, *Do You Feel Like I Do?* – 'I first met Graham Nash and Allan Clarke [when] the two of them would come into the dressing room, Graham with his black Gibson acoustic, and they'd sing Buddy Holly songs. Those two voices, Allan and Graham... I was speechless. They were so good and with such ease.'

Appearances on *Top of the Pops, All Systems Freeman, Tarbuck's Back* and *Dee Time*, along with European promotional appearances on German, Danish and Belgian TV networks, saw the new single re-establish the band back in the upper echelons of the UK charts, topping out at #7 during an eleven-week run, whilst also charting in at least sixteen other countries. Then, sandwiched in between promotional appearances and plans for the next overseas tour, the group managed to squeeze in a series of further recording sessions back at the EMI studios, with the next potential album release in mind.

'Tomorrow When It Comes', predominantly an Allan Clarke composition, saw the band once again try to take their sound to a new level, with a heavier guitar effect, accompanied by prominent bass and drum fills. The song was also later offered to a group known as The Stack, but no recording was ever officially issued. Meanwhile, Graham's contributions included the contemplative 'Relax', which saw him take the experimental style he had developed during the *Butterfly* sessions, including the phased vocal effects, and walk a similar path of lightweight reflection. They even made a rough but abortive attempt at cutting a version of the song Graham had composed the previous summer, during his vacation in Morocco. He felt that 'Marrakesh Express' was another step in the right direction for where the band should be heading. The other members, along with Ron Richards, disagreed but cut the backing track all the same. It remained in the vaults, as did the other new tracks.

The spring of 1968 saw the group embark on another foreign excursion, this time taking in Japan for two live appearances, their first visit to the Far East. A performance at the two-thousand seat Shibuya Kokaido in Tokyo on 24th April was followed the next evening by a show at the nearby Otemachi Sankei Hall, another regular performing venue for many travelling western musicians.

*Stop! Stop! Stop! / Just One Look / I'm Alive / Look Through Any Window / I Can't Let Go / Bus Stop / Carrie Anne / On A Carousel / Jennifer Eccles / Dear Eloise / Butterfly / The Times They Are A-Changin' / A Taste Of Honey*

24th April 1968
Shinuya Kokaido setlist

Whilst in Japan, they also made some guest appearances on the Kyoto television network, performing live vocals to pre-recorded tracks on 'Bus Stop', 'Stop! Stop! Stop!' and 'Jennifer Eccles'. The group are known to have appeared on at least two shows, including *Hit Parade*, but surviving detail remains scarce.

Following this latest overseas venture, they returned home, only to go straight out on tour once again, crisscrossing the familiar width and breadth of the UK. This time, it was a twelve-date package tour with a difference.

What might be labelled the snob tour of 1968 opens its doors to the general public in Shrewsbury on Friday, May 17. Only three acts will be on the bill. The Hollies – now way up on the normal pop group; the Scaffold – with their distinctive brand of sartorial jollity; and Paul Jones – with his ethereal brand of satirical elegance. This will be the premiere of the first of the new-look tours.

'We planned it ourselves and chose the people we wanted to be with,' Hollies drummer Bobby Elliot explained. 'We thought people were tired of seeing endless groups, so we decided to have only three especially good acts and give them time to present themselves properly.'

*Disc & Music Echo*
May 1968

In addition to having their two chosen support acts accompany them on the road, they also took along the Mike Vickers Orchestra to each venue, trusting the now-established arranger with the duty of representing a fuller sound on the stage, thus matching the lush recordings featured on recent vinyl releases.

Scaffold member Mike McCartney now recalls, 'I first came across The Hollies in 1967. I didn't see them at the Cavern at all. I only went there to see our kid play, so I first met The Hollies on *Top of the Pops*, in Manchester, as an act just going on. We would have seen them, they would have seen us, trying to dodge cameras. Those things would travel a million miles an hour, trying to knock over the teenage audience! Then I got to know Graham, just in the business, as it were. We had a similar sense of humour…

'The first time we would have worked together was that tour. They liked us, The Scaffold, because we weren't a threat. We were a comedy, singalong group.'[78]

With The Hollies dressed in white stage suits, with an ominous cabaret-styled bow tie or two also on show at some venues, the tour was a huge success in the eyes of both critics and concert attendees. Sticking predominantly to the recent setlists but removing 'Dear Eloise' and replacing it with a returning 'King Midas In Reverse', The Hollies closed the show each night to stunning effect. With an impressive lighting backdrop projection, and Vickers' orchestral arrangements to the fore, the band ran through the gamut of hits along with the now-familiar 'Butterfly' and 'The Times They Are A-Changin''. New songs also added included renditions of Peter, Paul and Mary's 'Puff The Magic Dragon' and Roger Miller's 'Dang Me', before they finished each performance with 'Blowin' In The Wind'. Graham even responded to enquiries about their take on the Dylan tune by informing the journalist from the *New Musical Express* that they were considering cutting a version for their next single. Indeed, soon afterwards, they performed the song live on the *Bobby Gentry* TV show, taped for the BBC, and followed that three months later by taking it into the studio. The version cut that day subsequently remained in the vaults for the time being, excepting for two B-side appearances in Sweden and Germany.

Despite his reservations over where the band were heading and the lack of positivity he was receiving in return towards his own intentions for them, Graham was strikingly upbeat following the opening show of the tour, thrilled that the audience came to listen to the music and see the presentation, as opposed to the screamers of old.

'They listened, man, didn't they?' he enthused to anyone who would listen. 'That was the most important thing. They listened. Now, on the next tour, we'll be able to go out there and do something really different.'

Clearly, those fourteen- and fifteen-year-old fans who had previously followed the group around the country were maturing and growing older with the band as well. And yet, despite the optimism in evidence, Graham still had too many issues to hold within, choosing to unburden himself in the *New Musical Express* just prior to the tour commencing. It couldn't have been the best of timing:

'I believe in a completely different musical direction to that in which The Hollies are going. I also need to be alone a lot to get the best out of myself as a songwriter. It's very stimulating for me and it's something I enjoy.

'I can't say if I'll be leaving The Hollies soon. All I know is that last year I came close to it twice and it could happen at any time.'

Allan would later recall touring with The Scaffold for other reasons: 'We became great friends with them, and the rarest Hollies recording was one we did with The Scaffold. It was a recording that we did on Newcastle station, in a singing booth, in 1968 and it was actually myself and Graham, and The Scaffold in there, and we sang 'Tiptoe Through The Tulips'. Apparently, there's only one copy of that and [Scaffold member] Roger McGough has it...' [45]

'Those crazy nights on tour with the Hollies!' responded McGough recently, when asked about the tour for this book. 'I wish I could lay on a feast of rock 'n' roll memories but, alas, it was all too dim and distant. I also wish I did have the copy of 'Tiptoe...' but I have no recollection [of it]...'

Elaborating one step further, Mike McCartney today recalls that 'we played Scotland, somewhere on the east coast, and after we've done the gig, we were going to go back to Liverpool or Manchester, but Allan, Graham and the three of us had heard about this thing in Newcastle. It was a new drink called Newcastle Brown! Being professional rock 'n' rollers, we had to check it out. Just the five of us. We had this young, impetuous attitude and we said, "let's just go for it!" So, we got on this train to go home, but we had to stop off in Newcastle, *en route*, to test this Newcastle Brown. Now, we get to Newcastle station and there was this little one-man record booth on the platform. You put in some money and out came this floppy record and, being in showbusiness, we said, "Come on! We gotta make a record!" So, there were the five of us, crammed into this one-man booth, and we decided to sing Tiny Tim's 'Tiptoe Through The Tulips'! And, remember, we did this *before* we got to the pub!

'I think John Gorman (the third member of the trio) had the record, but I think he may have lost it now,' he continues, before finally adding with a laugh, 'or he sold it on eBay for millions!'[78]

The May 24th show, held at the Lewisham Odeon in south-east London, was even taped by EMI, using a basic mobile 2-track recording facility. The initial idea was to release a live recording as the next LP in place of any forthcoming studio releases. Alas, the band were not happy with the results, citing the performances substandard on an artistic level and that the tapes were spoiled by the sound of screaming girls (not everyone was listening intently, it seems...). The limitations of the 2-track facility were also noticeably evident.

When The Hollies hit Lewisham Odeon on Friday, the pop world was there to see them. Paul McCartney and Monkee Micky Dolenz were among the strangely quiet audience who listened intently to what was undoubtedly the best sound ever to come from a cinema package tour.

The odd screamer was uncomfortably out of place and the applause was manual rather than vocal, and the net result was immense gratification.

*Disc & Music Echo*
June 1968

'We played Lewisham and they were all there, McCartney, the lot,' noted Allan in *Rave* magazine. 'I wish they hadn't told me. I felt we had to show them something and it put me right down. And because I worried about it, I did a bad show. I know I could have done better.'

Portions of the surviving tapes were subsequently released many years later as part of a multi-CD set; *The Clarke, Hicks & Nash Years*, highlighting the band at the top of their game. The precise instrumentation and razor-sharp harmonies, with the fully orchestrated 'King Midas In Reverse', despite the slightly off-key trumpets, gave the impression of a band at their peak.

Then, just a matter of days after the final show of the tour, held in the Midlands city of Derby, *Disc & Music Echo* ran an article that seemed to sense the end was near.

Graham Nash, leading light behind The Hollies, is to split from the group to record his own solo album. 'This album is something I've been thinking about for a long time. I am staying with the group, of course, it's just that I must do this album to satisfy myself and if I hadn't been able to do it, I would have quit to do it. I'm not really interested in what the rest of The Hollies think about it – I'm going to do it.'

Whilst on the road, Graham had been building up a catalogue of new compositions, songs that, in his words, were "very personal, very un-Hollies type". Titles such as 'Lady Of The Island' and 'Right Between The Eyes' seemed to flow out of him. He also made plans to travel to New York the following month to work independently with The Fool, the Dutch design group who had previously designed the *Evolution* LP packaging, and to start sessions for his proposed album. Nevertheless, despite his grand plans becoming very public knowledge, no further announcements were forthcoming. However, he did find the time to strike out alone once again. This time, it was providing backing vocals at a Donovan recording session, held during May at London's Olympic Studios where, alongside Mike McCartney/McGear, he contributed to the delightful round of harmonies during the close of 'Happiness Runs'.

A further series of tentative Hollies recording sessions, with Graham's full participation, were undertaken during the spring and summer months, all with the ominous shadow hanging overhead. Many contained the familiar Hollies-sound running throughout the sessions – 'Like Every Time Before', 'Man With No Expression' and 'Do The Best You Can' were all polished, upbeat and cheerful, with 'Man With No Expression' being a particularly strong cut. This tune had been written by a friend of Graham's, singer-songwriter Terry Reid, back in the early 1960s (and originally entitled 'Without Expression'). Adapted by Graham for The Hollies' version, Terry generously gave Graham a co-credit in acknowledgement of his latter contribution.

'That song is one of my favourites,' notes Bobby. 'It's just right for the period. But Ron didn't really seem to take to it, and Allan had his own ideas. And it was that period where I felt it all sort of pulling apart.' [42]

Around this time, the band also laid down an updated studio rendition of the concert staple 'A Taste Of Honey', another early 1960s composition which showed that, with a strong arrangement, The Hollies could swing in such a fashion that it made one wonder what they *couldn't* do. A similar swing arrangement, complete with a big and bold brass accompaniment, was also attempted when they cut the Bob Dylan favourite 'Blowin' in the Wind', featuring two of Bobby's jazz heroes, Ronnie Scott and Ronnie Ross. This took the band further into unchartered territories that didn't sit altogether comfortably with what they or their fan base were used to. Graham Nash, in particular, was noticeably appalled by the production, calling it "slick, saccharine and Las Vegasy". When members of the band suggested that they record a full album of Dylan covers, despite Nash's initial acceptance of the concept, it was (according to *Wild Tales*) the final factor that "broke the camel's back".

'That was it as far as I was concerned. I was convinced The Hollies had lost their focus. No more Dylan. I put my foot down.' [1]

One other new Clarke-Hicks-Nash composition that they also took into the studio during this period was called 'Survival Of The Fittest', a title suggested to the trio by Bobby, who was urging his bandmates to contribute together, as a team once more.

''Survival Of The Fittest' was written in the Forrester Hotel in Stockholm,' Bobby later recounted to BBC radio's Mark Radcliffe. 'We knew that Graham was pretty much well on his way but we were all still friendly and so I said, "You guys, get some writing done" and I pushed them into this room and said, "Don't come out 'til you write something!" and they wrote this. 'Survival Of The Fittest' doesn't come into the lyric at all, but that was my idea of the title because it was the very last song that the songwriting team wrote together and I thought, *well, let's see who survives the longest after this…'*

The song's lyrics related to the tale of a female artist, forced to perform in public against her inner wishes – "*She's so empty inside, lies to herself and the public…*" words that quite possibly came directly from Graham, reflecting his feelings and situation at that particular point in time. Unfortunately, the song would remain unreleased for now.

In August, Graham went back to the US, alone, and spent time with Crosby, Stills and Joni Mitchell. His relationship with his wife, Rose, was crumbling, and his fascination with this Canadian songstress was deepening. He had recently moved out of the flat he shared with Rose and he was now a man on the town, enjoying the fruits of being a single rock star.

A series of additional foreign visits were also arranged for the band during the heady, hazy summer of '68. Firstly, the band undertook a brief return to Sweden between 25th July and 5th August, where they had maintained a loyal following since they had first broken through, culminating with a #1 hit on the Swedish charts with 'Very Last Day'. Their visit this time around was particularly notable, as they were supported during their performances by a newly formed Swedish band, Bamboo, fronted by the Stockholm-born vocalist Mikael Rickfors. Blessed with a resonating Scott Walker-esque vocal range, and a talented guitarist and songwriter to boot, Rickfors, and his bandmates, had seen two 45 releases issued via the Swedish distribution arm of the Parlophone label, which no doubt hastened their connection to their UK counterparts. Whilst neither release saw a huge success, the talents of the strikingly handsome frontman, both vocally and musically (he composed the B-sides to both releases), shone through and were duly noted by the British contingent. Tony, in particular, was taken by the band and subsequently offered to produce them in the studio. Soon after, he sent them a proposed new composition and they even went to London to record it at a later date, but the results weren't deemed of a strong enough quality and the connection went no further. For now.

In August, The Hollies travelled to Yugoslavia to participate in the third International Pop Festival, an annual three-day music competition, similar in fashion to the Samremo Festival in Italy in which the band had competed the previous year. Held in the city of Split over the weekend of the 9th-11th (and not to be confused with the First European International Pop Festival, held three months earlier in Rome, or even the previous year's Monterey International Pop Festival), The Hollies, along with Julie Felix, were billed as non-competing guest artists for the first night of the festival, and eight songs from their performance were subsequently broadcast across the prime Yugoslav TV channel.

Dressed in matching suits at Graham's suggestion – to appeal to a more mature audience – and topped off with bow ties, the image that The Hollies presented to the festival audience was rapidly becoming out of sync with the times, and the band were veering dangerously close to the middle-of-the-road "establishment" that was so mocked by many of the rock elite. As a whole, The Hollies had never portrayed themselves as an image-conscious act, thusly avoiding the pitfalls of categorisation but, ironically, the newly acquired suits and bow ties went against all of the credibility and "hipness" that Graham stood for. Just five months later, four bedraggled long-haired Liverpudlians gathered together on the rooftops in Savile Row, near the centre of London, and for the first time in several years played a live set as a band, highlighting the direction that they had travelled, and where rock music was *really* at. The Hollies, meanwhile, churned out a set for their Yugoslavian hosts consisting of a selection of pop hits and decidedly bland cover tunes, opting to avoid the marvellous selection of self-composed works they had amassed in recent years. How puzzling is it that, instead of options from *Butterfly, Evolution* or *For Certain Because...* they chose to perform uninspiring renditions of 'Stewball', 'Dang Me' and The Weavers' folk standard (also covered by both Jimmie Rodgers and Peter, Paul and Mary), 'Kisses Sweeter Than Wine', a song that was omitted from the televised broadcast (as was the closing encore of 'Bus Stop'). They even threw in the odd piece of comedic schtick for the undoubtedly bemused audience, the majority of whom, to date, would have only been familiar with the band via Parlophone-Yugoslavia releases of 'Stop! Stop! Stop!', 'Carrie Anne' and 'Jennifer Eccles'.

With Tony and Graham alternating between guitars and banjos, the quintet still put in a fine performance for their audience, with the hokey sounds of the recently recorded 'Do The Best You Can' (credited to the Clarke-Hicks-Nash songwriting team and issued as a single in some European territories), featuring the duelling banjos of the two frontmen. Meanwhile, whilst the principal focus may have fallen on Allan, singing, swaying, snapping his fingers and wailing away on the harmonica, both Bernie and Bobby also got to shine on 'A Taste Of Honey', with Bernie's fingers dancing up and down the fretwork and Bobby simply powerhousing away behind the frontline. Despite the unity that the band were happily showing on stage, jesting and smiling, it was still a notable point when, during Allan's introduction to 'Jennifer Eccles', Graham slid in a subtle "*boo*" as a quiet side note. He still didn't approve of having to play the number.

Having returned to the UK, the group were then treated to the sight of a new collection from the EMI/Parlophone label, pulling together most of the hit singles to date on a newly compiled LP, climbing up the charts. The collection, entitled *Hollies' Greatest*, eventually peaked at the very pinnacle of the lists, a first for the band and, much to Graham's chagrin, only went to highlight the popularity of The Hollies as a singles act. To Graham, this was a further step backwards in history, looking over the shoulder, as opposed to the continual desire he possessed to keep advancing forwards. Nevertheless, a six-month run in the upper reaches of the charts, including seven weeks holding the pole position, fending off the advances of Cream, The Bee Gees, The Moody Blues, Tom Jones and the soundtrack from Disney's *Jungle Book*, saw the band back at the centre of public attention.

Of note, an error at EMI saw an incorrect (and previously unreleased) version of 'Yes, I Will' included on the stereo version of the LP by mistake. Featuring an alternative guitar break by Tony, along with a distinctly differing vocal introduction, the album (unnoticed until the record was in the stores) was subsequently snapped up by collectors and completists alike, contributing significantly to the record collections of those who had all and everything issued to date. Not that the group had time to dwell on such minor issues, as they still had a steady supply of commitments to fulfil, although the distinctly non-salubrious, smoke-filled surroundings of the two-thousand capacity Batley Variety Club, in West Yorkshire, would hardly have added a smile to the face of the burgeoning rock musician.

Between the dates of the 18th and the 24th of August 1968, The Hollies returned to the northern mecca of the cabaret circuit, and the unofficially labelled "Las Vegas of the North", the Variety Club in Batley, twenty miles south of Leeds. Dressed in their hauntingly regular white stage suits and ties, the group entertained the northern masses, all sitting at neatly lined up tables, pint glasses and baskets of fried chicken and chips stacked up before them, with a short set of hits and singalong cover tunes. It was a mind-numbing take-the-money-and-run scenario, giving the group little time to reflect on the situation with due diligence, reduced instead to simply lining up the one-line gags with a steady flow. Yet, the band recognised the importance of such gigs, and praised the circuit to the media:

'We do a lot of cabaret these days. We only play the best clubs and we're building into a star cabaret act. We like it because we're not screamed at. If people sit back and listen, they hear a lot more. Maybe the kids enjoy screaming but they'd enjoy it more if they listened.'

Allan Clarke

*Rave*: 1968

Returning to his hotel room each night, high on the performing buzz but morally subdued, Graham would pour himself into his songwriting, developing the intimate tunes he was currently and steadily working on alone. Unfortunately, much like many of his other recent compositions, the current song he was working on, the folky 'Teach Your Children', fell on the deaf ears of his bandmates and those of their producer.

Allan would later comment to the UK press, 'All of Graham's new songs are very slow and very boring. He wants to go all soppy artistic and beautiful...'

Following the conclusion of their residency in Batley, the band returned south and on 28th August they entered the Abbey Road studios for, what would turn out to be, the final recording session with the present hit-making five-man line-up. With top keyboard session player Nicky Hopkins along for the ride (fresh from his recent studio activities alongside The Beatles, cutting the tracks for John Lennon's 'Revolution'), the band tackled a new composition by Tony Hazzard, a successful British hit songwriter with Top

20 credits for Manfred Mann and Herman's Hermits to his name. It would go on to be The Hollies' eighteenth Top 30 UK hit.

'After 'Jennifer Eccles', we all had a meeting and said, "Let's find a song as good as 'I'm Alive', because that's the only number one we've had. We found a good song called 'Listen To Me', and we did it in our own style. I think it will be the best we've ever made.' (Allan Clarke: *Rave* 1968)

> *"Have you ever wondered why, when everything goes wrong*
> *Nobody stops to lend a hand, nobody seems to care"*
>
> 'Listen To Me'
> Words and Music by Tony Hazard

'Listen To Me' b/w 'Do the Best You Can' (Parlophone R5733) entered the UK Top 30 charts on 8th October, and gradually built up sales before peaking four weeks later at the number 11 spot. With Graham's vocals overdubbed on three individual parts – co-lead, high harmony and counter vocal – it may well have climbed higher had the band been available to promote the release further, but Graham Nash had instead chosen to return Stateside once again, to develop his friendships across the Atlantic, and the promotional push was lost. A further series of TV appearances did take place once Graham had returned home, but the momentum had swiftly dissipated, and by now Graham knew inside where his priorities lay – and it was no longer in the UK. It was just a matter of time as to when and where.

*Colour Me Pop* was a British music televised programme broadcast on BBC2 between 1968 and 1969. Designed to celebrate the new introduction of colour to British television screens (for those who could afford it), it showcased half-hour sets by many popular pop and rock groups of the period, including Fleetwood Mac, The Tremeloes, The Kinks, Small Faces and The Moody Blues amongst numerous others. On 7th September, the weekly show broadcast thirty minutes of The Hollies in performance, featuring the band running through fourteen of their songs, albeit some lip-synched whilst others were undertaken completely live. Sadly, as was the BBC policy of the era, the taped recording of the show was scrapped shortly afterwards (following a December '68 re-run) and no colour footage is known to survive, although a black and white telerecording circulates amongst collectors to this day. Appearances on *Top of the Pops*, *Time for Blackburn* and *Once More with Felix* followed, before the band headed off to Europe on 27<sup>th</sup> September for a further series of live appearances and a TV guest spot on the Dutch TV show, *Twein*. Visits to Sweden and Belgium rounded out the promotional jaunt, culminating on 3<sup>rd</sup> October in Brussels where they also filmed a short series of promotional videos for TV circulation ('Stop! Stop! Stop!', 'Blowin' In The Wind', 'Do The Best You Can' and 'Listen To Me'). However, a proposed tour of the US for October was postponed at short notice.

Having lost much of the impetus they had built up Stateside over the preceding year, and with the Epic 45 releases of 'King Midas In Reverse', 'Dear Eloise', 'Jennifer Eccles' and 'Do The Best You Can' all failing to bother the *Billboard* Top 30 placings, the group cancelled the visit, with a scheduled 12<sup>th</sup> October date at New York's legendary Fillmore East venue filled by The Turtles instead. Certainly, the disruption surrounding Graham's continuing dissatisfaction was causing internal friction within the band, to the extent that the proposed idea of recording an entire album of Bob Dylan compositions, largely a notion pushed forward by Tony, was also thrown into confusion once Graham openly objected to the idea. Having put himself through the brassy reworking of 'Blowin' In The Wind', he was initially open to the concept but then, upon hearing the proposed new arrangements for the remaining choices, he baulked, choosing to attend a recording date for the upcoming 45 for The Scaffold, as opposed to attending the initial *Hollies Sing Dylan* sessions.

''Lily the Pink' was originally a filthy, disgusting rugby song,' stated Mike McCartney in conversation with the author, when recalling the song they cut at that session. 'We sat down and we rewrote the words, and I restructured the song, with just funny little verses. Now, The Hollies had just had this big hit called 'Jennifer Eccles' and so we did this little bit taking the piss out of them. I rang Graham and said, "We're taking the piss out of The Hollies and we're recording it in Abbey Road. Do you want to come and sing it?" And he said, "Yeah! I'm free. I'll be there." Sure enough, he comes along...'

Jennifer Eccles had terrible freckles...

In addition, whilst the rest of the band were busy in the studios, cutting the early tracks for the proposed new album during the first week of November, Graham was also holed up in a small flat in Moscow Road, West London, in the company of David Crosby and Stephen Stills, who had flown into the UK with the sole intention of getting Graham to commit to a future in America, alongside them and away from The Hollies. Even John Sebastian from The Lovin' Spoonful journeyed across the ocean to join them for a while, adding yet further weight behind the drive. That did it. Following a week or two of harmonising, composing and smoking vast amounts of pot together, and even submitting to an audition with Apple Records – who rejected the act after the cocksure Stills unduly annoyed Beatle George by requesting that McCartney produce them, as opposed to Harrison himself – Graham subsequently made it formal and his departure from the band was duly announced to the press. Reluctant to face his bandmates face-to-face, Graham had relayed the news to Ron Richards first, who then passed it on to his bandmates before sharing it with the media. A group meeting took place shortly afterwards, whereupon Bernie, clearly upset by the revelations, blurted out, 'Do you think you're irreplaceable?' Nash just looked back at him and nonchalantly shrugged his shoulders.

The established US trade magazine *Record World*, upon announcing the news of the impending split, saw fit to suggest that the new trio may even link up with Eric Clapton and release a *Super Sessions* album (as Stills had previously undertaken with Mike Bloomfield and Al Kooper) but that contractual issues may hinder their development. Blinded by the music, Crosby, Stills and Nash ploughed on...

So, it's finally happened, and thousands are still reeling from the shock. Graham Nash is going it alone...

The last time The Hollies play together in their present format will be on December 8, at a charity show at the London Palladium. After that, Graham will go his own way.

Allan Clarke commented, 'Graham was not completely satisfied with what he was doing with us. He thinks he can do better on his own, and we wish him the best of luck. We just want to keep on being The Hollies, but there are no hard feelings.'

Tony Hicks also regrets the split. 'We've been together for something like five or six years, but it was really very simple. It had to happen, just because of what Graham wanted to do. He wanted to work with his friends, and most of his friends are in America. That's where he wants to be. We'll be getting someone else. He'll have to have a very high voice, but without going into falsetto. Like Graham...'

*Melody Maker*
November 1968

At one stage, Graham, realising the hurt he was causing to his oldest and closest friend, offered Allan the opportunity to come Stateside with him, but that was probably no more than a heartfelt gesture. What could Allan truly bring to the already close-knit circle of LA friends that Graham had built up around him? And, unlike the disillusioned Nash, Allan wasn't going to uproot or simply walk away from his family.

'I took it as a personal thing,' Clarke was to later respond. 'I always thought we'd be together the rest of our lives. I relied a lot on our friendship. I was in a state of shock.'[2]

Agreeing to fulfil his commitments to the band, which included a visit to Germany to promote 'Listen To Me' on the German TV shows *Beat Club* (13th November) and *Die Drehscheibe* (14th November), and then participating in a London Palladium charity concert during December, Graham would formally part company with The Hollies on 8th December 1968. Footage of the band filmed romping in a park in Bremen, West Germany for the *Die Drehscheibe* show, was the last time they were caught on film together.

Tony, meanwhile, had also been spending some of his time striking out alone. At one stage during early 1968, he appeared in the musical feature film, *Popdown*. Directed and self-financed by American filmmaker Keith Marshall, this was a social satire told against a background of modern-day London society, with little dialogue of note, but which used a set of space characters to illustrate the decadence of the cosmopolitan surroundings. For his part, Tony briefly appeared onscreen as a singing minstrel, and graced the screen alongside several other British musicians and bands, including Brian Auger and Julie Driscoll, Don Partridge, Dantalian's Chariot (featuring Andy Summers and Zoot Money) and The Idle Race (Jeff Lynne) – but the film was so obscure that it barely garnered any significant publicity, resulting in it being cut to a mere fifty-four minutes in length for its theatrical release towards the end of the year. Unfortunately, a number of the featured musical excerpts were also included in the cull, and the footage disappeared into cult status and the bottomless *whatever happened to* files soon after.

Not that Tony was the only Hollie looking at such a venture. It was also in early '68 that Graham had expressed an interest in striking out into the world of movie soundtracks. Alongside three rising pop stars, the Gibb brothers, the idea of composing the music for *Wonderwall*, a new psychedelically inspired film from first-time director Joe Massot, had been directed towards him. However, despite his initial curiosity over the project, neither party took the option any further and the responsibility for the soundtrack eventually fell into the lap of George Harrison.

Three weeks later and the London Palladium "Save Rave" concert, a multi-talented affair put together to raise funds for the Invalid Children's Aid Association, saw The Hollies performing a four-song set comprised of 'Carrie Anne', 'Dang Me', 'Blowin' In The Wind' and 'A Taste Of Honey', whilst sharing the stage with Scott Walker, The Easybeats, The Scaffold, Madeline Bell, The Love Affair, The Bonzo Dog Doo-Dah Band and The Echoes. The menacing presence of David Crosby backstage, hovering ominously, dressed in his trademark leather cape and Italian-made hat, hardly eased the tense atmosphere for Allan, Tony, Bernie and Bobby either. Allan had taken it hard that his longest and closest friend was leaving the band, leaving him, and he held Crosby partially to blame.

This charity show had been an entry in the band's schedule for a considerable period by now, and Graham had initially envisaged a higher profile of artists participating – Beatles, Hendrix and Stones amongst them – with a nationwide TV broadcast included, but such grand and imaginative plans never came to fruition, despite the vast publicity generated for the event and the ensuing success of the show. Nevertheless, two days after the final curtain fell in Argyll Street, Graham simply walked away from his British life, his home, his crumbling marriage and his former band, on a flight bound for Los Angeles with David Crosby, and a new challenge. Stephen Stills followed shortly afterwards. Negotiations over contracts were ongoing, and Dick James had generously torn up the publishing deal that Graham was tied into. Three days later, The Scaffold hit the top of the UK charts with their novelty hit, 'Lily The Pink', featuring the uncredited vocals of Graham Nash singing the lyrical references to Jennifer Eccles.

'To this day, everyone accepts that that was Roger McGough,' laughs Mike McCartney. 'But, listen to it again. It's just *so* Graham Nash!'

Graham, it appears, wasn't leaving the UK behind that easily…

THE *NEW MUSICAL EXPRESS* 1968 POLL WINNERS
Category: British Vocal Group

| | |
|---|---|
| 1. The Beatles | 7. The Jimi Hendrix Experience |
| 2. The Hollies | 8. Cream |

3. The Rolling Stones
4. The Bee Gees
5. The Shadows
6. The Tremeloes

9. Love Affair
10. The Who
11. Small Faces
12. The Dave Clark Five

Titelfoto: Jean-Marie Périer · Rücktitel: Pictorial Press

# The Hollies

Es gibt sie nicht mehr. Leider. Natürlich werden die Hollies
weitermachen. Aber ihr bisheriger Boß Graham Nash wird
nicht mehr dabeisein. Er stieg „aus musikalischen Gründen"
aus. BRAVO bringt für alle Hollies-Fans das letzte Bild der
Original-Besetzung: Tony, Alan, Graham, Bobby, Ben

# PART TWO

# CHAPTER SIXTEEN

---

# "LOOKING ROUND FOR SOMEONE NEW..."

By the winter of 1968, the music scene had shifted to a darker, colder place. The rainbows and rose petals that had wafted over the grass-infused melodramas of 1967 had turned into a stark, white vision of uncertainty. Across the ocean, the real-time effects of the ongoing Vietnam crisis, the assassinations of Martin Luther King and Robert Kennedy, the student riots and clashes in Chicago and the election of Richard Nixon to the White House were dominating the world's media. Visions of peace and love promoted by idealists of the youth generation were dissipating amongst the smoke, the tears and the lies. On UK home soil, race relations were prominently reported in the press, civil rights, the trade descriptions act... and the musical act who had shaped the 1960s continued to experiment and diversify, shifting yet further away from their mop-topped image of yore. Returning from an Indian ashram hiatus, they recorded *The Beatles*, a 2-LP set featuring heavy rock, folk, blues, music hall, ballads and even hints of the avant-garde and electronic experimentation. The contrast of the plain white sleeve packaging with the extravagance of the *Sergeant Pepper* cover from the previous year could not be more pronounced. No longer just a collection of songs, albums had now become artistic statements.

Performances within long-players were also becoming wilder and more varied. Much of it was raw and underproduced, void of the fuzzy, trippy overtones that psychedelia had sprinkled over it during the ensuing months of that summer of love. In addition to The Beatles and their vast collaborative – and individual – double vinyl release, The Kinks had foisted their *Village Green Preservation Society* upon the world, Hendrix had issued *Electric Ladyland*, The Rolling Stones were preparing *Beggars Banquet*, and the Monkees were still steadily moving up a degree with *Head*. *Cruising With Reuben & The Jets*, *Astral Weeks*, *Waiting For The Sun*, *The Fantastic Expedition of Dillard & Clark*, *In Search of The Lost Chord*, *Music From the Big Pink*...

With hindsight, it's perhaps easy to reflect on why the previous year's *Butterfly* LP failed. It was probably released too late in the calendar for that halcyon summer's "pop" market, lost in the pre-Christmas festive activities, whilst following on too closely to the release of the *Evolution* offering. It also clearly suffered from a degree of lukewarm promotion from EMI and reluctant acceptance from the media, both of whom were still too heavily focussed on the ongoing success of *Sergeant Pepper* to see what they had in their hands. Neither Ron Richards nor the band members themselves were really working from the same sheet as Graham Nash. Tony Hicks, the second driving force in the studio, and the one who stepped up to the mark once Graham's commitment began to waver, was clearly unimpressed at the album's relative failure, and decided enough was enough. It was time to fold up the kaftan, put it away and, months before the fab four officially announced it to the world, get back to where they once belonged.

Now, a full twelve months since *Butterfly* had taken flight or, rather, had failed to, was a follow-up release comprising an entire selection of Bob Dylan covers the solution? That remains open to much discussion, but the general concept certainly wasn't a return to the tried and tested Hollie-formula, and it was enough to drive in the final spike that engulfed the Nash-Hollies division.

'I was convinced The Hollies had lost their focus', Graham was to summarise in the *New Musical Express*. 'The LP idea was bad, in my opinion, because The Hollies sound is not enough for it. We argued about it and got nowhere.'[1/72]

The initial sessions for what would become *Hollies Sing Dylan* had commenced during the first week of November 1968 when the basic tracks for eleven Dylan compositions were worked upon. Session guitarist Alan Parker was brought in to fill out the sound on at least one song ('I Shall Be Released') where Graham's rhythm guitar would have plugged in, and over the course of the next few months they would periodically return to work on the project, intertwining with a series of recordings with the next single in mind.

Early January had seen the band revisit the Chappell Studios in Bond Street and attempt a recording of Chip Taylor's delightful 'Angel Of The Morning', previously a 1968 hit for Merrilee Rush, along with a version of Roger Miller's 'Dang Me'. Clearly, the foursome were confident enough to continue recording as a quartet, with Allan more than a capable enough vocalist in supplying the higher register harmonies in the studio. In fact, a US media article at the time even went as far as suggesting that the band were considering the options as a four-piece. However, from a touring standpoint, it made perfect sense to fill the void that Graham's departure had created, and thus continue to deliver the trademark three-part Hollie-sound in concert. Subsequently, priority was soon enough afforded to finding a suitable replacement.

'I went to church when I was small, and I used to be in the choir when I was four. It was at a church called St Agnes. I couldn't even read, but I could sing. They put me on the end and I just used to stand there and sing the tunes. I was a choirboy until I was nine years old.'

Terry Sylvester

Terence James Silvester (the "y" would come later) had been born on 8th January 1947 in Allerton, a suburb of Liverpool, to James A. Silvester and his wife Ivy, née Davis. His family lived no more than a hundred yards from the McCartney doorstep in Forthlin Road, and Terry grew up with the familiar sight of one of the two McCartney brothers casually walking past his front door.

'I used to have to walk past their house too, Paul's house, to get to the bus stop to get into the city of Liverpool. I remember many times when I was only twelve or thirteen, listening to the music as I went past the house. I could hear the drums. That was The Beatles rehearsing.'[27]

With Terry clearly making an impression on his daily walk along the terraced street, Mike McCartney now recalls, 'He would be going past and I'd say to our kid [brother Paul], "Look, there goes a rocker!" As a young lad, he would regularly go past our house to the flats at the end.'[78]

Terry attended both Lidderdale Road and Dovedale Road schools during his formative years, and by the time he was in his early teens (leaving the Morrison Secondary School for Boys in Rose Lane, Allerton at aged just fourteen), he was working as an apprentice panel beater at a local garage, J. Davies. The business was managed by Peter Harrison, whose brother was also a friend of the McCartney boys. However, his career there was short-lived as music became more and more important to him.

Influenced by his father, who played the trombone in a police jazz band, Terry took up playing music for himself at an early age. Purchasing his first guitar from a local pawn shop, he formed his first group along with two former classmates, Mike Gregory on bass and John Kinrade on lead guitar.

Mike Gregory later recalled for *Mersey Beat*, 'A teacher at our school started a guitar class after school hours, and John and Terry came along to these classes but not for long because they already knew quite a few chords. Then we all used to go and sit in the shed in Greenbank Park along with Joey Molland [later of Badfinger]. Joey had a home-made guitar, made by his brother, and we all used to gawp at him because he could play 'Guitar Boogie Shuffle' to a fairly high standard.

'I can't really remember how we came to get the idea of forming a group – that came after we left school, but only just – we were all about fifteen years old. We were still congregating in the park but before we knew it, we were round at John's house learning Shadows' instrumentals. John and Terry were really good for their ages, so I was given the ultimatum that if I wanted to be in the band, I had to be the bass player. They both had Futurama electric guitars already.'

Adding drummer Johnny Foster (Ringo Starr's cousin) to the line-up, to be replaced shortly afterwards by Peter Clarke, this young band, initially calling themselves The Mexicans, followed by the M Squad (named after a late 1950s US TV series), finally settled on The Escorts for a name, and went on to achieve a sizeable following throughout the clubs and coffee houses of Liverpool. They could regularly be found at some of the more popular venues around the city – the Mardi Gras, Downbeat, the Iron Door, the Peppermint Lounge, the Blue Angel…

'One day we were working at the Majestic Ballroom in Birkenhead when Bob Wooler approached us and said how much he enjoyed it, and would we like to work at the Cavern? We were so excited, as we saw that as being the first steps to making it, as all the best groups were playing there.'

In the ensuing years, The Escorts would play over one hundred lunchtime and evening sessions at the Cavern, supporting such high calibre bands as The Mersey Beats, The Rolling Stones and Gerry and The Pacemakers. Club manager Ray McFall even used to hand them the keys to the venue after lunch so they could leave their kit set up and rehearse before playing the first set in the evening. However, perhaps their most notable appearance on the dark, dank stage was on the 3rd of August 1963, when they supported The Beatles at their last ever Cavern appearance. Shortly afterwards, they appeared at the Non-Stop Beat show, held at the city's Stanley Stadium, sharing the billing with many top artists of the day, including The Hollies.

In a *Mersey Beat* poll, held later that year, The Escorts were voted the ninth most popular group in the city, no mean feat for such a young line-up in a city of such musical talent.

Mike continued, 'Later that year we entered a talent competition [the Lancashire & Cheshire Beat Group Contest], held at the Philharmonic Hall along with eighty other bands, including some very popular and later to be famous ones, and we won it. Bob Wooler, George Harrison and Ringo, along with Decca A&R man Dick Rowe, were the judges. We did an original arrangement – a harmony version of 'Blue Moon', which got us marks for originality. Right afterwards we were whisked off to the Granada TV Studios where we performed 'Blue Moon' again on the *Granada Reports* show. Then we went back to the Blue Angel to celebrate. We turned professional the next day.'

The prize for winning the competition was the offer of a management deal with a London impresario named Harry Lowe, along with a recording contract with Decca Records. Unfortunately, it later transpired that the label was only offering a recording test, and not a contract, and they subsequently failed to take up an option on the group. Soon enough, with Lowe offering the band little support or promotion, they switched management to Jim Ireland, who not only owned a number of popular Liverpool venues but also looked after the Swinging Blue Jeans. Under his guidance, they secured a recording deal with the Fontana label.

A nationwide theatre tour followed, running throughout March 1964, accompanying Cilla Black, Gene Pitney, The Swinging Blue Jeans, The Remo Four and headliner Billy J. Kramer on stage. On the 21st of the month, whilst playing at the Guildford Odeon, The Hollies also made a guest appearance for one night only, replacing The Swinging Blue Jeans.

'We opened the show,' recalled Mike Gregory, 'and only had to do fifteen minutes, so we had all night to get up to mischief. The main thing that John and Terry got up to was lying in the pit with peashooters and firing peas at Gene Pitney when he was down on his knees singing to the girls!'

The Escorts' first single was a cover of Larry Williams' 'Dizzy Miss Lizzy' b/w 'All I Want Is You', released in April 1964 (Fontana TF453), some sixteen months before The Beatles released their own version, but it failed to chart. In July, the group cut their second single, 'The One To Cry' b/w 'Tell Me Baby' (Fontana TF474), which peaked in the UK charts at #49 before sliding away.

The group subsequently made two appearances on TV's *Ready Steady Go!* show that summer, the first occasion on 12<sup>th</sup> June, promoting their second 45, and appearing alongside The Dave Clark Five, Peter and Gordon and Dusty Springfield.

The boys' current disc 'The One To Cry' is selling three times as fast as their first disc 'Dizzy Miss Lizzy' and they are hoping that it will make a chart showing. The group is just back from a highly successful three-day tour of Scotland.

'We were mobbed in Glasgow,' John (Kinrade) said. 'We couldn't play our full spots as Terry Sylvester and I were dragged off the stage. Terry even lost his shoes, and I had to be passed over the crowd of girls, football style.'

After playing two dates in Glasgow and one in Perth, the boys travelled down to Leicester and then to Surrey before returning to Liverpool. 'We'll be playing at local venues mostly during the next week or so,' said John.

Talking about the group's recent "Ready Steady Go!" appearance, John said that he and the rest of the group didn't even manage to see it. He explained, 'We dashed to catch a plane home after recording the show but there weren't any seat vacancies, and we had to wait until 10.30pm to get seats. Then storms delayed us, so we didn't get home until the early hours of the morning. If we'd have come home in the van, we'd have been home hours earlier.'

*Mersey Beat*
July 1964

Despite the lack of significant record sales, the touring continued, and during the summer of 1965 they made their first trip overseas, staying a month in Germany. The manager of the infamous Star-Club in Hamburg, situated along the notorious Reeperbahn section of the city, had previously requested the band to play in his venue, but at the time they were too young to get work permits so the offer was shelved. Nevertheless, by the summer of '65, they had obtained the necessary documentation and were booked to play at a Munich club called the Hit House, located in the Schwabing district. During their time there, The Hollies came to headline for a series of performances, resulting in Allan Clarke and Graham Nash joining the group on stage.

'I got laryngitis through singing such long hours,' Mike adds, 'and Graham helped us out by singing my harmonies on some of the songs. That's where the connection with Terry came from.'

Three more singles followed during 1965 and 1966, including covers of The Drifters' 1964 recording, 'I Don't Want To Go On Without You', along with an English rendition of 'Je t'appartiens', a French composition dating back to the 1950s and later popularised by The Everly Brothers as 'Let it Be Me'. Unfortunately, neither version charted. The third release, 'C'mon Home Baby', written by American songsmiths Dick and Don Addrisi, also failed to register with the record-buying public.

Because The Escorts and The Swinging Blue Jeans shared the same manager, it became a natural move for Terry when Ralph Ellis, rhythm guitarist in the hit-making Blue Jeans, decided to leave the line-up, and in 1966, with a young family to support, Terry switched allegiances.

'The Escorts weren't too impressed,' Terry later noted, 'but it was a great step up for me because they were all set. They'd had hit records, they were doing tours of Sweden, Denmark, Germany… so, for me, I'd made it!'[28]

New Swinging Blue Jeans rhythm guitarist and vocalist Terry Sylvester has fitted in with the group's style within a very short time. At Beaconsfield Youth Club last week, The Blue Jeans were battling against a dead audience, but Terry showed he was a useful guitarist and vocalist, as well as being very popular with the birds. This looks like one personnel change that's going to work.

UK Press Review 1966

Unfortunately, by then, The Swinging Blue Jeans' star was waning. The band had been one of the prime exponents of the original Merseybeat sound, achieving Top 3 status with their smash hit 'Hippy Hippy Shake', a cover of the 1959 Chan Romero composition. However, success was brief, and as the 1960s progressed, The Blue Jeans, in a similar fashion to many of their Mersey contemporaries, got left behind. They still maintained a healthy touring popularity, enough to sustain them through these leaner years, but despite a continuing run of singles releases on the HMV label during Terry's stint as guitarist and vocalist – 'Sandy' (a delightful cover of the Buzz Cason-Bucky Wilkin composition, featuring Terry on lead vocals), 'Rumours, Gossips, Words Untrue' and 'Tremblin'', the latter essentially a solo recording by the band's co-founder Ray Ennis – their hit-making days were behind them. Soon enough, the northern cabaret circuit beckoned... and another opportunity fell at Terry's feet.

> The new Hollie – a replacement for Graham Nash – will be a singer who has already had a hit record. His name will be announced officially by the group at a reception in London today.
>
> Said Hollies manager Robin Britten on Tuesday: 'It is still very much a last-minute decision. We've got it down to three people, but we won't know for certain until each has actually sung with The Hollies in the studio tomorrow night. All I can say is that of the three, two are from groups who have had hits and the other is a solo star who has had a hit.'
>
> *Disc & Music Echo*
> January 1969

Only the taxman knows how much Terry Sylvester has earned over the past year. But over the next twelve months he stands to make around £33,000. Terry is the replacement for Graham Nash with The Hollies and when I met him this week, he seemed delighted, and a little anxious, at having won the job from some ninety applicants.

Terry, a 22-year-old from Liverpool, spent three years with The Escorts, followed by three with The Swinging Blue Jeans – his notice with the Blue Jeans expires on January 31.

'I met The Hollies in August 1965, when I was in Germany with the Escorts,' he told me. 'I didn't really expect to get this job, but I came down and had a sort of personality interview with Robin

Britten, The Hollies' manager. Then I did an audition singing with Allan and Tony and then another day in the studio for the benefit of the recording manager.'

Terry, who names his favourite singer as Tony Bennett and group as The Association, will be taking over the high note role with The Hollies.

'I shan't be playing much guitar,' he told me. 'I shall just stand there with the acoustic guitar and maybe play on a couple of numbers.'

*Melody Maker*
January 1969

Bobby Elliott would later confirm in the same article how the final choice came about: 'We had about ninety applicants and we got it down to three, and then two. We then went into the studio and the other chap had to do a lot of rehearsing to get things right. Terry went in and just did it straight off.'

Allan Clarke was also clearly delighted with the choice, offering a further insight as to how Terry's name came into contention: 'Things should be better now that Graham has left,' he noted. 'If there is one unhappy person in a group it is bound to upset you. When the big blow came and Graham left, we had started trying to find a new singer when a slip of paper came through my door saying Terry would like the job. I thought, *why didn't I think of him before?* In Germany, we were all Everly Brothers fans, and with The Escorts he was doing those high Everly harmonics…'

'I remember the day I joined,' Terry later added. 'We had a reception at the Westbury Hotel in London [16th January 1969], and it was all a big secret. Our manager, Robin Britten, arranged this whole thing. Nobody knew who the new Hollie was, so we just built the whole thing up. The next minute the doors opened, and all the press were there – every big newspaper in the UK. Here's the new Hollie! For me, it was just a dream come true…'[28]

Robin Britten, looking at the position from a business perspective, was also clearly relieved. 'We had to cancel three months of work when Graham left, including a Palladium date and an American tour. I reckon that was over £30,000 worth of work. Now we are planning a college tour for February, March and April, and we will probably also do some concerts, about six at major venues like the Royal Festival Hall and Manchester's Free Trade Hall. Then there is also a Swedish tour and we also plan to go to Israel. Finally, we are going to do quite a bit of cabaret in the major clubs up north.' (*Melody Maker*)

Having undertaken a vocal test with Ron Richards and EMI studio engineer Alan Parsons before his appointment was announced, Terry Sylvester's first official recording session as a Hollie took place on 27th January 1969. Over the next forty-eight hours, the newly constituted line-up committed two songs to tape that would ultimately make up both sides of the next 45 release. Shunning the ambitious direction and lavish productions of the recent Nash-led era, the band reverted back to their pop roots, cutting a new composition by Allan Clarke (and published by recently renamed ALTO Music), 'Not That Way At All'. The result was a relief for all, highlighting the new, smooth vocal harmony blend that Terry now brought into the group. The second offering was a song written by seasoned writers Geoff Stephens and Tony Macauley – a mid-tempo, bright and breezy offering they had entitled 'Sorry Suzanne'.

Stephens had been behind a great number of UK chart successes prior to co-composing this particular tune and had seen his work recorded by artists such as The Applejacks ('Tell Me When'), Dave Berry ('The Crying Game'), The New Vaudeville Band ('Winchester Cathedral'), Manfred Mann ('Semi-Detached Suburban Mr James') and Herman's Hermits ('A Kind Of Hush'), amongst others. Likewise, Macauley was the man behind hits for The Foundations ('Baby Now That I've Found You' and 'Build Me Up Buttercup'), along with The 5th Dimension ('(Last Night) I Didn't Get To Sleep At All'). The combination of their talents was ideal for creating the required hit for the rejuvenated Hollies.

'I went up to Tony Macauley's office,' recalled Tony, 'and when he played me [the demo], I knew we would have to record it. We wanted something we could do by ourselves. 'Sorry Suzanne' is just The Hollies, there's nobody else on it. Sometimes an orchestra or extra session musicians can add to the effect, but for this single, which was so important for us, we didn't want anybody else on it. It was just what we wanted.' (*New Musical Express:* April 1969)

To aid the launch of the forthcoming release, the band also filmed a promotional video for the Stephens-Macauley tune, confirmed as the A-side for the intended single. Dressed in the matching white suits and ties, the footage was simply the band filmed miming to the song, positioned on a darkened sound stage, although the opening shot (and, subsequently, the closing one) of a solo Tony Hicks, *sans* band, playing his guitar, was a seemingly surreal introduction to the new formation. Certainly, by early 1969, the development of the promotional film was far more advanced than this unimaginatively filmed production offered (directed by band road manager Rod Shields) and, despite the commercial success that the release would deliver, the image they portrayed here was one of a band in visual turmoil, still uncertain of exactly where their position lay within the realms of credibility.

The 1968 *New Musical Express* reader's poll had seen The Hollies rise to the lofty number two position in the UK fan faves category (no prizes for guessing who still maintained the top slot for the sixth consecutive year), but with Graham now having departed, and the psychedelic period almost ancient history in musical terms, The Hollies were stagnating in an image rut. The beads and flowing paisley had long gone, leaving them adrift in the white cabaret suits, drifting farther and farther away from where the "hip" crowds gathered in their faded denim and battered cowboy boots, with their unkempt shoulder-length hair and beards. When the feeling took hold, Lennon and McCartney still knew how to be rock stars, Jagger knew how to strut, and the Davies brothers, in between the sibling arguments, knew how to be stylish. Unfortunately, and despite The Hollies' unquestionable ability to match any of these bands when it came to perform their music, they had no get-out clause concerning presentation. Even after all of these years, and despite the impressive catalogue of music they held within their grasp, they still represented "clean-cut" to the nth degree.

Not that they were alone in their predicament. Several bands stood firmly beside them when it came to the image stakes, or lack of such. The end of the decade was surely divided by the decision to either appeal to the masses and go for the family-friendly presentable appearance, or to head in the opposite direction, aiming for the credibility vote, and risk non-acceptance. A huge chasm was developing within the music industry. Very few bands of notable acclaim achieved the best of both worlds in the UK charts back in the late '60s – Beatles and Stones excepted – and The Hollies, by keeping their faith in commerciality, stepped warily, and perhaps unknowingly, towards the safer environment, populated by Marmalade, Love Affair and Amen Corner. That is not to put down such acts, but The Hollies, for all of their ability and talent, deserved to be accepted and duly recognised in the upper echelons of the UK music rankings – and not just as a current fan fave. One can only compare such a scenario, once again, across the ocean, with the rise and fall of American band The Beach Boys. Similarly reduced to a mass public non-acceptance of their recent album releases – *Smiley Smile, Wild Honey* and *Friends* – and currently to be found touring the college circuit in matching white suits, whilst contemporaries such as The Byrds, The Rascals and the Arthur Lee-led Love dressed as they pleased, cut "cool" albums and appealed to the new wave of the post-hippie generation.

The second week of February 1969 saw Terry make his debut stage performances as a member of The Hollies. Entertaining the university crowds in Cardiff, followed by a second show the following night in Swansea, gave him the opportunity for a couple of low-key appearances, away from the media spotlight of a big city show, contributing to a setlist heavy on the hits, but also notable for featuring a selection from the forthcoming Dylan-themed album. Nevertheless, it was still a daunting prospect for him:

'I've gone through a few fits of nervousness already,' he would comment in the *New Musical Express*. 'First came the interview for the job. I was so anxious I marched straight into the office and told them I thought I was the ideal man for the job! After I heard I was to join The Hollies I realised just what it meant, and I really started worrying. Then came the first recording sessions. It was unbelievable, [but] it went so well, and the sessions were finished ahead of schedule. Then came the first live gig. I was petrified! The strain built up as we were late going on, but Allan told me to just concentrate on the vocals and feel my way through the songs and not to worry about the chat bit. It all went very smoothly, and we went straight into 'Stop! Stop! Stop!' without any trouble and I was over the first hurdle. However, it was difficult getting out of the habit of just singing along to Hollies hits now I had to actually sing them properly!'

'The worst thing about joining was having to follow someone like Graham Nash,' he would also later remark to journalist Julie Webb. 'I didn't quite know what people expected of me, or what the others in the group expected of me...'

With any initial concerns swiftly laid to rest following his successful appearances both on stage and in the studio, thoughts turned again to completing the upcoming album, on hold for the past few weeks during the initial transition period.

'Now we must get down to some good rehearsing,' Bobby was to comment in *Melody Maker*. 'We have got to finish our new album. It's a tribute to Bob Dylan and they are all Dylan songs. We finished the backing tracks in November and have been waiting to get the three voices on.'

For one member of the band, however, it was to be a longer period of unsettling downtime. As a non-singing member of the group, Bernie Calvert had little to contribute to the recording sessions once the instrumental tracks had been laid down. Even in concert, the need for any vocal input from the quiet bass player was deemed unnecessary, although surviving photographs from Bernie's pre-Hollies days as bass player for the Ivan D. Juniors suggest that he was more than capable of adding his vocals to the mix. Nevertheless, with the three-part Hollie harmonies dominating their instantly recognisable sound, Bernie often had more time on his hands than the three frontmen. Subsequently, during early February of 1969, Bernie found himself back in the recording studios cutting a series of instrumental tracks, but this time with an unfamiliar group of bandmates around him.

The Bread and Beer Band came together at the start of the year, the result of former Decca Records PR man Tony King conceiving the idea of cutting an album, under his own co-production, featuring some of the UK's finest session players. Together they would record, in King's mind, a "mad album of instrumentals".

Tony King: 'I called on Reg Dwight, Bernie Calvert, Roger Pope, Caleb Quaye, Liza Strike and her husband, and two Jamaican percussionists who were introduced to the sessions when we did some recording over at Abbey Road. We had such a laugh doing them, and afterwards at the local pub!' [25]

'The sessions were not supposed to lead to anything significant,' adds guitarist Quaye. 'We had no money, which is why we called ourselves The Bread and Beer Band. All of it was down to Tony King, who instigated the project, and it was just a one-off that was never intended to be anything more than what it was, a lot of fun and the opportunity to make some money.'[25]

Whilst King was full of praise for the enthusiasm of the participants, the piano-playing Reg Dwight being one, he noted that Bernie was of a slightly more subdued nature, "but a great bass player".

'At the time I was considered a hot session musician,' notes Bernie. 'I had played with other artists such as Simon Dupree and The Big Sound, and on many other sessions done at AIR.'[25]

According to King, the two Jamaican percussionists he had brought into the Abbey Road sessions, credited as Rolfo and Lennox Jackson, were the same players who had earlier contributed the steel drums to the Hollies' 'Carrie Anne' session – and whilst this has never been confirmed (and seems highly unlikely), Bernie recalls them as 'super cool Jamaicans who, on one of the songs, were trying to get a reggae feel going. I didn't play reggae and they were telling me what to do, which I was a bit edgy about. I didn't like that very much, but I met them halfway. I just couldn't feel it the way they did.' [25]

Twelve psychedelic jazz-fused tracks were cut during the sessions, co-produced by Tony King and Chris Thomas, with Bernie's bass mixed heavily to the fore, but, officially, only one single was ever released to the market: 'The Dick Barton Theme (The Devil's Gallop)' b/w 'Breakdown Blues' (Decca F12891). The B-side, a full-blooded, lengthy piano-guitar-bass-driven jam session, bore the songwriting co-credit of Caleb Quaye-Bernie Calvert-Reg Dwight-Lennox Jackson and highlighted the abilities of each player to the maximum. However, the remaining ten cuts intended for the follow-up album, including instrumental covers of 'Zorba The Greek', 'Needles And Pins' and 'If I Were A Carpenter', along with part-vocal takes of 'The Letter' and 'Mellow Yellow', were sadly shelved when the proposed release of the long-player was cancelled, although the recordings were later unofficially circulated on both vinyl and compact disc once Reg Dwight's popularity rocketed skywards. He became the rocket man. Reg/Elton now owns the studio masters to the sessions, but The Bread and Beer Band were to be heard no more.

Ever keen to keep his fingers in all pies, Allan also struck out alone during the early months of 1969, albeit briefly, to produce a one-off demonstration 45 for a previously unknown act labelled The Warm Sensation. The resulting single, pressed on Columbia, 'I'll Be Proud Of You' b/w 'The Clown' (with both titles published by GRALTO), was standard brass-filled pop fare for the times, and swiftly disappeared. There are no records to indicate as to whether it received a general release.

Now, with Bernie returning to the fold, and Allan having fulfilled obligations, and following the culmination of a short series of university gigs (joining up with The Moody Blues and Fairport Convention for a 21st February performance at the Sheffield campus), along with a round of the usual promotional TV spots for 'Sorry Suzanne' – including *Dee Time* and *Top of the Pops* – The Hollies settled back at Abbey Road to complete the vocal overdubs for their own upcoming album. They also added a completely new vocal track to the previously cut 'Blowin' In The Wind', subsequently wiping Graham's contribution and adding Terry to the mix. Allan's lead certainly sounded slicker on the updated rendition.

A live recording of the song, with the full accompaniment of the Paul Kuhn Orchestra, was taped during a various artists Gala Performance held in Berlin, shortly afterwards. The recording appeared on the LP *Gala Abend der Schallplatte Pop 1969* (TST 76-266), but was never originally issued on a commercial level, appearing only as a limited German promotional release. Despite its rarity status, it was only in 2014 that this live version finally emerged in the collector's community, appearing as a bonus track on a Hollies Japanese re-issue CD.

By the 4th of March, the album sessions were completed, and the tracks were mixed and scheduled by EMI/Parlophone for a 2nd May release as *Hollies Sing Dylan* (PMC/PCS7078), coupled with a US issue shortly afterwards, albeit retitled for the Epic Records release as *Words and Music by Bob Dylan*. In the meantime, 'Sorry Suzanne' had appeared as the band's nineteenth UK single, going on to follow the pattern set by the previous releases, comfortably breaking into the chart lists. The 45 reached the Top 10 in at least eleven countries around the globe, hitting #3 in the UK and reaching the top spot in South Africa, Poland and Switzerland, although, once again, the band's reputation in the US took a further hit when the single limped to a lowly number 56 in *Billboard*, despite the continuing publicity pursued by Epic Records.

In the native land of Great Britain, The Hollies' single 'Sorry Suzanne' has become a rousing success. In fact, it's one of the Top 5 records there. 'Sorry Suzanne' is also generating as much positive excitement – if not more – right here on the shores of America. With strong airplay on Top-40 stations, and lots of action on the Top-100 charts. And all of this is backed with good solid sales to make one glorious single.

Epic Records promotion. 1969

Further televised guest appearances promoting 'Sorry Suzanne' followed, with slots on *This is Tom Jones*, German TV's *Beat Club* and *Evening Gala of Discs*, a Dutch airing on *Jam TV* and further appearances on *Top of the Pops*. With each viewing and performance, it became more apparent how, despite it coming across as a very simplistic pop song, it was never an easy arrangement to perform. With its distinctive, individual vocal parts – Clarke, then Clarke-Hicks and finally, Clarke-Hicks-Sylvester (with specific parts by Clarke-Sylvester) – each had to hit their respective vocal mark spot-on. The song never stopped its full-on flow, and there was certainly no room for error or hesitation in such an arrangement, something that the band, now with Terry integrating himself within, strove to achieve.

Then, on 30th March, the group appeared at the Golders Green BBC TV Theatre, a recently converted 700-seat venue in North London, to tape their very first BBC TV Special, *The Hollies in Concert*.

Broadcast to the nation in full colour on the UK's secondary BBC2 network, at 9.15pm, on the 3rd of May 1969, if The Hollies were ever in doubt over their continuing acceptability to the British public, then this was the sign that all remained well. It was wholesome, professional and still retained that familiar "Hollies sound". The newly revised line-up was clearly working out for the better...

'We had two and a half months of looking about for a person who could replace Graham,' Allan was to say during an interview with *Melody Maker*. '[He had to] fit in the group and be tuned in to the musical aims of The Hollies. It was frightening. There was a stage when the group nearly broke up and I had to think about what I was going to do in the future. I had considered going solo, because after all I have a family to support. Fortunately for the group, after many auditions and much searching, along came Terry Sylvester.

'Terry had been playing guitar and singing with Liverpool's Swinging Blue Jeans and fitted perfectly into The Hollies' mould of happy, melodic music. It was uncanny how well he fitted in. He's a hard worker and he believes in what the group is trying to do.

'Graham left because his musical ideas, and the rest of the group's, conflicted. We wanted someone who would want to play Hollies music, the music we have been playing since we started. Terry's working wonders. He's gradually changing and moulding himself into the group. He's smartening himself up and he's now got something worthwhile to work for. We've been working in suits for a year now. I'm happy because I love being smart. When the hippy thing was in, we dressed like that. We jumped on the bandwagon then, and I thought afterwards we were wrong. That's not our scene. I'm happier with the suits.'

# He Ain't Heavy... He's My Brother

Music by BOBBY SCOTT  Lyric by BOB RUSSELL

Recorded by
**THE HOLLIES**
on Parlophone

# CHAPTER SEVENTEEN

# IT'S A LONG, LONG ROAD...

The Hollies are to stage their own major concert presentation at London's Royal Festival Hall on Friday, June 27. The event will be titled "An Evening with The Hollies" and the group's entire act will be recorded for later release by Parlophone as a live album. An 11-piece orchestra directed by Mike Vickers will accompany The Hollies, who will be on stage for well over an hour.

In order to make this a special Hollies day, the group is planning a full-scale convention for its fan club. Fans will have the opportunity of meeting all members of the group before travelling to the Festival Hall for its concert.

*New Musical Express*
February 1969

Plans for such an ambitious live project never came to fruition, but fans of the band were treated to the 40-minute TV Special during May, the same month that saw the band's new *Hollies Sing Dylan* album appear in the stores.

Heavy on songs from the new release, the TV Special was a slick affair, with the newly formed harmony trio providing an accomplished sheen to the proceedings. Terry's higher register came across as a lot smoother and less piercing than Graham's had and, as the watching public could hear for themselves, made the blend so much sweeter.

'When Terry took over from Graham,' Allan would recall during a 2019 interview for BBC Wales, 'he fitted in so well, and his harmonies were just as good as Graham's. They were softer but they seemed to mould in a different way to the previous harmonies. He was a good guy to get at that particular time.'[23]

Overall, the performance was perfect for a primetime BBC audience, with nice clean suits, alarmingly large bow ties and a non-threatening vibe, all played out before a politely applauding audience. But it was almost as far away from rock 'n' roll as one could get. With musical accompaniment from the competent, yet rather staid, Arthur Greenslade Orchestra, with the arrangements by both Greenslade himself along with Mike Vickers, it swayed, it sashayed, but at no time did it get down and dirty. Even the hits played out before the cameras, either as stand-alone performances ('Carrie Anne' or 'Stop! Stop! Stop!') or as part of a medley ('Just One Look', 'Bus Stop', 'On A Carousel' and 'Sorry Suzanne') were clinical, routine renditions of near-perfect pop. Where was the Allan, Tony, Bobby and Bernie that had given us 'Have You Ever Loved Somebody', 'Try It' and 'Open Up Your Eyes'? Were the brief, downtrodden engagements on the cabaret circuit getting into the bloodstream, setting the standard and becoming the norm? Terry was routinely introduced to the cabaret regime shortly after the filming of the TV Special, when the band spent a week in the grand surroundings of the Showboat Social Club, located in Middlesbrough, the week commencing 13th April.

Allan Clarke (in *Melody Maker*): 'We find now that the cabaret act is our strongest area rather than doing a string of hits. That's why we do songs like 'Blowin' In The Wind' and 'A Taste Of Honey'. We find that the audience really appreciates the things like this we do, and it's better for us, too.'

Given the fractious events that preceded the recording sessions for the *Hollies Sing Dylan* album, its subsequent UK success upon release was surely a victorious moment for the band, and in particular for Tony, who was the principal driving force behind the conception. Tony was, by now, becoming a central figure behind the key decisions the band made. Robin Britten, seated behind the manager's desk, may well have held the formal title, and placed his signature on the contracts, but the band themselves, headed by Tony, were now strongly instrumental in much of the decision-making process. In turn, Bobby had also stepped up, sharing the load and taking on the additional reins as archivist and dealing with their increasing catalogue.

Allan, meanwhile, from an outside perspective, was also seen as holding a key role. Bernie and Terry remained as salaried employees of Hollies Ltd – vitally important, yes, but salaried nonetheless – but Allan was still very much perceived as the group frontman. He was the band's focal point. It was a position he had rightfully regained following Graham's departure. Yet, behind the scenes, he was suffering. He reportedly wished for little more than the lead vocalist role, and at his own behest kept the decision-making and managerial positions at arm's length.

Still hurting from the departure of his closest musical companion, he seemed lost at times during performances over this period, and his confidence appeared to be of a more subdued nature.

'I had always been the number two and I liked that situation,' he would comment in the *New Musical Express*. 'I'm a pint and darts man myself. For a while I fell in love with Graham's ideas. Maybe for a while I really believed them, or perhaps I was simply scared he would leave The Hollies. At any cost, I thought Graham and I must stick together. But it didn't take very long before I realised that wasn't me at all. I didn't understand what it was all about. While I was dabbling in meditation, I was wearing the kaftan and beads and I went up to Salford one day and one of the boys came up with a big grin on his face. I was so self-conscious. I suddenly realised that I was only wearing the outfit because everybody else was. I went straight home and got into a suit. I realised that it wasn't me at all.'

He was proud of his northern roots, finding solace in a regular beer, or something stronger, as a way to relax and take his mind off more pressing matters. Nevertheless, like it or not, the Top 3 success of the *Hollies Sing Dylan* album put the band very much back in the spotlight, all the more surprising given the relative failure of the previous LP, and the lack of any accompanying 45 from the release to promote it further.

Overall, the album was a mixed affair and whilst Bob Dylan wasn't always known for his commerciality, it continues to court discussion and divide to this very day. With the folky 'When The Ship Comes In', complete with its jaunty banjo-filled arrangement, setting the sleek tone from the start, the way the band set about the recording sessions, adapting an upbeat, finely polished approach, certainly raised questions over Graham's initial opinions on the theme.

'I Want You', 'I'll Be Your Baby Tonight' and 'Quit Your Low Down Ways', with the latter offering an impressively wild acoustic guitar solo (along with

Bobby's slick shuffling accompaniment), all gave the listener a thoroughly enjoyable audible ride, whilst their take on the widely covered 'Wheels On Fire' (a then-recent hit for Brian Auger and Julie Driscoll) maintained the trademark Hollie-frontline harmony vocals right from the powerful opening salvo.

'The things to listen out for on this one,' suggested Tony to *NME* journalist Gordon Coxhill, when listening back to the driving Dylan/Danko composition, 'are Bernie's fine organ playing and Bobby doing his nut on the drums. There's a great sustained effort near the end which is very fast and very difficult.'

Nevertheless, if there was one failing for the collection, it was once the shiny slab of vinyl was flipped over and, immediately after the jazz-folk-country fusions of 'Quit Your Low Down Ways', the listener had to endure mediocre covers of songs that were all-too-familiar by now. Dylan himself had popularised 'The Times They Are A-Changin'' to the extent that no one could compete with his original version, and The Byrds had already made 'All I Really Want To Do' and 'My Back Pages' pretty much their own (although, ironically, it had been former US session singer Cher who had achieved the biggest hit on the *Billboard* chart lists with her rendition of the former). In 1966, Manfred Mann had also taken 'Just Like A Woman' into the UK Top10.

To close the album, The Hollies then opted to cut their own interpretation of 'Mighty Quinn', originally conceived by Dylan back in 1967 as 'Quinn the Eskimo (The Mighty Quinn)'. However, despite the new Dixieland rearrangement, the song was already overly familiar due to the astonishing success that another recent cover version by Manfred Mann had achieved – a Top 10 hit in numerous countries around the globe, including such a placing in the US *Billboard* chart, along with the number one slot in the UK. To many, The Hollies' versions paled in comparison to these widely recognised recordings and, despite the original approach utilised, and the impressive accompanying sales figures, they suffered in the eyes and ears of the media accordingly.

That said, a number of noted rock journalists and "progressive" music magazines almost *begrudgingly* acknowledged the album's worth:

The Hollies, an institution in British rock since the very early Beatle days, have always been among the most conservative of English groups. This conservatism began to bring their nominal leader, rhythm-guitarist and singer-of-high-harmonies Graham Nash, down.

'Let's do a Hollies Sing Dylan album,' said the other Hollies. 'Let's not,' said Graham. 'We're not capable of doing his material justice.'

The results: the Nash-less Hollies and this album, which, depending on your perspective, is either (1) everything Graham warned it would be, that is, frequently insensitive to Dylan's material and a bit too predictably Hollies-commercial, or (2) a flying gas.

Well yes, the new Hollies, featuring Terry Sylvester in Nash's spot, are generally oblivious to the sort of ironic nuances that characterise many of the Dylan songs they have chosen (without much imagination, it should be noted. The commerciality of nearly everything included has been previously demonstrated by someone or other). But here is the place to mention that this album must be taken on its own terms; there isn't a down arrangement on this album, and absolutely everything included gets the same unabashedly exuberant, gloriously unpretentious and commercial treatment, associations notwithstanding.

For those who are keeping score, Nash's absence isn't even noticeable, in such fine form vocally are Clarke, Hicks, and Sylvester.

In short, I love this album and, as always, I love The Hollies. You're sure to be utterly knocked out. It's simple and happy rock and roll at its very best.

*Rolling Stone* Magazine
1969


'We have been fans of Dylan for ages, but I wouldn't call it a tribute to him. We thought his melodies would lend themselves to the arrangements we had in mind. I think they worked out very well. It is a new dimension for us and could be the first of several similar ideas. I'm proud of it and if it sells well, I'll be very pleased.'

Tony Hicks
*New Musical Express*
April 1969


To help promote the album, the band filmed two promotional appearances during the initial month of release, lip-synching to both 'Blowin' In The Wind' and 'All I Really Want To Do' although, upon airing on Dutch TV for a televised slot alongside Scottish singer Lulu, the 'Blowin' In The Wind' segment had a notably racy addition to the footage – a partly naked couple caressing and making out with flesh aplenty. Then again, the eyes of many a fan would have not been immediately drawn to the raunchy images before them anyway – but to the man sitting behind the drum kit instead. An unfamiliar face? Not so, it appears, for during this period Bobby had taken on the decision to disguise his notably receding hairline, duly abandoning the succession of hats and caps that had adorned his cranium to date, by sporting the first in a series of hairpieces that would atop his balding pate over the coming years. Certainly, the array of hats he had worn throughout the preceding years had earned that feel of notable familiarity about him. A certain elegance and style. One notable concert appearance in earlier times, when an ever-eager fan had rushed the stage and stolen the hat off his head (causing Bobby to down sticks and chase the perpetrator), may have given him pause for thought – although, in reality, whilst it may have made not a dent of difference to the music, it was clearly a move to make himself more credible and comfortable in the rock music fraternity. Indeed, over the subsequent decade, it would elaborately alternate in length and, at stages, varying shades of colour – but such was the man's immense talents it raised but a smile amongst the knowing… and little more.

Further TV appearances swiftly followed, including *This is Tom Jones* (for the US ABC Network) and *Julie Felix in Concert*, a 25-minute special taped for the BBC at the Golders Green Theatre, before they headed back out on the road for their first overseas visit with their new musical partner alongside. A seventeen-date visit to Sweden ensued, earning an astronomical (for the time) £1,000 per night for each performance (reported in the media as being an all-time record fee for a British act in Scandinavia). A further European visit was also scheduled for the summer but, before they took the fight to the continent once again, they spent a select few days in Abbey Road, laying down tracks for the proposed follow-up to *Hollies Sing Dylan*. One particular tune, first attempted on 25th June, was of particular interest to the band as it highlighted a complete change in direction for them, musically.

As a unit, they had always included ballads within their repertoire. Some were no more than gentle love songs, sentimental affairs with little intensity, whilst others had relied on grand studio production to bring out the pathos and feeling within the composition. This time was different.

Once again, it was Tony Hicks, trawling the publishing offices of London's Soho district, who uncovered the song, initially cut in demo form by the American co-songwriter himself, Bobby Scott (who had earlier composed the Sam Cooke hit 'Chain Gang', along with The Hollies' concert favourite, 'A Taste Of Honey'). Written in collaboration with Bob Russell, a fellow US composer who was suffering from lymphoma at the time (and who passed away shortly afterwards), the song had first been cut by Kelly Gordon in early 1969, and then subsequently rejected by Bill Medley (who then cut a later version), The Association and Joe Cocker, but it was when Russell's son-in-law, who was living in London at the time, began hawking the demo around publishers' offices that it was brought to the attention of the astute Mr Hicks.

'Yes, I pulled 'He Ain't Heavy, He's My Brother' out of a publisher's,' recalled Tony, 'but simply because it was a good song. I wasn't consciously looking for a different direction for The Hollies, or a change in any other way. I used to go into a publisher's [Cyril Shane] on Baker Street and listen to twenty or thirty songs and just bring out the ones that appealed to me, and then play them to Ron Richards. I heard the song and it just appealed to me. There was no great excitement. The band then listened and said, "it's quite pleasant," but the attitude was "let's give it a try."' [7]

Hearing the bubbling potential that the song had to offer, Ron Richards agreed that the band should record it, and even though there was no rhythm section on the initial demo, Ron wanted to retain the emotion that he heard upon playing it. In particular, he was struck by the piano arrangement, and although Bernie Calvert had contributed a lot of piano and keyboards to various Hollies recordings to date, the choice for this track was to bring in a quality session player.

'I'm not a world-class player,' suggested Bernie. 'I just do what I can do.' [25]

Utilising the studio piano skills of Reg Dwight, at a costly rate of £12 per hour, the track was swiftly laid down in a matter of minutes.

'When Reg came in, we didn't know whether Ron had given him the demo beforehand, but he certainly knew it when he came in,' continued Bernie. 'We all sat around the piano and I got my bass part organised with Reg, and with Bob Elliott, who was in a little booth laying down his drum part. We only did a few takes of it, because Reg was such a good keyboard player, we didn't need much practise. It was basically bass, drums and piano, and that was it. It was that simple.'[25]

With a satisfactory instrumental take on the shelf, along with the backing tracks for a series of new, self-composed songs – including 'Do You Believe In Love 'and 'Please Sign Your Letters', both credited to the newly founded Sylvester-Clarke-Hicks songwriting trio, 'Please Let Me Please' (Clarke-Hicks) and two new solo efforts from Tony and Allan ("Cos You Like To Love Me' and 'Goodbye Tomorrow') – the band were undoubtedly in a positive frame of mind. Although *Hollies Sing Dylan* had barely lasted two months in the UK album charts, sessions for its successor had started well, and when the first week of August saw the vocal sessions and orchestral sweetening completed on 'He Ain't Heavy, He's My Brother', even their cautious producer was to confidently state that 'this is a big hit record for you, boys.'

Although the completed version featured no guitar at all, it was filled out by a lush orchestral arrangement by Johnny Scott, along with a concluding choral section, handled by The Mike Sammes Singers, a seasoned troupe of session vocalists who had graced many a Top 10 album and single to date.

'That was a fabulous song,' remembered Allan. 'That just came out of the blue. We thought that, maybe, ballads weren't our thing at that time, but the actual message of the song got through to us. We thought *we've got to give this song a chance*. It was just beautifully orchestrated and the production on it was marvellous...'[6]

'Ron Richards could spot a winner,' states Bernie. 'It all takes some organising as you don't book an orchestra until you have the backing track, but Ron was superb at that.'[25]

'What I basically used to do with all of their tracks,' commented Ron, 'was that I used to record the rhythm section first. Purely a basic hi-hat, bass drum, snare with no frills. Then [I would] lay on the vocals and anything else that was needed. I'd have Allan singing a guide vocal during the rhythm tracks. I always insisted that the vocals go on after the rhythm track, before I added anything else. After the vocals were laid on, I'd see what holes we had before I let Bobby do any filling, and certainly before any orchestra.' [70]

The song also saw Allan Clarke, who was suffering from a slight head cold on the day of recording that gave his vocal an even more emotive edge, provide some brief harmonica, followed by one of his finest moving lead vocal performances. Terry's high harmony voice also added a mature quality to the frontline vocal trio.

As Ron Richards later put it: 'It was one of the best things they ever did...'

With the current round of recording sessions completed, along with one more UK TV appearance taped for *Tarbuck's Back*, the band repacked their suitcases and headed back out across the English Channel, bound for Ostend in Belgium – although not before Tony had accepted an invite as a backstage guest for The Rolling Stones' performance at London's Hyde Park on 5th July. For their first public appearance in almost two years, this huge outdoor concert was planned as a vast publicity introduction for the Stones' new guitarist, Mick Taylor, although the death of his predecessor, Brian Jones, two days previously, brought about a sombre mood hovering over the day's events. That mood, coupled with the sight of Jagger's poetic readings, delivered whilst wearing a flamboyant white Mr Fish dress, followed by thousands of dead butterflies being "released" on stage, all from airtight cardboard boxes, highlighted the charade and pomposity that the upper tiers of rock 'n' roll were rapidly developing. It was, as the Rolling Stones had previously stated themselves, fast becoming a *Rock and Roll Circus*. The Hollies, however, seemed intent on following their own path...

An extensive tour of Switzerland, Spain, Germany, Denmark, Norway and Finland followed, with the group appearing at the recently opened 1,000 capacity Barbarella Club in Palma, on the Spanish island of Mallorca on 15th August. That same weekend, 4,000 miles to the west, Graham Nash stepped out on stage with his new bandmates in front of (as estimates still suggest) 400,000 bedraggled, mud-soaked attendees at the Bethal Rock Festival – An Aquarian Exposition, held on a dairy farm in upstate New York. Nowadays known as the Woodstock Festival (albeit forty miles away from the actual town that gave it its name), the event changed music forever, and the Crosby, Stills, Nash... and, occasionally, Young, legend was born.

'This is the second time we've ever played in front of people, man... we're scared shitless!' So said Stephen Stills.

On a less grand scale, on 28th August, The Hollies' touring party reached Finland where, during a visit to the capital city of Helsinki, they undertook a performance for a future televised broadcast. This 30-minute "special" was shot in front of a somewhat muted audience, judging by the lack of any audible participation (and possibly even just the film crew and production team), with the familiar studio recordings later overdubbed onto the footage due to a series of technical issues affecting the live performances. Only

Allan's between-song patter and introductions survive from the original audio recordings that day, and the band themselves, dressed in a matching abomination of flared trousers, long waistcoats and wide-collared shirts, appeared tired and weary from the punishing schedule as they meekly played along to the selected eight songs, with Allan, in particular, looking a drawn, embattled characterisation of his former self.

Stop! Stop! Stop! / This Wheel's On Fire / Quit Your Lowdown Ways / I'll Be Your Baby Tonight / When The Ship Comes In / He Ain't Heavy, He's My Brother / Sorry Suzanne / Blowin' In The Wind

Live in Helsinki: 1969

From Helsinki, they flew on to Basel in Switzerland, before culminating the tour with televised recordings in Zurich (for the *Hits a Go Go* show) and across the German border in Stuttgart (*4-3-2-1 Hot and Sweet*). By the time the second week in September came around, they were back in London, once again entrenched in the Abbey Road Studios, working on a series of further new recordings. They also committed to a Hollies Fan Club Convention, held on 20th September, at EMI's Manchester Square office block in London (home of The Beatles' legendary stairwell photoshoot), where they mingled and chatted with a select fortunate few who had made the journey into the city centre.

During September, they briefly broke off from cutting their own songs as they toyed with the idea of doing further conceptual collections, this time intending to focus on either favoured country and western songs or folk material.

'We love making albums,' Bernie Calvert was quoted as commenting in a 1969 article. 'I know I personally enjoy them. We are very involved in one at the moment, contributing our own material. This is The Hollies singing their own material, and we are devoting a lot of time and attention to it. We are also doing an album of country and western numbers. Not hillbilly stuff, but commercial country and western done in The Hollies style.'

Four tracks were attempted during mid-September – 'Louisiana Man' and another take on 'Dang Me', both songs they had previously performed on UK TV with Graham the year before, along with Don Rollins' 'The Race Is On' and Neil Diamond's 'Kentucky Woman'. However, after concluding that more "tribute" sets may well be getting too unoriginal in the eyes of both media and public, they abandoned the idea and returned to their own material. Now, with the sessions once again resuming a clear direction, the band members were committing to an album comprised solely of their own compositions. It was a complete turnabout in approach to that of the successful Top 3 predecessor, and that indeed was a significant aspect for at least one member of the line-up.

Allan Clarke's self-assurance had been severely rocked by the departure of his childhood friend, but by recommitting to be the central focus once again, lead vocals and centre stage without Graham, and by taking the young Terry Sylvester under his wing, his confidence and, subsequently, his songwriting began to redeploy. To date, Terry hadn't honed any of his potential writing abilities, and it was through Allan's experience and guidance that his talents began to also bear fruit.

The first song that Terry had brought to The Hollies' table was a delicate ballad entitled 'Gloria Swansong' (a play on the name of 1920s actress, Gloria Swanson), although once Allan had stepped in and helped him out with the composition, and it was taken into the studios during those early September sessions with Johnny Scott arranging an orchestra around it, the song simply took flight.

'Allan and I have become a songwriting inspiration to each other,' Terry was to comment in conversation with Alan Smith of the *NME*. 'He particularly helps me because he can translate the basic ideas I have into the final stage. He's also got a better idea of words than I have. I did one bit of a number in which I had words about "Prince Charming". Now I look back, they were diabolically corny. However, Allan let me down slowly and he said: "Well, I don't see Prince Charming for this one. I see swans. So, we did swans – and the result is 'Gloria Swansong' and it's all the better for it.'

'The only song from that LP that we performed live in that period was 'Gloria Swansong',' recalled Bobby. 'And if a song can survive in a Hollies' setlist then it's a good song.'[30]

Paired with a simple acoustic composition from Allan, the poetically styled balladeering 'Marigold', the joint 5-minute presentation was a particular highlight amongst the newer tracks, confirming the band's desire to stamp their own authority on their next release, without the cloying tweeness that had often dominated earlier albums. Sadly, on the finished product, a rather slipshod edit between the two songs, with a complete change in the audible ambience from one to another, emphasised the technical differences in production between the two adjoining numbers. For all of his abilities and expertise, this one appeared to go unchallenged by Ron Richards.

Of the dozen new songs that would eventually appear on the next album release, Terry would contribute his songwriting to six of them, all co-written between himself and Allan (with two gaining additional assistance from Tony), confirming the guiding light that mentor Allan was offering. By comparison, Allan's own songwriting skills, often far too easily overlooked in the grand scheme of Holliedom, brought forth an impressive ten of the eventual twelve selections. Tony, meanwhile, settled for a minor role when it came to putting pen and notation to paper for this particular project, content in his leading role when it came to studio work, or for trawling around the Tin Pan Alley areas of London, always on the search for external contributions.

That said, when the next 45 was issued, it was a Hicks composition that graced the flipside of the single, the thoroughly enjoyable yet slightly awkward "Cos You Like To Love Me", with its rushed pop phrasings and out-of-place harmonium break. However, there was never any question over the lead side of the new release, with the glorious 'He Ain't Heavy, He's My Brother' rolling out of the blocks on 19th September 1969 (Parlophone R5806). Entering the Top 40 two weeks later and climbing up to its peak of the number 3 position one month after that, it was only halted in its ascendance by American singer Lou Christie and 'I'm Gonna Make You Mine', along with the saccharine-coated million-seller 'Sugar Sugar' by the cartoon-creation, non-existent Archies. For all their attempts at reaching out for a new audience, diversifying their sound and cutting a full album of Bob Dylan compositions, The Hollies' hit-making potential continued unabated. Incredibly, this was their twentieth consecutive UK hit single for the Parlophone label, and the run showed no signs of slowing down. The success wasn't restricted to home shores either. Australia, Canada, Germany, New Zealand, South Africa, Malaysia, Norway and, most notably, the United States all afforded a place in their respective Top Tens to the single, with a strong showing at the number 7 position in *Billboard* being their first break back into the US Top 20 since 'Carrie Anne', almost three years previous.

The Hollies: 'He Ain't Heavy, He's My Brother' (Parlophone R5806)

Bang goes the happy-go-lucky Hollies and in comes a blues-orientated scene, beautifully led by Allan Clarke and all very slow and moody and doomy, come to that.

Story of sadness, with harmonica splurges, and some of those excitingly high-flying Hollie harmonies. Really this is tremendous stuff –one of the real value singles. If it isn't a smash biggie, then justice has gone for good. MASSIVE SELLER

UK Press Review

Needless to say, the promotional bandwagon followed on, with several appearances on *Top of the Pops*, along with guest slots on *The Vera Lynn Show, This is Tom Jones* (aired in both the UK and the US) and the popular Amsterdam-based show *Doebidoe*. Then, on 30th October, the band were once again given free rein over the TV airwaves to tape another televised special, albeit this time airing two weeks later on BBC2 at the distinctly non-social time of 11.45pm, just before the daily shutdown (the UK still turned off TV viewing during the night back in 1969). By this time, most young fans would have already turned in for the night – with no VCRs on hand to tape it and watch later.

*Friday Line-Up Presents: Pop into Bed (A Musical Nightcap with The Hollies)* was reportedly partially filmed during their recent sojourn in Sweden. It featured the band miming to a succession of songs taken from their upcoming album, to be entitled *Hollies Sing Hollies,* and the footage was then also interwoven with several artistic sequences filmed, ostensibly, to enhance the viewing experience.

'It was very nice of the television company to give us the opportunity of doing this,' commented Tony to the Swedish media at the time. 'Instead of just putting us in a studio and doing half an hour of studio shots, they allowed us to do some filming outside, which tied in with the actual tracks on the LP. There's one called 'Gloria Swansong' where we did some shots of a swan on a lake, which fitted in very beautifully with the song. The actual studio shots that we did were as good as could be expected, considering we had to rush through it...'[34]

Such was the BBC's unforgiving lack of foresight during this golden era, the tapes were subsequently wiped almost immediately after broadcast, and evidence of such artistic nature no longer survives in the archives, although it has since been confirmed that songs performed were 'Goodbye

Tomorrow', 'Marigold', 'Soldier's Dilemma', 'Look At Life', 'Gloria Swansong' and 'Reflections Of A Time Long Past'.

The group also made further TV appearances on *Dee Time* and *The Cilla Black Show*, dutifully made with the sole purpose of publicising their recent Top 3 hit and the release of the new album. Yet, despite the positivity surrounding the November UK release of the LP (in stereo only) – following on from the success of both *Hollies Sing Dylan* and the current 45 – along with the increased televised airtime, *Hollies Sing Hollies* suffered a severe sales setback, failing the register once again on the LP chart listings at home. It was yet another puzzling twist, albeit perhaps not unexpected. Had the band seen the achievements of *Hollies Sing Dylan* as a sign of their unwavering draw and support, with *Butterfly* but a blip on their track record? Did neither they nor EMI Records truly believe that the impact of not including 'He Ain't Heavy, He's My Brother' was negligible? Surely, the silver-disc award-winning 45 would have given the album a significant sales boost. Indeed, when the release appeared Stateside a few months later, retitled after the 45 and with the hit included (but 'Gloria Swansong' omitted), it gave the band their second Top 40 entry into the *Billboard* album charts. There seems little logic behind the decision.

> Currently riding high in the Top 10 of the best-selling singles charts with their 'He Ain't Heavy, He's My Brother' hit, The Hollies will soon equal that success on the LP charts with this powerful album follow-up. Here they offer such exciting items as 'Do You Believe In Love', 'Why Didn't You Believe' and 'Please Let Me Please'.
>
> *Billboard Magazine*

Certainly, the choice of material included on the UK edition, bar the exclusion of the single, was of exceptional quality. Visiting the UK shortly after the album's release, Graham Nash reportedly commented, 'If we'd been recording material like this, I'd never have left...!' However, had Nash contributed to any such sessions, then it's of much debate as to whether the album would have sounded so much of a 'group' effort. Allan's revitalised offerings were both unrestricted and truly outstanding, and Terry was both finding his feet and his voice with comparative ease. Meanwhile, Tony, Bobby and Bernie were cutting the instrumental tracks with a wealth of expertise and precision.

If anything, without Graham around, both Allan and, to a lesser degree, Tony emerged as notably more mature songwriters on the release. With 'Marigold' and the anti-war stance on 'Soldier's Dilemma', plus the two heartfelt reactions over Nash's exit with 'Goodbye Tomorrow' and 'My Life is Over With You', Allan cut a solitary and yet accomplished figurehead. Tony, meanwhile, provided the supportive, Buddy Holly-esque 'Don"t Give Up Easily', which featured an early Moog synthesiser – possibly the very same machine that George Harrison had recently imported into the Abbey Road Studios whilst The Beatles were working on their next release.

Allan and Terry combined once more to bring in the bouncy 'You Love 'Cos You Like It', initially written with pop starlet Clodagh Rodgers in mind, whilst Tony also stepped forward to take a rare lead vocal on the exquisitely arranged Clarke-Sylvester song 'Look At Life', later recalling;

'This was very rare for me. I know I'm not a very good singer, so I never pushed myself, but there was one particular song which we wrote when we were in Sweden, called 'Look At Life', and the meaning of the song was just trying to get people to take more advantage out of what is free in life. Not to get all hung up and get aggravations about… well, things which are just generally aggravating. I say we wrote it in Sweden particularly because it is one of the most beautiful countries in the world and it just inspired us to write.'[34]

When reflecting on his own contributions, Allan recounted, 'When Graham left The Hollies it was one of the most depressing moments of my life. How can I deny it, breaking up hurt. As I sat at home, utterly depressed, I wrote a song to pass the time. It's called 'My Life Is Over With You'. It's just a number about two people going their own ways. You can take it straight or as a romantic thing towards a girl, but let's be honest – I'd lost a great and lifelong friend and I was obviously writing about the experience.

'Graham came over here a couple of weeks ago and heard the LP. He said nothing while it played. Then when it finished, he looked up and said, "Why weren't we doing that two years ago? Why?"'

Bernie too also made a significant impact, coming in the form of a lavish orchestral piece that he had recently composed. Whilst some may question the inclusion of such an instrumental work, 'Reflections Of A Time Long Past' showed that the band were prepared to step away from the restricting boundaries that the vocal-pop tag came with.

'I can't seem to express myself with words,' Bernie commented in a conversation with *Mirabelle* teen magazine. 'I'm planning to team up with someone in the group who writes lyrics. I am ambitious but within the framework of the group. We've still got a lot of enthusiasm within the five of us which hasn't been tapped. I think it was the new blood that Terry brought in that fired us with this enthusiasm.'

In fact, the prospect of Bernie working outside of the band, on his own project, had even been mooted during mid-1968, prior to his external contributions to The Bread and Beer Band, but the general concept had never become anything more than talk.

He continued: 'I do worry slightly about the next five years, about the continuing success of the outfit, so I'm trying to expand my scope for writing.'

'I think we have definitely made quite a big step forward with this record,' was Tony's comment to the *New Musical Express* at the same time. 'That will bring in a new variation on everything. We have really widened our listening public.'

Sadly, it didn't play out in record sales, potentially hurt by the record's presentation. Whilst critical prog-favourites The Moody Blues and Jethro Tull were toying with lavishly created gatefold sleeves, Eric Clapton's *Blind Faith* was courting controversy with a cover featuring a naked eleven-year-old girl, and their former bandmate was lining himself up on a battered couch, along a sun-kissed Hollywood Boulevard, dressed down in denim and black cowboy boots, The Hollies, by comparison, were seen seated on garish yellow linoleum, wearing matching brown slacks, slip-on shoes, flared white-collared patterned shirts and cheesy grins. Allan, looking the worse for wear, had his hand unceremoniously placed between Tony's legs, whilst the bewigged Bobby looked like he'd rather be anywhere else but seated before the photographer. For all their musical efforts, The Hollies were now truly out of sync with the times.

For the first time, the record was presented in an expansive gatefold sleeve, offering up a more casual image of the band within. But, to view the inner spread, one had to *purchase* the album – and that meant being handed that front sleeve across the counter. Not many were prepared to go that far...

# CHAPTER EIGHTEEN

# NO ONE'S GONNA CHANGE OUR WORLD...

As the turn of the decade approached, The Hollies were considered very much a part of the British entertainment establishment. Since rock 'n' roll had first invaded the shores of Blighty and had subsequently mellowed out into varying forms of "beat" music, The Hollies had always been at the forefront. Eight years down the line and they were still reaching the higher peaks of the singles charts across the globe and selling out concert venues week by week. It was a phenomenal accomplishment, and the band members were duly recognised for their feats. Allan Clarke was accepted as having one of the finest lead vocal talents in the business, whilst the instrumental abilities of Messrs Hicks and Elliott were highly regarded amongst their peers throughout the industry. In addition, Calvert and the newly acquired Sylvester were no slouches with their contributions either. Although the five band members didn't live in glorified splendour, high up in ivory towers or turret-festooned castles or mansions, success had brought them a comfortable lifestyle and a sense of business acumen.

Allan, by now a happily married father of two, lived with his wife Jeni and their two boys in the affluent Hampstead district of North London. Tony, meanwhile, spent much of his time commuting around the world from his mews house in Knightsbridge, just around the corner from Harrods – although he too would soon move into a larger house in St John's Wood, close to Abbey Road, where he would share his time with '60s fashion model Jane Lumb. Always cautious with his money, Tony had developed an acute awareness of business strategy, going back to the first influx of wealth when he and Graham had financed Manchester's Pygmalia clothing boutique. In more recent times, he had invested in Gordon Mills' management company that oversaw the phenomenal rise of Tom Jones and Engelbert Humperdinck, whilst also purchasing shares in a London photographic agency, responsible for handling David Bailey amongst others.

'I find it a great enjoyment rushing out to buy *The Times* every morning and checking the prices,' he was quoted as saying. 'I do take gambles because I can't be bothered to study too closely, but I've done very well so far.' (*New Musical Express*)

Whilst sharing a penthouse flat in London for when business needs dictated, both Bobby and Bernie defied the urge to permanently move south, maintaining their northern heritage and opting to keep their roots firmly in the familiar surroundings of Burnley, Lancashire – Bobby in partnership with Tony's sister Maureen, whom he had been dating since the turn of the previous decade. Even the youthful twenty-two-year-old Terry Sylvester, who had barely been in the band for twelve months, could now afford to upgrade his living space, moving into a spacious Hampstead abode near to Allan, with his wife, Lynda, and their young son, Paul. It was a good life for them, even if many of the photographs that appeared during this period showed the weariness behind the eyes of certain members. Yet it was proving a constant battle to keep the band in the public's attention, such was the shifting focus of the industry.

The era of the "beat group" had long since faded, and many names that had once dominated the chart lists alongside that of The Hollies – Freddie and The Dreamers, Billy J Kramer, The Searchers, Gerry and The Pacemakers – had dropped from the front pages and were reduced to touring the northern cabaret circuits or knuckling down and making a living appearing in the lucrative pantomime season. Other acts, such as The Dave Clark Five, The Tremeloes and Herman's Hermits, had managed to maintain a career just that little longer, each adding to their impressive lists of chart facts, but they too were beginning to foresee the nails finally being driven in. It was by no means an easy feat to survive the pitfalls of the public's fickle taste.

Then again, it was often more than just down to the purchasing habits of the British population. Living in the back pockets of each other, day in, day out, crammed into the back of tiny transit vans for years can drive a serious wedge between even the most loyal of bandmates. By late 1969, The Beatles' empire was rapidly crumbling around them, the egos and the business dealings clashing, with John Lennon announcing to his bandmates his intention to quit as early as September that year. The Rolling Stones had endured the departure of one of their founding members, whilst the quarrelsome Kinks fought through the kontroversy of a US banishment and a declining if not loyal popularity. The Animals, The Move, Small Faces… they all had moments of power and glory but very few came through intact and, in some cases, certain individuals didn't come through at all.

Then, as the swinging '60s faded away into the history books, disproportionately consigned to the memory as little more than a halcyon summer of colours and bubbles, other bands took up the mantle.

The Moody Blues had stepped out of the remnants of Brum Beat, found two new frontmen, discovered the universe and took flight. Likewise, The Yardbirds, then later The New Yardbirds – rising back out of the ashes with a rock god at the fore, turned up the amplifier to eleven and rechristened themselves as Led Zeppelin. Pink Floyd resurrected their career, Fairport Convention fused folk with rock, emphasising the folk aspect – whilst Jethro Tull did the same, albeit opting to push harder on the rock pedal.

Across the ocean, the 1969 gathering at Bethel, NY had defined what would become known as the Woodstock Generation, and the rise of the thoughtful acoustic singer-songwriter fought hard to be heard above the rhythmic chooglin' of Creedence Clearwater Revival, the Latin influences of Santana, the eclectic rootsy sound of The Band or the downright loud 'n' dirty barrage of the MC5. Earlier groundbreaking acts such as The Byrds, The Lovin' Spoonful, The Mamas and The Papas and The Turtles had fallen away, and a new breed of musician followed on behind. Graham Nash, now a quarter of one of the most popular and acclaimed musical acts of the era, was right at the epicentre of it all, living the hedonistic lifestyle of a Los Angeles superstar (although he was to relocate to San Francisco shortly afterwards). The ego was very much far from dead…

Influences across the vast musical divide were spread far and wide, occasionally coming together to form vast cities of youth counterculture, either at the tribal gatherings of Woodstock, Altamont or, in the UK, at the legendary Isle of Wight musical festivals. The inaugural 1968 gathering on the usually serene island, located just off the English south coast, had seen

San Francisco's Jefferson Airplane headline the event, playing to a crowd of around ten thousand or so. Two years later, with Jimi Hendrix, The Doors, The Who and The Moodies performing on the stage, over half a million attendees swarmed across the small divide of water separating the island from the mainland. However, for one of the top-selling acts of the previous decade, an act still unanimously acclaimed by their peer group worldwide, and one that was placed ninth on the list of weeks spent in the UK singles charts that entire decade – 231 weeks – there was no slot on the bill. The Hollies, by virtue of their own unwillingness to portray an "image", or to bow to any pressures of expectation, were largely ignored by the burgeoning rock music fraternity. Their music may have moved on from the Gouldman-penned simplicity of everyday suburban lifestyles, but the clean-cut persona remained.

'The Hollies have never followed any trend,' Tony remarked in *New Musical Express*, one of the few credible music papers that still offered column space to the band. 'Images and gimmicks, they all die in the end. I can only really listen to the kind of music we might do. I am not a fanatical listener [but] I like the kind of stuff Graham is now doing. I bought all four Cream albums and I love Jethro Tull – they are really great.'

When asked why the band persisted with stage uniforms and suits, he responded, 'Because so few other groups do. The Hollies are run like a business. We all have an equal say at meetings and are ready to listen to another's point of view. Everyone can see where the money comes from and where it goes...'

By the end of November 1969, with the *Hollies Sing Hollies* barely going stale in the record racks, the band were already contemplating the next album, working on a series of initial sessions at Abbey Road. The cycle was endless. A swift visit over to the European continent towards the end of the month, followed by a week in cabaret at the Batley Variety Club, set the tone for the remainder of the year. On 14th December, they taped an appearance at the Yorkshire TV Studios in Leeds for a televised broadcast, airing over the seasonal period, that paid tribute to the work of EMI producer George Martin. Entitled *With A Little Help From My Friends*, this hour-long spectacular saw the neatly suited and booted Hollies pay tribute to George alongside other established names in entertainment, including Ringo Starr, Lulu, Dudley Moore and Spike Milligan. Then, that same month saw a significant release in The Hollies' canon, albeit one that possibly escaped the attention of many fans and collectors.

By that point, the 1968 recording of 'Wings' had been one of the great lost recordings of The Hollies. Composed in the main by Allan, with contributions from Graham, the song had been cut at Abbey Road during January of 1968 but had lain dormant in the studio vaults since then. When the prospect of contributing to an upcoming charity album was first mooted, Ron Richards proposed offering the forgotten recording as The Hollies' donation to the project. So it was that 'Wings' first appeared on a various artists compilation entitled *No One's Gonna Change Our World*, a collection assembled by comedian Spike Milligan and released in the UK on 12th December 1969 for the benefit of the World Wildlife Fund. With liner notes by the charity's patron, the Duke of Edinburgh, the release became more widely known by collectors as the original location for The Beatles' song 'Across the Universe', and its title was adapted from that particular song's lyrics. Nevertheless, The Hollies' contribution was a much-lauded critical inclusion, and the album (issued on the Regal Starline label SRS-5013) became a soon-sought-after collectable release.

A cover version, relabelled 'Wings (Why Do They Want Us To Walk)', as recorded by the unlikely pairing of Rod McKuen and Rock Hudson, appeared as a single in May of 1970 on the Warner Brothers label but, wisely, it didn't sell well and the less said, the better.

Rounding the year off and seeing out the 1960s, the group appeared on the European TV Special *Pop Go the Sixties*, a 75-minute co-production between the UK's BBC and Germany's ZDF broadcasting companies that aired on TV various channels across the continent on New Year's Eve. Several prominent artists from across the decade were featured, all from the UK (excepting German easy-listening pianist Horst Jankowski), and each took to performing one or more of their hit singles (although some of the selected acts, such as The Beatles, were shown via archive footage). For The Hollies' segment, the group were filmed at the BBC's Television Centre in London, two weeks previously (19th December), performing a live vocal rendition of *He Ain't Heavy, He's My Brother*. Allan, looking far healthier and more relaxed than he had for a long time, turned in an excellent vocal, whilst, interestingly, Bernie sat in on Reg Dwight's piano stool and Tony took on the bass guitar role. It was a fine way to end the year – and the decade, especially once the annual poll results came in from the *New Musical Express*, considered by many to offer the most accurate opinion of current musings.

## THE *NEW MUSICAL EXPRESS* 1969 POLL WINNERS

*Category: British Vocal Group*
1. The Beatles
2. The Rolling Stones
3. The Hollies
4. Fleetwood Mac
5. The Moody Blues

*Category: World Vocal Group*
1. The Beatles
2. The Rolling Stones
3. The Beach Boys
4. The Hollies
5. Creedence Clearwater Revival

Dear Members,

Thank you all very much for your Christmas cards – between us the boys and I received nearly enough to wallpaper the office. Terry also sends his thanks for the birthday cards which he hopes to find waiting for him when he comes into the office again!

From what I've heard, the boys all spent Christmas quietly at home. Terry, Lynda and Paul went to Liverpool, but just before Christmas Terry had been given one of the many injections that he had to have before leaving the country. This meant not only was his arm swollen, but he couldn't drink at all. He and Bernie went to a football match on Boxing Day – Liverpool v Burnley. Liverpool won 5-1, so Bernie wasn't too happy.

You must have realised by now that The Hollies have definitely gone to Australia as I said they might, last month. Allan, Terry, Bernie, Bobby, Rod and Derek left at 8am on Monday 5th January, flying via Frankfurt, Istanbul, Beirut and other places, and eventually arriving in Sydney on the 7th – a total of 42 hours flying time. Robin and Tony left England on the 3rd and took the shorter route via Los Angeles. This was for two reasons – firstly, because Robin wanted to arrive early in order to check that everything was all right, and secondly, because Tony hasn't been too well. As he took the shorter route and will have had a few days extra rest on arrival in Sydney, I should think he'll be fit and well by the time The Hollies start their 3-week cabaret appearance at "Chequers". All the boys have promised to send postcards.

Best Wishes
Lynne (Wheeler)
Fan Club Secretary

## CHAPTER NINETEEN

# I CAN'T TELL THE BOTTOM FROM THE TOP...

Australia 1970. Despite the success story that The Hollies had achieved down under, ten Top 20 hits to date, this was to be the first time that they had boarded a plane and headed for the southern hemisphere. A tour had previously been planned for the summer of 1967 but had to be cancelled following Bobby's flirtation with the shadows of death, and so this particular visit, a three-week residency at a popular Sydney club, was a first for the so-called Manchester boys.

Chequers enjoyed the reputation of being one of the finest nightclubs and entertainment venues in the world. Visiting dignitaries from the US cited it as superior to even the best that America could offer – including those that dominated the New York nightlife, such as the Copacabana and Latin Quarter. However, despite the big money it could generate to entice the world's premium performers to appear on its stage – Sammy Davis Jr, Liza Minnelli, Shirley Bassey – and a £7,500 weekly pay-out for jazz legend Sarah Vaughan, the club was renowned for its seedy underworld liaisons, with links between local Sydney gangsters and the American Mafia engraved into the brickwork. Thus, to pay The Hollies to travel halfway around the globe, put them up in luxury individual suites for three weeks, and to offer them unlimited use of a 72' motor yacht, captain and crew included, was fairly small change for such a "prestigious" booking.

The club itself was only small, enough for approximately 500 guests, but the contract requested The Hollies play two shows per day for the period of their residency, 7.30pm and midnight, and so plenty of paying punters had the opportunity to see them perform on the ornately surrounded stage.

On stage, they are as good vocally as on any one of their discs, which is something only The Beatles and Beach Boys can do.

'He Ain't Heavy, He's My Brother', 'I'll Be Your Baby Tonight', 'Dang Me' and 'Stewball' brought the house down.

Solid voices of unerring instinct, with great stage presentation – that's The Hollies. They are brilliant and generated much professional steam at their debut. The crowd was stimulated to a tingle of excitement.

Reviews of the Chequers residency
*The Hollies Official Fan Club Newsletter*

Much of their remaining time in Sydney was spent undertaking the promotional rounds of the radio stations, chatting to the local DJs and presenters, although they did also make an appearance on *Bandstand*, a popular and long-running Australian TV show, based on the format and success of the US show *American Bandstand*. Hosted by the radio and television newsreader Brian Henderson, the show had seen many fine artists grace the studio set over the years, including the pre-fame days of both Olivia Newton-John and The Bee Gees. The Hollies, upon taping their appearance (airing a short while later, on 7th February), performed a live-vocal six-song set comprised of 'He Ain't Heavy, He's My Brother', 'Carrie Anne', 'Just Like A Woman', 'Stop! Stop! Stop!', 'A Taste Of Honey' and 'Blowin' In The Wind', along with a medley comprising of 'Bus Stop', 'Just One Look', 'I'm Alive' and 'Sorry Suzanne'. Neatly presented, switching between white and dark suits, what was most surprising about the overall appearance was how they chose to stick to the old tried and tested setlist, and other than the recent single (a Top 10 hit across the varying Australian chart lists), they opted to completely ignore the *Hollies Sing Hollies* album, offering no support to its recent release, but instead continuing to play two songs from the previous *Hollies Sing Dylan* LP. Australia was one country that, surely, would have been open to hearing the new developments and musical turns of the band, far away from the media baggage that they carried with them on home shores. Didn't 'Don't Give Up Easily', 'Soldier's Dilemma' or, perhaps most obviously, 'Please Let Me Please' just lend themselves to the stage show? Apparently not...

Then, with the three-week stint completed, and just before boarding the long flight back home to England, they briefly diverted to Brisbane's Festival Hall for a show, and then on to Adelaide where they also managed to squeeze in an appearance at the Memorial Drive Park on 1st February, performing a concert supported by Australian acts Johnny Farnham, Travis Wellington Hedge and local band The Harts.

Carrie Anne / Medley (Bus Stop – I'm Alive – Just One Look) / Just Like A Woman / You Ain't Goin' Nowhere / I'll Be Your Baby Tonight / Stewball / Sorry Suzanne / Reflections Of A Time Long Past / He Ain't Heavy, He's My Brother / A Taste Of Honey / Blowin' In The Wind

Unfortunately, for reasons which remain unclear, Farnham (later, a hugely successful 1980s hit-maker) faced the ignominy of being booed off the stage that evening.

With a further series of international appearances scheduled on the horizon – although a Canadian tour (intended to follow on directly after Australia) was cancelled at short notice – the group returned to Abbey Road studios almost as soon as they had returned to the UK. With the need to keep the impetus in motion, and issuing a follow-up single to 'He Ain't Heavy, He's My Brother' a priority, they regrouped under the watchful eyes of Ron Richards during the middle of March to cut a series of songs, the first of which, surprisingly (at Ron's suggestion), was a reworking of 'Wings'. With the potential single in mind, the band tackled an updated rendition of the song – the original of which was still very much a rarity in Hollies collecting circles – but this time featuring Terry's prominent high harmony instead of Graham. The same 1968 instrumental track was utilised. Unfortunately, to date, that rendition remains in the vaults, and emphasis was instead placed upon a new composition by the British-Australian songwriting partnership of Guy Fletcher and Doug Flett, that also saw the return of Reg Dwight to the recording sessions. By this stage, Reg had taken to referring to himself by a new name (albeit not legally yet)... Elton John.

'I Can't Tell The Bottom From The Top' saw The Hollies repeat the format of the previous 45, not only with the additional keyboard assistance but also with Johnny Scott's orchestration accompaniment over another slow-paced melodramatic ballad. Without wishing to pigeon-hole themselves, it was clearly a move that suited the band, although another ballad that they had wished to pursue slipped through their grasp. That one was a new composition by Elton himself, entitled 'Your Song'.

Tony Hicks: 'I was in Ron Richards' office, and he played the demo of 'Your Song'. I thought, *Yeah, I'd love to record that*, so we got back to Dick James the publisher and he said, "Well, to be honest, the American record company are quite keen on that, with Elton trying to break in America. It will probably come to nothing and, obviously, Elton would love you to do it." But, of course, it was a big success for him, so we never ended up getting it…'[69]

Whilst not quite as distinctive as 'He Ain't Heavy…', 'I Can't Tell The Bottom From The Top' was still a strong number that saw both Allan Clarke's lead vocal and the tight Clarke-Hicks-Sylvester harmonies shine in what is a powerfully built, well-crafted song. Initially, however, neither Bobby Elliot nor Allan Clarke were convinced, with Bobby later commenting that the acoustic guitar was out of time with his percussive playing (a 2003 remix controversially omitted the acoustic guitar track entirely).

'Everything's okay, but life is just kind of rolling along nicely,' Allan would comment to the *New Musical Express*. 'If the single made it into the Top 30 – fine, but from my own point of view maybe not having a hit would be the inspiration I'd appreciate right now. After we left the studio, I just felt that [the song] hadn't really worked out.

'I've been recording on my own a little recently, finishing off a musical with my brother-in-law and Terry Sylvester. It's an unusual thing. The project is turning out a lot bigger than I thought it would. But it's like a challenge and that's what I like. I'll always get satisfaction being a Hollie but right now there's a kind of nagging thing in my mind that keeps telling me to do something else. That's why the musical is some kind of outlet…'

Other songs attempted during this run in Abbey Road included an updated take on 'Survival Of The Fittest', the 1968 Clarke-Hicks-Nash composition that the band had earlier attempted during Graham's final throes as a band member. This new version even incorporated much of the

1968 backing track, with Nash on acoustic guitar, and simply overdubbed some new instrumental work, along with Terry's harmony lines. Also taped were the singalong, harmonica-driven Tony Hicks composition 'Dandelion Wine' and another delightful, heavily orchestrated instrumental from Bernie, the visionary thematic melody of '(No More) Snow On Heather Moor'.

'Snow On Heather Moor' was later retitled 'Thoughts In The Night', Bernie was to later recall, 'because a friend of mine wrote some beautiful lyrics to it. 'Snow...' was just the working title. It was recorded to follow up 'Reflections Of A Time Long Past' from the *Hollies Sing Hollies* album, and that one had been so well received that we actually played it when we were touring with the orchestra. We featured that on stage, as an instrumental, and got such a tremendous response from our audiences at that time, so it seemed like a good idea. I felt 'Snow On Heather Moor' was even nicer and I had the privilege of mixing it myself. I missed out on a couple of sessions, due to illness, where the boys had a go at mixing it, but when I went down and heard it, I commented that I was unhappy about it, so they left me to remix it and I felt that I got a delightful track at the end of the day. Unfortunately, as in all cases, the selection of material that went on the albums was left to arbitration amongst ourselves and the producer and it never made it onto the following album, but it gave me a lot of pleasure to do that...'[36]

Another entry into the studio log for that series of sessions included the title 'Bobby's Prologue', although that item was no more than a short recitation from the drummer, perhaps all too aware of how Graeme Edge, the drummer for the high-flying Moody Blues, successfully introduced his own "cosmic" poetic readings onto their own million-selling albums. The initial intention was indeed to place the recitation at the start of the next album, offering a sardonic introduction to the otherwise serious project but, progressive as it may have seemed, that concept, along with the use of Bernie's gloriously constructed theme, never came to pass.

'That was simply me reciting poetry,' confirmed Bobby. 'It's something I've been doing for years, a piece by Sir Walter Scott. We were going to whack it straight into one of the songs. In the end, though, we didn't include it on the album. It was just something I did to make the guys laugh.'[56]

One week later and it was back out on the road for a ten-date tour of Germany and Austria, visiting Hanover, Dortmund, Colne, Duisburg,

Oberhausen, Mannheim, Nuremburg, Frankfurt, Vienna and Berlin, all accompanied en route by a twelve-piece German orchestra.

The first show was in Hanover. We arrived there to find ourselves six inches deep in snow – a surprise because the weather was so nice when we left England. Tony Prince, the Luxembourg DJ, flew over to compere the show and was very entertaining indeed.

The Hollies act has been described so many times that I only have to say it was as usual – all superb. The boys became a little unhappy towards the end of the act because the audience will not stay in their seats. 3,000 people clustered around the edge of the stage, and they sang 'Blowin' In The Wind' with at least 100 people trying to sit on their feet! However, as I've said before, this is the highest compliment a German audience can pay an artiste, and it's an incredible sight to see. We are taking stronger security precautions now, though, just in case someone should get hurt.

*The Hollies Official Fan Club Newsletter*
April 1970

'Professionalism could very well be a word The Hollies invented,' confessed Tony Prince when reviewing the tour shortly afterwards. 'Just before the show, The Hollies ran through a new song which Tony Hicks had just written and were busy getting down to the smaller but important details of the arrangement. As they worked away, a camera team took some film of them for a German TV show and a world-famous photographer used up dozens of films for a top German magazine.

'Then at each concert I compered for them, I saw the perfect audience. They joined in when The Hollies offered fun, they were serious when the group was, and enthusiastic throughout – right to the point of shouting themselves hoarse for encores and rushing the stage for autographs on the last triumphant note. I myself conducted the orchestra with a Coke bottle and giggled when I stood on my head to introduce the "Greatest Harmony Group in the World"!'

The Hollies are one of the very few groups which survived from the first years of beat [sic]. How they managed this became obvious last evening at the Philharmonic. They stuck to their happy style but nevertheless progressed excellently. But this one-hour show was more than just a brilliant performance of the world hits. The Hollies proved to be true entertainers.

German Press Review (translated)<br>April 1970

Following the tour, the band headed back home to commence a brief round of promotion for the new single, including appearances on *Top of the Pops* and *Not Only But Also*. Issued as Parlophone R5837, 'I Can't Tell The Bottom From The Top', paired with Allan Clarke's sublimely jaunty and humorous 'Mad Professor Blyth' (taped towards the end of the previous year), entered the UK Top 40 on 18th April, debuting at number 44 before advancing with a steady climb into the Top 10, finally stalling at the number 7 position during its ten-week run. Curiously, an alternative mix of the single was released in Australia on a latter-day Music for Pleasure compilation release. Whilst essentially the same recording, the strings overdubs were notably different to the familiar 45 release.

Media reviews of the single were largely positive, although some publications took it upon themselves to criticise both the release and the band itself, with one clearly misguided journalist writing for the *Peterborough Citizen,* "It's a bit slower than their usual stuff but it's still the same old, boring, repetitive Hollies!"

They also taped a return appearance on the *Julie Felix Show* (previously *Once More with Felix*), surprisingly performing a previously unheard Tony Hicks composition, the excellent 'Lady Please', a tune they had taken into Abbey Road the previous November but, to date, were still sitting on, potentially as an inclusion on the next album. Subsequently, it was largely unfamiliar to many viewers and fans and a potential promotional sales opportunity was missed, particularly in light of the fact that the second offering taped for the appearance, a duet with Felix on Tom Paxton's 'Going To The Zoo', a comical if somewhat embarrassing affair, did absolutely nothing for the band's integrity.

With Terry now comfortably fitting into his role and playing an increasingly developing part within the set-up, the group then ventured back across the ocean to the US to introduce American audiences to the new line-up. After yet more familiar-sounding tales of delayed visas, they flew out with BEA two days late, in two separate parties, over the afternoon and evening of 23$^{rd}$ April, arriving in New York the following day, with the first show scheduled for the vast, brand-new Hampton Coliseum, down in Virginia on the 25$^{th}$.

It was to be the usual round of punishing schedules for such a tour, as the five band members, along with Robin Britten and their two road crew, Rod and Derek, travelled hundreds, and even thousands, of miles on a daily basis, jumping from venue to venue, city to city. Chicago, over seven hundred miles to the north, was next on the agenda, followed by a series of college gigs in and around Michigan and Ohio. A flight even further north came next, flying across the border into Canada and appearing at the 6,000-seat Ottawa Auditorium, before they resumed a succession of shows in the US with sold-out college appearances in Albany, Bangor and Washington DC. However, at one point on the tour, such was the poor planning that it reached the stage whereupon several of the shows had to be cancelled, due to the overly long crisscrossing distances between venues.

Gradually, the band also began to introduce changes to their setlists, including a number of alternative cover versions to sit alongside the hits, whilst gradually dropping some of the older favourites. One of the first new additions, much to the delight of a rapturous American audience, was a simple piano-led version of The Beatles' newly released 'Let It Be'. With Bernie supplying the lone piano accompaniment, and Bobby taking an off-stage break, the trio of Hollie-harmonies rang out over the audiences each night, leaving them spellbound. With 'He Ain't Heavy, He's My Brother' still occupying a position in the US *Billboard* Hot 100, nineteen weeks and counting, it was a prime opportunity to reinstall the faith that their many loyal fans still held for them in the USA, despite their erratic chart success so far. The band even found the time to appear on the short-lived ABC-TV show *Get It Together*, co-hosted by their old friend Cass Elliott, performing the hit (airing in the final episode of the short run, later that year).

Then, after a couple of rest days, during which time Terry and Tony jetted into New York City to purchase some new guitars, they flew down for the penultimate show on the tour, one thousand miles south-westerly, appearing at Arkansas State University, before rounding it all off with a show at Florida's impressive West Palm Beach auditorium. Overall, the tour had been a huge success, but such is the size of the expansive continent that, in reality, the dozen or so shows undertaken, along with minimal TV and promotional opportunities, did little to raise their profile across the entire vastness of the US and, despite the runaway success of 'He Ain't Heavy, He's My Brother', when its successor appeared, 'I Can't Tell The Bottom From The Top' (Epic 5-10613), it peaked at a disappointing #82 position in *Billboard*.

The next set of recording sessions, upon touching back down in London on 11th May, took place soon after, and this ultimately completed the tracks for what would be the next album, provisionally entitled *Moving Finger*. Tony in particular, who was contributing significantly to the songwriting this time around, was incredibly enthusiastic as a result of the initial recording, prior to the final mixes, effusing to the press, 'It's really going to be something and will knock spots off any of our previous albums. It's really more what's happening today. There are certain audiences who only go for Jethro Tull and Crosby, Stills & Nash, and I'm sure this material will pull them as well.

'It opens with Bobby trying a piece of poetry, which is tongue in cheek, but basically the rest of the album is very serious with strong ideals. It's opinions and observations on what's going on around us.'

And yet, despite the recent sessions potentially taking the band into new exploratory territories and, perhaps, finally waking them up to where the music was now at – if only they could adapt the image too – they still had many pre-booked appearances to fulfil, and much of their key income in the UK, like it or not, was generated from the cabaret circuit. So, it came as no surprise to find them back on the treadmill during the first week of June, just four weeks since playing to sell-out auditoriums and universities across the US.

Following on from a lone college gig in Coventry, the band headed into Birmingham city centre where, for one week, they performed their popular-yet-routine cabaret act at the Dolce Vita Club (opened by actor and comedian Lance Percival) and the Cavendish Club, located in nearby Yardley, supported by a local band named Sunstroke. It appears that the white suits weren't ready to be consigned to the wardrobe just yet. Expanding their UK repertoire, they subsequently worked both 'Gloria Swansong' and the still-unreleased 'Lady Please' into the shorter setlist, and such was the response to their rendition of 'Let It Be' during the American tour that that one also found a position within the show. A petition was even run by members of the Hollies Fan Club requesting that the band record and release their version of the McCartney ballad. Unfortunately, the request went unheeded.

One further appearance in Oxford, at Keble College, brought the current round of touring and recording to a halt, allowing the band the luxury of a July break.

It was also during this period that the musical project Allan had been working on, alongside his brother-in-law John Bowstead, had seen fruition – albeit in a very limited way. John, the brother of Allan's wife, Jeni, and a burgeoning member of the '60s UK pop art scene, had initially conceived the stage production, a project he entitled *Oh Flux!,* as an imaginary *Alice in Wonderland*-styled piece, and he had engaged Allan to provide the musical landscape to accompany his conceptual visions. Working alongside Terry Sylvester, John and Allan then copyrighted a series of new compositions that they intended to use in the production, with the co-collaborations listed as 'Critical Inquisition', 'He Threw In A Diminished Seventh', 'Love Makes The World Go Round', 'There's No Business Like It' and 'Welcome To Our Show'. In addition, 'Chicken Out And The Channel', 'Life Is Next To Something Else' and 'Thing Of Beauty' were listed solely as Bowstead-Clarke compositions, whilst the Clarke-Sylvester partnership also offered up some new tunes. Cutting the tracks with Terry, and utilising the rhythm section of bassist Dee Murray and drummer Nigel Olsson, Allan even produced the songs that were to be heard during each stage performance. Sadly, all of his efforts amounted to little as, following a five-day preview run at the small Gulbenkian Theatre in Canterbury during May of that year, the show went no further.

Allan: 'We put it on at the Gulbenkian Theatre at the University of Kent, and it got rave reviews. We then got a call from an impresario called Robert Stigwood, who later managed The Bee Gees, and he said that he wanted to put the play on in the West End. A few weeks later, Robert called and said that another musical had come along and that they were going to go with that one instead of ours. I thought, *Shit, what's that called then?!* It was *Jesus Christ Superstar*! I asked Robert who wrote it and he said that it was a guy called Tim Rice. Tim used to be the tea boy at EMI!'[31]

Any future intentions for the project fizzled away... permanently. The recordings still reside in Allan's personal archive to this day.

Having spent much of July resting up after the busy preceding weeks and months, with the five members scattering to various locations across Europe and the UK (Allan and family flew to Portugal, Bobby and Maureen spent time in Wales, whilst Bernie drove his sports car and his girlfriend down to

Cornwall – Terry and Tony simply relaxed at their respective homes), the band regrouped and resumed duties during the final week of the month. First up was the taping of an appearance for the *It's Lulu* TV show on the 26th of July (airing on 1st August), followed by an Abbey Road recording session on the 29th and then a performance at the glitzy Blackpool Opera House on 2nd August. Finally, for now, they resumed cabaret duties with a week at the Golden Garter Club in Wythenshawe, Manchester on the 3rd, a venue they had first graced the previous July.

Acclaimed 1960s singer-songwriter Gene Pitney, who had first encountered members of The Hollies back in 1964, later summarised the smoky atmosphere of the northern cabaret circuit, and of the Golden Garter in particular, recalling, 'It was a huge club in its day. It was fantastic. It was a smoke-filled, drinking atmosphere and a late-night show. Sometimes it was like looking through a haze to see your audience. And it got pretty rowdy at times, but it was fun. Those kind of shows always had a tremendous amount of bouncers. There were ladies who would rush the stage and grab whatever they could from you!'[32]

Certainly, for the majority of performers who regularly frequented these smoke-filled venues during lengthy seasonal runs, often filled to the rafters with paying customers, the intense exposure could easily cause issues with their vocal abilities, and for Allan in particular, performing two shows a night in such hostile environments, these dates often caused him severe issues and challenges. The week recently spent in the hot and humid climes of Sydney's Chequers nightclub, with the constant air conditioning aiming to maintain a steady temperature, had threatened the group's appearance when, after one week in the venue, Allan had lost his voice. Subsequently, he spent the remainder of the run on a diet of various pills and injections, with a personal dehumidifier installed in his room, hoping to revitalise his dried, weary vocal cords. The thick cabaret smoke only made it harder.

With the constant battle to keep the group relevant and within the public's attention span, and with EMI keen to keep the momentum going, another 45 was placed on the label's release schedule for the 18th of September. Cut during the 29th July session, this next release was a song penned by the successful Roger Cook-Roger Greenaway duo, a pairing previously known professionally as David and Jonathan (who had achieved success back in the mid-'60s with a cover of Paul McCartney's 'Michelle', followed by their own self-composed hit 'Lovers Of The World Unite'). Cook had then gone on to be a co-founder of the popular UK act Blue Mink, releasing a succession of successful pop-orientated singles for the Phillips label such as 'Melting Pot' and 'Good Morning Freedom'. Combining their talents with Tony Macauley ('Sorry Suzanne'), the trio came up with the social commentary of 'Gasoline Alley Bred'. A fine work, highlighting the social differences between the well-heeled and those from the English working classes, those struggling to find a penny to rub together, Blue Mink also cut their own version during the same period, featured on their 1970 *Our World* LP, with Roger Cook's lead successfully blending with the soulful vocals of fellow band member Madeline Bell. For The Hollies' tasteful rendition, the lead vocals were handled by Allan, with Terry supplying the supporting lines on the second verse.

Nevertheless, the media reviews were mixed:

Play it once and there are no doubts about its immediate commerciality. Play it again and the nuances and the subtle changes of both tempo and volume are that much more apparent. It's a sign of the times. Whereas The Hollies once went for the obviously commercial, they now experiment. Longish, but interest-holding. It's well up to the standards set over the past.

*Record Mirror*
September 1970


The Hollies reach a peak – of boredom!
This must be the most boring tune they've ever tackled. Superbly done, and they sing in tune and all that, but if this is a hit, I'll retire to a pebble farm in the Azores…

Kenny Everett
*Disc & Music Echo*
September 1970


Whilst the band were waiting for the song to get a worldwide release, they briefly crossed back over the North Sea for a short five-day visit to Scandinavia, taking in performances in Karlstad, Stockholm, Furuvik and Gothenburg in Sweden, with a fifth show added in for Helsinki in Finland.

All four of these Swedish shows undertaken were played within the folk parks, popular outdoor venues that could be found scattered throughout the country, benefitting from rural settings, and filled with funfairs and entertainment shows, many of which had to shut down for the period of the big shows so as not to interrupt the sound system. Interestingly, 'Gasoline Alley Bred' was issued in Sweden three weeks earlier than anywhere else, to capitalise on the visit, although, somewhat surprisingly, it wasn't a big success there. Then again, a typesetting issue on the hastily cropped picture sleeve, and also on the label, listing it as 'Gasoline Alley Bread', couldn't have helped the local Scandinavians understand the interpretation.

Despite a curiously top-heavy treble mix that drained all power from Bobby's sublime drumming, The Hollies' first stereo UK single appeared to be set for another rapid ascent up the charts and yet, upon a worldwide release, and notwithstanding a strong performance on the BBC's flagship *Top of the Pops* (a first, in that they finally stepped out of the suits and appeared in casual dress – causing howls of protest and letters of dissent to be mailed in to the fan club), the single surprisingly stalled outside the Top 10, finding its eventual peak at #14. It also missed out in the US as well, failing to register at all in *Billboard*, although it did manage a modicum of international success elsewhere, including the #6 position in Poland and #2 in Singapore. Despite a round of further TV appearances in the UK, including *Champagne on Ice, The Bobbie Gentry Show* and, lastly, *The Rolf Harris Show* (where a dispute over the lyrics to 'Lady Please' forced a change in the two-song choice), the 45's failure to break into the Top 10 is surprising, given the selection of several mediocre releases that filled the upper reaches and, for whatever reason, caught the public attention to a greater level – Bobby Bloom, The Poppy Family, Hot Chocolate, Roger Whittaker... and Des O'Connor. A brief two-day visit to Germany, to tape another TV appearance, also failed to deliver, as the single was neglected there as well.

This release would mark the final time that The Hollies would actually break into the UK Top 20 for a considerable period. Subsequent releases would falter, and it wouldn't be until early 1974 that they would bother the higher levels of the lists again. The long, continuous run of chart successes, twenty-one in a row, had finally come to a close...

# CHAPTER TWENTY

# DON'T GET SUNBURNT...

Confessions Of The Mind, the tenth long-playing album issued by The Hollies, appeared on the record racks on 13th November. Following a change of title, instigated by the inclusion of a new composition by Tony Hicks, and a decision going against including Bobby's poetic recitation, the album quickly garnered favour amongst the close-knit community of fans and followers for the wide range of recordings and styles featured within. Once again, all of the songs were composed by the band members themselves, highlighting their increasing maturity as songwriters, although it was noticeable how Allan and Tony were no longer working together creatively, distancing their relationship, offering up a succession of solo works instead or, in Allan's case, in partnership with Terry. Terry, in his own right, was also adding to the band's overall strength as individual composers.

Two of the Clarke-Sylvester songs came about as a result of the *Oh Flux!* musical, with both 'Isn't It Nice' (full of dense, wonderful harmonies) and the heavier, bluesy 'Perfect Lady Housewife', featuring the newly rechristened Elton John wailing away on Hammond organ, bringing a new sophisticated approach to their sessions. The eleven performances captured onto tape were of a far more complex and diverse nature than that which they had cut before, with the lengthy Hicks-composed title track taking the listener through a variety of moods, time changes and atmospheric feelings that showed their development, both as composers and artists. Simply put, they had taken the progressive stance intonated on the preceding *Hollies Sing*

*Hollies* collection but moved it up a notch. Certainly, Tony's abilities shone through with his varying selection of stringed solos.

> An outstanding album on which all of the songs are good. The impeccable vocals are particularly effective and the imaginative arrangements by Johnny Scott are a cut above the kind of things one hears with most groups.
>
> *Reveille*
> November 1970

Although, as was still the norm, no single was taken from the release to help promote the album further, there were unquestionably two or three potential inclusions that could comfortably have graced a seven-inch piece of EMI vinyl. Tony's 'Little Girl' and 'Lady Please', or the upbeat Clarke-Sylvester 'Man Without A Heart' (a Top 30 hit in Holland), all had the commerciality to succeed, as did the impressive Hicks work, 'Too Young To Be Married' – a song Tony had been working on for a considerable period. Composed during the summer of 1969, and initially taken into the recording studios the following September (and eventually completed during early May 1970), the song ultimately went on to great success when EMI-Australia followed their instincts and successfully released it as a single the following year.

'We can't go on putting out happy singalong type songs,' commented Tony to *Disc & Music Echo*. 'Commercial songs still sell well but we feel that we've passed that stage. They're all right for groups like Pickettywitch and White Plains, but not for us.

'Our songwriting has also undergone change. I used to write about love mainly, but now I choose more general subjects. I'm writing about worldly affairs and more important issues. They mean so much more.'

Perhaps by way of taking their approach more seriously, and by dropping the cheesy sleeve photograph scenario, the album (issued as Parlophone PCS7116) went on to gain a reasonable level of achievement, outselling its predecessor and reaching the UK Top 30. Packaged in a plain black and white cover, conceived by EMI promotions manager Terry Walker, void of any band image, and with the lyrics printed on the reverse side (à la *Sergeant Pepper*), *Confessions Of The Mind* stands out in the Hollies catalogue as being a turning point whereupon it appeared that they were successfully attempting a move away from being the hit-making, besuited, clean-cut favourites of the early days, and taking on the mantle of a serious rock band. And yet, despite their best intentions and some of their finest recordings being cut during this period, The Hollies had by now become an anachronism in a world of progressive album-oriented music. The non-image they had crafted for so long, paired with the middle-of-the-road appeal of the *Hollies Sing Dylan* release, the cabaret dates and the bow ties, had torn away the credibility to those who actually listened and purchased such grandiose productions. The fans who squealed at their concerts, or the parents who happily hummed along to 'He Ain't Heavy, He's My Brother', were simply not going to fully appreciate the underlying artistic arrangements that went into Allan's acoustic 'Separated', a true gem of tablas, sitars and misplaced hollers of enthusiasm, or the delicate lyrical intentions of Tony's 'Frightened Lady', a composition that came out of hearing about the increasing tensions within the American political scene, and one that took on more resonance following the recent events that the band had experienced for themselves, during their own recent visit to the USA.

'We had played Kent University, Ohio, the day after the riot in which six people were shot,' Allan was to recall during an interview for *Record Mirror*. 'The atmosphere there was very tense. Everybody was very edgy and even though nothing happened while we were there, I was glad to get away.'

Overall, the commerciality in the music was still there. It was always there, bubbling away underneath, and the band never turned their backs on their 45 hit-making potential, but the albums had now developed into artistic statements – two years after Graham Nash had tried to convince the world of their value. But who was really listening now?

The subsequent cabaret bookings that the band commenced during the closing months of 1970, filling out the smoky halls of Sheffield's Bailey Club, Stockton's Tito's, the Club Latino in South Shields or the familiar surroundings of the Batley Variety Club, were not going to be ringing out to the sounds of the 5-minute title track, that was for certain, although for their non-cabaret appearances, playing to the younger university audiences, the band did try to widen the appeal.

Asked by the *New Musical Express* why the band hadn't performed on a full UK tour for a considerable period, Allan responded, 'We will do one when we are ready. If we did it at this moment, we would die a death. If we keep on the way we are going I think we would be able to go into the Manchester Free Trade Hall and fill it.

'The people we are after are the ones who don't buy our records now. We were classed as bubblegum, but now we have changed, and it is the other kind of audience we want to grab hold of.'

For the university gigs, the succession of classic '60s hits was reduced further, seeing them incorporated into one quickly run-through medley, allowing them time to concentrate on the newer tunes such as 'Too Young To Be Married', 'Gloria Swansong', 'Lady Please' and 'Isn't It Nice', and their popular version of 'Let It Be' remained a regular favourite as well. They also briefly toyed with a cover of Elton John's 'Country Comfort', along with an a cappella rendition of an old 1800s seas shanty, 'Blood Red Roses' – a song that Tony had recently discovered on an Ian Matthews LP.

Then again, such was the commercial impact of 'He Ain't Heavy, He's My Brother' that it was almost inevitable that this particular song was going to bring each show to a dramatic climax night after night, regardless of the venue or audience age spectrum. That song, alone, had placed the band into the very establishment against which much of the youth culture was rebelling – and such was the dichotomy in which their split personality had now placed them.

For the North American issue of the album, the originally proposed title was retained and the Epic Records release of the *Moving Finger* album, whilst not as successful in the charts as it was at home, still generated a position in the lower regions of the Top 200 LP lists. Substituting the two closing songs on the UK version – 'Separated' and 'I Wanna Shout' with 'Gasoline Alley Bred' and 'Gloria Swansong' (omitted from the previous US release), the collection was another equally satisfying gathering, unhampered by the change in track selection or the newly designed packaging (hand-signing the individual letters of the album title on the front and a lengthy essay on the rear, penned by respected journalist-singer-songwriter Morgan Ames).

The Hollies is a group that knows what it's doing and has a lot to do. They know music and have much to say with it. They continue to be one of the most influential forces in pop music, and this album is a fine representation of their impact. Hold onto it.

Morgan Ames
*Moving Finger* sleevenotes
Epic Records 1970

With production duties afforded to the man who was continually their guiding light in the studio, Ron Richards, the album in either format remains compulsive listening and stands as an important benchmark in the band's catalogue.

'The most important thing for The Hollies is that the songs they record have a strong melody,' commented Ron at the time. 'But recently we have been moving away from that as the main criterion into the sort of songs where the lyrics really matter. This change has been helped along by the changes which have happened in the group. The only two members who originally started out are Allan and Tony, and this has meant that there has been a constant injection of new ideas, which is essential for survival.

'People think that The Hollies have a built-in following which automatically sends their records up the charts. I don't believe this. We have to prove ourselves with each record. Normally, we all collect songs which we like and then play them in a sort of *Juke Box Jury* session, where I pronounce the final judgement. The Hollies are judged purely on each record they produce.' (*Record Mirror*: September 1970)

*

On 23rd November, 1970, Tony Hicks made an unannounced guest appearance on the children's BBC TV show *Blue Peter*. Using his guitar skills, he successfully demonstrated a new style of portable radio microphone for the instrument that allowed the user to walk freely around, whilst playing, and without the need for trailing electrical cords. Unfortunately, and despite his generosity in giving up his time to demonstrate such equipment, the TV show's resident studio dog felt otherwise and duly bit into his leg, tearing his trousers in the process. The perils of live TV...

*

The arrival of another new year saw the group once again fly out on the long journey to Australia, playing a series of shows across the country, whilst also taking in two appearances in New Zealand beforehand. Following the conclusion of the tour, they would then fly home via South-East Asia, performing a further series of concerts across the continent *en route*.

Departing from London's Heathrow Airport on 22nd January 1971, and journeying via the North Pole, Los Angeles and Tahiti, the group touched down in Auckland on the morning of the 24th, three days before the opening show of the tour. Greeted by a sea of press reporters and media frenzy, the band acclimatised for a short period before travelling on to the New Zealand capital city of Wellington, where the first concert was scheduled. Such was the huge demand for the group that they even managed to squeeze in a TV appearance beforehand, taping an unplanned 20-minute special for the New Zealand Broadcasting Corporation (NZBC) network prior to the opening night.

On the strength of their live performance alone, The Hollies will remain top in their field for a long time to come. Rarely has Wellington seen a more exciting pop act than that which the five-man English group turned on for a packed house in the Town Hall last night. This was one occasion where no time was lost getting through to their audience in the preliminary stages of the act. It was all systems go from their opening selection of early Hollie hits to their final encore – a furious rendition of the Chuck Berry standard, 'Too Much Monkey Business'.

The reception accorded the group was one of the most enthusiastic seen here for a long time.

*The Dominion*
January 1971

27th January 1971: Town Hall, Wellington, New Zealand
28th January 1971: Western Springs Stadium, Auckland, New Zealand
29th January 1971: Festival Hall, Melbourne, Australia
31st January 1971: Capitol Theatre, Sydney, Australia
2nd February 1971: Festival Hall, Brisbane, Australia
4th February 1971: Civic Theatre, Canberra, Australia
5th February 1971: Memorial Drive Park, Adelaide, Australia
6th February 1971: Perry Lake Stadium, Perth, Australia

Performing a setlist which included a succession of popular releases that had seen Top 20 success in both New Zealand and Australia, the group worked these into a show that intertwined the hits with a collection of newly added material, filling each venue to rapturous applause night after night.

Stunning *a cappella* renditions of 'Amazing Grace' and 'Blood Red Roses' framed the by-now-familiar version of 'Let It Be', whilst a nod of the head to their former bandmate came about with a version of the Crosby, Stills, Nash & Young arrangement of Joni Mitchell's 'Woodstock'.

These, paired with performances of 'Gloria Swansong' and the recently released 'Too Young To Be Married' (a song that went on to top both the New Zealand and Australian charts later that summer), filled out the halls and stadiums each night, all courtesy of the group's impressive PA system they had brought along, especially for the tour.

Carrie Anne / Just One Look / Bus Stop / Stop! Stop! Stop! / Sorry Suzanne / Gasoline Alley Bred / Amazing Grace / Let It Be / Blood Red Roses / Woodstock / Gloria Swansong / Too Young To Be Married / He Ain't Heavy, He's My Brother / On A Carousel / Too Much Monkey Business

Following the sell-out second performance in the sweltering 90-degree heat of Auckland, the group moved on to Australia where, in between the continuing run of successful shows, they were followed around by ABC-TV director Bruce Wilson and his camera crew, who captured the five-man line-up, both on and off stage for yet another upcoming 60-minute TV Special.

Tour manager, Rod Shields: 'Apart from The Hollies seen performing on stage, during the next few days we filmed sequences with a beach buggy, surfboarding – in which Allan got a black eye and Tony caught a cold – and Bernie acting a role in a surfboard factory, purchasing boards for the rest of the boys.

'During one of the days filming, ABC organised a barbeque out in the bush and Terry and Tony, who had taken their acoustic guitars along, started playing, and Allan, quite spontaneously, started singing about the things around him. In particular, the beautiful red gum tree which they were sitting beneath. All this was quite unrehearsed, and it was filmed just as it happened...'[33]

Filming would continue for the duration of the short tour, with the results airing shortly afterwards as the ABC broadcast *Don't Get Sunburnt* (a play on the fact that both Allan and Terry had suffered severe sunburn whilst filming on the beach), although, due to various contractual reasons, the special never received a worldwide distribution, with the final cut residing in the vaults to this very day, unseen by many. Meanwhile, each performance continued to be greeted with wild enthusiasm as they travelled across the vast country, with many local radio stations forced to request that any hopeful attendees stay away unless they had a valid ticket for the evening performances, such was the media and public demand to see the band appearing.

An enthusiastic crowd of more than 8,000 last night welcomed the British pop group to Adelaide for their second visit in less than twelve months. England's Hollies held a capacity audience in the palm of their hand from the moment they leapt onto the stage at Memorial Drive last night.

*The Adelaide Advertiser*
February 1971

Then, following the sell-out Australian leg of the tour, and a four-day break in the schedule (taking in some sunbathing, snorkelling and fishing), the band took in new territories once more, venturing to South-East Asia where they played sold-out performances in Djakarta, Singapore, Kuala Lumpur and finally, Hong Kong.

Playing shows in the Indonesian capital city of Djakarta was a first for a western rock band, and the demand was so high that tickets for the two shows, held in the city's 10,000-seat sports stadium, were exchanging hands for up to seven times their face value, but the band duly gave a performance that warranted such interest and devotion, playing to a rapturous reception throughout. The continuing adulation followed them for the remainder of the schedule, even generating the support of a local band of Malaysian Hell's Angels who afforded the quintet the honour of a motorcycle escort back to their hotel, following the successful second show in the populous city of Singapore.

Notably, the second of these Singapore performances was captured onto audiotape, courtesy of Bobby Elliott who, during an afternoon's shopping excursion, had purchased a stereo cassette recorder, positioning it next to the stage that very evening. Rumours abounded that the resulting recording would eventually surface officially on vinyl, but it was all to little avail, as the general poor quality of the recording suggested otherwise.

Even sceptics of currently accepted popular music would probably agree that The Hollies are five accomplished performers. Their fans who bought every seat for the group's two shows in Hong Kong's City Hall seemed convinced. Fortunately, for the Hall's management, the pop fans generally keep to their seats and show their enthusiasm with palm-blistering clapping, shouts and screams. But at the end of the show there was a rush to the front of the hall to get autographs.

Hong Kong Press Review<br>February 1971

Returning home shortly afterwards, the group took little time to rest, opting instead to continue with daily demands by immediately taping an appearance for BBC's *Top of the Pops*, guesting on the show's new "album slot" – a break from the usual hit single-format, whereupon one band or solo artist each week was given the opportunity to perform two more obscure songs from their recent album release. For their appearance, The Hollies chose to perform two tracks from the *Confessions Of The Mind* album; the opening number, 'Survival Of The Fittest', along with Tony's 'Too Young To Be Married'. This latter tune reportedly caused a great deal of consternation during the actual filming when the televised audience, dancing mindlessly before the cameras, were brought to an open-mouthed standstill when the lyrics turned to *having a baby*. This was new territory for "rock" lyrics...

Filming completed, it was then straight over to Holland to tape a 25-minute appearance for *Jam* TV which included a rare-televised slot for the lengthy album title track (sadly, the footage seemingly no longer exists). Then, 11ᵗʰ March saw them resume the UK cabaret schedule with a show in Derby, before gracing the newly constructed hallways of AIR Recording Studios for the first time, intent on continuing the run of chart successes.

Following the foundation of AIR (Associated Independent Recording) by George Martin, John Burgess, Peter Sullivan and Ron Richards back in 1965, the business had thrived from a production perspective, operating from a series of recording studios in and around London. The payback of such a set-up was beneficial for all, in that AIR would fund the production costs of new releases, relieving record labels of the outlay and, in return, they would take a royalty on the eventual sales. For the artists they worked with, they had the reassurance that some of the very best in the business were overseeing their recording sessions. Then, with the October 1970 construction of a four-studio complex in Oxford Street, right in the very epicentre of the London shopping district (located in an unused banqueting suite, up on the fourth floor of the Peter Robinson department store), AIR took a huge leap forward. Comprised of two large studios, alongside two smaller ones, and a selection of soundproof booths, impressive Bösendorfer grand pianos, and the very latest studio technology – a 24-track recording and 48-track mixing console, custom-designed by Neve to AIR's specification – the building soon became the go-to facility for many top artists of the day. The larger studios were often booked out for months in advance and, as did so many others, The Hollies soon found themselves at odds with other bands, fighting for studio time. Pink Floyd were also in residence during that same period, cutting tracks for what would become the *Meddle* album. Roxy Music and Queen would follow in soon after.

'Hey Willy', a new song composed by Allan Clarke, in collaboration with the Greenaway and Cook partnership, was the first song The Hollies would cut in the new studios, a location in which they would spend much of the coming weeks, rolling into months, as they toiled on new music together. A much heavier composition than they had worked on before, driven by a heavy, repetitive guitar riff and thundering bass line, coupled with some tinkling ivories courtesy of session pianist Roger Coulam (co-founder of Blue Mink), leaving Allan to power through the vocals, breaking into falsetto at times as he raised both his game and pitch. Issued as Parlophone R5905 (paired with the lyrically smart and racially observant 'Row The Boat Together'), the recording initially entered the charts the following May but, after spending just four weeks rising to a peak of #22, the role was reversed and it surprisingly began a gradual descent, before dropping away altogether – and that was despite the song garnering the recognition of John Lennon in the music press.

'It will shoot up the chart like a rocket...' John reportedly noted, either in faint praise of the recording or resigned acceptance as to The Hollies' continuing success. Clearly, he was misguided, as were others;

I'd heard The Hollies doing great things but this – it fair takes the breath away. I am staggered. This is rock and roll; it's loud, it's heavy, it's gritty, bluesy, raucous and absolutely brilliant. A number one smash hit – no doubts.

*Disc & Music Echo*
April 1971

As to whether the composition refers in any way to Graham Nash, whose nickname in the band had always been *Willy*, that remains fully unclear, even fifty years after the event. It may well have been purely coincidental, and Allan has both confirmed and denied it over the ensuing years (co-writer Roger Cook has always categoricaly denied it), but the relative failure of the song as a single release, given the band's previous chart history, came as a surprise to many as it continued the downward spiral started by 'Gasoline Alley Bred'.

At the same time, Epic Records in America opted to release an edited version of 'Survival Of The Fittest' (omitting the third verse and hastening the fade), taken off their *Moving Finger* collection, as a US 45 release. But, despite several positive press reviews, the single failed to gain much airplay and suffered the same fate that had befallen many of their US releases, failing to register in *Billboard*.

> The cheerful flashiness of The Hollies' style doesn't quite match the lyric in this new single, but the brilliance should make it a fast-rising favourite with Top 40 listeners.
>
> *Cashbox*
> April 1971

Late March had seen the band back out on the European circuit once again, playing five nights across Germany. Unfortunately, a pre-tour performance in Amsterdam had to be cancelled, as Allan was suffering from a back injury he had sustained in Australia. Nevertheless, he had sufficiently recovered within the space of a week and the German tour went ahead as planned.

> The Hollies will be the first group to perform in East and West Berlin on consecutive days! They will succeed in temporarily breaking down the Berlin Wall when, on March 8th, they star in their own 45-minute live radio show in East Berlin – then, the following day, they cross into the Allied sector to give a concert in the Philharmonic Hall.

Manager Robin Britten told the NME that he has also asked the London Royal Festival Hall for its first available date, in order that The Hollies can star in concert there.

*New Musical Express*
March 1971

25th March 1971: Offenbach, Germany
26th March 1971: Saarbrucken, Germany
27th March 1971: Stuttgart, Germany
28th March 1971: East Berlin, Germany
29th March 1971: West Berlin, Germany
30th March 1971: Braunschweg, Germany

With a few adjustments to the selection they had performed down under, the band played a 45-minute set, reintroducing 'I Can't Tell The Bottom From The Top', along with renditions of Tony's 'Frightened Lady' and a recent Neil Young composition, 'Only Love Can Break Your Heart', a song supposedly written for his friend, Graham Nash, to help him over the heartbreak of his recent split from lover Joni Mitchell. Needless to say, the reviews from the German media were unanimous in their praise.

The following month, they made a triumphant and long-overdue return to their hometown, making a now all-too-rare concert appearance at Manchester's Free Trade Hall on 25th April. Having concentrated solely on cabaret audiences in the UK for far too long, this concert was duly heralded accordingly, with the review in the *Disc & Music Echo* thusly stating, "Hail the conquering Hollies! Henceforth the greatest harmony group in the world. Their triumphant rapturous return to the UK concert platform proved beyond any shadow of a doubt that musically they're among the best live acts around. They sang superbly. Presentation is painstakingly professional. Funny without being frivolous. All the time aware that they're musicians, there to entertain."

With hindsight, it seems surprising that the band made so few concert appearances in the UK during this particular period. As Allan had previously noted in conversation with the *New Musical Express*, they were changing, trying to put their music across to a new audience. British cabaret was all well and good for filling the coffers, but the appeal of the shorter sets in smoke-filled lounges was uninviting for many. He would later elucidate further with *Melody Maker*:

'Cabaret was like being put out to pasture. It was good for the bread and things like that. It was a spate The Hollies went through because we were the type of group that appealed to everybody. We'd pack 'em in and we'd go down so well anyway. It was easy. I just get fed up with singing all the hits, night in night out, y'know? I was just like a dummy. Pull my string and I'm off for an hour. I think with the cabaret audience they just sit there, and they want to be reminded, but with the concert audience you've got to be spot-on, because they're intense. They sit on the edge of their chair and they say, "Right, entertain me." With a cabaret audience half of them are pissed anyway so all they are after is a good night, clap their hands and stamp their feet...'

Ironically, immediately after the Manchester performance, the band settled back into cabaret with a week-long residency at the Fiesta Club in Sheffield. Then there was the university circuit – for those who truly appreciated much of the current progressive music scene – but this was also restrictive for its audience accessibility. Not everyone could gain access to these smaller student venues, and with the band stepping out of their recognised comfort zone with the recent album releases, coupled with the heavier drive of the current 45 (given its debut live outing in Manchester), the opportunities to see them live in a concert setting were becoming increasingly restricted. The UK music scene was undoubtedly shifting unceremoniously away from the "pop group" era, and unless you were prepared to popularise the burgeoning teen-glam market that was beginning to flourish, and would soon dominate the press, then you needed to be working to be seen and heard. One couldn't sustain by *Top of The Pops* appearance alone.

A further appearance on the UK's flagship music show took place soon after, scheduled to promote the release of 'Hey Willy', and their appearance alone was one that would linger long in the memory. It was a world away from the neat suits and boots image that they were known for. With flowing shoulder-length hair, Allan took it upon himself to dress in buckskin, tasselled high boots and a brown open-necked shirt complete with a wide buckled belt. Tony, meanwhile, smartly suited in a brown jacket and tie, topped his appearance off with a recently grown moustache that seemed bizarrely at odds with the familiar much-loved, youthful image. The fact that Bernie was sitting stage right, tinkling away on the piano, with Terry handling the unfamiliar bass guitar role, was lost on many. That casual appearance had also been evident the previous week when German television had aired footage of the band performing 'Too Young to Be Married', filmed for their own monthly ZDF-broadcast *Disco* TV show (a word that didn't resound with the same connotations that it would a few years later). Their performance that day was marred somewhat by the sight and sound of the host and the audience cheerfully clapping along, despite the serious connotations portrayed within the lyrics. Moustache duty for that particular taping was officially handled by Allan…

THIS IS ONLY 3:19 SECONDS
OF THE HOLLIES NEW ALBUM.

FM freaks around the country are being delightfully blasted with air play of The Hollies singing "Long Cool Woman in a Black Dress." S 10871

For those of you who lack a vivid imagination this photo should do very nicely when you hear the song again.

Of course the group that spawned Graham Nash. And the group that has been voted England's second best group. And the group that has constantly been in the mainstream of American music offers more than just one great song on their new album.

In fact there are 11 songs on The Hollies' new album. 11 songs that create something you won't ever have to imagine.

A good time.

**The Hollies are back with their new Epic album "Distant Light."**

*Also available on tape

® "EPIC" MARCA REG. T.M. PRINTED IN U.S.A.

# CHAPTER TWENTY-ONE

---

# MY TEMPERATURE STARTED TO RISE...

Throughout these spring months of 1971, venturing into the early summer, the group had been constantly finding time at the Oxford Street AIR Studios to record a series of songs that would ultimately make up the next album. Maintaining the more progressive approach of their recent recordings, the band had stockpiled a series of new compositions, evenly spread amongst the principal songwriters. However, such was the division now between them, often choosing to work with external songwriters and friends instead, that the ALTO Publishing brand (previously GRALTO) was quietly laid to rest. Allan Clarke's songs were now being published by his own Timtobe Music – named after his two sons, whilst Tony Hicks, writing alongside his friend, fellow singer-songwriter Kenny Lynch, published his works as T.H. Music. Terry, meanwhile, in liaison with manager Robin Britten, created Charlotte Music Publishing for his songs.

Another contributing factor to this period was that long-time producer Ron Richards fell ill during 1971, forcing his absence from the studios, and so the band members themselves took on the role of self-producing, working alongside AIR engineer John Punter.

'Dad had a severe nervous breakdown as a result of overwork,' recounted Ron's son, Andrew Pratley, during a recent conversation. 'He was recovering but he was not firing on all cylinders. In the studio, he was still in command.

He was able to distance himself from all that as he was so absorbed, but he was a bit of a mess outside it. He used to suffer with his nerves and was drinking too much. He would throw up in the toilet before he had to go into the studio. He was a bag of nerves before the session but as soon as he stepped into the studio complex, be it Abbey Road or AIR, he was in complete command.

'Dad gave the doctors the runaround and he thought he could deal with it himself. The reality was he needed a lot of help, but the right sort of help didn't exist back then, and even if it did, he wasn't ready to engage with it.'

Subsequently, it came as no surprise when the finished product appeared, during mid-autumn, that a lot of the natural Hollie-sound was missing. Gone were the dominant harmonies on many of the finished songs, scaled back to virtually unnoticeable levels, and replaced at times by a soulful, often mournful gospel feel. It was the sound of a maturing band, brought about, unquestionably, by the shift of focus within the industry.

'The 1970s was a challenging period for the Hollies,' continued Andrew, reflecting on the experiences his father encountered. 'Apart from what was happening in the music scene, which was becoming all about making albums rather than singles, there were two significant events that affected the band and their recordings. Firstly, the absence of Graham Nash, who had taken the right decision to follow his musical inclinations. Dad rated Graham very highly and was sorry to see him go. They nevertheless maintained a friendly relationship, with Graham and Neil Young coming over to our London home, and Dad visiting Graham in LA.

'The event that precipitated his breakdown was Gordon Mills' [unsuccessful] proposed takeover of AIR. My dad was the only one of the four directors who was wholly against it. The others wanted to sell their stake. There was quite a wrangle of it. He said that AIR was his baby and he wasn't going to sell it to anyone. It was also doing very well, and he had lots of plans to turn it into a major player. I can understand it from the other's perspective, as none of them were really businessmen, but Dad parted company with AIR and went freelance.

'This had two impacts regarding the Hollies. Dad was no longer at the height of his powers and neither did he have the level of control in the studio he enjoyed in the 1960s when he set the musical agenda. By the '70s he was employed by the Hollies and had to be more careful in what he said to them. It meant he had frustrations he could not address, such as the Bernie problem.

'The electric bass during the 1970s became ever more important since you couldn't do the kind of rhythm tracks required unless you had a terrific bass guitar player. This was very limiting. Bobby was always a great drummer and with better support from the bass department would have been stretched much more to everyone's benefit. Terry was a capable singer but, according to my father, was not a musical virtuoso. This again was limiting. Tony was a fine guitarist, but he also had his limitations. This was an era of massed guitars. Another top-class guitar player of a different style to Tony would have been a big help. The Hollies did use session players but didn't always choose the right ones. My father had been used to using session players like Jimmy Page, Ginger Baker, John Paul Jones, Elton John and John McLaughlin to name but a few, but The Hollies chose what was considered the second team in my father's eyes when they could have got the best. This all meant my father used orchestras increasingly, and especially arrangers who were Young Turks rather than the established guys, in order to make things musically interesting. Dad hated what he termed "fish and chip music", done by arrangers who were basically hacks.'

High summer 1971 had seen the group lined up to perform at two Mediterranean festivals, notably in the holiday hotspots of Benidorm in south-eastern Spain, and on the island of Ibiza.

Whilst the first show went ahead without incident, The Hollies' concert at the 8,000-seat Ibiza Bullring venue, situated on the sun-kissed island, was cancelled by local organisers just fifteen minutes before the band were due to take to the stage, due to an undisclosed intervention by the Spanish Musicians' Union.

Top British pop group The Hollies flew into London yesterday seething over the treatment they received on the Spanish island of Ibiza. The group were to have given a one-night show (but) when the engineers tried to set up their equipment attendants sprayed it with a hose. Fans were told that the concert had been cancelled because none of the stars had turned up. Damage to the equipment, which was worth £20,000, has still to be assessed.

*Daily Mirror*
July 1971

Robin Britten, furious with the festival organisers, vowed that the band would never perform again in Spain. Instead, the band returned home and took up a week-long residency at the newly opened Barbarella's Club in Birmingham. Performing under a dazzling display of glitzy spotlights, surrounded by the grey Birmingham skyline, was no substitute for the Spanish sunshine, but the week proved a successful outing, as did a subsequent show in Sutton Coldfield, along with a short university tour that was scheduled for October, performing in Nottingham (supported by Slade), Bradford, Loughborough, Aberystwyth, Manchester and Oxford.

EMI UK has launched an experiment in promotion with the creation of the field team. Headed by Terry Walker, formerly an EMI repertoire manager, the team will give specific coverage to selected artists. It will concentrate his initial efforts on promoting the forthcoming Hollies' university tour. The team's function will encompass most aspects of promotion. Said Walker: 'We will select two or three albums each month and give them full coverage. The artist selected will be from the progressive pop field most likely to appeal to the campus audience.

'Whenever it is possible, we will send white label copies of albums to social secretaries a month ahead of release so they can judge our act for themselves. The idea is to act as a liaison between the company, universities and the artists' management. Special emphasis will be given to artists on tour.'

The Hollies will be the first assignment for the team, working in liaison with the Harold Davidson organisation, which is promoting the tour. Walker will be printing 2,000 extra posters in addition to the 4,000 copies due to be sent to dealers. The extra copies would be distributed to universities.

EMI Promotional Publicity
*Billboard*
August 1971

For the first time, the band also recruited some additional sidemen to fill out the stage production, with an organist and two saxophonists adding to the sound. They also managed to find the time to pre-record an hour-long BBC radio special, *Meet The Hollies*, taped on 25th July and subsequently airing over the August bank holiday weekend. Comprising interviews, hits and three songs from their upcoming eleventh studio album (performed partially live over a selection of pre-recorded studio tracks), the show was also notable for Bobby playing an excerpt from the live audio he had taped at the Singapore National Theatre.

Of the three songs featured from the upcoming album, the variation of new styles was immediately evident. Two songs by the recently formed Hicks-Lynch partnership highlighted the potential that such a pairing had, although Allan's over-emphasis on his pseudo-American accent on the otherwise excellent, gospel-influenced 'What A Life I've Led' was certainly a talking point. With Madeline Bell, Liza Strike and Doris Troy adding their distinctive bluesy voices to the studio backing vocals, this was a real departure from the formula group sound, as was the characteristic use of a pedal-steel guitar (played in the studio by Mick Abrahams). The second Hicks-Lynch offering was the moody and atmospheric 'Look What We've Got', a song that featured the external contributions of Procol Harum's Gary Brooker on piano, and session player (and former schoolmate of Bobby) Jimmy Jewell supplying a saxophone solo. However, the most significant song played in the show was a recently recorded composition, credited to the Clarke-Cook-Greenaway trio, that Allan had initially planned for a project he was quietly conceiving in the back of his mind.

'It was actually just Clarke and Cook,' explained Terry, 'but Cook and Greenaway were partners and used to put both names on all songs, even if they weren't involved in the project.'[49]

Roger Cook later recalled to the *Tennessean* newspaper that they had returned to their office one day, after a particularly heavy lunchtime drinking session, and decided it would be fun to write a song about prohibition and all the bad scenes surrounding it. So, pens in hand, they concocted a story about an FBI raid and a barroom singer, dressed provocatively in a black dress.

Allan Clarke would later elaborate, 'I was in their offices one day and Roger Cook, who I knew was in Blue Mink, so we had met each other, just said, "D'you fancy writing a song?" I said, "Yeah, why not." We were there with a bottle of brandy and a few other things, and we said, "Well, what shall we write about?" He said, "I've got this little bit of an idea, and it goes like this..."and I said, "That's really good. Just put a bit of chunk-chunk-chunk..." and we just got into it. Out of that came 'Long Cool Woman...'.

'It was a throwaway track. It was loose and it had this driving guitar rhythm when we did it.'[69]

When the band eventually took it into the studio, 'Long Cool Woman (In A Black Dress)' developed into an up-tempo, pure rock 'n' roll number. As with the original concept, it was cut loosely, void of any band harmonies whatsoever, with Allan striking a solo pose out front; alone, excepting for an electric guitar slung around his neck from which he picked out the opening guitar riff.

'Normally, when you have Tony Hicks on hand you don't need anyone else on guitar, but that happened because I devised the riff, so I got to play it,' Allan later confessed. 'That one was a throwaway, and we never put on a harmony vocal.[12]

'When Ron Richards first heard it, he tried to make me redo the vocals, complaining that he couldn't hear what I was singing. But I said, leave it, it's only an album track. Thank God he saw it that way because if he had seen it as more than that, it would have been a completely different recording!'[5]

Much like that of his fellow bandmates, Allan's songwriting ability was continuously developing and evolving. His initial spurt at composing, working alongside his childhood friend Graham Nash, had seen a succession of 2-minute candy floss anthems but, as time had passed, his confidence and abilities had begun to grow. By the time that Graham had started to distance himself from the band, choosing to work alone, Allan was almost forced to do likewise and, without his closest musical companion and ally, his true identity as a writer began to flourish. Initially starting with his own works on the mid-'60s albums, with compositions such as 'High Classed', 'Lullaby To Tim', 'Would You Believe' and 'Charlie And Fred', he was undoubtedly exploring his capabilities as a composer, but as his confidence grew, his wings took flight and the influences around him grew ever stronger, as did his skills as a true songwriter, albeit one that has often been unfairly overlooked.

Discussing his influences in the media, he expressed an admiration for Creedence Clearwater Revival, Blood Sweat & Tears, Elton John and, most notably, Crosby, Stills, Nash & Young. Clearly, any bad feelings were, by now, distant memories;

'I haven't seen them play live yet, but I'm really looking forward to that,' he would comment to the *NME* when discussing his friend's recent successes. 'I like the album *Déjà Vu* because it's different. The harmonies are beautiful and it's just perfect. I couldn't find any fault with it.'

And Elton? 'I've known him for a long time. I think he's an individual. He doesn't sound like anyone else, he's fresh.'

With the mixing of the completed sessions now in the hands of Ron Richards, still frail, but deeming himself fit enough to return to work after his lengthy lay-off, the band set about promoting the upcoming release further by taping a guest appearance on *It's Lulu* for the BBC. Taken by the reception that 'Long Cool Woman (In A Black Dress)' was receiving, they performed it again for the cameras, along with another new tune, a Clarke-Macauley composition entitled 'A Little Thing Like Love'.

Released on 8ᵗʰ October 1971 (Parlophone PAS10005), *Distant Light* came packaged in a memorable gatefold sleeve featuring a detailed external woodland summer scene, painted by a youthful twenty-year-old artist named Colin Elgie (the original of which ended up in the personal collection of Rod Shields). Study the sleeve with a curious mind and all kinds of objects and mysterious figures take shape in the reflections of the water, although all meaning is open to conjecture.

When asked about the artwork during research on this book, the artist recalled, 'This was painted when I worked with the record cover design group, Hipgnosis, which I did from 1971 through to about 1983. I did the *Distant Light* cover as one of my first designs when I started with them. I remember that the initial idea came from Storm Thorgensen [who, along with Aubrey Powell, was one of the founders of the company]. To be honest, I really can't remember what all the imagery and symbolism in the design was meant to represent. I remember that some of it was to do with renewal, rebirth… that sort of thing – for example, the lizard shedding its skin. As for the imagery in the pond reflections, it may have been inspired by the song lyrics, but I can't remember in detail what they were. It was painted in gouache onto watercolour board.'

The inside spread was a two-fold collection of band images, captured on camera at a recent Tony Hicks house party, and artistically gathered together as a collage by the design studio Hipgnosis (who had also worked with Pink Floyd, The Nice, The Electric Light Orchestra – and later Led Zeppelin, 10cc, Wings and Genesis). It was certainly the group's most ambitious release to date, and there were soon discussions taking place over which songs to take off it and issue as 45 singles – an option that had always previously been vetoed in the past.

You could use the word sensational about The Hollies' new album, "Distant Light" and not be far wide of the mark. Apart from the ever-present musicianship, the sensation lies in a large proportion of the material and to an extent in the choice of writers. "Distant Light" represents a consistently successful pop group trying hard to capture a wider section of the market. They haven't missed on record as yet, either albums or singles, but there's been a tendency to put them in one specific category. Now we can forget that category. On this album, there's a fair helping of the more typical Hollies' approach, but then they'd be criminally insane to go the whole hog. But they also move into an adventurous, deep, provocative area of music and emerge triumphant.

*Record Mirror*
October 1971

Commencing with two of the new Hicks-Lynch compositions, 'What A Life I've Led' and 'Look What We've Got', the collection immediately grabbed the listener's attention by simply sounding *not* like it should. This was not the accepted or *expected* sound of The Hollies. The overall production, the arrangements, the composing... this was something else altogether. Musically, the five-man band were already recognised and acknowledged by their peers throughout the industry for their strengths and abilities, and it was clear that, even with the use of additional sidemen (Gary Brooker, Mick Abrahams, Jimmy Jewell, John Peter Robinson...), they were putting all those to good use here.

Tony and Kenny Lynch contributed to the larger portion of songwriting duties, with five of their collaborations included amongst the eventual eleven-song selection. The remaining six cuts were shared between Allan (three collaborations and one solo offering) and Terry (two solo works and one with Allan). Of these, the styles ranged from Allan's progressive rock stance on 'Hold On', featuring Robinson's wild organ solo over a backdrop of Floyd-ish female vocals, via Terry's bare Lennon-styled 'Pull Down The Blind', through to the more familiar acoustic pop fare of the Hicks-Lynch 'To Do With Love'. Other notable highlights came in the form of Terry's calming ballad, 'Cable Car', the daring venture into Moody Blues-familiarity with the drawn-out effects in 'You Know The Score' and, finally, Tony and Kenny's impressive album closer, 'Long Dark Road', featuring Allan's distinctive lead vocal alongside further guest contributions from Gary Brooker. And then there was 'Long Cool Woman (In A Black Dress)', Allan's pulsating slab of pure rock 'n' roll that Terry didn't even get to appear on, much to his consternation when discussing the album with *Record Mirror* editor, Peter Jones:

'That's the difference this time,' he remarked. 'We just didn't crowd people in the studio for the sake of it. I wasn't even on this one!' How ironic would that turn out to be?

In a later interview with *Disc & Music Echo*, Terry also commented on how he had found his time as the new member of The Hollies and how it had helped his writing come to fruition: 'If I hadn't joined, I can't imagine what I'd be doing now. I'd made twelve records and never had a hit! Now I've got everything I ever wanted, and it's a wonderful feeling. I'm very happy.

'I wrote before, but never seriously. Simply because there was no incentive. Nobody to confide with and ask what they thought of my efforts. That's where Allan has been of assistance...'

One cannot overlook the significant contributions that both Bobby and Bernie also brought to the sessions either, each holding down their role effectively, blossoming where demands necessitated. In Ron Richards' eyes, Bernie may have had his limitations, certainly on a technical level, but his playing was always solid and reliable.

At one point during the recording, Bernie was actually taken ill, and Tony stepped in to fill the bass duties, but Bernie's deft fretwork on 'A Little Thing Like Love' certainly brings into question Ron's doubts. Meanwhile, Bobby's consummate professionalism, underpinning the rhythm throughout the entire album, driving the instrumental support on the more up-tempo songs such as 'Hold On' and 'To Do With Love', only went to justify his standing amongst his peers. The "drummer's drummer" many referred to him as. He didn't just maintain the timekeeping; he *was* the timekeeping.

Indeed, whilst initially envisaged as a more Jerry Reed-styled country/ rockabilly recording, it had been Bobby who had first suggested slowing down the tempo of 'Long Cool Woman (In A Black Dress)' and tackling it with a more Creedence-styled swamp-rock sound, and it was Bernie who had then suggested that they utilise an echo on the vocal to get the hollow feel of the lone voice.

'I remember the afternoon we played it,' recalled Bernie, when reminiscing over 'Long Cool Woman...' during a taped interview with US

Hollies collector, Mark Ritucci. 'We actually did the backing track between, maybe, 2:30 in the afternoon and 5:00 o'clock in the evening. It laid down very quickly and easily. Allan had that guitar riff, which was great to play along with on bass, and the drum feel was just right from the word go. When we broke for our evening refreshment, at about 5:30, I remember Bob was a little bit hesitant that the feel, or the tightness of the track, might not have been complete, and we thought that we may come back in the evening after we felt a little bit looser, and record it again. But when we came back from our break and played it to fresh ears it sounded dynamite! And all it needed, of course, was the lead vocal which Allan duly put down that evening...'

This was a fully functioning five-man band without question and, quite clearly, EMI was hoping for big things from this new album, as were the band themselves. They even ventured back into the AIR studios almost immediately after the release of the album, cutting a working version of another new Tony Hicks composition, 'Oh Granny', that was never intended for release (it was later issued in error on an EMI-MFP collection, in lieu of a later Terry Sylvester-led rendition) – but then, just three weeks after the album first appeared in the stores... the bombshell dropped.

Allan Clarke is Quitting The Hollies

Allan Clarke, founder member and lead singer of The Hollies announced this week that he is quitting the group before the end of the year. He will, however, continue with the outfit until all its existing commitments have been fulfilled. The Hollies are at present engaged in a university tour of Britain and Allan's final date with them will be a cabaret week at Batley Variety Club starting December 12.

Clarke explained that he has long had an ambition to cut a solo album and this is something he feels he cannot do while still part of the group. He sees the solo LP as the first step towards a solo career. Meanwhile, the remaining Hollies have been quick to stress that the group will continue.

*New Musical Express*
October 1971


Allan had been harbouring the idea of recording a solo album for a while now. Having seen the success story that had befallen Graham Nash since his departure and, having suffered the insecurities of not having his best friend working alongside him, he saw the opportunity to gather a collection of songs that he personally wanted to cut as an ideal solution and as a sideline to his work with the band. He had no immediate desire to strike out alone, despite rumoured stories of others whispering in his ear that he too could become a big solo star. After all, he *was* the sound of The Hollies to many.

'About that time,' Terry Sylvester was to be quoted in the *Los Angeles Free Press*, 'Allan was getting a little bit, I won't say restless, probably even more strange. He was being influenced by a lot of people outside the group. While we rehearsed, you could sense it. I think basically he was listening to people outside of us who were saying, "Why don't you go solo or make a solo album?"'

'In August of '71 we were going over the conditions of the new contracts,' Allan responded at the time. 'We wanted a clause giving everyone his individual freedom in case he wanted to make other recordings. Everyone agreed on it. Two months later, just before the contracts were due to be signed, I remarked that I wanted to record my solo album...'[66]

Nevertheless, having put his proposal to the band, it was deemed as a non-workable option. With Tony Hicks the key decision-maker in the unit, and the driving force behind the group as an entity, there was no compromise in the concept, and it was subsequently put to Allan that he either commit to the group or quit. There was no room for side projects, regardless of the simple fact that, as a co-founder of the band, he was the sole survivor of the original quintet that had first announced The Hollies on stage, back in December of 1962.

'Making a solo album is something I have to get out of my system,' he would continue in the *New Musical Express*. 'I have a lot of songs that I want to get down in my own way. So, I asked the group if I could do an album and single, to enhance myself for three- or four-years' time. But they said no. I can understand their point of view, but I was very upset by their saying no. I was taken aback by that. I don't see how making a solo album would have interfered with the group. If I was going to go out on my own, it would have done but that was not my idea.'

'I saw how well Graham was doing in the States, so I thought, *I'd like a bit of that*,' he later added. 'I didn't want to leave, and I had no idea if I'd be successful, but I decided to take the chance.'[5]

'It was a matter of his parting more in sorrow than anger,' recounted Robin Britten in a *Melody Maker* interview. 'But it was just one of those things. When a man wants to go solo there's no point in trying to stop him. The Hollies have always worked as a unit, once a person decides he wishes to pursue a solo career then it is to no one's advantage to put obstacles in his way. But when the lead singer leaves, the problem of a replacement is really horrifying. Of course, we were immediately inundated with applicants, so we had to do some weeding out. We asked people to give details of their professional experience, to send in a photo or either tape or a demo record.'

Promotion on the album was effectively suspended for the time being, with the sole exception of Tony and Robin flying out to Germany and Luxembourg to participate in a series of radio interviews. The option of initially promoting a single in the UK was also abandoned, although the Hansa Records label (who had been releasing The Hollies' material in Germany since 1967) saw fit to issue 'Long Cool Woman (In A Black Dress)' b/w 'What A Life I've Led' as a German 45 the following January, a subsequent result following the success of Tony's brief visit. Such was the positive reception to it that the single dutifully climbed into the German Top 20. Parlophone in the UK then followed suit but, without promotion, the record soon stalled.

Nevertheless, despite the significant setback, the album continued to receive a further succession of largely positive reviews in the music press:

The evergreen Hollies are still as consistent as ever. They are back with eleven brand new tracks and Tony Hicks' influence is evident throughout. This is quite possibly the best album they've yet made, for it contains more depth and is less instant than much of the earlier work. The group harmonies are still unmistakable and intelligent use of echo adds a touch of welcome nostalgia.

*Sounds*
October 1971


As agreed, in as much the same vein as Graham had done before, Allan remained in the band in order to fulfil the contractual obligations already on the schedule which, following the completion of the university tour, would amount to no more than a week-long December cabaret residency at the Batley Variety Club in West Yorkshire. By then, the search for his replacement was nearing completion – if it hadn't already done so.

*"The search goes on for a new singer"*, read the headlines in the January 1972 edition of the *Hollies Official Fan Club Newsletter*. "Although the group have several people in mind for the job there is no definite news that I can pass on to you at present".

Terry later recalled meeting Carl Wayne, who had recently exited The Move, to discuss the idea of his taking Allan's place, but the notion never came to fruition. Instead, their attentions were drawn farther afield:

> The Hollies management was left with quite a problem on their hands when lead singer Allan Clarke left the group last December to concentrate on a solo career. They had to find another singer with a good voice and good face and image because The Hollies, being a very well-established group, could not afford to go wrong with their choice.
>
> They auditioned more than eighty people but either their voices weren't up to standard or they didn't fit the image. Luckily, Tony Hicks remembered a certain concert the group had done with a Swedish group called Bamboo in Stockholm, a few years previously.
>
> He recalled a young man called Mikael Rickfors and so the big search began. Agents, working on the group's behalf, flew to Sweden and tracked down the much-wanted singer.
>
> *Mirabelle*
> January 1972

Per Mikael Rickfors had been born in Stockholm, the capital city of Sweden, on 4th December 1948. The only boy, alongside three sisters, born to Per Gunnar and Elisabet Rickfors, the handsome blond youngster initially grew up with a love for art, the results of which saw him attending a nearby art college for three years during the mid-1960s, studying oil painting. Nevertheless, a passion for music was also in the bloodstream, with particular favourites such as The Four Tops, The Band and the New Orleans-based blind blues vocalist Snooks Eaglin influencing his musical direction.

His first group had been at the tender age of just ten when he played around with Mike's Skiffle Group, and by the time he reached his late teens, he was also an accomplished guitarist and pianist and had already made his first professional appearance. With the arrival of the mid-'60s boom, he co-founded the extremely popular Stockholm-based quintet Bamboo who, upon signing to the Swedish division of EMI-Parlophone, released two singles on the label during the latter part of the decade. Fortunately for Mikael, as a promotional tie-in, the band were offered the opportunity to support fellow Parlophone artists The Hollies during one of their own Scandinavian tours.

Despite the popularity of Bamboo, neither of their 45 releases – a retitled cover of Phil Spector's 1958 hit for the Teddy Bears, 'To Know You Is To Love You', backed with the Rickfors-composed 'Touch', and 'Everybody's Gone Home' b/w 'Can't You Come To Me' (another Rickfors-penned B-side) – were successful and, following the departure of one key member of the line-up, the band folded during 1970.

Later that year, Mikael released a series of four Swedish language solo 45s on the Mercury Records label, the first of which was a version of the Bacharach-David tune 'Everybody Is Out of Town (Finns Du Kvar I Stan Annu)', paired with a rendition of Elton John's 'Your Song'. He had also just joined up as lead singer with another local band, their eyes fixed firmly on success when he got the call.

'Before I left school, I knew I wanted to be a singer,' Mikael would comment to *Mirabelle* in one of his earliest interviews as a Hollie (albeit in broken English as the language didn't come fluently to him). 'I was interested in blues music and had started a blues band. I was also a solo singer for a short while and I had two hit records released only in Sweden. I didn't enjoy being solo. It's a very lonely life and contrary to what people might think, I don't feel you have a lot of freedom to work with. In many ways, you are restricted. Working in a group is much more fun.'

Having taken the call, The Hollies invited Mikael over to London to meet the band and to work through a few songs in the studio, to ensure he fitted in as well as Tony had envisaged. Not all were convinced over the decision, with Bobby having distinct reservations about Mikael's suitability, and one of the songs purportedly attempted was a version of 'I Can't Tell The Bottom From The Top', for which, initially, Mikael had difficulty finding the correct key – opting to follow Allan's rendition and its higher register. Nevertheless, once the song was attempted for a second time, with Mikael finding his own balance, then it all came good – at least in the eyes of their overseeing producer.

According to Bobby's later recollections, and without any further discussion with the bewildered band members who were watching on from the control booth, Ron Richards pronounced that Mikael was "in" and, despite his vocal being far bluesier, grittier and deeper in tone than Allan's, Ron concluded that Mikael fitted exactly with what the band were looking for. Whilst the Swede's attempts to cover the early hits may well have ruffled a few feathers once the band took them on the road, it was deemed that this approach at a new progressive stance was ideal for their current music. Still unconvinced, Bobby's immediate thoughts turned to: *How on earth is this going to work? Is this guy the only option?*

'Ron had told him he was in, and now the deed was done so we had to make it work…'[39]

It then became a case of finding the timing and opportunity to release the news.

'It was like being in a James Bond film,' said Tony. 'We didn't want the news to sneak out until we knew Mikael had a work permit. At the same time, we wanted to let everyone know who our new singer was going to be, so it was all rather difficult.'

In the meantime, whilst waiting for the correct documentation to arrive, The Hollies, now with Mikael alongside, returned to the AIR Studios with Ron to work on the first single with the new line-up.

Just before Allan's December departure, the remaining four members had commenced work on two new recordings. One of these was, in fact, a case of simply sweetening and adding a new lead vocal onto the song 'Oh Granny', previously taped with Allan two months earlier, and for this take, Terry stepped forward and handled the vocal. The second song, however, was a brand-new composition, with the band once again returning to the talents and composing abilities of Chip Taylor for 'The Baby'. A heavily orchestrated number with Terry's harmonies, Tony's electric sitar arrangement and Bobby's percussion heavily to the fore, accompanied by strings arranged by Richard Hewson, it was another total departure in sound for the band, and it took a further late December session to complete the song (along with a 10th January sweetening date), with Mikael now supplying his soulful lead vocals to the recording. In fact, when it came to publicly present the new member to the world's press, during a January reception held at the Westbury Hotel in Mayfair, 'The Baby' was played to the waiting crowd, just prior to the band entering the room – and no one realised the singer wasn't English.

That said, from a studio production and an engineering perspective, Mikael's inability to fully comprehend and enunciate the English language was to become a major stumbling block going forward, with many arduous hours utilised whilst he adapted his phrasings from his native tongue.

'When I first got the offer to join the group,' Mikael would comment to the *New Musical Express*, 'I was worried in case they wanted to play all the old songs and expected me to sing them like Allan Clarke. But that would be very hard to do. Although we plan to still include some of the old numbers on stage, I think 'The Baby' is the first of a new batch of material. The rest will come from the next album. As yet, I've only heard a few of the songs planned…

'The only thing decided is that each track should be able to stand up in its own right as a single. We can't help but sound different, but how the change will show itself is not known yet.'

With support from Robin Britten, Mikael took up residency in a flat near Chelsea, in west London, and flew his girlfriend out to join him as he attempted to adjust to the sudden change in lifestyle. His rugged good looks made him an immediate target for the female-orientated teen-zines and fashion world and, within weeks of his appointment, his face was gracing the pages of *Mirabelle*, *Jackie* and *Woman's Own*; smiling denim-clad images, strolling through Carnaby Street, the King's Road, Trafalgar Square and Piccadilly.

'I just love London, the whole feeling of the place,' *Jackie* was to report. 'I love drinking, and English pubs have such a special atmosphere. They're great places for meeting people. The clubs I like too – I've been to the Speakeasy quite a few times since I've been here, and the rest of the boys have been really looking after me and showing me around. Shopping is very good too. I'm truly very happy to be here, and believe me, I even like the weather. I know I'm going to love living here and working in England, and I know I'll find it much easier when I know the language.'

The enforced arrival of a new frontline vocalist wasn't the only significant change for The Hollies during early 1972. Having spent the previous decade as part of the EMI/Parlophone roster, it came as a surprise when the new single release of 'The Baby' appeared on the distinctive red label of the rival Polydor company. The reason behind the move was clear, according to *Reveille* (11th February 1972):

The reason they have changed labels is simple – a guarantee of £100,000 over three years, which does not cover their records released in America, Germany, Spain, Austria and Australasia.

With Ron Richards continuing to work as an independent producer, and not tied down to a specific label as he was when the band had first signed with EMI, the Polydor contract gave the band the freedom they desired, moving forward with their new style of music. This change of label, after a healthy ten years with EMI, was instigated by former EMI employee John Fruin, now head at Polydor, who knew that The Hollies' brand was far greater than that of any individual member, and who believed that the band still had mileage in them, despite the departure of Clarke. In another move, former EMI/RAK promotions man, Terry Walker, also joined up with The Hollies' management team, linking up with Robin Britten to help keep their profile in the media spotlight.

At Robin's insistence, the new contract was negotiated to give the band the best deal possible, separating the European union into varying distribution aspects to highlight their popularity. EMI, meanwhile, retained the distribution in Australia, New Zealand and the Far East, whilst CBS/Epic continued in the USA and Canada, but for the UK (along with the European territories), with a new vocalist and a new label, it was a new start…

# CHAPTER TWENTY-TWO

# "HALF FORGOTTEN IN THE PASSING OF TIME..."

Tony Hicks says The Hollies can't appear again yet – 'because we only know one number.' Apparently, new member Mikael Rickfors only had time to rehearse 'The Baby' single.

*Disc & Music Echo*
February 1972

The Hollies: 'The Baby' (Polydor 2058-199)
And The Hollies jump yet another giant hurdle to live another day. There were many who thought that these lads would never survive the departure of Graham Nash... but they were wrong. There were even more who thought they were completely dead without Allan Clarke, thereby losing both their main voices... but wrong again. Mikael Rickfors is the new man from Scandinavia, and he marks a totally new chapter. Gone is the old high-flying harmony sound, although there's still plenty of harmony in the chorus of this Chip Taylor song. In its place comes a cracked, soulful voice and a great voice. It'll take many times to appreciate these are not The Hollies you knew and loved but virtually a new group, with a new sound. Once you come to terms with that, you'll find this record will grow and grow.

*Disc & Music Echo*
February 1972

I can find nothing negative to say about this record. It is one of those perfect songs which has you straining to memorise the words so that you can sing it again on the way to work. Their harmonies blazed with emotion and new singer Mikael Rickfors proves himself far more than just a pretty face. The arrangement too is a masterpiece of understated climax.

*The Times*
February 1972

In early February, the band taped a promotional video for the single, ensuring their debut for Polydor achieved maximum exposure around the globe, and then on the 17th, they debuted the release in the UK on *Top of the Pops,* followed shortly afterwards by the first airing of the promotional video on the Dutch *TopPop* show. Further heavyweight support came courtesy of the many popular radio stations, with both BBC Radio One and Radio Luxemburg giving the release significant airtime. And yet, despite the promotional push from the new label, with an additional series of advertisements appearing across the media and the press, the release wasn't as universally successful as many would have hoped. Maybe it was too different a style for the band? Maybe the familiar Clarke-led sounds were too obviously absent for their faithful record-buying following? Whatever the reasoning, the single (paired with the recently updated version of 'Oh Granny') limped to a disappointing #26 during an all-too-brief six-week run in a UK chart list that was led by such established names as Harry Nilsson, Don McLean, Paul Simon, The New Seekers and The Supremes. It is also worth noting that, featuring heavily in the charts the week that 'The Baby' reached its peak position, were the early frontrunners representing the new UK glam scene. For the next few years, the charts would be full of hit after hit by the likes of Slade, T. Rex and Sweet. It would no longer be easy breaking into a list dominated by such teen-fed fun as 'Poppa Joe', 'Look Wot You Dun' and 'Telegram Sam'. The following year would see yet another band enter the fray – Mud, featuring the Guildford-born bass player, Raymond Stiles.

Elsewhere, 'The Baby' missed out on a US *Billboard* position but did manage to chart in a variety of different countries, including making #8 in Holland, 21 in New Zealand, 23 in Germany, 12 in Rickfors' native Sweden, along with a lowly 73 in Australia.

Not to be outdone by their departing money-makers, EMI Records then chose to issue a second LP of hits, *Greatest Hits Volume 2*, aimed to repeat the success of the chart-topping forerunner and comprising a further selection of singles recorded for their Parlophone label. This 12-track collection, compiled with the assistance of Allan Clarke, was a mismatch, juggling of songs from across the years, with the opening 'Gasoline Alley Bred' sitting uncomfortably alongside a rare alternative stereo mix of the 1963 hit 'Searchin', and the relatively unsuccessful 1965 45, 'If I Needed Someone', preceding 'I Can't Tell The Bottom From The Top' from early 1970. The selection also included several non-UK releases that had achieved a certain level of success elsewhere – 'Too Young To Be Married' and 'Blowin' In The Wind' – but EMI had to drop plans to feature the still-collectable 'After The Fox' recording due to contractual issues with United Artists. Despite their good intentions, the LP failed to ignite the public interest and, more importantly, empty their wallets. It also failed to chart.

Following their successful promotional visit to Germany, both Tony and Robin Britten then jetted off to New York, specifically to raise the profile on the somewhat lapsed Stateside interest in the band. Whilst they were there, with his keen ears ever open to new music, Tony took the opportunity to visit a number of key publishing houses, listening and uncovering new songs and demos that he found of interest. Armed with stacks of acetates, he returned to the UK four days later, intent on selecting proposals for the band's next studio album. The first with Mikael, and for their new record label.

The next month saw the band commence rehearsals with Mikael, focussing on putting together a full show suitable for live performances, along with try-outs for the upcoming recording dates. Initially, it was just Tony, Terry and Mikael practising their harmonies together and working out the vocal arrangements in Tony's north London home. Then, once they felt they had those down perfectly, Bobby and Bernie were brought in so the instrumental side could be worked upon together in the peaceful surroundings of the red-bricked village hall in Cholesbury, a quiet retreat near to Ron Richards' hometown in Chesham.

Early on, it was decided that Mikael's contributions to the early hits would be kept minimal, with Terry taking the lead on 'On A Carousel' and Tony handling 'Carrie Anne'. Mikael was just given 'Bus Stop' to work on.

'We didn't bring him into the old stuff too much,' Tony was to say. 'He had enough on his plate with the newer things anyway' (*Disc & Music Echo*).

By mid-April, rehearsals were paying sufficient dividends to allow the group to move into the studios to start tracking and laying down the instruments on their chosen songs. Reverting to the tree-lined suburbs of St John's Wood, and settling back inside the familiar surroundings of Abbey Road Studio 2, the quintet spent the next four weeks holed up in the famed studio, cutting a series of new works, briefly breaking over the Easter period to allow promotional visits to both Paris and Ghent. It was in the Belgian city that they taped an appearance on the popular TV show *Slalem*, as well as undertaking an interview for a further televised slot. But, with commitments completed, it was soon back inside the hallowed walls and corridors of Abbey Road.

Unfortunately, Ron Richards once again distanced himself from the new round of sessions, partially due to his ongoing health issues, but he also harboured concerns over the way the band were now working; rehearsing and recording at their leisure. Taking their time. He was from the bygone era of cut-it-quick-and-move-on and didn't appreciate the relaxed pace. The members themselves felt otherwise and, without wishing to bring to a halt the positive feelings they had over the material, they continued without him, taking on the production role for themselves, with long-time recording engineer Peter Bown still seated behind the mixing desk.

'Mikael Rickfors had a very distinct voice,' recalled Bernie Calvert, when reminiscing about this particular era. '[It was] very different from Allan Clarke so a lot of work was going on between himself, Tony Hicks and Terry Sylvester in maintaining The Hollies' sound. Also, because Ron decided to leave us to our own devices, we spent more time on the tracks. They were very relaxed. Mikael was a very quiet, retiring sort of guy but he loved his music. He loved playing and we also were able to swap instruments. Mikael played bass on a couple of tracks and gave me the opportunity to play keyboards, so it was a different experience with him, but rewarding nonetheless.'[69]

Meanwhile, confident with the results of the rehearsals, Robin Britten began to put together the first tour that would subsequently introduce Mikael as a Hollie to a paying audience. A twelve-date South East Asia tour was proposed for July, following the route of the previous visit to the area, and venues in Indonesia, Hong Kong, Kuala Lumpur and Singapore were pencilled into the schedule. There was even discussion about taking the tour on to Japan afterwards. Unfortunately, availability and scheduling at the venues in question couldn't be aligned and the projected idea was duly postponed. Instead, following a return visit to perform on Germany's *Disco* show, lip-synching to 'The Baby', the group resumed their recording patterns.

An initial release date for the upcoming album, provisionally a ten-track collection entitled *Touch*, was listed for July but, due to conflicting interests with a recently released album by The Supremes, also labelled *Touch*, the scheduled release date was cancelled. Then, following a further visit to the US, whereupon Tony once again returned with a series of demo recordings (this time gathered from Nashville), the band decided to rework the proposed selection, taking a heavier approach and removing one of the early inclusions – a gentle Rickfors-led ballad called 'Papa Rain' – and undertake further studio sessions.

*Touch / Words Don't Come Easy / Jesus Was A Crossmaker / Magic Woman Touch / Down River / Delaware Taggett & The Outlaw Boys / Romany / Papa Rain / Lizzy And The Rainman / Blue In The Morning*
1972 *Touch* album
Original proposed track running order

Of the initial choices, five of the proposed songs were composed by a young British songwriter by the name of Colin Horton-Jennings. A former member and lead vocalist of the progressive rock band The Greatest Show On Earth, a group conceived by the Harvest Records label as a UK equivalent to the horn-based sound of Blood Sweat & Tears and Chicago, Colin had fronted the group for their two albums released during 1970. The second of these albums, *The Going's Easy*, had featured a song entitled 'Magic Woman Touch', a co-write with fellow band member Norman Watt-Roy (later a member of Ian Dury's Blockheads), and one that was duly covered by The Hollies during the May recording sessions.

Following the disbandment of The Greatest Show On Earth, and hearing of Allan Clarke's departure, Colin had applied to join The Hollies but, as had so many, lost out to Mikael Rickfors. Nevertheless, Tony, in particular, was struck by his songwriting ability and introduced his work into the band's sessions.

'We did two or three albums in a row using all our own songs,' commented Bernie in an edition of the US-based *Words & Music* magazine. 'So now we've decided to do some other people's, just to change back a bit.

'If you write a song yourself, then you usually have some ego trip about the way it should be done and that can get in the way of making the best possible music.'

In addition to covering the delightful 'Magic Woman Touch' (recorded with two different arrangements by the group), Colin was also responsible for 'Papa Rain', the introspective 'Words Don't Come Easy', the funky 'Delaware Taggett & The Outlaw Boys' and the grandiose 'Romany', a song that borrowed a little of its style and subsequent arrangement from that of Crosby, Stills, Nash & Young. Certainly, the dense harmonies, the Crosby-esque melody and nautical theme, accompanied by the Stills-style muted guitar pattern drew a considerable comparison. But then, such was the worldwide acclaim of the California-based quartet that few bands *could* now ignore them.

Other songs to come out of the sessions included the unissued 'Summer Side Of Life', a cover of David Ackles' 'Down River', and renditions of Judee Sills' tender 'Jesus Was A Crossmaker' and 'Lizzy And The Rainman', the latter being a composition from the American country pairing of Kenny O'Dell and Larry Henley. Together, these final two choices were perfect vehicles for Terry's mellow vocals. And yet, having seen the two previous Hollies' albums comprised solely of self-composed songs, it was an interesting decision that saw only two coming from the band members themselves this time around. Tony and his regular writing partner Kenny Lynch had brought forth 'Blue In The Morning' (another composition that leant heavily on the CSNY influence), whilst the initially proposed title track, 'Touch', was a Rickfors song, initially cut and released back in 1968 by his Swedish band, Bamboo. In addition, a third song taped during the album sessions, a new Terry Sylvester-David Gordon tune entitled 'Indian Girl', would soon find its way onto a single B-side. Nevertheless, by the time the additional July and August sessions were completed, which brought another four new cuts into the mix, the song selection they had at their disposal was deemed sufficient enough to draw the sessions to a final conclusion and prepare the final choice for the album, now scheduled for an 8th October release under a new title, *Romany*.

Late summer 1972 had seen the BBC broadcast an episode of their current documentary series *The Succeeders*. A 30-minute programme, airing in the north-west region of the UK, this was a short-lived series that focussed on success stories emanating from that particular region of the country. This specific episode, shown only on BBC North-West during the late evening of 15th August, was notable for concentrating on the northern roots of The Hollies and, amongst the highlights on offer, a brief montage of home footage, never seen in public before. Shot by Rod Shields on his personal movie camera, much of it whilst accompanying the group on tour, the sequences included TV rehearsals, the 1968 Japanese visit and various excerpts from the Swedish and Australian tours. The band were then interviewed by host Peter Harrison, discussing their career to date, before culminating with a studio performance featuring songs from the upcoming album.

This was, presumably, one in a series of promotional jaunts in the lead-up to the album but, during research on this very book, it became harshly evident how little survives in the television vaults.

That month also saw the release of a new single by Tony's songwriting partner, Kenny Lynch, 'A Better Place'. Lynch had released a succession of successful pop singles during the early part of the preceding decade but had been concentrating on his songwriting abilities of late. Having signed a new recording deal with Atlantic Records, Kenny revitalised his singing career with this 45, the first of three releases that he would issue over the coming years on the label, all featuring the writing credits of the Hicks-Lynch partnership. Sadly, none would achieve any significant success, despite the contributions of Tony and, on occasion, his bandmates (with Terry, Mikael and Tony all offering up background vocals on this session). The Hollies would also cut their own version of this particular song the following year, for the *Out On The Road* album.

A similar fate had befallen the efforts of the duo when they wrote a single for Cilla Black. Issued the previous year on the Parlophone label, the delightful 'Faded Images' (Hicks-Lynch) saw a limited distribution as a 45 in both Sweden and New Zealand (a reasonable Top 20 hit), but elsewhere had to settle as the opening track of her 1971 *Images* LP.

After a further delay, *Romany* finally saw a release during the first week of November 1972. A revised twelve-track collection, now including several of the additional US songs that Tony had recently uncovered in Nashville, the album was an impressive gathering. Opening with one of the recent additions, the heavier AOR-feel of 'Won't We Feel Good That Morning' – written by Michael Leslie Davies and William Davidson (credited to Day-Leslie, and mis-pressed on the sleeve as 'Won't You Feel Good That Morning'), and featuring a co-lead vocal between Mikael and Tony, the LP was well received by much of the world's media, garnering mostly positive reviews amongst the press. With the heavy Gretsch guitar riffs of 'Slow Down' (a further Davies-Davidson offering) added in alongside the album closer, 'Courage Of Your Convictions', a recent work by American composers Randy Cullers and Alan Rush, these last-minute additions further acceded to the Americanised approach of the album.

As Bobby later noted for the *Hollies Official Fan Club Newsletter*, 'When our friends from Epic Records in America heard 'Courage Of Your Convictions', they thought it would be the ideal follow-up single for us. The words are quite interesting, and a nice guitar riff runs through this song. It's a good dancer.'

Now poised for a determined onslaught on the album charts is The Hollies' new Polydor long-player called "Romany". Many arduous recording hours have gone into the production of this album and the originally conceived format of "slow and tasteful" has been changed to "up-tempo and GO", with the taking out of some lesser impact songs and the inclusion of others calculated to better please the rockers. A sure-fire best-seller in true Hollies tradition!

Always an interesting group, but this album is more interesting than usual. The first one without Allan Clarke and with Mikael Rickfors. The Rickfors voice is quite outstanding in a bluesy-edged dramatic way, and his faint Swedish accent adds to, rather than detracts from, the overall sound. 'Won't You Feel Good That Morning' is a fine opener, up-tempo and energetic, gradually working into the old Hollies' style of harmonies. 'Slow Down' is a fiery opener for side two, and the title track a good slice of where the Hollies are at now. A summing up? The basic sound has changed, naturally enough, but those clean-cut and sharp-edged harmonies are still an integral part. A nice album, full of style.

UK Press Cuttings: 1972

"Romany" finds the Hollies once again in command of the charts, with every indication their success will continue. Rickfors, a deep-throated singer in the tradition of Alex Chilton, David Clayton-Thomas, et al., has adapted to the group, and submerged in their harmonies he becomes part of the traditional Hollies sound. That sound is in far greater evidence here than on just about any Hollies record since the days of 'Dear Eloise'.

Their current hit, 'Magic Woman Touch', is the fulfilment of every broken promise made by Crosby, Stills & Nash. And 'Won't We Feel Good', with its confident power and marvellous Easybeats licks, would make an ideal follow-up, although the obvious corporate choice is 'Courage of Your Convictions', a carbon copy of 'Long Cool Woman...' (despite the fact that it has a different author). The album's high calibre is maintained through 'Slow Down', 'Romany' and 'Blue in the Morning'. Even Judee Sill's 'Jesus Was a Crossmaker' comes out pleasant enough, proof that talent can overcome just about any odds. Not quite, though. 'Down River', a lifeless cadaver of misconceived songwriting in David Ackles' original version, is rendered here by Rickfors in a sort of slowed-down Engelbert Humperdinck voice – the worst atrocity since 'You Know the Score' on their last album.

But it's hard to hold a grudge against The Hollies, after such a generally wonderful album, after all the great records they've given us over these ten years, and especially because of the cherubic innocence they've managed to maintain through it all. Surely it wasn't their idea to record such an abysmal song; no doubt the spirit of Mickie Most put them up to it.

Greg Shaw
*Rolling Stone*

Like its predecessor, the LP came packaged in a lavish gatefold sleeve, with the young artist Colin Elgie once again utilising his concept from the front cover image of the *Distant Light* album, but updating it to encompass an alternative, colder season.

'The *Romany* cover came a year or so after *Distant Light*,' Colin confirms. 'But we decided to reprise the same layout, with the same character and woodland scene, but this time with a winter setting.'

'The lightly frosted pool shows that we're hoping the bad things have gone now,' commented an enigmatic Robin Britten at the time, reflecting on the imagery suggested in Elgie's artwork. 'We're hoping that things from years back can all be forgotten, that's why the boy is walking away from them. The two deer with their antlers locked in the background represent the clashes of opinions, which will always occur.'

Interestingly, one of the outtakes that didn't make the final song selection was a recent composition by American country-rock multi-instrumentalist Bernie Leadon, co-written alongside his new bandmate in The Eagles, Don Henley. Together, the newly formed band had taken their recording of the song 'Witchy Woman', featuring the distinctive voice of Henley, into the US Top 10. The Hollies' version, cut just five months after The Eagles' own recording, and with Mikael handling the vocals, was equally as satisfying but lost a little of the outlaw mystery and west coast *feel* in its translation.

Surprisingly, and perhaps even more so, given the acceptability The Hollies were gradually beginning to achieve with their more progressive work, the album failed to register on the UK charts, and with no British 45 taken from the selection to promote it further, it became lost in the pre-festive rush of annual compilations and Greatest Hits collections – *20 All-Time Hits of the 50s, 20 Star Tracks, 22 Dynamic Hits Vol.2, 20 Fantastic Hits* (*Volumes 1 and 2*), *Simon & Garfunkel's Greatest Hits, Best of Bread* – and the teen stars of the day (Donny Osmond, David Cassidy, The Jackson 5…).

Then, despite the lack of sales, and just as things were beginning to look promising for the new line-up, a strange phenomenon occurred – and a voice from the past came back to haunt them.

# CHAPTER TWENTY-THREE

# "IT'S NOT HIGH ENERGY ROCK 'N' ROLL..."

Having declared himself ready to return to work, but harbouring uncertainty over the group's current choice of material, Ron Richards had returned to the studios, armed with a new Cook-Greenaway composition that he was keen for the band to record as the next single. Taped at Abbey Road on 14th September, and delivered to Polydor shortly afterwards, 'If It Wasn't For The Reason' was a lightweight slab of commercial '70s pop, featuring the vocals of Terry and Mikael, perfectly moulded towards The Hollies' harmonies, accompanied by some exquisite Byrds-inspired jangling Hicks guitarwork. However, a furore had been building up on the other side of the Atlantic, following Epic Records' decision to reach back into the catalogue and issue a new 45 from the Allan Clarke-era. Such was the astonishing success it generated that the decision from Polydor to pull the proposed new release was understandable (citing a change of plans), given that EMI Records in the UK had chosen to follow suit and also belatedly re-issue the golden oldie, even though it was one that, at a mere fifteen months old, was barely a known classic.

'Long Cool Woman (In A Black Dress)' had first appeared as an album cut on the *Distant Light* release, albeit one that had barely made that selection, as Allan Clarke had initially foreseen it as appearing on a proposed solo album. But then, adult-orientated-rock DJs across North

America had started breaking it out for their radio playlists, getting more response with each play, thus forcing the hand of Epic Records to meet the demand and issue it belatedly as a single (Epic 10871) during the spring of '72. Perfect for US FM radio, the single flew up the *Billboard* Hot 100 charts, topping out at the #2 slot during an impressive thirteen-week run and earning the band their first million-selling US hit. As a result, copies of the *Distant Light* album also began selling in enormous quantities, with over 100,000 units shifting during the summer months alone, driving it up to within touching distance of the *Billboard* Top 20 album list. In addition to North America (where it even went one better and hit the prestigious top spot in the alternate *Cash Box* chart), the record also achieved significant success in a host of other territories. Following the US example, Canada and South Africa sent it right to the pinnacle of their respective charts, whilst in Australia and New Zealand, unsurprisingly, it also achieved Top 3 status. For both the band (promoting their new album with a new lead singer), and for their former frontman, it was a confusing scenario to be in. In fact, so much so that, with no band to promote the single on home shores – well, no band that featured the same lead singer – the UK re-release suffered the same fate the second time around, peaking at the lowly #32 position.

Polydor, meanwhile, having postponed their earlier plans for a new 45, then scheduled 'Magic Woman Touch' (b/w 'Indian Girl') as the forthcoming single release instead. But this unplanned success threw up other issues in turn. With an upcoming US tour on the horizon and looking to capitalise on the triumph of the million-selling hit, Allan Clarke put aside any earlier disappointments and proposed that he return for the tour, fronting the band as he had done for the original recording. Tony Hicks, however, had other thoughts and turned down the offer, opting to honour the touring schedule with the present five-man band and continue to promote their new material. It was a bold decision. With the new line-up rehearsed and ready to hit the road once more, there was an immediate demand from their loyal UK fan base to see the Hollies perform live once again, such had been the sporadic performances in their homeland of late. Yet, the big $$$ talked loudly and, unfortunately, whilst also keeping the news of Allan's offer out of the media and press reports, Rod Shields was forced to comment:

'The boys are preparing to start touring again and we have come up against a gigantic problem. When a group or an artist becomes internationally well known, and their records are more or less released simultaneously throughout the world, your fans want to see you and we have always believed in travelling the world to perform for our fans. We've just had a number one in the USA, and now Australia, and we are being besieged with offers to tour these countries. But you cannot simply go to these places for a few days or weeks – it is economically out of the question. A tour, to make any sense, has to last for four to six weeks. To put it in a nutshell, we can only be in one place at a time. It grieves the boys greatly that Great Britain, our home base, will have to wait until we are in a position to organise a full concert tour.' [33]

'I was a bit annoyed that I wasn't allowed to go to America to do the promotion of that,' confessed a disgruntled Allan. 'It being my song and me actually playing the guitar on it and writing it. It has no harmonies on it and it's really an Allan Clarke single, it's not a Hollies single, and it's so different from what The Hollies have done before...' [64]

The proposed five-week visit to the US was their longest overseas visit to date, taking in thirty-two shows during the tour, crisscrossing the state lines on twenty occasions, and playing in some of the vast cities for the very first time. With a setlist weighing heavily on newer material, and with supporting acts The Raspberries and current hit-making singer-songwriter Danny O'Keefe booked to accompany them *en route*, they flew out of Heathrow Airport on 11th October, destined for New York City.

13th October 1972: Music Fair, Valley Forge, PA
14th October 1972: University of North Carolina, Chapel Hill, NC
15th October 1972: Music Fair, Owings Mills, MD
17th October 1972: Palace Theatre, Albany, NY
19th October 1972: Kleinhans Music Hall, Buffalo, NY
20th October 1972: State College, Keene, NH
21st October 1972: University of Maine, Gorham, ME
22nd October 1972: Aquarius Theatre, Boston, MA
25th October 1972: State University, Raleigh, NC
26th October 1972: Dobyns-Bennett Dome, Kingsport, TN
27th October 1972: Park Centre, Charlotte, NC
29th October 1972: Memorial Auditorium, Spartanburg, SC
1st November 1972: Memorial Auditorium, Fayetteville, NC
3rd November 1972: Municipal Auditorium, Springfield, MA
4th November 1972: University of Rochester, Rochester, NY

5th November 1972: Philharmonic Hall, New York City, NY

6th November 1972: Kennedy Centre, Washington, DC

8th November 1972: Municipal Auditorium, Atlanta, GA

9th November 1972: Georgia Southern College, Statesboro, GA

10th November 1972: Venue undocumented, New Orleans, LA

11th November 1972: Venue undocumented, FL

12th November 1972: Auditorium Theatre, Chicago, IL

14th November 1972: Ford Auditorium, Detroit, MI

16th November 1972: Paramount Theatre, Portland, OR

17th November 1972: Armory Auditorium, Salem, OR

18th November 1972; Community Theatre, Berkeley, CA

19th November 1972: Community Concourse, San Diego, CA

22nd November 1972: Santa Monica Auditorium, Los Angeles, CA

'America was certainly better than last time, but there were some good and some bad,' Tony was to report back to *Disc & Music Echo*. 'Actually, the tour started off pretty shakily and got progressively worse for the next four nights, but after that, it pulled together.

'It was the first time we'd worked live with Mikael, and for a year as a group – but it was the same old story, though. We went over with the specific intention of doing some newer numbers off *Distant Light,* but they still wanted to hear the old things, like 'Carrie Anne'.'

A surviving audience recording from the show held at Kleinhans Music Hall in Buffalo certainly suggests that the band were facing a number of difficulties at some of the larger venues they were booked to play. At one stage, Tony can be heard commenting, "Did you all come in a taxi together?", referring to the poor attendance that particular evening. At the same concert, he also made reference to the vast distance between the audience and the stage, making it all the more difficult for them to build a connection. The audience responds with polite applause, but with little sincerity or enthusiasm throughout the set until 'Long Cool Woman (In A Black Dress)' is played out as the show's closing number.

Further issues also arose early on in the tour when support for one of the opening acts began to surpass that received for the headliners. Dave Smalley, bass player for the Cleveland-based band The Raspberries, would later claim: 'We smoked The Hollies in three straight shows. The audiences were alive with electricity when we played. The Hollies should have taken advantage of that, but instead they came out and played with little emotion. Somebody from their management told our manager that we had to slow the pace down over the last three songs of our set, or that they would cut us down from forty to thirty minutes, and just six songs. After that brief meeting, we knew that we were not long for the tour. We played one more show with them, then they booted us just before we were supposed to play at the New York Philharmonic Hall in New York. The problem was that most of the kids attending the shows were the younger teenagers. It was great for us but bad for them…'[37]

Terry Sylvester would, in more recent years, play down the controversy of the tour, insisting that The Raspberries were removed simply because "they weren't very good, and the promoter was getting complaints about them". Certain factors, however, would refute his later claims, with a series of mixed reviews, both good and bad, coming early on during the extensive schedule:

The Hollies: Eight years ago, a BIG group, second only to Paul and George and the rest of them. Then two lead singers walked out on them; Graham Nash (we all know where he went) and Allan Clarke. So here they are, back at the bottom of the ladder, and this is only the second concert they've played in a year.

They've got a new lead singer and brother, he can sing! A sultry Swede named Mikael Rickfors – he doesn't speak too much English but musically he fits right in with those nice ordinary boys from Manchester. And this strange new sound! Four songs in a row from their new album, "Distant Light", which is like nothing they've done before. You know, of course, they have to do some of the Golden Oldies, but have you ever heard anything like Mikael singing 'He Ain't Heavy, He's My Brother'? It really is something special. We may have witnessed, last Saturday night, the beginning of something rather special!

*The Daily Tar Heel*
Chapel Hill, NC
October 1972

Yet, from an audience perspective, watching the show from the front, it was clearly viewed from a different angle:

341

The Hollies only have to apologize to themselves and the 4,500 or so people who paid $6.00 for tickets and attended the show.

The show opened with a session from Seattle-based folk guitarist Danny O'Keefe, who nearly put the audience to sleep with one boring song after another. Next up, with the job of reviving the now near-comatose crowd, was the Cleveland-based pop-rock band The Raspberries. With the same excitement as Jan and Dean in their most popular days, the fab-looking guys with long hair blasted away with four consecutive fast-rocking songs.

With the crowd cheering wildly and standing, the band went into a rendition of 'Good Golly Miss Molly', which was played both fast and loud, with singer Eric Carmen belting out clear vocals. Lead guitarist Wally Bryson then switched over to The Beatles' 'Roll Over Beethoven' like a skilled surgeon as the band had the Chapel Hill audience stomping their feet-to-the-beat. For the grand finale, The Raspberries ripped 'Go All The Way' as loud as they could, while leaving the crowd drained at the end of their set.

Oh, The Hollies did finally get on stage. The English pop band were a very tired third act. The five-piece band lumbered through an uninspiring 45-minute set. Their once "high-and-bouncy" sound was just not there. The only time they got the Carolinians to respond was when they played their current hit 'Long Cool Woman...'. Otherwise, the one-time hit-makers bored the audience to sleep.

Chapel Hill, NC review
October 1972


Another scathing review from the University of Maine show held one week later in Gorham, Maine, noted that "the Hollies struggled to play through their first two songs. The booing became so loud that they stopped playing just one minute into their third song. Then, some of the fans in the audience started throwing "candy" raspberries at the band members on stage. It was an utter embarrassment for the British Boys..."

'The deal with The Hollies was that they had just changed their lead singer,' Raspberries' frontman Eric Carmen would later comment. 'Allan Clarke had left the group and it wasn't the same band. They were playing a lot of new material and people weren't digging them. They had imported a new lead singer from Sweden who couldn't speak English very well. They taught him their songs phonetically and a lot of people were disappointed to hear this very husky-throated Swedish singer singing 'Bus Stop' syllable by syllable. Their act is a cabaret act. It's not high-energy rock and roll. We were ending all our shows with 'Go All The Way', a Top 5 hit, which made it very tough for the Hollies to come on playing slow songs. They'd come on stage and play a couple of ballads from their *Distant Light* album and nobody knew what they were doing. They were very disappointed. As a result of this, they never said a word to us on the whole tour.

'With each subsequent gig, we got less room on stage and fewer lights. It was getting silly. I mean, we had ten feet on stage, front to back. Their drum set kept moving closer and closer to the edge of the stage, leaving us less and less room to set up. After six or seven dates, we were told to leave the tour. It got a lot of press in various places. The Hollies' people said, "Raspberries were blowing the show." Our people said, "The Hollies can't follow them."'[38]

Despite such negativity surrounding the initial performances, as the tour progressed, and the east coast rock 'n' roll drive and popularity of The Raspberries was cast aside, the positive aspects began to shine through. The audiences became more receptive to the quieter nature of a number of the songs, and Mikael began to fit in more comfortably alongside his new bandmates, although he still tended to remain stage left, often stepping back into the shadows with his guitar, preferring a role out of the spotlight.

Carrie Anne / You Know The Score / Pull Down The Blind / Look What We've Got / Only Love Can Break Your Heart / Words Don't Come Easy / Romany / Touch / Amazing Grace / Bus Stop / On A Carousel / Long Dark Road / He Ain't Heavy, He's My Brother / Long Cool Woman (In A Black Dress)

Let's make one thing perfectly clear, if you're going to shell out some green paper for an evening's entertainment, you want to get your money's worth, right? Then you couldn't possibly do much better than going to hear The Hollies in concert. The five-man group is pleasant to hear, fun to watch, and in all thoroughly entertaining.

*The New York Daily News*
November 1972

Mikael Rickfors, the quintet's new Swedish member, proved a big plus on vocals in such material as 'Amazing Grace' and 'He Ain't Heavy'. He also blended in well with excellent lead guitarist Tony Hicks and rhythm guitarist Terry Sylvester. The rock and roll numbers such as 'Bus Stop', 'On A Carousel' and 'Carrie Anne' stood out, as did 'Long Cool Woman', their recent Epic hit.

*Variety*
November 1972

Arriving in California on 18th November, the band played two sold-out shows in Berkeley and San Diego before they took to the stage for the final appearance on the tour. They were initially scheduled to fly up to Toronto, in Canada, on the 20th, where they would spend two days taping the CTV-broadcast *Rollin' on the River* TV show, fronted by Kenny Rogers and The First Edition, but, for whatever reason, this appearance seemingly never occurred. Subsequently, having had two days' rest, and with Billy Preston now added to the supporting role for the show at the Santa Monica Auditorium in Los Angeles, The Hollies brought the tour to a close. Unfortunately, the LA crowd at the 3,000-seat venue were very much a mixed gathering, with a large portion of the black audience leaving after Preston's supporting slot, but those who remained in attendance recalled how slick, professional and polished the band came across. However, within the media, there were still hurdles to cross:

Since Clarke's departure, there is no focal point; the members, except for drummer Elliott, change instruments and retain more of an equal, less specified function. Some of the songs they performed were boring, yet an even greater problem was the sequencing of the selections: too many consecutive slow songs, poor placement of hits. Their between-song patter was embarrassingly silly and indulgent.

The audience at Santa Monica Civic Auditorium was cold but polite as it waited for the band to recreate the spirit of the era of their early hits. It never happened. That failure concealed from view the group's amazingly complex history and its strong capacity for survival.

Harold Bronson
*Rolling Stone*

'That's our first concert tour of America in two and a half years, and it's proven such a success,' summed up a buoyant Rod Shields. 'The reaction to the concerts was great, and in the major cities of New York and Chicago the audiences gave the boys final tremendous ovations.' [3]

Whilst the tour had been in full flow, Epic Records had followed up the fruitful release of the 'Long Cool Woman (In A Black Dress)' 45, by issuing a second track from the *Distant Light* offering. Whilst not as immediately successful, the Hicks-Lynch-composed 'Long Dark Road' still achieved a reasonable rating in *Billboard*, hitting the #26 position and giving their profile a further lift across the nation. Unfortunately, the same couldn't be said back in their homeland, and upon duly arriving back in the UK following their lengthy US schedule, the band found that their current single, the Polydor release of 'Magic Woman Touch', had failed to even register in the chart lists. Under Rod Shields' direction, the group had filmed the recording session for the song before their American departure, and had subsequently edited the footage into a 3-minute promotional video, and whilst this had clearly benefited the release in other territories around the world (Top 10 in New Zealand and Holland, with lower placings in Canada, Germany and Australia), the film did little to enhance sales back home, despite its fascinating insight into the five-man band working together alongside recording engineer Peter Bown in the studio. Likewise, despite the promotional efforts of Polydor, the *Romany* album also failed to ignite interest in the UK and, in fact, saw greater success in the US, where, on the back of the tour, it climbed to a reasonable #84 position. A belated Epic issue of 'Magic Woman Touch' also saw US sales register with a #60 slot in *Billboard*.

Undaunted, and despite plans for a follow-up winter tour in Australia being cancelled – reportedly due to an overflow of UK bands performing down under at that time – the group immediately signed up for further promotional activity across the Atlantic, agreeing to return to the US in the new year to undertake some TV filming and take on some more live appearances, guesting with Canadian rock band The Guess Who.

With a restful few weeks scheduled over the Christmas period, and with recording activities temporarily placed on hold whilst they recovered from the tour, the final weeks of the year were spent relaxing, although they did briefly fly over to Amsterdam to tape an appearance on the Dutch *TopPop* show, performing 'Magic Woman Touch' and 'Won't We Feel Good That

Morning'. Then, as 1973 loomed into view, activities were once again put into gear with a series of Abbey Road recording sessions, cutting three brand-new compositions for future release; the Sylvester-Rickfors collaboration 'They Don't Realise I'm Down', the driving rock 'n' roll blues of the Hicks-Lynch 'Out On The Road', and a highly commercial solo composition from Mikael Rickfors, 'Don't Leave The Child Alone', a track energetically lifted by the immense sound of the three Hollie-harmonies. Nevertheless, following on from the light, polished production of the *Romany* album, these new tracks were deliberately cut with a rawer, rougher edge.

'I think it was a conscious decision to go heavier', Bernie recalls, 'because the consensus of opinion after *Romany* was that it was a little bit too polite. Personally, I thought it was a beautiful album and I still get more pleasure from listening to that one. I still enjoy it. The newer sessions sounded live. They weren't, but they were deliberately produced to be more raucous, sort of rockier...'[36]

However, putting aside any further recording plans for now, the group then set about filming an appearance on a brand-new BBC series in the UK, *They Sold A Million*, whereupon they played both 'He Ain't Heavy, He's My Brother' and 'Long Cool Woman (In A Black Dress)' for the very first episode. Then, with barely time to breathe, it was back once again across the ocean on a TWA direct flight bound for Los Angeles for the 30th January taping of *In Concert*, a fortnightly ABC-TV broadcast that aired simultaneously with an FM Radio show. Such was this innovative broadcast that it allowed the viewer to watch the show on their television set, whilst also listening at the same time to a stereo audio experience across the radio waves.

Filmed at the Santa Monica Civic Auditorium (the same venue that had seen the band complete their recent tour), The Hollies shared the show that week with The Guess Who and Billy Preston, each of whom were given a timed slot to perform before the gathered live audience, with a guaranteed 22-minute airtime upon transmission. Given the shorter opportunity to perform, The Hollies selected a setlist that included 'Long Dark Road' (with Tony on lead vocals and bass, Bernie on organ and Mikael providing a wailing harmonica, along with a screaming lead guitar solo at the end), 'Carrie Anne', 'Bus Stop', 'He Ain't Heavy, He's My Brother' and finally, to rapturous applause, Terry's moment in the spotlight, harnessing Allan Clarke's energy and taking on the lead for 'Long Cool Woman (In A Black Dress)'. All of these were featured in the final transmission – albeit with some additional vocal overdubs, taped a few days later (due to various audio and technical issues during the actual performance) – although a selection of other songs, including 'Romany', were also performed and subsequently filmed.

'We were disappointed that some of the newer songs weren't included,' Rod Shields was to later note when discussing the televised airing. 'But the final choice was in the hands of the TV network. 'Romany' was an outstanding performance, but I assume it was too slow for the overall programme…'[33]

One week later and following a quick cross-country flight to Peoria in Illinois to share a concert billing with country-rock band Mason Proffit at the Robertson Memorial Fieldhouse, the band were still basing themselves in the golden state, dividing their time between the Beverly Comstock hotel on Wilshire Boulevard, various press calls and social events. Taking full advantage of the LA nightlife, they hung around at Whisky a Go Go on the Sunset Strip where, according to the recollections of resident Hollywood groupie Dee Dee Keel in the tell-all book *Let's Spend The Night Together* (Pamela des Barres: Chicago Review Press), they also enjoyed the additional pleasures of what being a rock star brings. Tony also took the opportunity to fly north to San Francisco to briefly visit with Graham Nash. However, further commitments beckoned, and this time it was filming an appearance for the immensely popular NBC-broadcast *Midnight Special* TV show. Hosted by Johnny Rivers, the group turned in polished live vocal performances of 'Long Cool Woman (In A Black Dress)', 'Magic Woman Touch' and a truly powerful version of 'He Ain't Heavy, He's My Brother', airing shortly afterwards on 23rd February. One further televised US appearance also came along when CBS-TV aired a show entitled *Super Stars of Rock*, featuring the group performing 'Won't We Feel Good That Morning' and 'Touch', although both songs had been filmed prior to the US visit, back in London during December of '72.

Following the completion of their Los Angeles TV obligations, the band then flew out to the freezing temperatures of Fargo in North Dakota, joining up with Canada's hit-making The Guess Who two days later and appearing at the city's Memorial Auditorium. Holding 3,000 paying customers, it was reported that 5,000 turned up to see the show, with the local police force ushering away those without tickets.

The following day, 11th February, it was a three-hour flight down to neighbouring South Dakota and a show in Sioux Falls, after which their final appearance took place at the Metro Sports Arena in Minneapolis. By the evening of the 13th the majority of the touring party were landing back at London's Heathrow Airport, exhausted but undoubtedly elated, whilst others, including Terry and Tony, had allowed for a stopover in New York for additional business discussions. Six days later and the recording hiatus was deemed over as the band settled back into the studios of Abbey Road.

February 1973 also saw the release of a further 45 with a Hollies connection, when the Canadian-born vocalist, Denny Doherty, formerly with The Mamas and The Papas, issued a version of Terry's 'Indian Girl' in both the US and Canada. Originally recorded during the *Romany* LP sessions, The Hollies' version had recently appeared as the B-side on the 'Magic Woman Touch' UK Polydor single, and whilst perhaps not quite as lyrically strong as several of the other featured cuts on the album, it was most certainly a commercial tune that demanded greater airtime. Sadly, Doherty's version failed to offer it that, disappearing swiftly after release.

Another artist that had recently garnered the attention of the band was an American performer named Robert Tucker. Following their recent US trip, during which Tony and Terry were sufficiently impressed by his singer-songwriter abilities, they subsequently offered to bring him over to the UK so they could produce some tracks for him. Within the space of a month or two of their meeting, Tucker had flown into London and cut four rough recordings with the boys. Unfortunately, nothing was heard of this venture again.

Between 21st February and 15th March 1973, the quintet committed enough new material to tape to compile and ready the next album, the second with Mikael Rickfors as a band member, composer, musician and vocalist. As Bernie noted, the sound was purposely rougher around the edges, void of much of the polished studio sheen that had glossed over the preceding albums. It was a fresher approach, with production credits once again afforded to the band and Mikael's rich baritone cutting through the mix with clarity. The familiar band sound remained consistent; the harmonies were dense and powerful, even with a number of the inclusions being of a noticeably less commercial nature. However, all was not well within. Mikael Rickfors was noticeably uncomfortable with the situation he found himself in, both personally and professionally. Despite the initial impressions of living the life of a London-based rock star, he was finding it difficult to settle and adapt to a British lifestyle. He missed his Swedish home and family and flew back to his homeland whenever the opportunity allowed (he had recently spent Christmas back in Stockholm, and would return home again during the short Easter break), and the lonely hours that he and his girlfriend spent together in their Chelsea flat would plague him. On stage, despite his unquestionable ability to deliver what was required, he found it increasingly unsettling being placed centre spotlight, and more often than not, when the band reverted to a three-man frontline, it was Tony holding down the centre spot. Whenever possible, Mikael would seemingly disappear into the shadows of the side stage, void of any illuminating light. It was a compromise of sorts, but one that caused due concern, particularly in the eyes of Tony and Bobby, both of whom were all too aware of the importance of The Hollies' standing as live performers. In addition, much of the vocal studio work had to be compiled and edited together, due to Mikael's distinctive Swedish pronunciation coming across as too strong. Certain sections then had to be re-recorded and spliced in. It was far from ideal.

With the album ready to go, with just the running order and artwork to be decided upon, the band took off once more for a further series of overseas performances. Australia was first on the agenda, with three weeks during early May earmarked for live shows and radio promotions down under. Parlophone-Australia opted to release a new single to aid with the publicity, issuing one of the recent recordings, the Hicks-Lynch 'Slow Down, Go Down', a rare outing for a Sylvester lead on a 45, in advance of the visit (it peaked at a lowly #73).

Also helping to promote the tour, certain members then taped a series of radio promotional spots for broadcast in each of the cities they were due to play in. Primarily consisting of Bernie tinkling the ivories whilst Tony and Terry introduced the band to the listening audiences, the radio slots went a long way towards consolidating the bond between group and radio station, many of whom were sponsoring the shows in their particular city. Brisbane, Newcastle, Sydney, Melbourne and Adelaide all accommodated them as they played shows to rapturous audiences each night before they flew out across the vast country for their final performance, located on the western coastline in the city of Perth. A last-minute change of venue due to the inclement weather was a disappointing climax to the events, but the subsequent indoor show, delayed until a midnight start due to a classical concert taking place at the concert hall earlier that same evening, was again deemed a huge success although, overall, the group were not happy with how the tour had gone. Despite filling out venues in every city, issues with their equipment were causing frustration, and the performances felt lacklustre. In their own eyes, the dynamics were somehow missing, and the act was deemed as "scrappy" and lacking in effort, despite positive reviews in the media reports. In his autobiography, Bobby later referred to the fact that, earlier in the tour, he had noted in his diary, "show not so good, singer not making it. We obviously made an error in Mikael".[39]

Rod Shields: 'We all discussed the situation and the effort, or should I say lack of effort, that was evident in the performances and decided we knew what we had to do. When we returned home, a major rethink had to take place.'[33]

Departing from Melbourne Airport on 13th May, the band then flew out, via Honolulu, towards Los Angeles, from where they commenced the second leg of the tour, a further two weeks playing in the northern states of the US – Colorado, Montana, Wyoming, North and South Dakota, Iowa, Wisconsin and Indiana. That too was not without incident, with a typhoon ripping through the town of Evansville, Indiana shortly before the band were due to touch down, raising due concerns and rerouting with the flights. And then the concert itself, a co-headlining show with Canned Heat and Rare Earth, ran five hours behind schedule due to storm damage and power failure. Not that that put the waiting audience off:

Concert time was 2 o'clock in the afternoon. We finally arrived onstage at 7 o'clock. We had expected the audience to be totally fed up with the whole situation. They had been sitting there for six hours already. They were fantastic and weren't bothered at all with the technical problems. The boys put together a superb show. Tony excelled himself with some hilarious chatter to the audience and they loved it. The final three songs, 'Long Dark Road', 'He Ain't Heavy' and 'Long Cool Woman' built the act to a tremendous climax and the audience gave them a standing ovation as they walked from the stage.

*The Hollies Official Fan Club Newsletter*
June/July 1973

Arriving back at Manchester Airport soon after the final show, and following a few days' rest, Tony and Bobby met up in Tony's North London home to discuss the issues and concerns surrounding the tour. There had certainly been some successes during the five weeks on the road, and the audiences had, for the most part, been highly receptive to the band and the music, but changes clearly had to happen. Despite all of the mutual admiration for Mikael's talents, it was agreed that he wasn't the right man to lead the frontline. Swallowing their pride, they agreed to give their former bandmate a call…

It is possible that certain countries may be issuing the new LP at different times. The master tapes will be sent to all our recording outlets within the next few weeks when the final package is complete. The cover will be a folding album designed by the same team that did such a magnificent job on "Distant Light" and "Romany"; the inside will be two large colour pictures of the group performing live. On the left, as you open the cover will be a special picture taken from the stage of a theatre in Minneapolis on our last American visit. The second picture was taken from a 16mm movie film when the boys were filming in a London studio. The title of the album will be "Out On The Road' and the picture on the front will be a special painting with the boys' picture incorporated into it.

Rod Shields<br>
The Hollies Official Fan Club Newsletter

*Out On The Road*, the second Rickfors-fronted album cut by the group, now with a finalised track selection and presented within another Colin Elgie-Hipgnosis designed package (albeit with a far slicker, modern conception), was never issued as an album in England. In fact, despite Rod Shields' announcement, it wasn't scheduled for an official release anywhere once the group had decided on a new approach going forward. Instead, they opted to abandon the LP, regardless of the expense and the countless hours working on it. However, their German record label Hansa, along with Ariola Records, their Spanish counterpart, saw fit to issue the album before any other worldwide release, and before any final decisions had been confirmed, thus being the only countries who saw the LP appear on their rosters.

The April/May 1973 edition of the *Hollies Official Fan Club Newsletter* also ran a feature on the then-forthcoming release, with Bobby Elliott offering up his own opinions of each of the songs:

'Out On The Road': 'This is a rocker by Tony and his friend Kenny. The story is that of a rock musician who is playing and travelling most of his life, consequently, he misses out on a few things back home.'

'They Don't Realise I'm Down': 'Terry and Mike composition. It's a loose, mid-tempo thing, tied together by eights played on the piano by Bernie. Tony was on wah-wah guitar and uses it effectively, and there's room for some jiggery-pokery from drums and guitar before the fade.'

'The Last Wind': 'A Mikael composition about the sea, and the solitude of sailing. Acoustically based, it rises to Tony's guitar solo through a Leslie organ speaker. I use cymbal rolls and odd timpani beats to add to the picture. A truly magical song.'

'Mr Heartbreaker': 'By Mr Sylvester, sung by Terry "heartbreaker" himself. It gives a small insight into how a musician can feel when he's down and a long way from home.'

'Born A Man': 'Tony singing one of his own songs. A nice middle eight, backed up by ooh's and ah's and a tasteful guitar by Mr Hicks.'

'A Better Place': 'Another of Tony's songs. Mike sings of teaching people to love, which sounds fair enough. Tony uses electric sitar with wah-wah. Rocks along nicely.'

'Slow Down' – Go Down: 'Tony and Kenny composition. Up-tempo electric with a hint of banjo. Tells of a guy placing an order for a custom-built girl.'

'Don't Leave The Child Alone': 'Another Mikael contribution. Acoustic guitar sound, nice up-tempo, changing to half-time then back to full speed.'

'Nearer To You': 'Tony song with a reggae-type treatment. A recorder is featured in the intro and also in the solo.'

'Pick Up The Pieces': 'A sad Terry song on the complexities of love. Beautiful electric sitar by Tony, some ooh's and ah's, also electric piano by Bernie.'

'Transatlantic Westbound Jet': 'Written by Terry and myself when we were in the States, it expresses the exhilaration one experiences flying to the United States and playing concerts there. Terry begins on acoustic and it builds into an electric production with a harpsichord and a wah-wah playing a rhythm pattern underneath.'

Of note, neither of the two Terry Sylvester contributions featured – 'Mr Heartbreaker' and 'Pick Up The Pieces' – credit the co-writer on the songs, Terry's friend (and Marmalade frontman) Dean Ford. Later cover versions of both of these (solo releases by Ford and Sylvester respectively) corrected the oversight.

However, with the principal band members feeling that things were not working out with Mikael Rickfors who, in turn, was wanting to cut more album-orientated blues-influenced songs, an impasse had been reached. They were also concerned over the spiralling costs of the recording sessions, caused by Mikael's struggle with the English language. In addition, for all their current progression, they couldn't ignore the regular shout-outs in concert to play the old hits, which Mikael was loath to do, to the extent that, at one stage, he reportedly referred to them as "silly pop songs". Never undertaking any live appearances or significant promotional work in their homeland with the Rickfors line-up also raised issues. They failed to publicise any noteworthy release after the mediocre success of 'The Baby' to their loyal UK fan base and, as time went by, they began to realise the error of their ways; opting to accept that Ron Richards' sudden pronouncement, with Mikael as the "new Hollie", was a total misjudgement.

The forthcoming album release was cancelled and, at the urging of Don Ellis, head of Epic Records' A&R department, a meeting was arranged with Allan Clarke, to sound out the options available to them. Mikael subsequently received a call explaining the situation and informing him that his services were no longer required. He returned home to Stockholm, a much stronger artist for his Hollies experience, albeit chastened by his dismissal, going on to write a song a number of years later, 'Sailors Of The Heart' about his time with the band. Nevertheless, he also went on to enjoy much success at home as a solo artist.

For some time now, the boys have felt that all was not quite right between themselves concerning their live performances. This was brought home several times during the early part of the last Australian tour. The main problem has been the communication between Mikael and the rest of the group. During the last eighteen months the boys have only managed to record about twenty-four tracks. This is way below what is expected of us, and the group had been very aware of it.

Several weeks ago, we were asked to complete some material for a special Hollies anthology album for the USA, featuring The Hollies line-up before Mikael joined. After a lot of discussion during the latter part of this summer, Allan Clarke agreed with the rest of the boys to record these tracks together again. To cut a long story short, the atmosphere in the studio was so good, after a lot of heart-searching Allan is a Hollie again.[33]

# CHAPTER TWENTY-FOUR

---

# "THE HOLLIES NEED ME..."

Since leaving The Hollies during December of 1971, Allan Clarke had released two solo albums: *My Real Name Is 'arold*, issued by RCA Victor in 1972, and *Headroom*, released on EMI the following year. Neither had seen any significant success and Allan's vision of riding off into the sunset, built on the dreams of a successful solo career *à la* Graham Nash-style, had floundered pretty much from the start.

It was never going to be an easy option for him, stepping out into the spotlight alone, and similar visions of solo stardom from the likes of Carl Wayne (The Move), Dave Dee (Dave Dee, Dozy, Beaky, Mick & Tich) and Paul Jones (Manfred Mann) had all faced an equally daunting task, with each one falling at various stages of an independent existence. Carl Wayne, once of the riotous, hotel-trashing Move, had purposely moved into the cabaret circuit, undertaking insipid MOR lunchtime TV slots in between residencies, whilst Paul Jones, following a relatively successful launch into his own solo career, had swiftly changed direction once the hits dried up. And, despite a run of fourteen Top 30 hits with his former band, Dave Dee never once troubled the upper echelons of the charts once he had decided to strike out alone.

Unlike his childhood friend, who had a ready-made partnership waiting for him on the other side of the Atlantic upon his departure, and a queue of interested labels and management deals lining up for their signatures, such was the pulling power of the new triumvirate, Allan had no such luxuries. He left The Hollies with no record deal, no record producer and no supporting band awaiting him. Just the faith he had in his own music.

Following a series of unsuccessful pitches to various labels, the UK wing of RCA Victor, who were also responsible for releasing a solo album and a series of 45s for Carl Wayne, had seen the potential Allan still had to offer and had subsequently offered him a deal. He then put together a line-up of much respected British-based studio musicians who were more than eager to assist him with the new venture. Guitarist and songwriter Ray Glynn signed on, as did bass players Herbie Flowers and Dee Murray. Both Glynn and Murray had earlier encountered The Hollies when, back in 1965, as members of The Mirage, they had covered the "L. Ransford" song 'Go Away'. Another former acquaintance, drummer Tony Newman, who had earlier worked with The Hollies during Bobby's mid-'60s lay-off, stepped onto the drum stool for the majority of the sessions, and filling out the various studio dates were keyboard players Gary Brooker (pianist and frontman for Procol Harum) and Roger Coulam, along with guitarists Joe Moretti, Alan Parker and drummer Eric Dillon.

With seven new songs to his name, some composed in partnership with Ray Glynn and Herbie Flowers, others written alone, Allan took the compositions into the studio and, alongside engineer Alan Harris, self-produced his debut solo offering – *My Real Name is 'arold*. For the USA, he maintained his relationship with Epic Records and, perhaps hoping to capitalise on the then-current success of 'Long Cool Woman (In A Black Dress)', the LP was simultaneously issued Stateside.

Filled out with a selection of carefully chosen covers from the pens of Gerry Rafferty, Joe Egan and US singer-songwriter Kerry Chater, it was a strong, mature debut offering that was presented to the new label but, unfortunately, they did little to market the product, other than utilising a series of advertisements within the trade press. Despite the variety of styles than ran throughout the ten selections, kicking off with the impressive brass-dominated Clarke-Glynn-composed 'Ruby' (arranged by Richard Hewson), it failed to register significant sales across the store countertops.

Allan Clarke: "My Real Name is 'arold" (RCA SF 8283)
This is Allan Clarke striving to prove his talent as a solo performer, musician and songwriter. And he succeeds.

Painstakingly he has removed himself from The Hollies' image of block harmonies and pretty songs and come up with a collection and incorporates guts, ability, sound musicianship and emotion. Clarke's past should be forgotten. This is a brand-new spanking fresh start to another avenue of his career, not only as a writer-performer but as an astute producer. This is an exceptionally good set.

*New Musical Express*
1972

During this period, Allan also took time out to contribute harmonica to an obscure 45 release by Polydor act, Swampfox ('I've Got A Thing About You') and to Blue Mink's 1972 album, *A Time of Change*, a payback to his friendship with Mink members Coulam, Flowers and Parker, along with his occasional songwriting associate Roger Cook. A few months later, he would also receive production credits for a one-off session for the Liverpudlian quartet Colonel Bagshot, working together on the Polydor release of the Zeppelin-influenced 'Meet Down The Middle'.

A significantly higher profile partnership had also been undertaken the previous summer when, alongside Bee Gee Maurice Gibb, Allan had committed to tape a new composition entitled 'Maureen'. Working solely alongside Gibb and engineer Ric Holland they had cut the track at Island Studios in London but, sadly, despite the enjoyable nature of the sessions (as recounted to the author by Holland), the recording never went beyond an initial acetate pressing.

Nevertheless, perhaps the sole reason for *My Real Name Is 'arold*'s lack of success was the fact that, at times, Allan seemed unsure as to what direction his own music was aiming for, uncertain as to which styles he should incorporate.

Folk-styled acoustic numbers, electric rockers, brass arrangements, string-laden romantic ballads and the epic production on the self-penned 'Nature's Way Of Saying Goodbye' genuinely indicated how versatile he was but, as one UK press review wryly observed, he appeared to be an artist trying to jump on too many stools at once.

When discussing the album with journalist Tony Stewart in the *New Musical Express*, Allan noted, 'I've been wanting to do this for a long while. Not particularly to get away from harmony – I didn't really want to leave the group, but when I did, I thought, *This is it; you've got to be yourself.* I hope that's what's come over on the album. I was panicking a bit, but I did ask Graham to come over if he had any free time and give us a hand. All in all, I enjoyed doing

357

it, having to be one's own producer. I think I appreciate music more than I ever did, and I think I'm being more inventive than I ever was. I also think it's opened quite a lot of doors for me and I'm looking forward to the next one.'

Continuing in a similar vein in the newly renamed *Disc* (previously *Disc & Music Echo*), with the options for any potential hit singles in mind, he noted, 'The one that takes the overall verdict is 'You're Losing Me'. I really enjoyed doing that one, but my own personal favourite track is one I wrote about a year ago for The Hollies. It was typical Hollies, but they turned it down. They thought it was too commercial. It's called 'Baby It's Alright With Me'. The trouble with writing for the group as a whole was that you had to write commercially, so I was getting a little frustrated. On the *Distant Light* album I was writing for me personally.'

Both 'Ruby' (backed with the truly delightful 'Mary Skeffington') and the Kerry Chater-Renée Armand ballad 'You're Losing Me' (paired with the non-LP Clarke composition 'Coward By Name') were subsequently taken off the album and issued as single releases in various territories around the world, although only 'You're Losing Me' saw a UK release. Then again, neither generated any sales of significance, hindered somewhat by the noticeable lack of marketing activity. A promotional video was filmed for 'Ruby', but such was the scarcity of support from the record label that it swiftly disappeared. Without an actual working band behind him to promote the release, Allan failed to take the record on tour and publicise it. He was a notable face, with a notable voice, but the lack of public awareness for the album was surprising. But what did he really expect? The Hollies were constantly on the road during their heyday, promoting their records, and that's what drove the success. Once they took the foot off the UK pedal, concentrating on other markets, the success story at home withered. By not touring home shores with the newly issued *Romany* album, opting to take the $$$ and the live shows to other regions of the globe, acceptance, popularity and publicity were severely reduced.

Then again, maybe Allan wasn't in a fit enough state himself to promote the new record.

Loner Allan wins his toughest ever battle.
Allan Clarke – dark-eyed, gipsy-faced ex-singer with The Hollies has just resurfaced after fighting the toughest battle of his 31 years. For the trauma that followed when he quit The Hollies 18 months

ago left him so depressed and paranoid that he had a hard fight to hang on to his sanity.

It isn't difficult to understand. In the ten years he was with the group Allan sung on every one of those hit records. He even helped write a book on how to run a successful pop group. Then suddenly the great bust-up came. Just to rub a little salt into his wounds, The Hollies have since had two hits ('Long Cool Woman' and 'Long Dark Road'), which were both records he sang on before he left them.

'When I left The Hollies they said they wouldn't put out 'Long Cool Woman' as a single, but it got released. [The] first I knew about it was when a guy from CBS phones me from the States and says, "Hey, Allan, we got a hit on our hands." I thought he was talking about my solo record and I was knocked out until he told me the hit was 'Long Cool Woman', which no one even had the nerve to tell me The Hollies were putting out.

'This was when I started to get paranoid because I was looking in Billboard and there were The Hollies sitting there with a gold disc for my record.'

Gradually, it overwhelmed him. He says, 'I always said to myself I'd never go to a psychiatrist, but I'd got into a mental state where I think that talking to somebody with MD at the end of his name helped. It all happened six or eight months ago, and I've finished seeing him now.

'It was terrible. Everything used to be so easy for me with The Hollies and everything got screwed up. I'm completely sane now though, believe me, I just had the feeling that if I hadn't stayed in bed I would have died. It's very hard to get out of bed when you're mentally disarranged. You don't really want to get outside and face the big world.'

*The Daily Mirror*
1973

Disappointed by the lack of success the LP saw, the following year saw a refreshed Allan back at work in the studio, this time with an album arrangement courtesy of EMI Records, following RCA's rejection of the project. The resulting release, once again cut with a core studio team of Ray Glynn, Tony Newman and Dee Murray, was issued in the UK and Germany, but was notably without a US distribution deal, despite initial press reports indicating that it would appear Stateside as well. One noticeable addition was the arrival of former GRALTO songwriter (and another former associate of The Mirage), Kirk Duncan, providing keyboard accompaniment on many of the tunes.

> Allan Clarke has formed a working band and will be returning to live appearances from the beginning of March, starting with a short tour of Holland. The line-up is Clarke (vocals and guitar), Ray Glynn (lead guitar) and Kirk Duncan (piano and other keyboards).
>
> Clarke has also completed work on his second album, titled "Scaler". It will be issued in America in late April and the following month the band will tour the States. Negotiations are in hand to release the LP in Britain to coincide with personal appearances by the group during the next four months.
>
> *New Musical Express*
> February 1973

EMI had initially re-established contact with Allan in a bid to help them compile tracks for a second volume of Hollies hits, which had duly emerged in March of 1972, though failing to make a significant dent in the sales market. However, this helped bridge the departure of Allan from EMI's own artist roster and ultimately led to them re-signing him as a solo artist.

'[The second album] cost me around £15,000 and then RCA shelved it,' he would say soon afterwards. 'CBS also blew me out and, in the end, I had to buy the album off RCA so that EMI could release it. In all, I lost about £30,000 during that first year and with nothing coming back I got disillusioned to say the least.'

Released in July 1973, and retitled as *Headroom* (EMA-752), the LP was a significant step forward for the solo Clarke, who came across as having far greater confidence in his approach and, maybe, more importantly, he also appeared to have a focussed musical direction this time. Surrounded by a smaller band of musicians who, in turn, probably put less pressure on him than he had experienced with the debut set, the album saw a move more towards an Americanised AOR sound, with the Clarke-Glynn songs – such as 'Complete Controllable Man', 'Shift Lovin' Lady' and the country-blues of 'Fishin'" (featuring some outstanding guitar work by Ray Glynn, and some fine harmonica from Allan) all standing out. Another highlight came in the form of the majestic 'Who?', with its atmospheric arrangement and production, although when that became the (unsuccessful) single release that EMI chose to promote the album with, one wondered who made such a call. The most commercial offering on the release by far came in the form of 'Drift Away', a composition by American songwriter Mentor Williams (brother of the Academy and Grammy award-winning Paul Williams), but EMI dallied over the choice of 45, allowing the impact of Williams' work to transfer across to the US soul-pop performer Dobie Gray, who took 'Drift Away' into the *Billboard* Top 5, certifying its gold status with over one million sales. A huge missed opportunity.

Despite the rootsy-feel that ran throughout much of the album, Allan chose to close the record out with a grandiose updated version of his 1967 composition, 'Would You Believe', a song that had previously appeared on The Hollies' *Butterfly* album. Retitled as 'Would You Believe (Revisited)', the choice was a strange inclusion, at odds with much of the loose atmosphere of the preceding nine tracks, but it certainly added an imposing climax to the completed work.

With EMI's full support for the project, the record was issued in an elaborate gatefold sleeve, with the Rene Magritte-influenced artwork of Colin Elgie once again spread across the expansive packaging. Meanwhile, the inner sleeve noticeably presented individual images of the principal musicians, suggesting that Allan viewed this as more of an Allan Clarke Band project than a solo release. Not that it mattered in the long run as, despite the efforts of all concerned and the positive reviews it received, it sadly failed to shift in enough quantity to register any chart placing. Then again, there was no supporting work undertaken to promote it once plans for a tour had failed to materialise. Other than one impromptu solo appearance during early 1972, when he and Ray Glynn turned up at the Lanchester Polytechnic College Arts Festival in Coventry, armed with two acoustic guitars in true troubadour style, Allan never once took a solo show out on the road.

'I didn't have a band and I never performed on my own… ever. It never got to the point where people said to me, "Well, come to America and do a tour." People didn't know me, other than what I sang with The Hollies, so it would have been pointless actually going.' [23]

'The Hollies need me. Without the injection of my voice, you can forget The Hollies sound...'

Allan Clarke

*Melody Maker* 1973

One of the greatest groups of the last decade is back together again, after a two-year split. Sadly, not The Beatles, but a group who probably had, hit for hit, as much if not more success. The Hollies. When lead singer Allan Clarke left them it was a sad day for the group and their fans. Although The Hollies pressed on alone, as Terry Sylvester candidly says, 'Somehow it just wasn't right. I know members are always splitting from groups, but when your lead singer goes, it's a bit like having a head without a body.'

Allan was replaced by Mikael Rickfors, 'but although Mikael was good, he never felt or looked quite right, because he didn't speak any English, or hardly any.'

Despite the rather unsatisfactory state of affairs, The Hollies survived. They didn't have a lot of success in Britain, but they had a lot on the continent and also managed to breakthrough in America. Meanwhile, Allan hadn't managed to achieve the status he jointly shared with The Hollies, but his music was getting lots of airplay, gaining respect as an individual artist.

'One day Terry rang and said he wanted to talk to me. The boys wanted me to redo some vocals on some of the old numbers that would be released. Knowing the money is there in that kind of thing, and thinking it would be fun, I said, "Why not?" I was a bit nervous when we went into the studios, but it went really well...'

*Disc*

November 1973

Allan Clarke is reunited with The Hollies after quitting them two years ago to go solo. At the moment the reconciliation between Clarke and the rest of the group amounts to recording and there are no plans for Allan to go out on the road with them.

'Basically, I left The Hollies because they wouldn't allow me to do anything on my own. They couldn't face the fact that I might get success on my own talents,' explained Allan. 'They thought that when I became successful, I'd leave them anyway, so they just shortened the agony by forcing me to do one thing or the other. It was silly really because I wouldn't have left the group.

'I was in an incredible rush to record my first album and when it was finished, I realised it was a mistake. Terry was also unhappy with the way The Hollies were going and asked me if I'd be interested in doing some recording. Being in the position I am now, I'm pretty free to do whatever I choose, and I said yes. The musicians in the band aren't outstanding but their sound is and I'm hoping that we can perhaps develop it more. I'm hoping their schedules will be the same as mine, otherwise, nothing will come out of it. As it is, a friendship has still to come…'

*Melody Maker*
1973

In his autobiography, *It Ain't Heavy, It's My Story,* Bobby would later relate it as being Tony who first reconnected with Allan, whilst at the time Allan referred to it as Terry who initially reached out to him, and although the actual who, when and where is open to dispute, subject to whom is retelling the story, the facts are that Allan met up with Tony and Bobby at the Blenheim public house, along Loudoun Road in St John's Wood, soon after, and the discussion flowed freely. Despite Allan's suggestion that the close friendship may have initially been lacking, the possibilities of reconnecting on a professional level were still limitless. Allan agreed to come back to the band. However, whilst both parties actually needed each other, it was Clarke who held the trump card. He still wanted the flexibility to record his own material and issue solo releases under his own name and, providing he give The Hollies priority, the band were magnanimous in their agreement.

'I thought, Well, you've had no success of your own and this will mean a few extra thousand a year in your bank, so go ahead and see what you can get out of it,' Allan was to summarise at the time in the *New Musical Express*. 'But I think the main reason for going back was because I was getting bored with doing nothing. I preferred to go back to something I knew I could do something with. There was a better chance of getting somewhere with The Hollies and maybe I could use it as a vehicle to get myself in the public eye again.

'During those two years, The Hollies were very lucky to be able to go out and work, riding off the 'Long Cool Woman…' scene. I hate to keep bringing this up but that was the reason why they did the tours in America, and I was getting a bit pig sick about them riding on the back of it.'

Initially, Allan came back as a hired employee by Hollies Ltd., which allowed him the flexibility of running a parallel solo career. 'They hire me, they make the decisions and if I'm free I'll go along with it,' he would comment. The only party seemingly unsure about this arrangement was Robin Britten.

During his time away from the band, Allan had taken on a manager of his own, David Apps, a veteran of the 1960s music agency trade, and one who had worked with The Searchers, The Move, Bob Dylan and Simon & Garfunkel during the many various stages of his career. Robin now not only had to deal with the returning singer, who liked nothing more than to challenge the quiet, unassuming Hollies manager – more often than not under the influence of several or more beverages – but he now had the hard-lined Apps to deal with too. Nevertheless, with a fondness for the occasional tipple himself, and in between dividing his time between his other clients (including Gordon Waller, Paul Jones, Roy Orbison and Simon Dupree), Britten stoically dealt with what was thrown at him, pushing the band, time and time again, towards the easy money.

'We'd started out as a rock band,' Bobby noted. 'But the excitement that had made The Hollies great was being submerged under a tidal wave of middle-of-the-road-ness. Safe and suited, and with money in the bank, we'd become Robbo's puppets, and our hard-earned integrity and trust had been hijacked.'[39]

No records circulate as to the fate of the proposed re-recordings, but Epic Records in America were currently to be found compiling a new *Greatest Hits* collection for the group, potentially offering a home for the updated versions. Initially scheduled for an April 1973 release (but finally appearing in September), the twelve-track selection covered the US hits for both Imperial Records and Epic and, unlike the previous Imperial "hits" set, was made up completely of songs that US audiences would be familiar with, choosing only to omit 'Jennifer Eccles' from the final assortment. Clearly delighted that the label would also soon have brand- new material to promote, featuring the original lead singer, Epic Records shelved any plans to include the recent re-recordings and put out the hits album to much anticipation.

The Hollies: Greatest Hits (Epic KE-32061)

A fine collection from one of the pioneer bands of the British rock invasion, who always seems to have been vastly underrated. This set contains a representative cross-section of material from their first hit to their last major hit. All of the material features the fine harmony singing that has always been a trademark of The Hollies and also traces the band's development of songwriters, from early efforts such as 'Stop! Stop! Stop!' through to 'Long Cool Woman'. Most of the cuts include Graham Nash, founder member of the group, and all include the distinctive lead vocals of Allan Clarke (who, after leaving the group briefly, has now apparently returned). The Hollies' music always seemed deceptively simple, and it probably was in the beginning, but the development into a fine vertical band is seen well here.

*Billboard*
October 1973

'We were recording a collector's album of past hits for America,' confirmed Tony for *Record Mirror*, 'and Allan had come into the studio to help pre-record a couple of the tracks. It all went together very well, and we were all feeling good because it was going so well. It seemed a shame afterwards that we'd be packing it up again, so we decided to stick with it and carry on. There's no need to rush [the re-recordings] out now. We'll be doing a new album with Allan in the early autumn...'

Although the US release failed to hit the heights the label had hoped for, peaking at #157, it did justify the band's decision to keep attempting to break through to an American audience. The recent Rickfors-era tours had raised the band's profile once again, and the success (to whatever level) of 'Long Cool Woman (In A Black Dress)', 'Long Dark Road' and 'Magic Woman Touch' (also not included on the LP) showed that the lengthy visits were gradually paying off. But to what cost? The loss of a loyal home market? As Allan had recently learned only too well, if you don't go out on the road and play to your core audience, they will lose interest in what you are selling. The Hollies were now, as Bobby commented in his book, submerging themselves "under a tidal wave of middle-of-the-road-ness". Cabaret bookings had sucked the life out of their UK audience, and they were in danger of disappearing off the musical map on home soil.

The first signs of a new era came about with the release of the first single with Allan back in the band. 'The Day That Curly Billy Shot Down Crazy Sam McGee' (Polydor 2058-403) was another song driven by Allan's fascination with America and its western culture. If it wasn't the FBI, it was the Wild West.

'It was a song I had written two or three months before,' Allan recalled in *Disc*. 'There was no thought of The Hollies ever doing it. And even when we came to record it, it wasn't intended to be the single. But somehow it just happened!'

Taped at Abbey Road with Ron Richards during an early August session – on the same date as the excellent but lyrically evocative 'Mexico Gold' (the result of which saw it remain unreleased due to its questionable nature) – and rush-released for a 14th September 1973 launch (coupled with a new mix of the Hicks-Lynch 'Born A Man', previously cut for the *Out On The Road* album), the song was another driving Clarke-composed rocker, with a similar guitar-led introduction that had so successfully served the 'Long Cool Woman...' 45. Drenched in echo, with a thumping backbeat, perhaps the release suffered unfairly due to its uncanny comparison to the earlier hit. There can only be too much of a good thing. Nevertheless, pleased to hear Allan Clarke back fronting the band, the fan base drove the release up the British charts to a #24 peak and a six-week run in the fab forty list. Released worldwide to capitalise on the revitalised band, the single also charted around the world, going Top 10 in Belgium, New Zealand and the Netherlands (where it actually topped out at #1). Yet, surprisingly, the single failed to chart in America, where one would have assumed it was most likely to hit big.

The 27th of September saw the band make a long-overdue return to the BBC *Top of the Pops* studios, with a live vocal from a confident Allan Clarke, fronting the band on rhythm guitar, flanked either side by the boyish Terry and Tony. Dressed in a tasselled brown jacket, with his chest bared to the world, an earring dangling from his left lobe and his hair hanging down to his shoulders, the thirty-one-year-old Allan looked very much like the hardened rock star hero, albeit one now weary and drawn. He was never the golden-torsoed rock-god frontman that befell the status of Led Zeppelin and The Who – Plant and Daltrey already had that throne fully emblazoned with their names carved into it, but his bare-chested desire to be spoken of within the same revered tones was evident for all to see. As was the heady lifestyle he was now consuming, driven by an increasing intake of alcohol.

By comparison, his youthful guitar counterparts still came across as the handsome, chirpy northern lads they always were, joyfully smiling in their respective roles. Meanwhile, to the side, somewhere, you would always find Bernie, quietly plying his trade, looking like a 1970s insurance salesman, or the respectable delicatessen owner he would become in later life, with his heavy, albeit thinning, side parting and smart dress sense. And then there was Bobby. Powerhousing through each and every performance. Not quite in the Keith Moon-style of showmanship but enough to let the audience know that here was someone who really *understood* what he was doing. Yes, the hairpieces grew longer with each performance, a sign of moving with the times, but his approach was so slick, professional... and yet natural. It was no wonder that, shortly after their appearance on the BBC flagship show, Paul McCartney sidled up to him at the Abbey Road studios with the suggestion he may like to join up and fill the vacant drum stool in McCartney's own band, Wings. Undoubtedly flattered by the idea, Bobby politely declined, explaining that his gig was with The Hollies. Clearly, no one was going to tempt him away from *his* band.

A couple of weeks later, having crossed the Channel to Holland to film an appearance for the *TopPop* show, the band were once more firmly ensconced in the Abbey Road studios, reunited with Allan, and cutting tracks for what would become their reunion album. It would take the next three months before they were finally satisfied with the results and the LP was ready to be mixed, but the final selections were strong. A number of the chosen songs had previously been cut for inclusion on the preceding *Out On The Road* album, but with that release officially consigned to the vaults (excluding the limited distribution in certain countries), some of the compositions were deemed too good to pass on. They just needed to be recut with Allan's contributions replacing those of Mikael.

Terry's gently swaying 'Pick Up The Pieces' (once again omitting the co-credit for Dean Ford) was resurrected from the earlier sessions, with minimal changes (and "Again" added to the title), whilst both 'Transatlantic Westbound Jet' and the preceding title track, 'Out On The Road', were both totally rearranged and re-recorded.

'I pretty much wrote 'Transatlantic Westbound Jet',' Bobby later stated in conversation with Podcast researcher Jason Barnard. 'Nobody was really writing anything at that time, and we were staying over in LA, and there was a lot of to-ing and fro-ing on jets, TWA and all the rest of it, and I just wrote the lyrics. Tony wasn't interested in writing it with me, so I got Terry Sylvester and he la-la'd a few chords and put them down. It was just a device, I thought, to try and stimulate the other guys into getting back into writing quality stuff.'[42]

In addition, two more Clarke-Sylvester songs from the abandoned *Oh Flux!* stage show, 'Falling Calling' and the 1950s doo-wop influenced 'Love Makes The World Go Round', also made a rather belated reappearance. With the choice of 'Curly Billy' also scheduled for inclusion, that left just five new songs to be selected for the final line-up. Tony and Colin-Horton Jennings came together to contribute two of these – the first of which, the cheery Beatle-esque 'Down On The Run', featured the harmonica-playing of "Duffy" Power, a former British '60s rock 'n' roll performer from the Larry Parnes stable of artists, now turned session musician. (Allan, who usually undertook harmonica duties, was reportedly in Jamaica when the session was taking place.) Their second contribution, opening up the second side of the record, was the bluesy 'It's A Shame, It's A Game', this time featuring the additional saxophone work of Jimmy Jewell. Allan Clarke then added two more of his own works to the mix, the more familiar-sounding 'Don't Let Me Down', featuring some wonderful orchestral arrangements of Chris Gunning, along with the country-pop of 'Rubber Lucy'. Two further songs were also recorded mid-way through the sessions, but both remained unused for now; the Hicks-Lynch 'Tip Of The Iceberg', a lively, chugging rock 'n' roll number that didn't quite fit the slick sound the band were striving for, and a further rare addition to the Bobby Elliott songwriting catalogue, 'Burn Fire Burn' (aided in the studio by Bernie) that, whilst enjoyable enough, lacked the commercial appeal of the other potential songs. One final number, recorded towards the end of the studio run, was the harmonious 'No More Riders', a lively new Terry Sylvester composition written alongside Cat Stevens' elder brother, David Gordon, a partnership that had earlier composed 'Indian Girl' together. Despite not making the eventual album cut, it did make an appearance on the flip side of the next 45.

The group have already put down six tracks for an album that will be released as soon as possible, and Allan and Terry were unanimous in pronouncing that was the best thing they'd ever done.

'Although we always have made good albums, nobody ever bought them, except "The Hollies Greatest Hits" of course!' Terry said wryly. 'Strangely enough, the last one we made before we split, "Distant Light", was the most successful The Hollies ever had!'

'The split did us all a lot of good,' Allan affirmed. 'We have a better direction, my songwriting is stronger and our music is different. And above all, we're really into the music now.'

*Disc*
November 1973

# CHAPTER TWENTY-FIVE

# "SLEEP, SILENT ANGEL, GO TO SLEEP..."

One month into the album sessions, and with several recordings already committed to tape, fate then played its hand when the secretaries at AIR drew the attention of the band to an Albert Hammond-Mike Hazlewood song, initially cut by Hammond for his 1972 *It Never Rains In Southern California* album and covered the following year by Phil Everly on *Star-Spangled Springer*. Mike Pender of The Searchers had also learned of this song and was keen to do something with it. However, fellow-Searcher John McNally was reportedly not overly enamoured by the possibilities and they passed on it. Thus, utilising the same Duane Eddy-produced arrangement that Phil Everly had incorporated, The Hollies and Ron Richards initially took 'The Air That I Breathe' into the Abbey Road studios on 15th November 1973, with some additional guitar work overdubbed by Tony on 22nd November.

Songwriter Albert Hammond later explained the inspiration for the song: 'I just fell in love with a girl,' he said. 'We had some kind of short affair. She was the person who gave me shelter in Los Angeles when I didn't have any place to stay. I had no money, I had no Green Card, I couldn't work. I could have been homeless. I was just so lonely...'

The scenes of the vast city surrounding him hit hard. Unlike the other cities Hammond had lived in, everyone in LA has a car, so there's little socialising on the streets. And then there's the constant presence of the smog. You breathe it in.

'I just fell in love so bad, but I guess I needed to be with my family. So, I later sat down with Mike Hazlewood, and I said, "Mike, this is what's happened to me, and this is the person." I think Mike came up with the line, *"the air that I breathe".*[65]

Ron's son, Andrew, now recalls, 'I was lucky enough to be there when the song was recorded at Abbey Road. Chris Gunning did the arrangement. My dad was using him and Chris's friend Tony Hymas to do the orchestral arrangements. Tony later did the brilliantly symphonic arrangement for 'I'm Down'. Chris did the one for 'The Air That I Breathe'. I was also lucky enough to go to a briefing session at Tony's house to see how my father went about this part of the process with his arrangers. By this stage, having done it so often over so many years, he used to pick an arranger who he thought had the sort of orchestral handwriting he had in mind. He then gave the arranger a lot of freedom to pursue their ideas. He was always seeking fresh thinking rather than a competent hack-job. The arrangement delivered here by Chris was a real stunner, perfectly capturing the atmosphere of the song. Chris was the "Martini Man", having done the famous Martini commercial theme. These records were a real team effort and they followed a process that had been perfected over the years, which allowed all participants the time and space to make their contributions. Alan Parsons was the engineer…'[41]

This particularly strong number saw the inclusion of three of the band's essential core strengths played out; Clarke's assertive yet sincere lead vocal, the exquisite three-tiered harmonies (with Terry Sylvester's pathos-tinged higher range excelling), and Tony Hicks' emotive guitar- playing, notably on the distinctive introduction.

The Hollies' new single, a Hammond-Hazlewood composition – 'The Air That I Breathe' – is being rush-released by Polydor on Friday, January 25.

This week the group returned from television work in Holland and will consider offers to return to live performances. Their new album, "The Hollies", containing 11 tracks penned by the group, is to be released on February 10.

*Melody Maker*
January 1974

Selected as the next 45 release, 'The Air That I Breathe' b/w 'No More Riders', made steady progress up the UK singles chart upon release, taking seven weeks to reach its peak position of #2, bolstered by the usual heady mix of television appearances – *Top of the Pops, The Russell Harty Show, TopPop, The Eddy Go Round Show…*

Held off the top spot by the rather insipid 'Billy, Don't Be A Hero', as sung by Paper Lace, and surrounded by a list that included the glitter and teen-scene of The Bay City Rollers, Suzi Quatro, Barry Blue, David Bowie, Queen and their former business associate, Bernard Jewry/Shane Fenton (now performing under the guise of Alvin Stardust), it was a satisfying re-emergence at the top end of the hit parade.

The Hollies: 'The Air That I Breathe' (Polydor 2058-435)
A splendid single. It's a Hammond-Hazlewood song which somehow managed to be a disastrous flop for Phil Everly as a solo single. The Hollies, now restored to top form, and in super mood, do a superb job. Allan's voice is eloquently convincing. Slow-moving ballad with fine lyrics and some outstanding high-flying harmonies. Honestly, it's a smash single.

*Record Mirror*
February 1974

Hear only the first minute of this and you may well withdraw to the sitting room, feeling that The Hollies have made a pleasant enough single but hardly one to set brigands to pouring out of the mountains. Persevere and you'll see why I'm claiming that this is the best Hollies single since 'Look Through Any Window'.

The tempo is medium to slow, and the mood is brooding. Strings swoon in at 82 seconds and at exactly 103 seconds all those legendary harmonies come storming in, making CSN&Y sound about as thrilling as the Beverley Sisters. The sound is magnificent, the production near perfect.

*New Musical Express*
1974 review

'The definitive Hollies sound was three voices treble tracked, plus a lead vocal,' continued Andrew in conversation. 'Double tracking was something commonly used at the time. It effectively meant recording a voice twice – one voice singing in close harmony with the other. In the final mix, these vocal parts were melded together to give a fatter, more authoritative sound. With The Hollies, Dad took it a stage further. After Graham left, more emphasis was placed on Allan, and because his voice was so powerful and would cut through so strongly, my father decided to treble track the harmonies. Nobody did that at this point. In the Hollies' case, treble tracking made the harmonies more punchy and able to cope with Allan's powerful lead vocal track. So, what you are hearing on their records, if you include the lead vocal, are ten vocal parts. If the lead was double tracked, then it would be eleven. When I saw it being done, Tony did the lower parts, Allan the middle and Terry the higher ones. It was a difficult, meticulously done process.

'The vocals were often sung line by line when they were actually recorded. Sometimes it was done in even shorter bursts, word by word, depending on how difficult they were. To get that clean powerful sound it required precision and it took time and it had to be done just right. When it came to the final mix, Dad would handle the faders himself and mix it all by ear. He wouldn't let anyone else do it. It was very much his thing…'

'What happened with 'The Air That I Breathe', Ron was to say in later years, 'was that we recorded it and I went in to mix it, and I thought it was a bit too fast, the tempo. So, I put it on the old machine which slightly slowed it down and that's how we mastered it.'[70]

With the emergence of the teenage-orientated market in the UK charts, driven by the so-called "glam-era", it was never going to be easy re-establishing themselves as chart contenders. Outside of teenage loyalty to acts such as the afore-mentioned Rollers, or the doyens of clean-cut toothy wholesomeness, the Osmond family, the UK record buyers were a fickle bunch. One almost knew that the glitterazzi period of Sweet, T-Rex and The Glitter Band was but a passing phase, whilst the qualities that shone through the eyeliner of Bowie, Freddie Mercury, Steve Harley and Bryan Ferry were going to see them safely out the other side. But, for the more serious musician, there were new boys on the block, attempting to steal the crowns from the balding pates of former heroes.

By 1974, Manchester had a new bunch of readymade protagonists on the boil – ironically, a group made up of partial Hollies associates from years gone by. Within the next twelve months, 10cc, a quartet comprising two experimental ex-art students, alongside former Emperors of Rhythm and Mindbenders guitarist, Eric Stewart, and renowned '60s songwriter Graham Gouldman ('Bus Stop', 'Look Through Any Window'), would go on to become, in their own words, the UK darlings of this "thing called rock 'n' roll", establishing themselves with four sumptuous LPs and a succession of cleverly crafted Top 10 single releases. Likewise, fellow art-prog rockers Supertramp would begin their claim on world domination with *Crime of The Century*. In addition to that, the former Reg Dwight was nearing the pinnacle of his own 1970s achievements, dominating both singles and album charts on both sides of the Atlantic.

Meanwhile, the Brit-based LP lists would play regular hosts to the two Davids, Bowie and Cassidy, the excessively progressive meanderings of Emerson, Lake & Palmer and Yes, the funk of Stevie Wonder, the easy-listening of John Denver and The Carpenters, the boogie of the Quo and the Wolverhampton-based riotous pounding provided by Slade. And, of course, there was always the ominous presence of a solo Beatle or three, regardless of whom McCartney positioned on the vacant drum stool behind him. In the midst of all that, The Hollies released *Hollies* (Polydor 2383-262), on the back of the single success of 'The Air That I Breathe'.

Presented in a monochrome sleeve, featuring a striking image of the quintet with the only colour coming from their tinted eyes (a vast improvement on the previous occasion they last graced an album front cover), it was an impressive statement from the band, and one that placed them back into the long-playing charts for the first time in four years – although a pinnacle of #38 was never going to worry Elton and friends, high up in their glitterbox palaces.

This astonishing wave of revitalised success wasn't just restricted to UK shores either, with both single and album establishing themselves across the world. 'The Air That I Breathe' achieved Top 10 status in numerous territories, with Germany, Australia, Holland, New Zealand and the USA all placing it towards the top of their respective lists. Likewise, the LP was a notable success too, with the US even outdoing the UK in chart position, topping out at #28 in *Billboard*.

### Hollies (Polydor 2383-262)

They've been described as the most consistent group on the pop scene but, unlike their singles, The Hollies have never quite hit it off in the albums market. "Romany" was a fine, but unrecognised, effort, and now we have no flash design cover with the release of this one, simply titled "Hollies".

The album lives up to the true tradition of Hollie harmonies and it's the first group album to be released since the much-publicised return of Allan Clarke. It also includes the last and current Hollies' singles 'Curly Billy' and the Hammond-Hazlewood song 'The Air That I Breathe'.

If I had to pick one outstanding song, apart from the single, then it would be Sylvester's 'Pick Up The Pieces Again'. This guy could turn out as Britain's answer to David Gates!

The orchestral arrangements are very crisp, and Ron Richards as always excels with the production work. The album should do well.

*New Musical Express*
March 1974


When discussing the album with *Disc* for their 23rd February edition, Tony praised the contributions of Colin Horton-Jennings, clearly holding a great deal of respect for the singer-songwriter. So much so, that he was planning to do some more work with him soon, having just completed production on Colin's new album with his band Taggett.

'I'm almost embarrassed to admit it,' he would say. 'But I've just had a studio installed in my house. Of course, it's toytown compared to the big professional studios, but it's still good enough to produce master recording tapes. I have no yearning to make a solo album myself. Basically, I don't have that good a voice, but I'm going to have a bash at more producing. First of all, I'll probably do some more work with Colin. Perhaps we'll make another album. But apart from that, I've nothing much planned outside the group.'

One of Tony's earlier stabs at producing had been with a 1970 release on Columbia Records for British opera singer Joseph Ward. Released as a single, the 45 featured a bizarre cover of the Deep Purple song 'Hallelujah (I Am The Preacher)' on one side. The *Taggett* LP, however, was more in line with Tony's pop-rock standing.

Recorded at the Abbey Road and EMI studios, under the production guidance of Tony, and working alongside the engineering talents of Peter Bown and Alan Parsons, the Horton-Jennings-led *Taggett* album was a progressive-sounding collection of his own compositions, including the band's own take on 'Delaware Taggett & The Outlaw Boys'. Sadly, it garnered little attention and following a series of 45s taken from the album, the band folded soon after.

'People were saying nice things about my solo albums,' Allan was to say in an article – *Hot-Hit Hollies Bloom Once Again!* – printed in the daily *Sun* newspaper. 'The last was "Headroom", but nice things aren't enough in this business. I was comfortably off for money, but I missed having the boys behind me and an audience in front. The split came about because I felt that I didn't have enough freedom in the band. But that has changed now and I'm happy to be back. I will continue to make solo albums and the other Hollies will be doing their own things too.

'We wasted two years, I suppose, but only good has come out of them.'

Even whilst 'The Air That I Breathe' was still basking in its glory, and the subsequent *Hollies* album was making steady progress upwards, the band members were already thinking of future ventures. And Allan wasn't the only one contemplating spreading his wings. Encouraged by Robin Britten, with whom he had set up the Charlotte Music Publishing house, Terry Sylvester was also putting together the finishing touches to his own solo debut. One that he had high hopes for.

'They're thinking of releasing it on the 1st of June. It's my first solo single and I'm hoping it'll get to number one,' an enthusiastic Sylvester confessed to *Disc*. 'With The Hollies, we all have a lot of time on our hands, up to five or six months of the year, and I felt I had a little bit too much spare time, I was getting a bit lazy. Now, happily, we don't have to worry about getting around all the time to earn our bread and butter, so I've used the time to go to the studio and do my own thing.

'I find I'm listening to the words a lot more these days and that's why I take more notice of them in my own songs and they matter so much. In fact, most of the songs are written with The Hollies in mind. There have only been one or two that I've purposely kept back for myself...'

'I do want to become a solo artist eventually,' he continued in another interview. 'Obviously, The Hollies are going to pack up before I do but, who knows, we could go on for another five years for all we know. But, by that time, I should have established myself and then I can move on.' [40]

With an album on the cards as well, Terry was certainly hedging his bets for the security of a long-term career. Likewise, Allan was also adding the finishing touches to his next solo album, handed the flexibility to do so by the band upon his return. However, before any of the solo activities took precedent, The Hollies committed to taking their live show back on the road, around the suburbs of Britain, for the first full UK tour of non-cabaret appearances since the late '60s. It wasn't a particularly lengthy outing, eleven scheduled performances over a three-week period, but it was important to put the band as a performing entity back on the British map. That said, a week of cabaret, courtesy of Robin Britten and the Batley Variety Club, preceded the venture, and was hardly the warm-up they would have liked.

With support on the tour coming in the surprising form of James Griffin, co-founding member of the recently defunct best-selling US soft-rockers Bread, the venues were now far removed from the small theatre gigs they had played in during the extended package tour days. Although it was still a step too far for them to expect filling out the vast 10,000-seat cavern of Wembley Arena on their own, the choice of locations still included the impressive Free Trade Hall in Manchester, the Philharmonic Hall in Liverpool, the Winter Gardens in Bournemouth and the 2,000-seat Theatre Royal in London's Drury Lane. Having initially met Terry Sylvester at one of the many UK publishers in London during a promotional visit to the country, Griffin was keen to promote his newly issued solo album, *Breaking Up Is Easy* (also released on the Polydor label), and he agreed to sign on for the "special guest" spot on the tour.

11th May 1974: University of Leeds, Leeds
12th May 1974: Fairfield Halls, Croydon
20th May 1974: Free Trade Hall, Manchester
21st May 1974: St George's Hall, Bradford
23rd May 1974: Philharmonic Hall, Liverpool
24th May 1974: Bristol Hippodrome, Bristol
26th May 1974: Theatre Royal, Drury Lane, London
28th May 1974: Sheffield City Hall, Sheffield
29th May 1974: Apollo Theatre, Glasgow
1st June 1974: Winter Gardens, Bournemouth
2nd June 1974: Theatre Royal, Norwich

This was so nostalgic, it was almost like returning to church and finding the choir still sings 'Onward Christian Soldiers'. Allan Clarke said it all when he joked, 'We've got so many hits; you wouldn't believe it.'

Believe it or not, The Hollies still sound the same, even with a small orchestra rather vainly trying to make themselves heard over the solid rhythm of one of Britain's great bands.

As a return to concert work, after six years in comparative limbo, this must have been a strange gig for them. The audience was a mixture of kids through to matronly ladies and lacked the surge of a rock 'n' roll crowd. Nevertheless, they were an honest showbiz audience and The Hollies expertly wound them up to a thrilling and emotional finale.

*Record Mirror*
May 1974

If you fancy a trip down Memory Lane and see a very fine musical show into the bargain you can do no better than going to see The Hollies on their current British tour. The first part of The Hollies act consisted of several blasts from the past, old Hollies hits like 'Bus Stop', which Allan confessed to wanting to get out of the way 'because we've had so many.'

But the show wasn't totally composed of old hits. The group did a substantial amount of new material from the "Hollies" album, tracks like 'Pick Up The Pieces Again' and 'Don't Let Me Down'. They also did a couple of new hits: 'The Day That Curly Billy Shot Down Crazy Sam McGee' and 'The Air That I Breathe'.

Some surprising material included Lennon and McCartney's 'Let It Be' and Dylan's 'Blowin' In The Wind'. Both numbers were very well executed, as was the group's new single, 'Son Of A Rotten Gambler', which by their own admission they had never performed live before.

The show lasted well over an hour and a half – good value for anyone's money. One came away happy at seeing such a great show and satisfied at knowing that one of the best bands of the decade is still right up there at the top.

*Disc*
May 1974

'Son Of A Rotten Gambler' had been tracked in the studio, weeks prior to commencing the tour. Written by Chip Taylor once again, and with encouragement to record it from an enthusiastic Ron Richards, it was clearly an attempt to follow the big orchestrated ballad route that 'The Air That I Breathe' had afforded them. Sadly, the composition itself was so much weaker by comparison and it was only when the full harmonies kicked in, mid-way through, that the song took on a fully-fledged life of its own. Not too many listeners were prepared to listen that far, and despite a series of largely positive reviews, including that from the dry wit of BBC radio's John Peel, the subsequent single release floundered outside the UK charts, with only the Netherlands and the ever-loyal New Zealand bestowing it with a Top 20 placing.

The Hollies: 'Son Of A Rotten Gambler' (Polydor 2058-476)
Pick of the Week: Following such a fine single as 'The Air That I Breathe' is hard enough, but The Hollies sail in happily with this Chip Taylor song. It's another slowie of a ballad, and possibly not so instantly commercial, but it really builds gloriously and decisively. Once it's soaked in, it is quite brilliant. Chart cert.

*Record Mirror*
May 1974

I was out carousing until the medium-sized hours of the morning and am in no mood to review records. What I need in lieu of the vast pile of singles beneath my bilious eye is a soft hand, delivered to my fevered brow. But life being the harsh taskmistress that she is, soft hands are unlikely to be my lot, so I will address myself sulkily to The Hollies' follow-up to the epic 'The Air That I Breathe'.

I first heard 'Rotten Gambler' a day or so ago on some radio entertainment and I recollect thinking, amongst other things, "Oh dear." I communicated my fears to my newfound pal Terry Sylvester, and he said, "It'll grow on yers." He was right. It does grow on you, although perhaps not as forcefully as 'Air' grew on you.

As with 'Air', 'Rotten' builds slowly to a number of powerful climaxes and once again we have to wait for more than a minute and a half before we hear those magnificent Hollie harmonies. I venture to suggest that you'll be pleased with just about every second of the three-minutes-fifty-seconds or so that the tale of the activities of the offspring of the indifferent gamester takes in its unfolding.

9 out of 10 on the Richter scale

John Peel / *Sounds*

May 1974

'Dad loved the song,' recalls Andrew Pratley. 'He didn't always get it right. If he wasn't sure of a song, he would canvass opinion, but he always reserved the right to make the final decision. The Hollies accepted that because he was right many, many times – even after, when they had little real power in the matter. Their dependency on him musically was something all parties, including my father, were happy to understate for differing reasons. He asked me many times about what should be the next single. As a kid, I always liked up-tempo numbers and I usually made the wrong choice! I didn't like 'The Air That I Breathe', for instance!

'The Hollies came on my radar after The Beatles. By this stage, I was already a Beatles fan, playing them obsessively, but I remember liking The Hollies from the start. Right throughout the '60s, Dad was under pressure to come up with the goods for them. He chose the material and acted as their musical boss. I used to ask him to compare working with them to working with The Beatles. He said they weren't at their level. He used to encourage them to write songs but would search for songs for them from other sources. Songs were suggested by members of the band but in the end, he had to decide which were recorded and most importantly released as a single.

'Regarding 'Son Of A Rotten Gambler', I don't know why it didn't do well. There is no data which can tell you. Hit songs capture a mood or a time. There have been hit records that are little masterpieces of musical candy, but most singles are more like bad fast food. I don't remember any better material being around at the time. In those days, releasing singles was an event in the diary rather than something that could wait for the necessary inspiration. I think that fact had more to do with it...'[41]

One wonders what would have happened had the accompanying B-side, the funky Clarke-Sylvester 'Layin' To The Music', full of *boogaloos, itchy feet* and *dancin' to the beat*, been given the honour of gracing the lead side. Could The Hollies have been the ones to set the trend rolling for funked-up white boys struttin' their stuff? Or would we still have had to wait a full twelve months until the Gibb brothers got their jive talkin'? It's a thought.

On 19th May, during a break in touring responsibilities, the band filmed a guest appearance on the BBC comedy-variety show *Sez Les*, performing 'Son Of A Rotten Gambler' for the live studio audience, and although they clapped enthusiastically at the climax of the appearance, clearly they weren't moved enough to go out and buy a copy. Not that the failure of the 45 would have been high on the mind of guitarist Tony Hicks. He had more pressing matters to think about, as the end of April 1974 saw him marry his girlfriend, twenty-two-year-old Jane Dalton, in a quiet ceremony in Swyncombe, Oxfordshire. No longer was the baby-faced songwriter too young to be married…

# CHAPTER TWENTY-SIX

# "ANOTHER NIGHT, SATURDAY NIGHT..."

*Allan Clarke*, the third solo album issued by The Hollies frontman, appeared on the shelves during the summer of 1974, preceded by the advance release of a new single, a rather mediocre Roger Cook-Herbie Flowers pop song entitled 'Sideshow' (confusingly labelled as 'Side Show' on the album sleeve). Still under his solo arrangement with EMI, the single received a surprisingly positive review in *Disc*, accompanied as it was by a promotional video and a number of televised guest spots, despite it being a relatively weak offering for the initial launch.

Allan Clarke: "Sideshow" (EMI-2133)

Nice to see Allan Clarke's going to have a solo hit. As The Hollies have just had their biggest song for ages, and this is a good song written by Roger Cook and Herbie Flowers, I don't see how it can fail. It's a very memorable, fairly fast number with a catchy chorus. And it's Allan Clarke... that should be more than enough.

*Disc*
April 1974

The remaining eight tracks on the album, upon release, revealed the reasons behind the choice of single – as the lack of overall commerciality was startlingly evident throughout. Not that it was a lame offering, far from it, but it was immediately apparent how there were no real hooks from which to hang any promotion. And of even more significance was the eye-opening fact that there were no Allan Clarke compositions featured at all. Allan and his loyal team of session friends – Herbie Flowers, Tony Newman and Ray Glynn, along with keyboard player John Peter Robinson – working under the production guidance of Roger Cook, had pulled together and cut a series of cover tunes that, as individual recordings, stood strong but, as a collective, failed to hit the benchmark set by his previous releases.

Opening up with a tune by a young American singer-songwriter named Lindsey Buckingham, as featured on his obscure *Buckingham-Nicks* Polydor album (and a recently unsuccessful 45 release on both sides of the Atlantic), 'Don't Let Me Down Again' was a lively enough introduction, highlighted by the funk-driven bass and guitar riffs, the piano-playing of the multi-talented keyboardist-arranger Mike Moran, and swathed in the gospel-chorus of Madelaine Bell, Liza Strike, Vicki Brown and associated backing singers.

However, this was then followed by the first of five Roger Cook inclusions, none of which rose up to the levels of his previously known commercial successes.

The heavily weighted brass arrangements on 'Can't Get On', care of Lew Warburton and Jimmy Horowitz, completely dominated proceedings and effectively shunted Allan's otherwise excellent delivery to the side, and this, in turn, highlighted the deficiency with the entire release; the final mix and production simply failed to capitalise on the stronger aspects that each individual composition had underneath the surface.

By this period, Roger Cook was widely recognised for his abilities and success in the recording studios, and as a guiding influence behind bands such as Blue Mink, White Plains and The Fortunes. Nevertheless, with the guitars often buried too deep in the mix, fighting to be heard over the brass and bass, he appeared intent on over-emphasising the arrangements to the detriment of Allan's contributions, and the lack of any quality Clarke compositions was also a negative aspect, bearing in mind the nonentity of some of the choices.

The grand, yet overly wordy 'I Wanna Sail Into Your Life', the gentle 'New Americans' and the R&B drive of 'Send Me Some Lovin'', a 1957 hit for Little Richard (and featuring ex-Big Three/Merseybeats bassist Johnny Gustafson), were some of the more noteworthy highlights but, for many, the main focus fell on a composition from another upcoming American songwriter who, to date, had only released one underwhelming album; *Greetings From Asbury Park NJ*. Yet the potential that Bruce Springsteen had in his work was clearly evident to Allan, who homed in on the talented young New Jersey-born musician and his sacrilegious Jesus-in-the-Wild-West tale, 'If I Was The Priest'. Infused with lyrical tales that undoubtedly appealed to Allan's western infatuation, Springsteen had demoed the song a matter of months beforehand and, to the good fortune of all, a reel-to-reel had found its way to the Chappell Publishing house in London where Allan had first stumbled across it.

Since 'The Air That I Breathe' became a massive hit all around the world, The Hollies are suddenly big business again and everyone wants to see them. Allan's problem in life is getting away from The Hollies and their type of music. This one's done it though. "This one" is his third solo album called simply "Allan Clarke". I have to say it's as far removed the melodic music of The Hollies as chalk is from cheese.

The first track is 'Don't Let Me Down Again', with Allan's voice showing some of its rougher qualities. An excellent foretaste of what is to come. Many albums have a 'novelty' song and Bruce Springsteen contributes this with one for Allan's album. It's a fascinating song, placing religious characters in the song about the Wild West. I can't see the radio stations playing it, but a good song lyrically, nonetheless.

This latest offering is a very good album, with plenty of variety and lots of guts. If your reaction to Mr Clarke is "he ain't heavy, he's a Hollie", just listen to this.

*Disc*
August 1974

Cut at the AIR studios with the core line-up of Glynn, Flowers, Newman and Robinson, with additional piano contributions from Kirk Duncan, 'If I Was The Priest' still stands today as a towering highlight in Clarke's lengthy yet erratic solo career, despite many reviewers missing the underlying theme of the song. The actual recording session reportedly collapsed into disarray at one point, with Kirk Duncan openly questioning Allan's lead vocal, referring to it as an "unintelligible drawl". The result of this was that Duncan was unceremoniously removed from the proceedings and his contributions were reportedly wiped. Blue Mink-alumni Ann O'Dell was subsequently brought in to add an organ overdub. Nevertheless, all the time and effort appeared to be totally in vain as the LP, issued as *Allan Clarke* (EMC-3041), and packaged in a sleeve resplendent with an *extreme* close-up of his face, appeared and disappeared almost within the space of a few months, being completely removed from EMI's catalogue by the turn of the year.

For the third time, Allan's solo career faltered without due recognition, although it wasn't for want of trying – having scheduled a fourteen-date tour to promote the release.

Venues have now been confirmed for the first solo tour by Allan Clarke of The Hollies, plans for which have already been exclusively reported by NME. He is to play a dozen dates in this country as well as making two appearances at a Dutch festival. The object of the tour is to promote his new solo album "Allan Clarke", produced by Roger Cook, which EMI release on August 9th. The tour is parallel to Clarke's career with The Hollies and does not mean he is leaving the group.

Hollies' lead singer Allan Clarke has had to postpone plans for his solo tour this autumn due to pressing commitments with the band.

Clarke, whose solo album "Allan Clarke'" is released by EMI this week, hopes to have the tour rescheduled for the New Year.

*New Musical Express*
Press reports 1974

\*

Meanwhile, his fellow band member Terry Sylvester was also having an equally unglamorous introduction to the world of solo stardom. His debut 45 release, 'For The Peace Of All Mankind', a slab of sentimental, over-produced balladeering, appeared during July 1974 and despite garnering support from the BBC, and some positive reviews, it picked up little radio play elsewhere, failing to set the chart world alight...

Terry Sylvester: 'For The Peace Of All Mankind' (Polydor 205-8482)
Could one lone Hollie be presenting us with the 'My Sweet Lord' of

1974? Yes indeed, he could with this Hammond-Hazlewood comp that's every bit as good a mood piece as 'The Air That I Breathe'. The words make little sense but no matter. The melody is very lovely, and Terry more than does it justice. Top five, I predict, armed with the knowledge the gods at the Beeb have given it their blessing.

*Disc*

July 1974

...which is actually a great shame, as the remaining cuts intended for his debut album, all self-composed, were a fine set of recordings. Maintaining his studio partnership with Ron Richards, the admittedly syrupy selection crossed over into MOR territory at times, with the lush, swooping orchestral arrangements, care of soundtrack/TV ad specialist Chris Gunning, and the slick female backing vocals, stripping away any rock star credibility Terry had craved in his early years. Yet, it didn't try to disguise it. It was a studio-polished concoction, full of session players, and it played to an audience that was different from the music The Hollies provided.

'It's not a rock album at all,' he confessed to the *Adelaide Advertiser*. 'I used session musicians and a lot of orchestration on it. I felt like Frank Sinatra when I walked into the studio and saw all these musicians waiting for me to sing in front of them.'

Two of the stronger cuts were more familiar to fans of The Hollies, with polished, new reworkings of both 'Pick Up The Pieces Again' and 'Indian Girl', although, arguably, the most impressive cut on the eventually released collection came in the form of 'The Trees, The Flowers And The Shame', a new song Terry had written in partnership with his occasional songwriting partner David Gordon, which also benefitted from the contributions of studio engineer Alan Parsons (who would utilise some of the choral vocal techniques when launching his own project, two years later).

Unfortunately for Terry's many followers in his homeland, and to the dismay of the critics who had lauded his debut single, Polydor opted not to release the album in the UK or Europe, preferring to hand it over to Epic Records in the US and Canada, who subsequently released it under the title *Terry Sylvester* (KE-33076). Regrettably, the US charts were totally overloaded with teenage eye-candy at that time – David Cassidy, Donny Osmond, Andy and David Williams, Bobby Sherman, Rick Springfield, Tony DeFranco – and with a dreamy album sleeve photograph, caught on camera by David Bailey, it was apparent that this was exactly the market that the label and that of the overseeing guiding eye of Robin Britten were aiming for. Terry's youthful good looks were too good an opportunity for Robin to overlook, and he was convinced he saw solo stardom in the twinkling eyes. Sadly not. Regardless, the release failed to capture the passion or the purse strings of America (or Australia, where EMI put it out, albeit with a slightly alternative track selection), and it was subsequently lost in the melee.

Solo careers were always second priority with The Hollies. That was the agreement with Allan upon his return to the line-up, and although Terry was now also testing the waters of an individual career, the band soon reunited in the studio to consolidate the united front.

August 1974 saw the first tentative steps towards the next collection of new material with another composition by Bruce Springsteen falling under the vocal spell of Clarke and company – '4th Of July, Asbury Park (Sandy)'. Although the composer had already recorded and released the song for himself by this stage, issuing it on his second long-playing album, *The Wild, The Innocent & The E Street Shuffle,* during late 1973, public acceptance was wary of his talents during this early phase of his career, and his music wasn't widely recognised amongst the general populace. Nevertheless, his compositions were immediately recognised by Allan for what they were worth, and he brought this new song to the attention of the band soon after. Omitting much of the original visual lyrical narration, The Hollies' edited arrangement was smooth, the strings were prevalent, and the harmonies were full, but the grittiness that purveyed much of the original was absent. It became so much more of a love song than the east coast statement the composer had envisaged – but it was perfect commercial material and set the standard for much of the coming weeks.

'I came to Bruce Springsteen late,' admitted Tony, when guesting on BBC Radio's *Sounds on Sunday,* 'but I think he's great. He's the only person doing anything different. His lyrics are very interesting. They're not the kind you get straight away, you've got to think about it to suss out what he's getting at, but once you realise that, it goes in a really clever way. He says clever things, and his melodies are great. Everything is great – except he's over-produced!'

Of the new songs worked upon during this run of sessions, all but two came from the in-house songwriters themselves and, besides the Springsteen composition, only one other outside tune, the unused Colin

Horton-Jennings' Caribbean-flavoured 'Come Down To The Shore', broke through the all-encompassing grip that their own works had in the studio. Certainly, the refreshed partnership between Allan Clarke and Terry Sylvester dominated proceedings, with nine co-credits on the final release, although with Tony contributing to at least six of these it was a fully co-operational band effort as they toiled away together. Pulling two Clarke-Sylvester tunes from the earlier springtime sessions, the desperate romanticism of 'Lonely Hobo Lullaby' (later covered by Percy Sledge) and the anthemic 'Give Me Time', the band now had enough new material cut by the end of September to call a halt to proceedings, although the final song committed to tape, Clarke-Hicks-Sylvester's 'I'm Down' was, in fact, also issued as a 45 precursor to the forthcoming LP.

However, upon release during November (Polydor 2058-533), this polished yet melodramatic plodder, with orchestral arrangements by Tony Hymas (who had previously contributed some mellotron work to Allan's third solo album), was never going to lift the spirits of the UK nation, caught as it was in the grip of its first post-war recession, the ongoing Provisional IRA terrorist activities and the fall-out of a three-day working week. Britain, and much of the listening world, needed their moods and attitudes lifted above such despairing tales of abandonment, adoption and confusion. The UK charts had already seen enough mawkishness that year, courtesy of Terry Jacks' sorrowful goodbyes in 'Seasons In The Sun' and the depressing yarns of Paper Lace's Billy. Like them or not, the country needed the joyful twangs of David Essex's East-End London accent, The Rubettes' 1950s falsetto throwbacks or the neat jiving rhythms of Mud's 'Tiger Feet'. Failing that, the British public always had the singalong style of a bunch of furry-lined refuse collectors from Wimbledon to latch onto. Underground or overground. What they didn't need, or want, was The Hollies' new single, regardless of the epic qualities featured within the grooves. Not even the release of an accompanying promotional video, including one of the earliest public outings for Allan's striking newly permed hairstyle, or the support of BBC Radio's John Peel (who made it one of his "45s of the month"), could save the single. Then again, had the public or the radio DJs flipped the 45 over, they would have been confronted by the far more upbeat 'Hello Lady Goodbye', featuring some great hi-hat shuffling from Bobby, and a smooth bass riff from Bernie.

Elsewhere, the single achieved some degree of acceptability, courtesy of chart placings in New Zealand and Australia (#s 4 and 26 respectively), Holland (#21) and Germany (#23).

Towards the end of the year, Allan stepped out from the shadows of The Hollies once again, undertaking production duties on the comeback 45 for Gary Walker (aka Gary Leeds), former drummer with the Walker Brothers. Issued early the following year on the United Artists label, 'Hello, How Are You?' was a cover of an old 1968 recording by the Easybeats that, despite the dramatic, heavily orchestrated production from Allan, failed to revitalise his career.

The Hollies' sixteenth studio album, *Another Night*, was released in the UK (Polydor 2442-128) during February 1975, presented in a lavish gatefold sleeve, with a detailed illuminated city scene painting that clearly followed a guideline derivative of the discarded *Out On The Road* album. Again, the five band members were depicted on a billboard, high above the night-time neon imagery, whilst the track selection crossed between the gentler folk-tinged songs (the previously noted 'Lonely Hobo Lullaby' and 'Give Me Time'), some delightful ballads ('Lucy' and '4th Of July, Asbury Park'), the more adventurously arranged epic number ('Second Hand Hang-Ups') and heavier, blues-influenced rock songs ('Look Out Johnny', 'You Gave Me Life'). However, the opening number on the ten-track collection, and the song that gave the album its title, once more took the band into a gentle groove, displaying a penchant for some smooth rhythm & blues. As they had successfully proved with the previous year's 'Layin' To The Music', The Hollies had a capable familiarity about them when Bobby hit a shuffling pattern and Tony's pulsating chords struck a chunky rhythm.

As of early 1975, there were few predominantly white R&B bands of note breaking through into mass acceptance. The Average White Band were on the cusp of the big time, having seen the initial success of 1974's 'Pick Up The Pieces', whilst Barry, Robin and Maurice Gibb were turning the feel of their 1974 album, *Mr Natural*, into a more funky fusion with the subsequent *Main Course* collection. It was surely no coincidence that both of these acts were to be found working alongside renowned producer Arif Mardin. Meanwhile, over in San Francisco, the brassy Tower of Power had been plying their blue-eyed soul for a number of years before breaking through nationally. However, all of these acts were notably based out in America, despite some of their origins stretching from as far afield as Scotland,

Australia or the Isle of Man. Back in the UK, the scene was still shuffling along to the faux R&B-pop crossovers of Hot Chocolate, 5000 Volts and Leo Sayer.

The Hollies never took their brief ventures into dance territory to any great lengths – a miscalculated step into the disco genre was still to happen as of 1975 – but the urge to keep up to date with modern trends, technology and styles was often evident throughout their career – and never more so than with the Clarke-Hicks-Sylvester combination on 'Another Night', featuring studio engineer Alan Parsons playing Paul McCartney's Moog synthesiser (left overnight in the Abbey Road studios). Arranger and jazz pianist Tony Hymas also added some significant piano accompaniment to the session.

'That was a song we started when we were doing a television show in Holland,' Allan was to also comment on *Sounds on Sunday*. 'We started doing the album, and we had 'Sandy', and Ron Richards said yes, he liked that one, but could we go out and write some of our own stuff? That one was the first number that we finished together. From then on, it gave us a nice inspiration to write so we ploughed on and finished all the songs in a week. It's got a Steely Dan-type feel to it, which was down to Terry, who likes Steely Dan more than anyone else in the group.'

Talking to host Noel Edmonds, Allan continued, 'We wrote 'Give Me Time' the same time as we wrote 'Lonely Hobo…' I'd phoned up Terry and said, "What are you doing?" and he said, "Nothing much," so I said, "Let's meet at the office at one o'clock and we'll try and knock out a few songs." So, I told my wife, Jeni, I wouldn't be home until about nine, giving it a nice big space, and we sat down and within half an hour we'd finished them both! We then didn't know what to do with ourselves, so we went down the pub!'

'4th Of July, Asbury Park (Sandy)', now retitled for a Polydor single release as 'Sandy (4th Of July, Asbury Park)', was subsequently issued as the next UK single, although, by now, many territories around the world were choosing and issuing their own choices as the synchronising of releases became a futile action. Despite Polydor's faith in the song, the British public neglected to latch onto it, and a new Hollies 45 once more failed to achieve any notable chart placing, although 1975 did see both 'Lonely Hobo Lullaby' and 'Sandy (4th Of July, Asbury Park)' hit the charts in New Zealand, and 'Another Night' and 'Sandy' (using the abbreviated title) reach the lower levels in the *Billboard* lists (71 and 85, respectively). In turn, Germany also recognised the quality in the Springsteen composition, affording it a #22 placement in their own chart rundown, whilst a belated issue of 'Falling Calling', taken from the preceding *Hollies* album, would also achieve a reasonable #31 placement in the Dutch charts. That said, never again would a brand-new 45 release by The Hollies trouble the top tiers of the worldwide charts. The New Zealand record buyers would remain faithful to the band for another year or so, but with just two final Top 10 positions during 1976, even their loyalty would be brought to a saddening close.

The Hollies: "Another Night" (Polydor 2442-128)
In my humble opinion, The Hollies have always made first-class albums which unfortunately do not make the charts. The latest contribution on 33 1/3rpm is called "Another Night" and it isn't just another album. It displays not only their performing skills but their writing ones also. Sylvester, Clarke and Hicks have competently penned all the foot tappers and quasi-ballads, with the exception of the highly potent '4th Of July, Asbury Park' by Bruce Springsteen, who's currently being hailed as the new answer to Dylan. So, if you've always been a softie for The Hollies' faultless harmonies and "A" certificate lyrics, this golden platter will be very much enjoyed.

*Record Mirror*
February 1975

The *Another Night* album, despite the positive atmosphere surrounding its creation, didn't sell in the same quantities as one would have expected. Still coming down from the high of the recent success of the previous year, sales figures were definitely disappointing to many. Having made the Top 30 in New Zealand, it barely scraped into the *Billboard* lists, topping out at #123, whilst not making any indentation at all into the British charts.

'That is my favourite Hollies album,' Terry would later comment. 'If 'Sandy' had been a hit record, The Hollies would have been as big as The Bee Gees were in the same period. We were disappointed: we thought we'd done really well with "Another Night".' [5]

The Hollies: "Another Night" (Epic PE-33387)
Although they survived the sixties pretty much intact and with a substantial stack of notable hit records as their trophies, The Hollies

never became the objects of all-out critical esteem, as did a number of their fellow survivors of the British Invasion.

The problem obscuring the real worth of The Hollies was the group's anachronistic image as a standard "vocal group" in an era of self-contained, material-producing bands. Despite their image as seven-inchers in a 12-inch world, despite their long-standing inability to find a natural songwriter among their number, despite a trauma-inducing turnover in the star-lead-tenor department, The Hollies nevertheless made the jump across the decades and into grudging respectability. When they did "In Concert" two years ago, certain experienced pop-scene observers (myself included) were surprised to discover that The Hollies actually played their own instruments, and creditably at that. By that time, Tony Hicks, Terry Sylvester and gone-today, back-tomorrow Allan Clarke were writing most of the group's material, although the hits still came from borrowed tunes and The Hollies were – depending on one's orientation – either a deft singles machine or a still-vital institution.

Having won some status at long last, The Hollies have gained the aesthetic autonomy to demonstrate again the efficacy of doing what they do best: making recorded music firmly rooted in the pop tradition. "Another Night" resembles its predecessor, "Hollies", in its showcasing of the returned Allan Clarke in a context that emphasizes medium-tempo ballads and the captivating melodrama of those trademark harmonies. Lush orchestrations (which The Hollies have long – and unembarrassedly [sic] – favoured) combine with the harmonies to create a dense but still fluid effect, and they add a kick to the rhythm section as well. Producer Ron Richards, who's been working with the group for years, applies the proven aural designs with dispatch, and the group does what it does with total professionalism, making "Another Night" formula pop of the highest order.

The most dramatic variation on the formula is the group's selection for the album's one non-original (traditionally the hit single on a Hollies LP) of Bruce Springsteen's idiosyncratic 'Sandy'. They approach the seeming difficulty of interpreting the song in their inimitably brash way – by treating it as simply another tune and ploughing straight into it. Sure enough, their lack of reverence for "art" allows them to turn 'Sandy' into a vivid, poignant track that relates in equal measure to the writer's imagistic domain and to the appealingly eccentric world The Hollies themselves have been creating since 'Bus Stop' and 'Stop! Stop! Stop!' I wouldn't be at all surprised if they hand Springsteen his first hit single.

The ever-improving original material of Clarke, Sylvester and Hicks, the deftly mixed chemistry of formula and innovation, and the group's unique sense of their identity and limitations have combined to make this one of The Hollies' strongest efforts. They may never flirt with greatness, but it's for sure that The Hollies will always make the most of what they are.

Bud Scoppa (reprinted in full with permission)
*Phonograph Record*
February 1975

The lead-up to the album's worldwide release had seen the band make the long flight to Australia once again, performing a select few shows in the big cities across the country. A 23rd January appearance at the Festival Hall in Adelaide had seen them entertain the crowd with a set full of hits and near misses, although only two songs from the then-upcoming release were performed as a teaser:

I Can't Let Go / Just One Look / Look Through Any Window / I'm Down / I Can't Tell The Bottom From The Top / Bus Stop / The Day That Curly Billy Shot Down Crazy Sam McGee / Too Young To Be Married / Amazing Grace / Let It Be / Stop! Stop! Stop! / Carrie Anne / The Air That I Breathe / He Ain't Heavy, He's My Brother / Lucy / Long Cool Woman (In A Black Dress) / Blowin' In The Wind

Then, upon returning home and in between undertaking various televised guest slots, promoting the various singles in various European destinations – including *45* (UK), *Eddy Go Round* and *TopPop* (Holland) – they travelled on to Germany to film an appearance in an obscure German-made 90-minute TV movie, *Süd-Side-Story*, performing 'Long Cool Woman (In A Black Dress)' on a particularly windswept beach. Appearing in the final cut alongside The Rubettes, Olivia Newton-John and Alvin Stardust, with the production and distribution credits shared between the German-based ARD and the Dutch broadcasting company KRO, the film (directed by Peter Wester) detailed the story of a Hamburg-based group travelling through Germany down to Italy. Following its premiere on German TV on 1st March 1975, it was swiftly filed in the never-to-be-seen-again category, and promptly forgotten about. But that wasn't the end of the brief sojourn in Europe, and whilst on the continent, they also taped an impressive 30-minute *In Concert* TV special for Swiss TV. With additional support from keyboard player Pete Wingfield, the appearance was captured completely live for the cameras, with Bernie's piano-playing coming across particularly strikingly during 'I Can't Tell The Bottom From The Top' and 'I'm Down'. With Tony moving across to take on bass guitar duties at the appropriate times, Wingfield, in turn, delivered the synthesised string arrangements on the closing ballads, 'The Air That I Breathe' and 'He Ain't Heavy, He's My Brother', whilst also turning on some startling, electrified *beeps* and *whizzes* for 'Another Night'. All round, it was a strong performance by all, regardless of the seemingly non-committal, bored expressions across the faces of the watching studio audience.

With a week's residency at the Shakespeare Club in Fraser Street, Liverpool, just a mile from the site of the old Cavern Club, closing out February, the band then reconvened down at the Abbey Road studios to commence work on yet another Bruce Springsteen composition.

'I was introduced to Bruce Springsteen's music back in the early '70s,' commented Allan, 'when he was just coming on the scene. I went into Chappell Music where a friend of mine was running the publishing in that company and he said to me, "I've got this guy from America, and they've just sent me quite a few of his songs over and I think he's going to be quite big." So, we sat down and then he put the tape on and after listening to some brilliant music, I said, "Wow! Is there any chance of having any of these songs?" I chose three songs that I liked at that particular time, which were 'Born To Run', 'Sandy' and one called 'If I Were The Priest'. I was just sort of knocked out with the sound and the energy of 'Born To Run'.'[6]

Having already cut '4th Of July, Asbury Park (Sandy)' with The Hollies, and the magnificent 'If I Were The Priest' on his 1974 solo album, Allan was convinced about the quality and potential this third tune had to offer and, at his willing, the band took the song into the studio during March of 1975. Not all were convinced;

*(Above) Japanese 45rpm release*
*(Below) Colin Elgie's sleeve design for the 1971 Distant Light LP*

*(Above) The drummer's drummer, hard at work in the recording studio*

*Mikael Rickfors (Centre) steps into the spotlight role for the 1972* Romany *album*

*(Above) Dressed to kill, Allan steps out alone during the early 1970s*
*(Below) By 1974 he had returned to the band and the charts*

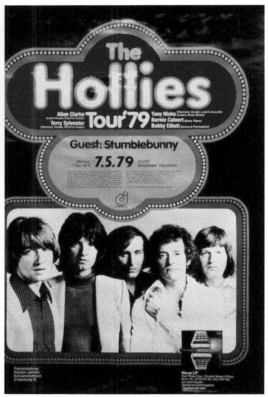

*(Top Left) Early 1970s Tony and Allan*

*(Below) Mid-70s and keyboard wizard Pete Wingfield joins the touring party*

*(Above) Reunited with Graham Nash and Eric Haydock for the 1981 appearance on Top of the Pops*

*(Below) A return to the Billboard Top 30 chart listings for the four-man line-up*

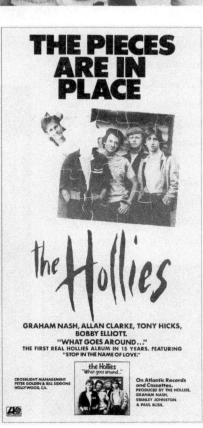

THE PIECES ARE IN PLACE

the Hollies

GRAHAM NASH, ALLAN CLARKE, TONY HICKS, BOBBY ELLIOTT.
"WHAT GOES AROUND..."
THE FIRST REAL HOLLIES ALBUM IN 15 YEARS. FEATURING "STOP IN THE NAME OF LOVE."

the Hollies
"What goes around..."

CROSSLIGHT MANAGEMENT
PETER GOLDIN & BILL SIDDONS
HOLLYWOOD, CA.

On Atlantic Records and Cassettes.
PRODUCED BY THE HOLLIES, GRAHAM NASH, STANLEY JOHNSTON & PAUL BLISS.

(Above and Below) The recording and touring line-up fluctuated during the 1980s and into the 90s –with Alan Coates, Durban Laverde, Denis Haines and Bernie Clarke.

(Right) Former frontman for The Move, Carl Wayne takes on the lead vocals as the group enters a new millennium

*(Above Left) Founding members Eric Haydock, Don Rathbone and Vic Steele reunite during 1991*
*(Left & Above Right) Allan, Bernie, Graham, Eric and Terry attend the infamous Rock and Roll Hall of Fame ceremony during 2006*
*(Below) Taking the applause, with Peter Howarth now out front*

*(Above & Right) Tony and Bobby still going strong during the 2018 Australian tour*
*(Below) Steve Lauri, Peter Howarth and Tony Hicks play out the trademark three-part Hollie harmonies*

Bobby Elliott: '[Allan] was in wannabe mode and had learned the song and every nuance of Bruce's vocal delivery. He wanted The Hollies to record it, but to me, this seemed misguided. I felt we ought to leave it alone. Allan disagreed and became angry. To console him, we went about laying a track, but it was a half-hearted affair and we never finished it…'[39]

Despite leaving the track incomplete, Allan was still determined to record a version of the song, ultimately taking it back into the studio a short while later and co-producing a solo version alongside Ray Glynn. With an arrangement by noted Irish composer Fiachra Trench, EMI belatedly issued the recording as a single later in the year (EMI-2352 – misspelling the composer as "Springstein"), backed with the Clarke-composed 'Why Don't You Call'. The release failed to sell.

'I took it back into the studios and I was very pleased with the outcome. I then took it to EMI who said, "This is a great job," but then they just sat on it. It was all ready to be released as a single and they went on strike. By the time they came back, unfortunately for me, Bruce had brought his version out. It was me against him. He won…'[6]

'The Hollies' version of 'Born to Run' was never finished,' indicates Andrew Pratley. 'I do remember the recording; it was really brilliant. This was before Springsteen's version came out. Allan was besotted with him. He wasn't alone.

'Bobby Elliot's drumming on it was awesome. The harmonies were also done on it, as well as the rhythm track. Dad brought back a reel-to-reel of it and I remember hearing it, full blast in our converted garage music room. We had studio monitors that Dad had bought from Tony Hicks, and it meant we could hear it properly. I have no idea what happened to the tape. My father said to me that Allan persuaded the rest of the band to leave the field open to Springsteen. Up to that point it was being thought of as a single, so I found it odd that Allan then did a version alone. It was a bit of a mystery. Maybe Allan just changed his mind.

'I have heard his subsequent version which is not a patch on what could have been with The Hollies. The Springsteen version was good, but I hold that this one had the makings of being better. The wonderful harmonies added a whole new dimension that no one yet has realized since.'[41]

Later research indicates that a completed vocal track was added to the recording, but that it still lacked the finalising instrumental flourishes. However, it is reportedly of useable quality.

'There were certainly egos and tensions around at that time,' Andrew continued in a later discussion with the author. 'I didn't see The Hollies in the studio when Dad wasn't there but I can vouchsafe that there was a difference of opinion within the band in the early 1970s. Allan certainly wanted to make them into a band that would appeal to the fans of Elton John and Chicago. He thought, as I did, that they were somewhat musically underpowered. Allan was especially entranced with Bruce Springsteen. I think Tony felt a bit threatened by this and Bobby always supported Tony. Allan used to lobby Dad and suggest material. Dad got on very well with Allan and rated him very highly. He was also conscious of Tony's views, which were more cautious. Tony, in the studio, was quiet and thoughtful. It should be noted that The Hollies never used other guitarists, like even The Beatles had. I think they missed a trick there by not doing that. Dad used orchestras as a way of having to deal with the Hollies' musical limitations. He was happy to do it, but I know he did find it frustrating. Bernie's bass-playing limitations especially frustrated him. But it should be remembered, at this stage, Dad was employed by the band and hence had a different relationship with them. He did have a lot of control but there were limits. In the '60s, he had complete control, although he was happy to accommodate Graham's wishes. Allan came much more to the fore when Graham left as they changed their vocal style. Had Graham stayed then the influence of Tony and Bobby would have been greatly diminished. I don't think in the case of The Hollies that they were so much a clash of strong egos as a clash of individuals who were insecure and were worried about their future. After all, they had had a brilliant run and they knew it was bound to come to an end. The question before everyone was how to keep their run going.'

Allan's lone solo outing wasn't the only external business he occupied himself with as, during this period, he spread his producer's wings once more, overseeing the sessions for a single by Australian singer Jeff Phillips and his United Artists release of 'Yesterday's Hero' b/w 'On The Road Again'. As befell much of his outside production work, the release saw little success.

Another potential diversion for the singer came about during the spring of 1975 when his name appeared on a list compiled by the progressive rock band Genesis. Peter Gabriel, the band's frontman, had recently informed his fellow bandmates of his intention to quit for a solo career and, although it hadn't yet been made public knowledge, the remaining members of the group let it be known amongst the music community that they were looking for a potential replacement and new lead singer. It remains uncertain as to whom contacted whom, or how far the idea progressed, but the name of "Allan Clarke (Hollies)" survives in existing documentation.

Following on from a week performing at Manchester's Golden Garter cabaret club, commencing 21st April 1975, the month of May saw The Hollies return Stateside once again, for their first series of US performances since Allan had rejoined the band. Playing a series of low-key promotional club shows on both sides of the country, most notably at LA's 500-seat Roxy Theatre, situated along the infamous Sunset Strip, and at New York's newly launched (and smaller) Bottom Line Club, located in Manhattan's Greenwich Village neighbourhood.

> Clarke looks and sounds just about as he did at the start and is the perfect lead singer, and when he harmonises with lead guitarist Tony Hicks and rhythm guitarist Terry Sylvester, the result is one of the most skilful and identifiable sounds in pop. In short, the seemingly ageless Hollies made a total triumphant return to the United States.
>
> *Billboard*
> May 1975

Following the first of the four shows at the Bottom Line, held on 9th May, the band were visited backstage by a clearly enthused Bruce Springsteen, who had dropped by to thank them for cutting a version of '4th Of July, Asbury Park (Sandy)'. Enthralled to finally meet him, Allan was still keen to praise him for his talents during the following evening's show: 'We had the pleasure of entertaining a really great guy last night by the name of Bruce Springsteen. I finally got to meet him. I don't know if you know about him, but he's a genius as far as I'm concerned. He makes nice albums and he writes beautiful songs…' The band then launched into a wonderful rendition of his composition to rapturous applause.

Performing a brief 50-minute set, featuring a surprising amount of '60s hits, they also included four songs featured on the recent album.

'We're going to continue now, and do what we came here for,' stated Allan, after completing the first salvo of golden oldies. 'That's to promote our latest album called "Another Night". We're going to do one now that was written especially for our recording manager, Ron Richards, who was an orphan. We wrote it about him. This one's called 'I'm Down'.

Having run through a strong version of the Clarke-Hicks-Sylvester tune, they then reeled off 'Another Night', 'Sandy' and 'Lucy' in quick succession, before finishing with a second barrage of hits, culminating in a rockin' rendition of 'Long Cool Woman (In A Black Dress)'.

Making good use of their time in the US, the band then taped a series of guest appearances for later broadcast across the nation. The popular syndicated chat shows *Dinah!* and *The Merv Griffin Show* both hosted the group, with the songs 'The Air That I Breathe', 'Another Night' and 'He Ain't Heavy, He's My Brother' appearing across the two shows. In addition, they also made a return visit to the *Midnight Special* studios in Burbank where they filmed three songs for the NBC cameras: 'Long Cool Woman (In A Black Dress)', 'Another Night' and 'Sandy'.

# WRITE ON

Words and Music by ALLAN CLARKE, TERRY SYLVESTER and TONY HICKS

As Recorded on EPIC Records by

# THE HOLLIES

Charles Hansen Distributor
EDUCATIONAL SHEET MUSIC & BOOKS, INC.
1860 Broadway / New York, New York 10023

G+W
Famous Music
Corporation
A GULF+WESTERN COMPANY

# CHAPTER TWENTY-SEVEN

# "I WOULD ROCK MY SOUL..."

With six months having passed since the band had last completed a series of sessions in the recording studios, 'Born To Run' notwithstanding, the early summer of 1975 found the group, once again, heads deep in concentration, working over a selection of new songs, with the follow-up to *Another Night* in mind.

Commencing with four new Clarke-Hicks-Sylvester compositions, 'Star', 'Stranger', 'Narida' and 'My Island', and utilising additional keyboard support in the shape of Pete Wingfield (currently high up in the charts himself at that time with his own 45 release, 'Eighteen With A Bullet'), Rod Argent and former Rubettes/Taggett clavinet and piano man Peter Arnesen, the initial sessions suggested a smoother direction for the band.

'My initial contact came about through working with the band Taggett, produced by Tony Hicks,' recalls Arnesen. 'Back in the '70s, I was a well-established studio musician in London, and I was booked for my input. Everyone had a certain style and character of playing. With The Hollies, we were given large leeway in interpretation and playing by the producers, and this was true of Ron Richards. When Ron was not involved in the production, it was Tony and Allan who were the driving force.

'I never actually met Pete Wingfield. We sort of traded off working with the band when the other was involved on other projects.'[50]

In keeping with the prevailing mood of the day, many of the tracks incorporated synthesised arrangements but even so, the quality of much of the songwriting was still there. 'Narida', in particular, with its lightweight funk groove and its sweet guitar soloing, was an encouraging sign, as was the focus placed on 'Star', with its faux-reggae rhythm and swirling synth-patterns, the latter courtesy of Rod Argent (co-founder of fellow-'60s hit-makers The Zombies). Other particular highlights came in the form of 'Stranger' and the distinctive country style of 'Sweet Country Calling'. However, the almost predictability of the arrangements on the smooth Latin sway of 'My Island', or the big ballad 'I Won't Move Over', brought the set down to a certain level of mediocrity, and even the impressively varied stylings of the lengthy 'Write On', with its subtle string arrangements from Tony Hymas, couldn't lift it up beyond a pleasant MOR status at times. As Bobby himself would later point out, the influence of 10cc's groundbreakingly mesmeric 'I'm Not In Love' just couldn't be hidden amongst the saccharine harmony wash of 'Love Is The Thing', the only track cut away from Abbey Road (at the Emison Studios in nearby Queensway), whilst the only true upbeat effort on the entire collection came in the form of 'Crocodile Woman (She Bites)', a number that still had less rock in it than a British seaside candy store. It was lively and bouncy, full of driving guitars, a pounding drumbeat and Pete Wingfield's tinkling ivories, but it was no more than good-time fun – a safe, plastic variety of true rock 'n' roll.

Subsequently, notwithstanding the polished quality that flowed effortlessly throughout these new recordings, there was nothing that jumped out as "hit" potential and although, upon release, the album was commercial enough (in some areas more so than others), all of the tracks blended in far too sweetly together. There was nothing that stood up, waving a Hollies' flag with pride, reminding the industry that they were still here. Still valid. Except, maybe... bringing the album to a close was the only non-original on the entire set, and one of the genuine overall successes from the entire sessions – a cover of American songwriter Randy Richards' anthemic 'There's Always Goodbye', a gorgeous string-laden ballad that had all of the potential to equal the past glory of 'He Ain't Heavy, He's My Brother' or 'The Air That I Breathe'. That said, wary of being labelled a big-ballad-band, the band wisely chose to avoid the scenario.

One other song attempted during these sessions, an Allan Clarke solo offering, was the lyrically impressive 'Samuel', a song that highlighted the influences that Springsteen was having on Allan as a composer, but, for reasons unclear, this was left incomplete – although Tony did finish off the instrumentation at a later date (adding some nylon string guitar work to the track during 1998 for an upcoming EMI compilation).

Pulling the final ten chosen songs together, the album eventually appeared during the opening month of the following year, a good seven months after the sessions had initially commenced. Issued by Polydor under the title of *Write On* (Polydor 2442-141) and packaged in a simple, plain angular white sleeve with gold lettering, the album notably bore the credit of A Hollies Production, with no mention at all of the overseeing eyes and ears of the loyal Ron Richards. Nevertheless, Bobby Elliott was later to comment to long-time fan (and reviewer for the Hollies' *Carousel* fanzine) Geoff Coles that Ron had, in fact, undertaken all of his usual production role for release, albeit uncredited. A strange omission?

I think The Hollies have lost their touch with this one. They used to have one of the most distinctive sounds in the business, as proved by the phenomenal string of hits they had. Now I'd find it difficult to identify them from this album. At the beginning they sound very like America, and by the end of it, they could be anybody. Perhaps it was just the old vitality that was missing.

*Record Mirror & Disc*
January 1976

This album proves how creative and diversified one band and its music can be. The Hollies are assisted by Pete '18 With A Bullet' Wingfield on this musical mixture of songs bordering on pop, country, reggae and funk. There are several tracks which could be winners but keep an ear open for the catchy 'Narida'.

*Girl About Town*
January 1976

Ageing pop stars can take comfort. If the Hollies set isn't their sharpest in years, then they've previously been denied due credit. This album perfectly illustrates Graham Nash's view of The Hollies – they don't need to be singing other people's songs. What The Hollies sing best is The Hollies, and all but one of these songs are by Clarke, Sylvester and Hicks.

There's no sign of flagging inspiration. Far from it. "Write

On" is one of the most skilfully released pop albums since "Honky Chateau", inducing the same reactions of surprise and admiration. On all 10 cuts, those gilded harmonies never lose their shine or the edge. And the instrumental work, augmented on all but one cut by Peter Wingfield, recall 10cc at their most inventive. Guys like The Hollies aren't supposed to play that good.

*National Rockstar*
January 1976

Resident BBC radio disc jockey Noel Edmonds made *Write On* his "album of the week" on his morning breakfast show, playing several tracks from it, and a number of televised promotional slots were scheduled to aid the promotion, although a late 1975 appearance on the popular teenage music show *Supersonic* shifted the focus back onto more successful times, with the band, fronted by a bare-chested Allan, performing live vocal versions of both 'Long Cool Woman (In A Black Dress)' and 'He Ain't Heavy, He's My Brother'.

Strangely, no UK single was lifted off the album initially, prior to the LP appearing, and it appeared to have little push from Polydor to drive sales. The result, unsurprisingly, was no chart placing on home shores, although New Zealand did honour it with Top 10 status, following the successful release of 'Star' b/w 'Stranger' as a 45. Germany, meanwhile, settled with issuing the title track as a single which, in turn, reached the #31 position on their national lists. South Africa also followed suit, pushing it up to #20 in their own hit lists. Perhaps unsatisfied with the hit potential on offer, Polydor (UK)'s attention focussed on another new recording, cut during the opening weeks of 1976, and opted to push the publicity machine towards that one instead.

Relocating out of North London during January and settling in for a two-day spell at The Manor recording studios in Oxfordshire alongside Pete Wingfield, The Hollies had recorded their melancholy rendition of an Emmylou Harris composition, 'Boulder To Birmingham'. Harris had released her own version of the song on her 1975 *Pieces of the Sky* album, and The Hollies' good friends The Walker Brothers had also included it on their *No Regrets* reunion LP, and so it came as a surprise to see The Hollies ignore the ballads of their recently issued *Write On* album and concentrate their focus towards this particular song instead. Nevertheless, with Alan Parsons now sitting in the producer's chair for these sessions, the band cut an admirably slick version of the song and handed it over to Polydor for approval.

'I never got paid for that,' Parsons would later comment. 'And I never produced anything else [for them], because they never asked. I was probably having too much success with Pilot and Cockney Rebel at the time.' [3]

Released as the next Hollies single during February of 1976, with an accompanying video filmed to aid potential sales, 'Boulder To Birmingham' b/w 'Crocodile Woman (She Bites)' continued the run of unsuccessful releases and saw little success on European soil, although undoubtedly much of the lyrical romanticism had been lost in the transition for the UK audiences. Why, they mused, would one travel from the glorious heights of Colorado's Rocky Mountain highs to the grey, overcast surroundings of a British Midlands former industrial city? Many, it appears, didn't realise that Birmingham was also a modern, vibrant metropolitan city in the state of Alabama, located in the shadow of the picturesque Appalachian region. Birmingham, UK, 125 miles to the north of London, was never the most chocolate-box of locations to be writing songs about. New Zealand, more understandingly, took the recording to their hearts, pushing it (b/w 'Write On') high into their Top 10.

One week after their visit to the Oxfordshire Manor Studio and the sextet (still with Pete Wingfield in the performing line-up) were flying high, jetting around the world for a short tour of New Zealand and Australia, where they were still enjoying much success. Sold-out performances in Dunedin, Christchurch, Wellington and Auckland followed, before a short flight over to Australia saw subsequent appearances in Brisbane, Sydney, Newcastle, Melbourne and Perth. The four-night run of shows held at the town hall, in Christchurch, New Zealand's second-largest city, were all recorded with a potential live LP release in mind, taped at considerable expense, and utilising the country's only sixteen-track mobile recording facility. An entire section of the 2,500-seat town hall roof had to be removed in order to lower in the recording console, carefully installed by a crane that dominated the city skyline.

However, in his 2020 autobiography, Bobby later recounted how much of the tour was dogged by Allan's ill health, the result of his excessive drinking and his love of the party lifestyle. Publicity shots from that period highlight how the now grizzled, lined appearance on the face of the thirty-three-year-old frontman and his ongoing tendency to live out and act the rockstar lifestyle, bronzed chest exposed to all onlookers, was often at odds with the safe, adult-orientated-pop-rock sounds that the group now regularly performed. Despite his wanting to play the role, The Hollies were never going to escape the past. They were never going to match the power of those who had successfully negotiated the route to true rock status; Led Zeppelin, The Who, Bad Company, The Rolling Stones – and how could you when, night after night, you were expected to churn out 'Bus Stop', 'Carrie Anne' and other milestones from the previous decade? Those pop-orientated tunes had brought the band considerable success and had put them on the musical map for all time, but the opportunity to develop their sound and become that serious rock band that Allan seemingly so desired had dissipated with the abandonment of the progressively themed work from the *Distant Light/Romany* era, followed by the subsequent MOR success of 'The Air That I Breathe'.

The Hollies could certainly stretch out when the desire took them, as their recordings of the self-composed 'You Know The Score' (*Distant Light*), 'Second Hand Hang-Ups' (*Another Night*) or the title track from *Write On* all justify, but under the domineering studio management of Tony and Bobby, the band seemed content to fill out their current repertoire with professional, slick but often soulless 3-minute songs.

Returning to the UK, they immediately carried on with the touring schedule, undertaking a seventeen-date jaunt around the provinces.

2nd March 1976: Bradford University
5th March 1976: Royal Albert Hall, London
7th March 1976: The Gaumont, Ipswich
8th March 1976: The Winter Gardens, Cleethorpes
9th March 1976: The Winter Gardens Cleethorpes
10th March 1976: The Fiesta Club, Sheffield
12th March 1976: The Capitol Theatre, Aberdeen
13th March 1976: The Apollo, Glasgow
15th March 1976: Jollees, Stoke-on-Trent
17th March 1976: The New Theatre, Oxford
18th March 1976: Club Double Diamond, Caerphilly
19th March 1976: Club Double Diamond, Caerphilly
20th March 1976: Club Double Diamond, Caerphilly

21$^{st}$ March 1976: The Winter Gardens, Bournemouth
25$^{th}$ March 1976: Baileys Club, Leicester
27$^{th}$ March 1976: Kings Country Club, Eastbourne
28$^{th}$ March 1976: The Theatre Royal, Norwich

The Hollies, one of the world's best harmony groups, have just started a British tour. Playing their first London date for seven years, they took the Royal Albert Hall by storm at the weekend – on a night of nostalgia and the promise of better things to come. And their new single 'Boulder To Birmingham' looks like adding to the long list of hits.

*Daily Mirror*
March 1976

The Hollies: 'Boulder to Birmingham' (Polydor 2058-694)
Big slow ballad which builds all the way. The Hollies harmonies are dazzlingly good, and this should be a massive hit. Sadly, though, these days there don't always seem to be many takers for Hollies' ballads, so it might not.

*Record Mirror & Disc*
March 1976

Meanwhile, Terry Sylvester, keeping his options open, juggled his time with the band alongside his increasing desire for a successful solo career. Having appeared without his bandmates for a solo appearance on *Supersonic* during the previous November, lip-synching to the 1974 recording of 'For The Peace Of All Mankind', Robin Britten and Polydor still saw endless opportunities to promote his career away from the band, scheduling his 1974 album for an upcoming UK relaunch, with a revised track selection. There was also talk of some solo live appearances.

'If you'd asked me three months ago, I'd have said, "I don't think so,"' he commented at the time to the newly combined *Record Mirror & Disc*. 'But now I'm not so sure. It might be really good. But I'll have to do it right and take an orchestra round with me.'

Terry Sylvester is like a long cold glass of Heineken; Revives, satisfies and refreshes parts others cannot reach.

Optimism flows from him like a turned-on hose pipe. No hang ups, put-downs, sideways frowns. No bull, he's a very un-plastic pop person. Terry Sylvester has been a Hollie since 1969 and will probably continue to be one until The Hollies finally rust up. But, by his own admission, a venture into the unknown world of the solo performer intrigued him – and if you make it, the dividends are far greater than merely reaping one-fifth of the honours in a five-man band. However, Terry looks upon his solo outing rather like a cat who's still got about eight more lives.

'It's a very exciting prospect for me,' he begins. 'But I know that if it falls through, I've always got the guys to fall back on. Perhaps, in a way that might work against me because I might try a little bit harder if I wasn't already in a band.'

*Record Mirror & Disc*
June 1976

Despite the recent downturn in The Hollies' chart successes, their former label, EMI Records, had seen fit to compile a new 2-LP gatefold set, featuring the very best from their time working together. *The History of The Hollies (24 Genuine Top Thirty Hits)* pulled together all of the best-selling hits from the early years into one lavishly packaged release. It did, however, opt to avoid any licensing issues with the Polydor label (hence the omission of 'The Air That I Breathe'), which undoubtedly harmed its full sales potential, leaving off their most recent, and one of their most successful hits.

Overlooking the notable involvement of Graham Nash, and choosing to utilise images of the current line-up on the outer sleeve instead (regardless of his input in eighteen of the featured twenty-four tracks), the gatefold sleeve was a visual treat for the record buyer; full of memorabilia and photos (with both Graham and Eric Haydock represented inside). With detailed sleevenotes from American journalist Toby Mamis, written at the request of Bobby, the release was by far the most definitive and chronological career collection to date – but one cannot help but think that, not only were the band themselves eradicating their album catalogue by opting to feature so little of the material in their concert setlists but that their record labels were content to do likewise.

Who, by the turn of 1976, other than the devoted long-time fans, was still familiar with the wondrously creative recordings from *For Certain Because…*, *Evolution* or *Butterfly*? Or the earlier beat-driven collections such as *In The Hollies Style* or, from 1965, *Hollies*? Or even the latter-day EMI releases, *Confessions Of The Mind* or *Distant Light*? It appeared that EMI, whilst holding the rights to these albums, were content only in marketing the hit singles, with scant attention paid to the remainder of the catalogue. The albums were mostly still in production, often appearing on budget labels with revised titles – *For Certain Because…* appeared on the Starline label as *Stop! Stop! Stop!*, *The Hollies* (from 1965) came out for the first time in stereo as *Reflection* on the Regal subsidiary, whilst *Evolution* was reissued simply as *The Hollies* on Music for Pleasure, so the music was there, but these butchered variations did little for the catalogue's credibility. On many occasions, there were no indications as to the origin of the songs featured, with no listing for the original release or title. In EMI's mind, The Hollies were never an album band anyway, and there was clearly no *Pet Sounds, Beggars Banquet* or *Sergeant Pepper* amongst them to continually press and market as they were initially intended. They had made their contributions to lining EMI's bank vaults by providing hit after hit of money-making pop perfection. And, just maybe, their lack of faith was justified when, upon release, even the *History Of* album (EMSP 650) failed to chart, despite an extensive press marketing promotion. Had the British record-buying public moved on *too* far? Then again, Decca Records in the UK had just achieved considerable success with the unauthorised issue of the 2-LP *Rolled Gold* set, pulling together for The Rolling Stones *exactly* what EMI had hoped for with their Hollies set. Who was now fooling who?

May 1976; and with publicity for their *Write On* album still hoping to drive sales for the stuttering collection (a belated April UK release of 'Star' as a single release had also faltered), the group participated in a new TV special, overseen by TV producer Mike Mansfield, the man behind the success of the popular weekly *Supersonic* show.

Filmed at the London Weekend Television studios in Kent House, on London's South Bank, *The Hollies* (aka *Superpop Hollies '76*) was, without question, one of the finest televised recordings that the band had undertaken in recent years. The vocals harmonies, particularly the higher register of Terry, were immaculate, and the featured eleven songs, interspersed by appearances from guest act R&J Stone (1975 RCA hit-makers with 'We

Do It'), were performed in such a fashion that, instrumentally, it showed what the endless years of performing live had achieved. Their musical chops were slick, accomplished and, with Bobby driving the pace with boundless energy and power, in perfect partnership with each other. Pete Wingfield's contributions, whilst now best placed in the *"that's what it was like in the '70s"* files, were best utilised when he was pounding away on the piano keys, kicking away the stool with enthusiasm (on 'Long Cool Woman (In A Black Dress)'), or when adding a synthesised string effect ('Sandy'). His tendency to add beeps and whizzes were once again an unnecessary distraction on some of the more up-tempo offerings when Tony's guitar could so easily have maintained the true essence of a Hollies sound, although for the delicate 'Love Is The Thing', the frontline trio opted to sing along to a pre-recorded track, such was the simple complexity of the arrangement. Restricting their performance to just two of their 1960s hits (a boogie-fied arrangement of 'Just One Look' and a faithful 'Carrie Anne') gave the band plenty of opportunity to plug the new album, with four of the tracks featured, including a stunning version of the title track.

Broadcast across the UK on 31st July and then distributed worldwide, the special failed to boost the album significantly, and the impetus to push it up the charts swiftly faded.

June had finally seen the release of Terry's solo album in the UK. Reworked, repackaged and retitled for the British market, and maintaining just six songs from the original 1974 release (sadly omitting the impressive 'The Trees, The Flowers And The Shame'). The new additions included some pleasing renditions of Stevie Wonder's 'I Believe (When I Fall In Love It Will Be Forever)', originally on Wonder's 1972 *Talking Book* LP, and 'Cable Car', from the *Distant Light* album. Of the remaining additions, it was his collaboration with Bread's former singer-guitarist James Griffin that stood out, combining and co-producing to great effect on the Paul Williams-Roger Nicholls song, 'Travellin' Boy' (previously a hit for Art Garfunkel).

Embracing such a compilation, the *I Believe* album certainly made for a far more enjoyable experience than that of the overly sweet, string- laden arrangements which had prevailed on the 1974 version. Pulling the Stevie Wonder cover off the album as the chosen single, paired with his own 'It's Too Late', Terry still appeared optimistic over the album's potential success, despite the poor sales figures The Hollies had recently been achieving.

'We knew all along that that would be the single,' he would tell *Record Mirror & Disc* journalist Jan Iles. 'It was one of the strongest tracks. I'm pleased with the result, and some of the songs are great. You know sometimes I'll be listening to the radio and I'll hear something which is really great, and I think, *I wish I'd recorded that,* because it's musically exciting. I've had that feeling with a few of my own songs. They really knocked me out. I've been able to step outside myself and judge them objectively. I'm very optimistic.

'I had my first guitar at fourteen, turned pro at sixteen, and it wasn't until I joined The Hollies at twenty-two that things started happening for me. I mean, what's that, eight years? So, if I don't have a hit in the near future, I'm well prepared to give my solo career another eight years!'

Sitting in the producer's chair for two of the newer songs on the album, including the recently released 45, was EMI engineer Alan Parsons (it remains undocumented as to whether these were cut before, or after the unpaid 'Boulder To Birmingham' sessions) and, interestingly, Terry had previously worked alone with Alan when he had supplied a lead vocal for a new concept that was in the making – The Alan Parsons Project. Taped during the latter part of 1975, the long-playing *Tales of Mystery and Imagination* would be issued during the spring of 1976 with Terry supplying the lead voice on 'To One In Paradise' and backing on 'The Cask of Amontillado'.

Terry Sylvester: "I Believe" (Polydor 2383-394)
Terry Sylvester of The Hollies has just released his debut solo LP and a luscious one it is too. For a kick-off, it is beautifully arranged using melodic tunes, ripe enough for summer listening. Terry's writing clearly shows his adroitness for a pretty lyric and flair for honeyed tunes while his voice is ideal for the brand of material he's penned for the album.

Also featured is Terry's new single, Stevie Wonder's 'I Believe', which, although it is a good single isn't quite so suited to Terry's mellow super soft vocals as some of his own stuff. I reckon 'Pick Up The Pieces Again' with a strong hook and fluid guitar solo would have been a better single.

*Record Mirror & Disc*
July 1976

Further TV appearances on BBC2's *Mike Reid Show* in September, and two consecutive days on LWT's *Supersonic* show shortly afterwards, embarrassingly lip-synching direct to the camera for the teen-dreamy 'End Of The Line', did little to further aid promotion, and without any significant sales of note, Terry's dream of solo stardom, and that of Robin Britten's, effectively ended there.

He did go on to commit a series of further solo recordings to tape during his Hollies' residency, with two more Polydor 45 singles appearing in 1978, one of which – '(Too Bad) Lucy Jane' – was a fine work that could have benefitted even further from the Hollies treatment. But, paired with the self-composed 'Undecided', it sadly followed a similar path to its predecessors. For the remaining cuts, 'Silver And Gold', 'Realistic Situation' and the unreleased 'Is There A Way', there was equally no commercial success in sight.

Not to be outdone, Allan Clarke was also in the process of putting together his next solo album. Having offered up the majority of his recent compositions to The Hollies for their sessions, this fourth solo affair featured eleven new recordings, ten of which were cover versions of other composers' works, whilst the eleventh track, most bizarrely, was an elaborately orchestrated summary of the previous ten inclusions!

Ranging from Bruce Springsteen's 'Blinded By The Light', through works by Janis Ian, Melissa Manchester, Junior Campbell, Iain Sutherland and Dan Fogelberg, it was an eclectic selection, slickly produced for an American market.

Having met the German-born, Los Angeles-based producer Spencer Proffer at United Artists Records, it was put to him that, to appeal to US audiences he needed to have a more American-sounding approach. To achieve this, Clarke agreed to cut the next album in Los Angeles, using a top LA session team, with seasoned pro Jimmie Haskell undertaking all of the arrangements. Excited by the prospect, and opting to exclude any of his own compositions, Allan and his new producer then set about choosing the songs to cut.

'Spencer Proffer and I did sit down and choose all these songs, and the ones that really stood out to me were 'Stand By Me', and 'The Long Way' by Dan Fogelberg, who I always admired. When I first heard it, I thought, *I'd like to sing that song, I think that I can do a decent job on that.* I think it came out really well. It's that type of song that has a really good sentiment about it. I loved it.'

With EMI in the UK electing to issue Iain Sutherland's 'Living In Love' as the chosen advance single release, and Asylum Records in America (who had picked up the US distribution tab) opting to go with the commercial Nicky Chinn-Mike Chapman song, 'If You Think You Know How To Love Me' (a recent UK Top 10 hit for Smokie), the release was pushed out in the summer of 1976 as the *I've Got Time* LP. Sadly, with hindsight, and despite the reluctance of EMI to promote another Bruce Springsteen composition, 'Blinded By The Light' was, perhaps, the more obvious choice for a promotional tool. When Allan told his Hampstead neighbour, keyboard player Manfred Mann, that EMI had no plans to select his recording of the tune for a single, Mann took it upon himself to cut and issue it with his own Earth Band, earning them a worldwide Top 10 smash. *I've Got Time*, meanwhile, suffered the ignominy of following the previous Clarke solo albums to the store bargain bins shortly after release.

One other footnote to Allan's solo excursions of 1976 was his credit on the October release of an obscure 45 by Jeff B. Clark. Issued on the Epic label in the UK, this self-composed single by Clark, 'Roll Your Own' b/w 'Home In The Country', listed the pairing of Allan Clarke and Ray Glynn as co-producers on both tracks, alongside Rod Turner. However, little else, if anything, appears to have come from these sessions.

# CHAPTER TWENTY-EIGHT

# "DRAGGIN' MY HEELS..."

The summer of 1976 was a turning point for Great Britain. Amid the sweltering temperatures of a rare heat wave, the second hottest on record, the UK music industry was at the start of a new revolution. Whilst much of the industry was focussed on the rise to the mainstream of the disco movement, with the sounds of The Hues Corporation, Carl Douglas and George McCrae dominating the airwaves, the British youth were rising up. Disconnecting themselves from the established BBC radio playlists, disenchanted with the elaborate stage presentations, elongated guitar solos and twiddly keyboard prog-monstrosities of the established rock music scene, casting the likes of Yes, Genesis, Pink Floyd and Emerson, Lake & Palmer aside as outdated dinosaurs, they began to strip the music down to the basics, vociferously sticking two fingers up to the government, the monarchy, even their parents – and anyone else who stood in their way. And not only did the prog-rockers take a hit. Many of the new breed tore down the mantles bestowed upon the earlier, acceptable regimes of The Beatles, Cliff Richard and mid-'60s Elvis – preferring to honour the early aggression of The Kinks, The Who and The Rolling Stones. They absorbed the hard-core glam scene that had evolved out of the clubs over in New York City and Detroit, where the likes of The Stooges, fronted by Iggy Pop, and the New York Dolls prowled the stages, and name-checked Brit-glam icons such as Marc Bolan and David Bowie.

That summer, British new wave punk band The Damned played their first-ever show, supporting The Sex Pistols, a London-based quartet that had arisen out of the social dissatisfaction going on around them. They played fast, they played hard, but they played with a passion – and they despised the "superficial" disco scene and all that came with it.

For established acts, those who had plied their trade over the past decade, establishing a contemporary audience became a significant challenge. The sudden rise of British new wave, punk and pub-rock was engulfing all they had worked so hard for. The record labels, always out to earn a quick £££, were jumping on the bandwagon, signing up these three-chord wonders without a care. It was almost Merseybeat revisited. When The Beatles had landed on the tarmac at JFK Airport in February 1964, and British Beatlemania was launched Stateside, every record label across the States was signing up virtually anyone who held a guitar and had a British accent. Now, twelve years later, it seemed as if the same scenario was happening again on UK shores. And if the major labels headed by the cigar-smoking '40s and '50s generation weren't interested, there were new, independent companies springing up seemingly everywhere. It was turning full circle and the competition was Stiff.

Caught in the crossfire, as undoubtedly many of their peers and contemporaries were, The Hollies ploughed on, following their hearts and recording what they believed to be the best music they had available, regardless of style or genre. Tony Hicks, when asked by *Melody Maker* for his views on the established 1970s rock stars, responded, 'Yes, Genesis, Queen, 10cc… I admire them greatly, but I don't like them. They are products of overdubbing, and they are not raw enough. I think Steely Dan are tremendous, and there's something about the music of America [the group] that I'll always buy, and even though I don't need to listen to it before, I know I'll enjoy it.

'For the first six or seven years of our career, it was important to be free, because it was the days when the kids were jumping about and screaming and that. It was very enthusiastic. That's it; that sums them up. I think the fans are probably about the same today. The kids were looking more for excitement than sound…'

Indeed, underneath the success in which all five of the principal band members now bathed, they were all original punks themselves. Born into the first wave of beat music (The Fourtones, The Emperors of Rhythm, The Dolphins), they eschewed the popular dance bands and the cheesy vocalists of the late '50s and '60s – Frankie Vaughan, Johnny Ray, Dickie

Valentine – achieving their own levels of fame, before they too evolved, becoming that same establishment. A great number of their musical peer group duly recognised that fact, unwaveringly accepting of their part in the new movement and, often belatedly, attempting to adapt their music accordingly (the most famous example being Fleetwood Mac's turnaround from *Rumours* to *Tusk*). Others seemed to let it pass them by, mistakenly continuing to follow the mirrored disco ball as it bounced merrily along, oblivious to the holes in the road over which they would soon trip, stumble and fall. Others still wavered somewhere in between.

Regardless of Tony's views, mid-1976 found The Hollies doing just that. More and more, they were stepping back from the raw, free approach that they had proudly delivered during their early careers, intent on delivering a range of styles – yet uncomfortably stuck between a rock and a hard place. They were now working on a series of new recordings, some of which were smooth, dance-orientated cuts that skirted around the edges of disco, daringly hanging their wide open-necked collars, leisure suits and white flares onto the bass hooks and hi-hat shuffles. Not that they were moving completely away from the rock 'n' roll sounds they grew up with, as the inclusion of the self-composed 'Russian Roulette', 'Louise' and, in particular, '48 Hour Parole' would testify. They still knew where to find the guitar-driven power chords – more so than with the previous *Write On* album – but the commercial aspect was misplaced. Crucially, the "Hollies Sound" began to noticeably change, as Allan's voice began to dominate the previously more balanced blend of voices on these new recordings.

It was almost as if, in the aftermath of punk's arrival, they were subconsciously trying to roughen it up on a number of the new tunes, unwittingly drawing in inspiration from outside. The trance-like arrangement of 'Be With You', a number put onto tape deep into the album's recording sessions, suggested more than a little external influence with mid-'60s band The Herd and their 1967 Top 20 hit 'Paradise Lost', a fact Tony later put down to being "coincidental". But the result of this mismatched mix in style was that much of the studio emphasis then went towards the remaining songs – which included the likes of 'Lady Of The Night', 'Draggin' My Heels', the haunting, soulful 'Thanks For The Memories' (featuring a prominent harmony lower from Tony) and… dare it even be mentioned here, 'Wiggle That Wotsit'. All infused with a groove that defied the truest of Hollie traditions.

'That was a terrible song!' Allan Clarke was to later claim, when referring to the aforesaid wiggling abomination. 'I don't like to say that I had anything to do with the writing of that song, honestly. We were experimenting with different sounds and different ways of writing songs. That's what those albums were more or less about. We thought that we had a chance of getting hits with the newer songs we were making because they were different and more in the American way, but it wasn't meant to be. The songs are still there, though, and they still sound great.'[47]

'It was a gamble,' he would continue in a separate interview. 'Everyone in the late '70s went into glam rock and disco-type stuff. You had to change with the times if you wanted to stay in the business…'[43]

Recording sessions were held at the Basing Street Studios, located in London's affluent Notting Hill district, where, with Ron Richards absent once again, the band oversaw the production duties themselves. With a succession of studio musicians filling out the sound; keyboard player Peter Arnesen, percussionist Chris Karan (from The Dudley Moore Trio) and a brass section made up of Jimmy Jewell, John Mumford and Henry Lowther, the result was that the numbers were smooth, rhythmic, stereotypical and utterly void of soul.

Not that this was any fault of the band. The Hollies were never blue-eyed soul boys, but they had simply churned out a series of flavourless, danceable recordings – which unfortunately fell a long way short of 'You Should Be Dancing', 'Play That Funky Music' or 'Lowdown'.

Rounding out the sessions towards the end of August, with fourteen new songs committed to tape, it was an uneven collection that was finally submitted to Polydor for approval as the next LP, ten of which would make the final selection. Nevertheless, the label clearly saw some potential in the product and scheduled it for release over the festive season of 1976.

The band next flew out to Germany for a short series of concerts.

24th September 1976: Glockenhalle, Bremen
25th September 1976: Musikhalle, Hamburg
27th September 1976: Schloß Kiel, Kiel
28th September 1976: Stadthalle, Braunschweig
29th September 1976: Hochschule der Künste, Berlin
30th September 1976: Hochschule der Künste, Berlin
1st October 1976: Rhein-Ruhr-Halle, Duisburg

2nd October 1976: Messehalle, Köln
5th October 1976: Liederhalle, Stuttgart

A member of the audience at the Messehalle in Köln taped the show and whilst the surviving audio is of particularly lo-fi quality, it remains interesting to note that, in addition to promoting the upcoming album with lively performances of two of the newer tunes, 'Daddy Don't Mind' and 'Draggin' My Heels', they also retained a couple of the songs from the earlier unsuccessful *Write On* release.

I Can't Let Go / Just One Look / Sandy (4th Of July, Asbury Park) / Another Night / Bus Stop / Write On / Daddy Don't Mind / Draggin' My Heels / My Island / I'm Down / Stop! Stop! Stop! / Long Cool Woman (In A Black Dress) / Carrie Anne / The Air That I Breathe / Too Young To Be Married / He Ain't Heavy, He's My Brother

Gearing up for the launch of the release, the next stop-off point was in Holland where they filmed an appearance on the AVRO broadcast of the *TopPop* show, airing on 16th October. With Allan dressed all in white, contrasting against Tony's all-red outfit, the band lip-synched their way through one of the more successful songs on the forthcoming release, the rhythmic 'Daddy Don't Mind'. Fusing the essence of the dance-orientated composition with Tony's rock guitar patterns and a novel trombone break courtesy of 1950s big-band player Wally Smith, this was selected as the first single to be issued from the sessions, and the one most likely to put the band back in the charts. Perhaps the sight of these now-seasoned musicians, swaying to the beat, whilst singing about "*Sass 'E' Frass*" and "*Joe 'D' Glow, headin' out to the picture show*" was a touch too far for the public to consume? Nonetheless, issued as Polydor 2058-779 (b/w the throwaway beat of the country-styled 'C'Mon'), the single bravely charted the Top 40s of Holland, Belgium and Germany, but sadly lacked any sales of note on home soil.

Taped during the same *TopPop* appearance, but held back for airing, the band also gamely played along to what is now generally accepted by many as the absolute nadir of their collective recording career. With the band caught off guard, much to their amusement and disgust, the television production team started the playback without any countdown, leaving Terry and Tony in a fit of laughter and Allan shaking his head in disapproval before Bobby picks up the hi-hat shuffle and the band kicks into the embarrassing job of lip-synching to 'Wiggle That Wotsit'. Complete with its *"ring-a-ding-a-ling, rub-a-dub-hug-me, shakin' that shimmy"* lyrics, this slab of Clarke-Hicks-Sylvester composed white-disco-funk highlights the sad lack of direction that the group were lost in during this period. When the *Russian Roulette* album eventually appeared during December of 1976, this song was placed as the album introduction, swiftly followed by the all-out guitar rock of '48 Hour Parole', thus isolating either those who were inexplicably drawn in by the dance grooves – or never even reaching the ears of the rock fans, repulsed by the syncopated beats of too much wiggling.

Having seen the disapproving reaction to the debut single from the set, Polydor then saw fit to issue 'Wiggle That Wotsit' as a 45 (coupled with the Jamaican rhythms of the non-LP 'Corrine') within a month of its predecessor. Somehow, the ever-loyal New Zealand following deemed it suitable enough to bestow on it a Top 20 position although, once again, UK buyers ignored it.

'Corrine', meanwhile, moulded similarly to the unreleased 1974 cut 'Come Down To The Shore', had been recorded back in July of '76 and had evolved out of the earlier collaboration between Allan and Maurice Gibb, 'Maureen', taped five years previously (and later demoed by the band themselves).

*"Maureen Maureen, I love you. Maureen, say you'll be mine"*

'Maureen' (unreleased)
Allan Clarke & Maurice Gibb. 1971

With promotion completed in Europe, they then took a long gruelling flight out to Canada, where they undertook a further two weeks of live performances, playing various venues throughout Ontario, Saskatchewan and British Columbia, before returning home in time for the album launch.

The Hollies: "Russian Roulette" (Polydor 2383-421)
There's no doubt that this is a good album. The production is immaculate, and the songs are attractive, and their performance is just as professional as we've come to expect. And yet there seems to be something missing. Maybe it's just too well done. After a while, you tend to forget there's a group there at all! But, having said that,

favourite tracks are 'Draggin' My Heels' and 'Daddy Don't Mind'. I also like 'Thanks For The Memories' which is cooler, with its cool harmonies, and 'Lady Of The Night' with its lovely sax playing. The rest don't really rise out of the ordinary and that's a shame because the band with their talent and experience are capable of far more than just ordinary.

*Record Mirror & Disc*
December 1976

Packaged in a black sleeve designed by the Hipgnosis team (in direct contrast to the white sleeve on the predecessor), featuring a bizarre cartoon-like drawn image of a fish in a cocktail glass, the album went on to receive a similar fate to that of the two preceding singles. A subsequent guest slot on the televised Saturday afternoon music show *Supersonic* followed. However, performing impressive live versions of 'Daddy Don't Mind', complete with additional keyboard players and a percussionist, and an extended lengthy take of the Latin-styled 'Draggin' My Heels', with wild piano and synth solos from Pete Wingfield, seemingly did little to impress the teenage audience who, having sat through Andy Fairweather-Low and Brotherhood of Man, were probably all waiting to empty their lung capacity and commence high-decibel screaming at current boy-band faves Flintlock. One can only wonder what fellow guest stars Mud, and their bassist Ray Stiles thought of The Hollies' newly found rhythms.

The remaining years of the decade were to follow in a similar fashion. Recording sessions would be followed by promotional or live appearances which, in turn, would be followed by an album or single release. Further promotional work would then ensue. Allan would soon achieve critical acclaim by following Terry's example, contributing vocals to the second Alan Parsons Project LP, *I Robot* (on the track 'Breakdown'), but having seen the lack of chart success the previous three Hollies albums had achieved, one could hardly have gone into 1977 with the expectation that, once again, they would grace the upper reaches of the UK album charts.

Some territories around the world still offered them hope, and they still managed to maintain a loyal following in the southern hemisphere, whilst the USA remained sceptical, even after all of these years.

One interesting collection that did appear Stateside was the Epic compilation, "*Everything You Wanted To Hear By The Hollies But Were Afraid To Ask*, a twelve-track gathering pressed for promotional purposes during 1977 (AS-138). Featuring a selection of songs from across the years, ranging from 'Just One Look' and 'Bus Stop' through to 'Long Dark Road', 'Sandy' and 'Another Night', it remains unclear as to whether this was manufactured solely for radio circulation or was ever intended to be an actual official release. Nevertheless, it remains a collectable curio to this day.

> The Hollies are survivors. They have weathered well over a decade of, at times, cataclysmic changes in popular music, tastes and purposes. They have been able to keep sailing where so many other lesser talents have foundered and sunk, simply because all through their evolution, they have maintained a standard of taste and clarity of purpose that is apparent here in cut after cut. They have retained their musical image intact throughout all sorts of changes whether it be the depletion of group members, the addition of new studio techniques or production changes, or even the direction of their own ideas.
>
> We have seen them weather many different seasons in the past and can expect them to be with us for many seasons to come. The Hollies are definitely not deciduous. They're evergreen.
>
> Gerard Quigley
> Epic Records Promotional Sleevenotes

Neither *Write On* nor *Russian Roulette* had warranted an individual release in the US by Epic Records, and the subsequent combined effort of the *Clarke, Hicks, Sylvester, Calvert, Elliott* LP (Epic PE-34714) – a neatly packaged compilation, with an artistically hand-drawn sleeve and featuring tracks from the last three UK studio albums – fared poorly across the vast nation upon release in April of '77. A syndicated broadcast of the band performing 'Daddy Don't Mind' (along with 'Just One Look'), filmed on the set of the UK's *Supersonic* show, had been shown across the States during the early weeks of the year, airing on a series entitled *Twiggy's Jukebox*, featuring the former Brit-model. However, any sales of the US collection certainly weren't going to be aided by the appearance, due in no doubt to the fact that the song in question wasn't scheduled to appear on the LP – and wasn't currently available in the US! 'Draggin' My Heels' was the eventual, and unsuccessful, song of choice by Epic for the 45, along with an exceedingly rare, 6-minute promotional 12-inch disco mix (Epic ASD-37) – which actually charted in Canada.

Nevertheless, when Polydor first mooted the idea of releasing the recent live tapes on record, taped the previous January in New Zealand, punters would hardly have been racing to the bookmakers to place odds on the album being a success.

*

Ever since the late Richie Valens' record label had posthumously issued the *In Concert at Pacoima Jr. High* LP, widely regarded as the first "live" LP from the rock 'n' roll era, hundreds of recordings taken from live performances had been issued on record, many to great critical acclaim. The jazz scene had been benefitting from live recordings for untold years, but when rock 'n' roll first hit, many remained wary as to the quality of such instrumentation in a live setting. Coupled with that, the audience reaction to the sights and sounds of a rock 'n' roll concert was so much *louder*, drowning out much of what could be caught on tape.

The Beach Boys were one of the earliest "live" examples to top the US charts with their 1964 *Concert* LP, with other '60s artists swiftly following suit – James Brown, The Yardbirds, Otis Redding and The Rolling Stones to name but a few of the timely ones. By the turn of the decade, the list was increasing further still, as the concerts themselves were expanding into mammoth one-hour, then two-hour sets. Double live albums, sold at a premium price by the labels, and sometimes even treble sets, were fast becoming the norm.

In America, The Grateful Dead, The Allman Brothers, Lynyrd Skynyrd, CSNY and countless others capitalised on the popularity of the concept, whilst the jazz-rock band Chicago even took the multi-disc set to extremes by releasing the 4-LP *At Carnegie Hall (Chicago IV)* box-set, which achieved Top 3 *Billboard* status. By the middle of the decade, with sales exceeding those of many regular studio LPs, both *Wings Over America* and *Frampton Comes Alive* were achieving multi-platinum sales figures. Meanwhile, in the UK, it was often the more easy-listening of artists who benefitted from live sales during the early years, with Cliff Richard, Frank Sinatra and The George Mitchell Minstrels, along with the many early Vegas-era releases from Elvis, seeing success. This was before more rock-orientated artists like Van Morrison, Joe Cocker, The Who and Deep Purple stepped in and drove the format forward.

For their part, The Hollies had taped a number of their live appearances over the years, most notably their set performed at the Lewisham Odeon back in 1968 which nearly, but not quite, saw an official release. Subsequently, to date, there had been no examples of their live musicianship issued on record, bar one lone offering ('Blowin' In The Wind'), despite the many sell-out tours throughout the years. Therefore, Polydor's faith in the band seemed rather questionable when they formally announced a new *Live Hits* album, compiled from the New Zealand recordings of 1976, with an expensive TV campaign to back it. Issued initially in German as *Hollies Live*, with imported copies arriving in the UK soon afterwards, Polydor UK provided a promotional budget in the region of £100,000 to cover the costs of their British launch.

With a televised advertisement commencing with a simple voiceover stating, *This man is NOT going to join in with "Hollies Live Hits"*, the ad then focussed on the image of an elderly gentleman, sitting alone, trying to resist the catchy selection of Hollies hits playing around him. Gradually, his foot starts to tap, and he starts to move, culminating with him rushing out to join a large swaying crowd, with the punchline booming out, *"You can't help joining in with The Hollies"*.

For whatever reason, Polydor chose to utilise a frame from the TV advert for the actual album sleeve, ignoring the far superior packaging of the German release, complete with a colour insert. Instead, they highlighted the band in various stages of a-movin' and a-groovin', surrounded by the cheering, swaying crowd of TV extras. Whilst amicably smiling, Tony Hicks was reportedly not pleased with the way the promotional launch was turning out on that particular day, and, viewing the sleeve with hindsight, one can understand his frustrations. This was a singalong karaoke-sleeve, twenty years before that phrase spread across the world, and it only went to re-emphasise how far The Hollies were drifting away from reality, in terms of musical credibility. In a world where the 2-LP *Frampton Comes Alive* was spending an entire year on the chart lists, presented in a gatefold sleeve, with detailed notes included, *Hollies Live Hits* (released during March 1977 as Polydor 2353-428) was meagre in comparison. A single LP, clawing in at fifty-five minutes in length (leaving off two of the songs recorded at the shows

– 'Boulder To Birmingham' and 'Amazing Grace'), the featured track listing ran through the familiar gamut of hits and popular concert showstoppers – particularly those that had seen chart success in New Zealand, whilst also featuring a selection of tunes from the then-recent *Write On* release.

What is simply amazing, however, taking all of the above into consideration, is exactly how successful the promotional campaign proved to be – driving sales of the release through the roof, culminating in a #4 position in the official UK album charts during its twelve-week run.

Audibly, the sound left much to be desired, with the final mix being too thin at times and Allan's lead vocals set too far back, but the performances were nigh on perfect, with the harmonies cutting through the wafer-thin sound with precision.

Across the Atlantic, Epic Records chose to pass on any US release, although Canada also picked up on the option, issuing the release on the Columbia label and duplicating the presentation of the classier German issue. This, in turn, prompted other territories to distribute the album and duplicate the same sleeve, adorned with a live photograph, with a number of countries even affording it either gatefold status or with the additional picture insert. Nowhere, however, could quite equal the astonishing success of the UK edition, despite the appalling packaging.

Not wishing to sit back on their laurels, the band immediately went back into the Basing Street studios to cut a new track, intended as the follow-up single, hoping to keep the fires burning. The song in question, 'Hello To Romance', somewhat surprisingly, was another mid-tempo ballad that did nothing to excite the fan base after the success of the upbeat *Live Hits* LP. One cannot deny the class and the polished production on the song, and the orchestral arrangements, along with session man Tony Coe's saxophone solo, were quite exquisite. Clocking in at a fraction over the 5-minute mark, the Clarke-Hicks-Sylvester composition soon became a band favourite, with Terry confirming in recent years, 'That is a brilliant song. So well crafted. Anybody with a sense of music or romance must appreciate that, surely…' [5]

Paired with the heavier, gutsier guitar-flavoured '48 Hour Parole', this could so easily have been promoted as a double A-side, thus pleasing all followers of the band, regardless of style or favouritism. Unfortunately, the flipside was lost to the media, and with an edited 'Hello To Romance' (Polydor 2058-880) receiving scant attention, bar the occasional plug on BBC Radio

2, a station deemed suitable for the more easy-listening audiences, the single unceremoniously flopped. It was fast becoming a familiar tale. Three years had now passed since The Hollies had last graced the UK singles charts. Ten years previously they had sustained over ten straight Top 20 hits in a row during a similar period. How the times had changed.

'I was discontented with what was happening from 1975 onwards for several years,' Allan would later admit. 'There were lots of internal things wrong, though nothing that the public saw, because there was always work there and we were still touring and recording.'[5]

Allan himself was suffering personally. It was now a well-known fact within the inner circles of the band how much the drink was affecting him. A tour of Germany had followed on from the recent sessions, with the singer still unable to curb his consumption. The cigarettes weren't helping either as he struggled to maintain the vocal powers needed with every performance. Nevertheless, having negotiated the demands of the road, the five group members continued with their busy schedules, recommencing work at the Basing Street studios during May, alongside Pete Wingfield, Peter Arnesen and Jimmy Jewell, on what would ultimately become their seventeenth UK studio album. Sessions were drawn out, and it would take a full four months to complete the proposed recordings, but with another short visit across to Europe, followed by a flight to South America booked in for September, they toiled to complete the sessions before taking to the skies.

Ten new songs were put down onto tape during this period, although two of these would remain off the proposed new LP selection, replaced by two of the earlier, unsuccessful 45s. And why were 'Hello To Romance' and the earlier 'Boulder To Birmingham' even considered for the final track selection? A dearth of potential hit material appears to be one reason behind it. Nearly all of the newer songs were considerably weaker in comparison. Bland, keyboard-based ballads, or mid-tempo at best, with little to differentiate between them, with only two strong upbeat numbers hidden amongst the pack.

The first recording dates gave forth the upbeat synth-guitar-pop of the excellent 'Crossfire' and the unashamedly Springsteen-influence of 'Burn Out', both featuring some scintillating guitar riffs from Tony and some solid rhythm from Bernie. 'Crossfire' came across as one of the stronger cuts from the sessions, although the unnerving predictability of the composition itself still left it wanting. But wanting what exactly? A stronger hook, a twist in the melody? *Anything* to take it away from the annoying norm of banality. A harsh overview, but the bottom line is that, even with such notable moments of interest, these compositions were still all-too-predictable. One could almost anticipate where each song was heading before the bridge even kicked in.

These were then followed by the broody, Steely Dan jazz-inspired moods on 'Let It Pour' and the sweet harmony-big-balladry of 'Amnesty', the latter being the only non-Clarke-Hicks-Sylvester tune amongst the newly recorded selection – and it went downhill from there. 'Caracas', with its Latino-fused saxophone arrangement, was but a pleasant homage to the rhythms of Venezuela (where they were due to appear a few weeks later), whilst 'What Am I Gonna Do', 'Feet On The Ground', 'Writing on the Wall' and the bluesy 'Clown Service' were all full of studio production and strong arrangements, but little substance, all negotiating the instantly forgettable melodies with an apparent lack of diligence. The songwriting was uninspired, with the threesome combining to offer nothing of any meaningful depth, leaving it considerably short of their previously high standards. Overall, the slick production was clinical, and it was all, dare it be said – too clean-cut.

July of 1977 saw The Hollies appearing on the latest 45 by Tony's friend and former songwriter partner Kenny Lynch. The fourth of Kenny's solo single releases emanating from the partnership, 'Is It True What They Say About Georgia', a Chip Taylor composition, appeared as a Polydor single in both the UK and Germany, backed with a further Hicks-Lynch tune, the Three Dog Night-soundalike 'Nightmares'. Both songs featured the distinctive "Hollies Ltd" credit on the label and, although uncredited, bore all the trademark sound of the band as support for Kenny in the studio. Although unsuccessful as a release, thus bringing the Hicks-Lynch partnership to a sad conclusion, Kenny's follow-up 45 (released two years later on the tiny Satil label) was a co-write with Colin Horton-Jennings. One connection led to another and a new songwriting partnership was born.

At the same time, breaking away from their own sessions to promote what they had accumulated so far, The Hollies briefly flew out to Holland, performing a further time on *TopPop* and milking every last promotional note out of the 'Hello To Romance' 45. Continuing into Germany (and returning to the *Disco* show), they then debuted the Danny Douma composition 'Amnesty' as the follow-up single. Selected as the best of the choices available, with its breathtaking *a cappella* intro, and sticking to the tried and tested mid-tempo balladeering formula (and paired with the far livelier 'Crossfire'), this appeared during July as the next official 45 (Polydor 2058-906) and swiftly disappeared into obscurity virtually everywhere – failing to register in even their most loyal of markets.

With the tracks fully completed, leaving just the final mix to be finished, the band gathered themselves together and once more ventured back out onto the road. Australian band Sherbet, still high on the success of the previous year's global smash hit 'Howzat', acted as support band for the duration of the trip, which started in Bad Salzuflen, located in north-west Germany.

Having sold out a week's worth of German shows, The Hollies then ventured halfway across the world, flying down to Venezuela in Concorde, where they were greeted by huge crowds, loyal to the popular *Los Hollies* releases, issued in their country via the Odeon and Polydor labels. Booked to perform two shows at the vast 20,000-seat Poliedro de Caracas, a huge indoor arena situated in the country's capital city of Caracas. Bobby would later reveal some of their exploits in his insightful autobiography. Then, having flown home in the not quite so luxurious surroundings of a battered DC-10, within days they had rejoined Sherbet back on the touring circuit, this time up in Scandinavia. Commencing with a performance at the majestic outdoor Tivoli theme park in Copenhagen, they then journeyed on to Norway to play a series of shows in Trondheim, Oslo, Bergen and Stavanger, visiting the country for only the second time in their career, before finishing up in the Swedish capital of Stockholm. Playing at the impressive Concert Hall in the city, the band were greeted backstage by the smiling and forgiving face of Mikael Rickfors who, despite being uncomfortably snubbed by Allan Clarke, turning his back on his temporary replacement, was gentlemanly enough to accept an apology from Allan in later years.

'Apology accepted. Allan was a bit boorish at the time,' Mikael would comment to Sweden's *Rock 'n' Roll Magazine*, 'but the situation might have been a bit awkward.'

Then, after a few days' rest, the full touring party was out across the Atlantic once more, this time flying northwards towards Canada where, with additional support for a struggling Allan coming along in the form of his wife, Jeni, successful shows in Vancouver, Calgary, Winnipeg, Thunder Bay, Edmonton, Saskatoon, London and Toronto, finishing at Montreal's 3,000-seat Salle Wilfrid-Pelletier complex, brought the crowds out each night.

One final notable moment came along before the year was out when, having returned home from North America, the band revisited Germany for the third time that year, this time arriving in Hamburg to film an upcoming TV spectacular, *Silvester Tanzparty* (New Year Dance Party), an annual New Year's Eve extravanganza broadcast throughout West Germany. After a day's rehearsal, The Hollies were filmed for the show, lip-synching to four songs before a dancing, high-heels-and-tuxedo-dressed middle-aged crowd, more intent on drinking and shimmying than focussing on the music.

'Burn Out', 'I'm Down', 'Long Cool Woman (In A Black Dress)' and 'Write On' were all caught on camera that day, but the band were clearly just going through the motions, tired after an exhausting few months.

Having toyed with the album title of *Amnesty*, the new long-playing release was duly labelled *A Crazy Steal*, a lyric within the song 'Hello To Romance', and scheduled for a spring 1978 issue.

With the various previously released singles added to the final selection, and the slick drive of 'Crossfire' left by the kerbside, it was a decidedly middle-of-the-road affair that eventually hit the record racks and then the bargain bins during March that year. And the front sleeve packaging wasn't much better.

Bernie recalls: 'That was a difficult period for the band. Allan was going through another unsettled period within himself. We had a great deal of problems. We were touring in Germany and the album was finished and the record company was pushing to get the product on the market, so therefore the cover was rushed. It was photographed in a sports stadium somewhere in Germany…' (the Stadthalle in Bremerhaven), '…and consequently the whole thing was very much a rushed package, so to speak.

'The single tracks were probably included as fillers in retrospect, although I don't remember any arguments or debate about it at the time. It just seemed like Polydor wanted to get the product on the market. I wasn't particularly impressed with the album or the cover…'[36]

Using Bobby's idea of a drinks machine as a prop, the group posed in walking mode for no apparent reason, with a time-travelling effect blurred around them. It was most unsatisfactory, and without the benefit of a current hit single to publicise it, much of the emphasis was placed upon the unsuccessful 'Boulder to Birmingham', 'Hello To Romance' and 'Amnesty' singles. Issued worldwide, with a belated Epic 1978 release in the US, it failed to chart anywhere, which was a tragedy as it thus lost the impetus that *Live Hits* had pushed back in their favour, although it certainly didn't help when, during the initial burst of promotion, Allan Clarke turned around and announced his departure once more…

The Hollies: "A Crazy Steal" (Epic 35334)
Allan Clarke, lead vocalist, is here and The Hollies' patented harmonies are intact. This LP consists of ten cuts ranging from the usual rockers to a cover of Emmylou Harris' 'Boulder To Birmingham' that indicates the lads are still very much in tune with contemporary harmony. Instrumentation ranges from semi-lush to sparse but is all grounded in rock.

*Billboard*
August 1978

The Hollies: "A Crazy Steal" (Polydor 2383-474)
Perhaps it's no surprise about Allan Clarke quitting The Hollies yet again. After all, fifteen years is a hellava long time and "A Crazy Steal" is an awfully long drag to listen to. If only the group would stick to their old policy of recording other people's songs, maybe they would turn out a decent album. But eight of the ten tracks are Clarke, Tony Hicks and Terry Sylvester compositions which fail on several levels. All acceptable pop pulp. Each carry something of a melody, a hook line or two, Clarke's searing top notes and rich harmonies, but only the two non-Hollie tracks, 'Amnesty' and 'Boulder To Birmingham' have that "play it again, Sam" appeal.

If, as the title suggests, the group have become bankrupt of ideas, then Clarke has not left them a moment too soon. But hold your breath and see if 1971 repeats itself again. Remember what happened when 'Long Cool Woman In A Red [sic] Dress' made it to number one in the States?

*Record Mirror*
April 1978

# CHAPTER TWENTY-NINE

# "SOUNDS THAT GREW OUT OF THE NORTH..."

Early March had seen The Hollies meet up with successful American producer John Boylan, who had flown into London to discuss the option of creating new music alongside the band. Having worked earlier on in his career with The Association (overseeing their much-acclaimed eponymous 1969 LP), Linda Ronstadt and Pure Prairie League, as well as being the man credited with helping bring The Eagles together, he had recently gained considerable praise through his sleek production work of The Little River Band and, more prominently, with Boston, and was deemed much-sought-after in his role.

The group members were in a positive frame of mind after the meeting and were, in Bobby's words, 'excited about recording in America.' Certainly, the prospects opened up several opportunities for them. Unfortunately, Allan didn't see the options in the same light and, meeting up with Robin, Tony, Bobby, Bernie and Terry the following day, he promptly announced his decision to walk away once again. The possibility of a Boylan-connection began to crumble there and then.

There was no further explanation offered, but it was clear to those in attendance that Allan's head and health were not in a good place. He was growing frustrated once again, feeling that the band had reneged on their agreement to allow him time for his solo projects. Added to this, there was the hidden fact that, unbeknownst to his bandmates at the time, he was already working on another solo effort, spending time in Los Angeles with producer Spencer Proffer. His mind had clearly been turned once more, and the prospect of individual stardom was again raising its ugly head.

Whilst in Los Angeles, he had recently contributed to a recording session by LA soft-rockers Buckeye, offering backing vocal support on their eponymous album (on the track 'Poor Cheater'), whilst the first fruit from his own solo push had initially come in the form of a Proffer-produced 45 single, issued by Polydor back in January, although, presumably, at the time there were no further indications to his unaware bandmates as to any additional ongoing sessions.

The A-side, the rousing 'I Don't Know When I'm Beat', was a co-write between Allan and Brit-born songwriter Gary Benson. Benson, a Top 20 hit-maker himself ('Don't Throw It All Away' – 1975 on State Records), had first met Allan when he had been the opening act for a Hollies performance in Germany. Striking up a rapport, they had soon linked up, writing together surreptitiously, specifically for Clarke's solo career, and a number of their collaborations would appear on his upcoming releases.

'Gary is a very prolific songwriter and when I write with him, we write for me. It's not like he's writing a Gary Benson song. He got me writing again after two or three years. I didn't want to pick up my guitar and he showed me the light.'[73]

Although the single (Polydor 2058-979), backed with the pleasantly orchestrated ballad 'The Passenger', had failed to register any significant sales, the partnership with Benson was encouraged, resulting in a second collaborative offering on 28th April. Again produced by Proffer, this second issue, 'I'm Betting My Life On You' b/w 'I Wasn't Born Yesterday' (Polydor 2059-025), followed suit, achieving a similar lack of interest in the UK. However, over on American shores, the release of the debut 45, retitled as '(I Will Be Your) Shadow In The Street' (Atlantic Records-3459), featuring the impressive guitar work of seasoned session player Ben Benay, gave Allan his first real taste of individual success, peaking in the *Billboard* charts at #41. By no means a smash hit, the signs were certainly encouraging as the new album was being quietly prepared.

With Spencer Proffer again utilising some of the very best session stalwarts – Benay, Mike Porcaro, David Kemper and Tom Hensley, and with Jay Graydon helping out with the basic arrangements, the *I Wasn't Born*

*Yesterday* LP, Clarke's fifth independent release, appeared later that year. Surprisingly – and despite the second Polydor 45 promoting the then-upcoming release, it appeared on the small Aura label in the UK. Polydor maintained the distribution rights around much of Europe and Japan, and Atlantic Records held on to the US and Canada sales, but in the UK, Spain and Portugal, it was farmed out to the small, newly founded independent label, with distribution handled initially by Anchor Records, then via Pye. Needless to say, the promotional potential was also somewhat reduced by the switch, with Aura's budget significantly smaller than the might of Polydor, and yet the music held within the grooves was anything but lighter. Comprising ten Clarke-compositions, paired with two distinct collaborating partnerships – six with Gary Benson, four with producer Proffer (three of which also included the contributions of backing vocalist Randy Bishop) – the album sounded so much more cohesive as an entity, geared towards an American market, devoid of most of the synthesised sound that was pervading much of The Hollies' current output.

'My producer, Spencer Proffer and I sat down before the recording,' Allan would later recount. 'Because he wasn't involved with the first three albums, we tried to reflect on what I'd done wrong. He said, "Let's try the right approach. You have got to write the songs because you sing your own songs better than you sing anybody else's."'[73]

The sweet sound that ran throughout 'I'm Betting My Life On You', with its gentle country overtones, was a prime example of the Stateside influence on, what is essentially, a British-born Clarke-Benson composition. That said, the adventurous construction of 'The Man Who Manufactures Daydreams' was a brave attempt to add a bit of '70s prog-air-guitar pomposity into the equation, mixed with the drive of a typical Asbury Park anthem. In turn, 'No Prisoner Taken (Light Brigade)' was simply crying out for the full Clarke-Hicks-Sylvester harmony treatment.

The jaunty commerciality of 'Light Of My Smiles' is, perhaps, the one song that sounds out of place in the collection, with a distinctive Euro-beat sounding chorus, but with the album closing out with the excellent Clarke-Benson 'Off The Record', featuring another supreme vocal performance, tight harmonies and scorching guitars, the set pulled strongly together as a complete package. With hindsight, one can see that this hinted at the direction that maybe The Hollies should have been heading towards, as opposed to the endless approach of increasingly stale and predictably melodramatic ballads. Despite the resulting lack of any subsequent commercial success (even in the US, where hopes had been high), *I Wasn't Born Yesterday* was a significant personal achievement and highlighted the fact that, afforded the correct approach and production, Allan's creative work could still be so very relevant. And yet, as with many of his previous solo outings, the apparent lack of promotional work undertaken by Allan himself certainly hindered the potential for the release. Despite the launch of two promotional videos (for 'I Wasn't Born Yesterday' and 'I'm Betting My Life On You'), there was no MTV or similar publicity machine during that era that could continually grind these in constant rotation. To succeed, it needed that extra personal promotion from the artist to consolidate any initial flurry of interest and, outside of an initial proposal for a three-week US solo tour, nothing came to fruition. Then again, not everyone appreciated the results with the same enthusiasm, and the hardened "serious" music journalists were quick to pounce:

Allan Clarke is all whiney projection. Buffered by Nash et al., that whine could be a bracing instrument. On his own, Clarke's shrillness of tone is matched by a shrillness of approach, and the album is hardly tolerable. There are songs that conceivably could have been Hollie tri-annual ballad hits – 'I'm Betting My Life On You' and '(I Will Be Your) Shadow In The Street' – but otherwise, Clarke's LP is pure dentist's drill. He also fancies himself a composer, but he's not content to recycle sentimental axioms. Clarke, from the fussy, frantic title song to the sub-Zevon excursion into some metaphorical "valley of destiny" on 'No Prisoner Taken (Light Brigade)', is guilty of overreach. "We need some new blood," he shrieks. "Let's keep the sheets clean! Stop this confusion, we need a transfusion." (What?)

'The Man Who Manufactures Daydreams' is as bad as its title, and 'Light Of My Smiles' is the silliest theatrical conceit since something or other by Leo Sayer, but the nadir is reached on the closer, 'Off The Record', which is hilarious vitriol.

Clarke bolted The Hollies once before, only to return; if there's still an opening for a lead singer, and if he truly wasn't born yesterday, he'd be wise to apply for the slot.

*Creem*
October 1978

One can only sympathise with his plight, and hindsight is often beneficial. The gulf between *A Crazy Steal* and *I Wasn't Born Yesterday* was a chasm, and yet the democracy of the five-man band was always going to win out against the personal wishes and demands of one individual.

'That album [*A Crazy Steal*] took a long time to record,' Allan was to recall to *Trouser Press* magazine. 'Even the cover took three months to get together. There was no guidance and I wasn't really a guide. I had no direction. I had nobody up there telling me what to do, so there's no way I could guide them. There has to be somebody behind every group, and we didn't have anybody. There's no way The Hollies could ever take to one person as boss. In the end I gave up my position on the board of directors and my vote within the corporation.

'The only song I wanted on the *Crazy Steal* album was 'Writing On The Wall' and I had to force them to record it. I should have left with Graham. I should have listened to him all along. You know you could knock your head against the wall just so many times before you start bleeding. There's no way I'm going to spill my brains out for anybody other than myself anymore.'

How ironic was it then that, with Allan's well-executed, credible solo offering ready for release, EMI Records in the UK then chose that moment to promote the goldmine of hits at their disposal and take a look backwards at past glories again, drawing the public attention away from the now. On home soil, the limited promotional budget of the UK's Aura Records had no chance against the might of the EMI publicity machine.

June 1978 and EMI Records prepared a huge promotional campaign, built upon the success they had achieved with the 1976 release of The Beach Boys' *20 Golden Greats* album. Simple, effective packaging that caught their attention, but filled top to toe with hit after hit, The Beach Boys LP hit the very summit of the UK charts during those hot, sun-kissed summer months and remained in the list for an astonishing eighty-five weeks. Driven by an extensive TV and media campaign, it capitalised on the public's desire to look back to simpler times, rekindle memories of their youth, and compile them all into one neat conceptual package. Realising that they had hit upon a rich seam of super-sales status, the label swiftly followed up with Glen Campbell's *20 Golden Greats* (also reaching #1) The Shadows (#1), Diana Ross (#2), Buddy Holly (#1), Frank Sinatra (#4), Nat "King" Cole (#1) and Cliff Richard (with his chart-topping 2-LP *40 Golden Greats*), before attention turned to the band still widely recognised as Manchester's finest exports.

"*20 Great Sounds That Grew Out Of The North*" ran the byline on the front cover, superimposed over the perplexing image of a smoky industrial north, billowing clouds of pollution, silhouetted against a golden sunset. However, the music within the sleeve was immediately identifiable. Twenty classic recordings, a succession of hits, presented in such a way that left the listener breathless as one smash followed another. The only downside appeared to be the random way that the selection was compiled, and from a chronological perspective, it must have had the obsessive biting at their fingernails as 1971 gave way to 1964 which, in turn, led into 1970.

Assisted by a television advertisement that defied logic, EMI's marketing department switched into overdrive, pushing sales to the maximum and driving the album up to the number 2 position – although the twenty-week run in the Top 100 was considerably shorter than some of the previous EMI campaigns.

The Hollies: "20 Golden Greats" (EMTV-11)

Over the years, The Hollies' records have tended to fall into one of three categories: the bright, snappy early '60s pop put together from the same ingredients used by The Beatles, only minus the genius and plus a heavy Coasters influence; the impossibly dippy playground of mild-psychedelic pop that bubbled to the surface before Graham Nash took off in search of creative satisfaction, hip credibility and large amounts of readily negotiable currency; and the godawful cabaret emoting-pop that followed 'He Ain't Heavy, He's My Brother' and lasted up until the present day, if not longer.

This album carries large chunks of each of these aspects of their oeuvre, and since it opens up with 'The Air That I Breathe' and ends with 'He Ain't Heavy' you can tell which tracks'll crop up on the massive spate of TV commercials which the release of EMI's "20 Golden Greats" invariably calls forth. It contains most of the essential Hollies hits and most of the garf. The tracks are assembled in an irritatingly random manner, with no regard for either chronology or continuity.

Best bits: the early stuff like 'Stay', 'Just One Look' and 'I'm Alive'

434

and some tinny exuberance in the shape of 'I Can't Let Go' and 'Here I Go Again'. The real standouts, however, are the claustrophobically erotic 'Stop! Stop! Stop!', the coolly menacing 'We're Through' and the amazing 'Bus Stop'.

One note about the north country packaging: they have got to be kidding.

*New Musical Express*
August 1978

The TV advert that actually appeared on the UK screens during the summer of '78 was not the one that the label had initially storyboarded, and it held little relevance for the band, the songs or… anything. Comprised of forty-five seconds of stock wrestling footage, humorously linked to the song lyrics ('The Air That I Breathe', for instance, showed wrestlers in a chokehold), how that was related to the music appears totally incomprehensible. The original concept for the ad wasn't much better but, with a £50,000 budget, it at least focussed on the band's heritage. The agency charged with filming the project reportedly shot footage of stereotypical northern characters and cobbled streets and houses, harking back to the band's Manchester roots – but EMI remained unimpressed with the results, and at short notice compiled the wrestling footage to meet the schedule. With a £200,000 campaign at their beckoning, the album was launched successfully (with the Polydor label also benefitting financially from licensing out 'The Air That I Breathe' to their EMI rivals) and once again gave The Hollies a lifeline for their stuttering career.

The Hollies: "20 Golden Greats" (EMTV-11)
20 tracks are here, every one a winner, mostly emphasising the good quality of Allan Clarke's vocals and the above-average musicianship. It was sugary pop with a sheer gloss. The harmonies of Nash and Allan Clarke sat at the top of a precise, slightly antiseptic sound that churned out all the hits featured on this album.

'Stay', 'Carrie Anne', 'I Can't Let Go', 'Bus Stop', 'Gasoline Alley Bred', 'On A Carousel', 'Just One Look' and many more all came hygienically wrapped and each sounding too similar. But the formula was hugely successful, and fans fell heavily for the tight harmonies allied to incredibly catchy hook-lines. 15 years on, they still sound tight and professional and the songs will stand forever, evocative of an era.

But are they relevant to 1978, I hear you ask? Well, a massive advertising campaign on television is about to tell you they are. Today, as in 1963, The Hollies are "product" – however, you can dance to them.

*Melody Maker*
August 1978

With the future of The Hollies jeopardised again, following the departure of Allan Clarke, the need to find a replacement was once again brought back to the table. The slim possibility of resurrecting the John Boylan-produced sessions was still an option, with some tentative Los Angeles dates for June or July pencilled in, and so various names were duly suggested for the frontman role, including Alan Merrill, the former vocalist with 1970s hit-making trio The Arrows (and co-writer of the classic 'I Love Rock 'n' Roll'). However, the band seemed in no rush to commit and the Los Angeles opportunity quietly faded away. Terry later suggested that he and Tony also approached Dean Ford, whose own band, Marmalade, had recently split up, but Ford declined the offer.

Terry: 'The first thing we did was contact various people we had in mind, some of whom were quite well known. Then Tony and I had a sort of singsong with them in our office. It was very informal sort of thing, just to feel out the vocal style of particular people. The thing is, we're not actually looking for someone who sounds like Allan – we're looking for somebody who can sing with Tony and I. The first person we tried was very close to it, and is probably not out of the running, but we'll carry on looking a little bit longer. We don't need to panic. There must be somebody out there who fancies their chances, although it's got to be someone who has a lot of experience. We don't want a rank amateur...'[48]

August had seen the remaining quartet venture back into the Abbey Road studio and cut the track for a new Gary Brooker and (uncredited) Keith Reid ballad, 'Harlequin', with Brooker himself helping out and supplying a delightful guide vocal. At one point during the session, Bobby Elliott became unwell and so Brooker brought in fellow ex-Procol Harum drummer B.J. Wilson to assist, although, upon completion, the tape was returned to the studio vaults for the time being.

'I thought it was outstanding, with Gary doing the vocals,' Bernie was later to comment, and there was subsequently a suggestion that Gary himself, having recently seen his own band disintegrate through a recent lack of commercial success, may step in to fill the void left by Allan's parting.

'We considered that,' Tony would confirm, 'but I think Gary had moved on and was probably not ready to go back on the road. I remember visiting him around that time, and he took me to quite a flourishing public house nearby, which he either owned outright or part-owned. I think he was quite happy to be doing that and the odd gig here and there, as opposed to being a professional touring musician.'[5]

Another strong contender to fill the void was Strawbs frontman Dave Cousins, with Tony going on to actually offer him a berth in the line-up, but that option failed to come to fruition once it became apparent, during early October, that Allan wanted to return. As to whether it was a kneejerk reaction to the lack of success his latest solo venture had afforded him and, having seen the current EMI compilation shifting vast quantities across the sales desk, he was prepared to crawl back, tail between legs, remains unclear, but the band members were open to the possibility. A healthy band meeting took place shortly afterwards, whereupon Allan was duly reinstated into the line-up. But a certain amount of trepidation went into the decision. Who was to say that the uncertainties over whatever issues he had wouldn't arise again? Would his ongoing battle with alcohol give cause for further concern? Nevertheless, for now, The Hollies resumed operations.

Another face at the recent meeting had been Ron Richards who, despite his own health issues in recent years, was also keen to resume activities in the studio with them. Yet, behind the smiles, all knew this would be Ron's last role in the recording studios with them before he retired; health and age having finally caught up with him. Nevertheless, everyone, it seemed, was keen to try once again to reignite the magic. Subsequently, within a matter of days of reconnecting, the familiar five-man band and their long-time producer reunited in the studio.

Ignoring the drive and the rock-influenced themes that ran through Allan's recent solo album sessions (had the band themselves actually listened to it?), the all-too-familiar sound soon enough permeated the studio control booth as sessions resumed, with the band intentionally concentrating on the well-trodden, tried-and-tested ballads formula.

Six new songs were started on, commencing with two compositions by British singer-songwriter Murray Head; 'Say It Ain't So Joe' (misspelt as "Jo" on the Hollies' eventual release, and recently covered by Roger Daltrey) and 'When I'm Yours', both originally featured on Head's own 1975 LP *Say It Ain't So*. Ignoring the acoustic, mid-tempo arrangements of Head's own renditions, The Hollies slowed down both songs, taking them into the pre-prepared piano-based balladeering territory that they were becoming so locked down with. The harmony sound was still luscious, rich and fulfilling, notably on 'Say It Ain't So Joe', but the content lacked inspiration. Another of the newer offerings was a co-write between former associate Tony Hymas and Peter Brown, a partnership that had previously worked together as part of Jack Bruce's backline support (Brown was co-composer on many of Cream's biggest successes), entitled 'Something To Live For', a pulsating number that had been suggested to Ron by his son Andrew. It had previously appeared on the Jack Bruce Band's 1977 album *How's Tricks*.

'I have always had a soft spot for this track,' Andrew notes today. 'It was written by Tony Hymas and Pete Brown, and Tony played keyboards and did the arrangement. Dad identified with the sentiments of this song. Life had been difficult for him during this period and prior to each day of recording, he was often physically sick. He was suffering badly with both anxiety and nerves, and what I admired about him, then and now, was that once he was in the studio you would never have known it. It was the one place where he felt secure.

'My task at this time was to sift through demo tapes for potential material, offering it up to my father for him to knock back or approve. He would then take it to the studio for the band to see if it was something they could work with. This song was one of a number that appeared on the album that I put forward to him...'[41]

Two further Hymas-Brown songs were cut during that period, along with a third composition by Peter Brown alone – and whilst 'Song Of The Sun' and the Sylvester-sung 'Boys In The Band' both had a mid-tempo funk within the arrangement, neither were of strong enough quality to stand out. And therein lies the issue. With the predictability of 'Stormy Waters', the (then-unreleased) 'Lovin' You Ain't Easy' and the heavily dramatic theatre-based tune 'It's In Every One Of Us' (initially released by the songwriter David Pomeranz back in 1975 and later utilised for the London stage musical *Time*) filling out the sessions, it was left to the remaining two inclusions to lift the eventually released product out of the balladeering doldrums. Terry

Sylvester added his lead vocals, along with Allan Clarke's backing, to the joyful 'Harlequin' (although Gary Brooker's guide vocal can be audibly heard during the fade), whilst the only band original, the futuristic Allan Clarke-Gary Benson collaboration, 'Satellite Three', brought out the band's progressive soft-rock instincts, with its synthesised arrangements and Tony's sweet guitar solo. One further tune, Gary Benson's 'Sanctuary', with its highly infectious chorus, was omitted from the final product which, given its commerciality, was truly puzzling, as it was exactly what the sessions were lacking. When Polydor opted to issue the Hymas-Brown 'Something To Live For' as the advance 45 during March of 1979, one could almost sense the impending lack of support and subsequent failure that it would endure.

> The Hollies 'Something To Live For' Polydor (POSP-35)
> World-weary defeat set in mounting melodrama. Terminally depressing.
>
> *Melody Maker* 1979

With the chosen ten-track collection appearing the following spring as *5317704* (Polydor2442-160), The Hollies had achieved exactly what they had set out to do. An album chock-full of slow-to-mid-tempo arrangements, superbly performed, with a polished production from Ron – but ultimately it was an album that achieved nothing, charting nowhere. Polished to a sophisticated sheen and yet, surrounded by a society that was trying to define new meaning, it was unquestionably bland. One could almost sense that the recent upheavals of the disco phase, and the overwhelming growth of the adult-orientated rock regime, had sucked the life and passion out of the band's integrity. *Russian Roulette, A Crazy Steal* and now *5317704*; the same feeling flowed across the three-album set.

Taking its name from the word HOLLIES – type the numbers 5-3-1-7-7-0-4 on to a calculator keypad and turn it upside down – the LP reeked of the late '70s establishment, unsure of how to respond to the current new wave idiom, driven by technology and of an idealistic yet outdated futuristic vision.

'That was Bobby's idea,' Tony admitted, when reminiscing over the title. 'He has this rather lovely country cottage and he spends quite a lot of time in it, and he obviously has nothing better to do there than play with calculators!'

'Actually, that was me,' countered Terry in a separate interview. 'I was dabbling with my son's calculator one day and, you know you can write certain things on calculators like "hello" and "shell oil", and I was just mucking about and I realised you can write the word "hollies" by turning the thing upside down. And I thought, *hey, that's good!* That was a couple of years ago now, and I thought one day... I didn't want to just steam in and say, "We have to record an album to fit with this!" but I thought one day... that'll come in handy...'

The sleeve design, initiated by Rod Shields and fashioned by Jack Wood (the creator of numerous works for the budget Music for Pleasure label, before his involvement with the rock medium – Status Quo, Thin Lizzy, Godley & Creme), seemed to say it all. Lined up alongside such newer creations as The Jam's *Setting Sons*, XTC's *Drums and Wires*, Blondie's *Eat to the Beat* and The Police's *Regatta De Blanc*, it only went to emphasise how The Hollies were completely out of touch, both musically and visually, despite the LP remaining a firm latter-day favourite amongst the Hollies' fan circle.

As a Hollies Album Archive blog would later summarise, "This album works best really as a mood piece, one full of reflection and seriousness rather than the energy and dynamism of old, and that annoys as many listeners as it thrills".[44]

Once again, they had failed to fully capitalise on the publicity and success of the preceding album, in this case, *20 Golden Greats*, reconfirming the unthinkable notion that they were fast becoming irrelevant to the current industry, and a future consignment to the nostalgia circuit. It was a bittersweet culmination to their final recording sessions with Ron Richards. Beloved and respected for their past, dismissed and ignored for the present. And what of the future?

'I'll tell you what,' Ron was to stoically remark when referencing the *5317704* LP, 'it's a brilliant album, but it never got any promotion.'[70]

'In the '70s, I became quite ill and had to give up work, so everything I was doing had to stop. I was sorry in many ways, but it was also time. These things run in a cycle and when the cycle stops it's time to do something different. They were exciting days, very exciting, but you can't live in the past.'

Ron Richards
*Carousel* Fanzine 1991

To promote the album, and to celebrate the success of EMI's top-selling compilation, the band took to the road once more, bringing Peter Arnesen along as supporting keyboard player. Following an initial week-long residency at the popular Wakefield Theatre Club (preceding notable appearances by both Tina Turner and The Jacksons at the Yorkshire venue), they undertook a series of shows up and down the country:

18th March 1979: New Theatre, Southport
19th March 1979: New Theatre, Oxford
20th March 1979: Colston Hall, Bristol
21st March 1979: Winter Gardens, Bournemouth
23rd March 1979: The Odeon, Birmingham
24th March 1979: The Gaumont, Ipswich
25th March 1979: Fairfield Hall, Croydon (2 shows)
27th March 1979: Conference Centre, Wembley, London
28th March 1979: Conference Centre, Wembley, London
29th March 1979: Conference Centre, Wembley, London
31st March 1979: Capital Theatre, Aberdeen
1st April 1979: The Odeon, Edinburgh

...followed shortly afterwards by a visit across to Germany, with a further tour of Canada also scheduled in. Touching down in Mainz for the opening night of the German leg, all seemed fine until Allan arrived with his personal manager, David Apps, in tow, setting the mood down a notch before subsequently announcing he was turning tail and flying back to the UK, unable to commit to such a strenuous tour. Chaos ensued. Fortunately for the paying audience, already filling out the venue, he didn't follow through with the suggestion and, despite the opening shows leaving the band on tenterhooks – would he, wouldn't he? – the first two nights continued without incident. Then, on the third night, whilst appearing at the 2,000-seat Beethovenhalle, located on the shores of the Rhine in Bonn, Allan walked off stage after the opening few numbers, leaving Terry and Tony totally unprepared, but able to cover his vocals as best they could. Issues were coming to a head, with Allan then being informed by doctors that he must now rest for the sake of his health. Nevertheless, with commitments to be met, the tour progressed. On some nights, Allan was there; on others, he wasn't, with Terry taking the centre spot for appearances in Kassel, Heilbronn, Nuremberg and Hof.

Finally, after a run of shows in Berlin, Hanover and Hamburg, in no fit state to continue, on the further advice of his doctor and those around him, and with the band despairing, Allan returned home to the UK, suffering from a nervous breakdown. David White, the lead vocalist for Stumblebunny, the American support band on the UK/German tour, offered his support and so, with Terry, Tony and David supplying the vocals, the schedule was concluded with muddled appearances in Aachen, Essen, Munich, Augsburg, Manheim, Köln and Munster.

Two weeks later and with a new arrival, keyboard player Paul Bliss, now filling a role in the live band, The Hollies, minus Allan, returned to both Munich and Baden to film guest appearances on the TV shows *Pop '79* and *Plattenküche*. For both shows, they performed the Sylvester-fronted 'Harlequin', a current Polydor single in the country (and notable for only featuring the images of Tony, Terry, Bobby and Bernie on the front picture sleeve).

Meanwhile, back in England, Allan Clarke had taken things into his own hands. Aware of the damage he was doing to himself and his young family, and on the advice of medical specialists, he had checked himself into a rehabilitation clinic, intent on curing his excessive alcohol intake. It had been a long time coming.

'Over excess for a long time very much took its toll,' Allan would later reflect for a 2019 *Sunday Express* article. 'Just drink, not drugs. You get to a point where you're drinking and drinking and wake up the next morning not knowing how much you've had. If I didn't stop drinking, I'd have lost everything. I'd die and didn't want that. So, in 1979, I stopped. I became a changed man. I'd had fifteen rock 'n' roll years and it took all that to get it out of my system.'

He remained in the clinic for several weeks, weaning himself off his reliance on alcohol. The Hollies, meanwhile, continued with their touring schedule, with Tony, Terry, Bobby and Bernie flying out across the Atlantic to Canada during June to honour arrangements. Accompanied by Paul Bliss performing on stage with them, adding his harmony into the mix from behind the keyboards, it soon became apparent that a full overseas tour without Allan was not the best option.

'We got Paul Bliss,' recalls Bernie, 'and he helped us out on a very protracted tour of Canada, which we ultimately cancelled because we just weren't getting the kind of reviews or audience response that we would have got with Allan there. [We felt] it was better to terminate the tour than jeopardise the future of the band because no one knew quite what the future held at that point...'[36]

Returning home, with the outstanding Canadian dates cancelled and unsure of what would happen next, the band laid low for the remainder of the summer months.

Birmingham born singer-songwriter-keyboard-player Paul Bliss had only recently broken into the frontline of the music industry, having previously worked as the bass player in the mid-'70s band Dog Soldier. Despite his 1978 debut album, *Dinner With Raoul* (credited to The Bliss Band and produced by ex-Steely Dan alumni Jeff "Skunk" Baxter, with vocal assistance from Michael McDonald), along with the follow-up *Neon Smiles*, both failing to set the charts alight, he was gradually building up a reputation for his abilities. A fairly recent convert to keyboards, with his live debut behind the synthesiser stack being as a member of the David Essex touring band, his appointment with The Hollies would continue for a number of years.

September 1979 had seen the band testing the murky waters once more. With Allan out of his rehab isolation, seemingly clean and healthy, The Hollies committed to one week at the Birmingham Night Owl, a small, intimate venue that proved ideal for cabaret-style shows for which Robin Britten so loved to add to his diary. They followed that up with a similar residency at the Golden Garter in Manchester during the first week of October. Shortly afterwards, during November, they linked up with songwriter and producer Mike Batt and began cutting tracks together, firstly at Wessex Studios in Highbury, North London, followed by dates at both Lansdowne Studios and Abbey Road.

'I first met Tony Hicks socially,' Batt recounted during 2020. 'It was quite early on in my career, maybe 1971, but around 1980 Polydor asked me to write and produce three songs for The Hollies.'

Two tracks were initially worked upon together, both of which were composed by the Wombling hit-maker, although one of these, the thoroughly enjoyable 'Can't Lie No More', a song that harkened back to the traditional harmony sound of the band, sadly remained in the can for a further twenty-four years. The second number, 'Soldier's Song', a heavily orchestrated epic featuring the London Symphony Orchestra, alongside a powerful Allan

Clarke lead, with the Clarke-Hicks-Sylvester harmonies adding to the effect, was clearly a Batt-conceived production to the max. With a barely audible Hicks-guitar solo being the only significant contribution from the band, instrumentally, it was never really a *Hollies* product in more than name. Yet, Polydor thought otherwise, seeing only the hit potential of the collaboration as the key indicator. Issued as a Polydor single (2059-246) during April of 1980, their faith was duly justified as the release climbed to a reasonable, but unspectacular, #58 in the charts, their first UK "hit" for six years. The band even took to performing the song live and on TV, with an appearance on the UK series *Starburst*, accompanied by Peter Arnesen, airing later that year.

'Mike was a perfectionist,' Tony was to note. 'I have nothing but praise for the things we did with him. He's a great character to be in the studio with. He knows exactly what he wants from you and that makes it very easy.'[5]

The third collaboration with Batt had also taken place during February, with the partnership now meeting up at Odyssey Studios in central London. Once again, they chose to record a new Batt composition, 'If The Lights Go Out', but this time it was *all* Hollies caught on the tape, in both vocal and performance. With Bobby driving the beat and Tony's distinctive guitar dominant throughout, the frontline harmonies rang out like a chorus of bells – reminding the listener of how and what The Hollies should be sounding like, given the right material to work with.

*5317704* had been a well-produced, polished affair, but it simply wasn't the true sound of The Hollies' passion. This was. It was The Hollies' sound for a 1980s generation. And yet, inexplicably, the "listener" never had such an opportunity to judge for themselves as no sooner was this vibrant, upbeat number committed to tape than it was locked away, remaining unreleased for a further number of years...

It remains a tragedy that The Hollies-Batt partnership fizzled out then and there. It could have brought forth so much more, but Batt held total control in the studio, to the extent that he reportedly even tried reworking some of the band's harmonies, although it was to little avail. By now, they knew what sounded best for them. Simply put, he was possibly too much of a force of nature to work collaboratively with them on an entire album.

# CHAPTER THIRTY

# "THEN YOU'D KNOW WHY I FEEL BLUE..."

With the arrival of the new decade, it was a time to reflect. The past few years had seen a plethora of differing music styles breaking through, as they each fought to establish a foothold in the aftermath of punk. The impact of the movement had left a defining mark, as it diversified into the alternate worlds of indie music – new wave, ska, two-tone, mod revivalist – all benefitting from the punk scene that had gatecrashed the industry with such vitriol, passion and originality just a few years before. Disco had died but had evolved into the differing worlds of funk and hip-hop. Meanwhile, the leftovers from the 1960s beat scene, those who had set the benchmark all those years ago, the originators, were left to fend for themselves amongst the slim pickings of chart successes. The four individual Beatles were still acknowledged and accepted as the true icons of their time, with even the reclusive John Lennon beginning to show signs of willingness to participate in activities outside of his Dakota building homestead, but long gone were the days of chart dominance. The Rolling Stones still held court as the greatest rock 'n' roll band of all time, despite their limitations in keeping up with an ever-changing industry. The Who, suffering from the fallout of Keith Moon's recent death, were struggling to re-establish their identity, whilst The Kinks, basking in a revitalised American glory with their *Low Budget* album, couldn't get the time of day on home soil. For their part, The Hollies, who had fought tooth and nail alongside these bands as one of the UK's most consistent chart acts of the '60s, were also still rolling along, albeit at a quieter, more sedate pace – living off the fruitful payments of the northern cabaret circuit as opposed to selling out Madison Square Garden. Try as they might, they simply could no longer compete with the best-selling acts of 1979, many of whom, ironically, maintained a familiar wholesome image – The Electric Light Orchestra, The Bee Gees, Supertramp and ABBA included.

With a clean outlook and a new sense of purpose, early 1980 saw Allan Clarke take the opportunity of a break in the Hollies' schedule to begin work on another solo album. Keen to progress the previous sessions undertaken with Spencer Proffer, he returned to Los Angeles and settled in at Proffer's own Pasha Music Studio, located along Melrose Avenue in Hollywood. Once again drawing on the talents of some of LA's finest session team – Mike Porcaro and Lee Sklar on bass, David Kemper on drums, Richard Bennet and Doug Rhone on guitar and Tom Hensley on keyboards (many of these had worked together before, as a part of Neil Diamond's regular backup band) – and pulling together another gathering of Clarke-Benson compositions, the sessions resulted in a fine AOR album, with rock music and rock instrumentation at the core. Thankfully, there were little synthesised influences running through the tapes.

With the central focus for the promotion placed upon the Clarke-Benson song 'Slipstream', issued as the lead-off single, the album appeared in two formats during the early summer of 1980. In the US, Canada, Australia, Germany and Japan, the album was issued via Elektra-WEA (and on Mercury in Germany), entitled *Legendary Heroes* and presented in a traditional, progressive-rock styled artwork, whereas in the UK, Netherlands and Spain, it appeared on Aura Records as *The Only One*, featuring a harder-edged, new-wave style sleeve.

The ten-song selection remained the same throughout the differing versions, albeit in a slightly differing sequence, although, overall, the product appeared slightly tougher than much of the smooth LA-rock of its predecessor. Certainly, on 'Brandenburg Plaza', an updated variation on the arrangements of 'Long Cool Woman (In A Black Dress)', Allan showed his rougher side, growling and spitting out the lyrics with venom. That is not to say the album doesn't have its tender moments, and with the lengthy

6-minute 'Stairway-To-Heaven'-ish-sounding 'The Survivor', featuring Aussie guitarist Billy Thorpe, Allan delivered an opening reading that could grace any prog-rock concept with ease before the drum break kicked in and took it into pure '80s LA pout-rock.

Two songs also came about as a result of the songwriting between Clarke and Proffer; 'Imagination's Child' and 'Legendary Heroes', both melodically strong and yet overly lyrical, but it was with the Gary Benson solo contribution, 'Sanctuary', that the album reached its pinnacle. Previously recorded, but unused by The Hollies during the *5317704* sessions, this slower gospel-rock arrangement shone through and highlighted the quality of the composition.

Whilst undertaking little in the way of personal appearances for the album, Allan did visit the German TV studios to tape an appearance on the show *Plattenküche*, lip-synching to the 'Slipstream' single, during June of that year. Despite the 45 making headway, notably into the *Billboard* chart lists where it reached the #70 position, it soon disappeared, taking the album along with it.

With the Los Angeles sessions completed, Allan swiftly returned to the UK and his commitments with The Hollies – and that meant back into the studios to start work on a new "theme" project. In as much the same vein as Tony Hicks had been the instigator and driving force behind the creation of the *Hollies Sing Dylan* album, back in 1969, eleven years later found Allan Clarke suggesting an album comprised of Buddy Holly covers. After all, if it became as successful as the Dylan release then it would surely have been a wise choice.

It remains open to conjecture as to whether all of the band members were in favour of the move, but tackling the project was agreed upon, producing themselves and, in a similar fashion to the 1969 release, putting their own spin on the arrangements. Sadly, it was 1980, and that meant much of the industry was focussed heavily upon the over-use of synthesisers, to the detriment of the more traditional rock-familiarity of guitar-drum-bass recordings. Forty years later, much of what was taped during that era hasn't always held up upon review.

Between May and July that year, the band worked together at both Odyssey and Utopia studios in London, committing their updated renditions to tape. First up was a version of a song that they had previously recorded and released, back in 1966 for the *Would You Believe?* LP – 'Take Your Time'. With Pete Wingfield and Peter Arnesen both drafted in individually to add the electronic keyboard wash over the recordings, it was a polished vocal performance by the frontline trio that filled out the sessions, but it was so heavily synth-influenced that it took away so much of the basic dynamics that made the original recordings so special. The synth-solo on 'Peggy Sue', the opening number of the released LP, set the tone of what lay ahead – and, at times, it wasn't pleasant. That said, the second song cut in the studios, 'Wishing', a song posthumously released by Buddy's label in 1963, did maintain much of The Hollies' musical ethos, with some nice Hicks guitar lines, whilst the strength of both the guitar arrangement and the harmonies on 'Love's Made A Fool Of You' made this a highly enjoyable listen. The new arrangements on 'Heartbeat' and 'Tell Me How' also raised the enjoyment factor, whilst the "live" feel that ran throughout the Glitter Band stomp of both 'Midnight Shift' and 'Think It Over', featuring the horn section of Dave Caswell, Reg Brooks, Ron Astbury and Merseybeat veteran Howie Casey, showed that some of this concept could have worked really successfully had they applied it throughout the sessions. As for the downbeat boogie arrangement of 'That'll Be The Day', it was certainly an interesting new take on the song, for good or for bad, and would be copied virtually identically four years later by Status Quo, for their Top 10 update of Dion's 'The Wanderer'.

As to be expected, the singing remained impeccable throughout (just listen to the glorious fadeout on 'What To Do', featuring a rare guest vocal from Pete Wingfield, supplying the bass tones) but, sadly, much of the media focus went towards the new versions of the classic hits. How would these new arrangements work on those oh-so-familiar golden oldies? Not too well, it seemed – with 'It Doesn't Matter Anymore', 'I'm Gonna Love You Too' and 'Maybe Baby' joining 'Peggy Sue' on the synth-dominated pile, and the three-chord riffs of 'That'll Be The Day' opening it up to the scathing criticism it duly received.

On paper, the idea of The Hollies recording nothing but an album of Holly songs is fascinating. On vinyl, though, it turns into something stiffer than an embalmed corpse. You would have thought The Hollies would learn from previous mistakes. "The Hollies Sing Dylan" project was what made Graham Nash cry "enough" and join forces with Crosby and Stills.

It isn't that The Hollies butcher the Holly originals, their versions are, on the whole, respectful but the album is an undistinguished tribute to one of rock's seminal figures, adding little or nothing to the originals. The sad thing is that somebody fresh listening to this album would find little here to make them want to trace the Holly material back to source.

*Melody Maker*
1980

'We were searching for an idea,' Terry would later say. 'We didn't just want to go into the studio with ten songs and say, "Here's a new album," so we changed the songs around. There was a couple of ways we could have approached it. We could have just gone in and copied the originals, but there's really not much point in doing that. Possibly we went over the top a little bit, but we did what we thought was best at the time.

'We shouldn't have produced it ourselves. We should have got a producer to do it, but we thought it was a good formula and we figured it would be successful. We thought a lot of people would want to hear it – but a lot of people didn't want to hear it! That surprised me…'[46]

Released in October 1980 by Polydor (POLTV-12), with a brief TV campaign launched to accompany it, and preceded by the issue of 'Heartbeat' b/w 'Take Your Time' and 'Reprise' (a strange closing piece on the accompanying album that consisted merely of edited snippets of each track, compiled for promotional purposes), the public failed to respond positively to either release and the album bombed in the retail outlets throughout the UK and Europe, whilst also failing to chart in Australia. In addition, the collection did not even warrant a release in the US, with Epic having finally dropped the band from the label the previous year. Televised appearances on the BBC's *Friday Night, Saturday Morning* and the Dutch shows *TopPop* and *TeleBingo*, lip-synching to 'Heartbeat' and 'That'll Be The Day', were also unsuccessful in raising awareness. Interestingly, the synth-led 'Peggy Sue' actually picked up a fair bit of UK radio airplay at the time, more so than 'Heartbeat', being such a radically different take on the original, but Polydor failed to react to this and the opportunity passed. If anything, these TV appearances were more notable amongst the fan community for being some of the first public appearances of Bobby's acceptance of baldness, finally discarding the morning wigging rituals and gracefully donning the caps of old.

Note: The Beach Boys had also recently revisited Holly's catalogue, and their 1978 version of 'Peggy Sue' had actually charted in the US, Canada and Australia, which may well have hindered any international possibilities The Hollies may have had. You can only have so much of a good thing...

Following a series of shows in Germany, fifteen performances running from 19th September through until 5th October, the remainder of the year was played out quietly, and it wasn't until the following spring that the band resumed activity in the recording studio. But they also had other matters on their minds during that period.

Mike Batt had been the first to bring it to their attention. During a playback session for 'Soldier's Song', Batt had aired his opinion that The Hollies were being held back by the management of Robin Britten. Times had changed, but Britten was still content to book them out on the northern cabaret circuit occasionally, failing to look further afield and search out new opportunities. It was an outdated approach for a band that still had new music flowing through them. Many of their peers and contemporaries lived off the circuit. It was good money for little effort, but The Hollies still had so much more going for them. Robin had not been well in recent months, but Allan, Tony and Bobby were still unhappy over his management style. That, in turn, caused internal friction with Terry Sylvester who, with Robin as his personal manager, wanted to stay loyal to his long-term friend. Bernie Calvert also had reservations against such actions.

In the meantime, the group had a session booked at Odyssey Studios during mid-April 1981. Tracking a new composition by British-born composer Steve Thompson, who also accompanied the band in the studio on piano, 'I Don't Understand You' (also demoed by Colin Blunstone) was a mediocre offering at best. Neither Bobby Elliott nor Terry Sylvester was overly keen on the composition. Nevertheless, the arrangement the band now proposed had the potential to turn it into a pleasant slice of '80s pop, with an eye on the next single release. Paul McCartney was approached to see if he would be interested in sitting in the producer's chair for them. Sadly, due to commitments with his own *Tug Of War* sessions, he was unavailable but, at one point, Bruce Welch, the legendary rhythm guitarist, producer and arranger for The Shadows and, latterly the man credited with overseeing Cliff Richard's return to the top of the charts after many years in the wilderness, was brought in to produce the song. (His company also handled Steve Thompson's publishing.) Having not been present during the first date, Welch subsequently stated that he didn't like the performance, he didn't like the studio – and he also didn't think much of the piano- or bass-playing. If he was going to work with the band, he wanted to bring in his own players.

It was harsh, particularly on Bernie Calvert, who had remained a loyal, trustworthy member of the band for over fourteen years. To find himself suddenly cast aside from a recording session on the words of a producer was a bitter pill to swallow. Tony, loyal to his former Dolphins bandmate, refused to consider replacing Bernie on a permanent basis, as had been Welch's recommendation, but acceded to his demands that they look elsewhere to complete the sessions at hand.

'The "Buddy Holly" album was the last thing I ever did with the band,' Bernie later noted, when discussing his eventual departure from the line-up, 'apart from an attempt at a track that Bruce Welch was producing for us. That was what helped to instigate my departure from the band. Bruce pulled a session at one stage, saying he was unhappy with the style of keyboard-playing and the style of bass-playing, and he wanted to employ a couple of session musicians who he thought would be better for the track. So, instead, I found myself stood at the railway station waiting to travel back home whilst the other guys were in the studio, recording with another bass player. It was something that had never happened before, and I must admit I felt a little bit disillusioned about it at that stage….'[36]

Relocating to Shadows' drummer Brian Bennett's Honeyhill recording studio in the quieter surroundings of Radlett, Hertfordshire the following month, and bringing in Shadows' sidemen Alan Jones on bass and Cliff Hall on keyboards, the backing track was recut by Tony, Terry and Bobby, with Allan supplying a guide vocal and Bruce Welch seated behind the control desk. Two further sessions for the song, scheduled to add the final vocal tracks, would also take place during June, the first of which would have even greater repercussions.

Meanwhile, a meeting was arranged during May at Robin Britten's Bryanston Mews West office, located just north of Marble Arch in central London. Allan, Tony and Bobby duly informed Robin that his services were no longer required, against the wishes of Terry Sylvester and a non-committal Bernie. From his perspective, Terry believed that Robin deserved far greater respect for his loyal twelve years of service, especially in light of having overseen their increased royalty payments, but to the united front of Allan, Tony and Bobby, that wasn't enough. They felt the band needed invigorating, and a new lease of energy.

Bobby's 2020 autobiography, *It Ain't Heavy, It's My Story*, recounts the situation in greater detail but, in essence, Robin was relieved of his duties – much to his relief. The band would oversee much of their own management responsibilities going forward.

Reconvening at Honeyhill on the 1st of June proved to be a fateful day. Welch was a taskmaster in the studio and after a pressurised few hours of vocals and overdubs, both Tony and Terry retired to the nearby alehouse to wind down. Tempers were fraught after the long, gruelling session. Following a reputedly heated exchange of words in which, as Tony would later recount, Terry began to put forth his strong opinions, emphasising his own importance within the band structure, Tony briskly responded, suggesting he either be quiet or 'You know where the door is.' With frustrations simmering, Terry reportedly shook on it... and walked. There were undoubtedly other contributing factors involved that evening but, as neither party present has divulged what actually took place in detail, one can only speculate. And that is often unwise. That 1st June recording session in Radlett was Terry Sylvester's final contribution to his twelve-and-a-half-year Hollies career.

'Terry phoned me up and said he was very unhappy about the way Bruce Welch was working,' recalled Bernie, 'and it had led to some heated argument and friction within the group. He said, "I'm going to leave," and I said, "To be honest, Terry, I've been thinking about that as well."'

One other significant contributing factor in Terry's departure appears to be the lack of live performances the band had lined up at the time. Allan was still not fully ready to commit to life back out on the road after his recent rehabilitation and wanted to cut back on appearances and, much to Terry's annoyance, Robin Britten had subsequently been avoiding making any bookings in the diary. This was somewhat ironic in that he was still acting as Terry's personal manager and would continue to do so.

'I loved performing on stage,' Terry would say, 'so when the idea to stop touring came up, I thought what was the point of staying on?' He also added at a later date, 'Robin was not only a great manager, but also a really good friend, so I was really unhappy about that. I didn't think we were capable of managing ourselves. Allan was still making his annual threat to leave. All of these things combined, and I decided to leave.'[3/5]

One week later, Bernie Calvert also resigned from the band.

Bernie Calvert, bass guitarist with The Hollies, said farewell to the pop scene yesterday.

'After 15 fantastic years with the group, my heart is no longer in the job,' he explained. 'I'm disillusioned, tired of living out of a suitcase, and feel I can no longer give music the full works.'

*Unidentified Press Source*
1981

'I left because I had made a conscious decision some six months earlier that I was going to try and establish a future for myself outside of the music industry,' Bernie summarised, many years later. 'I was in a bad place at that moment in time. My first marriage was on the rocks and I was blaming music for all my ills and I decided that I would make a move and change the course of my life. I felt I'd reached a crossroads. I was only thirty-seven at the time, but I felt that by the time I was forty I really wanted to know where I was going.

'Terry left the band at the same time as me. I think he is a super guy, and I've really got tremendous respect for him. He made some superb solo product, but it seemed like you get to make hit records with The Hollies but outside of that, nobody seems to want to know you. I was never a virtuoso bass player. I never thought I played well enough to be employed as a full-time session musician. I felt I did a good job for The Hollies, but outside of that, I was certainly no wonder bass player. Therefore, I had to establish myself in some other career.

'Terry, I think, had an artistic dispute. He disliked the song that Bruce Welch was attempting to produce, and he felt that the band had lost direction. And so did I. I think that we both felt we didn't know where we were going as a band. There were no engagements on the books and the future looked a little bit bleak at the time. It was all very unsettled, and we seemed to have lost respect for each other. I think basically it was just familiarity breeding contempt. It's sad it should come to that after such a lengthy career, but these things happen, and they happen for a reason. The solution seems to be that somebody or something has got to give, and what actually gave at that time was Terry and I…'[36/69]

'It was just something that happened,' summarised Terry, ten years or so later. "'There was nothing in the book as far as touring was concerned, Bruce Welch was producing for us and, to put it mildly, the songs we were recording at that time weren't that good! There wasn't really anything happening. Bernie and I left at the same time. We didn't have a manager, Robin Britten wasn't with us anymore, so the whole thing seemed to be fading away. People leave jobs and do other things and there was no bitterness really. And that's the end of it." [18]

# PART THREE

# CHAPTER THIRTY-ONE

# "STOP! IN THE NAME OF LOVE..."

For a band so recognisable for their harmonies, and the sheer joy that many of their early recordings had brought to the ears of the population, the late 1970s, and the approach of another new decade, were troubling times for The Hollies. The music they had been recording in recent times was of a more mature and far more sophisticated nature. Yet, it appeared that they were treading water, seeking only to repeat the formula by persisting in what was proving an ever-elusive search for another 'He Ain't Heavy...' or 'The Air That I Breathe'.

With Tony Hicks being very much the driving force in this pursuit, Bobby Elliott riding shotgun alongside, it was apparent there was now simply too much drama caught up in the music. What was truly needed was a fresh, up-beat approach, giving the group a positive direction and new commerciality. The Hollies should be above mediocre or synthesised rehash.

It remained a positive factor that, to date, they hadn't felt the need to revert to compiling nauseating, fun-filled party albums, or sink to the dreaded signs of familiarity – the seasonal festive affair – but, many of their current sessions displayed a noticeable lack of Hicks' fretwork and Elliott drive – a trademark Hollies' sound – too often phased back in favour of synthesisers, orchestration, or guest musicians – and, in turn, that led them to drift further away on the public radar.

Thankfully, despite this, they did manage to retain a certain level of public affection by, in essence, remaining true to themselves. Their vast catalogue of past hits, spanning over a decade in length, was too deeply ingrained into the nation's psyche to dismiss them entirely, and, by not constantly trying to reinvent themselves, their audience largely stayed loyal. The dalliance with disco, or with Allan's determination to be seen with a credible Americanised "rock'" sound, may have raised a few eyebrows, but the underlying Hollie-ethos; the harmonies, the strong pop melody, remained firm. They just needed the correct material to work with. The falsehood of melodrama and the electronic wash that prevailed through much of the *Buddy Holly* LP, and that of its predecessors, was not what made the Hollie heart beat…

With both Terry Sylvester and Bernie Calvert having walked away from the band, it gave the remaining core trio the opportunity for a rethink, and a restructure. The solid and reliable if unspectacular bass rhythm provided by Bernie had proven to be a perfect foil for Bobby across the years, whilst, without question, the higher harmonies of Terry had come as a godsend following the departure of Graham Nash. His smooth vocal partnership with Allan, and when Tony chimed in too, had seen the band come through numerous ups and downs, and maintain their dignity throughout all that had been thrown at them – even whilst wiggling their wotsits. Also, for more than a fleeting moment, Terry's compositional talents had shone brightly in the line-up, either as a partner to Allan or as a solo (or with external assistance). More often than not, the times he had stepped up to the front microphone and taken lead had been a revelation, breaking up the familiarity of Allan's distinctive tones. And that is possibly where some of the recent studio albums had fallen down. As magnificent a frontman as Allan was, the variety of the voices throughout the years, from Graham's leads on *Evolution* and *Butterfly*, through Tony's occasional meanderings to the fore, to Terry's moments under the spotlight – 'Cable Car', 'Indian Girl', 'Pick Up the Pieces Again' – had all given a certain diversity and originality to the mixture. With Allan so dominant on the recent releases, that variety had been missing. Now, without the backup and contributions from their errant partners, the immediate future looked uncertain.

First on the agenda for the reduced Hollies was the completion of the Bruce Welch-produced 'I Don't Understand You', and with the additional assistance of singer-songwriter Labi Siffre adding in a higher harmony to complement Allan's and Tony's lower ranges (a fact of which Welch has no recollection), a session on 18th June finished off the recording. However, certain members remained unimpressed with the result and it was immediately placed upon the shelf, where, for unclear reasons, it duly remained. One month later and the trio once more found themselves in the studio together, albeit this time in the more familiar surroundings of Abbey Road, where they recorded two new works – both featuring Alan Jones standing in Bernie's shoes once again.

With vocal assistance this time coming in the shape of songwriter John Miles, widely recognised for his Alan Parsons-produced Top 5 hit 'Music', they cut the Miles composition 'Carrie'. A much more progressive attempt at a 1980s rock song, with plenty of guitar in the mix, and filled out with a descending opening arrangement that ABBA would have been proud of, the drawback was the lack of *that* familiar Hollie-sound. With Miles himself providing the distinct high falsetto vocals, there was no true vocal blend evident. The same smooth fusion that the combination of Clarke-Hicks-Nash/Sylvester had so comfortably produced was gone. With Terry's departure, had the moment finally passed?

A rare guitar-led instrumental, 'Driver', from the pens and picks of Allan and Tony, completed this brief round of sessions but, with Polydor unimpressed with the results, both recordings were returned to the vaults for now. Instead, attention was now turned to yet another new project that had fallen in front of Tony and Bobby. One that would have interesting repercussions for the fans of the band, dating back to the Nash era.

*

'Stars on 45' (known as Starsound in the UK) was a Dutch-based novelty music craze, briefly very popular throughout Europe and later on in the United States and Australia during 1981. The brainchild of Jaap Eggermont, formerly an early founding member of the rock band Golden Earring (prior to their smash hit 'Radar Love'), the music consisted solely of studio session musicians, under his direction, recreating classic hit songs of years gone by as accurately as possible, combining them into medleys, held together with a continuous tempo and underlying drum track. It was big-time classic party material, and the first release, pulling together a selection of Beatles songs, became a huge hit, charting in at least a dozen countries around the world (including hitting the #1 slot in *Billboard*). Needless to say, to follow up such an immediate success became paramount and, soon enough, a succession of further releases was in the pipeline ('Stars on 45 – More Stars', featuring a similar collection of ABBA soundalikes was the next hit).

Working under the assumption that the music of The Hollies may be utilised for a future reworking (although no evidence suggests they were), and instead of letting the opportunity pass by and handing out the glory elsewhere, Tony and Bobby combined their thoughts, and the continuing relationship with their former label, into compiling their own version of a beat-driven medley of their hits.

'Everyone we saw in the street seemed to say, "Why don't you do it?" So, we thought, why not?' Tony explained to the *New Musical Express*. 'If we hadn't done it, somebody else would.'

Utilising the original EMI master tapes from the EMI vaults, thus avoiding any unnecessary re-recording or extensive studio time, the duo compiled snippets of their various 1960s golden moments, spliced them together (adding vari-speed to synchronise the rhythm) and topped it off by mixing the 5-minute edit down to a 4-track recorder, allowing them to fill out the remaining three tracks with electronic beats and handclaps.

It was clever, it was audacious, and importantly – it was successful... but to the dedicated Hollies' fan, it was no more than an abomination. Entitled 'Holliedaze', with a selection of further edits compiled into the secondary 'Holliepops' on the flip-side, EMI issued the monster during the late summer of 1981, watching it successfully break into the UK Top 30 for a seven-week run, with a peak of #28. Regardless of the quality of the original material, the repetitive drumbeat, and the unnatural way that one song blended into the next, made it an uncomfortable listen – but one that was ideal for a party atmosphere. Had The Hollies, in desperation, finally sold out? Was a Christmas album next on the horizon? Thankfully, not so...

The Hollies: 'Holliedaze' / 'Holliepops' (EMI-5229)
Just One Look – Here I Go Again – I'm Alive – I Can't Let Go – Long
Cool Woman (In A Black Dress) – Bus Stop – Carrie Anne
b/w Stay – Yes, I Will – Look Through Any Window – On A Carousel
– Jennifer Eccles – Listen To Me – He Ain't Heavy, He's My Brother

As the single made its ascent up the UK charts – 60-36-36-28 – a long-overdue return to the BBC *Top of the Pops* studio was called for. At one point it was suggested that, having been on the original recordings of (almost) every track on the 45, a certain Graham Nash, now living in superstar luxury in Los Angeles and Hawaii, may like to appear alongside his former bandmates. Tony reached out. Word also went out, via Bobby, to the group's original bass player, Eric Haydock – and so it was that, when their appearance aired on BBC1 on 10th September (one day after the taping), the five hit-making Hollies of the '60s were reunited on the small TV soundstage, lip-synching and playing along to their medley of singles for the first time in fifteen years.

Throughout the many passing years, the relationship between the two former Ordsall Board Primary School pupils had been strained, and both Allan and Graham would go on to admit that, initially, their approach to the 1981 reunion had been wary. But, as they talked, and posed for pictures before the enquiring press photographers, they relaxed, and old friendships were rekindled.

Graham Nash: 'It was a little tentative with Allan at first. It was the first time I'd seen him since splitting from the band. I definitely felt an edge, an undercurrent that quickly ebbed away. It was time to move on. He looked good, and his voice was great…'[1]

'When CSN became a success and there were articles on them in the paper, I never read them,' Allan duly admitted. 'I wanted to shut Graham out of my life completely. I could have ended up a very bitter man if I hadn't had some degree of success myself and if I hadn't gone through a particular period of growth. Then, as the years passed, I was anxious to sing with him again…'[2]

Regardless of the press reports noted above, Graham and Allan had actually spent some time together during the mid-'70s when, having just rejoined the band after his own solo sojourn, Allan had visited Graham in Los Angeles.

'I had spent a couple of days with him. He was still as spaced out as ever,' Allan had chuckled in conversation with *Melody Maker* at the time. 'But he seemed to have got it all together, and he was a happy man.'

It is 15 years since The Hollies pop group were at the peak of their fame. But now they're getting together for a special performance on BBC TV's "Top of the Pops" for their golden hits are climbing the charts again in the form of a medley record called 'Holliedaze'.

Back from America is millionaire Graham Nash, who left the

group in 1968 to sing in America with Crosby, Stills, Nash and Young. Three of the originals, Allan Clarke, Tony Hicks and Bobby Elliott, still perform as The Hollies.

*The Daily Express*
September 1981

'Bobby approached me on this one,' Eric Haydock was to comment during a 1990 interview with the *Carousel* fanzine. 'I had seen him socially a couple of times and he just rang me up one day and said, "Do you fancy a gig?" I said, "Well, what is it?" and he said, "Ol' Nash is coming over..." which flabbergasted me as you can imagine, after all these years. Then, when we did get together, it was very touching. I really did enjoy it.'

With his Hawaiian shirt unbuttoned to the chest, the suntanned Nash looked strangely at odds with his paler colleagues – Allan in his neatly collared tee-shirt and fatherly slacks, Tony, still defying the ageing process, with Bobby and a grey-haired Eric barely visible behind, but it was reportedly a happy atmosphere backstage at the BBC studios in White City, West London. And none more so when, the following day, Allan, Graham, Tony and Bobby reunited at the Audio International Studios in Marylebone, to undertake work on a brand-new recording together. Eric, meanwhile, reportedly uncomfortable with playing in a modern style on any new recordings (or so the media would comment), was thanked for his services, paid his flat £150 performing fee by the BBC and caught the train back north.

The session at which Graham joined his former bandmates wasn't initially intended to lead on to anything. He initially tagged along just to watch. The group had the studio booked to cut a new composition by Alan Tarney, Tom Snow and Trevor Spencer called 'Something Ain't Right', but when Graham voluntarily stood around the microphone with Allan and Tony once more, it just seemed so natural.

With the multi-talented Alan Tarney (hot off recent successes with Leo Sayer, Cliff Richard and Barbara Dickson) producing the session and contributing to the majority of the instrumentation himself (keyboard, rhythm guitar, bass), the trio supplied their harmonies alongside Allan's lead vocals, and small talk then tentatively ventured towards undertaking further work together. A new album was mentioned, to which Graham responded:

'I wouldn't mind joining in on the album. Let's see what happens and decide where we go from there.'[1]

With commitments back in America with CSN, and completion on their upcoming *Daylight Again* album scheduled, Graham agreed to commence working with his former bandmates the following year once all obligations had been fulfilled. He then flew back to America's sunshine state. Allan, however, still not fully comfortable with Graham's sudden re-emergence, was initially hesitant to the suggestion:

'I didn't really want Graham to become involved again, if I'm honest,' he recalls. 'I wasn't very happy about the boys making the decision that Graham should come back and record with us, because as far as I was concerned, [the sessions] were going great anyway. But I was voted against, so I had to go along with it. What I couldn't understand was *why* he wanted to do it.'[63]

Just before reuniting with Graham, the trio had recorded another new composition at Abbey Road, but any further developments with it had been sidetracked, following the surprising success of the 'Holliedaze' release. 'Take My Love And Run' had been composed by veteran keyboard player Brian Chatton, a former member of The Warriors (whom Graham and Tony had assisted in the studio, back in the 1960s) and a founding member of Flaming Youth (alongside a pre-Genesis Phil Collins). Written in partnership with fellow John Miles acquaintance, Barry Black, this synth-dominated "80's-pop" song had been tracked by The Hollies back in early September, with Chatton producing, supplying backing vocals and sitting in on keyboards.

'It was the Dick James Publishing staff that played it to them,' recalls Chatton from his home in Los Angeles. 'But they insisted I played on it and produce it for them as well…'

A lively-enough tune that fitted in nicely with the chart hits that Bucks Fizz, Human League and Soft Cell were churning out but, upon release, it became evident that it also lacked the accompanying visual appeal that such popular acts at that time utilised. Where was the glossy, artistic promotional video? Subsequently, despite several televised appearances (*London Night Out, The Russell Harty Show* and a brief feature on *Nationwide*), the single release of the song (POSP-379), b/w 'Driver', failed to register with buyers – although it wasn't for the want of trying on Polydor's behalf, cleverly utilising a picture of the reunited band with Nash and Haydock in the line-up (from *the Top of the Pops* taping) on the 7" picture sleeve of the release. They even went to the limits of publicising newspaper advertisements, claiming that the original quintet had reunited for the recording. It would be The Hollies' final release on the label. With the band frustrated at Polydor's inability to get a hit, and their rejection of the John Miles-produced sessions, they parted company.

By this time, needing to fill out their onstage sound, The Hollies had added a number of new faces into their performing line-up. Both Chatton and Paul Bliss had assisted them during recent TV appearances, with Bliss remaining onboard for a while longer, whilst bass player Steve Stroud and rhythm guitarist-vocalist Alan Coates would also soon accompany them, helping to fill the void on stage and in the studio.

'I first became involved with The Hollies when a very shady character by the name of John Bates asked me in a pub on the Old Kent Road, when I was with my own band Sprinkler,' Stroud was to tell Martin Hockley in *Carousel* fanzine. 'He said, "Do you want a job with The Hollies?" I said, "Of course, doesn't everybody?" He was a friend of Tony Hicks and he was serious!'

In the meantime, with the single following the same pattern as many of its predecessors, the novelty value of 'Holliedaze' excluded, the new year turned to focus on the upcoming album sessions, although the possibility of also working with Thin Lizzy founder, the irrepressible Phil Lynott, was also mooted in the *New Musical Express* during this period. Sadly, that tantalising option never fell within the public's grasp.

In early January 1982, Allan flew out to the US, spending a week on the west coast, discussing plans with Graham who, as promised, returned to the UK himself during early spring to help oversee the initial recording of the backing tracks, held at the White House Studios in Reading.

Hollies keyboard sideman Paul Bliss took control of much of the instrumentation on the new songs, co-producing the tracks, six of which were either composed or co-composed by himself. Surprisingly, with such focus on the reunited quartet, with Graham's headlining status still worthy of attention in the media ratings, and the composing abilities of the group members within, the band opted to cover a selection of non-originals, in addition to reworking two golden oldies from the 1960s (including one of their own hits). On top of that, they utilised three recent recordings by the band: Alan Tarney's 'Something Ain't Right' from the inaugural Nash-reunion session, Brian Chatton's 'Take My Love And Run' and Mike Batt's excellent 'If The Lights Go Out', simply overdubbing new layers onto the latter two existing tracks.

'The Hollies were always a great interpretive band,' noted Graham at the time. 'For this album, we decided to choose songs we liked to sing that had a certain space for vocal harmonies.'[2]

'After we had agreed to do the project,' added Tony, 'I used to ring Graham up in Hawaii and play him songs over the phone. We had some great material by our keyboard player, Paul Bliss, and the whole experience was really enjoyable.'[56]

One final track selected, a beautiful seafaring ballad entitled 'Let Her Go Down' had been composed by British folk musician Peter Knight, and included on *Sails of Silver*, an album released by his band Steeleye Span, two years previously. Unfortunately, Bliss's unnecessary overuse of the synthesiser strings stripped away much of the acoustic delights that had appeared on the original, although a biting but all-too-brief Hicks guitar solo offered some redemption.

Having completed a further round of sessions on the tracks during May, this time at the Riverside Studios in Hammersmith, Allan, Tony and Bobby then flew out to Los Angeles during June, settling in at Graham's own Rudy Records studio in Hollywood to supply vocal tracks and additional instrumental overdubs. Outside, and down the street from the studio, the band could clearly see the massive billboards dominating the Sunset Boulevard skyline, advertising all of the big new albums. Just maybe…

Scheduled touring commitments from both parties – The Hollies and Crosby, Stills & Nash – enforced sporadic sessions undertaken on the album as it slowly progressed, and it would be early 1983 before the final mixdown could take place.

In the interim, The Hollies gradually began to book up live appearances once more, having cut down on commitments in recent years at Allan's request. The 23rd February 1982 had seen them accept an invitation to perform at the annual winter Carnival celebrations in Mainz, Germany (two years after 10cc had stormed the festival). With both Steve Stroud and Alan Coates making their live debut appearances with the band, handling bass guitar, rhythm and harmonies, the band ran through twenty songs for the enthusiastic crowd, starting with two of the early hits and then running through a wide selection, including excerpts from *Another Night, Write On* and *Russian Roulette*. They also debuted one of the choices from the upcoming release, Alan Tarney's 'Something Ain't Right'. Stroud's playing may not have impressed purist aficionados of the band, with his 1980s style of plucking the heavy strings, but the overall quality of the performance couldn't be ignored. Taped via the soundboard mixing desk for a German radio broadcast, this was the live album that the band should have released, a full unedited performance with all members in superb form. Ironically, both 'Write On' and 'Blowin' In The Wind' did eventually appear on later European releases.

Some of the songs may have been rearranged for the modern audience, with the synthesised keyboards of Messrs Bliss and Arnesen changing the feel of many of the classic hits ('Just One Look' was totally rearranged for the show and would reappear in a similar style on the studio album shortly afterwards) but when they let rip during the extended instrumental section of 'Draggin' My Heels', followed by an oh-so-sweet solo from Tony, it took the band onto a higher level altogether. And that was before they had the audacity to turn in an incredible 11-minute rendition of 'Long Cool Woman (In A Black Dress)'. It was noticeable, however, that some of the selection had the key slightly lowered, enabling Allan to hit the higher ranges easier.

I Can't Let Go / Just One Look / Another Night / Sandy / Bus Stop / Draggin' My Heels / Write On / Something Ain't Right / Medley (Stay – Look Through Any Window – Sorry Suzanne – I'm Alive) / Take My Love And Run / King Midas In Reverse / Too Young To Be Married / On A Carousel / Carrie Anne / The Air That I Breathe / Soldier's Song / He Ain't Heavy, He's My Brother / Blowin' In The Wind / Johnny B Goode / Long Cool Woman (In A Black Dress)

Following their return from Los Angeles, July saw the band travel abroad once again, making a welcoming return visit to Sweden, before undertaking a series of sporadic UK appearances towards the end of the year.

Allan, meanwhile, also took the opportunity to briefly dive back into his solo career, cutting ties with Spencer Proffer and remaining in the UK to record two new songs with his songwriting partner Gary Benson, who also produced the sessions. The resulting two songs, 'Someone Else Will' and 'Castles In The Wind', were both delightful compositions, produced and arranged without the excessive need for synthesisers. Sadly, both were released on the relatively unknown (and short-lived) Forever Records label during September, and garnered little press or media attention, swiftly disappearing into obscurity.

Delaying the reunion project further, Graham then had his own promotional work to deal with, undertaking the next CSN Summer 1982 tour with a three-week run of US shows. On top of that, promotion surrounding their successful *Daylight Again* album had a further autumn/fall tour in the pipeline, whilst the recent achievement of Graham's composition, 'Wasted On The Way', a Top 10 hit in *Billboard*, ensured that their flame continued to burn brightly. So much so, that one wonders how much commitment Graham was prepared to offer up to the Hollies album. His dedication to the partnership with David Crosby and Stephen Stills was undeniable, and he was simultaneously working and editing a new live video and LP – *Allies* – for the trio at the same time as the Hollies project was gradually taking shape.

'The Hollies are unfinished business with me,' he would tell the *Los Angeles Times*. 'It's the same guys I worked with in the '60s. It's a chance to go back to my roots. I like Hollies' music. It's pleasant pop music, you know, but it's not like CSN music. CSN music means more to me. CSN music is like a god, a sinister god. It haunts me. No matter what I do, I have to go back to it.'[2]

It was clearly a healing process for Graham. Friendships to be rekindled, old damages to be repaired. After all, this was not his full-time job, so quite why he went along with this collection of synthetic synth-pop-pap without demonstrating some form of heavyweight powerplay remains unclear. Or did he? Was he partly responsible for the song selection? Was he content with going through the motions and creating this updated form of instantaneous music? Outside of the harmonies, was this even art?

Graham had been through the full 1960s ride with his friends, and they had seen it all together. Since that point, he had seen what the true "rock" lifestyle was all about. Something that Allan had appeared to be constantly striving for. Graham lived it daily back in his golden land of palm trees, sunshine and harmonies.

'I felt a bit out of my depth, as Graham is like a fucking superstar to me. I hadn't seen him since I left…' summarised Eric Haydock, after the recent *Top of the Pops* reunion.

One only has to take a listen to the recent music being created by his Stateside partnership – 'Wasted On The Way', 'Delta', 'Shadow Captain',

'Southern Cross' and the exquisite Nash-composed 'Cathedral', and then compare it to the Paul Bliss compositions, 'Casualty', 'I Got What I Want' and 'Say You'll Be Mine', all governed by a cataclysmic catastrophe of synthesised overdubs.

Bliss was certainly a talented composer, as the gently hypnotic ballad 'Someone Else's Eyes' suggested. With Graham contributing some beautiful harmonies to the dense layering, the song had all the ingredients to be something very special – until the mood was completely shattered by the songwriter once again, adding a mid-song synth-break to the arrangement. Where was the Tony Hicks flowing guitar solo we were waiting for?

Nevertheless, following a further round of LA-based vocal sessions at Rudy Records during February of 1983, overseen by producer (and longtime Nash cohort) Stanley Johnston, the new songs for the album were completed. Additional vocal work was also undertaken on both 'If The Lights Go Out' and 'Take My Love And Run', adding them into the final selection, and the album was scheduled for release under the title of *What Goes Around*, with distribution handled by Warners/Atlantic, for the early summer of '83.

Recalling the additional overdubs for his composition, Brian Chatton notes, 'Apparently, Graham wanted to be on it too and so I believe he sent his harmony voice across to the UK somehow and it was just added to the original mix.'

Essentially so, although there are other small variations between the two versions, with Allan's lead vocal slightly differing, whilst the tempo was also adjusted.

The central focus on the new album fell upon a nice, clean "pop" version of The Supremes' chart-topping hit from 1965, 'Stop! In The Name Of Love', and the band played heavily on its upcoming release during a brief visit to New Zealand and Australia, without Graham, immediately following the Hollywood sessions.

'We honestly don't know what to expect from the Australian audiences,' Allan was to say to the Australian *Sunday Press* in advance of the visit. 'We're a seven-member group now, including two synthesizer players, and only three of the original group members are left. On our way to Australia, we're stopping off at Los Angeles to put the finishing touches to our latest album. Paul Bliss, one of the group's keyboard players, has written four of the songs on the album and we'll be performing those on the tour...'

Playing a series of shows in Newcastle, Geelong, Albury and

Melbourne, preceded by an appearance on the popular Nine Network variety programme, *The Mike Walsh Show*, the band featured their rendition of the Holland-Dozier-Holland classic prominently during the visit. Unfortunately, issues with Allan's throat occurred mid-tour, a combination of humidity, dryness and air-conditioning, enforcing a couple of cancellations *en route*. Alan Coates was also noticeably absent on the tour, falling ill and unable to perform, so the band drafted in guitarist Jamie Moses, a musical acquaintance of Coates, as a temporary replacement.

Realistically, however, when issued as a single (WEA U-9888), backed with the non-LP 'Musical Pictures' (another pleasing piano-led ballad from Paul Bliss, crying out for some Hicks-magic), the recording lacked the impact and punch that had graced the Motown original, many moons before, and it also clearly lacked any soul. The vocals were strong, and Allan comfortably tackled the lead, but it was devoid of the intensity the composition deserved despite, finally, Tony getting to briefly let loose with a slick guitar solo. From an outside viewpoint, 'If The Lights Go Out' appeared to be a far stronger option to promote the LP. It was upbeat, highly commercial and not so reliant on the electronic tendencies that were bubbling underneath the Bliss-production of the '60s classic –which was more than could be said for the remaining keyboard-dominated album tracks; 'Casualty', 'Say You'll Be Mine', 'I Got What I Want' and the truly awful reworking of 'Just One Look', featuring the tacky 1980s rearrangement recently suggested at the Mainz concert. Combined, these not only lacked impact, punch, soul and intensity, but they also lacked everything in between.

Offering to help with the initial publicity for the album, Graham duly appeared on a selection of European and US TV shows (*Vorsicht Musik* and *American Bandstand*) as the band launched the single and album. They even combined to film a promotional video for the single, achieving some prestigious MTV airplay as a result, although the quartet appeared only sparingly throughout its visual Nash-led anti-war message. However, despite the despair from many of the band's long-time fans, horrified over the direction the band were taking and mostly disappointed that the reunion had come to little more than a glossy 1980s synthesised facsimile, the publicity paid off in several countries around the world, pushing the single up to a respectable #29 in *Billboard*, #31 in Canada's *RPM* charts and Top 100 spots in Australia and Germany. It also achieved Top 10 status in the unlikely surrounding of Brazil's Hot 100. Likewise, the LP also scraped into the *Billboard* best-selling album lists.

'We feel really good about this album,' Graham was to continuously state in press interviews. 'It was a lot of fun to make.'

That said, much of the press was less generous with their praise.

Unfortunately, neither release saw any success in the UK, with the media still unsure as to how they viewed the band. They always drew considerable respect for their catalogue, but perhaps the public was all too wary of the new wave image timidly portrayed on the 7" picture sleeve, with Graham, Allan, Tony and Bobby adorned in their sneakers, braces and cropped-sleeved tee-shirts. The Hollies?

A follow-up release in some regions, the perfect pairing of 'If The Lights Go Out' b/w 'Someone Else's Eyes', surprisingly failed to match the success, although, perhaps, by that point, the novelty of the revitalised '60s icons had waned.

With Graham committed to another CSN European tour that summer, further promotional work was restricted, but he did find the opportunity to link up with his Hollies bandmates again for some live performances in the US during the latter part of the summer.

It is worth pointing out here that the short tour had provisionally been placed on the group's schedule back in April, thusly dismissing later claims that Graham's availability was only made possible due to David Crosby's imminent incarceration for drug-related issues. Crosby would not face the prospects of prison life until his first hearing in June, by which time The Hollies 1983 American Tour had been confirmed.

With touring support from Paul Bliss, Steve Stroud, Alan Coates and additional keyboard player Denis Haines, and remaining on the eastern side of the country, the band fitted in a selection of shows in Ohio, New York, North Carolina and Illinois, whilst also venturing across the border to Ontario for one performance. A west coast leg was cancelled due to poor ticket sales, with a show at LA's 6,000-seat Universal Amphitheatre only generating around 300 sales. Sadly, a number of eastern shows also had to be rescheduled to smaller venues, as tickets were particularly slow in certain regions. The Hollies, it appears, did not have the pulling power of their halcyon days, even with Graham Nash back in the line-up.

A polished recording from a performance at the Kings Island Amusement Park in Cincinnati, held on 2nd September, would later surface in bootleg form as *Hello Graham Nash*, highlighting the bands continuing professionalism. An official release would eventually appear in 1997, fourteen years after the event, initially entitled *Archive Alive!* (later appearing as *Reunion*, with the addition of two extra tracks).

Whilst adding selections from the newly released album to the setlist, 'Casualty', 'If The Lights Go Out', 'Someone Else's Eyes' (which featured a delightful guitar solo replacing the studio synthesiser) and 'Stop! In The Name Of Love', along with two of Graham's finest post-Hollie moments (presumably to appease the hollers from the pro-Nash crowd) – 'Wasted On The Way' and 'Teach Your Children' – the loss of such concert-pleasers as 'Draggin' My Heels', 'Another Night' and 'Too Young To Be Married' was a jolt for the usual upbeat feel of the show. Another noticeable point was Graham's reticence to offer up some of his lead lines on a number of the old tunes, handing Allan the lead vocals on 'On A Carousel' – although, undoubtedly, a lack of rehearsal time had some implications.

Psychodrama loomed when the original 1960s members of the Hollies – Allan Clarke, Graham Nash, Tony Hicks and Bobby Elliott – performed Tuesday at the Bottom Line. The group has made a reunion album and is touring the United States with four backup musicians; its New York show was moved from Radio City Music Hall to the 400-seat Bottom Line.

After leaving the Hollies in 1968, Mr Nash went on to considerably more renown as part of Crosby, Stills & Nash. But the Hollies were Mr Clarke's band – he sang lead vocals on virtually all of their hits – and Mr Nash's presence made him uneasy.

'He's a millionaire, and we're broke,' Mr Clarke said, pointing to Mr Nash. For his part, Mr Nash interrupted Mr Clarke almost every time he spoke. Mr Hicks, on lead guitar, and Mr Elliott, a staunch drummer, tried to ignore the friction.

Mr Clarke's tension soured his high tenor and the vocal harmonies in the first part of the set. Luckily, that was where material from the new album was, washed-out remakes of soul hits and songs by the band's co-producer, Paul Bliss, that are ill-suited to the Hollies' delicate three-tenor blend.

After a pair of Crosby, Stills & Nash songs, with reworked harmonies, Mr Clarke relaxed, and the set turned to the Hollies' hits from the late 1960s and the early '70s. Among schmaltzy ballads and the dulcet whimsy of "Carrie Anne" and "Stop! Stop! Stop!", the one surprise was the angry "King Midas in Reverse" from 1967.

*New York Times*
August 1983

When questioned in the *New Musical Express* over the change of direction, both Allan and Tony were defensive in their response, acknowledging that their records now sell, "certainly not to the kids. It's to people in our age bracket, who came up with us in the '60s.

'If you start asking questions about bands in the Top 20, I wouldn't be able to answer you. We've been going for eighteen years. We went through all the kids-running-after-us stuff. How did we cope with all the other trends while we were being The Hollies? We carried on. We have to be professional entertainers now.'

Even with the relative dismissal of the album from both media and public alike, one collectable item that did result from the chaos was an obscure New Zealand 45 release of 'Stop! In The Name Of Love'. This was the only country that placed the charming, yet otherwise unreleased, Hollies version of Steeleye Span's 'Let Her Go Down' as the B-side. Even stranger was the fact that it was EMI/Parlophone who initially released it (NZP-3586), despite the band being contracted to Warner's for distribution. Realising the error, EMI withdrew the single and Warner's reissued it (WEA-2598647) – but it still sold relatively few copies.

Following the culmination of the US tour, Graham returned to the family home in Hawaii, all plans on hold whilst awaiting the outcome of David Crosby's future (Crosby would eventually spend five months in Huntsville Correctional Facility in Texas). His Hollie-bandmates, now once again *former*-bandmates, flew back to the UK, with no immediate plans to continue the reunion.

# THE HOLLIES
## IN CONCERT

Enjoy 90 of Rock 'n Roll's sweetest minutes as original Hollies members Graham Nash, Allan Clarke, Bobby Elliott and Tony Hicks reunite. Recorded live in concert. Hear live versions of the songs that made the Hollies one of rock's most influential bands.

"Bus Stop"
"He Ain't Heavy (He's My Brother)"
"Stop Stop Stop"
"The Air That I Breathe"
"Long Cool Woman (In A Black Dress)"

**Plus**
"If The Lights Go Out"
"Stop In The Name Of Love"
"Casualty"
"Just One Look"
From the Hollies' new LP
"What Goes Around..."
on Atlantic Records.

The weekend of October 14-16

Produced exclusively for The Source by Starfleet Blair Inc.

Sponsored, in part, by Budweiser and The U.S. Navy.

# CHAPTER THIRTY-TWO

# "THIS IS IT..."

With the mixed reaction to the Nash-reunion ringing in their ears, the trio that now comprised The Hollies stepped into 1984 with a degree of trepidation. They had no current record label, having signed off with Polydor, and the arrangement with WEA being for the one-off reunion. The US tour had suffered from poor ticket sales in many key regions, and the possibilities of further extensive touring with Graham had been abandoned once their erstwhile partner returned to his full-time occupation: West Coast rock star. That said, they were still coming down off a Top 30 *Billboard* hit, and the tour of New Zealand and Australia, although not generating the pandemonium of previous years, still provided enough interest to confirm their ongoing popularity on foreign shores.

January 1984 saw one final burst of reunion nostalgia when they travelled across to Los Angeles to test the waters once again in Graham's Rudy Records studio, cutting vocals on a composition listed as 'Don't Close Your Eyes'. Sadly, the song remained incomplete, despite Tony Hicks commenting in later years (for a concert programme), 'That was a lovely song that we really should go back and finish off one day...'

Whilst enjoying the Los Angeles hospitality with Graham, they also took part in two televised guest appearances for US TV, the first of which was a one-off live concert at the Hollywood Palladium, filmed on 13th January and broadcast the following month as part of the NBC-TV spectacular *Supernight of Rock 'n' Roll*, a two-hour musical extravaganza, produced by legendary TV icon Dick Clark. For their part, The Hollies only got to appear briefly on stage and, despite the billing prominently highlighting "Graham Nash and The Hollies" – which must have raised more than a few questions – were only given the opportunity to perform two songs. Nevertheless, with Allan, Graham and a smiling Tony all performing their original vocal parts on the classic 'Carrie Anne', and with Bobby providing the beat and two of Graham's session associates helping out (bassist Philip Chen and Kim Bullard on keyboards), it was a wonderful and fitting climax to the reunion – despite the noticeably poor audio on the final broadcast, with sound producer Stanley Johnson mixing Graham's voice far too prominently.

The second spot saw them appear on the US syndicated TV show *Solid Gold* (airing three months later), once again accompanied by Graham, Chen and Bullard lip-synching to both 'Long Cool Woman (In A Black Dress)' and 'The Air That I Breathe', neither of which, ironically, had featured Graham on the original recordings.

Nevertheless, despite such highs, the following few years would be lean times, as the band returned to the UK and Europe, *sans*-Nash (regardless of many UK articles at the time stating that he would indeed be taking part in some forthcoming shows), continuing to ply their trade in a low-key manner, with smaller regional tours – such as the brief four-date visit to Sweden during April – interspersed with sporadic recording sessions appearing throughout the schedules.

Whilst out on the road, The Hollies' concert reviews always stayed positive, but with little or no new product to promote, excepting the *What Goes Around* album, the band were often going through the same routines, retreading the past with reverence, accompanied by Stroud, Coates and the recently acquired Denis Haines, fresh from a supporting role in Gary Numan's phenomenal electro-pop successes (and, until recently, half of the Polydor act, Hale and Haines). On occasion, Peter Arnesen would resume his spot behind the bank of keyboards too, but all three of the regular supporting team were now being regarded as "official" Hollies by the core trio. Opinions on a postcard, please…

Of all the bill-topping bands which emerged from Merseyside and Manchester a couple of decades ago, The Hollies were and are recognised as one of the most accomplished.

The real tragedy is that so many of their rivals, so many lesser groups from the '60s, are touring today with little or nothing left of their original talent. In the rare case of The Hollies, some key people are still there to front the 1984 line-up most ably and extend the useful life span of this distinctive and distinguished band.

Behind the songwriting duo of Clarke and Hicks is stalwart drummer Bobby Elliott, plus a further quartet of young enthusiastic musicians. The current combination lets The Hollies retain their strength and even enhance the instrumental side of things in terms of club and concert appearances.

Throughout the act, Clarke works extensively with his guitarist sidekick Tony Hicks. Together they display a fine combination of confidence and long-term experience as they parade their self-penned hits ranging from 'Carrie Anne' to 'Stop! Stop! Stop!'

Other interesting elements of the 1984 stage show include a segment playing tribute to Graham Nash, presented in acoustic trio format, a rip-roaring rock 'n' roll finale and a lighting plot which sets all the sounds in a series of effective rainbows.

*The Stage & Television Today*
April 1984

Television also provided a steady supply of work for The Hollies, and the band appeared to remain in popular demand for shows across the continent. A 1984 appearance on the Danish DR-TV broadcast *Eldorado* (filmed during late 1983) offered up a live vocal take of 'Stop! In The Name Of Love', with the full contingent of touring members behind, including both Peter Arnesen and Denis Haines on keyboards, whilst German TV gave forth later appearances on *Flashlights* and *Music Convoy*. These two shows, taped towards the end of the year, featured lip-synched performances of 'I Got What I Want', a German single selected from the *What Goes Around* album. Ideally suited for the Euro-synth-pop market, this release, on the WEA label, failed to connect even in their most loyal of locations. Shortly after the Danish recording, Peter Arnesen left The Hollies line-up for personal reasons.

'I reluctantly stepped away from the band when I decided to leave the UK on a permanent basis in the '80s,' he recalls today. 'Partly because of personal reasons, unconnected with the band, and partly in order to pursue a career in higher education. As far as my highlights in the studio and on the road go, for me it was all magic. I enjoyed it all…' [50]

Despite the loss of the ever-reliable sideman, such was the band's continuing popularity in Germany that they were even given their own TV Special during 1984, a throwback to past glories when this was positively the norm. This time around, however, the cross-pollination of 1980s fashions, lighting and staging, mixed with a series of classic '60s and '70s songs – 'Bus Stop', 'On A Carousel', 'Long Cool Woman (In A Black Dress)', 'He Ain't Heavy, He's My Brother' and 'The Air That I Breathe' (along with the two recent singles) – made for thirty minutes of uncomfortable viewing, with Allan's pirouetting and neatly trimmed hairstyle (finally abandoning the remnants of his curly perm) clearly at odds with, and a generation apart from, his youthful new bandmates. Both Coates and Haines in particular, dressed in modern trends ("BOY" branded tracksuit trousers), looked suitably out of place, surrounded by the mature, advancing years of Allan, Tony and Bobby.

For his part, Haines would go on to reach further into the German market by releasing a solo synth-pop single on the Polydor-Germany label that same year.

A November 1984 visit to the Abbey Road studios, their first session in the hallowed halls for several years, gave little further encouragement, with just two future B-sides emanating from the date. 'You're All Woman' was another fateful dig into the realms of synth-pop, and 'You Give Me Strength' was a rather unadventurous journey into middle-of-the-road territory, albeit one that was very smoothly produced and performed. Surprisingly, bearing in mind the lack of composing that the band had undertaken themselves in recent years, both of these came from the collaborative pens of Allan and Tony, paired with Peter Vale (hit songwriter for Sheena Easton). One can only wonder how deep this collaboration went, as the personal relationship between Allan and Tony had never been strong at the best of times in more recent years. Both men recognised the abilities of the other and afforded due credit for their musical partner's contributions, but Allan had never overlooked the dismissive response from Tony at his suggestion of a solo career, instead, informing him that he had to leave the group in order to pursue such a move. In return, Tony was all too aware of the issues that Allan had carried around with him during the latter half of the 1970s, and the unreliability that came with it – the results of which had come to a head during the 1979 tour of Germany. It was an uneasy truce, driven by power and ego, and the indefatigable belief that, when the group were on top of their game, there were very few who could better the line-up. One only had to listen to or see such moments of spectacular glory, when the band had truly been on fire, to understand why they suffered gladly. Despite the unforgiving factor that the key members were getting long in the tooth, the youthful appearances were fading and the hairlines were thinning (all except Tony's), few could match them for vocal or instrumental prowess.

Allan and Peter Vale also collaborated on another tune around this period, another heavily synthesised recording, taped by Allan during a solo session (which leads one to assume that the previous recordings may well have also originated from the same Clarke-Vale sessions). 'Two Shadows', along with the otherwise undocumented 'So Long', was drenched in excessive electronic overdubs (unlike the simple delights of his previous solo outing) and remained unreleased. He also undertook some further solo work alongside David Holland, drummer with heavy rock outfit Judas Priest, but that too remained unheard.

1985 would see further group recording during the late winter months, going into early spring, but, without a clear objective in mind, only one single would appear – the May 1985 issue on Columbia Records, 'Too Many Hearts Get Broken', a big-ballad release from the pens of Allan Clarke, Peter Vale and Vale's songwriting partner, Mick Leeson. Paired with 'You're All Woman' on the 7" single, with production from the same in-house team, and given the bonus of an additional 12" release and the inclusion of a third track (Billy Bremner's 'Laughter Turns To Tears'), the release failed to gain significant airplay and support in either format, resulting in yet another chart failure. Certainly, 'Laughter Turns To Tears', an enjoyable cover of the former Rockpile songwriter-guitarist Bremner's own 1982 version of the song, may have been a stronger choice for the lead side and, in fact, was originally scheduled to be the chosen single. Then again, the 1980s was a time for the big ballad (Foreigner, Heart, Toto etc.), and so the heart-rending combination from Clarke-Vale-Leeson won the day. Mind you, the overall feel of 'Too Many Hearts Get Broken' wasn't helped by the use of a drum programme at the session in place of Bobby's regular kit, and the absence of Alan Coates' increasingly distinctive high harmony was also a contributing factor to the unfamiliar sound.

The next new 45 release, again on Columbia, wouldn't appear for another twenty months. Until then, the band would have to make a living solely on touring, with the occasional TV appearance – all built on a solid foundation of golden oldies.

> The Hollies, at The Cresset, Bretton, on Saturday, proved they are still as popular as ever. The screaming teenagers of earlier days were replaced by a more mature audience, but a string of old and new hits still managed to bring them to their feet with a touch of hysteria. Although the group has spent years on the circuit, their songs have never gone out of fashion and classics like 'The Air That I Breathe' showed their showmanship and resulted in a standing ovation.
>
> The Sovereign Hall is not the ideal place for concerts, but the small size helped create an informal atmosphere. The sound was good and gave everybody a gentle reminder of the days when it was possible to distinguish the words in pop songs.
>
> The mixture of ballads, pop and rock left the audience shouting for more and even a half-hour encore did not satisfy them. The night belonged to their heroes.
>
> May 1985<br>Concert Review

A performance held at the Magnum Centre in Irvine, Scotland, during June of 1985, was recorded and broadcast on Radio Clyde soon after, but later attempts to have it officially released sadly failed.

The partnership with Columbia Records had come about through negotiations with EMI, The Hollies' former label with whom they still maintained close ties. The UK arm of Columbia was independent of its US CBS-operated counterpart and was overseen (and subsequently phased out) by EMI Records during the 1980s, a period when The Hollies really needed the support to keep the band alive and successful. Unfortunately, the group was in a creative slump at that particular period, and opportunities were few and far between, and so it came as no surprise that, following the two further unsuccessful 1987 releases, 'This Is It' and 'Reunion Of The Heart', even the might of EMI/Columbia could do no more for the band's ailing sales figures, and the partnership folded.

'This Is It' hadn't been the initial choice for the second Columbia release; that honour had fallen to a song that had been cut during March and April of 1986 and was a far grittier, punchier recording than those recently attempted. Entitled 'Hard To Forget', featuring significant studio contributions from the three touring band members, was a synth-driven arrangement but contained some biting Hicks-guitar running throughout. It lacked the distinctive Hollie-harmonies but, with additional vocals in the studio from Alan Coates, it was highly commercially acceptable material for the period. However, after a UK TV appearance on the Tyne-Tees broadcast show *Nightline*, during which the band debuted the song (lip-synching to the studio track) – along with 'Carrie Anne' – the proposed single was removed from the release schedules – assuming it had even reached the Columbia Records desks by then…

'We only finished it a couple of days ago,' Allan was to say to presenter Anna Raeburn, 'so this is the first airing of it. It will be out in a couple of weeks. The release date has yet to be unfolded to us.'

'That's because the record company haven't heard it yet…' interjected Tony.

Allan then turned to Tony, much to the amusement of the studio audience and his watching bandmates, politely enquiring, 'What's it called again?'

No explanation has ever been put forward as to who decided against issuing the recording, or indeed why, but instead of the new Hollies 45 gracing the racks, a further period of uncertainty followed, filled out only by the constant touring, much of it overseas.

1986 saw visits to Iceland, their first performances in Reykjavik for over a decade, followed by a series of August appearances in Norway, playing six shows in Alesund, Bergen, Stavanger, Tromso, Mysen and Oslo (a visit that was interrupted due to Alan Coates being struck down with appendicitis). Then, in September, they returned to the recording studios, this time at the Maison Rouge Studios in Fulham where, working with producer Graham Sacher, they cut two new tracks, the aforesaid 'This Is It' and 'Reunion Of The Heart', both composed by the Welsh-born songwriter Maldwyn Pope.

'I was being managed by Larry Page at the time,' Pope recalled during 2020 when questioned about the connection. 'He also managed The Kinks and The Troggs. He got me a publishing deal with Granada TV, who were trying to expand their publishing arm, and I think it was either Larry or Roland Rogers at Granada that started playing Graham Sacher my songs.

He liked what he heard, but the problem I had was that Cliff Richard also wanted to record 'Reunion Of The Heart' and, possibly, 'This Is It'. At the time, Cliff was more successful than The Hollies, but mid-project, he changed producers to Alan Tarney, who ended up writing most of the new album [*Always Guaranteed*] himself. In the end, Cliff's version of 'Reunion…' ended up as a B-side on a 12" single.

'I remember hearing The Hollies tracks down the phone. I had grown up with them, and I also loved the fact they covered some early Bruce Springsteen songs. They appeared on quite a few TV shows at the time, performing both of my songs but, sadly, neither song dented the charts.'

'This Is It', the first of the Pope compositions to appear publicly, featured an upbeat guitar-synth arrangement similar to the abandoned 'Hard To Forget', and was driven by a typical 1980s pounding crisp drumbeat. Melodically, it was pleasant enough, but the lead vocal just didn't sound like Allan. It required little of the Clarke power or vocal range which, from a Hollies' perspective, is where it fell flat. Paired with the 1984 recording of 'You Gave Me Strength', the single flatlined, despite primetime televised promotion on the BBC's *Wogan* and *Pamela Armstrong Show*. Heavy promotion was also undertaken at concert venues, with each seat having an advertising flyer for the single placed on it, prior to the concert. Unfortunately, no one told the band, and they omitted the song from the setlists for much of the subsequent tour!

The follow-up release of 'Reunion Of The Heart', which took the band back into soft-rock ballad territory, did no better, despite it offering Allan a little more range to vocalise with. Then again, at times, it sounded more like a Clarke solo release, void of any noticeable band harmonies except for a female choral backing. An appearance on the Anne Diamond-fronted TV series *The Birthday Show* did little to help.

'We only put things out we believe in,' stated Allan, during a televised interview at the time. 'Those we think had got half a chance of getting there. We're in the studios quite a lot but most of the stuff we do we're not pleased with, so we don't put it out. We wait for the right one to come along.'

To support the releases, the band resumed their touring duties, undertaking a lengthy thirty-date jaunt around the UK, although, having recently appointed official Hollie-status upon Messrs Stroud, Coates and Haines, it was interesting to note that the promotional artwork for the tour only featured the images of Clarke, Hicks and Elliott. Possibly a sense of uncertainly was prevailing over the backline team as, having covered for him during the 1983 tour of New Zealand and Australia, guitarist Jamie Moses again stepped in at one point to cover for an absent Coates.

Discussing his stand-in duties, Jamie recalls today, 'The connection was via Alan Coates and Steve Stroud, both of whom were in a terrific band called Sprinkler, who I sometimes played with at their gigs at the Green Man and the Thomas A'Becket in London's Old Kent Road.

'To this day, I can't remember exactly where I played with The Hollies, but I know Australia and New Zealand was in there. I also recollect another tour or two with them in Scandinavia and the Middle East. I do remember being in a speedboat with Stroudy in Abu Dhabi and driving it with my teeth. Also, to this day, I still owe Allan Clarke £1 million after losing a game of pool to him!'

Both Moses and Alan Coates later joined up in the band Broken English who, briefly, received some recognition and chart success, in between Hollie-commitments, with their 1987 Top 20 hit (composed by founding member Steve Elson) 'Comin' On Strong'.

By this stage, Steve Stroud had also moved away from The Hollies, signing on with Cliff Richard's touring line-up instead. In his position came Ray Stiles, taking over the bass mantle with aplomb. Having seen success close up, Ray knew all about the trials and tribulations of being a "pop" star. His previous band, Mud, had achieved fourteen Top 20 UK hits, including three #1s during the hectic 1970s era.

For the *Carousel* fanzine, Ray would later recall how the offer came to join the band: 'After I left Mud, there was four or five years where I didn't do a lot. I started a little group of my own and that was very regular work. We were on tour supporting Dionne Warwick and I got a call saying there's a band that wants you to do a tour with them. I found out that it was The Hollies and that I had been recommended, I presume, by the bass player who was with them at the time. But I thought, if I do this tour with them, I'd earn some money over a short period and then I'd come back and have lost all that I've built up, so I turned it down. This would have been about 1984. Eventually, they came back to me because the bass player they had went away one time too often, so they said, "Right, you do it!"

'I was always a fan of The Hollies, and so were all of my friends. The way we all looked at it, The Hollies could actually play. They had this great drummer, a great vocalist and a great guitarist. It was all there.

'The first gig I ever did with them, which was in Bradford, always sticks with me because it was the first time that I'd met them. I'd met Tony, I had been to his house to run through some of the songs, but this was the first time I had met all the band together. It was kind of a strange sensation, me actually playing up there alongside these guys that I idolised.'

31st January 1987: The Royal Albert Hall, London
6th February 1987: The Royal Spa Centre, Leamington Spa
7th February 1987: The Cliffs Pavilion, Westcliff-on-Sea
13th February 1987: The Plaza, Exeter
14th February 1987: The Arts Centre, Poole
15th February 1987: The Fairfield Hall, Croydon
20th February 1987: The Royal Concert Hall, Nottingham
21st February 1987: The Ritz Theatre, Lincoln
22nd February 1987: The Theatre Royal, Norwich
25th February 1987: The Corn Exchange, Cambridge
26th February 1987: The White Rock Theatre, Hastings
27th February 1987: The Orchard, Dartford
28th February 1987: The Leisure Centre, Crawley
4th March 1987: The Hippodrome, Bristol
6th March 1987: The Apollo, Manchester
7th March 1987: The Southport Theatre, Southport
8th March 1987: The Grand Theatre, Wolverhampton
13th March 1987: The Guildhall, Preston
14th March 1987: The Harrogate Centre, Harrogate
15th March 1987: The Arcadia Theatre, Llandudno
27th March 1987: The Assembly Hall, Tunbridge Wells
28th March 1987: The Hexagon, Reading
29th March 1987: The Guildhall, Portsmouth
30th March 1987: The Derngate Centre, Northampton
3rd April 1987: The Capitol Theatre, Aberdeen
4th April 1987: The Playhouse, Edinburgh
5th April 1987: The Pavilion Theatre, Glasgow
10th April 1987: The Marlowe Theatre, Canterbury
11th April 1987: The Marlowe Theatre, Canterbury
12th April 1987: The Pavilion Theatre, Worthing

A large dose of nostalgia was just what the audience ordered as The Hollies turned back the musical clock 25 years at the Marlowe Theatre. For more than two hours, they charmed the sell-out crowd with songs spanning three decades on one of the last dates of their UK tour, and the expectant hundreds, mainly '60s diehards curious to see if time had caught up with the supergroup, were not disappointed.

From the moment The Hollies emerged dramatically on stage through the haze of dry ice and dazzle of laser beams, it seemed obvious they had lost none of their sparkle. Golden oldies were what the people had come to hear, and hit after hit was delivered with a crispness matched only by the rapturous applause which greeted the end of each song.

No one seemed to mind when lead singer Allan Clarke, one of the three original members in the line-up, coyly admitted the years had taken their toll on his ability to reach the higher notes.

During many songs he brought memories flooding back as he joined forces with Tony Hicks and newcomer Alan Coates in the three-part harmony which has become The Hollies' trademark as they rose to fame.

The standing ovation given to the group at the end of the performance was testimony to their continuing popularity.

*Herne Bay Gazette*
April 1987

After a brief rest following the culmination of the tour, the band took the long flight down under to undertake a series of shows around Australia, including a return visit to the 2,500-seat Melbourne Concert Hall.

'We're on the road about five months of the year,' commented Bobby when the band appeared on Channel 7's weekend show *Sounds Unlimited*, soon after arriving. 'We just finished a UK tour. That was very good. We started at the Albert Hall and packed that out. Then we had two weeks' rest before we came here...'

'We're not using support bands,' Tony added. 'We're doing the whole show ourselves. It's about two and a half hours, although we do have an interval in the middle. But in Brisbane on the first night, we got up to nearly three hours...' to which Allan exclaimed, 'We're just trying to beat Bruce Springsteen!'

'We do some of the songs pretty much as they were originally recorded in the '60s or the '70s,' continued Tony. 'Or if the mood feels right, the three frontline vocalists just take over with an acoustic guitar and we just throw a few around, but some of those early songs sound really good with sort of an '80s treatment…'

According to reports, a number of venues on the Australian tour were played out to considerably less than full houses, and the group were clearly in need of something to drive some focus back in their direction. Despite the impressive length of their concert appearances, giving more than value for money, the endless weeks of touring without any current hit product was considerably reducing the draw for the paying customer. And whatever it was they needed, they needed it soon.

Returning to the UK, within twelve months, they received just that.

# CHAPTER THIRTY-THREE

# "STAND BY ME..."

'We're halfway through an album!' Tony Hicks had announced from the stage, during the sell-out show at London's Royal Albert Hall at the start of the year. He sounded optimistic. Ten months later, and as the autumn leaves of 1987 began to fall, the band were once again without a record deal. The distribution arrangement with Columbia Records had borne little fruit and, after three unsuccessful releases for the media giant, they had parted ways, the proposed album plans never getting any farther than the prestigious floorboards of the South Kensington concert hall. Hushed words over a potential second *Hollies Live* album had also been whispered but had equally failed to find realisation. Instead, the group turned to resources outside of their native UK shores.

Whilst October saw former members Terry Sylvester and Bernie Calvert reunite to play a one-off show at the Old Loughtonions Hockey Club in Chigwell, Essex, entertaining the small gathering with a 50-minute run through of a few familiar hits, the current line-up of The Hollies were to be found on the European mainland, having reached an agreement with the Coconut Records label, a small independent German-based company founded in 1981, located in Hennef (Sieg) on the western side of the country. Based at the label's own Coconut Studios, the group initially added vocals to a pre-prepared track for 'Stand By Me', a new song co-composed by the label co-founder Tony Hendrik, alongside musical associates Jürgen Brinckmann, Hans Jürgen Fritz and Klaus-Dieter Gebauer. This driving slab of euro-pop, produced by the Brinckmann-Fritz-Gebauer triumvirate, complete with a wild saxophone solo, was originally taped for the soundtrack to the award-winning German-language film *Die Katze* (released in January of 1988). Having added their vocals during a visit to Köln, with Alan Coates filling out the harmonies once more, and then completing additional instrumental work at Abbey Road in London, it was duly issued during February as a Hollies German-only Coconut 45, distributed via Ariola.

The Hollies: "Stand By Me" (Coconut 109-664)
Almost constantly on tour, the Hollies even to this day experience a constant influx of new fans. With Allan Clarke (vocals), Bobby Elliott (drums), Tony Hicks (guitar, vocals) and Alan Coates (bass, vocals), The Hollies still produce their songs as fresh as they ever have.

And so their most recent recording, 'Stand By Me', has the best chance to get them back into the singles charts. This full-bodied pop song, which is also featured in the latest Götz Georg cinematic thriller "Die Katze", was featured in the top-rated ARD show "Formula 1", tipped as a likely hit.

Moreover, The Hollies were guests with 'Stand By Me' on the ZDF shows "Na Siehste" on 17th February and "Tele-As" on 25th February. In the spring of 1988, 'Stand By Me' can also be heard as the intro music of a new episode of the popular ARD crime series "The Investigator".

Coconut/Ariola Promotional Release

Despite the promotion and effort put into the release by both the group and the label, including an additional TV appearance on *Formel Eins* (a German 1980s equivalent of *Top of the Pops*), along with the inclusion on the Ariola Records *Die Katze* movie soundtrack, the single stuttered just outside the German GfK Top 50 charts.

The flip-side of the 45 had been another new recording, this time coming from the Allan Clarke and Gary Benson songwriting team. Partially cut at Denis Haines' home studio under the premise of a Clarke solo project, and finished at Abbey Road, 'For What It's Worth, I'm Sorry' fell somewhat short of hit material itself, due to the rather tame production and arrangement rendering it distinctly unmemorable (other than a keyboard solo referencing the harmonica intro to 'He Ain't Heavy, He's My Brother'), and destroying what was, potentially, a pleasant enough song underneath.

Down, but not broken, the band immediately returned to the studio in Hennef, cutting the backing tracks for two further songs during April of 1988, with production overseen by Tony Hendrik. Then, having fulfilled several concert bookings across the country, with Alan Coates once again filling out the vocal mix, attention moved across to St John's Wood in London where the vocals were layered down. 'Your Eyes', the first of the new tracks, was another Hendrik offering, pleasant but unspectacular adult-orientated rock, and yet most of the time and attention appeared to go into what would become the lead side for the next German 45.

Despite the increasing age gap between the reconstituted group members, the youthful Alan Coates was becoming an essential part of the team. His voice blended sweetly alongside the harmony mix of Allan and Tony, and whilst he was never going to integrate himself to the level of Nash- or Sylvester-status – progress and opportunity had changed rapidly since the heady 1960s and '70s pop-rock era – his contributions to the set-up highlighted his value and importance during such a rocky period.

'Alan is a lovely guy, he plays great guitar, he's a great harmony singer, and he's good to have around,' noted Bobby.

According to the detailed sleevenotes that later appeared in the EMI compilation *The Long Road Home*, Coates would always warm up at the band's live sound checks by breaking into the Nils Lofgren composition, 'Shine Silently', a track featured on the composer's *Nils* album from 1979 (and prior to him successfully joining Bruce Springsteen's E Street Band). A wonderful song, with a glorious hook line, ideal for the traditional sound of the Hollie-harmony, the band worked on it in the studios during April and May (having briefly toyed with it in a live setting). The plan was to issue it as an early summer 7" single (Coconut 109-981), with an extended mix, complete with a magnificent *a cappella* introduction, featuring on a 12" release (Coconut 60-981).

Built around a gentle guitar introduction, with some electronic percussion supporting Bobby's heavily echoed snare, the arrangement benefitted from a non-overindulgence in synthesisers and general keyboard wizardry. Too much had been lost in recent years to the effects of technology (the *What Goes Around* album being a perfect example), so it was good to hear The Hollies take it back to their core essentials.

Ray Stiles' bass-playing, in particular, stood out, running some nifty riffs along the neck, whilst Tony also put in a sweet solo, avoiding the need to overemphasise the opportunity to let loose.

With a 7" picture sleeve that confirmed the "official" line-up of Clarke, Hicks, Elliott and Coates, the group took to the promotional circuit to awaken attention towards their new release. Appearing on the German TV shows *Fernsehgarten* and *Die Pyramide* to promote the single, they turned in the professional appearances they were accustomed to, decked out in 1980s *Miami Vice* finery – the shades, the rolled-up jacket sleeves, shoulder pads.

However, back in the UK, something was stirring…

Sixteen years earlier, The Hollies had seen a massive boost to their fading reputation when, due to public demand, Epic Records in the US had seen fit to belatedly issue the twelve-month-old 'Long Cool Woman (In A Black Dress)' as a single, giving the band an instantaneous, and surprising, #2 hit across the country. Five years later, in a similar scenario (and this time on home soil), the *Hollies Live Hits* LP had rejuvenated interest in the ailing band when, following a massive TV campaign, the public had placed the release high up in the album charts.

Unbelievably, the same result happened again the following year when *20 Golden Greats* took the British public by storm and, high on a wave of nostalgia, placed them near the very pinnacle of the UK listings, topping out at #2.

Once? Yes, that was all very well. Twice? Impressive stuff indeed. Three times? Incredible, but surely no more than persistent good fortune? A fourth time? Surely not…

July 1988 had seen a new promotional 7" single appear on the EMI/ Parlophone label, re-pressed for marketing purposes from an earlier 1982 EMI 7" reissue programme (PMS-1001 from the Past Master Series), to coincide with a new television advertisement for Miller Lite beer.

Shipped to the publicity agents charged with promoting the beer, the agency then packaged the single up within a newly designed Miller Lite gatefold sleeve, which bore the words:

*£1.8 million to be spent on TV from August 8th to September 3rd.*

Miller Lite has captured the mood of today's more discriminating public. The clean light taste of Miller Lite is in harmony with the demand for a bright for a lighter lifestyle – heavy is out!

And now, in tune with the taste of today, Miller Lite introduces a great new advertising campaign.

In the tradition of Miller Lite's memorable original advertising, the new commercial speaks straight to the people who matter most.

Amusing, witty and, above all, attention-getting, the commercial includes the backing of the unforgettable classic 'He Ain't Heavy, He's My Brother' sung by The Hollies.

Just to remind you we included a copy of this great song with the comments of Miller Lite. Enjoy it.

The only thing heavy about this commercial is the advertising budget.

Presumably, EMI then sat back in their comfortable Manchester Square offices, believing that was all that was required of them. The single was duly distributed throughout the pubs and clubs around the country and folks were happy with their pint of the refreshing, chilled beverage. What no one could have imagined was the response from the general public once the TV advertising kicked in.

Needless to say, with such a heavy campaign built around it – and an amusing advertisement alongside – the British population took the song, now nineteen years old, back into their hearts. Realising the interest and demand for the single, EMI ramped up the pressing plants again and officially re-released the re-release (EM74) during late August of 1988. Within four weeks, it was sitting in the pole position of the UK charts, knocking Phil Collins and his version of 'Groovy Kind Of Love' off the top spot, remaining there the following week, before giving way to U2's 'Desire'. Continuously promoted on television screens across the country, night after night, the single remained in the Top 100 for over three months.

Reacting to the sudden demand with efficiency, and with the cash registers ringing in their ears, EMI immediately packaged an impressive 2-LP, 36-song set, *All The Hits & More: The Definitive Collection*. Also issued as a 40-track double compact disc selection, covering the years 1963-1980, it was an impressive aural delight as one hit rattled into another in chronological order. Even the latter-day period songs, which briefly took in the *Russian Roulette*, Mike Batt-era and (on the CD set) *Buddy Holly* releases, blended in nicely together, showing the progress and maturity of the band as the collection travelled through the years. Whilst not selling in huge quantities – after all, how many customers still needed such a collection after the incredible sales figures of *20 Golden Greats*? – it still achieved a respectable #51 placing in the UK.

Up to that point in time, there had been dozens of collections released of Hollies material, predominantly covering the clean-cut days of the 1960s hits. EMI, and latterly Polydor, had not only issued plenty under their own respective banners, at home and abroad (*Twenty Greatest Hits, 1963-1970, The Very Best, Long Cool Woman, The Other Side of The Hollies, Best of the EPs, Story of The Hollies, 40 Greatest Hits*), but had also licensed them out on numerous occasions to budget labels – resulting in cheaper, poorly packaged releases springing up in all four corners of the globe (*Hits of The Hollies, Listen to The Hollies, The Fantastic Hollies, In Gold, The Hollies Collection, Hottest Hits, Super Hits*).

Unlike The Beatles, who had ridden the crest of '60s mania alongside Manchester's finest exports, and who had vehemently controlled their output and subsequent releases through their own Apple label, The Hollies, under the management guidance of Robin Britten for many years, had pretty much left their record labels to do as they pleased. Within reason. Allan, Tony, Bobby – and, in earlier years, Graham, Eric, Bernie and Terry – had always maintained control over what was actually taken from the vaults. They owned the actual recordings – not only benefitting financially from the arrangements. They would only permit music they approved of into general circulation. So, it came to the delight of numerous Hollie collectors around the world when, on the reverse of the picture sleeve for the 'He Ain't Heavy, He's My Brother' re-issue, it listed the previously unreleased flip-side, 'Carrie' (from the 1981 John Miles-produced sessions), as coming from an imminent *Rarities* set.

When it did appear in November of 1988, *Rarities*, a 17-track collection, issued in LP, cassette and CD formats, compiled by the band's very own archivist, Mr Robert Elliott, and EMI producer Mike Heatley, brought a number of rarer tracks, along with many previously unreleased recordings, out into the public eye for the very first time. Encompassing the Nash, Sylvester and post-Sylvester years, the magnificent set only went to highlight the wealth of great material that the band kept locked away for varying reasons. 'Mexico Gold', 'Eleanor's Castle', 'Tomorrow When It Comes', 'Relax', 'Sanctuary', and the wonderful Rickfors-*Romany*-era outtake 'If It Wasn't For The Reason That I Love You' were, at times, breathtaking revelations and left the band's fan and collector circuit salivating for more.

Not that the band had too much time to reflect on such past glories, for during the autumn and early winter months of 1988 they were once again hard at work, promoting the surprise success of 'He Ain't Heavy…' to British audiences.

Live performances on the BBC's *Top of the Pops* for three consecutive weeks kept the band in the public eye, as did a televised appearance on behalf of the charity Sport Aid, participating in a massive outdoor concert held at Hillsborough Park in Sheffield on 11th September, performing alongside Big Country, Squeeze, The Proclaimers, Heaven 17, Womack & Womack and Eddy Grant.

They also had their own sell-out tour running throughout October to December, with each night culminating in three encores – plus the surprise inclusion of one particular cover song that would remain as a part of the setlist for several more years.

### The Guildhall, Preston

The Hollies packed the Guildhall with 2,500 people, one week after Des O'Connor only managed to pull in 500. But it was a very sedate affair, and the #1 hit 'He Ain't Heavy…' didn't come until the first of three encores when, at last, the middle-aged fans came to life. Singer Allan Clarke, who had the audience in stitches with his comic patter, said, 'If anyone had told us three months ago that we were going to be Number One, I wouldn't have believed them!'

Surprisingly, a cover version of Prince's 'Purple Rain' went down better than some of the band's own '60s originals, and keyboard wizard Denis Haines nearly stole the show with a spectacular medley of pop classics.

*The Sun*
October 1988

### The Royal Albert Hall, London

In a business where 25 weeks is a long time under the spotlight, The Hollies celebrate their Silver Jubilee with a chart-topping reissue of

'He Ain't Heavy, He's My Brother', aided by a beer commercial, and a two-month tour, which should have ended at the Royal Albert Hall on November 26, has had to be extended to meet popular demand.

A simulated November fog was followed by a green light as Allan Clarke, Tony Hicks, Bobby Elliott plus Alan Coates, Denis Haines and Ray Stiles came on stage. Clarke's distinctive, at times dramatic, voice was at its best on the poignant 'Soldier's Song', his black Spanish-like suit giving him a continental air. Then 'Stay' was the first of a batch of songs performed by just a frontline of Clarke, Coates and Hicks, their so distinctive Hollies' harmonies blending to good effect.

After 'Sorry Suzanne', The Hollies successfully trod the path between making it a nostalgia show and a contemporary affair by doing a nice job on Prince's 'Purple Rain', with the spotlight on the eternal youthful Hicks and his guitar.

Haines' superb keyboards work was a hit of the evening, and he really let go on 'Draggin' My Heels', which developed into a jam session. Then it was a hits medley with the group trying to please all the fans.

Clarke displayed his harmonica-playing and Tony his banjo skills before it was time for 'The Air That I Breathe' and 'He Ain't Heavy, He's My Brother', which was greeted with a standing ovation in places. After a rock and roll finale, The Hollies disappeared, leaving the fans wanting more.

*The Stage*
December 1988

However, despite the renewed interest in the band, built upon the success of the 'He Ain't Heavy, He's My Brother' re-release, which in turn resulted from the tie-in with Miller Lite, the reasonings didn't always sit comfortably with at least one member of the band – a recovering alcoholic.

'I didn't like that at all,' says Allan today. 'I'm no longer a drinking man myself, and they tried to portray us in the ad, with the long heavy coat and things like that… I thought it was a great advertising thing, but because it was for alcohol it didn't go with the sentiment of the song. It's a spiritual song, it a help-each-other song. I didn't write it. I wish I had, but the two guys who did write it got it straight, right the way through.

'It's about a place in America that does exist called Boys Town, where these guys take in all the orphans, educate them, and then they all leave at sixteen. They all have a ring, and on the ring there's an emblem of a guy carrying a child, and inside the ring there's a saying, "He ain't heavy, Lord, he's my brother". That's a true story. I'm glad that Tony found it on some publisher's desk. Those lyrics needed to be heard.'[45]

Hoping to capitalise on the success for themselves, EMI Records, somewhat unsurprisingly, picked the obvious contender as a follow-up re-release. Sadly, lightning didn't strike twice, or for a fifth time – that was too much to hope for – and 'The Air That I Breathe' limped to a lowly #60 on the back of all the recent publicity.

With the extended sell-out UK tour seeing out the remainder of the year, 1988 faded away, having left a few surprises *en route*, and the new year began with the six-man line-up of Clarke, Hicks, Elliott, Coates, Haines and Stiles reconvening at the Abbey Road studios to see if they could continue the momentum. Together they cut the gorgeous 'Find Me A Family', a song composed by Allan and Gary Benson to highlight the issues surrounding adoption and fostering throughout the UK. Utilised as the theme song to an ITV series, *Find A Family*, that was broadcast across the UK between 1989 and 1991, the song, and the televised programme, was an appeal to rehome disadvantaged children across the nation.

"Find Me A Family' wasn't originally written as a single,' explained Allan for the *Long Road Home* CD-box sleevenotes. 'I wrote that with different lyrics but then I was approached by ITV who were doing this programme, which was to help get children adopted. They wanted The Hollies to record a song for it, so I went to Gary and we changed the lyrics. ITV loved it and so did EMI.'

Coupled with the raunchy Clarke-Hicks rhythm of 'No Rules', dominated by a Hicks-fuelled grungy guitar blues riff, the combination was released through EMI on 13th February 1989, and peaked at #79 during a brief, frustrating two-week appearance in the UK charts.

'We were never convinced it was right as a single,' Tony was to recall. 'The song was good but because of the subject, it was a bit of a downer.'[5]

Yet, despite such reservations, the release deserved a far wider audience, and not just for charity purposes, as the overall performance was a fine return to form for a band who, in recent years, had been left gasping for air, clutching at straws to find an identity. Amongst those fortunate enough to make the purchase, it was a moment of discovery for many, and not just for the tender sentimentality of the lead side. The pseudo-ZZ Top boogie that graced the flip was just too frustrating – in that it needed to be longer, *far* longer, to explore such an exciting new territory for the band. It sounded like a simple studio throwaway, a studio jam – and it possibly was – tracked during one session on 10th January, but it held far more within its brief three minutes' running time. And it certainly showed that old dogs wouldn't die. This band still had life left in it. If only they would recognise it…

For the next few years, The Hollies relied heavily on touring commitments, as opportunities for new recordings became fewer and further between. As the last 45 had suggested, they still had the ability and passion when the willingness took them, but the drive to do it was, perhaps, forgotten in the need to survive.

At one point, revisiting their extensive catalogue and recording newly reworked versions of some of the hits was suggested. It was certainly a popular option at the time and, indeed, had been for a while, with a number of bands and artists choosing to follow such a route and avoid the excessive costs of licensing the original master tapes for new projects. As a result, a vast business of small, marketable record labels had popped up throughout all of Europe, whereupon, for the price of a television campaign, or even a newspaper advertisement, thousands of potential purchasers could be reached, all of whom would have the opportunity to obtain their favourite songs from a bygone era, as performed by the "original artists".

Alternatively, record stores had found themselves plagued by a surge of budget-price LPs and labels – Pickwick Records, K-Tel Records, Telstar, Arcade – all packaged cheaply and at prices everyone could afford, and – surprise, surprise – they all featured your favourite songs from a bygone era, and by the original artists! Of course, if the buyer were to pay close enough attention to the sleeve, they may well see the disclaimer, "These selections are re-recordings by the original artists, or by one or more members of the original group", which may have explained why a vast proportion of the recordings didn't sound… quite… right.

Nevertheless, a tie-in between The Hollies and the K-Tel label was discussed, with the temptation of extensive televised advertising included, but the deal stalled with the band unhappy about the financial offer. After dragging on for too long (and thankfully, for many a fan), the whole project was abandoned.

The final recording sessions of the decade had seen one last German-only single issued, the A-side of which, 'Baby Come Back', had been composed and produced by the Hamburg-based pairing of Hanno Harders and Holger-Julian Copp. Working alongside lyricist Gerald Heinemann, the collaboration had initially resulted in a television commercial for cat food, sung in German (with vocals by Copp). The song was then extended into a full English language variation, with lyrics by American poet Mary Susan Applegate (lyricist for the million-selling Jennifer Rush hit 'The Power Of Love'), before The Hollies contributed their vocal touch on top at the Abbey Road Studios. All of this added up to a German radio and airplay hit for the band when released on the WEA label, although the eventual chart peak of #58 was a disappointment in comparison.

Appearing on a couple of German television shows to promote the record, *Hit Parade* and *Eurotops*, the most notable feature was the fact that out of the official Hollies line-up, only Allan and Tony had made the journey across to film the two shows. Bobby was reportedly ill at the time, and so Canadian-born drummer Rennie Hatzke (a member of the popular German band Münchner Freiheit) sat in his place for the filming, and as Holger-Julian Copp had added his vocals to the original harmony mix, and was a familiar face to the watching German viewers, he also appeared alongside, playing rhythm guitar and lip-synching the harmony lines. It made for confusing viewing.

Copp also appeared with Allan, Tony and Bobby in the official promotional video of the 45, filmed in the South of France at WEA's expense, although his appearance did little to aid sales for what is essentially three minutes of torturous Euro-pop. Moving on...

The B-side to the release was a different ball game altogether.

On 15th April 1989, ninety-six people had tragically died, crushed to death due to disastrous overcrowding at an English football match, held at the Hillsborough Stadium in the city of Sheffield. The match that day, a cup game between Liverpool FC and Nottingham Forest, was abandoned part-way through as many of the panicking supporters were squeezed against the surrounding barriers, unable to move as more and more fans pushed onto the terracing from behind. It was a terrible catastrophe. Unable to breathe, many bodies were laid out on the turf as they were pulled from the melee. Watching the game that day, safe in the upper seated levels of the stadium, was Terry Sylvester, an avid supporter of his hometown team.

The entire country was in shock as details of the day were revealed across the wire channels of the world. The public was openly moved, as was songwriter, guitarist and singer for The Hollies, Tony Hicks, who penned a moving tribute to the memory of those who perished. Co-credited to Allan Clarke, 'Hillsborough', featuring a rare mid-tempo outing for Tony's lead vocals, was uncomplicated and yet moving, taken in context. The direct simplicity of the composition, and that of the Hicks production, was all that needed to be said.

*

With a new decade having arrived, the fourth in which The Hollies were actually involved as a band, the music business was finally beginning to reassess and reflect upon the catalogue of recordings the original Manchester-based quintet had produced throughout the years. For far too long, the big hits had dominated the re-releases and the re-issues, with scant attention being paid to the vast wealth of material that lay dormant on long-deleted album releases. Finally, with the arrival of the reviving compact disc format back in the early part of the 1980s, the back catalogues from many of the great artists of the preceding decades were being re-examined, the sound was cleaned up, and they were lovingly (in the main) being re-issued to an eagerly awaiting public, keen to rediscover the sounds of the previous generation.

BGO Records, a small independent label in the UK specialising in classic rock, folk and jazz, were the first to realise the potential of the Hollies catalogue, outside of the innumerable EMI compilations that swamped the market. Over the course of the next few years, they would issue many of the band's original albums on both vinyl and compact disc, with both original mono and stereo editions (subject to format) quenching the thirst of both the curious and the devoted.

It was a good time to rediscover.

# CHAPTER THIRTY-FOUR

# "I NEVER MEANT TO CAUSE YOU ANY SORROW..."

It had been Tony Hicks who first came up with the concept of the band performing Prince's 'Purple Rain'. The opening guitar lick to the 1984 hit by Minneapolis' resident funkmaster, had been one that he was toying with during a pre-concert rehearsal two years previously, and the idea of performing the song in their show had appealed to the band. They also briefly worked up a version of Prince's 'When Doves Cry', but swiftly dropped that one from the set. Not that they needed to add external material into their shows; they had enough of their own to build upon but the general idea, and the arrangement they worked up for 'Purple Rain', allowing both Tony and Alan Coates the opportunity and space to deliver scintillating solos, sounded good. And the audiences duly agreed, giving the song a rapturous reception each night.

The Hollies had always utilised cover versions within live shows, to the frustration of many, to the enjoyment of others, and the 1980 tours were no different. Sandwiched in between medleys of their hits, along with a few that were deemed worthy of the full treatment, 'On A Carousel', 'Stop! Stop! Stop!' and a delightful new arrangement of 'We're Through', the new setlist incorporated renditions of rock 'n' roll favourites, 'Johnny B Goode', 'Heartbreak Hotel', 'Peggy Sue' and 'Maybe Baby', Graham's 'Wasted On The Way' and The Who's 'Pinball Wizard'. In addition to 'Purple Rain' there was also a wonderful arrangement of 'Whiter Shade Of Pale' that simply cried out for a recorded version.

Starting with a simple three-part vocal harmony, manoeuvering around the familiar theme of the timeless Procol Harum song, Allan then delivered a stunningly beautiful lead, accompanied only by the chiming sounds of Tony's guitar. It was only partway through the arrangement that Bobby's drums and Denis' synthesised organ rang out across the halls to tumultuous cheers.

Taking the show back out on the road again, with the returning Steve Stroud taking over the bass role once more, January and February saw them visiting regular haunts along the German circuit. They then followed this up with an extensive thirty-five-date tour around the UK, starting in Lincoln's Ritz Theatre on 1st March, immediately followed by a night at Wembley's Grand Hall. Having worked their way around the northern regions of Carlisle, Sunderland and Hull, down to the southerly coastal resorts of Portsmouth, Brighton and Bournemouth, they brought the tour to a close, once more, at London's Royal Albert Hall on 12th May, playing to a capacity crowd of 5,200 ecstatic fans. New product or not, the group always managed to turn on the power for their loyal following.

The spirit of Graham Nash lives on but there is a place in the '90s for a band with such a strong instinct for survival. Founder-member Nash quit as long ago as 1968, yet former schoolmate, Allan Clarke, lead singer, was still giving him a mention or two last night.

No one had any complaints about a set of more than two hours which features just about everything. No stage frills or mammoth right lighting rig but plenty of the usual chat and those distinctive harmonies.

Very polished, highly professional.

*Sheffield Star*
April 1990

Meanwhile, Allan Clarke was once again back in the recording studios. Even if the band had no clear intentions of resuming regular sessions as a unit, Allan still had his solo career which, although having kept it in check for the past eight years, he chose to reactivate during late 1989 and into early 1990.

Working with a provisional album title of *Spellbound*, entitled after one of his recent songs, and then relabelled as *Reasons To Believe*, Allan committed at least thirteen new recordings to tape, many of which had evolved from a series of demos he had worked upon with Denis Haines (also including a discarded version of 'When Doves Cry'). Cutting a nice balance between guitar-fed, adult-orientated rock, with a dash of modern synthesised technology, and comprising a selection of self-composed and external contributions, the proposed album moved towards completion and a May 1990 release date. However, unhappy with the final mixes, Allan and his co-producer, Tony Taverner, continued to tinker to their satisfaction, in between Hollie-commitments, working at the Great Linford Manor Studios near Milton Keynes, and delaying the issue until later in the year.

With no media announcements due on any forthcoming Hollies recording projects, it now seemed as if their recording career as a group was on a near-definite hiatus. Neither the band itself nor any recording label seemed hungry enough to commit to the financial implications of a fully-fledged new album. The money, it seemed, was in the constant touring machine. Subsequently, it came as a huge surprise to many, those fortunate enough to be attending the latter half of the recent UK tour, to find a brand-new, exclusive 12" record on offer at the merchandise stalls.

Unavailable in the stores (and before the luxury of online ordering), this limited edition 3-track vinyl and cassette offer suddenly appeared at the venues midway through the tour, featuring (due to fan demand) a studio version of 'Purple Rain', along with two further new cuts, 'Naomi' and 'Two Shadows'. All three songs had been committed to tape during a brief three-day period at Abbey Road during January and were presented in a limited run of only 500 units, packaged in a sleeve featuring black and white etched caricatures of the six band members.

The studio recording of 'Purple Rain' may have lacked a little of the impact that the live variation offered, with Allan supplying a deeper, nasal style to his vocal range, and the visual accompaniment was certainly absent, but fans and collectors leapt upon the release, nonetheless.

'Naomi' was a lightweight, Latin-tinged collaboration between Tony and his young son Paul, a budding musician and studio engineer himself, whilst 'Two Shadows', a leftover from the 1984 Allan Clarke-Peter Vale sessions, still suffered from its original electro-concept, albeit now in a slightly muted context. And if that wasn't enough to placate the dedicated, there was now one other piece of new "product" that Hollie-collectors had to fight to locate.

Pressed with even fewer copies made available (reportedly, less than 200 made it onto the collector's circuit), *Up Front Special Vol. 1: The Coconut Collection and More* was an unofficial 1990 CD issue, compiled by Ulli Eichblatt, the editor of The Hollies' *Up Front* German newsletter. This rarity pulled together all of the German Coconut recordings – including four different variations of 'Stand By Me' and the extended mix of 'Shine Silently', featuring the stunning a cappella intro. Padded out with a smattering of other recent rarities – extended dance mixes of 'Long Cool Woman (In A Black Dress)', 'Draggin' My Heels' and the backing track to 'Find Me A Family' – and despite the unofficial status that hung over it, the collection was recognised for what it was and was dutifully pounced upon by the hardcore collector.

Having just completed a four-day visit to the Middle East, the touring band suffered a recent blow when the talented Denis Haines decided to step away from the keyboard position, prior to the UK tour, opting to follow a route into studio work for television arrangement and composing. In his shoes, and following in the mighty footsteps of Wingfield and Arnesen, had come Dave Carey who, alongside Steve Stroud, had also contributed to the 'Purple Rain' sessions.

The Hollies' concert line-up had maintained a certain amount of fluidity during the preceding years, with both the keyboard and bass responsibilities fluctuating at times, from tour to tour. At one point during the mid-1980s, Venezuelan instrumentalist Durban Laverde had taken on the bass role as a Hollie for a series of UK dates, in between his commitments with Jimmy Page, whilst former Aztec Camera founder member Bernie Clarke had also been added to provide an additional keyboard role, prior to Haines' departure.

'Alan Coates and I had been signed to a publishing deal in 1979 and he asked me and Durban to do it,' Clarke would later recall. 'It was a whole tour of English dates, mostly Midlands We didn't have any rehearsals, just quick sketches of the songs on scraps of paper!'

Additionally, for one particularly notable tour, the band discarded the stringed bass completely, utilising Clarke as an additional keyboard player to handle the bass notes on his vast bank of keys. It wasn't a particularly successful venture and by 1991, a sense of stability had slowly begun to emerge, with Steve Stroud returning to his Cliff Richard obligations and the familiar sight of Ray Stiles back at the rear of the stage, bass guitar firmly in hand.

Allan Clarke, meanwhile, now with time on his hands after the current round of Hollies tours had been completed, had continued with the final mixes for his upcoming solo album. Making its appearance in Germany on the Polydor label during the late autumn of 1990, after several false starts, there were initially no confirmed plans for any further worldwide distribution. Eleven tracks appeared on the vinyl edition, with a bonus cut appearing on the CD. A thirteenth song appeared as the flip-side to the advance 45 release, the lead side of which was co-written by Hollie bandmate Alan Coates.

'Reasons To Believe In', the album opener, as well as being the lead-off 45, was a great piece of commercial AOR, featuring some fine Coates guitar work and a catchy chorus that drew the listener in. The accompanying B-side, 'Without Love', in a slightly poppier vein, saw composing credits going to Scottish brothers Iain and Gavin Sutherland, along with their former colleagues from the band Quiver, and highlighted how commercially driven this album was. The production by Allan and Tony Taverner was both clean and crisp, and the instrumentation – performed mainly by session player Steve Pigott – was equally as slick and polished. Ably accompanied by guitarists Alan Coates, Steve Byrd and Jim Williams, along with a gathering of experienced session vocalists – Alan Coates, Ray Calcutt, Carol Cook and Katie Humble (plus two of Allan's children, Toby and Piper) – Allan selected a strong collection of songs, including four of his own compositions – 'Spellbound', 'Catch 22 Situation', 'Caught in The Act' and 'Love Moves In Mysterious Ways' – all written in partnership with the reliable Gary Benson. However, with the two strongest cuts, 'Reasons To Believe In' and 'Spellbound', both falling short in the German singles market, the album saw little support and failed to garner any release elsewhere, with only German import copies reaching the stores on UK soil. Bowing out gracefully, that would be Allan's final solo release for nigh on thirty years.

He would remain active outside of The Hollies, participating in the filming of the second series of ITV's *Find A Family*, or even acting as treasurer for his local neighbourhood's parish church, but his solo career was effectively put out to pasture. Or so he thought.

For the remainder of the decade, The Hollies ploughed on in their interminable way. Touring took up a large portion of each new year, with the short-lived residency of Dave Carey soon coming to an end. Paul Bliss briefly returned to fill out the keyboard station before the Scottish-born ivory-tinkler Ian Parker (previously with The Tom Robinson Band and a regular sideman for Clannad) then came aboard to add his touches of magic to the sound, replacing Bliss, who had commitments elsewhere with The Moody Blues.

'I played with local rock bands in Ayrshire and then studied music at the Royal Scottish Academy of Music and Drama before moving to London in 1977,' comments Ian, when discussing his musical background. 'I started doing studio session work and then, after replying to an ad in the *New Musical Express*, joined The Tom Robinson Band. This was the height of the punk era, and it was really exciting to play with a band of that calibre. With TRB, I got to playing a lot of keyboard solos on Hammond and Moog and doing a lot of backing vocals. When I joined Clannad, I was more in the background but provided the big keyboard sounds and samples that bond the music together, as well as a lot of the harmonies.

'When I first joined The Hollies back in 1991, there were keyboard arrangements and sounds that the band were used to hearing, so I incorporated them with my own ideas, including a lot more Hammond organ. Generally, I tried to stay close to the parts that were on the records, including the wonderful orchestral arrangements of Johnny Scott on 'He Ain't Heavy', 'Midas', 'I Can't Tell The Bottom From The Top' and 'The Air That I Breathe'. I also started to interpret 'Sandy' a little bit different every night. Tony and Bobby are open to ideas…' [57]

Unfortunately, recording as a band remained intermittent. New compilations appeared as regular as clockwork, tying in nicely with the ongoing reissues of the original albums, courtesy of BGO Records. The latest batch included *Love Songs* (on EMI), *The Other Side Of… Plus* (on the See for Miles label) and the US release on Epic of *Anthology (From The Original Master Tapes)*. The latter two were particularly noteworthy for featuring rare additions to the catalogue; the original 1968 Nash-led version of 'Blowin' In The Wind' and a previously unreleased acoustic take of 'Magic Woman Touch' from 1972. Regardless, it was new material that the majority of fans wanted.

The summer 1991 edition of *Carousel* announced that Allan and Tony had ventured back into the Abbey Road studios to add their vocals to a various artists charity recording featuring, amongst the stellar line-up, Graham Nash. It was reportedly intended for the follow-up album to *Nobody's Child: Romanian Angel Appeal*, a various artists compilation, pulled together by George and Olivia Harrison. The proposed recording, 'That's Rock 'n' Roll-Ah' was seemingly never heard of again. There were also rumours that the band would reunite with Graham to record some new songs for a proposed multi-CD set, provisionally given the working title of *Treasured Hits and Hidden Treasures*, compiled for an American audience. Again, despite many stories circulating over the coming months, nothing appeared ready to proceed. In fact, the only new material to come out of The Hollies' camp that year was one that virtually no Hollie fan knew about…

The Shamrocks were, and remain, an unknown entity in rock 'n' roll circles. A Hamburg-based band, resident in the city's Chikago Bar and Nightclub, the one CD issued under their name, *Live Highlights,* appeared in 1991 and comprised twelve familiar cover songs (Beatles, Stones, Chuck Berry, etc.), cut in a raucous, live environment. Issued in Germany on the Repertoire label (Repertoire CD RET-8003), that is where their entry into the Rock Files starts and ends – excepting the fact that one of the band on that particular night, listed only as "Tony" on the sleeve, appeared to be none other than Mr Hicks, moonlighting with the group at the club for seemingly no other reason than to have a good time.

His contribution to the show may seem minimal at times, although his prominent slide guitar, particularly on their versions of 'Nutbush City Limits' and 'Jumping Jack Flash', adds a sweet touch.

A German-only vinyl and cassette rarity also appeared during this period, compiled by the German fan club as an alternative to printing the standard *Up Front* fanzine. Featuring a selection of news reports, interviews and rare recordings (including a live outtake of 'Long Cool Woman (In A Black Dress)' from the Shamrocks' Hamburg performance), this release soon disappeared into obscurity and remains highly desired to this day, featuring, as it does, a selection of previously unreleased recordings from a 1982 German Hollies show.

An extensive forty-date UK tour, running through until December, would see out much of the second half of 1991, with Allan debuting his new appearance, his long hair pulled back tightly into a ponytail, and a greying closely cut beard spreading out across his chin. It was also one of the first indications of the decreasing power of his vocal range, something that would cause him concern in the coming years.

> They weren't exactly squealing but just one look from Allan Clarke and the knees of the female adoration society at Wembley Grand Hall quivered. At 49, the vocalist in mustard-coloured designer suit and grey hair in a ponytail can still charm them.
>
> The main highs and lows of the evening lay with Clarke, depending on the degree of difficulty of the vocal lines. There was the occasional oddity, such as a brave attempt at a cover of Prince's 'Purple Rain', with a dry ice machine turning the stage into a dense fog.
>
> 'He Ain't Heavy, He's My Brother' brought a standing ovation. The enthusiastic crowd implored, 'Oh, won't you stay, just a little bit longer?', but it was time for the Horlicks.
>
> *The Daily Express*
> September 1991

At several venues along the route, the band set up recording facilities, using a 24-track mobile unit, and taped a number of the shows for a potential new *Hollies Live* album. The first fruits of this venture was a version of 'Another Night', that swiftly appeared as one of the tracks featured on a new German 4-track CD single, issued to promote Opel cars in the country – the payoff being that the motor company utilised 'The Air That I Breathe', the main focus of the single, on their TV advertisement for the cars. Bobby Elliott was reportedly handed the responsibility of listening to and selecting tracks for the proposed live album, and a version of 'Purple Rain', taped at the Harrogate International Centre on 29th November, would officially appear two years later – but, to much frustration, nothing else resulted from the venture.

1992, meanwhile, would prove to be a very uneventful year. Outside of the occasional live appearance, there was nothing of significance or notoriety within The Hollies' calendar.

The year had kicked off with a live appearance for the top-rated Dutch music radio and TV show *Goud Van Oud*, held before a vast 15,000 audience at the Brabanthal in 's-Hertogenbosch. Footage of the band performing both 'Bus Stop' and 'The Air That I Breathe' was later aired on the popular TV broadcast, whilst the remainder of the set (including covers of Chris Montez's 'Let's Dance', Jerry Lee Lewis' 'Great Balls Of Fire' and McGuinness Flint's folky-singalong 'When I'm Dead And Gone') appeared in full as an unofficial bootleg release soon afterwards. 'When I'm Dead And Gone 'actually appeared midway through the show, featured as part of an "unplugged" acoustic mini-set, as was the current trend for such interludes. With Tony on banjo and mandolin, Allan on acoustic guitar and harmonica and Alan Coates on acoustic guitar, the frontline trio provided a welcoming break to the standard concert format, also playing unaccompanied renditions of both 'If I Were The Priest' and the obscure 1966 B-side 'Running Through The Night'. Other than that, and a low-key run of return appearances at Savva's in South Wales, along with two dates in the distinctly non-salubrious surroundings of the Circus Tavern in Essex, the year passed quietly.

Taking advantage of the downtime, Alan Coates took the opportunity to cut and issue his own debut solo CD. A guitar-led instrumental collection entitled *Wings of Paradise*, rather misleadingly credited to Alan Baker, and distributed via the German Coconut label, its middle-of-the-road approach was smoother than the vast *autobahn* road system that ran throughout the country, and it did little to enhance his reputation amongst fans of the band.

One additional item that also appealed to the collectors that year was the arrival of another live bootleg recording, labelled as *Think Purple*, featuring sixty minutes of performance from the 1990 UK tour. In lieu of any other new material, this high-quality tape soon garnered support and collectability status within the close-knit fan circle. Then again, there was still hope clinging on for the US multi-CD set mentioned the previous year, whilst discussions were also in progress for a UK equivalent:

Founder Hollie Graham Nash is going back in the studio with his old mates for the first time in a decade. And he tells me he scuppered EMI Records' lacklustre plans to cash in on the Manchester group's 30th anniversary next year, by demanding they double the number of tracks to be released.

Says Graham, 'EMI was going to put out a 2-CD box set of The Hollies and I said, "Absolutely not – these guys have cut 500 songs, what do you mean, two? We're insisting on four CDs. For this anniversary, I'm going back in the studio with them and we're going to cut five or six more tracks.'

Alas, there are no plans for Graham to join the other three on a 40-date national tour in the spring, including the Manchester Apollo on May 13th.

*Manchester Evening News*
October 1992

1993 would be The Hollies' 30th anniversary. Few bands could match the longevity, creativity and still pull the crowds to their shows, without resorting to the endless miles of the nostalgia package tour route. Undoubtedly, this was partly down to the fact that the band were self-managed, now in liaison with London Management / Jimmy Smith Agency, who had been handling their affairs since the early 1980s. In agreement with Smith, who began to work with the band directly, they booked shows that they believed in, unlike the earlier days when Robin Britten would book the band either into an endless run of one-nighters or onto demoralising, week-long engagements in smoke-filled chicken-in-a-basket cabaret venues.

America's very own harmonymeisters, The Beach Boys, were one of the few equivalent bands who could claim such a lengthy feat, and their journey followed a very similar pattern to Clarke, Hicks, Elliott and co. Soon enough, their paths would converge on the banks of the River Rhine when the two bands appeared together during June at the Freillichtbuhne Loreley Amphitheatre in St Goarshausen, Germany.

'They're known as America's Hollies!' laughed Tony Hicks when questioned about their US counterparts.[18]

\*

Sadly, The Hollies' former manager, Robin Britten, had passed on in recent years. His health had been in rapid deterioration for a considerable period, despite being only fifty-six years of age, and his love and particularly his taste for the finer things in life had finally caught up with him during January of 1989, eight years after leaving The Hollies' employment.

\*

Approximately one-third of 1993 would be spent out on the road celebrating the 30th anniversary, and a slew of new products on the market would more than make up for the previous twelve months of relative silence.

First up on the market and in the music stores was a brand-new single, issued by EMI on vinyl and CD single format, followed up by EMI's official answer to the 30th anniversary celebrations.

Venturing back into the recording studios (owned by producer Mike Moran) during early January 1993, in what seemed like the first time in an eternity, Allan, Tony, Bobby, Alan, Ray and Ian cut two new recordings. Plans for the proposed studio work alongside Graham had, by now, fallen by the wayside, and the constant delays for a US multi-CD set had pushed the focus towards the upcoming UK collection.

First up was a song composed by US soft-rock heartthrob Richard Marx, 'Nothing Else But Love', a typical example of the big ballad, fist-clenching, heart-pumping rock so popular on the American AOR circuit back then. It only lacked the emphasis of the big hairstyle and the wild guitar solo to have it all.

The second song they tackled was created far more in the Hollies-mould – a catchy pop song, written by the UK's equivalent of Marx, albeit in a smaller package. Nik Kershaw had been an '80s pop star himself, enjoying a series of self-composed Top 10 hits before he began to develop his songwriting abilities, starting to successfully write for other artists. The song he offered up to The Hollies, the commercial-sounding 'The Woman I Love', exemplified the strong melody and instantaneous hook line that the band had specialised in back in their heyday. Allan would later comment that he felt a little uncomfortable with the subject matter, noting that 'I felt a bit silly singing that. I wasn't sure that the lyrics were suitable for a guy of fifty!'[5]

Regardless, when issued as an EMI single during March, 'The Woman I Love', paired with a live version of 'Purple Rain' (recorded during the 1991 UK tour), gave The Hollies their first UK Top 50 hit with a brand-new song for *nineteen* years, peaking at a reasonable #42. It was long overdue. But where *was* that *Hollies Live* album from the 1991 tour? Two years later, with the issue of 'Purple Rain', why hadn't the full set of recordings seen an official release?

'It's still forthcoming!' Bobby would tell *Carousel* contributor Uli Twelker. 'I mean, it's there. We've got too much material that's being released at the moment to contemplate anything, and we're on tour. So, we've still got to get in and mix it. We've got a good guy now called Tony Taverner. I hope that he's going to be involved in the mixing...'

Undertaking the usual round of televised guest spots to promote the release of 'The Woman I Love', coinciding with the launch of the lengthy scheduled UK tour, it all proved to the watching UK audience that this was a band who just wouldn't quit.

Travelling the width and breadth of the country once more, north to south, east to west, the band ran through the gamut of their recording history, although still entertaining the notion that their enthusiastic audiences were happy to hear them reproduce cover versions of other artists' hits. For this venture out, The Doors' 'Riders On The Storm' and even The Beatles' 'Please Please Me' were bandied about.

'We've stopped doing 'Whiter Shade Of Pale' now,' confirmed Tony in the same interview with Twelker. 'But just before the tour started, I was trying to think of something similar to 'Purple Rain'. A song that we can put our own trademark on, without anybody wondering, why are they doing that? And they're loving them. Particularly 'Riders On The Storm'. We don't do anything radical with it, other than the fact we do it—'

'We do it *our* way,' interrupted Allan. 'There is a certain percentage of people who probably wouldn't give 'Purple Rain' the time of day because of who it was done by. What I think, is that we make 'Purple Rain' acceptable to our fans and other people of that ilk, which is the same for 'Riders On The Storm'. I really don't understand the lyrics Jim Morrison wrote, he must have really been out of it when he wrote it, but we made it acceptable in a very positive way. We do it the Hollies way!'[18]

Allan Clarke is about to be a grandad; Tony is a big fan of "The Archers" and there's nothing Bobby likes better than mowing the lawn on a sunny afternoon. They sound like a crew of regulars at a Rotary Club dinner dance. But these three paragons of provincial virtue are members of one of the most successful pop groups in history – The Hollies. And this year they celebrate thirty years together, still packing them in on sell-out nationwide tours.

However, plenty has changed since the days when Allan Clarke, Bobby Elliott and Tony Hicks spent their nights at glitzy showbiz parties and rode around in limousines, pursued by screaming groupies.

Lead singer Allan, now fifty, admits he was a bit of a wild man in his pop heyday. But the likes of Mick Jagger and Bill Wyman would do well to heed Allan's growing-old-gracefully approach to stardom.

'All that madness is in the distant past,' he says. 'I tried drugs, but I didn't like them. I used to drink a lot and it became a problem and I knew I had to quit. Now I love the peace of the country and I'm looking forward to becoming a grandfather for the first time in August.'

Details of the seamier side of life on the road with The Hollies emerged five years ago when Eric Haydock, a member of the band in the early days, sold his story to a newspaper. He branded his fellow musicians as sex-mad bullies who once kept a nymphomaniac groupie hidden in a wardrobe. Flings with singer Marianne Faithfull and DJ Annie Nightingale were also alleged.

'He thought it'd embarrass us, but we were quite proud!' says Tony. 'There was a lot of truth in it, but we weren't a bunch of monks. Just don't talk about the wardrobe!'

*Today*
March 1993

By the end of March, with the band now a third of the way through their punishing schedule, EMI had finally gotten their new 30<sup>th</sup> Anniversary compilation CD out in the shops (CDEMTV-74), except, to the untold disappointment of many, it wasn't the multi-CD set that Graham Nash had hoped for. Other than it being a neatly presented 26-track single CD, it was ultimately little more than a shortened version of the previously issued 2-CD set *All The Hits & More: The Definitive Collection,* in new packaging, and with the added inclusion of the current hit. Alternatively, it could also be viewed as an expanded variation of *20 Golden Greats* – but whichever way you looked at it, it was another version of what most people already had. No additional extras or deep cuts to entice the curious or the obsessive. Nevertheless, with the hefty clout of a major televised campaign, *The Air That I Breathe: The Very Best of The Hollies,* still hit the #15 slot in the album charts with ease – but went no higher.

\*

May 1993 and Allan Clarke, Tony Hicks and Bobby Elliott stood on the small stage at the Grosvenor House Hotel in Park Lane, London, having just received the honour of a prestigious *Ivor Novello* award for their Outstanding Contribution to British Music. It was a worthy honour, and it was nice to see the band finally recognised for the input they had made into the nation's society.

*

Finally, after a succession of promises and delays, fans and collectors on the opposite side of the Atlantic were eventually treated to a new collection of Hollies releases. The much-discussed 3-CD set, now retitled *The Hollies 30th Anniversary Collection (1963-1993)*, courtesy of EMI (USA), had the additional pulling power of five previously unreleased recordings, dating back to the 1960s, one brand-new song, as well as both sides of the current 45. On top of that, and mixed in between the succession of more familiar tunes, came long-forgotten works such as the United Artists 45 'After The Fox', released in 1966 alongside Peter Sellers, and both sides of the obscure Italian single from 1967; 'Kill Me Quick' and 'We're Alive'. Of note, the version of 'Kill Me Quick' included here was the original stereo release of the song that included distinctive backup vocals. The original mono 45 release, from twenty-six years previously, had only featured Allan's lead vocal and had no backup vocals at all.

Of the previously unheard product, it was apparent why some of the tapes had laid undisturbed in the vaults for so long. Neither the 1963 recording of the uncredited 'I Understand', or the 1965 self-composed, sub-Freddie 'I Can't Get Nowhere With You' is comparable to the other works of that era, although the Byrd-ish jangle of 'She Gives Me Everything I Want' shows the direction that the band were heading towards as they turned away from the standardised beat sound of the mid-'60s. Likewise, the third Ransford composition, 'You In My Arms', with its pre-'Paint It Black' picked intro, shows a band that were prepared to attempt differing arrangements to emphasise their music. The fifth song dating back to the Nash era was the impressive 'Man With No Expression', Graham's collaboration with Terry Reid, and one that had suffered from the fallout of Graham's impending departure from the original line-up. Recut by Graham one year later as 'Horses Through A Rainstorm' alongside Crosby, Stills and Young as a potential inclusion for their then-upcoming 1970 *Déjà Vu* album (but ultimately unused), this had also recently appeared as an unreleased bonus on the Atlantic 4-CD *CSN* box – but The Hollies more acoustically arranged rendition won hands down for harmonies.

Richard Marx's 'Nothing Else But Love', cut in the studios five months previously, made up the last of the newer tracks on the collection.

Overseen by Ron Furmanek, EMI's resident CD researcher and compiler in the US, with a detailed discography included, it was a neatly presented package. Yet, unbeknownst to the band members, Furmanek had remixed a number of the original tracks, refining the stereo sound and making them easier on the ear for a modern US audience which, naturally, didn't go down well with Allan, Bobby and Tony.

'They tried to remix a whole lot of stuff,' recounted Allan. "Carrie Anne', 'King Midas In Reverse'. It was done without our knowledge. Even if we had known about it, we'd have said "no" in the first place. And it wasn't only us. There were guys at EMI who found that it had been done, and they were very annoyed about it.'

'It's like rewriting history,' added Bobby. 'It's cheating, isn't it?' [18]

Ron Furmanek later responded that The Hollies had actually liked his initial new mixes of the classic hits, but he believed that EMI in America, who were distributing the product, got cold feet and included only some of the cleaned-up cuts (mostly the B-sides), retaining the poor stereo mixes from previous years on the hits. Certainly, both Imperial Records and Epic in the US were guilty of bastardising variations of the mixes throughout the first decade of the band's career, overemphasising both echo and reverb to suit American taste. Nevertheless, and wherever the blame may lie, the actual song selection across the three discs, with the new rarities added, went some way towards appeasing devoted collectors, even if the mix debacle left a sour taste in the mouths of many. And, it must be noted, the collection still stands out as one of the finer reissue sets that has graced The Hollies' catalogue to date – and Ron Furmanek continues to work with the reissue programme to this very day.

With the UK shows completed, the six-man band took a brief respite from the constant touring, and other than the occasional performance (such as the show in St Goarshausen, Germany on 19th June with The Beach Boys), they rested up. However, come October and they were back out there once again, this time undertaking a second visit around Germany for a further sixteen shows during the next leg of the Anniversary Tour.

All told, 1993 had been a busy year for the band, and it was rounded off with an appearance on BBC TV's *Noel's Christmas Presents*, a show whereupon special "gift" surprises were handed out to deserving viewers. For their part, The Hollies made the day (the month, the year) for Brian Stubbles, a long-time fan of the band who suffered from spina bifida. Without warning, he returned home to find the band ready to perform for him in his back garden. Oh, the emotions of live television…

The success of the two compilation albums – critically and commercially, to certain degrees – the Top 50 achievement of the latest single and overwhelming public interest in the 30th Anniversary Tour, had kept The Hollies at the forefront of the media throughout much of the year. And who was to say, in 1993, that it wouldn't last for another thirty?

# CHAPTER THIRTY-FIVE

---

# "PEGGY SUE GOT MARRIED..."

It has been brought to our attention by a number of The Hollies' fans that they have seen The Hollies advertised at various locations and on purchasing tickets for the show have, in fact, not seen The Hollies, but Eric Haydock and his band. We are extremely concerned this happened.

Although we accept Eric was an original member of The Hollies, it was pointed out to him that he was not allowed to use the name The Hollies or Hollies either on its own, or with other names such as Eric Haydock's Hollies, and to this effect he signed an undertaking on 26th November 1992 confirming this. Regrettably, this undertaking has not been complied with.

The Hollies' legal representatives are currently taking this matter further.

Jimmy Smith

Spring 1994

Since his last encounter with his former bandmates, Eric had remained living in his hometown region of the UK, opening a music retail outlet, The New Rhythm Store, and making occasional live appearances as a member of The New Mindbenders, a band put together by two old stalwarts of the '60s and '70s scene, Michael Carroll and Peter Hughes (but with no connection to the original band). He had previously been a member of a local Stockport band, The Pressmen, back in the 1970s, but this was his first serious venture back into the world of touring, and together with Carroll and Hughes, he would journey around the clubs of Manchester and the north, playing a series of one-nighters, specialising in a '60s setlist filled out with Hollies hits ('I Can't Let Go', 'Yes, I Will', 'Here I Go Again' and 'Just One Look'). Eric even dusted off his old six-string bass that had seen him through many a tour with his original band.

A muck-raking 1988 interview with the UK newspaper *News of the World* had lifted the lid on his feelings towards his former bandmates, and there was certainly no love lost between them.

'I haven't had a bean since the day I left,' he would comment in print. 'Not one of the group has offered me a penny, yet I helped them to a career that has spanned twenty-five years.'

Subsequent years would see The New Mindbenders morph into the Eric Haydock Band and yet, despite the threat of legal action from The Hollies Ltd, promoters would continue to utilise the "Hollies" tagline at venues, even more so once the five-piece band began to expand their touring around the UK, Europe, Scandinavia, America and even Australia. The result was that during mid-1994, the group formally issued a writ against the former colleague.

'I'm very unhappy about the whole affair,' Eric continued. 'We were given the go-ahead by [The Hollies] to use the name Eric Haydock's Hollies. I was a founder member and they can't take my heritage away from me. The whole thing has been blown up out of proportion.'

The presence of Haydock would continue to grind away at the temperament of the surviving band members for the foreseeable, with the October 1997 Annual General Meeting for Hollies Ltd. attended by both Eric and his manager, James Cozens. Together, they worked through the company expenses, seeking remuneration on behalf of Eric, whilst also aiding former drummer Don Rathbone with previous outstanding royalty payments. Throughout much of the 1980s and on into the next decade, both Bernie Calvert and Terry Sylvester had received payments from the company, as had Graham Nash, but both Haydock and Rathbone had been noticeably absent from the fees and commissions payable.

However, for the performing entity that was The Hollies, the remainder of the 1990s passed by without much attention from the media. Certainly, at least, they received nowhere near the amount of publicity as that which had accompanied the 1993 tour.

Each year, the band would go out on a regular UK tour, playing to anywhere between twenty and forty venues, each one packed to the rafters with their loyal fan following, happy to hear the band churn out their many hits, mixing them in alongside the now-regular cover versions. Alongside 'Purple Rain', the mid-'90s setlists would also see such favourites as 'Born To Run', 'Norwegian Wood', 'Light My Fire', 'Woman' and 'Runaway' added into the two-hour stage routines. Additionally, the quarterly issues of the *Carousel* fan magazine continued to roll off the presses, keeping the well informed up to date with the band's movements, whilst reviewing the seemingly endless supply of new compilations that constantly appeared on UK shores from all over the planet.

As demands necessitated, the band would still add the occasional foreign visit to the schedule. 1994 would see a visit to the Far East, followed by a series of shows in Austria, whilst two years later they would break new ground by appearing in Namibia and South Africa, either side of two extensive UK tours.

However, recording opportunities were scarce. In a 1995 interview with the *Daily Express,* Allan commented that the band were contemplating cutting a new album of, as he referred to it, "classics", but the first sign of any new recordings was not quite so conventional.

On 30th August, the band entered the Granada studios in Manchester, accompanied by the cast of the long-running television soap *Coronation Street* where, together, they recorded a version of 'He Ain't Heavy, He's My Brother' for a TV cast album. Issued shortly afterwards on EMI, Allan's lead vocal was as perfect as ever, but the accompanying (and rather tuneless) chorus did make it sound like the band were playing in the snug at the Rover's Return. Yet, in between takes, Tony played his fellow band members a rare version of a recently discovered Buddy Holly demo, disclosing that the band had been asked to contribute to an upcoming tribute CD to the late rock 'n' roller and that Graham Nash had also been involved in the arrangements. Two weeks later, having relocated down south, this slightly more interesting proposition brought them back into the studios, this time at the Abbey Road facilities in St John's Wood.

When the option of first recording a tribute to Buddy Holly was suggested to Graham Nash, he immediately thought of a recording that he had heard a few years previously, following the release of the 1986 movie *Peggy Sue Got Married.*

'One of the producers for the film, Paul Gurian, had been given a demo of [the song] 'Peggy Sue Got Married' by Buddy's family,' recalled Graham. 'It was recorded on a tape recorder in his apartment in New York. It was fabulous. It was just Buddy on an acoustic guitar. I said in a perfect world I would get Phil Collins on drums, Paul on bass, George on guitar, and we would overdub the track. I could never work it out because everyone's schedule was much too tight. Then I thought, *Well, The Hollies could do this,* so I called Tony and Allan and Bobby, and they thought it was a great idea. I sent the track over and they put it into some Pro-Tools software and isolated his voice from his guitar and slowed it down and rearranged it slightly and then we overdubbed drums, bass and harmonies.'[51]

Bobby Elliott: 'Graham called us and told us that Decca Records in Nashville were putting together a tribute album to Buddy and we ended up being the only non-American act on there. Graham said if we isolate Buddy's voice, we could do 'Peggy Sue Got Married' with Buddy Holly. Ray Stiles is a whizz-kid and he managed to separate them and so we went into Abbey Road and recorded it.'[51]

Initially, Ray took the demo tape into his own Pelican Sound Studio set-up where, working alongside Tony and Ian Parker, they came up with a new arrangement, slowed down the speed and cleverly removed Buddy's acoustic guitar track, leaving just his vocals.

'At my studio, we have an assortment of digital recording and editing equipment,' explained Ray. 'So, over a couple of days, Ian and I set about sorting out the problems. We first recorded Ian's new backing track. This would be the framework for the whole song. Then we stretched Buddy's vocal track to the right length. We did this by using a digital editor. With careful manipulation, it enabled us to lengthen the timing of the song while maintaining the correct pitch of his voice.'[52]'

'It wasn't in any particular key, because there were no guitar tuners in those days,' added Tony. 'It was just short of A Flat. We decided to move that up to A, which improved it. Also, it was slightly out of time because Holly was just strumming away himself.'[53]

'Ian and I ended up with a clean and re-synced Buddy Holly vocal that fitted beautifully over the brand-new backing track,' summarised Ray. 'It was then down to Allan, Tony and Bob to decide if they thought our demo had worked, which they did. A few days later, we all found ourselves heading for the famous Abbey Road studios. After transferring the Buddy vocal directly to multitrack, Ian's basic track was laid down from the computer. Bob added live drums and then I recorded the bass.'

'I think we ended up with six guitar tracks,' continued Tony. 'A couple of electrics, acoustic and there's a very important one on there – an electric played through the Leslie speaker. Plugging it through an organ speaker gives you the swirling sound. If you listen to the recording, you probably think it's a Hammond organ playing. In fact, it's my guitar. Bobby went right back to the '60s and used a vintage, antique, very small Ludwig drum kit, the sort of thing everybody used then, and he did it live in the studio. And in the middle of all this, Graham arrived from the States, just as I was finishing the guitar parts. That just left us to do our vocals with Graham, Allan and myself, which we did all in a day and a half at Abbey Road studios.' [53]

Pelican Sound Studios' Dar Delta Plus was used to record a track by The Hollies for the Buddy Holly tribute album "Not Fade Away". The song, a new arrangement of 'Peggy Sue Got Married', is based around a 1958 recording of Holly singing and playing acoustic guitar in a hotel bedroom. Holly's performance was TimeWarped on the Delta to slow its tempo by 16% and WordFit automatic dialogue synchronisation was used on his vocal to match the feel of the new version.

The resulting timecoded DAT was transferred to a 24-track digital at Abbey Road Studio 2, which first hosted The Hollies in 1963, where the other parts were added, including the voice of original Hollies member Graham Nash, who flew in from the US for the session.

*Billboard*
March 1996

Ray: 'I half expected the three of them to sit down and discuss how to recreate that famous vocal blend. After all those years apart, it would be quite reasonable to expect them to need some time for rehearsal. But no! Allan just started singing his part, Graham added the unmistakable high harmony and Tony finished off with what are generally regarded the most difficult lines of all – the ones that no one else is singing, and there you have it, harmonies and a sound unlike any other.' [52]

Released as the opening track on the *Not Fade Away: Remembering*

*Buddy Holly* various artists compilation, issued by MCA Records that year, this version stood out for its smooth, modern style, complete with dense harmonies and a rip-roaring guitar solo – unlike the cod-reggae version attempted on the Hollies' *Buddy Holly* album from 1980. With credit in the studio also given to Tony Taverner, who sat at the desk alongside Ray for much of the session, it oozed commerciality. Unfortunately, MCA opted against issuing it as a single release, thus ensuring that anyone who wished to hear it had to purchase the full CD (it did later appear as a bonus track on a 1998 re-issue of the group's own *Buddy Holly* album on CD).

However, had any promotion been afforded to the song upon release during 1996 then the chances are they would have been without Ray Stiles alongside them on the stage. During the early part of the year, he was knocked off his motorcycle by a careless driver; the result of which was a broken pelvis and a shattered lower leg that ultimately had to be reconstructed and pinned back together, enforcing not only hospitalisation but an extended lay-off from the band. For the next six months, Steve Stroud, on a hiatus from his commitments with Cliff Richard, took the bass role once again, standing in for the duration of the spring '96 UK tour (although the proposed April visit to South Africa was postponed until September).

A remarkable event occurred on stage at the Barbican on Saturday night. The Hollies performed a duet with a pop icon who's been dead for more than 35 years. The icon I refer to is, of course, Buddy Holly and the song 'Peggy Sue Got Married'.

The duet was the result of many hours of technical wizardry which is becoming more and more popular. The effect was quite spooky, very well done, and I am sure, left the audience wanting more of the same in the future.

The Hollies were fortunate to be on stage at the Barbican, their previous two concerts at Preston and Derby had to be cancelled due to the lead singer Allan Clarke catching a cold and losing his voice. This was evident during the first couple of numbers but once the golden larynx had loosened up, the magic began to flow.

The second half was as exciting as the first and the audience were beginning to get in the swing of things by clapping along with all the songs. Rounding off the evening, and to make up for forgetting the verse to one song (I don't think many people noticed, and if they did they were very forgiving), Allan gave an impromptu solo on the harmonica.

To a standing ovation from the audience, they launched into an encore of 'Let's Dance' and 'Long Cool Woman (In A Black Dress).'

*Yorkshire Evening Press*
March 1996

The summer of 1996 saw Allan, Tony and Bobby sitting before a bank of cameras, reminiscing about their times at the Abbey Road Studios for a new 60-minute TV documentary. Broadcast two years later, *The Abbey Road Story* was the chance for viewers to glimpse some of what went on behind the scenes inside the world-famous building, although The Hollies' segment was reduced to a mere few minutes upon airing, showing the January 1967 'On A Carousel' vocal session, whilst the three members added in their thoughts.

'The Hollies were Abbey Road locals,' recounted Alan Parson for the camera. 'They always seemed to be around here!'

Sadly, that no longer seemed to be the case and the 'Peggy Sue Got Married' session would be one of the final times the band ventured within the hallways of the famed NW8 address.

As the decade drew towards its inevitable closure, reviews from the constant touring appeared to focus more and more on one thing: Allan's ability to deliver the vocals required for a two-hour performance each night.

1997 saw a thirty-date UK tour during the early winter months, preceded by a variety of outdoor summer shows and a journey across to the Channel Islands, and this was followed by a thirty-date run during the spring of the following year. July 1998 also saw them briefly in Denmark, appearing at the July Langelands Festival, performing a twenty-song set, heavy on hits, but also including renditions of 'When I'm Dead And Gone' and Buddy Holly's 'Rave On!' Needless to say, the long shows took their toll, and both the power and the range began to noticeably suffer.

1999 saw even longer spring and autumn tours across the country, along with a return visit to Scandinavia. Subsequently, the concerns surrounding his vocals were causing uncomfortable scenarios both on and off stage, with Ray Stiles – offering vocal support to Allan from the rear of the stage – visibly bearing some of the brunt of the vocalist's frustrations. The onstage rapport between Allan and Tony was also notably strained, and the added concerns over a back injury to Alan Coates only further hindered the smooth running of the show. At one stage, during a performance in King's Lynn, Coates was forced to contribute from behind the curtains, full of painkillers, lying prone but fully mic'd up, his guitar strapped across his chest. Layin' to the Music...

Backstage too, Allan Clarke was building an unfortunate reputation as a difficult character to deal with, outwardly complaining about the arrangements and venues, with the ever-loyal Rod Shields, working behind the scenes since 1964, allegedly passing comment that 75% of his time was now spent 'keeping Allan happy...' It was also noticeable to fans who attended the shows how, upon arriving on stage, Allan would always appear last, thirty seconds behind the others, milking the applause. Then again, in his defence, he was also having to endure a number of stressful situations enforced upon him at that particular point in time – and none more so than facing up to the fact that his own instrument, his golden voice, was shot.

Given the right scenario, Clarke could still deliver the goods, and at times his live performances were of the high standard that the group's following were accustomed to, but other times, not so.

'I was struggling to get those high notes,' admits Allan. 'We were even dropping keys and things like that and it was getting quite obvious. People were noticing. I had a chat with Tony and Bobby, and they said, "You're not really doing what we want you to do," and I can quite understand them discussing it with me. I wasn't really enjoying what I was doing. They were right. I was struggling. It was time to hang my vocal cords up...

'They actually said to me that they didn't know what they were going to do without me, and I said, "Well, if you are finding, maybe sometime in the future, you want me to do something then, who knows?" But that never happened.'[64]

His final studio performance came during the summer of 1999 when he supplied a lead vocal for the forthcoming solo album of Yes guitarist, Steve Howe. Delivering an emotional reading of Bob Dylan's 'Don't Think Twice, It's Alright', it was a highlight on the subsequent CD release, but the key was set considerably lower for him, and the strength in his tone had clearly gone.

Then, in a further blow, personal situations took over when his wife of thirty-five years, Jeni, was diagnosed with cancer for the second time. A previous scare, back in 1983, had proved worrying enough, but when it returned this time around, it prompted a firmer decision.

'Partway through the tour, she rang me up and told me it was cancer and that it was quite aggressive. So, I had to start rethinking my life.'[23]

'I had to be a strong guy,' he told the *Sunday Express* magazine. 'That's what you do. You don't walk away. Second time around, we really didn't know what was going to happen. At that time, I had problems with my vocal cords, which meant I could no longer hit the high notes. So, I decided to retire and that enabled me to spend more time with Jeni.'

Unfortunately, through the fault of no one, the timing couldn't have been worse. The band were at the closing stages of the winter tour when Allan left, walking away from the band following a performance at the Theatre Royal in Hanley, Stoke-on-Trent on 27th November 1999.

Here I Go Again / Jennifer Eccles / Just One Look / Sandy / Stay / After The Fox / Don't Let Me Down / Not That Way At All / Butterfly / Running Through The Night / I'm Alive / On A Carousel / I Can't Let Go / Yes, I Will / Sorry Suzanne / King Midas In Reverse / We're Through / Peggy Sue Got Married / Blackbird / Look Through Any Window / Bus Stop / Carrie Anne / Stop! Stop! Stop! / The Air That I Breathe / He Ain't Heavy, He's My Brother / Let's Dance / At The Hop / Long Cool Woman (In A Black Dress)

With a number of shows still to fulfil on the schedule, they turned to an old friend to see them through. The first approach had gone out to a friend of Ian Parker's, Peter Howarth, but he was contracted to appear in a musical biopic of Roy Orbison's life and was unavailable. Attention then turned to former Move frontman Carl Wayne, who was interested but reportedly turned the opportunity down, as he was unfamiliar with a lot of their work, with little time for rehearsal. Subsequently, John Miles stepped into the breach for the remaining few shows on the tour, sharing the lead vocals alongside Tony, Ray and Alan Coates.

'The few shows that John Miles did were very exciting, as he was very much a team player,' states Ian Parker. 'It made the other members of the band step forward more. His vocals and harmonies blended very smoothly with the band and he was a pleasure to work with.'[57]

'He was brilliant,' confirmed Bobby. 'We did four shows with him and that convinced us that we could carry on without Allan. But John is Tina Turner's musical director, so he was out the frame for a full-time job...'[5]

The year 2000 would prove a pivotal turning point in the band's history. Cutting ties with the past and starting a new journey into the future. After over thirty years of loyal service, touring manager, lighting and soundman, Rod Shields, had finally stepped down from his role. Now, with Allan's official retirement from the music business, there would be no third return to The Hollies, no reunion for the man who had helped found the group thirty-seven years before. Instead, with John Miles unavailable on a permanent basis, The Hollies once again called upon an old acquaintance and convinced him to step into the spotlight, putting on the lead vocalist shoes. One whom they had previously considered for the same role, twenty-eight years before, and then had just recently approached again, pre-Miles.

Colin David Tooley had been born on 18th August 1943 in the Winson Green suburb of Birmingham, deep in the British Midlands. Within a few years, the family had moved to Chipperfield Road in Hodge Hill, where Colin attended the local primary school on Stechford Road. Then, upon passing the 11-plus exam, he moved on up to Saltley Grammar School, near to where his parents ran the local grocery store.

By the late 1950s, with a love for music emerging, Colin had formed a skiffle group, The G-Men, who played in church halls and schools, before graduating to the nearby Curzon Coffee Bar. Colin also played the upright string bass in the band, although his talent and musicianship on the instrument have been brought into question.

'I first started singing when I was about fourteen in school bands,' he was reported as later telling the *Local London News*. 'I was influenced by the great rock and rollers of the day, people like Elvis and Chuck Berry.

'It was when I was attending Loughborough College, studying physical training and economics, that I decided on a career in music, so I turned professional and joined The Vikings. Like most other bands at the time, we went off to Germany.'

Originally known as Keith Powell and The Vikings, this band were already a well-established Birmingham-based act and, soon enough, upon joining them, Colin Tooley took on a persona to match his burgeoning rock 'n' roll status. Looking for a name that suited his newly appointed Viking significance, he adopted the Christian name of "Carl", one that he felt sounded distinctly Scandinavian enough for his image. For a surname, he took inspiration from one of the popular movie stars of the day; John

Wayne, and "Carl Wayne" was born. With their newly rechristened singer decked out in a distinguishing pink suit, the band renamed itself "Keith Powell, Carl Wayne and The Vikings" before a dispute with the then-leader, Powell, caused a rift and he quit. With Carl now as the sole frontman, the abbreviated Carl Wayne and The Vikings headed out to Hamburg for a six-month residency. However, whilst they toiled away the hours in darkened and often sordid nightclubs, something new was happening back home.

'While we were away, the whole Merseybeat thing happened – The Beatles had really taken over.'

After returning home and cutting a series of unsuccessful singles for the Pye label, and with a succession of personnel changes, the band split when their bass player, Chris "Ace" Kefford, mooted the idea of forming a new line-up with guitarist Trevor Burton from another band, The Mayfair Set, and multi-instrumentalist Roy Wood, from The Nightriders. Carl offered his services as vocalist, as did current Vikings drummer Bev Bevan. The Move was the result.

Between 1965 and 1969, with Carl out front as lead singer, The Move became one of the UK's leading chart acts. Initially signed to the Deram label, before switching to Regal Zonophone, the five-man band racked up five Top 10 hits, including the chart-topping 'Blackberry Way'.

Renowned for their wild-man stage antics, which often included Carl wreaking havoc with an axe as a prop, the group went down in the history books for having the very first record played on the BBC's new prime radio station, Radio One ('Flowers In The Rain'), although, gradually, the focus moved towards the band's principal songwriter, Roy Wood, often leaving Carl frustrated on the sidelines.

As the 1960s drew to a close, aware that Wood was also intent on setting up a new, orchestral rock project (The Electric Light Orchestra), Carl suggested to him that he could go ahead with the proposition whilst also continuing to write songs for The Move. Unfortunately, not only did Wood reject the notion, so did the other band members. Angry over the rejection and mortified by an onstage altercation between Wood and a member of their audience during a concert, Carl quit the band during January of 1970.

Calming down his stage presence, and putting away the axe, he subsequently adopted a smoother, middle-of-the-road solo approach, releasing one album (a 1972 eponymous release) and a slew of unsuccessful singles, many of which were geared directly towards the family-friendly television and cabaret career he had embraced. Eventually, this developed into a life in stage musicals before, with the turn of the new millennium, another opportunity presented itself to him.

'I was in *Blood Brothers* for six years but I still undertook a lot of session work as well,' he continued in conversation with the *Local London News*. 'Then, Allan Clarke, the original Hollies singer, decided to call it a day for various reasons, including his wife being very ill. I had worked with the current Hollies keyboard player on *Blood Brothers*. He suggested I take over. The rest of the Hollies didn't want to retire – it was their livelihood and they wanted to keep the band together. Another reason for asking me was they didn't want to become one of those horrendous old acts with a young singer! Hopefully, this will re-establish The Hollies as a good working band, not only with audiences but with record companies as well.'

Continuing the theme in a separate interview, he noted, 'I feel this is a new stage in their illustrious career, whilst respecting what has already been achieved. I am not joining The Hollies just to make up the numbers. The year 2000 gives us the opportunity to move forward, and rather than constantly refer to the past, there now exists enormous potential to record and succeed with new material. One of the things we are really hoping to do is a new album…

'I applaud Allan's extraordinary contribution to the success of The Hollies over many years and his decision to leave for personal reasons is admirable. I can never replace Allan Clarke; he *was* The Hollies during their hit-making peak. Allan was the heart, the soul and the voice of The Hollies for many, many years.' [9]

Having signed on, Carl's first performance was held at the Mercedes Event Centre in Sindelfingen, near Stuttgart in Germany on 7th July. The German audiences were immediately receptive to the new frontman as the band powered through a strong set, including 'Stay', 'Here I Go Again', 'Jennifer Eccles', 'Bus Stop', 'King Midas In Reverse', 'Sorry Suzanne', 'Blowin' In The Wind', 'Listen To Me', 'We're Through', 'Stop! Stop! Stop!', 'He Ain't Heavy, He's My Brother', 'The Air That I Breathe', 'Johnny B Goode', 'Let's Dance' and 'Long Cool Woman (In A Black Dress)'. For many, however, the highlight was when Carl stepped forward and delivered an exceptionally strong and moving performance on 'Soldier's Song'. Clearly, the years spent in cabaret had given his performance a far greater depth and power and, along with a formidable audience rapport that the crowds latched onto with joy, it was apparent from the start that the band had made a wise choice.

Returning to the UK, the new line-up debuted their show in the Suffolk county town of Ipswich, appearing at outdoor Christchurch Park on 29th July. Playing a slightly alternative selection, this show was notable for the first inclusion of Carl's chart-topper with The Move, 'Blackberry Way', a feat they would repeat regularly at most shows from here on in (often alternating with 'Flowers in The Rain', 'Fire Brigade' and 'I Can Hear The Grass Grow').

I Can't Let Go / Here I Go Again/ Jennifer Eccles / Bus Stop / I'm Alive / Sorry Suzanne / Yes, I Will / Just One Look / On A Carousel / Blowin' In The Wind / Carrie Anne / Stop! Stop! Stop! / The Air That I Breathe / He Ain't Heavy, He's My Brother / Blackberry Way / Long Cool Woman (In A Black Dress)

Shortly afterwards, they kicked off a lengthy thirty-seven-date venture around the country. Meanwhile, whilst their new partner was bedding himself in, centre stage, Tony and Bobby, in cooperation with their management agency, had other pressing matters on their minds.

For the past five years or so, The Eric Haydock Band, fronted by vocalist Michael Carroll, had been touring fairly constantly, picking up bookings around Europe and beyond. As the main draw in the act, Eric's history with The Hollies had gradually begun to take over setlists, and what had started as a New Mindbenders show, with a smattering of Hollies hits, had become more Hollie-centric in its direction. Subsequently, as the music of the more prestigious quintet began to take over, the promoters and the venues began to place The Hollies' name in bigger and bolder text on the adverts and flyers.

Despite previous warnings from the "official" band and their legal representatives, and the subsequent writ that followed, when the Haydock line-up arrived in Dortmund in Germany, during January 2000, followed by a springtime Australian tour, the "H"-word was still in prominent use. With Carroll and guitarist Peter Hughes, along with drummer Mike Copson and rhythm guitarist Graham Pollock standing alongside, Eric arrived down under during May and took on a series of low-key club dates in the cities of Sydney and Geelong, along with appearances in the Melbourne suburbs of Keysborough, Doncaster and Dandenong. They also managed a primetime guest slot on the *Denise* morning TV show, broadcast across the Seven

Network. With clearly no intention of halting any deception, it therefore came as no surprise that the Hicks-Elliott-led Hollies continued to pursue their legal rights and further their claims in court.

Members of the 1960's pop group The Hollies have asked the High Court to jail one of their founder members. They claimed bass player Eric Haydock has flouted a court order made in 1998 not to play under their name. They also claim that Peter Hughes plays with Mr Haydock in a group calling itself Eric Haydock's Hollies and music manager James Cozens helps set up gigs. Mr Haydock formed the group in Manchester with Allan Clarke and Graham Nash but left in 1966. Stephen Glover QC, representing the band, told Mr Justice Etherton: "The view of the complainants is that British prisons are full enough, and they wish no imprisonment to occur to any of the defendants, but they know of no other means of stopping this."

Despite being told only to refer to himself as ex-Hollies or former-Hollies bass player, he had formed the band called Eric Haydock's Hollies, it was claimed. All three men are aware of the earlier injunction which prevents Mr Haydock from using the band's name in this way. Breaches of the order included a tour of Australia in 1999, a concert in Denmark and shows across Britain.

The only original members of The Hollies' current line-up are guitarist Tony Hicks and drummer Bobby Elliott.

The case continues.

BBC News

# CHAPTER THIRTY-SIX

---

# "HOW DO I SURVIVE...?"

With Carl established into the band, and his acceptance amongst the loyal fan following eased by his own 1960s history, the tours continued – including overseas visits to Australia and New Zealand, where a recent 24-track *Hollies Greatest Hits* collection had displaced The Beatles' platinum-awarded "*1*" anthology from the top of the charts. Attention also turned towards new recordings. However, Carl was still very much his own man, taking on individual roles when the urge took him, although he always ensured that his solo work didn't conflict with the needs of the group.

During early 2002, just before the band headed out for a long-overdue North American tour, Carl contributed his vocals to a tribute album for Electric Light Orchestra founder member and Travelling Wilbury Jeff Lynne. He then also collaborated with Ulli Eichblatt, the editor for the German Hollies *Up Front* fan club, who was also known for being a producer of varying styles of dance music. Working together in Ulli's Blue Room Studio in Heilbronn, the duo conceived and produced a stunning new rendition of 'Soldiers Song' that showed the sheer power and phrasing of Carl's voice impeccably.

'In the past fifteen years, I've recorded with many people, but swear I've never met a more professional singer than Carl,' Ulli was to say. 'When I told him, "Carl, would you please try 'Soldier's Song' because we have to find the right level on the desk," I said to my engineer, "Just press the record-button."

In the end, Carl sang the song three times, but the very first recording was and still is the most impressive.

'It was more like fun than work. I couldn't stop him, whether it was 'White Christmas' or 'Blackberry Way', and he wanted to sing them in German too. He *wanted* to sing 'When The Boys Come Home', he *wanted* to sing 'He Ain't Heavy' and 'Sorry Suzanne'. Nothing could stop him!' [54]

However, with Eichblatt's status in the world of trance and dance music, it wasn't long before they soon ventured off into alternative territories, with Carl's distinctive voice on 'Blackberry Way' soon accompanied by the pounding dance rhythms of a synthesised beat. Credited to Et Cetera, the release took off in the sunshine holiday and party resorts of Majorca that summer.

Interestingly, this wasn't the first time that Eichblatt had taken the sound of The Hollies and included it within his hypnotic dance inclinations. Two years previously, in 2000, he had taken Allan Clarke's distinctive guitar riff to 'Long Cool Woman (In A Black Dress)' and, with Allan duly credited on the release, turned it into a dance floor Euro-hit, credited to Et Cetera *featuring* Allan Clarke. Allan had even assisted in promoting the song, miming his famous guitar riff on a number of televised appearances. The following year, they even repeated the process with a suitably slowed down German language version of 'He Ain't Heavy, He's My Brother', this time utilising Allan's harmonica intro. Neither recording featured any Hollie-vocals.

With Carl's recording duties completed, he then flew out across the ocean for the US tour, joining up with Tony, Bobby, Alan, Ray and Ian for a whistle-stop two-week jaunt, taking in many of the states along the eastern and mid-west side of the country, before following this up with several shows across the Canadian border in Quebec. An August stop-off at the Westbury Music Fair, thirty miles to the east of New York City, resulted in a wildly applauding crowd, clapping and stomping along in time for the 60-minute performance – notable for the inclusions of the Carl-fronted 'Stop! In The Name Of Love' and 'Peggy Sue Got Married', the return of 'Too Young To Be Married' and a beautiful, harmonic rendition of McCartney's 'Blackbird'. The show climaxed with a resounding 'Long Cool Woman (In A Black Dress)', their US #2 hit, as the closing number. Interestingly, they dropped any representation of Carl's former band from the setlist, seeing that none of the UK Top 10 hits by The Move had achieved any significant recognition across the Atlantic.

Nevertheless, upon their return home from the successful visit, all commitments were temporarily placed on hold, including a proposed visit to Germany along with the annual UK Autumn Tour, when Carl was suddenly hospitalised with concerning throat issues.

'A month after returning from our recent American tour, I experienced difficulty swallowing,' he reported at the time. 'I had various tests and it was discovered that I had an oesophageal blockage, which doctors have stressed needs operating on immediately. Sadly, this has meant I will be unavailable for the forthcoming tour and all my other commitments while I recover. This is a huge disappointment, but I have been told I need to make a full recovery before I can resume my career and return for the rescheduled tour in the New Year. I look forward to seeing you all on tour during 2003.'[54]

What Carl hadn't revealed was the seriousness of the issue. He had been diagnosed with oesophageal cancer, a form of the disease that affects the gullet, and is usually found in the later stages when there is no known cure, only regular treatment. However, chances of survival are often increased with surgery and for Carl this was the only option.

During January of the following year, with Carl resting and recuperating after his operation, the band took to the stage in Germany, with two scheduled shows featuring session vocalist and former backup singer for Tom Jones, Ian Harrison, taking on frontline duties. A capable enough singer, his youthful, mohawk-shaven head and gangly stage persona sadly appeared at odds with the band's mature image. Nevertheless, the show must go on, and Harrison's unquestionable ability and amiable last-minute availability ensured that the legions of fans weren't disappointed. Bobby Elliott, meanwhile, had also considered the possibility of bringing another old hand back on board to fill the temporary vacancy:

'When Carl had to have his operation, I spoke to Graham [Nash] with the thought of him coming over to fill in,' Bobby said to the *Eastern Daily Press*. 'People would have liked to have seen that and it would have been quite an event for him to tour with us. Unfortunately, he was doing a book tour of the States and had some dates to do with David and Stephen, but he would like to have done it. That would have been quite something.'

Then, perhaps somewhat surprisingly after such a short period of time, but with doctors pleased with his response to the treatment, Carl returned to the stage. His first show had been a tentative appearance at a low-key Roy Wood concert, held at London's Roadhouse Club on 21st December 2002.

Reuniting with his former bandmate, the duo had run through a selection of classic Move hits before a rapturous audience. However, come the new year, he was now feeling strong enough to take to the concert circuit on a regular basis and, shortly afterwards, with his vocal strength rapidly improving, the dedicated pro returned to his Hollies duties, resuming the official touring schedule. Commencing the opening night of their 40th Anniversary Tour with an appearance in St Albans on 26th February, the evening activities saw the sextet back on form, the show culminating in a rousing finale, with all three present and former bands represented – with Mud's stomping 'Tiger Feet' (for Ray) leading the charge, swiftly followed by The Move's 'I Can Hear The Grass Grow' (Carl) and The Hollies' 'He Ain't Heavy, He's My Brother' closing out.

Yet, even as the tour progressed, which was followed by further overseas visits to Belgium, Germany, Denmark and Switzerland, Carl began to feel the band's continuing lack of direction a constant source of irritation to him.

'These are great songs to sing, and therefore it's usually a very successful evening,' he went on record as saying. 'The sound and lights are good, the members of the group are pleasant and talented, and the shows are usually sold out and the response is great. But the worst thing is the band's failure to progress. They just seem content to plod on and play the same songs and venues that they've been playing for so many years when we should be recording new material and playing bigger but fewer venues. They're nice blokes, so I just enjoy the shows, but I do find this aspect very frustrating.

'They're one of the three most important British groups of the early 1960s, along with The Beatles and The Stones, but they just didn't really achieve their true potential following the departure of Graham Nash.' [55]

As of early 2003, The Hollies still had high hopes of resurrecting their recording career, and during February that year, they made some tentative steps back into the studios at Abbey Road to cut one new song, with the ominous 40th anniversary hanging heavy in the air.

'How Do I Survive', a Paul Bliss composition, updated the traditional Hollie-sound, without holding on to the cloyingly stereotypical trademarks that many of the long-term 1960s survivors still displayed. It was definitely a song for the now, and a clear redemption for Bliss after the *What Goes Around* atrocities. It was near Hall & Oates-styled, blue-eyed soul perfection – but not quite, and yet it must have breathed delight into not only Carl but the entire band.

'It was a last-minute thing,' reported Bobby. 'We just shot into Abbey Road. I came down from the North, met up with the other guys and we just did it very quickly. But The Hollies usually work under pressure, to a deadline. We're very pleased with the new song. Everybody seems to like it.'

Nevertheless, it was just a fleeting glimpse of the promise suggested, and when it subsequently debuted on yet another compilation, EMI's newly constructed but all-too-familiar-looking 40th Anniversary *Greatest Hits* 2-CD set, the writing was on the wall.

There was talk of further sessions for EMI with, purportedly, Carl's former bandmate Roy Wood offering up some songs for them, but a difference of opinion over financial agreements curtailed such a project. Ray Stiles had even been turning away a lucrative income on his home studio, rejecting offers of leasing it out to other clients, in the hope that The Hollies would move in and resurrect their recording career, but the prospect of an album only dragged on further still, causing a rift between Ray and Carl over the proposition.

The March release of the current *Greatest Hits* collection put the band back into the LP charts once more, with a surprising peak of #21 – surprising in that, on the face of it, it differed little from previous collections (with the exception of the one new recording). However, underneath the generic sleeve image of white, puffy clouds was a forty-seven-song set filled, for the first time, with true stereo mixes of all the UK hits, which was a sheer delight for many of the band's loyal following, some of who had even been partially involved with the track selection process and the accompanying detailed booklet. And yet, the interest status in this set was surpassed ten-fold by the October issue of a new six-CD collection that followed from EMI. *The Long Road Home 1963-2003* was a truly fascinating, carefully constructed 136-song collection, compiling hits, deeper cuts, unreleased outtakes and live recordings from across the years. Packaged in splendid style, complete with a detailed fifty-six-page booklet, with extensive liner notes by acclaimed music journalist Peter Doggett (from where this very book has drawn a great deal of information), this gathering was a near-perfect representation of the previous four decades, receiving rave reviews for its presentation and integrity. But it begged the question – would there, or could there, be anything noteworthy to follow? Or was this the final hurrah?

Taking them across the country, the UK 40th Anniversary Tour resulted in them spending a good proportion of the year on the road... and 2004 looked to start in similar fashion, with a setlist pleasing to most aspects of their following:

I'm Alive / Here I Go Again / Jennifer Eccles / Yes, I Will / On A Carousel / Sandy / Listen To Me / I Can't Tell The Bottom From The Top / I Can't Let Go / We're Through / Fire Brigade / Look Through Any Window / Blowin' In The Wind / Long Cool Woman (In A Black Dress) / Sorry Suzanne / Just One Look / The Baby / Soldier's Song / Gasoline Alley Bred / Too Young To Be Married / Bus Stop / Blackberry Way / Carrie Anne / Stop! Stop! Stop! / The Air That I Breathe / I Can Hear the Grass Grow / Tiger Feet / He Ain't Heavy, He's My Brother / It's In Everyone Of Us

As the journey progressed around the UK, all appeared to be fine; the band were on song and the audiences were loving it, bathing in the nostalgia as the hits endlessly flowed. Carl was outwardly showing no ill effects from his recent hospitalisation, although at times, unbeknownst to the audience, the ongoing concerns over his diagnosis had him using an intravenous aid to see him through some of the rigorous touring schedules. But then, concertgoers who attended the show on 21st August in Nottingham were a little taken aback to find Ian Harrison once again standing in for Carl. Tony Hicks explained to the crowd that their popular frontman was unwell and unable to perform but said little more on the subject. The truth is, even the band members themselves didn't realise exactly how serious Carl's ailment had become.

Having made an appearance with the band at an earlier show on 10th July 2004 in Norway, where he had entertained the enthralled crowds with a scintillating performance, he had returned home to rest and undertake a series of further routine check-ups. However, the cancer had taken hold once again and his condition deteriorated rapidly, and by August he had returned to hospital. Tony Hicks visited him there and was shocked to see how viciously the disease had taken hold.

Shortly afterwards, with little warning, at the age of just sixty-one, Carl Wayne passed away in his sleep. It was 31st August 2004. He left behind a wife and son.

Speaking to BBC West Midlands Radio soon after, The Hollies' agent, Jimmy Smith, commented, 'We are shocked by it because we didn't expect it to be so sudden. We have got a tour in the autumn and he was looking forward to coming back and joining us. His wife called me on Friday to say he was ill but wanted to keep it quiet while there was hope, and we were all hoping.'

Meanwhile, speaking to BBC News, Bobby Elliot said: 'The Hollies and the world of music have lost a shining star, a true professional. It is a very sad day for the band. Our thoughts and prayers go out to his wife Susan, son Jack and all of his family. Carl was a fearless performer and a powerhouse singer. It has been an honour to work with him.

'I'm sorry that we didn't make an album with him. He was a great frontman and such a great character. I shall remember his five years with The Hollies with great pride and affection.'

# CHAPTER THIRTY-SEVEN

# "STAYING POWER..."

W ith the tragic loss of Carl Wayne, The Hollies' future was once again placed at an uncertain crossroads. Left without a lead singer, the band had the simple option of calling it a day – or finding a swift replacement. To seasoned performers such as Bobby and Tony, who had known little more than a life on the road for the past forty years, the choice was fairly straightforward. The Hollies' legacy demanded that they carried the name forward. They were still very much a headlining act, one who could carry a two-hour show without hesitation, albeit no longer quite in the same league as some of their illustrious counterparts who were treading the boards during the initial opening years of the millennium.

Bon Jovi, U2 and Springsteen could all still sell out arena tours with ease, whilst the modern heavyweight acts such as Metallica, Red Hot Chilli Peppers and rapper Eminem were shifting CDs by the armful across the counter. Garth Brooks, Michael Jackson, Britney Spears and the re-emergence of Carlos Santana... the musical diversity that was dominating the industry at that time was phenomenal, but for many of the artists and bands who had been setting foot on the world's stages for the past four decades, there was still a healthy living to be made amongst the competition.

Paul McCartney could still sell out stadiums and arenas at the drop of a hat, whilst The Beach Boys, in varying degrees of line-ups, as a collective or as solo performers (subject to lawsuit status), were still continuously on the road and in the compilation charts. And The Rolling Stones? When the urge took them, they were arguably still the greatest rock 'n' roll band out there, as the recent *Voodoo Lounge, Bridges to Babylon* and *Licks* tours proved (each outing grossing in the region of $300 million apiece).

For The Hollies, a band who could continue to fill venues the size of London's Royal Albert Hall, it was a case of finding a suitable frontman who could charismatically follow on from both Allan Clarke and Carl Wayne. Someone who could hold both the stage and the audience and do the music justice. The band's catalogue would, and always will, sell itself.

Unlike Carl Wayne, who had brought with him decades of experience, and a public persona already established through many years of headlining status, the man they opted to go with was not a name familiar to many. Although he was known throughout much of the UK music business for his supporting roles with Cliff Richard and The Who, and for his theatre work on *Only the Lonely* and *Robin, Prince of Sherwood*, Peter Howarth was a relatively unknown entity in Hollies circles, despite having been offered the frontman slot previously, following Allan Clarke's departure.

Born in the seaside town of Blackpool, Lancashire, birthplace of Graham Nash amongst many others, Peter arrived in the world on 3rd May 1960, just shy of three years before the newly christened Hollies would enter the hallowed hallways of the Abbey Road recording studios for the first time.

After developing a love of music early on, taking classical guitar lessons at the tender age of just seven, he soon enough began to consider a career in the music industry as a possibility, with the ensuing years consolidating such impassioned dreams with a role as a session singer and guitarist. He formed his own band, Sahara, during the 1980s (subsequently releasing the album *Observation*) before going on to add his vocals to releases by Joe Longthorne, Elkie Brooks, Michael Ball and Madeleine Bell.

In 2001, having recently finished a run in the West End, appearing in the Roy Orbison tribute show *Only the Lonely*, he appeared as part of a male backing chorus, alongside Carl Wayne, supporting Kylie Minogue for the EMI release of her 'Your Disco Needs You' single. By now, he was also firmly established as one of Cliff Richard's backing troupe, appearing on a succession of best-selling recordings and world tours – often appearing alongside Cliff's resident bass player Steve Stroud.

'When I was asked to join The Hollies in 2004, it was a huge honour,' Peter would say on his website (*peterhowarth.com*). 'The Hollies are part of rock 'n' roll history and it is a privilege to be part of such a special institution.'

Debuting the new line-up in the German city of Muenster on 2nd October 2004, supported by The Rubettes and fellow '60s survivors The Tremeloes, it was apparent how Peter immediately brought his own approach to the show, taking to the stage with comfortable ease and winning over many (although not all) of the group's loyal followers with his charm and confidence. Noted German journalist and long-term Hollies aficionado, Uli Twelker, gave the newcomer his seal of approval.

'"Peter looks and sounds good." This is how drummer Bobby Elliott had announced Howarth. On this October night in Muenster, both credits were verified in seconds. Howarth has the power, charisma and precision to replace Allan Clarke; he can pass as a young Clarkey, without imitating him in the slightest. And with the first chorus of the opening 'I'm Alive', the Hollies' harmony triangle, their new Howarth-Hicks-Coates-combination, sounded clearer and more genuine than any time during the last decade.'[58]

With the endorsement of his new bandmates, Peter also adapted several of the arrangements to suit his vocal abilities, without being detrimental to the Hollies sound originated by his predecessors.

Ian Parker: 'When Carl joined, he was very much a frontman who liked to be out front. He had great stage presence and the audience really liked him. Carl's voice was uniquely different, so the delivery of the songs was uniquely his own. We did some of the Move songs in the set; 'Blackberry Way', 'Flowers In The Rain' and others, and they were great fun to play. When Peter joined, he contributed some wonderful new arrangements – a solo acoustic version of 'Here I Go Again', an acoustic version of 'Sandy' with harmonies and keyboards, and a semi-acoustic arrangement of 'I Can't Tell The Bottom From The Top'. He quickly took command of the centre stage with his soaring vocal range and great stage presence, and I believe the vocal blend of the current line-up delivers beautifully the famous Hollies vocal harmony sound.'[57]

A follow-up show one week later in Munich, sharing the stage with Smokie, Suzi Quatro, Sweet and The Tremeloes, confirmed Peter's suitability and adaptability for the role, although by the time they hit the stage for an appearance in Austria on the 23rd, followed by the first in a series of winter UK shows, another change in the line-up had occurred.

For the past twenty-two years, Alan Coates had been one of the unsung heroes of The Hollies' stage shows. From his debut with the band at the 1982

Mainz Festival in Germany, as a mullet-haired, (relatively) youthful twenty-nine-year-old, through to the recent German shows with Peter Howarth, he had supplied the high tenor range with apparent ease, filling in where Graham and Terry had gone before, and blending in comfortably alongside Allan, Tony and Carl. However, as the years passed, and the hairline receded, his work outside of the band, building up a burgeoning composition and publishing company with his wife, singer and actress Kim Goody, began to take precedence. Developing a career for writing and producing commercials and television jingles proved a lucrative option – so much so that when The Hollies kicked off their 2004 UK tour at the small 500-seat Hafren Theatre in Powys, Wales, Alan was no longer a touring member of the band. In his place, stage right in the frontline harmony trio, stood Steve Lauri, a guitarist and harmony singer with strong connections to many of the recent touring members of The Hollies.

Initially starting his career as a latter-day touring member of the '70s disco outfit 5000 Volts, contributing guitar and vocals to their stage performances across Europe, Steve then joined up with Bonnie Tyler's band before, inevitably, he ended up as the featured guitarist in resident pub specialists Sprinkler (former London bolthole for Steve Stroud, Alan Coates and Jamie Moses). Later stints alongside Stroud in the Bucks Fizz touring group, followed by a three-year run with Cliff Richard, performing with both Stroud and Peter Howarth, ensured his ability was receiving the attention it deserved.

Having then furthered his reputation playing alongside David Essex, Elaine Paige and a spin-off of the original Glitter Band, Steve then began to add session duties to his résumé, often spending his time working at Ray Stiles' Pelican Sound Studio. It subsequently came as little surprise when a recommendation to fill in on the current Hollies touring schedule came his way. Whilst not a natural high tenor, as Graham, Terry and Alan had been, his falsetto vocal slotted sweetly into the mix, filled out by the additional input of Ray Stiles and Ian Parker, with Ray often supplying much of the higher register from the rear of the stage.

However, with the memory of Carl still very much in their minds and hearts, it appeared only fitting that the band should honour his memory with a moving tribute during the first tour without him. Stepping to the front of the stage, Ray would deliver an emotional rendition of 'Flowers In The Rain', offering up his own homage to his former comrade, perhaps by way of easing the hurt that their dispute over studio sessions had caused.

> Whenever I stop to think about The Hollies in any way, it's always the period spent with Carl that seems to come to mind first. The Hollies have always been a great live band – always willing to try something new, never willing to just sit back and live on reputation and past achievements. When "Charlie" [Carl] came in, he brought something exciting, a new way forward.
>
> Carl and I had differences – these things happen in bands – but we always sorted it out and I know that he respected me as much as I did him. As far as I'm concerned, I have been honoured and privileged to work with a great professional, a great singer and a lovely man. [54]
>
> Ray Stiles. 2004

With a stable line-up now in place – original stalwarts Tony Hicks and Bobby Elliott, along with Peter Howarth, Ray Stiles, Ian Parker and Steve Lauri, the new-look Hollies consolidated their reputation together by hitting the road for the regular three-month period, every year, playing the hits to the thousands of devoted fans, both new and old, young and elderly, who attended the shows across the country, and occasionally Europe.

In 2005, the first recorded evidence that the band were still intent on moving forward became known, with the surprise EMI CD single release of 'Hope' b/w 'Shine On Me', two brand-new recordings taped at Pelican Sound Studios, with the production credits given to both Ray and Ian.

With the lead side co-written by Ray's former Mud bandmate, Rob Davis (co-writer of many Top 10 hits in recent years, including Kylie Minogue's 'Can't Get You Out Of My Head'), the new recordings were clean, precise and yet, maybe, a little too clinical in their sound. There was no clear indication of the traditional Hollies familiarity at the core and, with Peter Howarth yet to establish his vocal sound within the band, this could so easily have been a pleasing, modern solo recording by the singer. Likewise, the accompanying 'Shine On Me', co-written by Brit-songsmiths Cliff Masterson, Mark Read and Robert Hart, was another fine example of modern technology; a catchy hook line – but little else. The performances were perfect, the production was polished – but the overall combination was just lacking the magic.

Nevertheless, on the outer sleevenotes to the release, it stated that both tracks were taken from a forthcoming album *Staying Power*, to be released in February 2006. Unbelievably, after almost twenty-five years, The Hollies were back with a brand-new album.

As Bobby was to relate to journalist Spencer Leigh for *Record Collector* magazine, 'Ray Stiles, our bass player, has been with us for twenty years, but he was with Mud and his best friend is (Mud guitarist) Rob Davis. He had these songs that Rob had written, and they were good, and we had more by Mark Read. Ray has a studio, so we thought we would do two or three of them and take them to EMI. They said that we didn't need to come to Abbey Road because the quality was fine, so we spent all last summer recording at Ray's, being fed by his lovely wife, and we had a great time! We didn't even consider doing any covers, as we had so many new ones to choose from.' [15]

In a 2005 article in *Carousel* magazine, it became apparent how differently the collection was actually recorded, in comparison to earlier times. No longer were the band all in the studio together, creating the album as a unit. Instead, Ray Stiles fronted the project from his home studio, with each band member coming in separately to add in their individual parts.

'Ian would start the process off by laying down three or four song arrangements on piano, using click tracks and a guide synth bass,' Ray would comment in print. 'After balancing these, I made a CD and sent it to Tony who worked out what he wanted to play. With the tracks well on the way with regard to guitars, it was time for Bob to come down to the studio to replace the tempo clicks with his drums.

'On the vocal side, there were no problems. Pete is such a fine singer and knows exactly how he wants to approach his song. Backing vocals were also a breeze. Steve took the top lines, Tony in the middle and Pete took the lower harmonies. We just worked them out in the studio and then recorded them straight away...'

Appearing in February 2006, *Staying Power* was the band's twenty-second full studio album, receiving a mixed reception across the fan community, some of whom were mightily impressed that the band could still churn out such quality – whilst others lamented the lack of inventiveness and dense harmonies and the lure of catchy pop.

How much can (or should) one expect from a band in its 43rd year of existence? Astonishingly, however, there is a huge amount to enjoy on this album, and so much that is new mixing with the old. The familiar Hollies sound has evolved into something a bit less distinctive – the harmonies here aren't nearly as special, and don't feel in any way unique – but all immensely accessible. New lead singer Peter Howarth, an alumnus of Cliff Richard's band, has a powerful voice that, when focused properly and with the right quality lyrics, does recall original Hollies lead vocalist Allan Clarke – and together, they generate a lean and powerful pop/rock sound, with lots of guitar and vocal hooks. The songwriting is also very strong throughout most of the album, and with the energy levels much higher than one expects from a band in its 43rd year, "Staying Power" seems a triply appropriate title. Indeed, this is the album they should have released for that 1983 reunion when they had all of the press attention on them.

Bruce Eder
*All Music* Review

A second single, the decidedly gorgeous 'So Damn Beautiful', composed by Mark Read and Graham Stack, whilst sounding uncannily like a Gary Barlow/Take That recording (Stack had previously written for the million-selling Manchester boy band), b/w 'Too Much Too Soon', was a pure delight and showed that the harmonies were still very much intact in the current formation, despite the unfamiliarity of the product.

With production occasionally wavering towards the plastic sounds of the new decade, with a pulsating drum programming replacing Bobby on several of the songs, it took compositions such as 'Break Me' and 'Touch Me' (both co-written by the same team of Rob Davis, Greg Alexander and Enrique Iglesias) to convince the potential audience that this was a band who, with over forty years of experience, actually knew their own instruments. These two tracks had previously appeared on Iglesias's own 2003 album, *7*, along with a third track featured here, 'Live It Up', confirming that it wasn't all computerised technology meeting every musical demand, and even when the faux synth-pop formula did start to dominate proceedings – the commercially-driven 'Suspended Animation' being a prime example – Tony was always on hand with a neat guitar lick or two to bring it back to reality.

Taking the album out on the road, however, they encountered a new series of hurdles. With over forty years of recordings, what to include and what to exclude?

Bobby, again in conversation with Spencer Leigh: 'I was working on the setlist this morning. It's a tricky job – how to fit in the new songs and which old ones to rest. Can we do an old song in an acoustic version for a change? We like to swap things around, although there are some songs like 'He Ain't Heavy, He's My Brother' that we have to do – and want to do. Lots of people come to see us every time we tour, so we have to include a few surprises.

'We have been ending our shows with 'Let Love Pass' for six months. People don't know the song but after 'He Ain't Heavy, He's My Brother', we do a little snatch of it *a cappella* with just the four guys. It's only short but it is magical, and it keeps the feel after 'He Ain't Heavy…' has finished. I love it.'[15]

Attempting to keep the setlist fresh was always a priority, particularly for the older hands who had played these songs hundreds, maybe thousands, of times. And it wasn't just for the band. They would often try out new arrangements of older songs to keep the audience interest alive as well, although some of the old favourites, previously adapted for a concert scenario, often worked better in their original form and needed no updating.

Ian Parker: 'We currently do an arrangement of 'On A Carousel', which either Paul Bliss or Peter Arnesen did in the mid-'80s, whilst I composed an overture to a new version of 'I'm Alive', with a new arrangement, which we used to play. We also did a very different version of 'Stay' with an overture I composed as well, along with differing arrangements of 'Long Cool Woman', 'Another Night' and 'Daddy Don't Mind', which would be attributable to either Paul Bliss, Peter Arnesen or Denis Haines.'[57]

It was also nice to see the vocals being shared around as well, with Ian often taking lead on 'We're Through' (whilst playing his "squeeze box"), Steve Lauri handling 'I Can't Tell The Bottom From The Top' and the line-up of Tony, Steve and Ray all contributing to 'Hey Willy' (a song that, according to Bobby, they never played live during Allan Clarke's run in the band). Later additions also saw Steve take on 'King Midas In Reverse'.

Immediately after the release of *Staying Power*, the media began to pick up on the band once again, with the German '60s and '70s specialist music magazine *Good Times* even going on to suggest that Paul Weller, hit songwriter for The Jam and The Style Council, was currently penning material for the next Hollies album. Ironically, whilst that wouldn't come to pass, Weller later contributed to the reunion album for another iconic '60s band, offering up 'Birth Of An Accidental Hipster' to The Monkees' 2016 album.

January 2006 had seen the band appear in concert at London's Café de Paris nightclub, an intimate 700-capacity venue from where the band broadcast their appearance across the internet. Performing a setlist that successfully crossed the broad division between the early hits and the more recent album, it showed the twenty-first-century Hollies embracing the new technology and reaching out to their vast fan base.

I'm Alive / Jennifer Eccles / Just One Look / On A Carousel / So Damn Beautiful / Bus Stop / The Baby / Emotions / Here I Go Again / Sandy / Look Through Any Window / Weakness / Stop! Stop! Stop! / Carrie Anne / Prove Me Wrong / The Air That I Breathe / Long Cool Woman (In A Black Dress) / Hope / He Ain't Heavy, He's My Brother / Let Love Pass

2006 also saw The Hollies immortalised within the Vocal Hall of Fame, a foundation dedicated to honouring the vocal contributions of many of rock 'n' roll's great icons. A long-overdue acknowledgement on American shores, the foundation was one in a long line of themed museums dedicated to various aspects of the industry, albeit one not under the same spotlight as the hugely commercial, but often criticised, Rock and Roll Hall of Fame. Nevertheless, the honour of such an award (sharing the nominations that year with The Moody Blues, The Byrds, The Lovin' Spoonful, Simon & Garfunkel, Bread and Queen) went away as quickly as it had come. Then again, Sharon, Pennsylvania, where the foundation and museum are based, is not a regular haunt along the tourist trail, and there was certainly no grand reunion to celebrate the honour.

Then, on 9th December, they filmed an appearance at the Sportpaleis near Antwerp, Belgium, which subsequently appeared in heavily edited form on an exclusive DVD release, *The Hollies Special Live Edition*, issued via the Hollies official website the following March. A combination from the Antwerp and Café De Paris performances, this 15-track limited DVD pressing also included, as an additional bonus, three lip-synched promotional performances, filmed at Shepperton Studios, from the *Staying Power* album – 'Break Me', 'Suspended Animation' and 'Prove Me Wrong'. For diehard fans only, the collection swiftly disappeared into collectable status, although at least it had made it onto the market. An earlier proposition of a *Live in*

*Concert* DVD release, filmed during a 2005 appearance at the Royal Albert Hall, was halted when EMI balked at the financial costs of the arrangement.

*

England, Scotland, Wales, Northern Ireland, Germany, Switzerland, Austria, Sweden, Netherlands, Belgium, Ireland... the countries and the cities racked up as the six-man band toured relentlessly during their allotted time together during the 2000s. It was by no means constant, and the members usually permitted three months each year for group duties, allowing the remainder of the time for individual projects. But for one member, however, The Hollies were never far from their mind:

'Being a director of Hollies Ltd is a full-time job,' admitted Bobby. 'There are always requests and enquiries from around the world on licensing songs from our catalogue. But sometimes I just play drums down the pub with local musicians. Performing is important to me, as long as it's fun..."[59]

However, even the long-standing drummer was forced to miss the occasional show, and when he suffered an accident at home, injuring his shoulder during 2008, the band were forced to bring in a replacement at short notice. Andy Downing, drummer for the Suzi Quatro Band, gamely deputised for a series of German shows that month.

The next series of studio recordings that appeared arrived during March of 2009 in the form of another brand new 11-track album, this time titled *Then, Now, Always*. There had been talk of an earlier follow-up to *Staying Power*, and Ray Stiles had been discussing songwriting sessions with his former Mud cohort, drummer Dave Mount. Sadly, during late 2006, Mount had taken his own life and the proposition ground to a halt. It would take a further three years before a follow-on saw the light of day.

Initially available only at venues during the summer 2009 UK tour, EMI Records then saw fit to pick up the option on *Then, Now, Always* and give it a wider distribution the following year, with the addition of one extra song.

Whilst the title may well have suggested a look back at previous days, with the familiar sound of the Hollie-harmonies ringing throughout, this release was very much like its predecessor; a product of modern crystal-clear technology, and the songwriting was much from the same group of composers – Rob Davis, Mark Read, Cliff Masterson, Robert Hart. This time, however, the product held together a little better. With production once again falling into the lap of the multi-talented Ray Stiles, he pulled together a collection that featured the band's instrumental abilities more prominently than recent attempts, although Tony's lead guitar was often mixed too far down, barely audible at times. Instead, the basic reliance on rhythm guitar, keyboards, drums and bass to provide much of the tracking was too often overly detrimental to the combined sound. The sub-boy-band anthem of Mark Read's 'I Would Fly' was one of the few opportunities afforded to Tony to shine, but following this with the bland, programmed nonsense of 'Coming Home', with Steve Lauri providing the lead vocals, effectively wiped out any lasting memories of the song. The pseudo-Santana feel of the Latin-tinged 'One Way Ticket' also had the potential to develop into something beyond the middle-of-the-road ambience that dictated the release. Sadly, the chance was not given to explore such a route, despite its obvious quality.

Of the featured standout inclusions, including a nice reworking of the delightful 2006 offering 'Too Much Too Soon', it was the opening number, 'Then, Now, Always (Dolphin Days)', co-written by Bobby Elliott and Mark Nelson, that gave the most excitement to fans of the band. Lyrically, Bobby's recollections of their early days were slightly twee – with memories of bus stops and carousels reminiscent of The Beach Boys' annoyingly endless tendencies to revisit their halcyon days of good vibrations, but with Tony handling a rare lead vocal, it offered a great deal of promise to the selection that followed.

'It was something I wanted to get off my chest,' said Bobby. 'My co-writer Mark Nelson is also an artist, who did the artwork for the album as well, and that is sort of where Tony and I, and to an extent Allan and Graham, came from. Those northern mill towns. We would come down from that millstone grit, we would come down from the hills, come down the M1 and through all the doubt and ridicule of "What're you going to do? You're not going to be a professional musician. You're from round here, you can't do that." You got all that, being put down, and I thought I'd get this off my chest. Sort of, this is where we are now. We were escaping from the tradition of Tony being an electrician and me being a mining mechanic. We escaped from that…'[69]

Unfortunately, despite this encouraging introduction, what really followed was a collection of similar-sounding Howarth-led recordings. It was a well-constructed gathering (with Bobby utilised to a greater extent than with the part-programmed sound of the predecessor) but, sadly, as with *Staying Power*, the compositions varied little from track to track. There was little diversity. The one other noteworthy inclusion, added onto the end of the EMI version of the album, was another Elliott-Nelson collaboration, 'She'd Kill For Me', which offered a slightly edgier, original arrangement than those that had preceded it. Written as a tribute to Maureen Hicks, with whom Bobby had been in a relationship since the original Dolphins-era, and subsequently married and remained with up until her sad passing in 2009, the song was a moving look back at their life together. Had the band pursued such a path, with great sweeping tempo changes, instead of settling for a selection of forgettable non-originals, it may have received greater acclaim amongst the fan collective, many of whom simply dismissed the final result as distinctly average. Nevertheless, any further publicity or success the album achieved was somewhat muted by a sequence of differing events that took place that year, and efforts towards promoting the new product were dwarfed once more, as their legacy once again took centre stage.

*Midas Touch: The Very Best of The Hollies* was a brand new 2-CD set, issued by EMI during February 2010. Another compilation, another run of promotional TV ads, and yet another Top 30 hit – #23 to be precise. The featured selection, including a newly remastered stereo version of 'King Midas In Reverse' (featuring a new set of percussive overdubs by Paul Hicks), also included two brand-new live recordings taped during 2009 (passable versions of 'The Baby' and 'I Would Fly'). Naturally, however, the focus as always fell onto the succession of hits that frustratingly flowed in non-chronological order and jumped haphazardly through the decades. Then again, the pleasing inclusion of both 'So Damn Beautiful' and 'Then, Now, Always (Dolphin Days)' may well have piqued the interest of the casual buyer, surrounding recent activities, and may well have benefitted sales of both *Staying Power* and *Now, Then, Always* – had another event not dominated the headlines that followed.

# CHAPTER THIRTY-EIGHT

# "THIS WASN'T SUPPOSED TO BE HAPPENING..."

'Look Through Any Window' was one of the most significant guitar riffs of the '60s, played by the very underrated and superb guitar player Tony Hicks. His beautiful guitar texture, along with his third harmony part, would complement one of the great two-voice harmony blends in rock history, Allan Clarke and Graham Nash, with one of rock's greatest inventive and solid rhythm sections in Bobby Elliott, Eric Haydock and Bernie Calvert, on amazing records like 'I'm Alive', 'Bus Stop', 'On A Carousel', 'I Can't Let Go', 'Carrie Anne' and their masterpiece of masterpieces, 'King Midas In Reverse'. Not to mention an entire second life of hits, once Terry Sylvester joined the group.

The Beatles would name their group after The Crickets, The Hollies after their lead singer, Buddy, and they would arrive on our shores with their British invasion brothers and sisters just in time to save my life. It is my distinct honour and pleasure to induct into The Rock and Roll Hall of Fame Allan Clarke, Graham Nash, Tony Hicks, Eric Haydock, Bobby Elliott, Bernie Calvert and Terry Sylvester. The Hollies…

Steven Van Zandt
*Rock and Roll Hall of Fame Awards*
March 10th, 2010

To many, the Rock and Roll Hall of Fame museum, located on the shores of Lake Erie in Cleveland, Ohio, along with the accompanying annual ceremony that purports to celebrate it, is a sham. A self-indulgent, self-centred glorification of the music industry, overseen by a gathering of journalists and music impresarios without a musical bone between them.

Certainly, it does court controversy, and when one sees reports of the annual nomination process deliberately avoiding the inclusion of influential 1950s doo-wop performers in favour of big-name rap artists who sell tickets, one can seriously doubt the credibility of such an establishment. And the Hall's credence that "the category is meant for recording artists and bands that have had influence and significance to the development and perpetuation of rock and roll" is significantly drawn into question when viewing some of the inductees and the absentees. Nevertheless, many artists who make the grade, and survive the nomination and voting process to step out onto the stage at the Waldorf-Astoria Hotel in New York, where the induction ceremony takes place, feel it is a recognition of their work, and validation of acceptance by the industry. Unlike some of the lesser foundations and honorary museums – and there are dozens of them in the US alone (The Vocal Hall of Fame, The Songwriters' Hall of Fame, The Musicians' Hall of Fame – *ad nauseam*) – the Cleveland establishment is the benchmark for all who care. Not that everyone approves of such an honour. The Sex Pistols had notoriously refused to attend the celebrations upon their induction, whilst Van Halen, Creedence Clearwater Revival and Blondie all failed to put bad feelings between the individual members behind them before taking to the stage. In more recent years, there have been several further publicity-hawking controversies but, in 2010, having seen nomination, voting and acceptance into the hallowed museum, The Hollies were invited to accept the honour at one of New York's finest hostelries. Possibly Graham Nash's friendship with the Hall's co-founder and *Rolling Stone* editor Jann Wenner may have swung events in their favour, but the recognition was well deserved, even in a country that had never *quite* taken The Hollies to its heart.

Allan Clarke, Graham Nash, Tony Hicks, Bobby Elliott, Eric Haydock, Bernie Calvert and Terry Sylvester were all sent invitations to attend (with only original drummer Don Rathbone and short-time vocalist Mikael Rickfors omitted from the classic era), but only five members took to the stage to receive the applause that night.

Since leaving The Hollies, there had been a variety of ups and downs for all of the former members. Graham Nash, living the high life of a jet-set rock star in the idyllic west-coast sunshine, had seen his fair share of critical acclaim and critical mauling in the ensuing years, following his departure back in 1968. His intermittent partnerships with David Crosby, Stephen Stills and Neil Young had achieved a succession of magnificent highs and despairing lows as the saga weaved its zigzagged pathway through an often barren world of harmony, love, drug abuse, platinum awards, sold-out stadium tours, disputes, despair and scandal.

There had been five solo albums to date; *Songs For Beginners, Wild Tales, Earth & Sky, Innocent Eyes* and *Songs For Survivors;* four more studio releases in partnership with David Crosby and eight with the CSN/CSNY collective. His humanitarian and photographic work had also afforded him much praise, even if his regular outpouring of political opinion had courted controversy at times. Indeed, he was due to be honoured by Her Majesty, Queen Elizabeth II shortly afterwards, and receive the award of an OBE. Yet, the occasional reunions with his former British bandmates had only gone to emphasise his view of his old band as lightweight plasticity, cruelly jibing them as little more than "pleasant pop music". To him, the adult themes of Crosby, Stills, Nash & Young was where his heart lay. That said, he remained immensely proud of his formative years, and of his rekindled friendship with his old school friend. To him, the forthcoming honour was a seal of approval for Allan, if nothing more.

By contrast, Allan Clarke had laid low since his retirement from the band during 1999, enjoying family life in the Northamptonshire countryside, with his loyal wife, Jeni, now recovered from her battles with cancer, by his side. Surrounded by an ever-expanding family – sons Tim and Toby, daughter Piper, and with an increasing brood of grandchildren – life was back on an even keel for him.

For Terry Sylvester, however, it had been a roller-coaster ride following his sudden 1981 departure. After leaving The Hollies, he had immediately set up a songwriting and publishing business, although the natural lure of the live performance soon drew him back. Instigated by a transatlantic telephone call from Robin Britten, still acting in a managerial capacity on behalf of Terry at the time, he partnered up with former Bread singer-songwriter-guitarist James Griffin, who had held down the support slot on The Hollies 1974 UK tour. Subsequently relocating to Memphis, Tennessee, where Griffin lived, the duo cut the 1982 *Griffin & Sylvester* album together, out of the small Daily Planet recording studios.

A slick 10-track offering released in Europe via Polydor Records (and later reissued with three additional bonus cuts), the album unfortunately suffered by taking Terry too far away from his comfort zone. Although he was often sidelined in Bread (due to the domineering presence of hit songwriter David Gates), James Griffin was a powerful force, steeped in Memphis blues, with an enormous soulful range to his voice. His mere presence overwhelmed Terry's contributions at times, and their ventures into the southern grit of 'Wolf River' and 'Rozanne' appeared at odds with Terry's softer-voiced inclusions. The central focus of the album and the featured single pulled from the release, 'Please Come Into My Life', was almost a mutual stand-off between the varying styles, and James and Terry promoted it heavily around Europe during the summer of 1982, but to little avail. Nevertheless, despite the album failing to take off, the duo continued to work together, off and on, throughout the coming years.

By the mid-'90s, Terry's performing and recording career were sporadic at best. He even took to working as an estate agent in the London area to help with finances, although a 1994 solo tour of Germany resulted in a new album, *I Believe In Love*, a collection of previously released songs, put together with some live recordings from the tour. Released with the assistance of Ulli Eichblatt, the album saw limited distribution on Eichblatt's Major Oak label.

Back across the Atlantic, where he was now spending much of his time, he once again started working closely with James Griffin. Initially scheduled to appear as a support act on Griffin's post-Bread reunion project, Bread Revisited (a concept that ultimately never took off), the partnership veered away, linking up with fellow hit-making singer-songwriter John Ford Coley, and thusly forming the Soft Rock Café triumvirate. US promoter and a close friend of Griffin, Jim Della Croce (who this author interviewed back in 2012 for a biography on Bread) recalled, 'Jimmy was very easy-going and if there was another opportunity to play music he was there. At that point, opportunities came up and one of those was the Soft Rock Café. Terry Sylvester came up with the name, and we started looking at the songs of The Hollies, Jimmy and Bread, England Dan and John Ford Coley, and we thought it would be great to combine all of these hits and put them into a package…'

The newly combined trio of Griffin, Sylvester and Coley commenced their partnership with an hour-long TV special on the US TNN Network, appearing on *Prime Time Country* during the latter part of the decade. TNN was going to be changing its programming schedule and offered Jim Della Croce the opportunity to showcase the band for the full sixty minutes before the changes took that particular show off the air for the last time, and the subsequent success of the show led to a promotional tour being booked. Performing before a live audience, the trio sang a number of their most recognisable hits on the TV special, including Griffin's Academy award-winning 'For All We Know' (a huge hit for The Carpenters), Coley's 'I Really Want To See You Tonight', perennial Bread favourites such as 'It Don't Matter To Me' and 'Everything I Own', and Terry's versions of 'He Ain't Heavy, He's My Brother' and 'Long Cool Woman (In A Black Dress)', all interspersed with chat with the show's host, Gary Chapman.

Then, starting off by selling the show in Las Vegas, the trio began successfully appearing at various corporate events and, whilst no studio recordings were ever to come to light, they was to prove a popular live attraction over the coming years. Although the partnership gradually faded away, one final Griffin-Sylvester songwriting collaboration appeared during 2003 when Griffin, shortly before his tragic passing from cancer, recorded the sublime 'High On A Hill In Marbella' for a solo project.

By the turn of the new millennium, Terry was living comfortably in Florida, making the occasional concert appearance, still working occasionally with John Ford Coley, whilst redeeming his royalties through the continuing sales of Hollies recordings. Nevertheless, he was more than happy with the opportunity to return to the Hollie-days at the ceremony.

For the two former bass-players, it had been a far quieter journey away from the spotlight of superstardom. Whilst Eric Haydock had recently been bouncing in between music store management, the legal tribulations that had resulted from the Eric Haydock Band saga, and more recent 1960s nostalgia trips as part of the newly formed Class of '64 band (alongside former Kinks drummer Mick Avory and The Tremeloes' Chip Hawkes), Bernie Calvert had virtually disappeared back into obscurity.

Other than playing as part of a local Christian group around the Manchester-Nelson district, Bernie's activities had been strictly non-musical for the best part of two decades. He had studied a catering course, ran a delicatessen, became a sales representative for Lion Foods and then became a technical sales manager for a packaging firm. His journey to New York for the awards would be a pleasant deviation back into his former life.

And as for Tony and Bobby…

'I've been in contact with them,' Graham was to comment to *Rolling Stone* magazine, 'and we are trying to work it out right now. They are very pleased. They are very honoured. They don't quite know what it is, because they are so European. But I think they understand the importance, not only because of their legacy of a band but also for record sales and future shows to be a member of the Rock and Roll Hall of Fame. I'm not sure it has sunk in yet, but I'm sure it will…'

Unfortunately, the current touring band were partway through their spring schedule, with sold-out bookings committed either side of the induction ceremony. Even with a month of prior warning, neither Tony nor Bobby was prepared to forfeit the shows for the sake of flying to New York. To a disbelieving Graham Nash, the choice was simple. Cancel the bookings, reschedule as and when. This was a once-in-a-lifetime opportunity, he told them. This was the Rock and Roll Hall of Fame calling!

'There was just no way we could get an alternative date for these venues,' Bobby would say when commenting about the dilemma for the BBC. 'We're just a bit hamstrung, but we couldn't get there. Our fans in this country are a priority. It's a great honour to be in the Rock and Roll Hall of Fame, no doubt about it. But it's just one of those things. What would we do?'

Original bassist Haydock later suggested that the reasons for Tony and Bobby refusing to attend went deeper than that. In Brian Southall's book, *The Hollies Story*, he was quoted as saying that they didn't travel across to New York 'because they found out I was going. It's as simple as that.' True or not – and only the two members who continually step out as Hollies know for certain – recent events surrounding the Hollies Ltd vs Haydock legal case were still fresh in the minds of many, as was his tell-all interview with the *News of the World*, and the duo may not have wished to confront their errant bassist face-to-face (a financial settlement was eventually agreed upon to resolve the legal dispute). The unfortunate result was that, instead of a reunited group celebrating together, Hicks and Elliott stuck to their guns and committed to the touring schedule, noting that 'Allan Clarke and Graham Nash are going to collect our awards.' And yet, even with the details surrounding the attendance controversially confirmed, the unfolding events on the day in question caused further reason for unsettlement.

Reportedly, Terry Sylvester, who now resided on the American side of the Atlantic, had flown in from doing a show in Ohio. Upon arrival in New York, he caught a cab to the hotel, expecting the rehearsals to be held there, as he had been informed.

'We all got letters saying that the tickets were paid and everything, and I was told to get there, I think it was a Monday night, but I got told to get there on the Sunday for rehearsals,' he recently recounted. 'But when I checked in at the Waldorf-Astoria, I asked if there was an envelope for me, and I was told "no". I didn't understand that because I was supposed to do a rehearsal the following day. Unfortunately, Graham Nash had taken control of the whole thing, as he didn't want anybody involved except him and Allan.' [61]

With Allan unable to deliver strong enough lead vocals for their expected performance, due to follow the band's acceptance speeches, Graham had drafted in popular young singers Pat Monahan (from the band Train) and Adam Levine and Jesse Carmichael (from Maroon 5) to handle the vocal responsibilities and help with the harmonies. With support from the house band, fronted by Paul Shaffer, it remains undocumented as to why someone closer to the band, or even Terry himself, wasn't afforded the role.

'It was fabulous. It really was,' Allan later recalled. 'There was a little bit of a worry that I wasn't going to be able to make it, and that Tony and Bobby weren't going to go, and I thought, *Well, you can't just say no to something like this*. But, at that particular time, I hadn't really been singing for the last twelve years. I mean, am I going to be able to do this? And Graham just said to me, "Just leave it all to me." That was good enough for me, so I said, "Let's do it." It's one of the best things that I've ever done, and I'll remember it for the rest of my life. It was just a magic evening...' [6]

Not that the evening was all harmonious, as a still bitter Terry Sylvester noted, 'We get to the actual induction and find that Allan and Graham and their families were on a table about one hundred yards from where me, Bernie Calvert and Eric Haydock were. We were the only ones that were all split up! He just wanted it to be the Allan Clarke-Graham Nash show.'

Following a lengthy introductory speech by Steven Van Zandt, Bruce Springsteen's right-hand man and a huge Hollies fan himself, the five members in attendance were all permitted to say a few words of thanks upon receiving their statuettes. It was nice to hear Graham give credit to the band's original drummer, Don Rathbone, in his speech, wishing him well against health battles, whilst Allan thanked Ron Richards for his contributions and Terry offered praise to Robin Britten. The absenteeism of both Tony and Bobby was also duly acknowledged, and Allan and Bernie warmly shook hands at one point, but the uncomfortable scenario that took place once Allan and Graham took to the performing stage was sad to see.

Having gotten through enthusiastic, if somewhat shambolic, renditions of 'Bus Stop' and 'Carrie Anne', with Levine and Carmichael sharing the spotlight, Monahan and Van Zandt then joined the line-up on stage as the instantly recognisable guitar riff of 'Long Cool Woman (In A Black Dress)' rang out across the auditorium.

Terry continued: 'Well, I'd had enough. We got our awards. I just thought the deal was they would sing 'Bus Stop' and 'Carrie Anne' and that was fine because I wasn't on those, and I was just ready to watch from the side. The next minute I heard the intro to 'Long Cool Woman' and I'm thinking, *What's going on here?* So, I went on and I just whispered in the guy's ear, "I'm singing the next verse."'

Strolling onto the stage from the wings, casually dressed in a football shirt and jeans (in contrast to the smart appearance of both Clarke and Nash), Terry began prowling around, dancing along to the beat, awaiting his opportunity. Then, having taken the mic off Monahan and having performed the second verse, he was then visibly snubbed by Allan, who took the microphone out of his hand, offering it back to their stand-in vocalist, who finished off the performance. Neither Haydock nor Calvert was anywhere in sight.

Terry: 'The worst thing was when I stepped back and just started trying to dance, Graham whispered in my ear, "Isn't this great?" and I just said, "Fuck off, it's not great!"' [61]

'Now, Tony and Bobby said they couldn't make it because they were working,' responded Allan, 'which I thought was a big mistake. They should have been there. It was a big thing. But everybody else was there. But for some unknown reason, Terry had got this in his head that we had fallen out with each other or something. He was quite off about the situation and I really can't understand why, but we kept apart. Then, when we got on stage and we did 'Long Cool Woman', which Terry wasn't even on, I saw him creep on stage and grab the microphone. I thought, *That's not right*, so I went and took the microphone back off him and gave it back. I just thought, *You did the wrong thing there, mate. There's a guy there helping me out with the song that you weren't even on. You had no right to do that.* I still don't understand the reason why he did that…'[63]

Unfortunately, in the intervening years, the onstage fallout has often overshadowed the relevance of the event, and it still rankles with Terry Sylvester to this day.

> There have been some suggestions that I was inappropriately dressed for the induction. No way. This is rock and roll. Since when did we dress like penguins to do a concert? My twenty-minute interview with "Rolling Stone" got me two words in the magazine regarding the induction. "Totally rude" were the words, and that's the way Graham Nash and Allan Clarke were to me. Allan ignored me throughout the evening. I have no idea why. I don't recall falling out with him. I didn't have a problem with Allan and Graham singing 'Carrie Anne' and 'Bus Stop' but why was Graham allowed to stay on stage on 'Long Cool Woman'? So, I decided to take things into my own hands and do the right thing for me.
>
> Terry Sylvester website
> 2010

Nevertheless, the fact that Allan took the time to honour Ron Richards in his speech was highly fitting at such an occasion, particularly taking into account the highly significant contributions that their former producer had made throughout much of their career. Sadly, Ron was not there to see it, having passed away just eleven months before.

### Ron Richards 22nd January 1929 – 30th April 2009

A modest man who did not push himself forward, Ron Richards was, nevertheless, one of the UK's top record producers. He produced such familiar records as 'Love Me Do' (The Beatles), 'You'll Never Walk Alone' (Gerry and The Pacemakers) and 'He Ain't Heavy, He's My Brother' (The Hollies), and when he sometimes saw others take the credit for what he'd done, he would simply say: 'I know what happened.'

Richards was calm and controlled in the studio, always smartly dressed in Savile Row suits. The only time he flew into a rage was in 1970 when he and The Hollies were sharing a studio with Phil

Spector, who was making George Harrison's album, "All Things Must Pass". He returned to the studio to find that Bobby Elliott's drum kit had been damaged. 'I wouldn't have been so angry if I'd known Spector carried a gun,' he wryly observed.

When Richards went to California in 1965, he talked to his American counterparts and discovered that they received royalties from their hit records. He convinced George Martin and John Burgess of EMI and Peter Sullivan of Decca (the godfather of one of his sons) that they should establish an independent production company. AIR became highly successful and there were bids for the company from the Dick James Organisation and MAM, but it was in 1974 that the founding partners found themselves divided. Martin, the chairman, favoured an offer from Chrysalis, while Richards, the managing director, was opposed. The stress of all these negotiations affected Richards's health and he left the company once the merger had taken place.

After that, Richards's career became something of an anti-climax. He did some independent production work, notably with Tom Paxton and Prelude, but he lost interest in the big picture. His final album was "5317704" with The Hollies in 1979. By then he felt that record production had become a young man's game. He enjoyed watching his family grow and pursued other interests, like photography and gardening.

*The Independent*
June 2009

Back in the UK, the current Hollies line-up, with Tony and Bobby still playing alongside their now-established partners, Peter, Ray, Ian and Steve, continued ever on. The year 2010 closed out with an appearance on the QVC TV channel, performing four songs before the cameras, still gamely promoting the *Then, Now, Always* release with lip-synched versions of 'She'd Kill For Me' and 'I Would Fly', alongside 'The Air That I Breathe' and 'He Ain't Heavy, He's My Brother'.

2011 then saw the release of a new film, issued on DVD to celebrate the music of the band. *Look Through Any Window: 1963-1975*, a two-hour presentation, was compiled by Reelin' In The Years Productions, a company that specialised in obtaining old musical footage and licensing it for distribution. With new interviews from Allan, Graham, Tony and Bobby also included, the film didn't attempt to tell the story of the band, but instead it concentrated on the musical aspects, focussing on the performances and the creation of their recorded output. It was a wonderful addition to the collection of any Hollies fan, and the bonus of the 'On A Carousel' recording session footage from 1967 was a pure delight to see, although the knowledge that the company in question also owned the rights to the long-forgotten 1971 Australian Don't Get Sunburnt TV special, but had no plans to do anything with it, was immensely galling.

A special promotional screening for the film took place at the 400-seat Aero Theatre in Santa Monica, prior to the official DVD release. Both Graham Nash and Allan Clarke attended the event and, following the screening, the duo took part in a discussion panel with the director, David Peck, along with professor and Grammy-winning music writer Rob Bowman, held before a cheering audience.

The following year saw the arrival of a new live collection, *Live Hits: We Got The Tunes!* a 2-CD set issued via the band's website, that had been taped during the recent spring tour. With a title influenced by a chance meeting between Tony and Oasis' vocalist and frontman, Liam Gallagher (or his brother, Noel, as some reports would have us believe), who reportedly shouted out across a supermarket in an instantly recognisable Manchester tone, "Love ya band, man! You got the fuckin' tunes…!", the twenty-four featured tracks, a combination of hits, deeper cuts and some of the more recent offerings, confirmed the quality that the band still put out each time they stepped out onto the world's stages. Certainly, some of the newer rearrangements deserved to be heard again, and perhaps none more so than, with its wonderful fresh approach, 'Look Through Any Window', featuring a distinctive Lynyrd Skynyrd-styled extended guitar outro, care of Tony and Steve.

Meanwhile, not to be outdone, EMI Records, who were still content to trawl through their archives, started issuing the definitive, three multi-disc sets that made up the 17-CD *Complete Hollies* collection. It was a fascinating aural journey from 1963 through to 1988. As was the equally enjoyable release, *The Hollies: Radio Fun,* a 32-track EMI compilation issued in partnership with the BBC, featuring various radio recordings spread throughout the years. Although frustratingly non-chronological, excerpts from old 1960s shows, such as *Saturday Club, Top Gear, The David Symonds*

*Show* and *This Must Be the Place,* only went to highlight how much the BBC did have stored away. An edited version of the same set was later re-issued under the title of *Live At the BBC* by Parlophone.

During December of 2012, another new recording of 'He Ain't Heavy, He's My Brother' appeared in the charts, this time credited to The Justice Collective. This updated version, issued as a CD single, a 7" vinyl or as a digital download, was primarily a charity release, featuring a huge list of celebrity names (including Paul McCartney, Gerry Marsden, Robbie Williams, Melanie C, Glenn Tilbrook, Paul Heaton, etc.), coming together to support the families of the 1989 Hillsborough football disaster. The recording went on to take the coveted Christmas #1 position in the UK charts, equalling the feat of The Hollies' 1988 re-issue. Although both Tony and Bobby briefly appeared on the video for the new rendition, purportedly adding a vocal track to the recording, neither was credited on the actual song session list.

For 2013, The Hollies' 50th anniversary took precedence. The tour that year was especially notable, for they not only took their show across the length and breadth of the UK, but they also revisited favoured hotspots such as Germany, New Zealand and Australia, performing a twenty-eight-song setlist that ran from 1963's 'Stay', through the decades, up to the recent title track from *Then, Now, Always.* Then, to celebrate the occasion further, albeit one year later, the EMI 3-CD set *50 At Fifty* appeared, featuring the bonus of a brand-new Bobby Elliott-Peter Howarth-Steve Vickers composition. Entitled 'Skylarks', this song was one of the most progressive-sounding works the band had produced for many a year and was greeted with near-universal acclaim.

Graham Nash's continuing career notwithstanding, it appeared to many that this may well have been the final new product that Hollies collectors had to concern themselves with. From a band perspective, as this is being written, that may well be so – the money was always in the touring, and no longer in the sales of new music. Nevertheless, if this is so, then it was with a fine song that they chose to bow out after fifty long years.

However, the man that co-founded the band all those years ago clearly had other thoughts in his mind, although it appears this was not his initial intention.

On 7th October 2011, Allan Clarke had appeared on stage at London's Royal Albert Hall, guesting with Graham Nash at a Crosby and Nash show at the wonderfully elegant venue. Although officially retired from the music industry, and without the range for taking the lead voice, he gamely stood alongside his childhood friend and together, with one united voice, they gave the rapturous audience a moving performance of 'Bus Stop'. Clearly thrilled by the reception he had received, he thought no more of it, other than revelling in the memory. Occasionally, he would still compose, writing down the words to songs that he presumed he would never record.

'Things just happen on their own,' he would say during a 2020 interview. 'It just so happens that one day, I was in my office and I decided I would write some lyrics and maybe start writing songs again. I have a friend in Los Angeles named Saul Davis. He's married to singer Carla Olson and we've known each other for many, many years. He had been trying to get me into the studio for the last thirty years to do a solo thing with him and Carla, but it had always been in my mind that I wouldn't be able to sing anymore. So, I figured what was the point? But I started writing these words down and they came rather quickly. One became a poem called 'A Love That Never Blooms', which I then sent off to Carla, and she put a song to it and sent it back. And though I liked what she had done, I didn't think it was the way I would have actually sung those words, and so I decided to put my own music to the lyrics, although I changed the title to 'I'm Only Sleeping'.' [62]

Then, during the latter end of 2017, Allan was diagnosed with prostate cancer. It was a bitter blow to the man who spent many recent years caring for his wife during her dalliances with the big "C". Fortunately for all, he responded well to treatment but, during therapy and recovery, with doctor's orders to rest and not take on anything strenuous, he began furthering up his writing again.

'What happened was that my son Toby showed me GarageBand on my computer, which is a recording studio really, and I began by getting two tracks up, and laying the formation of a song on it, which I felt very good about. I was pleasantly surprised I was able to do that!' [45/64]

Gradually, as his health and strength improved, he upped the ante and began to compose on a more serious level, having seen what the GarageBand app could do. With Toby guiding him through the modern technological aspect, Allan began adding guitars, bass and a guide vocal. Gradually, a form began to take shape. Keeping it in the family, his grandson Sam also added some lead guitar lines.

'I was singing four notes lower, but at least it still sounded like Allan Clarke,' he said.[62]

Sending the tracks off to Saul Davis in America only went to encourage him further still, and with a collection of around nine new songs to hand, he decided to call in some expert assistance – and that came in the shape of former Hollies keyboard wizard, Francis (formerly Denis) Haines.

'I'd worked with Francis previously on some demos in the late '80s, and I always thought he was a brilliant guy in doing arrangements and production. So, I asked him if he would help me make the songs sound a bit better. Well, he loved them, and we just had a great time in his studio. I just really enjoyed it because there was no pressure. I wasn't doing it for any other reason than just enjoying what I was doing.'[45]

Impressed with the polished versions cut in Haines' studio, Saul Davis then scheduled a meeting between Allan and the head of BMG Records, Hartwig Masuch, who, to Allan's absolute bewilderment, offered him a record deal.

'This wasn't supposed to be happening, but the whole thing took on a life of its own!'

With a full album now gearing up for release, and an advance single scheduled to precede it, the excitement amongst The Hollies' loyal following was palpable. It was simply not what anyone had expected. Allan included. But then, sadly, the excitement amongst the fan community was prematurely shattered when news began to filter through that, on 5th January 2019, at the age of 75, original bass player and co-founder of the band, Eric Haydock, had passed away peacefully at his home near Manchester. It was a shock to many. Although he had left the band early on in their career and had only intermittently appeared back in the limelight over the ensuing fifty-three years, he was still considered an essential part of The Hollies' core.

His style of playing, the wonderful riffs and runs he had conceived on his six-string bass, had defined the rhythm of many of the early hits, and his partnership with Bobby Elliott had formed the backbone of the band, leaving the frontline trio to do what they did best – provide the melodies and the harmonies to those classic moments from five decades or more before.

An official statement from Bobby Elliott followed soon after:

In the early 1960s, Eric was one of the finest bass players on the planet. Along with Tony, Eric and I were the rhythm section that created the springboard for Clarke, Hicks and Nash to launch that famous three-way Hollies harmony. On the early package tours, Dave Clark, The Kinks and artists of the period would watch from the wings as we effortlessly rocked the screaming theatre audiences into a frenzy.

Although Eric left The Hollies in 1966, I occasionally listen enthralled by our BBC and Abbey Road recording sessions and dear Eric masterfully playing his six-string bass.

Happy days.


Two weeks later and two of Eric's co-founding members were once again reunited on the stage, as Allan presented Graham with the UK's Americana Lifetime Achievement Award, held at London's Hackney Empire. A clearly moved Nash, who hadn't known that Allan was going to present him with the honour, not only thanked his friend, but also paid credit to his former bandmates, whilst also acknowledging the sad news of their original bass player's death.

Eric's funeral took place the day after.

# CHAPTER THIRTY-NINE

# "RESURGENCE..."

'I have a single release on the 12ᵗʰ of July and the album on the 20ᵗʰ
of September. The album title is "Resurgence" – the first single is
'Journey Of Regret'.

Statement from Allan Clarke

June 2019

With production credits shared between Francis Haines and Allan himself,
the first fruits of the new collaboration appeared online and in the stores
during early July. 'Journey Of Regret' was a fine introduction to Allan's new
vocal approach, demonstrating his deeper range, and whilst some may have
found the mellower tone not to their taste, or the country overtones that
drove the composition lacking in originality, others were only too delighted
to hear his voice coming through as strongly as it did. For a seventy-seven-
year-old man, who hadn't sung in any significant capacity for twenty years,
it was an astonishing turnaround.

The album that duly followed, packaged with a sculptured image of his
head on the front sleeve by his wife, Jeni, was surprisingly upbeat in places.
From the pounding drumbeats on 'You Broke My Heart' and 'Heart Of
Stone', both featuring some sweet guitar licks from grandson Sam, through
the bluesy 'The Door Is Slowly Closing' to the gentler and highly impressive
update of 'Don't Let Me Down' (as previously recorded by The Hollies back
in 1974), the recording showed that Allan was prepared to take risks and

step back into a serious rock vein, as opposed to the easier middle-of-the-road approach as befitting a gentleman of mature status.

Naturally, much of the focus fell onto the purposely entitled 'Long Cool Woman's Back In Town', a hard-edged slab of AOR that paid due recognition to earlier successes, complete with Allan's wailing harmonica, but the uninhibited success of this track alone only added further credence to the album overall.

Allan Clarke has a rich, bluesy vocal perfect for emotionally charged songs like 'You Broke My Heart' (one you could imagine Chris Farlowe having a go at) and the country single 'Journey Of Regret'. Certainly, a surprising comeback given Clarke's lack of recording activity of late, however, "Resurgence" is a decent set of tunes and fans will be pleased by this album.

*Get Ready to Rock* review

Clarke's distinctive voice is instantly recognisable on the opening track 'Journey of Regret', but slightly worn around the edges, which fits in perfectly with this edgy country tale that would easily have fit into Cash's American body of work.

There's no evidence of a DIY ethos here, and then again there is no over-production, which may have blighted some of his solo work; this album is all about the songs… and the songs alone.

Clarke appears to have embraced the Americana ethos with both hands; using that type of imagery, and occasional twang, to great effect on 'Hearts of Stone', 'I'll Just Keep on Walking' and the deeply personal 'I'm Coming Home', which errs on the folkier side of the spectrum; and will touch your heart in the most unexpected fashion.

The only nod in the direction of Allan Clarke's Hollies days is a song called 'Long Cool Woman's Back in Town' and the world is a better place for this bittersweet alt. country-rocker, featuring some spine-shivering harmonica from the man himself.

*The Rocking Magpie* review

Though the songs bear little resemblance to the music made with The Hollies, or, for that matter, even to his efforts on his own, the songs still resonate with effusive accessibility that proves his pop chops are still intact.

*Goldmine* review

One of 2019's most unexpected albums is also one of its most exhilarating. As Allan says himself: 'It's given me a new lease of life in doing something I thought I'd never do again.'

*Maximum Volume* review

Rather surprisingly, Allan ploughed headlong into the promotion surrounding the September release, availing himself to countless radio interviews, both localised and national (including *The Johnnie Walker Show, Aled Jones, Jools Holland*), and even releasing a series of videos from his own YouTube channel, discussing how he and Francis Haines had created the album. Needless to say, much of the talk was angled towards future live appearances and a return to concert performing, but, for now, Allan ruled out the possibility, hesitant to rely on the unquestionable demand upon him to use the "classics" to flesh out his setlist.

'I'm not that Allan Clarke anymore,' he noted. 'Those high notes aren't there anymore. I can't go out and do two and a half hours. I know Bruce Springsteen does it all the time, but he doesn't have to go that high!'[62]

All told, by the turn of the year, *Resurgence* had gone to receive an astonishing level of acceptance and, despite a lack of significant chart success, Allan was clearly thrilled by the reviews – if still a little bewildered by it all. His thoughts naturally began to turn towards future recordings. His continuing friendship with Graham Nash turned the process towards a collaboration of sorts and the duo even started discussing the options available to them, across the great divide of the Atlantic. But then, the music world wasn't prepared for what hit it during the late winter and early spring of 2020. No one was.

As the terrible Covid-19 pandemic swept across the globe, the music business was put on hold. The entire population of the planet was effectively put on hold. The touring Hollies band postponed all scheduled concert appearances, including a long-overdue return tour to the US, as the world sat and waited, often in self-isolation. There was little else that could be done. One of the few positive aspects that was to arrive out of the catastrophe – and that is not a word used lightly – was the strength of the human race pulling together. The support given to the frontline workers, those who put themselves in the face of danger on a daily basis, to help, care and support the needy, was seen as a necessity, and many turned to charitable functions in order to offer their own small gift of thanks. For many of us, we could only watch. And pray. But for many musicians across the planet, those also stuck at home due to restrictions on movement, in their lounges, kitchens and bedrooms, they took to keeping the music alive and raising the spirits of all affected by the scene unfolding upon mankind.

From his apartment in New York, Graham Nash broadcast a short, acoustic set by way of supporting the cause, whilst Allan Clarke, equally affected by what was going on, recorded a charitable single, donating any proceeds from those watching to aid the NHS workers.

Allan: 'I asked my producer and good friend Francis Haines if he would do a piano piece of 'He Ain't Heavy' for me, in a lower key, as all the years that I had sung that song I always felt that every time it was not a message from me, but from the two guys that wrote the song. I mean, they must have had some inspiration from somewhere to write that sort of lyric, which means a lot to helping people in the world who can't help themselves.

'When I actually got the piano piece, the way that Francis had done it was so different to what I was used to, that it actually made me feel more emotional about the song and, maybe, I was able to put in that emotion as I did it, in my lower voice. I hope that the people like it, they can download it for themselves, they can stream it, or they can donate whatever they can towards the NHS. It doesn't matter how much; every little bit is very important …'[64]

The 2020 version of 'He Ain't Heavy, He's My Brother', with its simple piano accompaniment, was a symbol of unity. It wasn't cut to be compared to the original version, recorded and released by The Hollies half a century beforehand; it was recorded solely for its meaning. Support one and all. After all, we ain't heavy; we are all brothers, sisters, sons and daughters. We are one…

For their part, The Hollies also came together, so to speak. During May 2020, the current six-man band combined via individual internet links, during self-imposed isolation, to offer a video rendition of 'The Air That I Breathe'. With their respective parts played directly from their homes, *The Hollies: Unlocked* also offered their fans the opportunity to join in, coming together as a series of personalised video contributions at the climax of the song. It was a classy performance, but one that had a little wind taken out of its sails by unnecessary comparisons to Allan Clarke's own Covid-related offering. This wasn't a time for cruel jibes. It was a time for coming together. A united front. But the barbs still felt sharp.

Today, the varying factors of the hit-making band remain divided. The chasm that separated them at the 2010 New York Hall of Fame ceremony only appears to have widened with time, and whilst the tight-knit inner circle remains silent on such matters, words are spouted that suggest disharmony remains in some circles.

Of the famed line-up, Allan Clarke and Graham Nash remain close, as do Terry Sylvester and the reclusive Bernie Calvert, whilst the ongoing strong musical partnership between Tony Hicks and Bobby Elliott ensures the band's name continues ever onwards – but the chances of any of these divisive factors reuniting appear to fade with each passing day.

2017 saw Graham Nash openly suggesting that he had been offered the opportunity for a reformed band to play a show together, exclusively for the BBC, but nothing came of it. And even if they did; would it pull in a large enough audience? Certainly, the loyal following the band has retained over the years would be there, as would much of the world's music media, enthused by the return of Clarke and the opportunity to see the original three-way harmonies chiming out once again, but as Allan has mentioned on numerous occasions in recent years, he could no longer provide the range or the power to perform all the hits from a bygone era. And without Allan up there, pouring it out, what would be the point? Egos would never permit the original band playing second fiddle to the current line-up, and unless they could offer a guarantee of packing out the largest of venues, night after night, the £££ simply wouldn't be talking loudly enough to even consider such an option. And the bitter truth is, for The Hollies, for all their credibility and reputation for being one of the finest UK bands to rise out of the 1960s beat boom and survive, a reunion of sorts wouldn't generate such significant ticket sales. They could, and still do, sell out the Royal Albert Hall, and a one-off televised reunion could do the maths and the magic, but could the pride be swallowed? And would you still believe?

'That will never happen,' states Allan today.[62]

Ironically, one of the last social gatherings of former members, away from the stage spotlights, came about back in November 1991, when three of the *original* Hollies – Eric Haydock, Don Rathbone and Vic Steele –

had come together for the evening during the launch of Alan Lawson's *It Happened In Manchester* reference book.

Throughout the years, since 1963, the music of The Hollies, be it as a group or as individuals, has touched so many. They may not have had the cultural impact that The Beatles bestowed upon the world, or Elvis, or Sinatra, and in certain regions they may not have even matched the commercial success of The Dave Clark Five or Herman's Hermits, but for millions of record buyers, millions of concertgoers, millions of music *fans* across the planet, they have given, and continue to give, countless hours of joy.

'The music was light-hearted but not lightweight, and its spirit was contagious,' wrote journalist Mitchell Cohen in recent years. 'The Hollies made pop ecstatic.'[67]

Between 1963 and 1970, The Hollies had more Top 20 British hits than any other group except for The Beatles. More than The Rolling Stones, The Kinks or Manfred Mann, twice as many as The Who, The Small Faces, The Searchers or The Dave Clark Five, three times as many as The Yardbirds, The Move or The Troggs. And yet they didn't stop there. The hits realistically dried up after 1974, but the longevity of their career remains almost unparalleled. And, perhaps more importantly, it remains largely untarnished, influencing a tide of international artists and bands throughout the many years that have followed – from the late 1980s Manchester vibe of The Stone Roses, through to the American power-pop of The Posies and Jellyfish.

Darian Sahanaja, founding member of fellow US power-poppers The Wondermints (and, more recently, musical arranger for Brian Wilson's touring band), who contributed to the excellent 1995 Hollies' tribute CD *Sing Hollies In Reverse* (Eggbert Records), reflects:

'I remember a television ad that ran in the mid-'70s for a British Invasion LP compilation where short snippets of songs were played. The six or seven seconds of The Hollies' 'Look Through Any Window' had nearly the same effect on my twelve-year-old brain as 'I Get Around' did only a few years earlier. The harmonic sophistication left me dizzy and hungry for more. And boy, did they have more. A lot more.

'The Hollies had top-notch songwriting, impeccable musicianship – Bobby Elliott is my favourite of all the British Big Beat drummers – and a vocal harmony blend as unique as The Beach Boys. My bandmate Nick Walusko and I liked to refer to them as the Raphaels of '60s pop music, meaning that they may not have been the ground-breaking innovators that The Beatles and Michelangelo were, but they were the best at bringing all the signature elements of a movement together to create pieces of very high quality.'

Even a musician of the stature of the late US-born singer-songwriter Dan Fogelberg cited The Hollies as being one of the earliest influences on his career. Likewise, Elvis Costello has also been interviewed in recent years, professing a deep admiration for them from an early age.

Maybe that is their legacy and, just perhaps, that is the reason why the classic line-up is best left as a celebration of a bygone era.

Back in July 1974, just days before her own sad passing, "Mama" Cass Elliott, in conversation with the BBC's Brian Matthew for a *My Top Twelve* radio special, named 'King Midas In Reverse' as one of her personal choices.

There are still recordings which lie in the vaults, unheard to this day and, at the time of writing, rumours abound of potential new rarities sets being unleashed upon us. Maybe that is the way we will continually get to hear and refresh our minds of these wonderful talents. Tony and Bobby guard the catalogue with a strong hand and nothing gets issued without the approval of Hollies Ltd. Nevertheless, the BMI files suggest titles such as 'Love Emergency' (Clarke-Benson), 'Nightminds' (Clarke-Hicks-Sylvester), 'Takes A Strong Man' (Clarke-Benson) and the intriguingly entitled 'Spaghetti Western' (Clarke-Hicks-Painter) all survive either on tape or as written notation. Of course, there also remain a number of known titles intriguingly listed amongst the various sessionographies that circulate; titles that the audience have only read about for years but have never had the opportunity to hear.

As one famous song so eloquently says, "...*listen to me, I'll sing a song to change your mind*". And all it took?

Just one look...

# SELECTED DISCOGRAPHY

## UK Singles

*1963 Parlophone releases*
(Ain't That) Just Like Me / Hey What's Wrong With Me (R5030)
Searchin' / Whole World Over – (R5052)
Stay / Now's The Time – (R5077)

*1964 Parlophone releases*
Just One Look / Keep Off That Friend Of Mine (R5104)
Here I Go Again / Baby That's All (R5137)
We're Through / Come On Back (R51780

*1965 Parlophone releases*
Yes, I Will / Nobody (R5232)
I'm Alive / You Know He Did (R5287)
Look Through Any Window / So Lonely (R5322)
If I Needed Someone / I've Got A Way Of My Own (R5392)

*1966 Parlophone releases except where noted*
I Can't Let Go / Running Through The Night (R5409)
Bus Stop / Don't Run And Hide (R5469)
After The Fox / (non-Hollies B-side) (United Artists UP 1152)
Stop! Stop! Stop! / It's You (R5508)

*1967 Parlophone releases*
On A Carousel / All The World Is Love (R5562)
Carrie Anne / Signs That Will Never Change (R5602)
King Midas In Reverse / Everything Is Sunshine (R5637)

*1968 Parlophone releases*
Jennifer Eccles / Open Up Your Eyes (R5680)
Listen To Me / Do The Best You Can (R5733)

*1969 Parlophone releases*
Sorry Suzanne / Not That Way At All (R5765)
He Ain't Heavy, He's My Brother / 'Cos You Like To Love Me (R5806)

*1970 Parlophone releases*
I Can't Tell The Bottom From The Top / Mad Professor Blyth
(R5837)
Gasoline Alley Bred / Dandelion Wine (R5862)

*1971 Parlophone release*
Hey Willy / Row The Boat Together (R5905)

*1972 Polydor & Parlophone releases*
The Baby / Oh Granny (2058 199)
Long Cool Woman (In A Black Dress) / Cable Car (R5939)
Magic Woman Touch / Indian Girl (2058 289)

*1973 Polydor release*
The Day That Curly Billy Shot Down Crazy Sam McGee /
Born A Man (2058 403)

*1974 Polydor releases*
The Air That I Breathe / No More Riders (2058 435)
Son Of A Rotten Gambler / Layin' To The Music (2058 476)
I'm Down / Hello Lady Goodbye (2058 533)

*1975 Polydor release*
Sandy / Second Hand Hang-Ups (2058 595)

*1976 Polydor releases*
Boulder To Birmingham / Crocodile Woman (She Bites) (2058 694)
Star / Love Is The Thing (2058 719)
Daddy Don't Mind / C'mon (2058 779)
Wiggle That Wotsit / Corrine (2058 799)

*1977 Polydor releases*
Hello To Romance / 48 Hour Parole (2058 880)
Amnesty / Crossfire (2058 906)

*1979 Polydor releases*
Something To Live For / Song Of The Sun (POSP 35)
Also issued as a 12" single with The Air That I Breathe (POSPX 35)

1980 *Polydor releases*
Soldier's Song / Draggin' My Heels (2059 246)
Heartbeat / Take Your Time / Reprise (POSP 175)

*1981 EMI & Polydor releases*
Holliedaze / Holliepops (EMI 5229)
Take My Love And Run / Driver (POSP 379)

*1983 WEA release*
Stop! In The Name Of Love / Musical Pictures (WEA U 9888)

*1985 Columbia release*
Too Many Hearts Get Broken / You're All Woman (DB 9110)
Also issued as a 12" single with Laugher Turns To Tears (12DB 9110)

*1987 Columbia releases*
This Is It / You Gave Me Strength (DB 9146)
Reunion Of The Heart / Too Many Hearts Get Broken (DB 9151)

*1988 EMI releases*
He Ain't Heavy, He's My Brother / Carrie (EM74)
The Air That I Breathe / We're Through (EM 80)
*1989 EMI release*
Find Me A Family / No Rules (EM 86)

*1990 Exclusive Hollies release*
Purple Rain / Naomi / Two Shadows (SRT 9OLS 2407)

*1993 EMI release*
The Woman I Love / Purple Rain (Live) (EM 264)

*2005 EMI release*
Hope/Shine On Me (340 6232)

*2006 EMI release*
So Damn Beautiful / Too Much Too Soon (354 0642)

# UK ALBUMS

Stay with The Hollies
*Released: January 1964 / Parlophone (PMC 1220 / PCS 3054)*
I'm Talking About You / Mr Moonlight / You Better Move On / Lucille / Baby Don't Cry / Memphis / Stay / Rockin' Robin / Watcha Gonna Do 'Bout It / Do You Love Me / It's Only Make Believe / What Kind Of Girl Are You / Little Lover / Candy Man

In The Hollies Style
*Released: November 1964 / Parlophone (PMC 1235)*
Nitty Gritty / Something's Got A Hold On Me / Don't You Know / To You My Love / It's In Her Kiss / Time For Love / What Kind Of Boy / Too Much Monkey Business / Thought Of You Last Night / Please Don't Feel Too Bad / Come On Home / You'll Be Mine / Set Me Free
* The stereo release was not issued until 1967 under the alternative title Vintage Hollies *(World Records ST-979)*

Hollies
*Released: September 1965 / Parlophone (PMC 1261)*
Very Last Day / You Must Believe Me / Put Yourself In My Place / Down
The Line / That's My Desire / Too Many People / Lawdy Miss Clawdy
/ When I Come Home To You / Fortune Teller / So Lonely / I've Been
Wrong / Mickey's Monkey
\* The stereo release was not issued until 1969 under the alternative title
Reflection *(Regal Starline SRS 5008)*

Would You Believe?
*Released: June 1966 / Parlophone (PMC 7008)*
I Take What I Want / Hard Hard Year / That's How Strong My Love Is /
Sweet Little Sixteen / Oriental Sadness / I Am A Rock / Take Your Time
/ Don't You Even Care (What's Gonna Happen To Me?) / Fifi The Flea /
Stewball / I've Got A Way Of My Own / I Can't Let Go
\* The stereo release was not issued until the spring of 1967 *(Parlophone
PCS 7008)*

For Certain Because
*Released: December 1966 / Parlophone (PMC/PCS 7011)*
What's Wrong With The Way I Live / Pay You Back With Interest / Tell
Me To My Face / Clown / Suspicious Look In Your Eyes / It's You / High
Classed / Peculiar Situation / What Went Wrong / Crusader / Don't
Even Think About Changing / Stop! Stop! Stop!

Evolution
*Released: June 1967 / Parlophone (PMC/PCS 7022)*
Then The Heartaches Begin / Stop Right There / Water On The Brain
/ Lullaby To Tim / Have You Ever Loved Somebody / You Need Love /
Rain On The Window / Heading For A Fall / Ye Olde Toffee Shoppe /
When Your Light's Turned On / Leave Me / The Games We Play

Butterfly
*Released: November 1967 / Parlophone (PMC/PCS 7039)*
Dear Eloise / Away, Away, Away / Maker / Pegasus / Would You Believe
/ Wishyouawish / Postcard / Charlie And Fred / Try It / Elevated
Observations? / Step Inside / Butterfly

Hollies Sing Dylan
*Released: May 1969 / Parlophone (PMC/PCS 7078)*
When The Ship Comes In / I'll Be Your Baby Tonight / I Want You / Wheels On Fire / I Shall Be Released / Blowin' In The Wind / Quit Your Low Down Ways / Just Like A Woman / The Times They Are A Changin' / All I Really Want To Do / My Back Pages / Mighty Quinn

Hollies Sing Hollies
*Released: November 1969 / Parlophone (PCS 7092)*
Why Didn't You Believe? / Don't Give Up Easily / Look At Life / Please Sign Your Letters / My Life Is Over With You / Please Let Me Please / Do You Believe In Love / Soldier's Dilemma / Marigold / Gloria Swansong / You Love 'Cos You Like It / Reflections Of A Time Long Past / Goodbye Tomorrow

Confessions Of The Mind
*Released: November 1970 / Parlophone (PCS 7116)*
Survival Of The Fittest / Man Without A Heart / Little Girl / Isn't It Nice / Perfect Lady Housewife / Confessions Of A Mind / Lady Please / Frightened Lady / Too Young To Be Married / Separated / I Wanna Shout

Distant Light
*Released: October 1971 / Parlophone (PAS 10005)*
What A Life I've Led / Look What We've Got / Hold On / Pull Down The Blind / To Do With Love / Promised Land / Long Cool Woman (In A Black Dress) / You Know The Score / Cable Car / A Little Thing Like Love / Long Dark Road

Romany
*Released: November 1972 / Polydor (2383 144)*
Won't You Feel Good That Morning / Touch / Words Don't Come Easy / Magic Woman Touch / Lizzy And The Rainman / Down River / Slow Down / Delaware Taggett & The Outlaw Boys / Jesus Was A Crossmaker / Romany / Blue In The Morning / Courage Of Your Convictions

Hollies
*Released: March 1974 / Polydor (2383 262)*
Falling Calling / Down On The Run / Don't Let Me Down / Love Makes The World Go Around / The Day That Curly Billy Shot Down Crazy Sam McGee / It's A Shame, It's A Game / Rubber Lucy / Pick Up The Pieces Again / Transatlantic Westbound Jet / Out On The Road / The Air That I Breathe

Another Night
*Released: February 1975/ Polydor (2442 128)*
Another Night / 4th Of July, Asbury Park (Sandy) / Lonely Hobo Lullabye / Second Hand Hang-Ups / Time Machine Jive / I'm Down / Look Out Johnny (There's A Monkey On Your Back) / Give Me Time / You Gave Me Life (With That Look In Your Eyes) / Lucy

Write On
*Released: January 1976 / Polydor (2442 141)*
Star / Write On / Sweet Country Calling / Love Is The Thing / I Won't Move Over / Narida / Stranger / Crocodile Woman / My Island / There's Always Goodbye

Russian Roulette
*Released: December 1976 / Polydor (2383 421)*
Wiggle That Wotsit / 48 Hour Parole / Thanks For The Memories / My Love / Lady Of The Night / Russian Roulette / Draggin' My Heels / Louise / Be With You / Daddy Don't Mind

Hollies. Live Hits
*Released: March 1977 / Polydor (2383 428)*
I Can't Let Go / Just One Look / I Can't Tell The Bottom From The Top / Bus Stop / Another Night / 4th Of July, Asbury Park (Sandy) / Star / My Island / I'm Down / Stop! Stop! Stop! / Long Cool Woman (In A Black Dress) / Carrie Anne / The Air That I Breathe / Too Young To Be Married / He Ain't Heavy, He's My Brother

A Crazy Steal
*Released: March 1978 / Polydor (2383 474)*

Writing On The Wall / What Am I Gonna Do / Let It Pour / Burn Out / Hello To Romance / Amnesty / Caracas / Boulder To Birmingham / Clown Service / Feet On The Ground

5317704
*Released: March 1979 / Polydor (2442 160)*
Say It Ain't So Jo / Maybe It's Dawn / Song Of The Sun / Harlequin / When I'm Yours / Something To Live For / Stormy Waters / Boys In The Band / Satellite Three / It's In Everyone Of Us

Buddy Holly
*Released: October 1980 / Polydor (POLTV 12)*
Peggy Sue / Wishing / Loves Made A Fool Of You / Take Your Time / Heartbeat / Tell Me How / Think It Over / Maybe Baby / Midnight Shift / I'm Gonna Love You Too / Peggy Sue Got Married / What To Do / That'll Be The Day / It Doesn't Matter Anymore / Everyday / Reprise

What Goes Around…
*Released: July 1983 / WEA (25 0139 1)*
Casualty / Take My Love And Run / Say You'll Be Mine / Something Ain't Right / If The Lights Go Out / Stop! In The Name Of Love / I Got What I Want / Just One Look / Someone Else's Eyes / Having A Good Time

Archive Alive
*Released: 1997 / Connoisseur Collection (NSP CD 518)*
I Can't Let Go (Live) / Just One Look (Live) / Bus Stop (Live) / On A Carousel (Live) / Look Through Any Window (Live) / King Midas In Reverse (Live) / Wasted On The Way (Live) / Teach Your Children (Live) / Soldier's Song (Live) / Stop! Stop! Stop! (Live) / The Air That I Breathe (Live) / Carrie Anne (Live) / Stop! In The Name Of Love (Live) / He Ain't Heavy, He's My Brother (Live) / Long Cool Woman (In A Black Dress) (Live)
* Re-issued in 2005 as Reunion with the addition of Casualty (Live) and Someone Else's Eyes (Live) *(Snapper SMACD 919)*

Staying Power
*Released: February 2006 / EMI (09463-559832-2)*
Hope / So Damn Beautiful / Prove Me Wrong / Break Me / Shine On Me / Suspended Animation / Touch Me / Emotions / Weakness / Live It Up / Yesterday's Gone / Let Love Pass

Then, Now, Always
*Released: 2009 / Hollies Distribution (5317704)*
Then, Now, Always (Dolphin Days) / If You See Her / One Touch / Passengers / I Would Fly / Coming Home / I Lied / One Way Ticket / Too Much Too Soon / Unforgivable / Hearts Don't Lie
* Re-issued in March 2010 with the addition of She'd Kill For Me *(EMI 50999-9175022-8)*

Hollies Live Hits: We Got The Tunes!
*Released: March 2013 / Hollies Distribution (B00C5HAJAC)*
The Day That Curly Billy Shot Down Crazy Sam McGee / I Can't Let Go / Jennifer Eccles / Yes, I Will / On A Carousel / Then, Now, Always (Dolphin Days) / Sandy / King Midas in Reverse / Look Through Any Window / Very Last Day / Emotions / The Baby / Bus Stop / Sorry Suzanne / Stewball / I Can't Tell the Bottom From The Top / Weakness / Just One Look / Stay / Long Cool Woman (In A Black Dress) / Carrie Anne / Stop! Stop! Stop! / He Ain't Heavy, He's My Brother / The Air That I Breathe

# UK COMPILATION ALBUMS

Greatest Hits
*Released: August 1968 / Parlophone (PMC/PCS 7057)*
I Can't Let Go / Bus Stop / We're Through / Carrie Anne / Here I Go Again / King Midas In Reverse / Yes, I Will / I'm Alive / Just One Look / On A Carousel / Stay / Look Through Any Window / Stop! Stop! Stop! / Jennifer Eccles

Greatest Hits Vol.2
*Released: March 1972 / Parlophone (PCS 7148)*

Gasoline Alley Bred / Searchin' / Listen To Me / Too Young To Be Married / Dear Eloise / He Ain't Heavy, He's My Brother / Hey Willy / Just Like Me / Sorry Suzanne / If I Needed Someone / I Can't Tell The Bottom From The Top / Blowin' In The Wind

History Of The Hollies (24 Genuine Top 30 Hits)
*Released: 1975 / EMI (EMSP 650)*
24-track collection

20 Golden Greats
*Released: July 1978 / EMI (EMTV 11)*
20-track collection

The EP Collection
*Released: 1987 / See For Miles Records (See 94)*
22-track collection

All The Hits And More
*Released 1988 / EMI (EM/CDEMS 1301)*
36-track LP / 40-track CD collection

Rarities
*Released: 1988 / EMI (EMS 1311 / CDP 7912972)*
Carrie / Mexico Gold / If It Wasn't For The Reason That I Love You / Louisiana Man / She Looked My Way / Eleanor's Castle / Here In My Dreams / Sanctuary / Relax / Tomorrow When It Comes / Open Up Your Eyes / The Times They Are A-Changin' / Look Through Any Window (French Version) / After The Fox / Non Prego Per Me / Like Every Time Before / Wings

The Air That I Breathe: The Very Best
*Released: 1993 / EMI (CDEMTV 74)*
26-track collection

Hollies At Abbey Road 1963-1966
*Released: 1997 / EMI (CD Abbey 103)*
28-track collection

Hollies At Abbey Road 1966-1970
*Released: 1998 / EMI (72434-934502-7)*
24-track collection

Hollies At Abbey Road 1973-1989
*Released: 1998 / EMI (72434-964342-0)*
20-track collection

Greatest Hits
*Released: March 2003 / EMI (72435-820122-2)*
47-track collection including: How Do I Survive

The Long Road Home
*Released: 2003 / EMI (07243-5848562-2)*
136-track, 6-CD box set including hits, album tracks, various rarities and previously unreleased recordings

Midas Touch: The Very Best
*Released: 2010 /EMI (50999-6082272-7)*
48-track collection including: The Baby (Live) and I Would Fly (Live)

Radio Fun
*Released: May 2012 / EMI (440 7702)*
Here I Go Again    (Live) / Jennifer Eccles (Live) / Bus Stop (Live) / I've Got A Way Of My Own (Live) / Wings (Live) / Step Inside (Live) / Wishyouawish (Live) / Shake (Live) / Put Yourself In My Place (Live) / Ride Your Pony (Live) / I Take What I Want (Live) / Little Bitty Pretty One (Live) / Away Away Away (Live) / Charlie And Fred (Live) / I Can't Let Go (Live) / Hard Hard Year (Live) / If I Needed Someone (Live) / That's How Strong My Love Is (Live) / To You My Love (Live) / So Lonely (Live) / Something's Got A Hold On Me (Live) / Nobody (Live) / Set Me Free (Live) / She Said Yeah (Live) / You Must Believe Me (Live) / Lawdy Miss Clawdy (Live) / Too Many People (Live) / Look Through Any Window (Live) / Too Young To Be Married (Live) / I'm Alive (Live) / The Games We Play (Live) / He Ain't Heavy, He's My Brother (Live)

50 At Fifty
*Released: 2014 / Parlophone (82564223541)*
50-track collection including: On A Carousel (Live) / Then, Now, Always
(Dolphin Days) (Live) / Skylarks

# WORLDWIDE ALBUMS

Here I Go Again (US Release)
*Released: June 1964 / Imperial (LP 9265 / LP 12265)*
US variation of debut album (alternative track listing)

Hear! Here! (US Release)
*Released: November 1965 / Imperial (LP 9299 / LP 12299)*
US variation of The Hollies' third album (alternative track listing)

Beat Group! (US Release)
*Released: May 1966 / Imperial (LP 9312 / LP 12312)*
US variation of Would You Believe album (alternative track listing)

Bus Stop (US Release)
*Released: October 1966 / Imperial LP 9330 / LP 12330)*
Collection of previously unreleased US tracks

Stop! Stop! Stop! (US Release)
*Released: December 1966 / Imperial (LP 93369 / LP 12339)*
US release of For Certain Because... album

Greatest Hits (US Release)
*Released: May 1967 / Imperial (LP 9350 / LP 12350)*
Bus Stop / Pay You Back With Interest / Here I Go Again / Tell Me To
My Face / I'm Alive / Look Through Any Window / Stop! Stop! Stop! /
Whatcha Gonna Do 'Bout It / Just One Look / Memphis / I Can't Let Go
/ On A Carousel

Evolution (US Release)
*Released: June 1967 / Epic (LN 24315 / BN 26315)*
US variation of Evolution album (alternative track listing)

Dear Eloise / King Midas In Reverse (US Release)
*Released: November 1967 / Epic (LN 24344 / BN 26344)*
US variation of Butterfly album (alternative track listing)

He Ain't Heavy, He's My Brother (US Release)
*Released: December 1969 / Epic (BN 26538)*
US variation of Hollies Sing Hollies album (alternative track listing)

Moving Finger (US release)
*Released: December 1970 / Epic (E 30255)*
US variation of Confessions Of The Mind album (alternative track listing)

Greatest Hits (US Release)
*Released: April 1973 / Epic (KE 32061)*
Bus Stop / Carrie Anne / Stop! Stop! Stop! / Look Through Any Window / Dear Eloise / Long Cool Woman (In A Black Dress) / He Ain't Heavy, He's My Brother / Just One Look / King Midas In Reverse / Pay You Back with Interest / Long Dark Road / On A Carousel

Out On The Road (German Release)
*Released: 1973 / Hansa (871191IT)*
Out On The Road / A Better Place / They Don't Realise I'm Down / The Last Wind / Mr. Heartbreaker / I Was Born A Man / Slow Down – Go Down / Don't Leave The Child Alone / Nearer To You / Pick Up The Pieces / Trans-Atlantic West Bound Jet

Clarke, Hicks, Sylvester, Calvert, Elliott (US Release)
*Released: 1977 / Epic (34714)*
10-track collection featuring songs from Another Night, Write On and Russian Roulette

The Hollies (Australian Release)
*Released: 1978: Axis Records (Axis-6361)*
14-track collection including the otherwise unavailable outtake of Poison Ivy

Epic Anthology: From The Original Master Tapes (US Release)
*Released: 1990 / Epic (EGK 46161)*
20-track collection including: Magic Woman Touch (previously unreleased acoustic version)

Up Front Special Vol.1 : The Coconut Collection (German Release)
*Released: 1990 / Coconut (260448000)*
Stand By Me (Special Dance Version) / Stand By Me (Abbey Road Version) / Stand By Me (Radio Dub Version) / Stand By Me (Instrumental Version) / Shine Silently (Special 12" Version) / Shine Silently (7" Mix) / Your Eyes (Special 12" Mix) / Your Eyes (7" Mix) / For What It's Worth, I'm Sorry (7" Mix) / Long Cool Woman (12" Remix) / Find Me A Family (Instrumental Version) / Draggin' My Heels (Special Disco Version)

30th Anniversary Collection 1963-1993 (US Release)
*Released: 1993 / EMI USA (E2 99917)*
57-track collection including: I Understand, I Can't Get Nowhere With You, She Gives Me Everything I Want, You In My Arms, Man With No Expression, Nothing Else But Love, Purple Rain (Live)

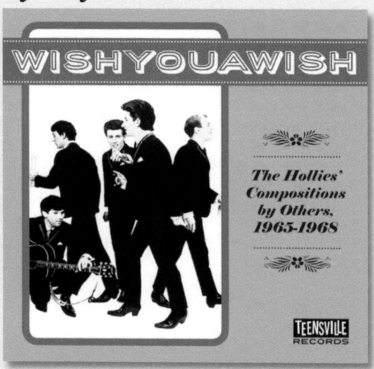

# CREDITS &
# ACKNOWLEDGEMENTS

Although this is an unofficial biography, I would duly like to offer my appreciation, and dedicate it to Allan, Graham, Eric, Don, Tony, Bobby, Bernie and Terry...
along with Vic, Mikael, Alan, Steve, Denis, Ray, Ian, Carl, Peter and Steve – and all the others who have stepped aboard and sailed on the good ship *Hollie* (Tony's M & N, Pete, Hans-Peter, Paul, Jamie, Ian H, Dave, John...)

Thank you to the following kind folk for contributing, however large or small it may have been (directly or indirectly);

Dean James Adshead, Peter Arnesen, Karl Baker, Jason Barnard, Mike Batt, Laura Beeby, Jane Bozian, James Byatt, Steven Casto, Brian Chatton, Peter Checksfield, Linda Cleveland, Geoff Coles, Colin Elgie, Vic Farrell, Jerry Fuentes, Ian Greensmith, Peter Howarth, Iain Lee, Derek Leong, Helen Macdonald, Tony Marsden, Mike McCartney, Roger McGough, Mark Meinhart, Ann Moses, Jamie Moses, Paul Mylnarz, Tony Newman, Olaf Owre, Ian Parker, Maldwyn Pope, Andrew R Pratley, Domenic Priore, Derek Quinn, Don & Stella Rathbone, Mark Ritucci, Chrissy Rowan, Ian Rusten, Darian Sahanaja, Bud Scoppa, Simon Smith, Kaoru Soejima, Janet Stevens, Anthony Strelley, David Summers, John Truman, Richie Unterberger, Klaas Veenstra, Klaus Voorman, Dave Watkinson, Ash Wells, Simon Wordsworth

With SPECIAL THANKS to…

The invaluable eyes, memorabilia and staying power of Janet Stevens

The incredible knowledge of Geoff Coles – who often put words into my mouth, but they were good words, so I said 'em just the same

The meticulous research, the detailed attention and the informative tweaks of Simon Smith. Top man…

Don and Stella Rathbone for their generous hospitality, the treacle tart and loan of the "collection"

Vic Farrell/Steele for sharing his time and memories

Mike McCartney/McGear for his wonderful tales

The amazing scrapbook collection of Chrissy Rowan

The eagle eyes of Tony Marsden

Jane Bozian – all a bit lastminute.com, but no less important. Thank you…

My good friend Steven Casto for his early encouragement

All the knowledgeable Elevated Observations forum contributors (and those on any other forum I've stumbled across)

The *Carousel* Newsletter – edited and compiled by Martin Hockley, Chris and Sheila Bowen and their team (including the late Alan Pooley)

I also would like to recognise the thoughtful and insightful recollections of Andrew R Pratley

Finally, a huge 'thank you' to all of those who purchased the First Edition of this book. Without you all there wouldn't have been a Second Edition - and you wouldn't be reading this now…

# SOURCES

1. *Wild Tales* by Graham Nash (Penguin Books, 2013)
2. *Crosby, Stills & Nash* by Dave Zimmer (DaCapo Press, 1984)
3. *The Road Is Long: The Hollies Story* by Brian Southall (Poppublishing, 2015)
4. *It Happened In Manchester 1958-1965* by Alan Lawson (A Multimedia Publication, 1998)
5. *The Long Road Home* by Peter Doggett (EMI Records, 2003)
6. *Strange Brew Podcast* with Jason Barnard/Allan Clarke (2014)
7. *The Hollies Interviews* (Major Oak Productions, 1990)
8. *Things I Do For Love* by Eric Stewart (Apple E-book, 2017)
9. *Hollies.dk* The Unofficial Danish Hollies Site
10. *The Times* Newspaper (January 2019)
11. *The Cavern: The Most Famous Club in the World* by Spencer Leigh. (SAF Publishing, 2008)
12. *The History of The Hollies* by Bruce Eder (Goldmine Magazine, 1996)
13. *The Hollies.co.uk* The Official Website
14. The *Lancashire Telegraph.* Article by Gill Johnson (March 2008)
15. *Staying Power* by Spencer Leigh (*Record Collector* Magazine, 2006)
16. The *New Musical Express* Interview (April 1964)
17. *Look Through Any Window* (Reelin' In The Years DVD Production. 2011)
18. The Hollies' *Carousel* Newsletter. Various Editions
19. *The Story of The Hollies* by Bruinewoud & Rosendaal (Dutch Radio Series, 1995)

20. *CSNY: The Biography* by Peter Doggett (Bodley Head, 2019)
21. *It Happened in Laurel Canyon* by Harvey Kubernik (Musicconnection.com. 2019)
22. Interview with Tony Hicks by Nick Dent-Robinson (Pennyblackmusic.co.uk. 2013)
23. Interview with Allan Clarke by Aled Jones (BBC Wales, 2019)
24. Hollies Discussion Panel (Reelinintheyears.com. 2011)
25. *Tin Pan Alley: The Rise of Elton John* by Keith Hayward (Soundcheck Books, 2013)
26. Interview with Bernie Calvert by Jud Cost (Sundazed.com)
27. Interview with Terry Sylvester by Gary James (Classicbands.com 2017)
28. Interview with Terry Sylvester by Keith Hampshire (Terrysylvester.com)
29. Michael Cohen quote: Tintrunk.blogspot.com (2010)
30. *The Complete Hollies: CD Collection* (EMI Records, 2018)
31. Interview with Allan Clarke by Adam Coxon (Pennyblackmusic.co.uk 2019)
32. Gene Pitney quote: The Wythenshawe History & Heritage website
33. The *Hollies Official Fan Club Newsletter* edited by Lynne Wheeler/Rod Shields
34. Interview with Tony Hicks: *Poprama* (Swedish radio, 1969)
35. *The Hollies Tell You How to Run A Beat Group* (Daily Mirror Publications, 1964)
36. Interview with Bernie Calvert by Mark Ritucci
37. TheGearPage.net
38. *Eric Carmen: Marathon Man* by Bernie Hogya and Ken Sharp (Smashwords, 2011)
39. *It Ain't Heavy, It's My Story* by Bobby Elliott (Omnibus Press, 2020)
40. Interview with Terry Sylvester: *Nightbird & Co.* (US Army Reserve Promotional LP)
41. Comments from Andrew R Pratley, son of Ron Richards. Used with permission ©The author (2020)
42. *Strange Brew Podcast* with Jason Barnard/Bobby Elliott (2020)
43. *The Hollies: From Dylan to disco* by Imogen Harrison (Shindig Magazine, 2015)
44. Alan's Album Archive: Reflections of a Long Time Past (SpareRoom Studios, 2019)
45. Interview with Allan Clarke: *AJ on Your Radio* (242 Radio, Scotland, 2020)
46. Terry Sylvester Interview: c/o Mark Ritucci (1983)
47. Interview with Allan Clarke by Mike Ragogna (*Huffington Post*, 2011)
48. Unknown BBC Radio interview (1978)
49. Quote from Terry Sylvester: @terry_sylvester (Twitter account)
50. Comments from Peter Arnesen. Used with permission ©The author (2020)
51. *Buddy Holly: Learning the Game* by Spencer Leigh (McNidder & Grace Publishing, 2019)

52. *Buddy Holly & The Hollies* by Ray Stiles (The Hollies tour programme, 1996)

53. *Remembering Buddy Holly* by Robyn Flans (*Mix* Magazine, 1996)

54. *The Official Carl Wayne Website* by Helen Macdonald

55. Q&A with Carl Wayne compiled by Jo Rishton. *The Beat Goes On and On* magazine c/o *The Official Carl Wayne Website*

56. The Hollies Official UK Tour Programme (Various years)

57. Comments from Ian Parker. Used with permission ©The author (2020)

58. *The Hollies Concert Reviews* (Davideaves.co.uk)

59. Interviews with Bob Henrit and Bobby Elliott by Mark Forster (Mikedolbear. com. 2017)

60. Comments from Ian Brookes. Used with permission (2018)

61. *Ask Caswell: Conversation with Terry Sylvester* (Internet broadcast, 2020)

62. Interview with Allan Clarke by Lee Zimmerman (Goldmine, 2020)

63. Interview with Allan Clarke by Christian Swain (Pantheon Podcasts, 2019)

64. Interview with Allan Clarke by Danny Stoakes (Stoakes Media, 2020)

65. Quotes from Albert Hammond: *Behind the Hits* (Grand Central Publishing, 1986) and BBC Radio (1992)

66. *Why Allan Clarke left The Hollies* by Harold Bronson (*Rolling Stone* Magazine, 1973)

67. *Why The Hollies Still Matter* by Michell Cohen (Musicaficionado.com)

68. *Stone Alone* by Bill Wyman (Viking Publishing, 1990)

69. *They Ain't Heavy, They're The Hollies* Presented by Brian Matthew (BBC Radio Special, 2010)

70. *The Hollies Anthology: From the Master Tapes* (Epic Records CD sleevenotes, 1990)

71. *Heaven & Hell: My Life in The Eagles* by Don Felder (Weidenfield & Nicolson, 2007)

72. *Write On: The Illustrated Discography of The Hollies* by Manfred Schwanbeck & Peter Krause (Star Cluster, 2001)

73. *Allan Clarke, Survivor* by Janis Schacht (*Trouser Press* Magazine, July 1978)

74. *Ready Steady Go!: The Weekend Starts Here* by Andy Neill (BMG Books, 2020)

75. Quote from Rod Hill c/o Dave Wilkinson to the author (2020)

76. Quote from Vic Farrell to the author (2020)

77. The Don Rathbone memorabilia collection

78. Quote from Mike McCartney to the author (2020)

79. University UNT Digital Libraries 1967 recording

80. The Toggery Five Website (toggery-five.com)

All efforts have been made to credit excerpts, quotes and photographs wherever possible. If any have erroneously been missed, then please contact the author so that corrections can be made for future editions.

# FURTHER SOURCES OF INFORMATION & READING

*A Rock Legend from Hodge Hill* by William Dargue (Birmingham History, 2015)

*The Ultimate Biography of The Bee Gees: Tales Of The Brothers Gibb* by Melinda Bilyeu, Hector Cook & Andrew Môn Hughes (Omnibus Press, 2012)

*Billboard Book of Top 40 Hits* by Joel Whitburn (Guinness Press, 1983 edition)

*Billboard Book of Top 40 Albums* by Joel Whitburn (Omnibus Press, 1991 edition)

*Bread: A Sweet Surrender* by Malcolm C. Searles (Post Hill Press, 2019)

*British Beat 1960-1969* by Terry Rawlings (Omnibus Press, 2002)

*Channelling the Beat* by Peter Checksfield (CreateSpace Publishing Platform, 2018)

*Clowns, Lullabies and Butterflies* by Andy Morten (Marmalade Skies website)

*The Complete Book of British Charts* (Omnibus Press, 2000 edition)

*Do You Feel Like I Do?* By Peter Frampton (Hachette Books, 2020)

*Dream a Little Dream of Me: The Life of "Mama" Cass Elliott* by Eddi Fiegel (Sidgwick & Jackson, 2005)

*Elevated Observations* by Andy Morten (Shindig Magazine #15, March 2010)

*Exorcising Ghosts* by Dave Cousins (Witchwood Media, 2014)

*Faithfull* by Marianne Faithfull & David Dalton (Little, Brown & Co, 1994)

The Hollies Official Fan Club (Newsletter edited by Lynne Wheeler/Rod Shields)

*I'm Nearly Famous: Tales of a Likely Lad* by Tony Rivers (Private Publishing, 2015)

*Let's Stomp! American Music That Made the British Beat: 1954-1967* by Peter Checksfield (Independent Publishing, 2020)

*Meow! My Groovy Life With Tiger Beat's Teen Idols* by Ann Moses (Q Coding LLC, 2017)

*Papa John: An Autobiography by John Phillips & Jim Jerome* (Dolphin-Doubleday, 1986)

*Record Collector* Magazine (Diamond Publishing)
Ron Richards obituary by Spencer Leigh (Independent.co.uk)
*10cc: The Worst Band in the World* by Liam Newton (Rocket88, 2020)

…and *New Musical Express, Disc & Music Echo, Fabulous 208, Melody Maker, Record Mirror* and all of those other never-to-be-forgotten wonders of bygone music-reading madness. Thank you to the many editors, writers and journalists who helped contribute to the story over the years.

# WEBSITES

1960smusicmagazines.com, 45cat.com, BMI.com, Bradfordtimeline.co.uk Discogs.com, Elevatedobservations.proboards.com, Hollies.dk Hollies.co.uk, Manchesterbeat.com, Officialcharts.com Rocksbackpages.com, Setlist.fm Tsort. info, TVpopdiaries.co.uk

And, dare I forget them, Facebook, Wikipedia and YouTube all played their role too…

# PHOTOGRAPHIC CREDITS

All effort has been made to identify and credit the original photographer and/or source, but if there any notable omissions then please contact the author for future corrections. Credits/sources listed as known.

Front sleeve image of The Hollies c/o Pictorial Press/Alamy
Rear sleeve image of The Hollies c/o Don Rathbone Collection

Plate 1   Image of Ricky and Dane Young, source unknown
Image of The Dolphins, source unknown
Image of Cliff Bowes and The Arrows c/o Don Rathbone Collection
Image of The Emperors of Rhythm c/o Vic Farrell Collection

Plate 2   Image of Vic Steele and Eric Haydock c/o Vic Farrell Collection
Image of Allan Clarke c/o Don Rathbone Collection
Image of Graham Nash c/o Don Rathbone Collection
Image of The Hollies c/o Michael Ochs Archives

Plate 3   EMI/Parlophone Records Promotional Postcard
Image of Eric Haydock c/o Don Rathbone Collection
Image of The Hollies c/o Don Rathbone Collection

Plate 4   Advert of The Toggery: New Record Mirror, June 1963
Image of Allan Clarke and Graham Nash, source unknown
Image of Tony Hicks and Eric Haydock c/o BBC.co.uk

Image of Allan Clarke, source unknown

Plate 5  Front cover image: Record Mail, June 1964

Plate 6  Image of The Hollies c/o Abbey Road Studios

Image of The Hollies, source unknown

Plate 7  Image of the Hollies c/o Henry Diltz/Joe Butler

US Greatest Hits LP Sleeve: Imperial Records

Image of The Hollies c/o Frank Orrell Photography

Plate 8  Promotional postcard

Image of Terry Sylvester c/o Pictorial Press/Alamy

Image of the Hollies c/o Pictorial Press/Alamy

Plate 9  Image of Bobby Elliott c/o Pictorial Press/Alamy

Japanese 45 Sleeve: Odeon Records

UK Distant Light LP Sleeve: EMI/Parlophone Records

Image of The Hollies c/o Bravo/Pabel Moewig Publishing

Plate 10 US Promotional Poster: Epic Records

Plate 11 Image of Allan Clarke, source unknown

Image of The Hollies c/o Michael Putland/Hulton Archive

Plate 12 Image of Allan Clarke and Tony Hicks c/o Pictorial Press/Alamy

German Promotional Tour Poster

Image of The Hollies c/o Resources.stuff.co.nz

Plate 13 Image of The Hollies c/o PA Images

US 45 Sleeve: Atlantic Records

US Promotional Poster: Atlantic Records

Plate 14 Image of The Hollies: Promotional Press Photograph

German 45 Sleeve: Coconut Records

Image of The Hollies: 2001 Tour Flyer

Plate 15 Image of Eric Haydock, Don Rathbone and Vic Steele c/o Don Rathbone Collection

Image of Allan Clarke and Graham Nash c/o Kevin Kane/Getty Archives

Image of The Hollies c/o Jim Spellman/Getty Archives

Image of The Hollies c/o John Truman

Plate 16 All images c/o Anthony Strelley

# ABOUT THE AUTHOR

Malcolm C. Searles has lived and breathed in Chelmsford, Essex, forty miles to the north-east of London, for virtually his entire life; venturing out only occasionally to capture the warmth of vacation sunshine or to attend a concert or three in the nation's capital.

Happily married to Louise, with two grown-up sons, Sam and Matt, this is his third publication, following on from the biographical successes of *Bread: A Sweet Surrender (The Musical Journey of David Gates, James Griffin & Co.)* and *The Association: Cherish (The Story of America's First Folk-Rock Band)*. Further online written works include projects on The Beach Boys, The Monkees and Disney's very own Yachtsmen Quartet.

The story continues…

Lightning Source UK Ltd.
Milton Keynes UK
UKHW020729260422
402079UK00006B/608